The QuarkXPress 4.0 Handbook

Diane Burns

Sharyn Venit

D1456311

The QuarkXPress 4.0 Handbook

Diane Burns

Sharyn Venit

MIS:PRESS

A Division of
Henry Holt and Co., Inc.
New York

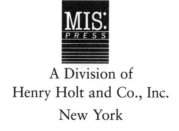

MIS:Press
A Division of Henry Holt and Company, Inc.
115 West 18th Street
New York, New York 10011
http://www.mispress.com

Copyright © 1998 by MIS:Press

Printed in the United States of America

All rights reserved. No part of this book may be reproduced or transmitted in any form or by any means, electronic or mechanical, including photocopying, recording, or by any information storage and retrieval system, without prior written permission from the Publisher. Contact the Publisher for information on foreign rights.

Limits of Liability and Disclaimer of Warranty

The Author and Publisher of this book have used their best efforts in preparing the book and the programs contained in it. These efforts include the development, research, and testing of the theories and programs to determine their effectiveness.

The Author and Publisher make no warranty of any kind, expressed or implied, with regard to these programs or the documentation contained in this book. The Author and Publisher shall not be liable in any event for incidental or consequential damages in connection with, or arising out of, the furnishing, performance, or use of these programs.

All products, names and services are trademarks or registered trademarks of their respective companies.

First Edition—1997

Library of Congress Cataloging-in-Publication Data

MIS:Press and M&T Books are available at special discounts for bulk purchases for sales promotions, premiums, and fundraising.

For details contact: Special Sales Director
MIS:Press and M&T Books
Divisions of Henry Holt and Company, Inc.
115 West 18th Street
New York, New York 10011

10 9 8 7 6 5 4 3 2 1

Associate Publisher: *Paul Farrell*
Managing Editor: *Shari Chappell*
Editor: *Andy Neusner*
Production Editor: *Danielle DeLucia*
Copy Edit Manager: *Karen Tongish*
Copy Editor: *Gwynne Jackson*

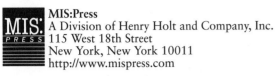

ACKNOWLEDGMENTS

The book you hold in your hands is the result of the efforts of many, many people. While it's impossible to name each and every individual who made a contribution, we would like to specifically acknowledge the help of several people from Quark, Inc. First and foremost we thank Fred Ebrahimi, President and CEO, for his support of this book since the first edition was written more than seven years ago. This edition could not have been completed without the help of Elizabeth Jones, Don Lohse and Amy Snelzter.

We'd also like to thank all the people at MIS:Press who made this book possible, and especially our editor, Andy Neusner, who guided it through both the editorial and production phases with endless patience and professionalism.

Finally, we thank you, our readers, and the QuarkXPress users who, over the years, have shared their insights on this very essential tool for all of us involved in publishing today.

FOREWORD

From the time Quark released the first version of QuarkXPress, our company has been committed to developing technologies that help advance the publishing world. Our users include staff from magazines, department stores, national and state associations, direct-mail companies, financial organizations, and catalog publishers around the globe who all share an interest in producing publications of the highest quality while maximizing productivity and minimizing costs. QuarkXPress has become part of a revolution in communication capabilities for nonprofit organizations helping to make this a better world, educational institutions working with our youth, small businesses struggling with profit margins, and special interest groups with information to share.

QuarkXPress 4.0 pushes the envelope of publishing capabilities further than ever before, on all platforms - MacOS, Windows 95, and Windows NT. New features such as Bézier drawing and text tools and features that help streamline long document production make QuarkXPress 4.0 a stand-alone virtuoso for all phases of document publication, from design to prepress. At the same time, it expands the range of formats supported for importing text and graphics from almost any other application that you or your clients use. In a time that has been named the Information Age, when printed and electronic communication is the primary "product" of human endeavor, QuarkXPress is increasingly the tool of choice.

We are very pleased about this book project. I have known and respected both writers for many years. I sought them out years ago as industry experts and experienced users of publishing tools to show them early versions of QuarkXPress, and collect their praises and criticisms. The real value of this book is that it incorporates the practical experiences and knowledge the authors have developed in their 12 years since they first became involved with desktop publishing. Herein they serve as your own "off the shelf" consultants.

-Fred Ebrahimi, President and CEO, Quark, Inc.

Contents

INTRODUCTION

QuarkXPress has become the world's leading publishing tool, commanding 70% to 90% of the high-end design and publishing market worldwide. The program is many things to many people, and it can be used for simple tasks, as well as complex ones.

There are many ways to master such a powerful program. Without question, one of the best ways to learn it is through hands-on experience, especially if you have a seasoned guide to help you. This book is not intended to replace practical experience with QuarkXPress but to supplement hands-on experience. Not a tutorial, this book is a reference and guide that will help you learn to "think like" QuarkXPress—it is not intended to be read cover to cover.

TIP: More experienced users may find it helpful to skim chapters for the tips, techniques, and special considerations offered. These are marked throughout the book by tip icons.

This book is divided into three sections:

- "Part I: QuarkXPress Essentials" covers basics that almost everyone who uses the program needs to know.
- "Part II: Publishing Long Documents" focuses on issues of interest to those involved in publishing longer documents, such as books or manuals.
- "Part III: Advanced Techniques" covers issues that are typically not faced by novice users, including special graphics features and color separations. This section also provides an overview using QuarkXPress for nontraditional media, such as CD-ROM or Internet publishing.

Because QuarkXPress is a truly cross-platform product, its features work the same way on Macintosh and Windows 95/NT systems. This book covers both platforms. Keyboard shortcuts for the Macintosh are followed by the corresponding Windows key command. For example, ⌘/CTRL.

What's New in 4.0

So much is new and different in version 4.0 that it's hard to know where to begin. Two areas, however, clearly stand out:

- New graphics capabilities have been added, including Bézier tools, text-paths, editable clipping paths, and the ability to convert type to outlines.

- Features have been added to make it easier to create long documents.

Quark has also improved existing features, adding those little touches here and there that have been requested over the years. An improved interface accommodates the new features nicely, but remains basically consistent with previous versions. Old-timers may feel overwhelmed at first but should find the transition relatively easy and the new functionality most welcome.

New Graphics Features

One of the most exciting aspects of version 4.0 are a slew of new graphics features. The addition of Bézier tools, along with the ability to create and edit clipping paths, will significantly change the work flow for QuarkXPress users. It will no longer be necessary to use illustration programs to perform a variety of routine tasks—drawing squiggly lines, converting type to outlines, or creating text on a path—nor will it be necessary to use programs like Adobe Photoshop to create clipping paths.

Bézier and freehand Bézier drawing tools for creating boxes, lines, and text-paths have been added. These tools work much like Bézier tools found in drawing programs such as Adobe Illustrator and CorelDRAW.

Version 4.0 allows you to convert type to editable paths in the form of picture boxes with the **Text to Box** command. Once text is converted to boxes, you can import pictures, apply a frame, and manipulate the shapes as you would any other picture box.

The **Merge** and **Split** commands, which have features that are similar to Illustrator's Pathfinder filters, let you combine complex shapes.

A new item type, the *text-path,* lets you draw straight or curved lines along which you can input text.

Used frequently to silhouette an image or render part of it transparent, clipping paths can now be created in QuarkXPress, eliminating the need to use an image-editing program.

You can create custom dashes and stripes, either numerically or graphically using slider bars. The **Dashes & Stripes** command is found under the Edit menu, and much like style sheets and colors, they become part of the menu of style choices for lines and box frames.

Long Document Features

For years, QuarkXPress users have had to rely on manual systems or third party XTension products to provide features necessary for long document production. Many of these features have been incorporated into version 4.0. A *Book* is a new type of QuarkXPress file that displays as a palette through which you can manage multiple files for printing and pagination. The Lists feature lets you generate any kind of list—including a Table of Contents—by collecting text, based on paragraph style sheets. An Index that lets you mark words and compile them into an index has also been added.

Other New Features

Other new features and enhancements include:

- Interface improvements, including tabbed dialog boxes.
- Character style sheets allow you to format individual text characters within a paragraph.
- A single column of text can be run around all sides of an image.
- The ability to append elements such as H&Js, Style Sheets, Colors, has been enhanced and made more flexible.
- Font and picture usage has been combined into one tabbed dialog box
- A number of limitations have been removed. You can now have thousands of paragraphs in a story and thousands of Style Sheets, H&Js, and Colors.
- You can anchor items of any shape, including Bézier boxes.
- New color models, including multi-ink colors that allow you to mix colors and PANTONE's Hexachrome colors used in "high-fidelity" printing.
- Color management is available through Kodak Digital Science Color Management System (CMS).
- The XTensions Manager lets you control which XTensions launch.
- The PPD Manager lets you control which PPD files are available to the program.
- Version 4.0 allows you to save documents in a format compatible with version 3.3.

These and other new features are covered throughout the book.

We hope you will enjoy this book and find it helpful in reaching what is, undoubtedly, your ultimate goal—to master the power of QuarkXPress!

PART ONE

QUARKXPRESS ESSENTIALS

1 The Basics

This chapter is geared toward those of you who are new to QuarkXPress and have not used the program very much. If you feel comfortable with the *basics* of the program, you can probably skip this chapter and move on to subsequent chapters. This chapter, as its name implies, sticks to the basics of QuarkXPress. We do assume, however, that you understand how to use your computer, keyboard, and mouse. We also assume you understand what the program is supposed to do, that is, page layout and design. This book is not about spreadsheets!

Getting Started

Before you start using any software program, you should be sure it's properly installed and that you know how to get it up and running. Refer to your QuarkXPress documentation for instructions on how to install the program correctly. Avoid the temptation to just start installation, without first reading about the various issues involved. For example, you may not need to use every XTension that comes with QuarkXPress 4.0, and since XTensions require additional memory, it's a good idea to install only those you'll need (or de-activate them using the XTensions Manager, found on the Utilities menu of QuarkXPress once it's installed).

Once you've installed the program, take advantage of the extensive online help that's available. On a Macintosh system, you'll find online help available in Apple Guide format, which you can display by simply pressing the Help key on your keyboard.

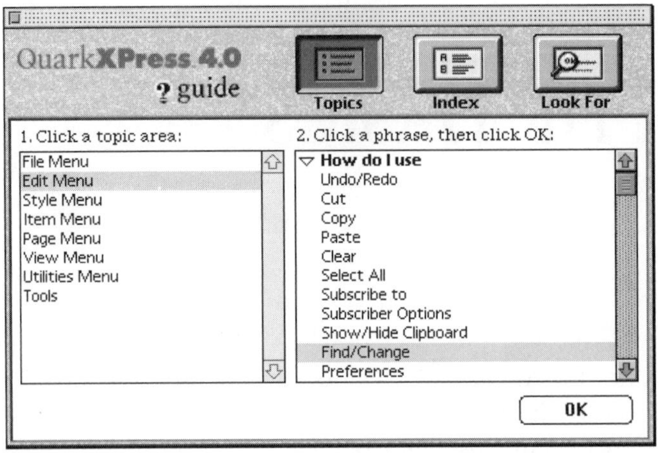

***Figure 1.1** QuarkXPress online help available on Apple Macintosh systems.*

On a Windows system, choose About QuarkXPress from the Help menu. You must have opted to install the online help files for them to be available, which is probably a good idea as you get up and running on version 4.0.

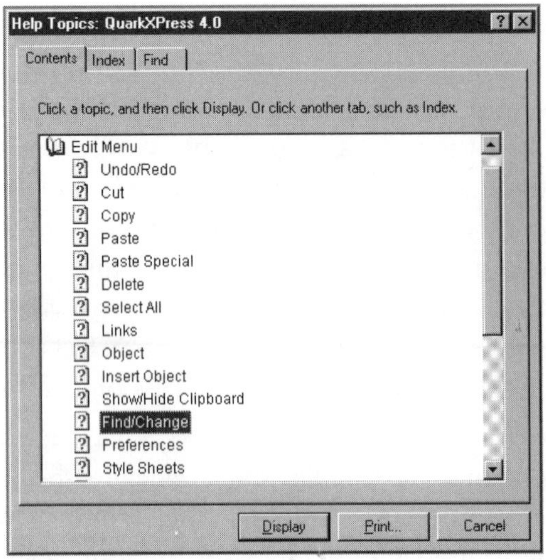

***Figure 1.2** QuarkXPress online help available on a Windows 95 system.*

Examining a QuarkXPress Document

Before we jump into the details, let's step back and take a look at a QuarkXPress document. It's important to understand the various components that make up a document, and from this overview we can learn a lot about the basic principles of using the program as well as the terminology that will become part of your QuarkXPress vocabulary. One of our goals is to make sure you're fluent in "Quark-ese."

Anatomy of a QuarkXPress Document

While it's possible to create a document using only the tools found in QuarkXPress, most real world documents contain text and graphics created in other programs. Face it, most editors would probably prefer to use a word processing program and don't really need QuarkXPress's graphics capabilities. Similarly, artists usually prefer to use Adobe Photoshop or something similar to create images. Figure 1.3 shows a typical page created in QuarkXPress.

Fashion Dolls

Fashion dolls live to dress and dress to live. Fashion victims all follow the quest for that perfect look.

Lorem ipsum dolor sit amet, consectetuer adipisc ing elit, sed diam nonummy nibh euismod tincidunt ut laoreet dolore magna aliquam erat volutpat. Ut wisi enim ad minim veniam, quis nostrud exerci tation ullamcorper suscipit lobortis nisl ut aliquip ex ea commodo consequat. Duis autem vel eum iriure dolor in hendrerit in vulputate velit esse molestie consequat, vel illum dolore eu.

Nulla facilisis at vero eros et accumsan et iusto odio dignissim qui blandit praesent luptatum zzril delenit augue duis dolore te feugait nulla facilisi. Lorem ipsum dolor sit amet, consectetuer adipiscing elit, sed diam nonummy nibh euismod tincidunt ut laoreet dolore magna aliquam erat volutpat.

Ut wisi enim ad minim veniam, quis nostrud exerci tation ullamcorper suscipit lobortis nisl ut aliquip ex ea commodo los esta consequat. Duis autem vel eum iriure dolor in hendrerit in vulputate velit esse molestie los esta consequat, vel illum dolore eu feugiat nulla facilisis at vero eros et accumsan et iusto odio dignissim qui blandit praesent luptatum zzril delenit augue duis dolore te feugait nulla facilisi. Nam liber

Tempor cum soluta nobis eleifend option congue nihil imperdiet doming id quod mazim placerat facer possim assum. Lorem ipsum dolor sit amet, consectetuer adipiscing elit, sed diam nonummy nibh euismod tincidunt ut laoreet dolore magna aliquam erat volutpat. Ut wisi enim ad minim veniam, quis nostrud exerci tation ullamcorper suscipit lobortis nisl ut

Sept/Oct Fashion Times 26

***Figure 1.3** Anatomy of a QuarkXPress page.*

Most of the text was written and edited in a word processing program (after being transmitted from the field, via modem) and then imported into QuarkXPress. The images were licensed and downloaded from a Web site, then brought into Adobe Photoshop, where they were edited and color adjustments were made. Some of the short text elements, such as the headline and subhead, were typed directly into QuarkXPress using the Text-path tool. Folios and automatic page numbering were set up on the document's *master pages*—special pages that contain elements that will appear on multiple document pages.

Document Pages

When viewed on screen, a QuarkXPress page looks pretty much the same as when printed, except that it is represented at screen resolution, usually about 72 dots per inch (dpi). The document page is shown in the *document window*, a standard window that can be resized and repositioned like any other window. You can have more than one document window open at a time, but the active document window usually displays on top of any other document windows (unless you have arranged them side by side). When you close a document window, you are closing the document.

On either side of the page is the *pasteboard*, which functions like an artist's drafting table, in that you can use it to store text, graphics and lines that can be positioned on to the document page as needed. The page image shows the outline of the edges of the paper; nonprinting dotted or color lines on the page indicate margins and columns. Optionally, rulers can be displayed at the top and right sides of the document window. The bottom left corner of the screen shows the current page-view percentage and the page number (Figure 1.4).

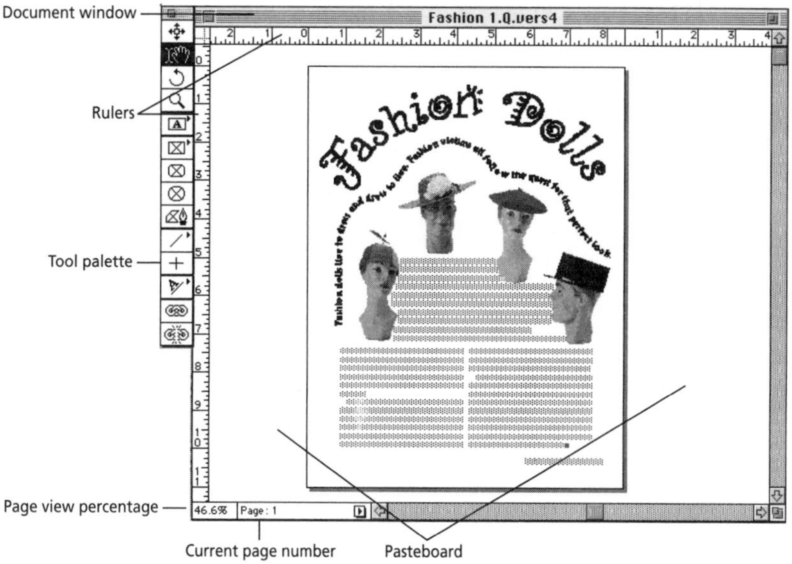

Figure 1.4 *The document window.*

Boxes, Lines, and Text-Paths

The basic building blocks of any QuarkXPress document—boxes, lines, or text-paths—are called *items*. They are drawn with QuarkXPress tools called *item creation* tools. We'll refer to items frequently throughout this book.

Boxes drawn using QuarkXPress tools can stand alone as empty graphic elements, or they can contain text or pictures. Text boxes on the first page of the newsletter shown in Figure 1.4 contain article text and folio text; the headline and banner were created with the Bézier text-path tool. The graphics were prepared in Adobe Photoshop, and imported into a rectangular picture box with a clipping path applied in QuarkXPress.

Examining QuarkXPress Palettes

QuarkXPress 4.0 has eight different palettes that provide various features and production aids. A *palette* behaves a little differently from a window in that it displays on top of all document windows. A palette is related to the active document only, but you can close any palette without closing the active document. Like windows, palettes can be moved anywhere on the screen by dragging on their title bars.

The Tool Palette

The QuarkXPress Tool palette is much like a conventional artist's assortment of drawing tools. Here, the pens, rulers, protractors, and X-acto knives of old are replaced by icons that perform the artist's work (Figure 1.5).

Like all QuarkXPress palettes, you can drag the Tool palette by its title bar to any position on the screen. You can close the palette by clicking on the **Close** box or selecting **View ➛ Hide Tools.** To redisplay the Tool palette after you close it, select **View ➛ Show Tools.**

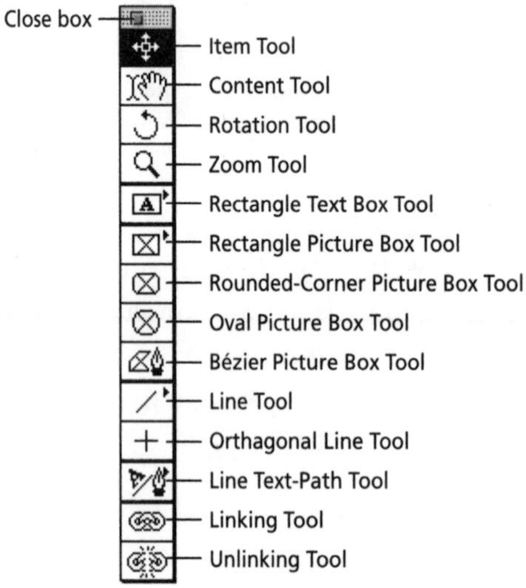

***Figure 1.5** The default Tool palette.*

Selecting a Tool

To select a tool from the Tool palette, click on its icon. The appearance of the cursor will change, depending on which tool is selected. Some tools have a small arrow in the upper-right-hand corner. These tools have pop-out menus that contain additional similar tools. To select a tool on a pop-out menu, drag and release the mouse over the tool you wish to use.

TIP You can add a tool from a pop-out menu to the main tool palette by holding down the **⌘/Ctrl** key while you select it. To remove a tool from the main tool palette, hold down the **⌘/Ctrl** key while clicking on the tool. At least one tool from each pop-out menu always remains on the palette.

TIP Some tools remain active until you deselect them by choosing another tool—the Item (✥), Content (☝), and Zoom (🔍) tools fall into this category. All the other tools revert to the Item tool or the Content tool as soon as they are used once. To keep the same tool active for repeated use, hold the **Option/Alt** key as you select it. The tool will then remain selected until you click on another tool.

Double-clicking on a tool brings up the Tool Preferences dialog box (described in Chapter 3, "Expanding the Document"), which enables you to set the default specifications for the Zoom (🔍) and Item Creation tools (boxes, lines, and text-paths) in the Tool palette.

General Tools

If you look carefully, you'll notice that the tool palette is divided into six sections, each separated by a line somewhat thicker than the lines that separate each tool. These represent logical divisions in the usage of different tools.

The first section of the Tool palette includes four general tools (Figure 1.6): the Item tool (✥), the Content tool (☝), the Rotation tool (↻), and the Zoom tool (🔍). Select the Item tool to move or resize items, clipping paths, or runaround paths. When the Item tool is selected, the cursor becomes an arrow (↖). It changes to a four-pointed arrow, or *mover pointer* (✥), when you position it over an item or path, and it changes to a pointing finger or resizing pointer (☜) when positioned over the handle of an active item or path.

***Figure 1.6** General tools include the Item, Content, Rotation, and Zoom tools.*

You need not select the Item tool from the Tool palette to move an item: With any tool selected, you can hold down the ⌘/CTRL key to temporarily activate the Item tool (✥) at any time. When you release the ⌘/CTRL key, the previously selected tool becomes active.

Although either the Item (✥) or Content tool (I☝) may be selected when you first import text or graphics, the Content tool must be selected to edit text and perform some modifications to pictures. When the Content tool is selected and the pointer is positioned in a text box, the pointer changes to an I-beam (I) for inserting and editing text; when positioned in a picture box, the pointer becomes the picture-mover pointer (☝).

To select text with the Content tool (I☝), position the I-beam beside a character inside an active text box and drag it to the end of the desired selection. Selected text is highlighted or reversed on the screen. Other methods of selecting a range of text are described in Chapter 4, "Word Processing."

The Rotation tool (↻) lets you rotate text boxes, picture boxes, lines, or active groups of boxes and lines, on a page. When this tool is selected, the pointer becomes a target symbol (⊕) at first, and an arrowhead (▸) indicates the direction of the rotation around the target point.

The Zoom tool (🔍) lets you change the scale at which you view the page. When this tool is selected, the pointer becomes a magnifying glass with a plus sign inside (⊕) for zooming in, or increasing the page-view percentage. By holding down the **Option/CTRL** key changes the tool to a magnifying glass with a minus sign inside (⊖) to zoom out, or decrease the page-view percentage.

Text and Picture Box Tools

On the default tool palette, the Text Box tool's pop-out menu contains seven tools for drawing boxes that will contain text. There are also seven Picture Box tools for drawing boxes of the same shapes that will contain graphics. The default tool palette arranges four Picture Box tools on the palette, with the three additional tools on a pop-out menu. Generally, the tool icon is the shape of the box that will be produced by drawing with that tool. Figure 1.7 shows each tool and the shapes they produce.

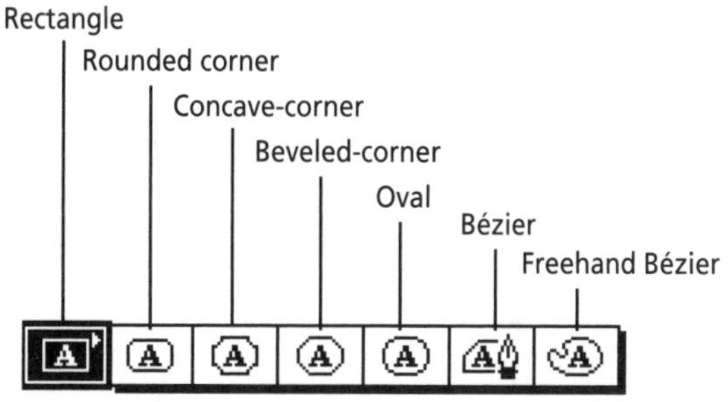

Figure 1.7 *The text box creation tools.*

When any of these tools is selected, the pointer becomes a crosshair (+), called the Item Creation pointer. Most tools create boxes by dragging the pointer on the page or pasteboard and releasing the mouse when the box is approximately the desired size. The Bézier tools are an exception. For more information on drawing Bézier shapes, see Chapter 6, "Graphics."

Line Tools

There are four tools for drawing lines (Figure 1.8). The Line tool creates straight lines at any angle, and the Orthogonal Line tool creates horizontal or vertical straight lines. The other two tools are used to create Bézier and freehand Bézier lines. As with the box tools, when a line tool is selected, the pointer becomes a crosshair (+). Straight lines are drawn by dragging the mouse and releasing when the line is approximately the desired length. For information on drawing Bézier lines, see Chapters 6, "Graphics."

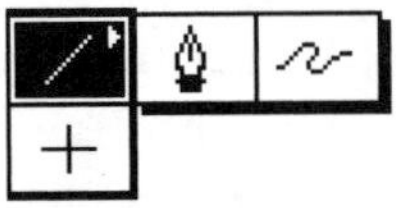

Figure 1.8 *The Line tools.*

Text-Path Tools

Like the Line tools, the four Text-Path tools (Figure 1.9) draw the same straight or Bézier lines but with an important difference: lines drawn with these tools can have text adjoined to them. This includes curved lines created with the Bézier tools, so that text can run along a curve, or even in a circle. For more information on working with text-paths, see Chapter 12, "Tips and Special Techniques."

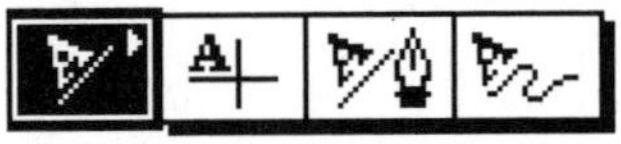

Figure 1.9 *The Text-Path tools.*

Linking Tools

The last two tools are called the Linking tool ( ) and the Unlinking tool ( ). Use these to direct the flow of text from one text box to another, as described in Chapter 3, "Expanding the Document."

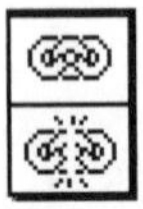

Figure 1.10 *The Linking tool (top) and Unlinking tool (bottom)*

The Measurements Palette

The Measurements palette (**View ➛ Show Measurements**) displays information about the currently active item on a page. The information on this interactive palette will change as you move, scale, or otherwise change an active item. You can also change the specifications of an item by making entries directly through the Measurements palette.

The Measurements palette provides a quick method for modifying many item and content attributes that can also be changed through menus and dialog boxes. The information can be changed in either area, but the Measurements palette is the fastest way to view or change values. This is a handy palette that we display and use all the time.

Like all other palettes, you can move the Measurements palette anywhere on the screen by dragging on its title bar, located on the left side of the palette. The contents of the palette will vary depending on the type of item selected, as shown in Figure 1.11.

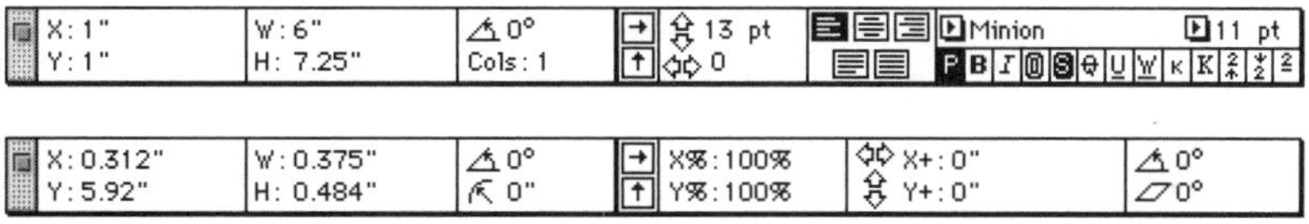

Figure 1.11 *Measurements palette when text box (top) and picture box (bottom) are active.*

When the Measurements palette is displayed, you can jump to its first field by pressing **⌘-Option-M/CTRL-ALT-M**, or you can activate any field by simply clicking on it. Once in this palette, as in dialog boxes, you can move through the fields by pressing the **Tab/CTRL-TAB** key, or press **Shift-Tab/SHIFT-CTRL-TAB** to tab in reverse order.

Make entries in the Measurements palette by editing the entry as text, using scrolling arrows to select values, or choosing from pop-up menus. To exit the palette and activate all changes, press **Return** or **Enter**, or click the mouse in the document window.

Changes made to the information on the left side of the palette (related to items, such as boxes and lines) are not reflected on the page until you exit the palette. Changes you make on the right side of the palette (related to the contents of active items) are implemented when you click on an icon in the Measurements palette or exit a field. You can exit the palette without implementing any changes by pressing **⌘-period/Esc**.

Entering Measurements

QuarkXPress offers unique flexibility in entering measurements. Regardless of the unit of measure that is currently displayed, you can enter a new value in inches, millimeters, centimeters, picas, points, or ciceros. To enter a measurement in units other than the current unit of measure, simply indicate the measurement system using the abbreviations listed in Table 1.1.

Table 1.1 *Measurement Units and their Abbreviations*

Units	Abbreviation	Example
Inches	"	1 "
Millimeters	mm	1 mm
Centimeters	cm	1 cm
Picas	p	1 p
		1p3 (one pica, three points)
Points	pt	1 pt
Ciceros	c	1 c
		1c3 (one cicero, three points)

TIP

You can enter most measurements in increments as fine as .001 inches, and you can enter font sizes from 2 to 720 points. You can also change an entry by adding or subtracting from the current value displayed in any field. For example, if the current measure is 4 inches, you can increase it by 1/4 inch by positioning the cursor after the 4 and typing **+.25**—you need not enter the unit of measure if it is the same as the current default measure. Similarly, you could increase the 4-inch measure by 2 picas and 3 points by typing **+2p3** after the 4. This comes in handy when you're trying to reposition or resize a box by a specific measure.

The Document Layout Palette

The Document Layout palette (**View ➛ Show Document Layout**) shows the master pages and document pages as icons (Figure 1.12). You can move the Document Layout palette around on the screen and resize it for a view of more page icons as your document grows.

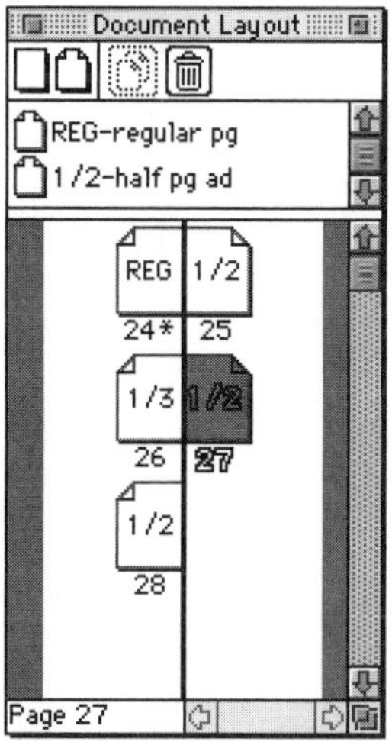

Figure 1.12 *The Document Layout palette.*

The icons at the top of this palette represent blank pages and master pages. If you have created more than one master page (up to 127 master pages per file are allowed), you can view the icons for various master pages either by clicking on the split bar and dragging it down, or by clicking on the arrows in the scroll bar adjacent to the master page icons. You will learn how to use these icons in Chapter 3, "Expanding the Document."

Document page icons are displayed in the lower area of the window. The line down the middle of the document page area indicates the binding edge of a facing-page document. The gray areas to the left and right of the document page icons represent a visual reminder of the 48-inch width, which is the maximum page width or spread width QuarkXPress allows. Each page icon shows the master that is applied to that page, with the page number shown underneath the icon. The active page is shown in outline type on the page icon in the palette.

You can double-click on a page icon in the Document Layout palette to display that page in the document window. The Document Layout palette can be used as an alternative to turning to pages by using various commands on the Page menu such as Previous, Next, or Go To. You can also delete pages by selecting the page icons and clicking the **Delete** icon (🗑) in the Document Layout palette.

The Style Sheets Palette

Style sheets provide a convenient way to automatically format text. The Style Sheets palette (**View ➛ Show Style Sheets**), shown in Figure 1.13, allows you to apply both Character and Paragraph style sheets to text easily. Use this palette as an alternative to applying styles via the Style ➛ Character Style Sheet or Style ➛ Paragraph Style Sheet commands.

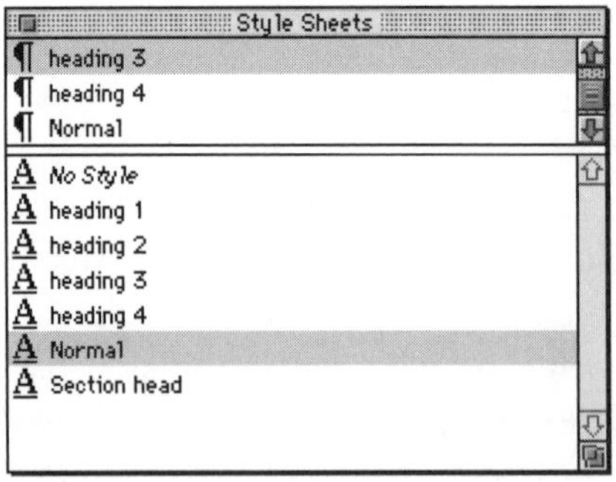

Figure 1.13 *The Style Sheets palette.*

The Style Sheets palette is not active unless the text I-beam pointer (I) has been clicked in a text box. The palette lists Character style sheets in the top of the palette, and Paragraph styles in the bottom half and may be resized to view long lists of style sheets. You can view a long list of character style sheets by either by clicking on the split bar and dragging it down, or by clicking on the arrows in the scroll bar adjacent to the character style sheets. To apply any style sheet, select the text you wish to format, then click on the appropriate style sheet name in the palette. You can learn more about how to use style sheets in Chapter 4, "Word Processing."

The Colors Palette

The Colors palette (**View ➛ Show Colors**) provides a convenient way of applying color to text, box backgrounds and frames, certain types of graphics, and lines. Using the Colors palette is the only way to apply a two-color blend to a box background. Figure 1.14 shows the Colors palette with the text box selected.

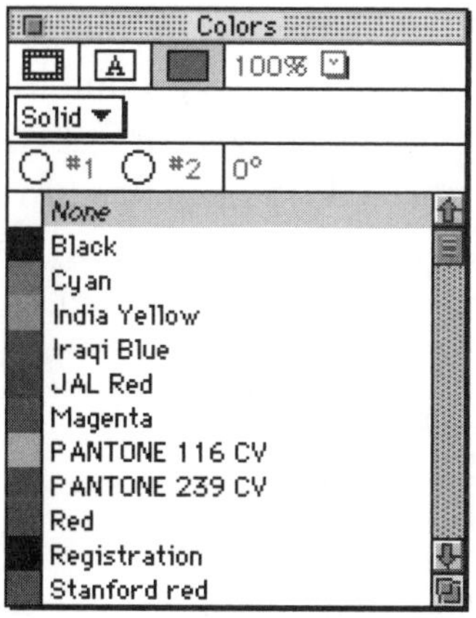

***Figure 1.14** The Colors palette when a text box is selected.*

To apply colors, choose one of the icons across the top of the palette, then choose a color and shade percentage. The icons across the top of the palette will change depending on what type of item is selected. If a text box is selected, for example, the icons across the top are, from left to right, for applying color to the text box frame, the text, or the text box background (Figure 1.13). An adjacent pop-up menu lets you assign a shade percentage, or you can type in any percentage. The palette lists all the colors created for the document under **Edit ➛ Colors.** The palette can be resized to view the color list, or you scroll up or down the list using the scroll arrows. For more information on using the Colors palette, see Chapter 7, "Color Basics."

The Trap Information Palette

The Trap Information palette (**View ➛ Show Trap Information**) allows you to specify the trapping relationship between adjacent colors on an item-by-item basis. Trapping between colors for an entire document is defined in the Edit Trap dialog box (**Edit ➛ Colors**), but those relationships may be changed on individual items using the Trap Information palette.

When a box is active, the Trap Information palette shows the trapping values for the color of the box background, the box contents and the box frame, including settings for gaps if a dashed frame is selected. If a line is selected, the palette shows the trapping specifications for the color of the line. Figure 1.15 shows how the palette looks when a framed text box is selected.

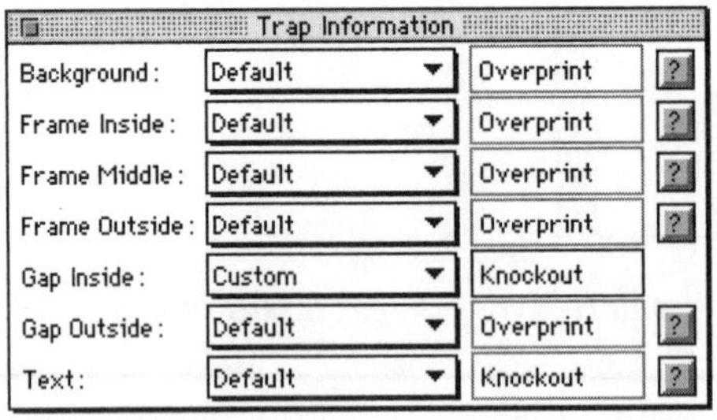

Figure 1.15 *The Trap Information palette when a framed text box is selected.*

Pop-up menus provide six different options for defining trapping relationships. See Chapter 13, "Printing Color Separations," for more information on trapping and preparing files for printing color separations.

The Lists Palette

The Lists palette (**View ➛ Show Lists**) displays lists created using the Edit ➛ Lists command. A list lets you designate a group of one or more style sheets that will duplicate all the text formatted in these style sheets to another location. One of the most common applications of this feature is to create a Table of Contents for a document or a book. Figure 1.16 shows the Lists palette.

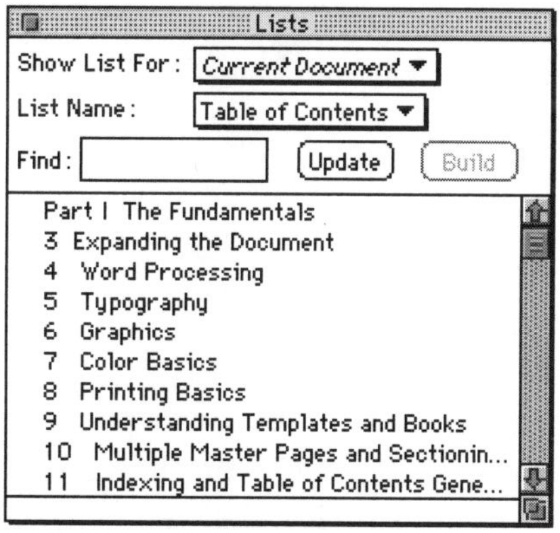

***Figure 1.16** The Lists palette.*

The Lists palette lets you choose any list from your current document or book that you wish to view. The lower portion of the palette displays all the text associated with the list you've designated. You can navigate in this text using the **Find** button in the palette; double-clicking text in the palette selects the text in your document. Once your list is in order, you can create a list by clicking on the **Build** button. For more information on working with lists, see Chapter 10, "Books, Lists and Indexing."

The Index Palette

The Index palette (**View ➛ Show Index**) is the primary tool used for building indexes for a document or book. You can use this palette (Figure 1.17) by selecting the word(s) in your document that you wish to index, then clicking the palette's **Add** button.

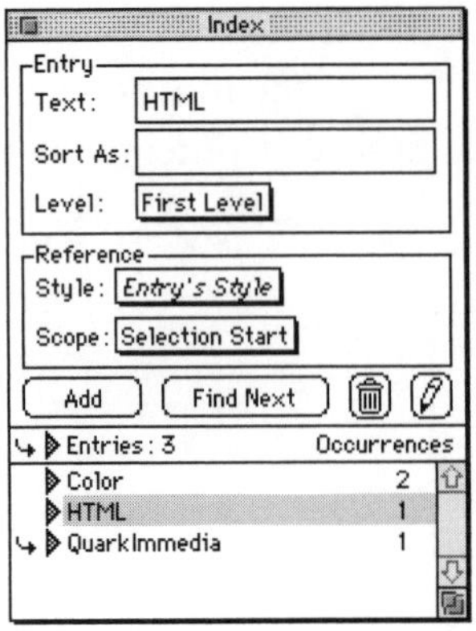

Figure 1.17 *The Index palette.*

As each word is added, it appears in the lower part of the palette, along with the number of occurrences of that entry. The page number on which the entry appears is displayed below the entry in the scroll list. To view the page number, click the triangle to the left of the entry. Once the Index palette contains all the words you wish to include, you can build the Index by choosing the **Utilities ➛ Build Index** command. For more information on Indexing, see Chapter 10, "Books, Lists and Indexing."

Examining QuarkXPress Menus

The menus in QuarkXPress have a logical organization to them. Understanding the general use of each menu can help you remember where to find commands as you are learning the program.

The File Menu

The File menu (Figure 1.18) includes commands that act on an entire file or document. These include commands to open, save, or print a file. QuarkXPress adds a Revert to Saved command that lets you cancel any changes you made to the document since you last saved it, by opening the last version that was saved to disk.

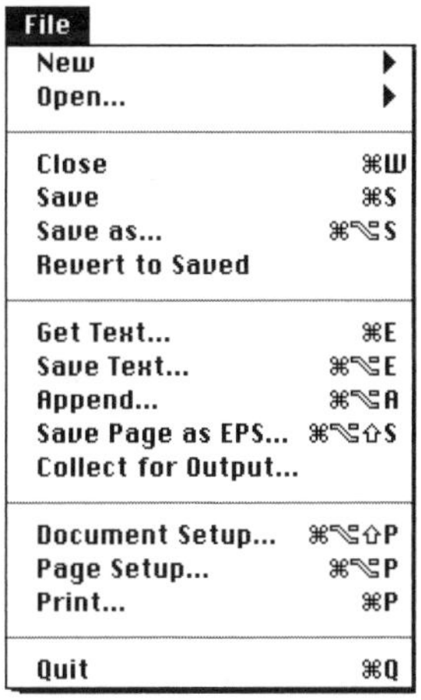

Figure 1.18 *The File menu.*

This menu also contains commands that relate to external file functions, such as Get Text or Get Picture files to import into a QuarkXPress text or picture box; Save Text from a QuarkXPress document to a text or word-processing file format; Save Page as EPS, which saves a QuarkXPress page as an EPS file; and Collect for Output, which collects your QuarkXPress document and all linked picture files into one folder for easy printing.

The Edit Menu

The Edit menu, like the File menu, includes editing commands that are commonly found in many programs, including Cut, Copy, and Paste. In addition, the Edit menu (Figure 1.19) contains commands to edit QuarkXPress elements—style sheets, colors, H&Js, lists, dashes and stripes, and print styles. Editing any of these items adds to the various lists containing them. For example, if you wanted to define a new style sheet for your document, you'd use the **Edit ➛ Style Sheets** command and the new style sheet would appear in the document's style sheet list.

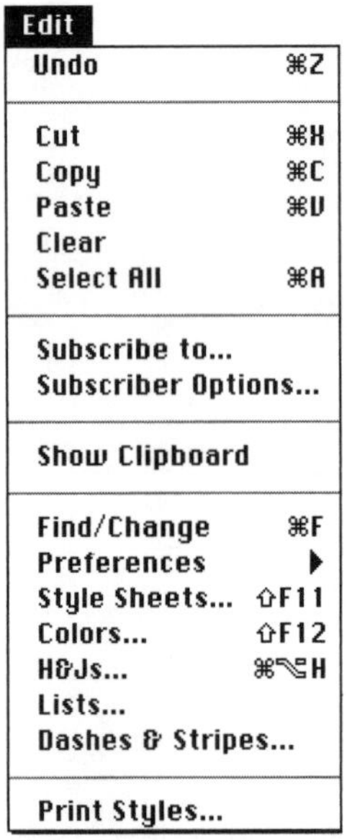

Figure 1.19 *The Edit menu.*

The Style Menu

The Style menu contains commands for changing the appearance of lines drawn in QuarkXPress, and the contents of a text or picture box (as opposed to the box itself). The commands on this dynamic menu change, depending on what type of QuarkXPress item you have selected (see Figure 1.20).

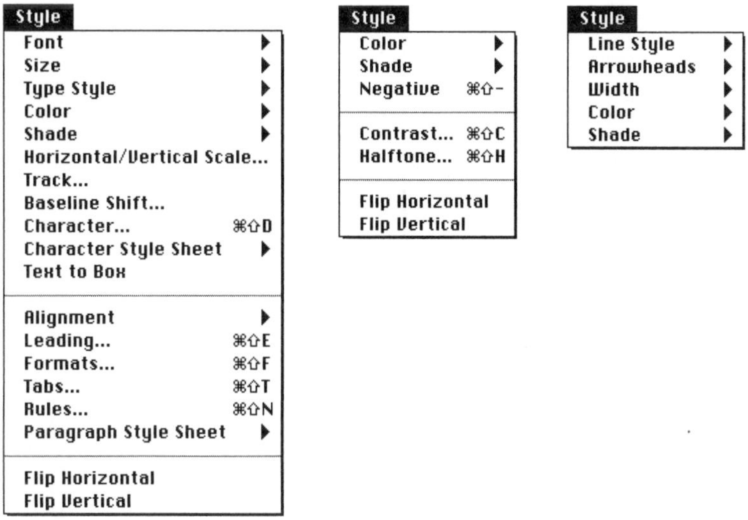

Figure 1.20 *Style menu when text box (left), picture box with an image (center), and line (right) are active and the Content tool is selected.*

When text is selected, the Style menu includes commands for all character and paragraph formatting, including tabs and rules. For pictures, the Style menu lets you apply color and contrast to certain types of graphics. When a line is selected, the Style menu lets you change the color, width, style and arrowhead endpoint styles of lines.

The Item Menu

The Item menu (Figure 1.21) contains commands that affect QuarkXPress items (as opposed to the *contents* of box items). Use the commands on this menu to change the size and shape of items, apply a frame to box items, or adjust the clipping or runaround paths on an item.

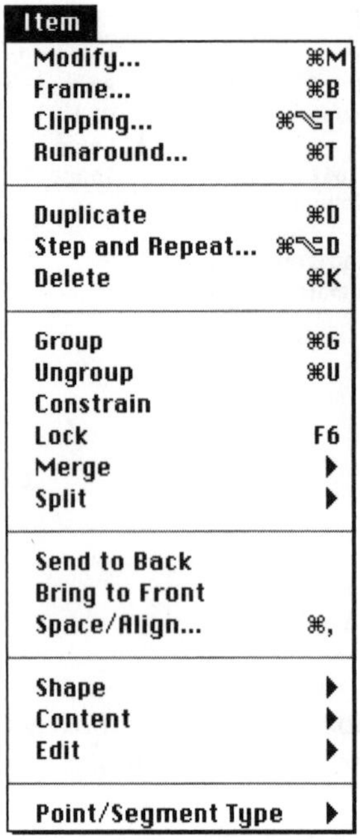

Figure 1.21 *The Item menu.*

The Item menu also includes commands for item-related functions, such as duplicating items, grouping or locking items, and moving an item to a different layer. The Merge and Split commands, for joining and splitting items, are found on this menu, along with commands for changing the shape or content of an item.

The Page Menu

The Page menu (Figure 1.22) handles page-related activities. This includes commands for inserting or deleting pages, and for turning to different pages.

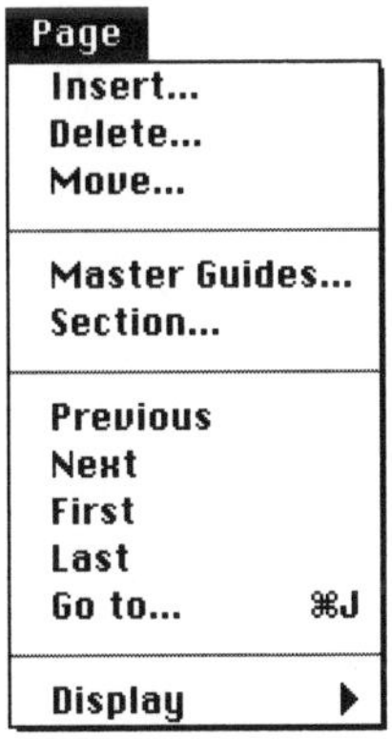

Figure 1.22 *The Page menu.*

The Page menu also contains the Section command, which is useful for changing the pagination within a document (such as numbering a preface with lowercase Roman numerals, then numbering regular book pages with Arabic numerals). When master pages are displayed, the Page menu contains the Master Guides command that help you change the margin and ruler guides on master pages and all the document pages using that master.

The View Menu

The View menu (Figure 1.23) contains commands that affect the view of a document in a window. This includes commands that change the zoom percentage at which a page is viewed, and commands for displaying or hiding guides, the baseline grid and invisible characters (characters that show spaces, tabs, paragraph returns and other nonprinting characters).

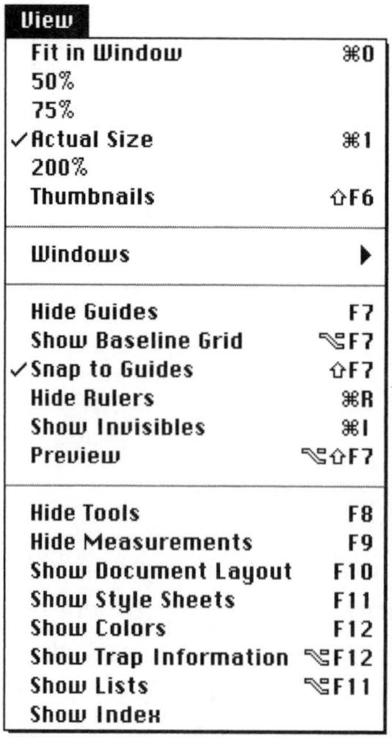

Figure 1.23 *The View Menu.*

The View menu also lets you display or hide any of QuarkXPress's eight palettes. None of these commands affects how the document looks when it is printed.

The Utilities Menu

The Utilities menu of Figure 1.24 includes commands for some wonderful extra things you can do with QuarkXPress. This includes some text-related functions, such as spell checking and building spell-checking dictionaries; and checking how QuarkXPress will hyphenate a word and building hyphenation exceptions.

Figure 1.24 *The Utilities menu.*

The Usage command lets you check all the fonts and pictures in your document, and change them if necessary. The XTensions Manager and PPD Manager let you control which XTensions and PPD (printer description) files, respectively, load with QuarkXPress. The Utilities menu also includes commands for building an index and editing font, tracking, and kerning values.

Summary

We told you we'd stick to the basics in this chapter! We hope you now have a working knowledge of "Quark-ese," and are well on your way to fluency. By reading through this chapter, and with a little hands-on experience with QuarkXPress, you should be ready to make the most of the rest of the book.

2 CREATING ONE PAGE

Let's take a closer look at the basic building blocks of QuarkXPress by analyzing the process of designing a one-page document. We're going to focus on the individual items used in building a QuarkXPress page, including text and picture boxes, lines, and text-paths. If you're relatively new to QuarkXPress, you may find it useful to read through each section of this chapter.

If you're a more experienced QuarkXPress user, you may just want to skim this chapter and look for tips, identified by the icon in the margins.

A big part of working with QuarkXPress, of course, involves dealing with multiple pages and longer documents, and we'll cover that in the next chapter, "Expanding the Document."

Setting Up a New Document

There are a couple of different ways you can set up a new QuarkXPress document. You can open up a brand new document, or you can open an existing document and change it. You'll probably find that you do both, depending on the circumstance.

Starting from Scratch

To create a new QuarkXPress document, select the **File ➛ New ➛ Document** (⌘-N/CTRL-N) command; the New Document dialog box will be displayed. This dialog box is where you'll specify the most basic characteristics of your document, including:

- the page size and orientation, and whether or not there will be facing page spreads;
- where margin and column guides are placed, along with specification of gutter width;
- and whether or not your document will use an Automatic Text box.

These entries are applied automatically to the first document page and the first master page of the document. Remember, every QuarkXPress document has at least one master page, whether you choose to use it or not!

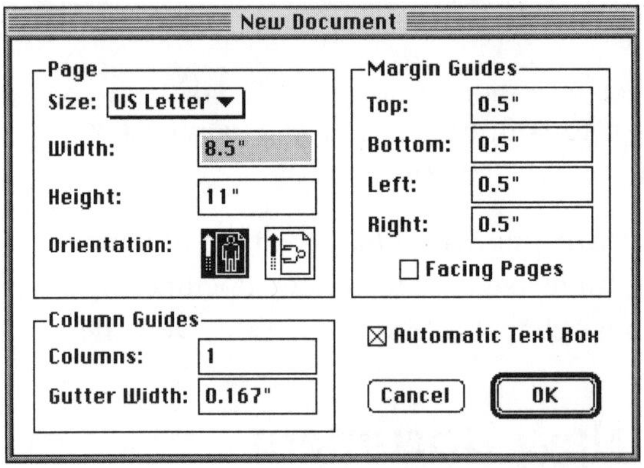

Figure 2.1 *The New Document dialog box determines the underlying characteristics of your page.*

Almost all of the settings you make in the New Document dialog box can be changed using different commands after you've begun to work on your document. But it's always easier to get it right from the start, isn't it?

QuarkXPress "remembers" the previous settings in the New Document dialog box, and when you create a new document, the settings will be those from the last new document you created. This is a great feature if you always create documents with the same specifications, but if you don't, you'll need to change the settings each time. It's easy to forget to change these settings, and suddenly have a letter-sized page on the screen when you really need tabloid size, for example. If all the settings are wrong, it may be easier to simply close the document and start over. Or, you may opt to change the settings from within the program, one by one—you cannot change all the settings using one command from within the document, and need to use a variety of commands. Changing the settings found in the New Document dialog box from within the document is discussed in the next sections.

Page Settings

Page settings determine the size and orientation of your document page. QuarkXPress offers five standard page sizes on a pop-up menu, or you can enter any custom size. Standard sizes include US Letter and US Legal, (commonly used American paper sizes); A4 Letter and B5 Letter (usually specified in millimeters) standard paper sizes in other countries; and tabloid, which is a small newspaper size.

You can see the five standard page measurements by clicking on each one and viewing the width and height measurements associated with each (Table 2.1):

Table 2.1 *Standard Page Measurments*

Setting	Dimensions
US Letter	8.5 × 11 inches
US Legal	8.5 × 14 inches
A4	210 × 297 millimeters (8.268 × 11.693 inches)
B5	176 × 250 millimeters (6.929 × 9.843 inches)
Tabloid	11 × 17 inches

Custom size can include any range from 1 inch by 1 inch up to 48 inches by 48 inches for a single-sided document (Figure 2.2). If Facing Pages is selected, the maximum page size is 24 inches by 48 inches (the total maximum is 48 inches, so if there are two pages, you have to divide 48 inches in half).

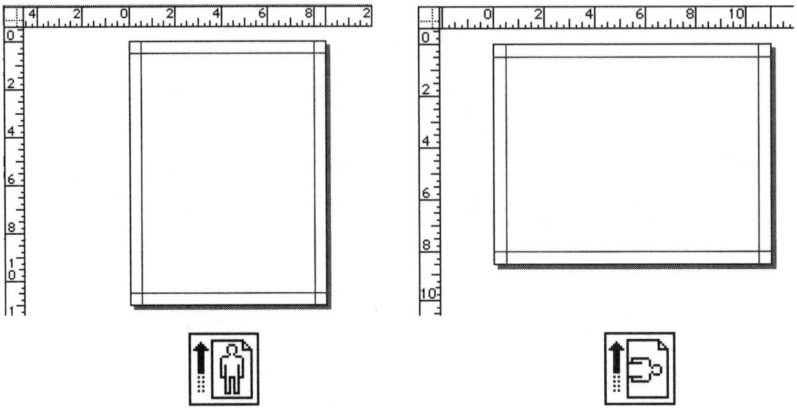

Figure 2.2 *Page orientation icons and their effects.*

The icons underneath the Width and Height entries indicate the orientation of a page in relation to the paper or other media onto which it will be printed. The icon on the left is for an upright, "tall," or "portrait" orientation; the icon on the right orients your page to a sideways, or "landscape," orientation.

TIP

The page-size measurement is always displayed in inches in the New Document dialog box, but you can enter values in any unit of measure, as long as you use the correct syntax (see the Table 1.1 for QuarkXPress measurement syntax). And, as with other measurement entries in QuarkXPress, you can change a page size value by typing in an added or subtracted value from the current setting, then pressing **Tab** or **Return.**

Keep in mind that the *page* size you specify in the New Document dialog box is not necessarily the size of the *paper* that you will be feeding into a laser printer or imagesetter. The page size determines the "trim" size of the page; i.e., its final publication size after going through an offset press and being trimmed to the correct size by the printer. This is the size the page will display onscreen, in the document window, and defines where trim marks, registration marks, and other marks will print when Registration is specified in the Document tab of the Print dialog box.

You may specify a page size smaller than the sheets of paper you print on, such as a business card, so it will display in the right size on-screen when you work on the design. And you can use the Registration Marks option in the Print command's dialog box to print crop marks that indicate where the pages will be trimmed and registration marks used in aligning color separations (Figure 2.3). You may proof the business card, however, on 8 1/2 × 11–inch laser paper. Or, you may specify a Tabloid size page, and print the large page out in two pieces on 8.5 × 11-inch sheets of paper, using the Tiling option of the Print command (see Chapter 8, "Printing Basics").

***Figure 2.3** Pages can be printed with crop marks and registration marks.*

TIP

If you decide to change the page size after you have started working on a document, use the **File ➝ Document Setup** command (Figure 2.4). You can use this command to change page size and orientation, and you can also add facing pages to a single-page layout.

Figure 2.4 *The Document Setup dialog box (**File → Document Setup**) lets you change page size after you have started working on your document.*

There a few things to think about if you change these settings after you have begun to work on your document. If you increase the page size, all items will retain their positions relative to the top left corner—that is, you will have wider white areas to the right and bottom edges of the page. If you decrease the page size to the point where an item no longer fits on the page, the item will extend onto the pasteboard (Figure 2.5).

Figure 2.5 *Items are forced onto the pasteboard when page size is decreased.*

The automatic text box, described later in this chapter, also changes size when you change the page width and height. Therefore, changing the page size will cause the text to reflow on all pages that use an automatic text box.

Margin Guide Settings

Margin guides create visible, but nonprinting guide lines on each edge of your page. The Margin Guide measurements entered in the New Document dialog box specify the distance from the edge of the page to where the guide will appear. Margin guides may or may not contain an automatic text box within; it depends on whether or not you check that option in the New Document dialog box.

Margin guides serve as guides only and do not affect the position of text except through their effect on the automatic text box, since margins determine the distance from the edges of the automatic text box to the edges of the page. You normally position running headers and footers (page numbers, for example) outside these margins, and outside the automatic text box. If you want no margin guides to appear, set all measurements to zero.

On a black-and-white monitor margin guides, like column guides, are represented as thin black lines; on a color monitor they display in the default color, blue, unless you change their color in the Display tab of the Application Preferences dialog box (**Edit ➛ Preferences ➛ Application**).

Like the page size, the margin guide values entered in the New Document dialog box apply to all pages of a document and to the default master page for the document. This is true, in fact, for all the settings in this dialog box.

TIP

If you wish to change the margin guides once you've started working on a document, it's a little trickier to figure out than changing the overall page size. The only way to change margin guides from within a document is to first view a master page (**Page ➛ Display ➛ Master**), then change the margins for individual master pages by selecting **Page ➛ Master Guides** and changing the measurements in the Master Guides dialog box.

Facing Pages

The Facing Pages option lets you create and view pages that will face each other in double-sided printing. This option provides you with both a left- and right-hand master page, as opposed to a single master page that is displayed when this option if not checked. Figure 2.6 illustrates both choices.

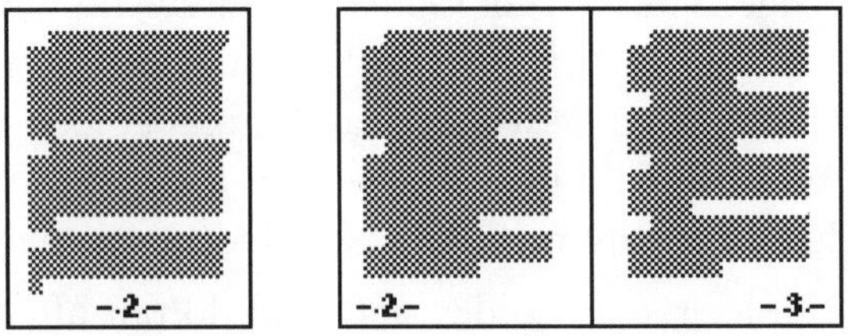

Figure 2.6 *Single-sided (left) versus facing-page (right) documents.*

If you create a new document as a single-sided document, the first master page will be a single-sided master and will remain so, even if you later change to Facing Pages through the **File ➛ Document Setup** command. If you do make a change to Facing Pages, however, you will be able to create single-sided *or* facing-page masters later.

The Facing Page option lets you specify inside and outside margins instead of left and right margins shown on a single-sided page. The Inside Margin measure applies to the right margin of left pages and the left margin of right pages. The inside margin is often set wider than the outside margin, to accommodate binding.

Single-sided and facing-page documents both offer the option of creating spreads—adjacent pages that will face each other across a fold in the final publication (Figure 2.7). Two facing pages are also a spread, separated by a bound edge rather than by a fold. Any QuarkXPress item—a text or picture box, a line, or a text-path—can run across pages in a spread.

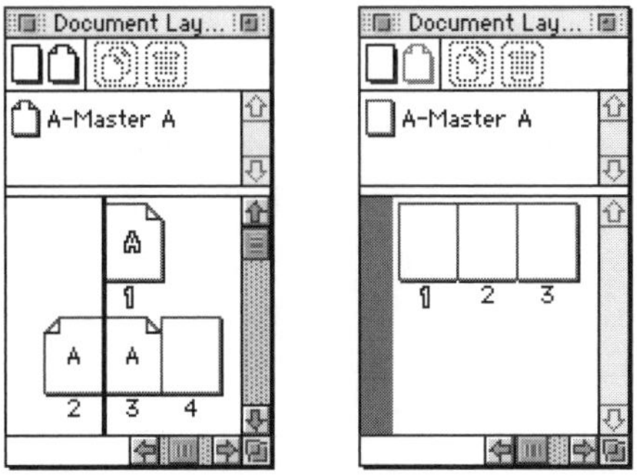

Figure 2.7 *Document Layout palette shows a facing-page document with a fold-out page spread (left) and a single-sided, three-fold brochure set up as a three-page spread (right).*

You can use the **File ➛ Document Setup** command to turn Facing Pages on or off, regardless of the option chosen in the New Document dialog box. However, to turn Facing Pages off once a document is set up, you must first delete all facing-page masters.

Column Guide Settings

Column guides are vertical guides that are displayed inside the margin guides. The default setting is 1 column. Like other entries, the number of columns you specify in the New Document dialog box applies to all pages of the document, unless you change the settings on individual master pages using the **Page ➛ Master Guides** command.

The number of columns you set in the New Document dialog box will apply to the first master page and also to the automatic text box, if you have specified that option. Column guides in an automatic text box define the width of text that is typed, imported, or pasted into the box.

QuarkXPress's default gutter width, the space between columns, is equal to 1 pica, or 0.167 inches. When you enter the number of columns and the amount of space you want between each column, QuarkXPress divides the page into equal columns between margins (Figure 2.8). You cannot, unfortunately, set the gutter to zero, which would be nice for making an underlying page grid; you must have a gutter of at least 3 points.

QuarkXPress imposes a maximum limit of 30 columns per box; the gutter width can be set from a minimum of 3 points up to a maximum of 288 points, or 4 inches. Therefore, the maximum number of columns allowed on a particular page is limited by the distance between the margins of the page and the space between the columns, and not just the 30-column maximum. In practice, you should rarely exceed this limit.

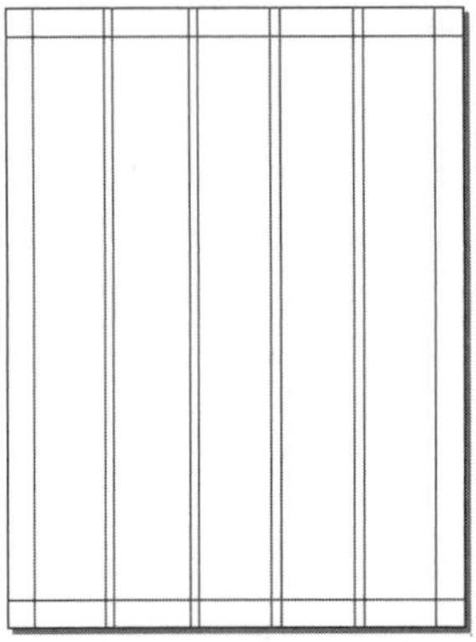

Figure 2.8 *QuarkXPress divides a page into columns of equal width, but always includes a gutter of at least 3 points.*

Automatic Text Box

The Automatic Text box is one that links text automatically from page to page. If Automatic Text Box is checked in the New Document dialog box, QuarkXPress will automatically create a text box with margins and columns as specified. This text box will appear on the first master page and on the first page of a new document. When you type or import text, pages will be added automatically as needed, until the entire text file is flowed in.

When text in the Automatic Text Box causes new pages to be added, the default setting is that pages will be added, one right after the other, starting from the page where you began to type or import the text. This is determined by the default Auto Page

Insertion preference setting, found in the General tab of the Document Preferences dialog box (**Edit ➛ Preferences ➛ Document**), which is set to End of Story. For more information on setting these preferences, see Chapter 3, "Expanding the Document."

If Automatic Text Box is not checked in the New Document dialog box, margin and column guides will be displayed on the pages, but no text box will be created. An automatic text box can be added to your document later using techniques described in Chapter 9, "Master Pages and Sectioning."

Using Other Documents

Many of us are involved in working with documents that are published on a regular basis, such as a magazine, or are otherwise similar in their basic characteristics in some way. If you are creating similar documents, it just doesn't make sense to start from scratch each time. It's best to borrow from another document, or a template, a special kind of QuarkXPress document that lets you reuse various elements in your document.

A template differs from a document in that you cannot save over it, and thus it will always be the same when you use it as a starting point for your document. When you use the Save command, a template always displays the Save As dialog box without a document name, so you cannot accidentally overwrite the original. Templates are explained in detail in Chapter 9, "Master Pages and Sectioning."

You can open any document or template by using the **File ➛ Open** (**⌘-O/CTRL-O**) command. If you use **File ➛ Open,** a dialog box is displayed that shows the list of available QuarkXPress files. When you click once on a document name to select it, the dialog box will display whether it is a document or a template file (Figure 2.9), along with the version number of QuarkXPress in which the document was created in and the latest version number in which it was saved. If the document or template has been saved in QuarkXPress version 3.2 or later with Include Preview checked On, a small thumbnail preview of the first page will display.

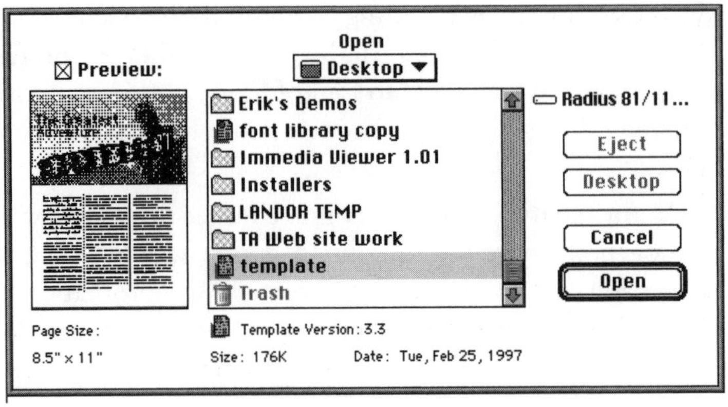

Figure 2.9 *Preview of a template in the Open dialog box.*

To open a file, click on the file name to highlight it, and then click on the **Open** button. You can also simply double-click on the file name of the document or template you want to open.

When you open a document or a template, QuarkXPress displays the first page of the document in the view scale in which the document was last saved. Once a document is open, you can modify it using all of the techniques described here and in subsequent chapters.

Viewing Pages on the Screen

The document window and the screen of your computer represent your digital drawing board, and QuarkXPress provides you with the means to work with this on-screen drawing board much as you might in the analog world, on a traditional paste-up board. For example, you can zoom into a page and look at items in great detail; lay down nonprinting guides and layout guides; and display palettes of tools as you need them. The following sections discuss how to use these production aids.

Changing the Document View Percentage

When you create a new QuarkXPress document, the page opens in 100% view, usually with only part of the page, the upper left corner, displayed on your screen. When you open an existing QuarkXPress document, it will open in the percentage view in which it was last saved. You can change your view of the page on the screen in several ways, and being able to change views quickly will make you more efficient working with QuarkXPress.

Using the View Menu

Using the View menu is often the least efficient way to change the view percentage, but it's still good to be familiar with the zoom options available on this menu. The first six commands in the View menu change the size of your view of the page—enlarging or reducing your view in fixed increments. You'll know which one is selected because you'll see a check mark beside the current percentage view.

The two commands from this menu that you'll find yourself using most often are Fit in Window (⌘-0/CTRL-0—zero, not the letter O) and Actual Size (⌘-1/CTRL-1). Notice they both have their keyboard combination shortcuts shown on the menu.

The percentage view you work in will change often, depending on your need at the moment. Fit in Window (⌘-0/CTRL-0) is a good view for checking and changing the position of objects on the page and for viewing facing pages or multiple-page spreads. Actual Size (⌘-1/CTRL-1) is the normal view for editing text and graphics. And, of course, the larger percentage views are good for working on fine details in your document, whether text or graphics. The Thumbnails view lets you see miniatures of all pages at once, but you cannot edit individual items on a page. You can, however, rearrange pages in Thumbnails view, as shown in Figure 2.10.

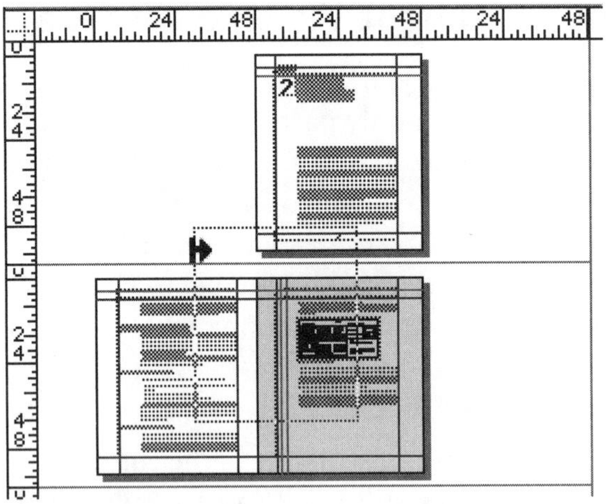

Figure 2.10 *Use Thumbnails view to rearrange pages.*

Using the View Percent Field

The percentage of the view scale at any given time is shown in the lower left corner of the document window. This field, called the View Percent field, is interactive: it not only shows what view you are currently in, but you can also type in the view percentage you wish to display (see Figure 2.11).

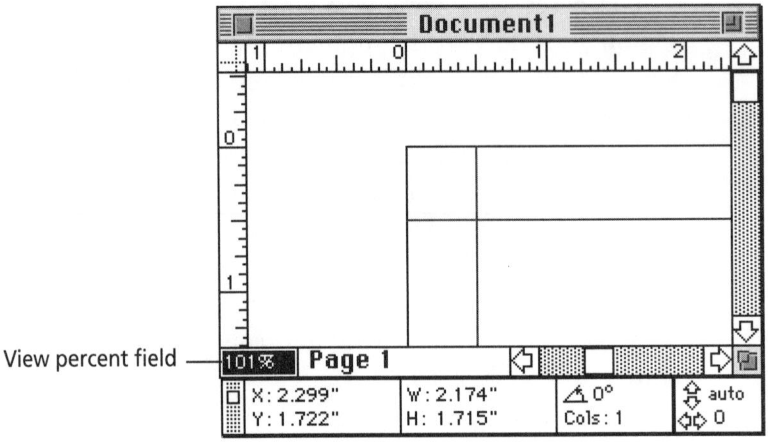

Figure 2.11 *You can type directly in the View Percent field.*

TIP

To quickly highlight the zoom percentage field, press **Control-V/CTRL-ALT-V,** and enter the scale view you prefer, from 10% to 800%. Type in **T** for Thumbnails view. Pressing **Return** or clicking in the document window causes the display to change to the scale indicated. At times, this method will be the fastest and most useful way to change the view of a page.

TIP

If you want to see many pages of your document at once, type in a small percentage, such as 15%. The display is similar to that shown the in Thumbnails view, but you can edit items when in this view, allowing you to easily move items from one page to another, for example. (Remember, you cannot edit items directly in Thumbnails view.)

Using the Zoom Tool

By far the quickest way to change the size of your view of the page is with the Zoom tool (🔍). With one click, you can zoom in to the part of the page you want to see in detail.

TIP

The most efficient way to use the Zoom tool (🔍) is to switch to it at any time by holding down the **Control/CTRL-SPACEBAR** key; the pointer will change to the Zoom tool pointer (🔍+) and you can click (right mouse button on Windows system) to enlarge the view. Press **Control-Option/CTRL-ALT-SPACEBAR** and click to reduce the view.

Alternatively, of course, you can choose the **Zoom** tool from the Tool palette, position the pointer over the portion of the page you want to enlarge, and click. To reduce the scale, hold down the **Option**/ALT key as you click the pointer on the page. The Zoom tool pointer shows a plus sign (🔍+) when you are enlarging, a minus sign (🔍−) when you are reducing, and is empty (🔍) when you are already at the maximum enlargement or minimum reduction. The current view percentage is displayed in the lower-left corner of the document window. The Zoom tool does not operate in Thumbnails view.

> **TIP** You can also drag the Zoom (🔍) tool to outline a rectangular area on a page; the area you select will enlarge to fill the screen. If you select a very small area on the screen, for example, the view percentage will be high.

The View Scale settings in the **Edit ➛ Preferences ➛ Tools** dialog box determine the range and increment of the view changes when you click with the Zoom tool selected. See Chapter 3, "Expanding the Document," for information on setting tool preferences.

Ruler Guides

In addition to margin and column guides, QuarkXPress provides ruler guides—non-printing guides that you "pull" from the horizontal or vertical ruler—that allow you to align items at any location on the document page or pasteboard. Once you position a ruler guide, you can use it to precisely align objects.

Ruler guides are best used when View ➛ Snap to Guides is checked on. When Snap to Guides is on, an item or an item creation pointer (+) snaps to a guide when you drag it within the Snap Distance.

The Snap Distance is specified in pixels, in the General tab of the Document Preferences dialog box (**Edit ➛ Preferences ➛ Document**). For more information on this and other Preferences that affect ruler guides—including specification of whether guides display on top of items or behind them—see the section on setting Preferences in Chapter 3, "Expanding the Document."

To position a ruler guide:

1. Place your mouse over the horizontal or vertical ruler and click.
2. When the ‡ pointer (from the horizontal ruler) or ⇹ pointer (from the vertical ruler) is displayed, drag the ruler guide into position on the page or pasteboard.

> **TIP** If you release a ruler guide over the pasteboard, the guide will extend across the pasteboard and all the pages in the spread; if you release a ruler guide over a page, it will only extend across that page.

If you wish to reposition a guide, simply click on the guide; when the ‡ or ↔ pointer appears, move it to a new position. As you click and drag on the ruler guide, the position of the guide is displayed in the Measurements palette.

If you wish to remove a ruler guide, drag it off the page. You can remove all the guides from a spread at once. To remove all the horizontal or vertical guides from the pasteboard, make sure the pasteboard is displayed in the upper left corner of the document window, then Option/ALT click on the horizontal or vertical ruler. To remove the all the ruler guides from a page in a spread, display the page so some part of it is in the upper left corner of the document window, then Option/ALT click on the horizontal or vertical ruler.

Ruler guides positioned on a master page will appear on all pages to which that master is applied. However, guides positioned on the master page pasteboard (which extend across all pages in the spread on the master page), unfortunately, will not display on the document pages to which that master is applied.

TIP

You can specify that a ruler guide display only at a specific zoom magnification. Hold down the **Shift** key while you drag the ruler guide into position, and the ruler guide will only display at the current zoom percentage or higher.

For example, with your document displayed at 400%, drag a ruler guide while holding the Shift key; the guide will display only at 400% or higher. When you zoom out to a view less than 400%, the guides disappear. This means you can have many guides available to fine tune your work, but you can view it without the guides in the way when you need to "step back" and admire your work!

Working with Nonprinting Elements

The next group of commands on the Page menu lets you control the snap-to effect of guides and display or hide different nonprinting elements when viewing a QuarkXPress document on-screen. (See Figure 2.12.) These elements include guides (margin guides, column guides, and ruler guides), the baseline grid, rulers, and invisible characters, such as carriage returns and tabs.

Hide Guides	F7
Show Baseline Grid	⌥F7
✓Snap to Guides	⇧F7
Hide Rulers	⌘R
Show Invisibles	⌘I

Figure 2.12 *View menu commands that show or hide nonprinting elements on a page.*

These commands are toggle commands that change in the menu when selected. In other words, if the guides are currently displayed, the command in the menu is Hide Guides. When you choose Hide Guides, for example, the command in the menu changes to Show Guides; the same is true for the other commands in this section of the View menu.

Show Guides displays or hides all margin, column, and ruler guides. When guides are hidden, only the handles on selected items will appear. To view the page as it will appear when printed, deselect all items by clicking in the margin of the page outside all items. Guides can have a snap-to effect that help you position items.

The **Show Baseline Grid** command displays a baseline grid as horizontal lines across the page. The increments of the baseline grid can be defined under the Paragraph tab of the Document Preferences dialog box (**Edit ➝ Preferences ➝ Document**). Text can then be forced to lock to this grid, by clicking the check box in the Paragraph Attributes dialog box. These options are discussed in more detail in Chapter 5, "Typography."

Use the **Show Rulers** command to display rulers that appear on the left side and top of the document window. The preset default is that rulers are displayed. The increments of the rulers can be defined by selecting units in the General tab of the Document Preferences dialog box (**Edit ➝ Preferences ➝ Document**), which is discussed in more detail in Chapter 3, "Expanding the Document."

Invisibles are all of the nonprinting characters, such as spaces, carriage returns, and tabs that can be typed as part of text, using the keyboard. **Show Invisibles** causes these characters to display. You may find it useful to display these characters, especially when typing directly in QuarkXPress, because it makes it easier to see exactly what you are typing. For example, accidentally typing in a space after a tab character will cause your text to be misaligned; it is difficult to see the extra space unless invisible characters are displayed. The default setting is that invisible characters are not displayed. All of QuarkXPress's invisible characters are discussed in detail in Chapter 4, "Word Processing."

Displaying Palettes

As we mentioned in the previous chapter, QuarkXPress offers several palettes that include tools and provide various aids to efficient production. Like the Show/Hide Guides commands, the commands to show or hide palettes act as a toggle switch. For example, when the Tool palette is already visible, the command on the menu reads Hide Tools. If the Tool palette is not visible on the screen, the command reads Show Tools.

The menu commands are most efficiently used only to show the palettes when they are not displayed, because you can easily close these palettes by clicking in the **Close** box on the title bar for each palette. Details on how to use each palette are covered in other chapters.

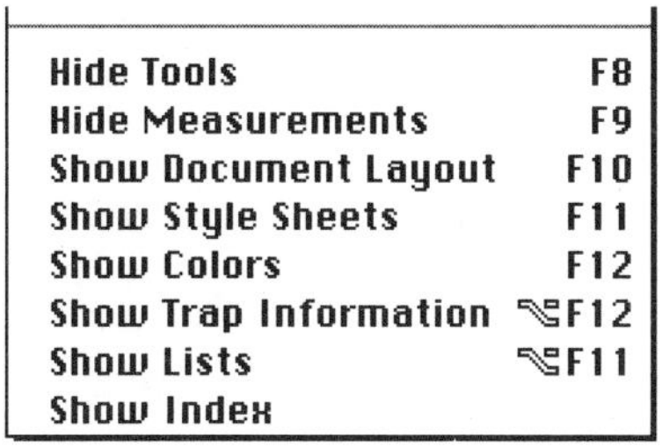

Figure 2.13 *Commands for displaying or hiding QuarkXPress palettes.*

When you first install QuarkXPress, the Tool and Measurements palettes are displayed along with the Index palette, if the Index Xtension has been loaded. The Tool and Measurements palettes are probably the two palettes most people are likely to use most often. Palettes remain displayed or hidden from the last time you used QuarkXPress, so as you use the program, the palettes *you* use most often will usually be displayed.

Creating and Modifying QuarkXPress Items

QuarkXPress *items*—text boxes, picture boxes, and lines—are the basic building blocks of any document. Before you can add text or a graphic to a page, for example, you must create a box to contain it. In the following sections, we'll show you how to work with QuarkXPress's items, from the basics of drawing items, to moving and re-sizing them, to changing their color and shape.

Our goal is in this section is that you have a clear understanding of how to work with different items by understanding the ways in which all items work in common. We'll try to draw on similarities among different items as much as possible.

More so than in previous versions, with QuarkXPress 4.0, the distinction between items (such as text versus picture boxes, for example) becomes somewhat less important, since for the first time, you can change the *content* of a box. Remember, too, that you can change the shape of a box to any other box shape. The addition of Bézier tools, which are primarily for drawing curves, gives the ability to make items of any shape, including those containing curves.

Creating Items

There are several different ways to distinguish different types of QuarkXPress items. Generally, there are boxes versus lines (including a new type of line item, text-paths), vector versus Bézier shapes, or text versus picture boxes. In this section we'll look less at the usual distinction made between text versus picture boxes, and more at the way items in general are created and modified.

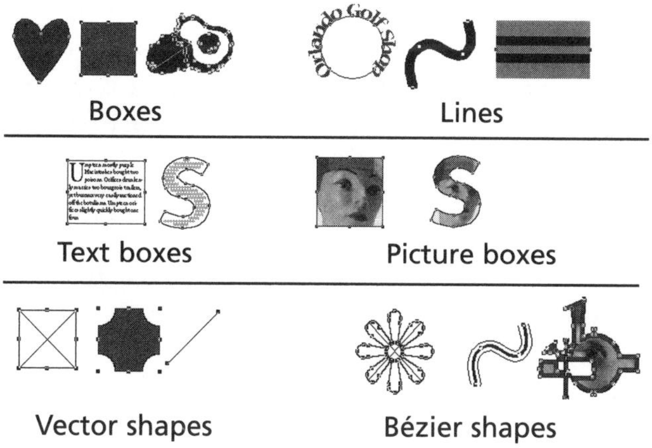

Figure 2.14 *There are different ways to categorize QuarkXPress items: boxes vs. lines, text vs. picture, or vector shape vs. Bézier shape.*

In previous versions of QuarkXPress, most tools were vector-based—good for drawing objects like rectangles, circles, or straight lines. The polygon tool was something of an exception to this, but with version 4.0, QuarkXPress adds the ability to draw curved shapes of any kind using Bézier tools.

Creating Vector Items

We really hate to use the word *vector* to describe these tools, but it's technically the most accurate term. (Quark's documentation sometimes uses the word *ordinary* for these types of graphics.) It means they are fixed shapes or objects, mostly made of straight lines, with no free-form curved lines. These tools include all tools except the Bézier tools. For a look at vector tool shapes, see Figure 2.15.

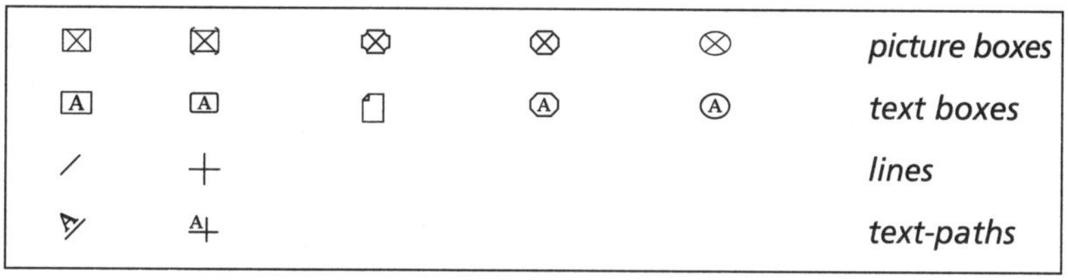

Figure 2.15 *All vector tool shapes are drawn using the same basic technique.*

To create a box with any of these tools, select the tool and position the Item Creation pointer (+) on the page. As you drag the pointer on the page, you create a box. The size of a box is displayed in the Measurements palette as you draw, if that palette is open.

TIP: Hold down the **Shift** key as you draw in order to constrain boxes to square shapes (for rectangular boxes) or circles (for oval boxes). When you release the mouse button the box is active, as indicated by its dark border and eight black "handles" (Figure 2.16).

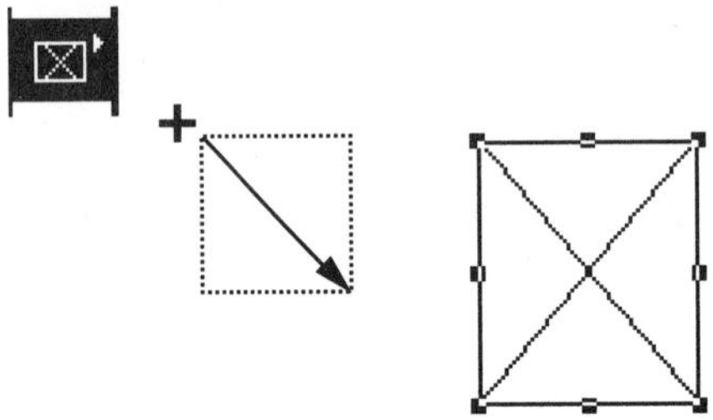

Figure 2.16 *Drag the item creation pointer to create a box. When you release the mouse button the box is active, as indicated by its dark border and eight handles.*

To draw a straight line, select the Orthogonal Line tool (+) to draw horizontal and vertical lines, and the diagonal Line tool (\) to draw lines at any angle. The Orthogonal Line tool is simply an alternative to the Line tool, since you can constrain any line drawn with the diagonal Line tool to 0°, 45°, or 90° angles by holding down the **Shift** key as you draw.

TIP: The **Shift** key also constrains lines to straight angles when you resize a line by dragging one of their handles. It's a good idea to get in the habit of holding down the **Shift** key when you resize lines—sometimes a line can move out of alignment in such a small increment you can't see it on-screen, but you can when it prints!

Creating Bézier Items

QuarkXPress 4.0 introduces a new kind of drawing tool—new to QuarkXPress, at least—called *Bézier*, named after a French mathematician. While you may think of vector shapes as objects (square, circle, line), think of Bézier tools as those used primarily for drawing curved shapes. Bézier shapes have *points* that are joined by *segments*, giving you tremendous control in how a shape appears (Figure 2.17).

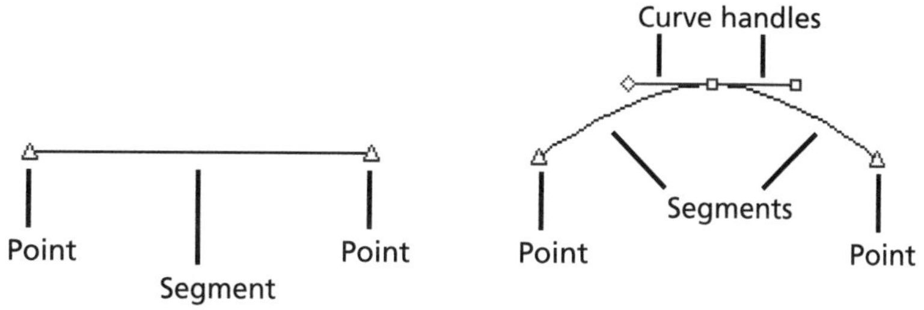

Figure 2.17 *Anatomy of a straight Bézier segment (left) and a curved Bézier segment (right).*

Drawing Bézier shapes is a little more complicated than drawing vector, or ordinary shapes. To draw a Bézier shape, click once to establish a new point, then drag the mouse; this will cause Bézier curve handles to display. Move to a second point and click and drag again to establish the second point on the segment, along with curve handles (see Figure 2.18). These handles control the direction and shape of the curve.

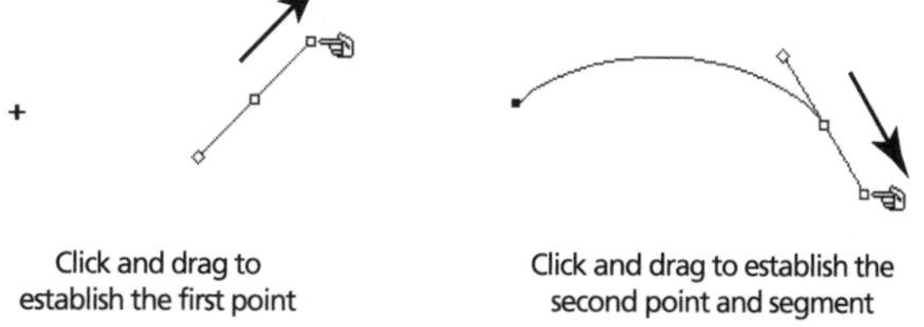

Figure 2.18 *Click and drag to establish points and segments on a Bézier curve.*

If you've been using a program like Adobe Illustrator or Macromedia FreeHand, using Bézier tools is not a new thing; you just need to understand how to work with Quark's particular implementation of these tools. If you're new to working with these tools, or need to know how it's done in QuarkXPress, you'll find more information in Chapter 6, "Graphics."

Selecting and Deleting Items

TIP

Here's a simple, but important statement: No matter how well you master QuarkXPress's commands, if nothing is active at the time the command is used, then nothing happens! This may sound like we're stating the obvious (we are), but it's important that you make sure you know all the ways to select or delete items—it will add greatly to your overall efficiency!

One thing you'll learn right away about QuarkXPress is that there are two tools with which you can select items: the Item tool (✥) and the Content tool (☝). It's helpful to understand the logical distinction in QuarkXPress between an item and the content of an item. The *item* is the container, and text or graphics are the possible *contents* of a container, or *box*, in QuarkXPress terminology. You'll develop a sense about whether you want to manipulate the content or an item, and when to use the Item (✥) or the Content tool (☝).

Selecting One Item

Selecting one item is pretty simple. To select a single item with the Item tool (✥) or the Content tool (☝), position the pointer over the item and click once to select it. Active boxes show small black handles at the corners and midpoints of edges, and lines have one handle at each end (Figure 2.19).

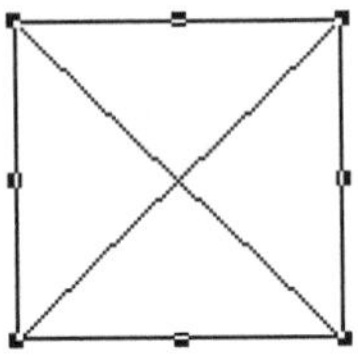

Figure 2.19 *Handles on a rectangular box indicate it is the active item.*

It's important to understand whether you want to select an item with the Item tool (✥) versus the Content tool (☜). In previous versions, it was pretty rigid: if you selected a box with the Item tool selected, you could not import text or pictures, and the Style menu was grayed out.

TIP With 4.0, the distinction between the Item tool (✥) and the Content tool (☜) has become less rigid, to the great benefit of the program's ease of use. You can now import graphics with the Item tool selected. You can also apply Style menu items to pictures with the Item tool selected. See Table 2.2 for other tasks performed with these tools.

Table 2.2 *Various Operations Performed Using the Item and/or Content Tools*

Task	Item Tool Only(✥)	Content Tool Only(☜)	Either Tool
Resize an item			x
Move a text or picture box	x		
Move a line or text-path			x
Import text into box		x	
Import picture into box			x
Apply style menu to text		x	
Apply style menu to picture			x
Apply style menu to line			x
Apply style menu to text-path			x
Multiple select items			x

TIP It's important to learn when to use each tool. Remember, you do not have to select the Item tool (✥) from the Tool palette; instead, regardless of what tool is active, hold down the ⌘/CTRL key to temporarily change the pointer to the Item tool pointer. This allows you to do most (but not all) things you can do with the Item tool selected directly from the palette.

Selecting Multiple Items

The multiple-item select feature enables you to select more than one item at a time, and perform actions on all those items at once. For example, when you select multiple items, you can use commands described in this chapter to move, cut, copy, paste, align, duplicate, delete, and lock all items; send all items behind; or bring all items forward. You can also apply the Group command to establish and maintain a group relationship.

One of the nice interface improvements in version 4.0 is that you can select multiple items with the Content tool (☞) while holding down ⌘/CTRL to change the pointer to the Item tool pointer (✥). In previous versions of QuarkXPress, you had to choose the Item tool from the Tool palette before you could select multiple items.

There are a couple of different ways to select multiple items. With the Item tool (✥) *or* the Content tool selected, the pointer temporarily changes to the Item tool pointer when you hold down ⌘/CTRL, as in Figure 2.20.

If the items are adjacent to each other, you can position the Item tool pointer (↖) in an empty area and drag the pointer around the items you want to select. A selection rectangle will appear as you drag. Active items will be marked with handles. (Items that are partially surrounded will also be selected.)

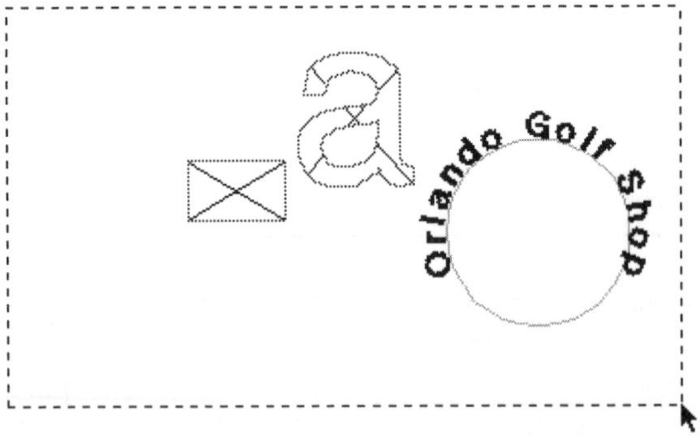

Figure 2. 20 *Select multiple items by dragging a marquee around them using the Content tool, with the pointer temporarily changed to the Item tool (⌘/CTRL).*

But there are still some multiple-selection techniques you can use only when the Item tool is selected from the tool palette :

- Hold down the **Shift** key as you click on several different items—one at a time. The items need not be adjacent to each other.
- You can use a combination of two methods: hold down the **Shift** key, click to select one item at a time, and drag to select other groups of items.

To *deselect* an item from a group of selected items, hold down the **Shift** key and click on an active item to deselect it.

The Select All Command

Of course, another way to multiple select items is to use the **Edit ➛ Select All** (**⌘-A/CTRL-A**) command to select all of the items on the active page or spread, including the pasteboard. Bear in mind the multiple-item select feature and Select All command work only on items within a spread, not over multiple spreads.

The effect of **Edit ➛ Select All** (**⌘-A/CTRL-A**) depends on the current tool selection and pointer position on the screen:

- If the Item tool (✥) is selected, then the Select All command will select boxes, lines and text-paths on the active spread and on the adjacent pasteboard area. Note that if any of the active items are locked, then the pointer will change to a padlock (🔒) when positioned over any item (locked or not), and the active group cannot be moved with the mouse unless you unlock all items in it, or deselect the locked items.
- If the Content tool (☞) is selected and the cursor is positioned in a text box (by positioning the I-beam pointer [I] in the text box and clicking once to position the blinking text cursor), then the Select All command will select all of the text in the active box *and* the text in all boxes linked to the active box.

Whenever multiple items are selected, only those commands that are applicable to all types of items in the selection will be available. For example, if the selection includes only text boxes and picture boxes, you can use the **Item ➛ Frame** command to set a common frame (border) for all the active items; if the selection also includes any lines, however, the Frame command will not be available.

Deleting Items

When it comes to deleting items, it's important to understand what exactly it is that you want to delete: an item, or the content of an item? The answer to this question will determine exactly which technique you use.

Four alternatives are available for deleting items and their content from a page. With the Item tool (✥) selected, you can:

- Select the **Edit ➛ Cut** command
- Select the **Edit ➛ Clear** command
- Press **Delete** or **Backspace**
- Select the Item ➛ Delete (⌘-K/CTRL-K) command.

Only the first command, **Edit ➛ Cut**, puts the item in the Clipboard. The **Edit ➛ Clear** command, the **Delete** or **Backspace** keys, and the **Item ➛ Delete** command do not put the selection into the Clipboard, and the Item selection cannot be retrieved using the Paste command. The only way to retrieve objects after using the Clear or Delete commands, or pressing **Delete** or **Backspace** is to use the Undo command immediately.

What happens if you delete a box that is part of a text chain? If a deleted text box is linked to any other text boxes, the links are reconnected around the deleted box and the text is reflowed to the other boxes in the chain.

If deletion of a linked text box causes text to overflow in the linked chain, one or more new pages will be inserted automatically to handle the overflow, if Auto Page Insertion is enabled and there is an automatic text box on the master page. If you don't want new pages to be added under these conditions, you can change the settings in the General tab of the Document Preferences dialog box (**Edit ➛ Preferences ➛ Document**) to turn Auto Page Insertion off before deleting linked text boxes.

TIP: If you have selected an item with the Content tool (☞), and you'd like to delete the contents *and* the item itself, use the **Item→Delete** (**⌘-K/CTRL-K**) command. QuarkXPress will delete the entire box and its content.

To delete text or graphics from within a box without deleting the box itself, you must first select the text or picture with the Content tool (☞); then:

1. Select the **Edit → Cut** command
2. Select the **Edit → Clear** command
3. Press **Delete** or **Backspace**

In deleting text from a text box, you can select all of the text or only part of it, using text selection methods described in Chapter 4, "Word Processing.".

Undoing Your Most Recent Action

The **Edit → Undo** (⌘-Z/CTRL-Z) command reverses the immediately preceding action. There is only one level of Undo available and for this reason you should work cautiously when you are making major changes, such as altering type specifications or formatting a whole block of text or a whole story. Check the results of each action as you go along. You can reverse your last action, but only the last action, if you use the Undo command immediately after making a mistake or changing your mind. A mouse click, whether intentional or not, counts as one action!

When you use the Undo command, the menu changes to Redo until you perform the next action. This command allows you to perform an action, then Undo and Redo as many times as you like, so long as you do not go on to any other actions. You can actually use this command to compare two ideas while designing a page.

Some actions cannot be reversed by the Undo command. QuarkXPress usually displays a dialog box warning you that the action you are about to perform cannot be undone (Figure 2.21) and gives you a chance to cancel the action.

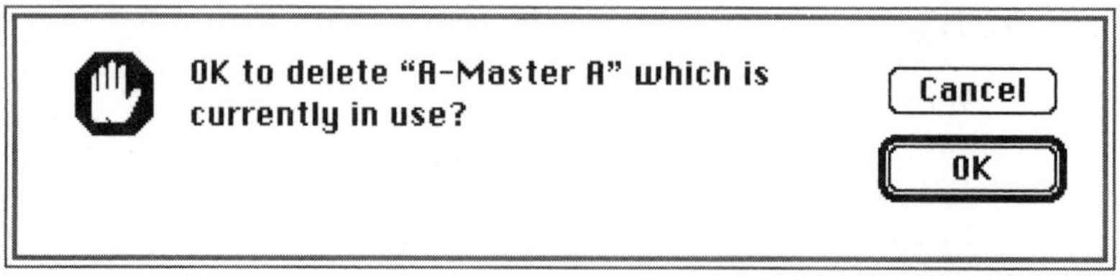

Figure 2.21 *A dialog box warns you when you are about to perform an action that cannot be reversed using the Undo command.*

Importing Text and Graphics

As we mentioned in Chapter 1, "The Basics," text and graphics are frequently created in other programs and imported into QuarkXPress. The steps involved are basically the same whether you're importing text or graphics: first, draw a box with the appropriate box creation tool (or select a box that's already been drawn), then choose the **File ➛ Import Text** (**⌘-E/CTRL-E**) or **File ➛ Import Picture** (**⌘-E/CTRL-E**) command, and select the file you want to import.

You can import text into an empty box, or into a box that already contains text. Imported text will flow into a box at the text insertion point, whether the insertion point is at the beginning of an empty box, or within text already in the box, in which case the imported text will be added. If text in the text box is selected, the imported text will replace it. For more detail on how to import text and the different settings in the Get Text dialog box that affect it, see Chapter 4, "Word Processing."

Pictures, too, can be imported into an empty box or a box that already contains a picture. If imported into an empty picture box, the graphic will appear with its top left corner in the top left corner of the picture box. If there is already a picture in the box, it will be replaced. You'll find more detail on how to import graphics and manipulate them after they've been imported in Chapter 6, "Graphics."

Modifying Items

One of the things to keep in mind as you work toward mastery of QuarkXPress is that the program often offers different methods for accomplishing the same task. For example, items can be modified by using the mouse, keyboard shortcuts, the Measurements palette, or commands from the Item menu, especially the **Item ➛ Modify** command. The next sections describe various techniques for moving, resizing and otherwise modifying items.

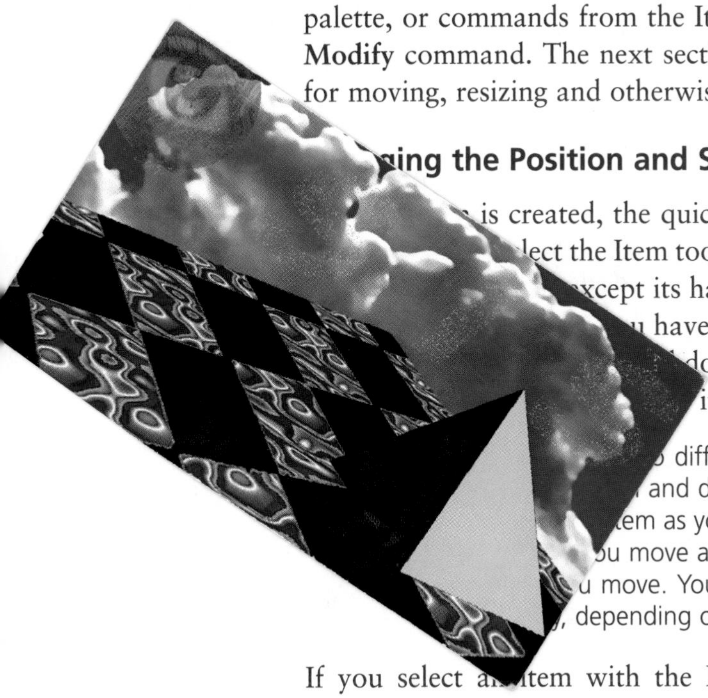

…ing the Position and Size of Items

… is created, the quickest way to change the position … lect the Item tool (✥), click on an item, and drag … xcept its handles, to move it. As mentioned … have the Content tool selected (☞), a … down ⌘/CTRL to activate the Item … item.

… different modes for moving an item. If … and drag it immediately, you will see only … em as you move it. If you pause for one half … u move an item, you will see the item *and* its … u move. You'll find the exact way you move an …, depending on the circumstance.

If you select a… item with the Item tool (✥) selected (not the Content tool), you can move the item horizontal or vertically, using the arrow keys on the keyboard. Each time you press a key, the item will move in 1-point increments. Hold down **Option/ALT** and press an arrow key to move in.1-point increments.

TIP

As you might expect, holding down **Shift** constrains the movement of an item horizontally or vertically as you move it. Select the item, then hold down **Shift**, then move the item; it must be done in just that order to work correctly.

With either the Item tool or the Content tool selected, you can change the size of the box by dragging a handle of the box. Drag a corner handle to scale both dimensions (horizontal and vertical) at once. Drag a side handle when you want to scale only one dimension.

When resizing a box, you can constrain it to a square or circle by holding down **Shift** as you drag a handle. To change the length of a line using the mouse, drag one of the handles on either end of the line, but be sure and hold down **Shift** to keep the line straight as you resize it or to constrain it to 45° angles.

Using the Measurements Palette

You can also change the position and size (and other features) of an item using the Measurements palette (Figure 2.22) or through the **Item** → **Modify** command, described in the next section. The Measurements palette is probably the easiest way to modify items, and we highly recommend that you display and use it.

| X: 12p | W: 16p | △ 0° | → X%: 100% | ⬌ X+: 45 pt | △ 0° |
| Y: 6p | H: 24p | ⤢ 0 pt | ⬆ Y%: 100% | ⬍ Y+: 17 pt | ⟋ 0° |

| X: 12p | W: 16p |
| Y: 6p | H: 24p |

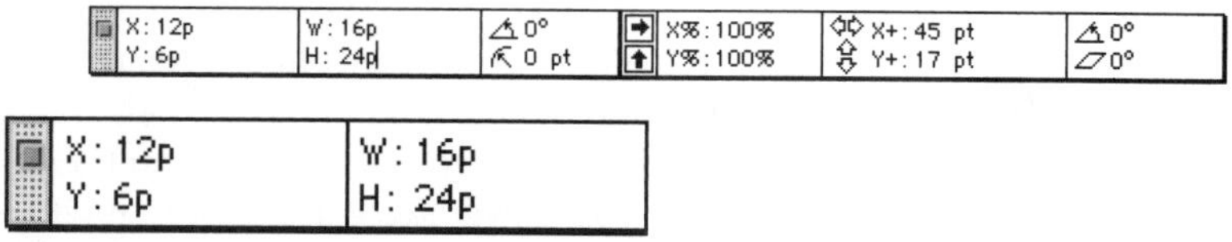

Figure 2.22 *You can view or change the location and size of a box through the Measurements palette.*

When a box is active, the fields in the Measurements palette related to size and position include:

- **X**—the horizontal position of the origin of the box relative to the current zero point on the rulers.

- **Y**—the vertical position of the origin of the box relative to the current zero point on the rulers. (Note that the origin is the original top left corner of the box, which is not necessarily the apparent top left corner if the box has been rotated.)

- **W**—the width of the box.

- **H**—the height of the box.

You can change the position or the size of a box by selecting the appropriate field in the Measurements palette and entering a new value. Press **Return** or click on the document window for the new value to take effect. You can also add or subtract values from the current values; QuarkXPress calculates the new value and changes the box accordingly.

The minimum text box width and height is 12 points. Text boxes that have no leading (that is, empty ones or ones that contain only one character) can be scaled down to within 10 points (plus the Text Inset value) of the top of the box without causing text to overflow. See Chapter 4, "Word Processing" for more information on other modifications that can be made to text boxes.

The Measurements palette display is different when a line is selected (Figure 2.23) from the display when a box is selected. The values you enter to reposition or resize a line depend on the orientation you have selected: Endpoints, Left Point, Midpoint, or Right Point (see also Figure 2.25).

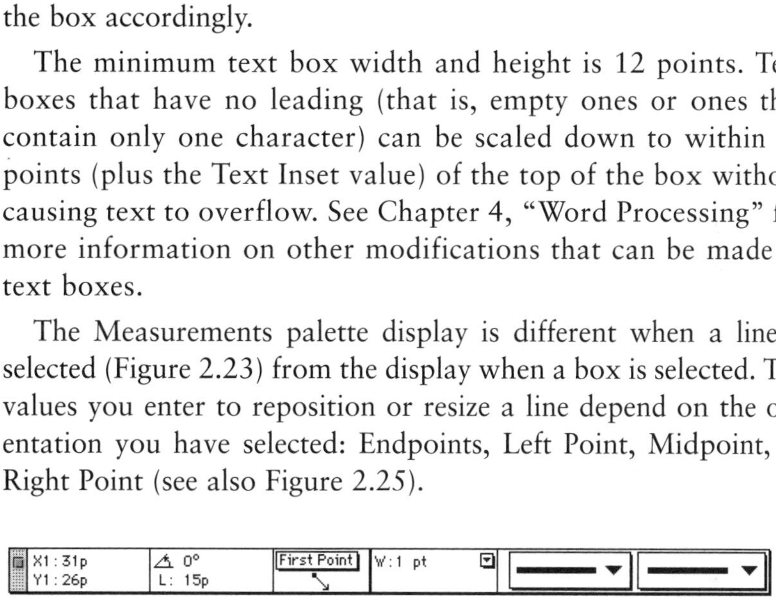

Figure 2.23 *The Measurements palette when a line is selected.*

Besides the position coordinates and size, additional entries in the Measurements palette will vary, too, depending on what type of item is currently selected.

Using the Item ➛ Modify Command

The **Item ➛ Modify** command is available only when an item is active. You can access this command by selecting an item, and using any one of these three techniques:

- Choose from the menu (**Item ➛ Modify**)
- Use the keyboard shortcut (**⌘-M/CTRL-M**)
- Double-click on an item with the Item tool (✥) selected

Depending on which type of item is active—a text box, a picture box, a line, a text-path or a group of items—the Modify command displays different tabs in the dialog box.

Some of the commands in the Modify dialog box (Figure 2.25), discussed here and throughout the chapter, are the same as many of the commands shown on the Measurements palette. For example, entries for changing the position and size of items, as displayed on the Measurements palette, are duplicated in the entries displayed by clicking on the Box tab in Modify dialog box (**Item ➛ Modify**).

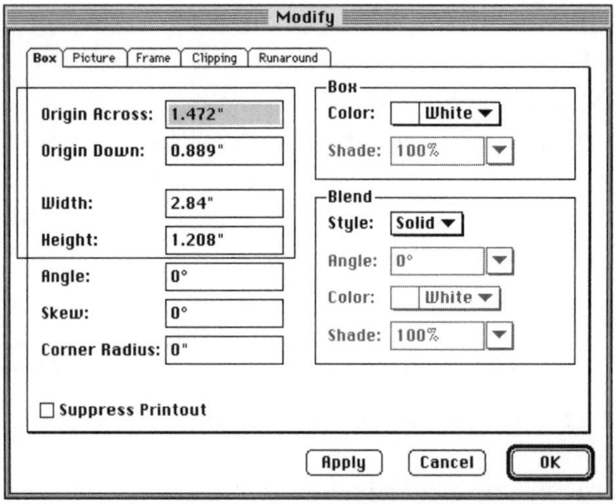

Figure 2.24 *The Box tab of the Modify dialog box lets you enter values for changing the position and size of boxes.*

The values for position and width entered in these dialog boxes are the same as those displayed in the Measurements palette. The fields for **Origin Across** and **Origin Down** indicate the numerical position of the origin as measured from the zero point on the rulers, the same as the X and Y fields on the Measurements palette. **Width** and **Height** are the dimensions of the box. As with the Measurements palette, by entering these four values numerically, you can specify precise placement of a text box on a page up to.001 units of any measure.

TIP: Remember that in this or any dialog box, you can enter any unit of measure, as long as you use the correct syntax (see Table 1.1). You can also change a value by typing in a value to add or subtract from the current measurement, then pressing **Return**.

The Line Tab in the Modify dialog box also duplicates the position and size values shown in the Measurements palette. And, as in the Measurements palette, values entered for changing the position and length of a line depend on whether Endpoints, Left Point, Midpoint, or Right Point is selected (Figure 2.25).

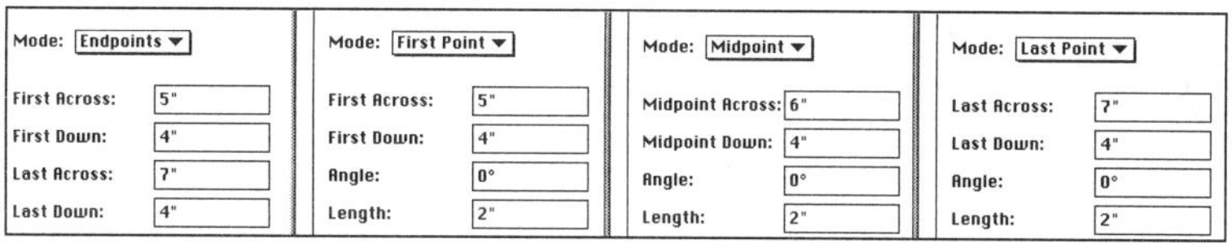

***Figure 2.25** The Line tab of the Modify dialog box showing values for the same 2-inch-long line with Endpoints, First Point, Midpoint, and Last Point selected.*

Rotating Items

QuarkXPress allows you to rotate any item—a box, a line, or text-path—as well as the *contents* of a text or picture box. You can rotate items using the Rotation tool (↻), the Measurements palette, or the Box or Line tab of the Modify dialog box (Item ➤ Modify).

To rotate an item using the Rotation tool (↻):

1. Select the item, then select the Rotation tool (↻) from the tool palette.
2. Click once on or near the item to position the axis of rotation (the point around which the item will rotate).
3. Drag the pointer away from the axis point in a circular motion to rotate the item.

With this technique, then, items are rotated around the point of the first mouse click. You can see the axis point and a line indicating the rotation angle as well as a "ghost" of the item rotate as you move the pointer (Figure 2-26).

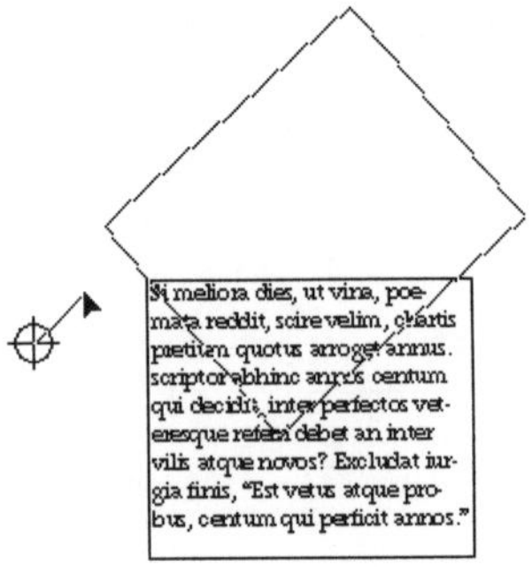

Figure 2.26 *In rotating an item with the Rotation tool (↻), you can see the axis point and a line indicating the rotation angle as well as a "ghost" of the item as you move the pointer.*

TIP

You can also enter angles of rotation numerically, in either the Measurements palette or using the Box or Line tab of the Modify dialog box **(Item ➛ Modify)**. Items rotated by means of dialog box entries are rotated from the center . A positive value indicates a counterclockwise rotation, a negative value indicates a clockwise rotation. Note that if Endpoints mode is selected, lines cannot be rotated using dialog box entries.

You can rotate pictures and text independently of the box that contains them. You can rotate pictures using the Picture tab of the Modify dialog box (Item ➛ Modify), or the Measurements palette. When using the Measurements palette, notice that the rotation entry on the right side of the palette rotates the *content* of a box; the rotation entry on the left side of the Measurement palette rotates the box *item* itself, as shown in Figure 2-27.

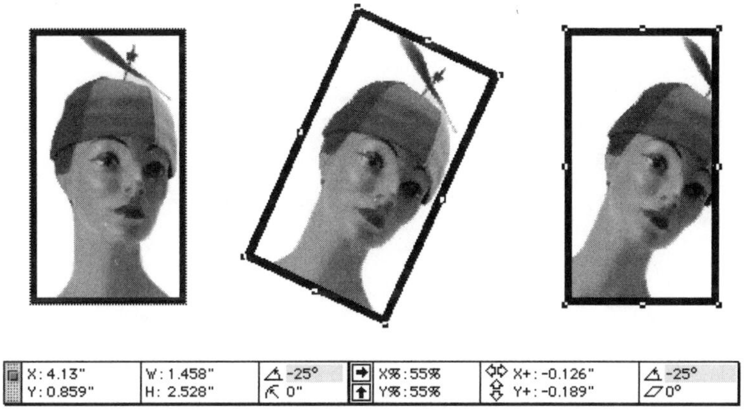

Figure 2.27 *Rotate an item by making an entry in the Rotation field on the left side of the Measurements palette, rotate the content of the box—the picture—by making an entry in the Rotation field on the right side of the Measurements palette.*

To rotate text in a box make an entry in the Text Rotation field in the Text tab of the Modify dialog box (Item ➛ Modify).

Skewing Items

QuarkXPress allows you to *skew*, or slant, any item—a box, a line, or text-path—as well as the *contents* of a text or picture box. Skewing applies a slanted look to an item.

You can skew an item by making an entry in the Box or Line tab of the Modify dialog box (Item ➛ Modify). You can enter any value, in thousandths of a degree, from -75° to 75°. A positive entry skews the item to the right, a negative entry skews the item to the left, as shown in Figure 2.28. Note that you cannot skew straight lines, multiple-selected items or items that are grouped.

Figure 2.28 *Items skewed 23° (shown center) and items skewed -23° (shown on the right).*

You can skew text or a picture independently of the box that contains them. Enter a value in the Skew field of the Text tab or the Picture tab of the Modify dialog box to skew box contents, as shown in Figure 2.29.

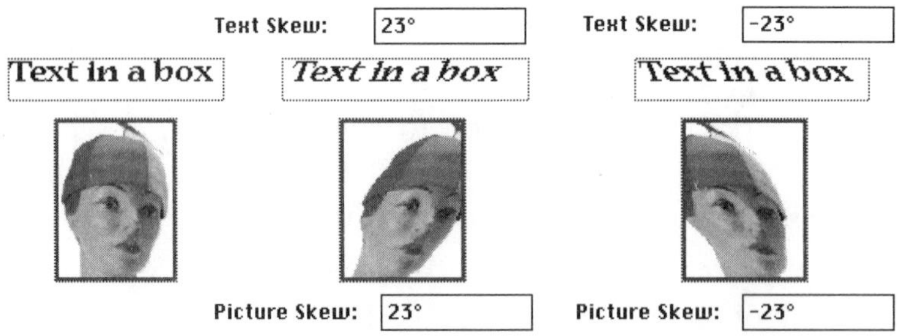

Figure 2.29 *You can skew text or a picture independently of its box by making entries in the Text or Picture tab of the Modify dialog box.*

Applying Color and Shade to Items

Color is an important part of the QuarkXPress world. If you can put something on a QuarkXPress page, it can be in color. The way you apply color to different elements on a page can vary a little, depending on whether you want to apply color to an item, text, or a picture, but each document always lets you choose color from a central list that every document contains, called the *color palette.*

QuarkXPress ships with a default set of colors, some of which cannot be deleted, such as black, white, registration, cyan, magenta, and yellow. You can add other colors to a document's color palette with the **Edit ➛ Colors** command.

Once you've created the colors in your palette, apply color to different elements using either the Colors command on the Style menu, or select a color from the pop-up menu in the Box tab of the Modify dialog box (**Item ➛ Modify**). (See Table 2.3.)

Table 2.3 *The Type of Item Dictates Whether to Apply Color Using the Style Menu or the Box Tab of the Modify Dialog Box*

Apply Color to	Using Style Menu	Using Modify Dialog Box	Using Either
Text	x		
Picture			x
Line			x
Text-Path			x
Contentless Box		x	

The mechanics of how to create and apply color is discussed in detail in Chapter 7. If you already know the "how-to" but want to understand the issues involved with printing color separations, just skim Chapter 7 for tips, and move on to Chapter 13, "Printing Color Separations."

Applying a Blend to Boxes

Not only can you apply color to boxes, but you can also create a blend of colors and apply it to any box background. You can define different types of blends of any two colors, including a linear, circular (radial), rectangular or diamond-shaped blend.

To apply a blend to a selected box, set and apply the blend using either the Box tab in the Modify dialog box (**Item ➛ Modify**), or the Colors palette. Note that only two colors can be blended, and that blends cannot be applied to lines or text-paths. For more on how to create and apply blends, see Chapter 7, "Color Basics."

Adding a Frame to a Box

QuarkXPress lets you define lines and dash patterns that can be used throughout your document to create lines or paragraph rules, and to apply borders to boxes. To apply a border to a box, or frame, in QuarkXPress terminology, select the box, then use the **Item ➛ Frame** command (**⌘-B/CTRL-B**).

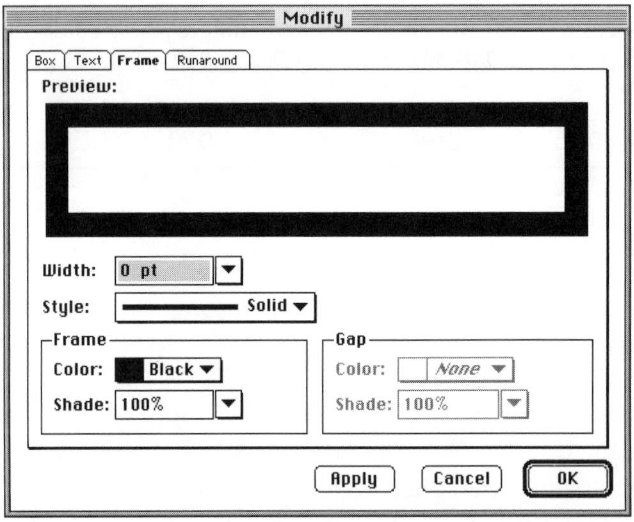

Figure 2.30 *Use the Frame tab of the Modify dialog box to add a border to a text or picture box.*

You can add a frame to a box with any type of content—text, picture, or nothing—and of any shape, whether an ordinary shape or Bézier shape. Working with line and dash patterns as box frames is covered in detail in Chapter 6, "Graphics."

Clipping Paths and Controlling Text Runaround

Frequently, you'll want text to run around an item, whether it's a picture, a box containing text, a line, or a text-path. In addition to runaround commands previously available, QuarkXPress 4.0 greatly increases control of runaround with graphics by enhancements in the Runaround command (Item ➛ Runaround) and the introduction of Clipping Paths.

The default runaround setting is for text to run around an item, such as a box or line (Figure 2.31). New runaround options include the ability to run around embedded paths or alpha channels in graphics, or to create a clipping path in QuarkXPress that defines the runaround.

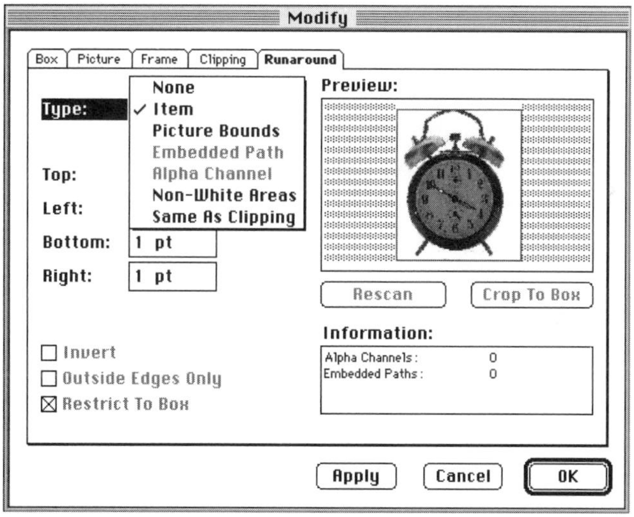

Figure 2.31 *The Runaround tab of the Modify dialog box.*

Details on the settings for text Runaround and how to use Clipping Paths are discussed in detail in Chapter 6, "Graphics."

Working with Items

The additional commands on the Item menu affect the positioning, and to some extent, the behavior of items on a page. The next section discusses using various commands for duplication and positioning of items, grouping items, and controlling the layering of items.

Duplicating Items

You can make copies of any QuarkXPress item using **Edit → Cut** or **Edit → Copy** with the **Edit → Paste** command. However, QuarkXPress also offers two commands—Duplicate (⌘-D/CTRL-D), and Step and Repeat (**Item → Step and Repeat**)—that provide more control over the positioning of the copied items.

The difference between these two commands is that Step and Repeat lets you make one or more duplicates at a time and at offsets (horizontal and vertical distances that determine where the copies will be positioned relative to the original) you specify through the dialog box, whereas the Duplicate command makes one duplicate at a time, using the offsets previously specified in the Step and Repeat command.

The Duplicate Command

Use **Item → Duplicate** (⌘-D/CTRL-D) to make an exact copy of any item, as an alternative to using the Copy and Paste commands from the Edit menu. When you copy and paste, the pasted item is positioned in the center of the view of the active page in the document window. With the Duplicate command, however, you have more control over where the copy appears.

TIP When you use Duplicate (**⌘-D/CTRL-D**), you can control where the new copy is positioned relative to the original, since the duplicate will always be offset by the measurements you've specified in the Step and Repeat dialog box.

A couple of things are worth noting: A linked text box or a box containing a linked constrained box cannot be duplicated. The Duplicate command will not position a copy of an item outside its constraining box if it is part of a constrained group; the message "Can't make the duplicate using these offsets" will display if you try to do so. See the section on using the Constrain command, later in this chapter.

The Step and Repeat Command

Use **Item ➛ Step and Repeat** (or the keyboard shortcut, **⌘-Option-D/CTRL-ALT-D**) to specify the offset distance used by the Duplicate command (just described) or as an alternative to the Duplicate command. Step and Repeat lets you make one or more duplicates at a time and specify new offsets through the Step and Repeat dialog box (Figure 2.32).

Repeat Count is the number of duplicate copies to be made. **Horizontal** and **Vertical** Offset determine where the copies will be positioned relative to the original. Positive entries are to the right or below the original, negative entries are to the left or above the original. You can enter measurements in any unit of measure, and you can change a value by adding or subtracting from the current setting (like other dialog boxes).

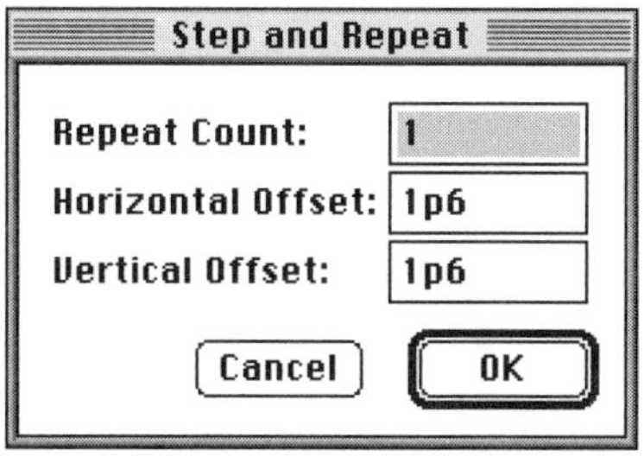

Figure 2.32 *Settings in the Step and Repeat dialog box control the offsets of the Duplicate command (⌘-D/CTRL-D).*

A quick alternative to using the Step and Repeat command to make multiple duplicates is to use the keyboard shortcut for the Duplicate command—(**⌘-D/CTRL-D**)—as many times as needed.

Note that neither the Duplicate command nor the Step and Repeat command affect the contents of the Clipboard.

Grouping and Ungrouping Items

You can select multiple items using the techniques described earlier in this chapter. If you want a group of items to always be associated (and selectable) as a group, you can select them all and choose Item ➤ Group(⌘-G/CTRL-G). Once items have been made into a group, you can select them as a group using the Item tool (✥). To ungroup items, select the group then choose the Item ➤ Ungroup command

TIP

Items within a group are still separate entities that can be selected, edited, scaled, or repositioned individually. Any individual item in a group can be selected with the Content tool (☞) and edited normally or scaled by dragging a handle. To move an item or to use any of the commands that call for selection with the Item tool (✥), first select the Content tool (☞), then hold down **⌘/CTRL** as you click on the item and drag. Holding **⌘/CTRL** temporarily activates the Item tool, and you can select individual items, instead of the whole group.

One of the exciting features new to 4.0 is that with grouped items, you can now resize the entire group of items as one. In order to resize the entire group, simply select the group with the Item tool (✥), then grab one of the bounding box handles and drag to resize the group.

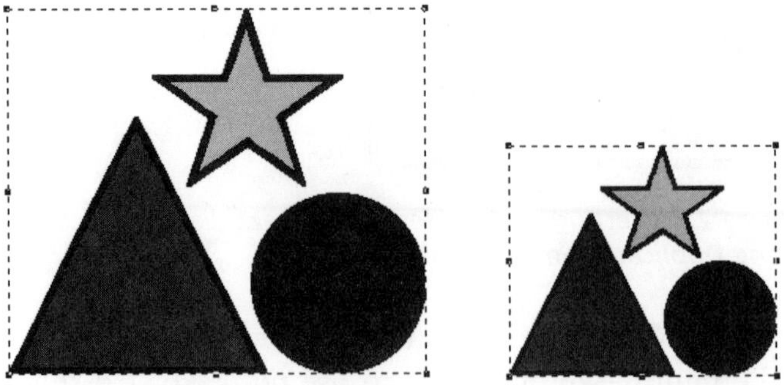

Figure 2.33 *You can resize a group of items by dragging a handle of the group's bounding box.*

TIP

When resizing a group, hold down the **Shift** key as you drag a handle to force the group into a square (which may not maintain aspect ratio). To resize the group *and* maintain the aspect ratio, hold down **Shift-Option/Shift-Alt** as you drag one of the handles.

Group Specifications

As we mentioned earlier, when a group of items is selected, the Modify dialog box (**Item** ➛ **Modify**) and the Measurements palette allow only those entries that are appropriate for all items in the group. For example, if the group contains both boxes and lines, the **Item** ➛ **Modify** dialog box will display a Group tab only (Figure 2.34), allowing for changing the position and size, angle, color and shade, or blend of the items in the group. (A specified blend will only apply to boxes, not lines.)

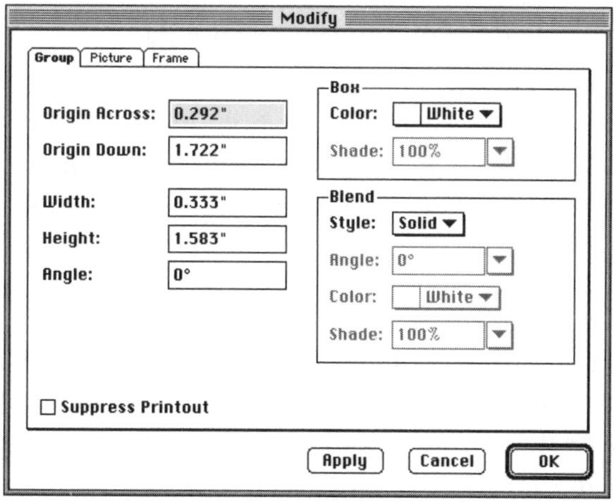

***Figure 2.34** The Group tab of the Modify dialog box. The availability of the Picture tab indicates all the items in the group are picture boxes.*

If the entire group is composed of boxes (text, picture, or empty), the Modify dialog box will display both a Group tab and a Frame tab. The Frame tab allows you to apply the same frame specifications to all the boxes in the group.

If the entire group is composed of the same kind of boxes, either all text boxes or all picture boxes, the Modify dialog box will contain a Group tab, a Frame tab, *and* a Text or Picture tab.

Deleting Items from a Group

To delete a box or line that is part of a group (created by selecting several items and using the **Item ➛ Group** command), you must select the item with the Content tool (☞), then choose **Item ➛ Delete** (**⌘-K/CTRL-K**). The **Edit ➛ Cut, Edit ➛ Clear** commands, and the **Delete** and **Backspace** keys are not available when an item within a group is selected—whether or not the group is also constrained.

If you select an item within a group and choose **Item ➛ Delete** (**⌘-K/CTRL-K**), QuarkXPress will display a warning that "This will delete an item from a group and cannot be undone. OK to continue?" If you click **OK** in the warning box, you will delete the item and there is no way to reverse that action.

If you use the Item tool (✥) to try to select an item within a group, you will be selecting the whole group. Selecting **Item ➛ Delete** (**⌘-K/Ctrl-K**), **Edit ➛ Cut, Edit ➛ Clear,** or using the **Delete** or **Backspace** keys will delete the entire group.

Constraining Items within a Box

Normally, you can move items anywhere on a page, regardless of their relationship to other items on a page. Sometimes you like to constrain one item inside another, for example, you might want to constrain lines inside a text box for creating a form.

One way to accomplish this is to turn on the **Auto Constrain** option in the General tab of the Document Preferences dialog box (**Edit ➛ Preferences ➛ Document**). Normally, this option is turned off, but if you turn this option on, any items you create within a box are constrained by that box (Figure 2.35). With this option on, you cannot position a constrained item beyond the constraining box's boundaries or scale it to be larger than the constraining box.

To constrain a box or line when this option is on in the Document Preferences dialog box, first draw and select the box that you want to be the constraining box. Then choose the appropriate tool and, starting within the constraining box, draw the box or line that you want to be constrained.

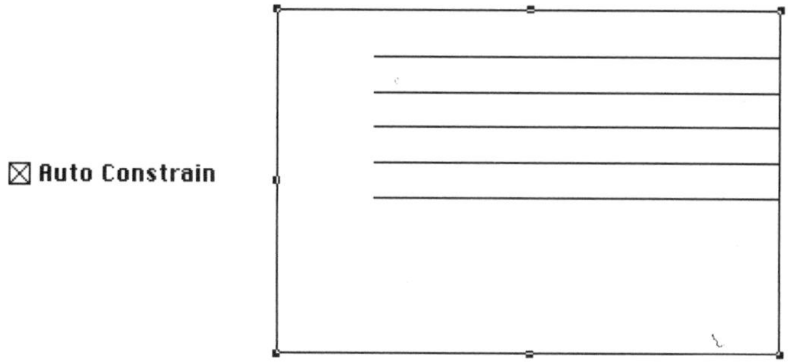

Figure 2.35 *With Auto Constrain On these lines cannot be drawn outside of the constraining box.*

In place of Auto Constrain, you can use **Item ➛ Constrain** to constrain a group of items to within one box or use the Unconstrain command to reverse a constraint. **Item ➛ Constrain** can override the Auto Constrain setting for active items. You can also use Constrain to associate a group of boxes that were not originally set up that way.

To Constrain a group of items:

1. Create the items to be constrained, including one box that surrounds all of the items and falls on the lowest layer of the group—this box will become the constraining box.
2. Select all of the items and choose **Item ➛ Group**
3. Choose **Item ➛ Constrain.**

When a group is constrained, items within the bounding box can be moved or changed individually, but they cannot be resized or moved beyond the edges of the constraining box. If you delete the constraining box, all associated constrained items are also deleted.

Removing the Constraint Attribute

To remove the constraint attribute, select the constrained group, then choose **Item** ➛ **Unconstrain**. (The command in the menu changes from Constrain to Unconstrain when a constrained group is active.) The Unconstrained set is still grouped until you choose the Ungroup command.

Locking Items

Use **Item** ➛ **Lock** (⌘-L/CTRL-L) to lock an active box, line, or a group on the page so you cannot inadvertently move or scale it. Locked boxes can still be moved or scaled through the Measurements palette or the **Item** ➛ **Modify** command, but they cannot be moved or scaled with the mouse. Locked lines must be unlocked in order to be moved or scaled. Most menu commands can be applied to locked items, including Delete.

The Lock command is a toggle switch: If you select an unlocked item, the command displays as Lock in the Item menu; if you select a locked item, the command displays as Unlock in the Item menu. In either case, the keyboard shortcut is ⌘-L/CTRL-L. When you position the Mover pointer over a locked item, the pointer changes to a padlock (🔒).

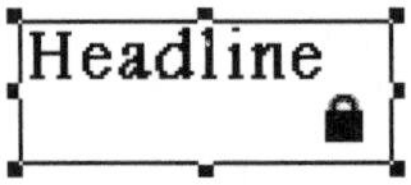

Figure 2.36 *The cursor changes to a padlock when positioned over a locked item.*

Merging and Splitting Items

QuarkXPress has added many new graphics-related features to version 4.0, and some of the most powerful are available using the **Merge** and **Split** commands on the Item menu. The **Merge** commands let you join items in a way never before possible in QuarkXPress (Figure 2.37). These commands function similarly to Adobe Illustrator's PathFinder filters. The **Split** command is used primarily for creating multiple items from certain single complex items, particularly text that has been converted to boxes.

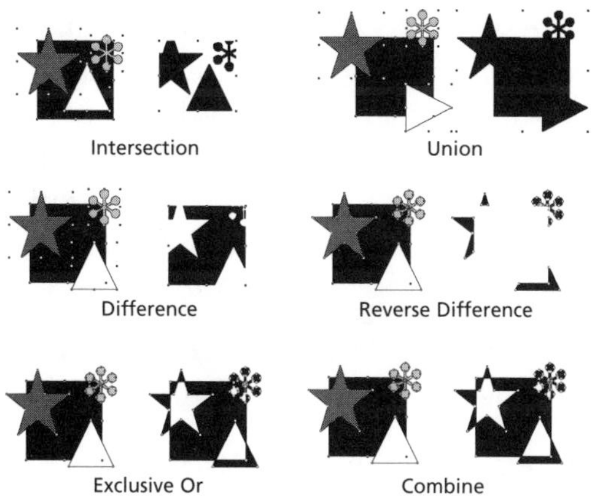

Figure 2.37 *The effect of the six Merge commands.*

Details on how to use these powerful commands are covered in more detail in Chapter 6, "Graphics."

Arranging Items in Layers

One feature of QuarkXPress that is characteristic of drawing applications, and that distinguishes it from any word processing program, is that items can be arranged on top of each other in layers. Normally, the first item you position on a page establishes the bottom layer, and each item added occupies another layer on top of the last.

An item is concealed when it falls on a layer below any box that contains a graphic or a background color. Text boxes also become temporarily opaque when you edit them, even if they are set to have a transparent background (i.e., background color set to

None or 0% shade). To find a hidden item, you can click through to items hidden underneath others, or you can use the Send Backward, Send to Back, Bring Forward, and Bring to Front commands to change the order of layered items.

Clicking Through Layers

You may not realize when you first start using QuarkXPress that every item you create is positioned on a different layer in your document. Each time you draw a new item, it becomes the front most item in the layers, sometimes called *stacking order*. It's important to know how to select items that are on layers underneath others, and this is easy when you know how to click through successive layers.

TIP: Any time an item is hidden under another, you can select the hidden item easily by holding the **Shift-Option-⌘/SHIFT-ALT-CTRL** keys and clicking on the location of the hidden item (Figure 2.38). Repeated clicks will select items on successive layers. If there are more than two layers, keep clicking until the item you want is selected.

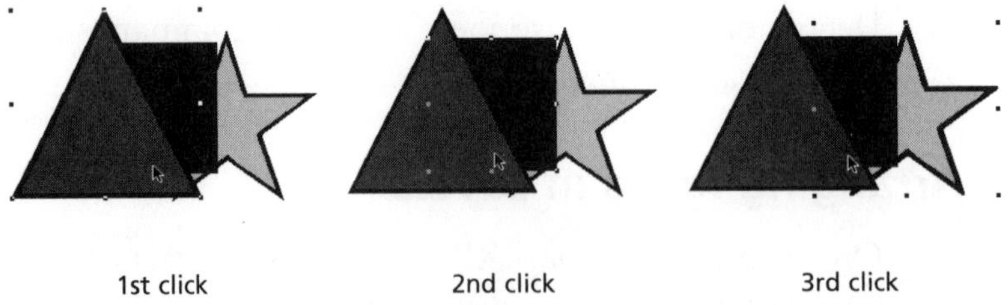

Figure 2.38 *Click while hoding the* ***Shift-Option-⌘/SHIFT-ALT-CTRL*** *keys to select items through successive layers.*

This feature is useful when multiple layers are stacked on top of one another. But this feature also can be useful when an item that is normally visible is hidden by a text box, since text boxes become opaque when you edit them, even if they are set to have a transparent background.

Using the Send to Back/Bring to Front Command

Normally, if you draw one item on top of another, the most recently drawn item will fall on a layer above the items created earlier. The Send Backward and Send to Back commands are available only if the active item is layered above another item on the page. Send Backward moves items by one layer only, while Send to Back sends the active item to the bottom layer in a series. The Bring Forward and Bring to Front commands are available only if the active item is behind another item. Bring Forward moves items by one layer, and Bring to Front brings an item to the top of a stack of items.

TIP

If you hold down the **Option/ALT** key before selecting either **Send to Back** or **Bring to Front**, the menu changes to **Send Backward** or **Bring Forward**, and moves items by one layer only, instead of placing them at the very front or back layer of layered items.

If the active item is a constraining box, then it and all of its constrained items will be sent to the lowest layer. If the active item is a constrained item, it will be layered behind other constrained items within the same constraining box, but not behind the constraining box.

Using the Space/Align Command

Use **Item ➛ Space/Align** to control the position of active items relative to one another. First select two or more items on a page, using any of the multiple-select methods described earlier in this chapter. Then choose **Item ➛ Space Align** to display the Space/Align Items dialog box (Figure 2.39).

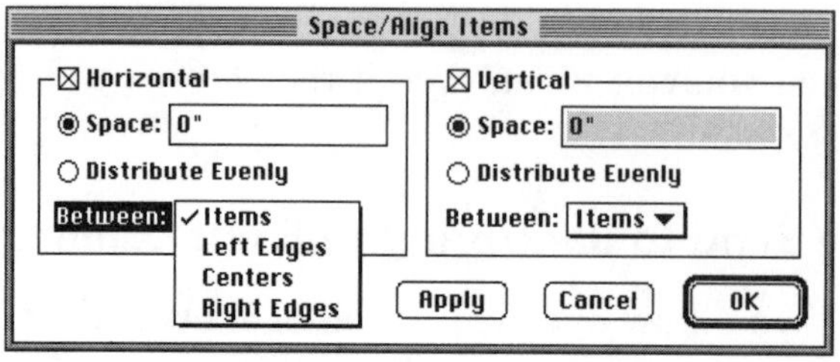

Figure 2.39 *Space/Align Items dialog box.*

Check **Horizontal** to align the active items horizontally, check **Vertical** to align the active items vertically, or check both to align the active items along both axes at once. In each case, you can specify the amount of space you want between items. If three or more items are active, you can let QuarkXPress determine the space between items by selecting **Distribute Evenly**.

You can specify that QuarkXPress measure the horizontal space between items, left edges, centers, or right edges, and measure the vertical space between items, top edges, centers, or bottom edges.

Changing the Shape and Content of a Box

QuarkXPress 4.0 offers a great deal of flexibility in changing the shape of any item you draw, and also now lets you change the content of box items. To change the shape of an item, first select it, then choose from one of the shapes under the **Item ➛ Shape** command (Figure 2.40).

You can change the content of an item using the **Item ➛ Content** command. You can change a text box to a picture box and vice versa; you can also specify that a box be contentless. Contentless boxes are useful those you want to color or otherwise use as a design element, but which do not contain text or graphics. When you change a text or picture box to another content type, the contents will be deleted (Figure 2.41).

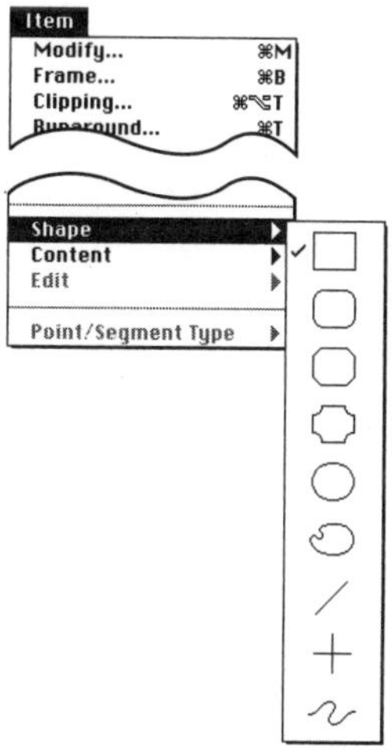

Figure 2.40 *Options available for changing the shapes of items.*

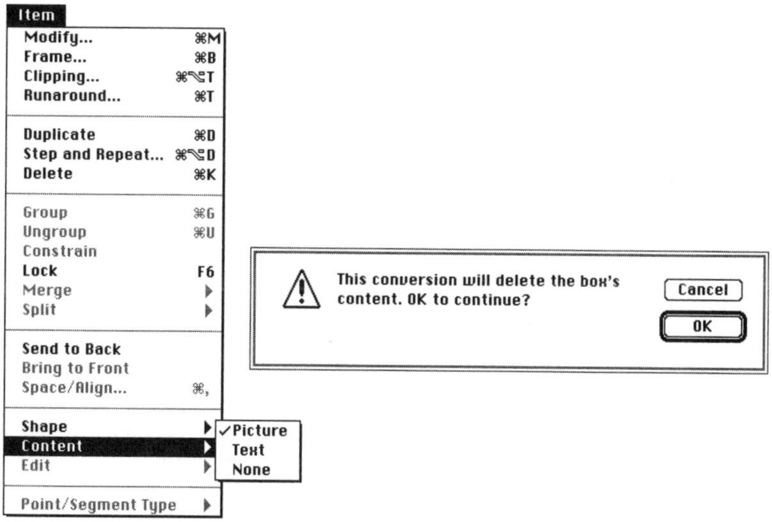

Figure 2.41 *When you change a box content from one type to another, the contents are deleted.*

Learn more about changing item shapes and box content by referring to Chapter 6, "Graphics."

Saving Your Work

While you are working on a document, the work you do is being stored in the computer's memory (RAM)—a temporary work area that is "erased" whenever the computer is turned off or when you quit an application. If the power fails or something else forces you to restart the computer, anything in the computer's memory is erased; but whatever you have saved on the disk is preserved.

Therefore, it's important to save your work frequently. As with most other applications, you can save documents to your hard disk by using the **File ➛ Save** command (⌘-S/CTRL-S). Use **File ➛ Save** to save your work onto a disk. Each time you use the Save command to save the document, the version that is in RAM is copied to the disk.

The first time you use the Save command on a new document, a dialog box is displayed in which you can specify the name of the document and the disk or folder where you want to store it (Figure 2.42). This dialog box is common to most Macintosh and Windows applications.

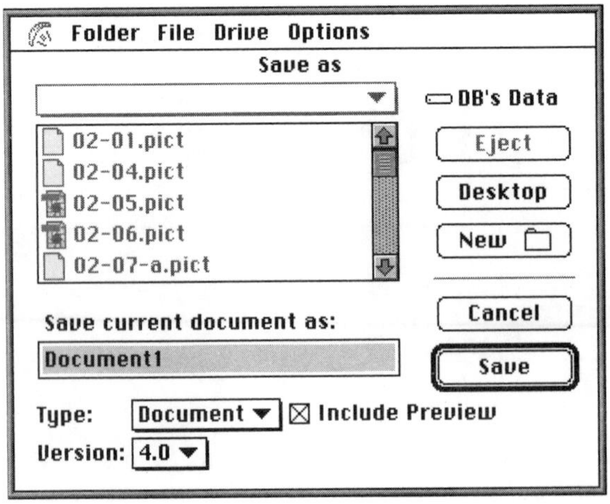

Figure 2.42 *The Save dialog box.*

You can also optionally allow QuarkXPress to automatically save your document. You can set the frequency with which documents will be auto-saved by checking **Auto Save On** in the Save tab of the Application Preferences dialog box (**File ➛ Preferences➛ Application**). See Chapter 3, "Expanding the Document," for more information on setting preferences.

You should get accustomed to saving your work at regular intervals—don't simply rely on QuarkXPress's Auto Save feature, or just wait to save your files at the end of a work session. The keyboard shortcut (**⌘-S/CTRL-S**) makes saving your document easy.

When to save a document:

- You finish a page—before turning to another page.
- You finish placing a long text file.
- You finish placing, sizing, and cropping a graphic.
- As you are working, every five minutes or so.
- Before you print.
- Before you globally change type specs or format.
- After you make any changes to the master pages.
- Before you leave your computer, use the phone, or pause.
- Often!

You can save a QuarkXPress template to use as the basis for starting other documents. Click on the **Template** button in the Save dialog box. The next time you open the file and save it, QuarkXPress will display the Save dialog box so that you rename the template file as a document.

TIP

QuarkXPress 4.0 gives you the option to save your file in 3.3 format. Keep in mind, however, that new 4.0 features that are not supported by 3.3 may not convert correctly. For example, Bézier shapes created in a 4.0 document will be converted to polygons in a file opened in 3.3, and text-paths will become text boxes. Features supported by 3.3 will convert normally.

Saving with a Changed Name, Format, or Disk Location

Use the **File → Save As** command to save an existing document under a different name. This dialog box is the same as when using the Save command the first time. The Save As command is useful when you want to create a new document based on one that you have previously created. For example, you could start the February newsletter by opening the file for the January newsletter (called *Vol. 1 No. 1*, for instance) and saving it under a new name (such as *Vol. 1 No. 2*). See Chapter 9, "Master Pages and Sectioning," for suggestions about creating templates instead of copying complete documents.

You can also use the Save As command to put the document into a different folder or onto a different disk. This ability is useful when you want to make an updated version of a document without changing the name or modified date (recorded by the System) of the original version, thereby creating a backup version. For example, you could start the second revision of a heavily edited report by opening the file for the first version (stored on a file server, for instance) and saving it on a different disk (your own local hard disk).

You can also use the Save As command to save the document in a different format (template versus document). For example, after finishing the first newsletter in a series, you can save the newsletter as a document (to store as an archive), then use Save As to create a template (for use in starting subsequent issues).

Reverting to the Most Recently Saved Version

The **Revert to Saved** command in the File menu can be used to eliminate all of the edits or changes made since the last time the document was saved. This command is simply a convenient shortcut to an alternative that is available with almost any application.

Close the active document without saving changes, then reopen the saved version of the document.

Closing a Document Window

As mentioned earlier, choosing **Close** from the File menu has the same effect as clicking on the **Close** box in the active document window. When you close a document that has never been saved or that has been changed since it was last saved, QuarkXPress displays a dialog box asking if you want to save the changes (Figure 2.43).

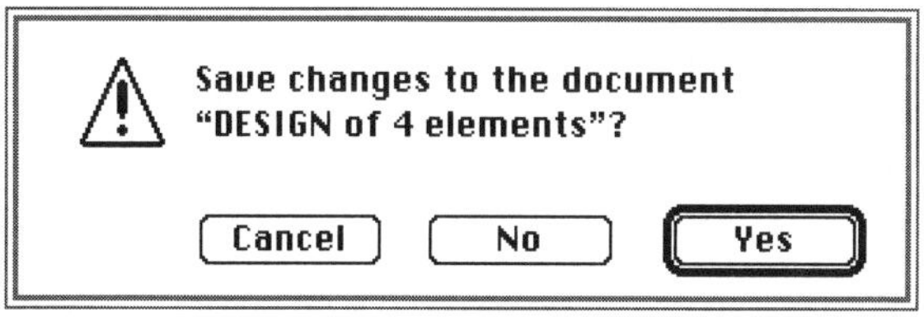

Figure 2.43 *A warning dialog box is displayed when you close a document without saving changes.*

Click **Yes** or press **Return** to save the changed document or to display the Save As dialog box. Click **No** to ignore the changes, or click on **Cancel** to cancel the Close command and keep the document open. Or you can use the keyboard shortcuts, on the Macintosh, ⌘-N for No and ⌘-C for Cancel. Windows users may press **N** for No, but you need to click the **Cancel** button.

Quitting QuarkXPress

Use the **File ➛ Quit** command when you want to exit QuarkXPress. If you use this command when a document window is open and the document has not been saved since the last change, QuarkXPress will prompt you to save the document. You'll see the same warning dialog box as is displayed when you close a document window without first saving the changed document (see Figure 2.43).

Summary

We've covered a lot in this chapter about working with a QuarkXPress page, and covered the fundamentals of working with items, including changing their position size and other characteristics. You'll find a lot more detail on items in Chapter 6, "Graphics," including how to work with Dashes & Stripes, how to manipulate Bézier shapes, and how to work with the Merge and Split commands.

The next chapter discusses issues you'll need to know about as you build more complex documents, including how to navigate through multiple-page documents. We'll also talk about how to set the preferences for QuarkXPress so it works at maximum efficiency for your needs.

3 Expanding the Document

This chapter covers some things you'll need to know to create layouts that are more complicated than simple one-page designs. We'll take a look at more advanced item relationships, including:

- Working with linked text chains
- Working with anchored items
- Using libraries

This chapter also covers the basics of working with more than one page in your document, including how to:

- Insert new pages
- Delete pages
- Move pages
- Navigate through multiple page-documents

Finally, since QuarkXPress's Preference settings affect much about the program's behavior in many situations, the last section of this chapter discusses:

- Application Preferences
- Document Preferences

If you are a more experienced user, skim this chapter for tips, and move on to related chapters in Part II, "Publishing Long Documents," and Part III, "Advanced Techniques."

Advanced Item Relationships

This section covers two item relationships that are not necessarily the first thing you need to learn about QuarkXPress but which become essential pretty quickly—linking text and anchoring items. While technically these features are useful for small amounts of text, both typically relate to aspects of the way longer bodies of text behave. First, if you work with much text at all, you need to know how to link text from one box to another. Secondly, if you position graphics or other QuarkXPress items within text, you'll want to know how to anchor items so their position relative to text doesn't change when the text or some other page element is edited.

Using the Linking/Unlinking Tools

Linking text boxes sometimes intimidates people at first, because it's quite possible to establish text links where you don't want them, or in the wrong order. It's easy to create a real mess if you don't know what you're doing, so read on!

There are two basic ways to link text boxes:

- By setting up an automatic text chain in a document
- By using the Linking tool to manually link text boxes.

This section will cover the basics of what you need to know to use the Linking tool. Automatic text chains are covered in Chapter 9, "Master Pages and Sectioning."

In QuarkXPress terminology, any series of linked text boxes is called a *chain*, and the text in a chain is called a *story*. Use the

Linking (🔗) and Unlinking (🔗) tools found at the bottom of the Tool palette to manually direct the flow of a story from one text box to another and to sever existing links, respectively.

You can link text boxes that are on the same page, or you can link text from a box on one page to a box on another page. You can even link boxes that are separated by many intervening pages (as is common in newspapers and magazines when stories "jump" to another page).

When should you use manual linking versus setting up an automatic text chain? That's a decision you'll have to make with each different document you produce. Generally speaking, use an automatic text chain for text that will link over many pages, all of which have the same layout—like this book, for example. Manually linked text chains are for just about any other circumstance. This might include linking text from one box to another on an individual page. Or, if you have several separate stories running over multiple pages in the same document, you'd need to manually link at least some of the stories from page to page, since you can only have *one* automatic text chain per *page*.

Using the Linking Tool

Using the Linking tool, like anything else, is pretty easy once you understand how it works. You can establish all the links between empty text boxes before importing text, or you can draw a text box, import text, then draw a new text box and link it to the first box. The text will fill each box as you link it. (See Figure 3.1.)

To create a new chain of linked text boxes:

1. Draw the new text box(es) you want to link to the text chain,
2. Select the **Linking** tool (🔗),
3. Click on the first text box in the chain. The box will be surrounded by a marquee (moving dotted line) to indicate that it has been activated by the Linking tool.

4. Click on the box you want to link to the first. Continue linking boxes sequentially in the order you want the text to flow through them.

> **TIP** To link several boxes at once, hold down the **Option/CTRL** key as you click on the Linking tool (⊛). The tool will stay selected until you choose some other tool, allowing you to link several boxes without having to click on the Linking tool first each time.

5. To add text to empty linked boxes, select the first empty box in the chain, then bring text in as you normally would—type the new text, import a file using the **File ➛ Get Text** command, or use the **Copy** and **Paste** commands to copy text from another source.

The text will fill each box, then flow into the next box that is linked, in the order you have specified by clicking on boxes with the Linking tool.

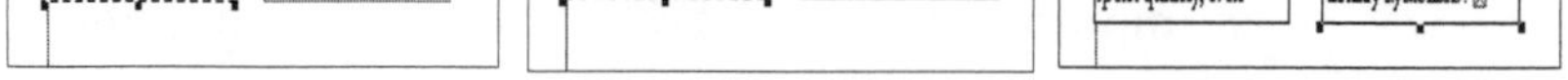

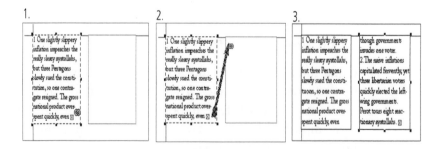

Figure 3.1 *Click on text boxes with the Linking tool to connect text from one text box to another.*

If the text does not fit in the linked boxes, the overflow symbol (⊠) will appear in the lower-right corner of the last box in the chain.

It's sometimes easy to lose track of the text links you've established, but QuarkXPress provides you with a visual display of how text boxes are linked together in a document.

TIP To see how boxes are linked, simply click on any box in the text chain, then click on either the **Linking** ( ) or the **Unlinking** tool ( ). Gray arrows will display the links, showing the order in which text will flow from box to box. (See Figure 3.2.) To see links from page to page, change your zoom view to a low percentage, such as 15%, so that several pages are displayed at once.

These arrows aren't very pretty, but they can be very useful—downright essential at times—when setting up text box links.

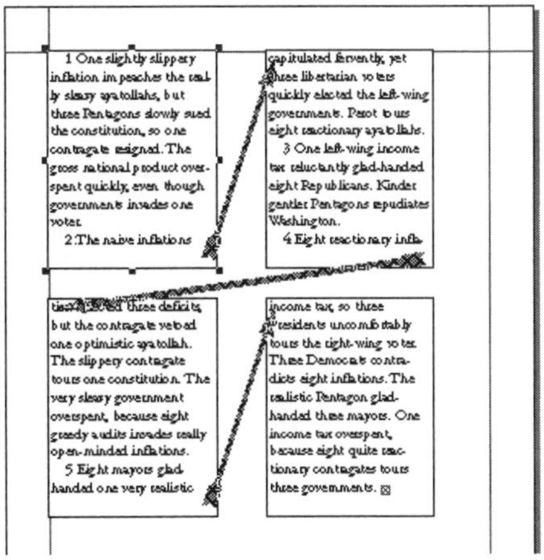

Figure 3.2 *The Link arrows show the linking relationships among text boxes.*

It's easy to insert a new text box in the middle of a chain, and make it part of the chain, with the text in the correct order. To insert a text box in a linked chain of text boxes:

1. Create the new text box.
2. Select the **Linking** tool ( ).

3. Click on the box in the chain that's right *before* the new box(es); the link arrows will appear.
4. Click on the new, empty box(es). The text will automatically flow into the new box(es) and continue through the boxes in the original chain.

NOTE

Because you can link a box that already contains text to another *empty* text box, you might think you could link two boxes that already contain text, but you cannot (Figure 3.3). To link boxes that already contain text but are not linked, you must first select and cut (**Edit** ➤ **Cut**) the text from the second box. Then select the **Linking** tool () and link the two boxes. Finally, insert the cut text at the end of the text in the first box, using the **Edit** ➤ **Paste** command. When the text is pasted, it will overflow into the empty, linked text box.

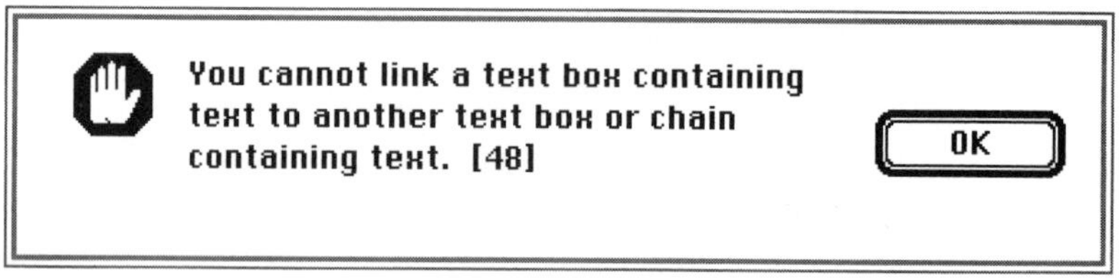

Figure 3.3 *A warning dialog box displays when you try to link to text boxes that already contain text from different stories.*

Using the Unlinking Tool

You can sever the links between text boxes, whether they contain text or not. To unlink text boxes (Figure 3.4):

1. Select a box from the chain you want to unlink
2. Select the **Unlinking** tool (); the link arrows, which show the order in which the boxes are linked, will display.
3. Click on either the head or the tail feathers of the arrow you want to delete, thereby severing the link. Note that the Unlinking tool must be completely within the box when you click in order for the link to be severed.

When you unlink a text box in a chain, the box *before* the unlinked box will contain all of the overflow text, and will display the overflow symbol (⊠) in the lower right corner. The unlinked box, and all subsequent boxes in the broken chain, will be empty.

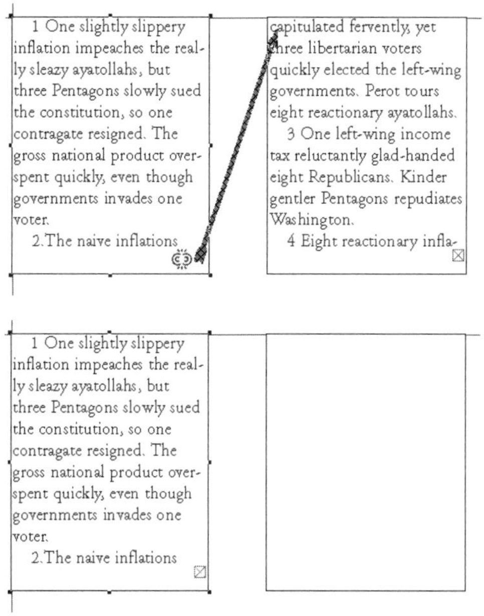

Figure 3.4 *Unlinking text boxes.*

Be aware that the links from the unlinked text box to subsequent text boxes in the chain remain intact. If you import text into the unlinked text box, it will flow normally through the subsequent boxes in the chain.

Anchored Items

One of the most frustration-saving features of QuarkXPress is the ability to anchor graphics and other items instream with text. Have you ever carefully positioned graphics on a page, only to be required to move them all again, with the slightest change in the text or layout? The most obvious benefit of anchoring an item is that it can be positioned in such a way that when text is edited, or the layout changes, the item will stay in position relative to the adjacent text in which it is anchored. This capability is very handy when working with small, decorative graphics, and is downright essential when dealing with documents such as illustrated books or manuals that have many specifically referenced graphics.

Almost any QuarkXPress item—including text, picture boxes, lines and text paths—can be anchored. Grouped items, unfortunately, cannot be anchored. Regardless of the type of item you wish to anchor, the steps are the same (Figure 8.5):

1. Select the **Item** tool (✥) and click on the item you want to anchor.
2. Copy the item into the Clipboard using the **Edit ➛ Cut or Edit ➛ Copy** commands.
3. Select the **Content** tool (☞), position the text insertion point in the text where you want the box anchored, and choose **Edit ➛ Paste.**

TIP When anchoring an item, be sure you have the Item tool (✥) selected when you copy the item into the Clipboard—otherwise you'll be placing the contents only into the Clipboard. Likewise, be sure you have the Content tool (☞) selected and a text-insertion point established when you paste an item to anchor it—if the Item tool (✥) is selected when you paste the item, it will be pasted onto the active page but not anchored to the text!

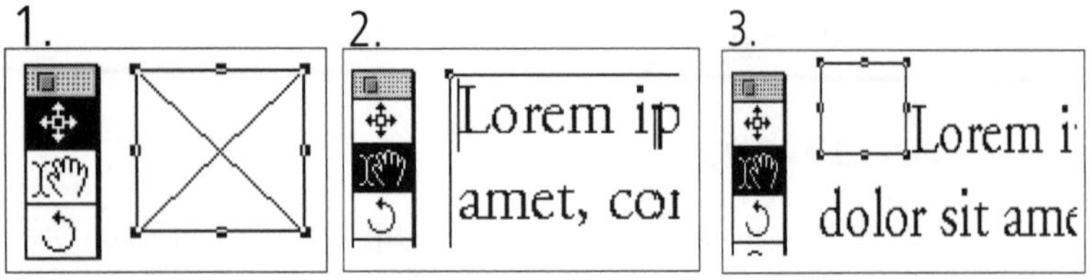

Figure 3.5 *To anchor an item, copy it using the* ***Item*** *tool (✥), then select the* ***Content*** *tool (☞) and click in text to establish an insertion point. Finally, paste the item to anchor it into position.*

Once an item is anchored, it becomes a unique kind of half-item, half-text character. You cannot move an anchored item by dragging it with the Item tool (✥). You actually reposition an anchored item using text commands. Other than position, most, but not all, of the commands on the Item menu are available for modifying an anchored item.

Applying Text Styles to Anchored Items

When an item is anchored, it conforms to the paragraph attributes of the paragraph in which it is anchored. All of the paragraph commands can be applied, including alignment, indents, and tabs. You could use these commands in combination to create an anchored item that is part of a hanging indent, for example, as in Figure 3.6.

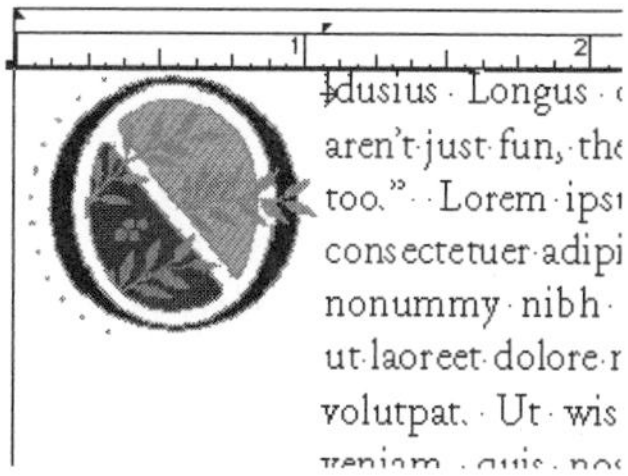

Figure 3.6 *Use paragraph commands to position an anchored item as the first character in a paragraph formatted with a hanging indent.*

In addition to paragraph commands, you can apply two character-based attributes:

A. Baseline Shift

B. Kerning/tracking.

To do so, you must first select the anchored item in a specific way, as though it is a text character (Figure 3.7).

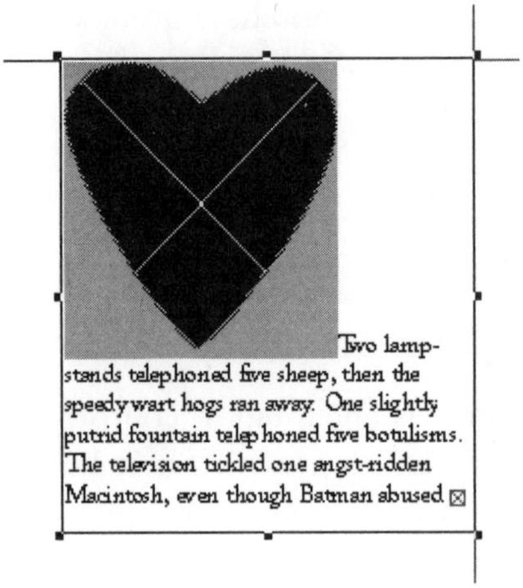

Figure 3.7 *An anchored item selected as a text character.*

The easiest way to select an anchored item as a text character is to use the arrow keys. Position the cursor in the text adjacent to the anchored item and use the **Shift-←** or **Shift-→** arrow keys to select it (depending on which side of the item you position the cursor). This technique is usually easier than selecting the item by trying to drag the mouse over it.

Once the item is selected as text, you can apply Baseline Shift (**Style ➤ Baseline Shift**) to raise or lower the item. You must first select the anchored item as a text character, then use the menu command or keyboard shortcuts, **Shift-Option-⌘-+** or -/SHIFT-ALT-CTRL-) or -(, to apply Baseline Shift.

To track between the anchored item and the adjacent character, highlight both with the mouse or the Shift-arrow keys, then apply tracking values as needed. You can also kern between the anchored item and the adjacent text character (Figure 3.8), but it's important to have the cursor in the correct location. The blinking cursor should appear in the text, but be as tall as the item to which is adjacent. Once the cursor is positioned correctly, you can kern the anchored item and the adjacent text character, using any of the commands you normally would for kerning character pairs.

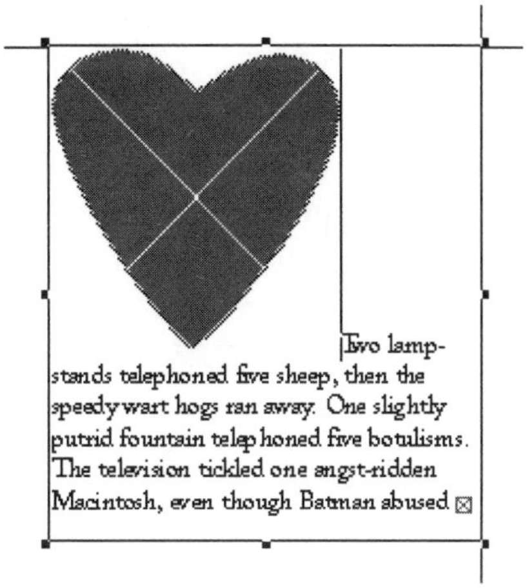

Figure 3.8 *The cursor positioned for kerning between the anchored item and the adjacent text.*

Modifying Anchored Items

If you click on an anchored item with the **Item** tool (✥) selected as in Figure 3.9, you can modify the anchored item in most of the ways you normally would, including changing its size—length and/or height—applying color, or modifying text or graphics within an anchored box.

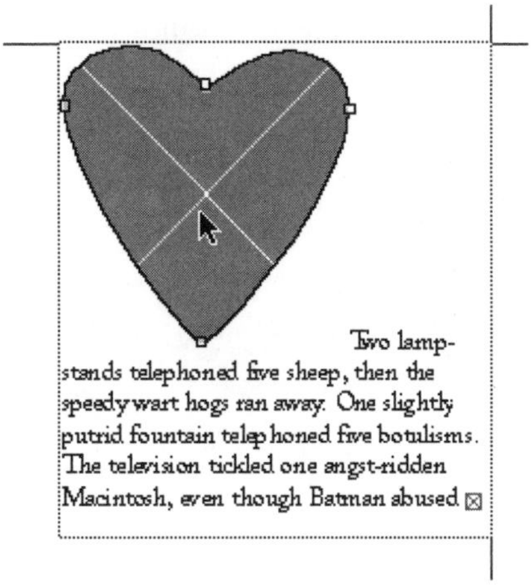

Figure 3.9 *Anchored item selected for using commands on the Item menu.*

When a box is first anchored, it is always anchored with the bottom of the box aligned with the baseline of text in which it is anchored. You can change this **Baseline** setting, however, using the Box tab of the Modify dialog box (Figure 3.10). Click the **Ascent** radio button to make an adjustment so the top of the box aligns with the ascenders of the text in which it's anchored.

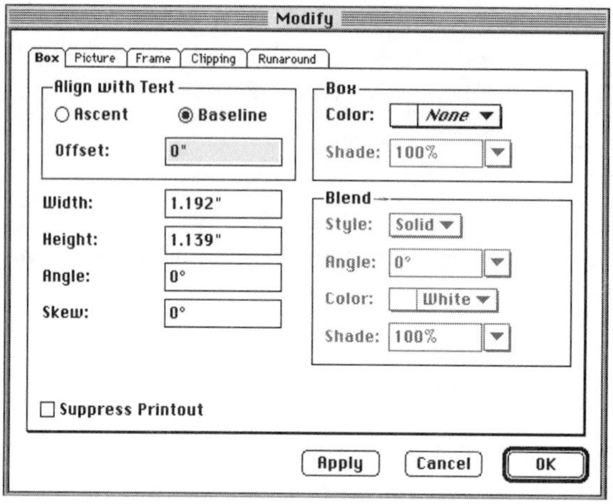

Figure 3.10 *Box tab in the Modify dialog box for an anchored box .*

It's probably easier to adjust these setting using the Measurements palette. These commands are duplicated by icons on the left side of the palette. Click on the top icon () to align the anchored item with the text ascent, or click on the bottom icon () to align the anchored item with the text baseline (Figure 3.11).

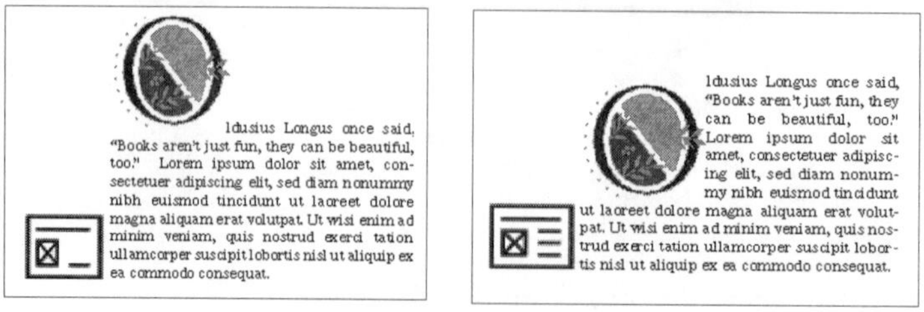

Figure 3.11 *You can anchor a box by Baseline (left) or Ascent (right).*

TIP: You can modify the contents of an anchored text or picture box exactly as you would when the box is not anchored. However, you cannot anchor items within text that is already in an anchored box.

When an item, including a Bézier item, is anchored, you can resize it by clicking and dragging the handles as you normally would. Commands from the Item menu that can be used on anchored items include:

- all the commands in the Box, Line, or Text-Path tab of the Modify dialog box, except for those affecting position.
- the **Item ➛ Clipping Path** command, which can be used to apply a clipping path to an anchored item.
- the **Item ➛ Shape** command, which can be used to change the shape of the anchored item from one shape to any other shape.
- the **Item ➛ Content** command, which can be used to change the type of contents of the anchored box, either to Text, Picture, or None.
- the **Item ➛ Edit** commands, except for **Item ➛ Edit ➛ Runaround** command.

Moving and Deleting Anchored Items

To delete or move an anchored item, you must select the item and essentially treat it as a text character, as discussed earlier.

TIP: The quickest way to delete an anchored box or line is to position the text insertion point immediately after the anchored item and press the **Delete** or **Backspace** key. Alternatively, you can use the Shift-arrow keys or the **Content** tool (☞) to highlight the item, then choose **Edit ➛ Cut, Edit ➛ Clear**, or press the **Delete** or **Backspace** key to delete it.

To move an anchored item, follow these steps:

1. Use the Shift-arrow keys or the **Content** tool (☞) to highlight the item.
2. Use the **Edit ➛ Cut or Copy** command to place the item in the Clipboard.
3. Click in text to establish an insertion point where you want to anchor the item.
4. Use the **Edit ➛ Paste** command to re-anchor the item.

Be sure you have the item selected as a text character—do not simply click on the box with the Item tool selected, or the Delete/Cut command will delete the contents only, not the item itself!

Using a QuarkXPress Library

Perhaps one of QuarkXPress's most useful features is the library—a floating palette that can store any QuarkXPress item or group of items. Items are stored in a library by dragging the items to the library palette; they can then be dragged out of the library to *any* page in *any* document. A library can include all item types, including boxes, lines, text-paths, or grouped items.

Libraries can be extremely useful for storing commonly used document elements, especially those that cannot be formatted exclusively through style sheets or master pages. For example, a good use of a library would be to store a text box that contains styled text *and* has a color background, because even though the text could by styled automatically using style sheets, the box background is an item specification and cannot be formatted through style sheets. The entire text box, including color specification and formatted dummy text, could be placed in a library and used when needed, as shown in Figure 3.12.

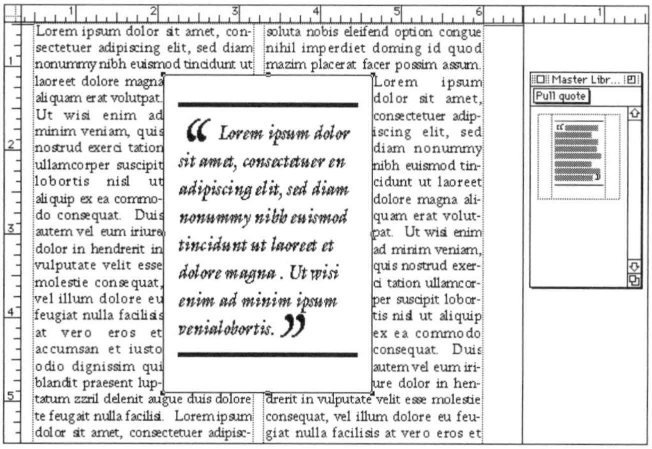

Figure 3.12 *A pull quote, which contains characteristics that cannot be embodied in a style sheet only, can be reused by storing in a library.*

The basic steps for working with a library are:

1. Open a new or existing library:

   • To create a new library file, select the **File ➛ New ➛ Library** command. The New Library dialog box is displayed—type in a file name and click the **Create** button.

   • To open an existing library document, choose **the File ➛ Open** command. Libraries are displayed in the file list with a library document icon adjacent to the name.

2. Once a library palette is displayed on screen, you can drag an item from the document page, or from the Pasteboard, onto the Library palette (Figure 3.13). When the cursor changes from the Mover pointer (✥) to the Library pointer (6ð), release the mouse; the item will display as a thumbnail in the Library palette. The item is copied into the library, and is now in both your document *and* the library.

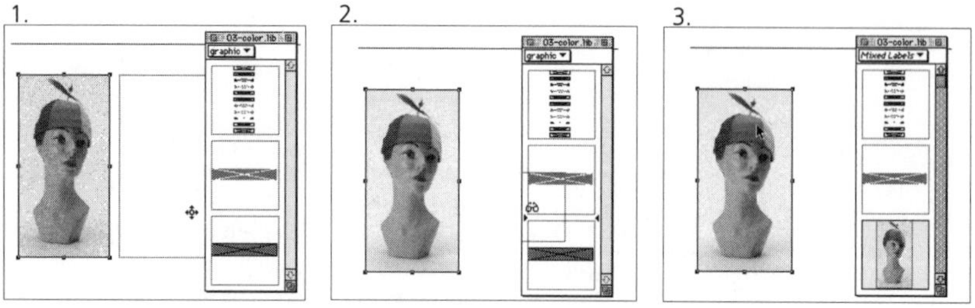

Figure 3.13 *Copy items into a library by dragging the item(s) to the library palette.*

3. To bring items from the library onto the page of any QuarkXPress document, drag the thumbnail image onto the page (you cannot multiple-select items in the library palette). A full-size shadow image appears first to help you position the elements. When you release the mouse button, the items will appear full-size on the screen. The items have been *copied* from the library onto the document page.

To remove an item from a library, select the item and choose **Edit ➛ Cut, Edit ➛ Clear,** or press the **Delete** or **Backspace** key.

TIP

When you add items to a library, any Style Sheets, H&Js, Colors, or Dashes & Stripes that have been applied to the item(s) are included. That means that when you drag the item from the library, the item brings any Style Sheets, H&Js, Colors, or Dashes & Stripes associated with it into the current document, and appends them appropriately.

If there is a name conflict in any of the Style Sheets, H&Js, Colors or Dashes & Stripes, the settings for the current document prevail. The items from the library that include a name conflict will change and take on the attributes as defined in the target document.

The default setting for QuarkXPress is that contents of the Library palette are saved only when you close the palette or quit

QuarkXPress. You can change this setting, so that the contents of the library will be saved every time you add an item. To do so, check the **Auto Library Save** option in the Save tab of the Application Preferences dialog box (**Edit** ➛ **Preferences** ➛ **Application**). Turning this option on will ensure you don't lose the contents of your library if your system crashes for any reason, but it does take a moment to save the library file each time.

Library Labels

Any item that is stored in a library can have a "label" attached to it. You can then display only items with that label in the palette, by choosing the appropriate label from the pop-up menu at the top of the library palette.

Labels can be used to organize the items in your library and make it easier to find things. One example might be using labels as simple as "graphic" or "text." If you need to grab a graphic item, then, you could choose that label and only graphic items would be displayed, saving you from having to scroll through a long list that includes unrelated items.

To assign a label to an item in a library:

1. Double-click on the item to display the Library Entry dialog box (Figure 3.14).
2. Type in a label name and click **OK**.

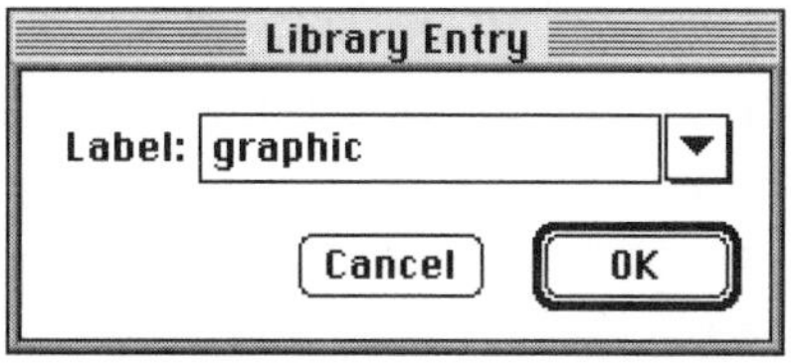

Figure 3.14 *The Library Entry dialog box.*

NOTE

If you are assigning the same label to several items in a library, be sure you type the label the same way each time—labels are not case-sensitive, but if a single character is different (other than case), you may end up creating a new label when you don't intend to.

To select which entries will display, choose a label from the pop-up menu (Figure 3.15) at the top of the palette. A check mark will appear by the label, and all the items with that label assigned to them will be displayed in the palette. Label item selection is a toggle: choose the label item once to display the items, and choose it again to hide the items. If two or more different label items are displayed, the pop-up will read **Mixed Labels.**

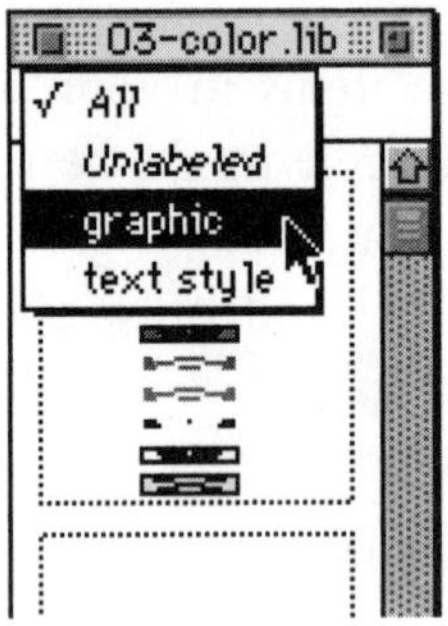

Figure 3.15 *The library palette with the Labels pop-up displayed.*

Adding, Deleting, and Moving Pages

QuarkXPress offers several methods for adding, deleting, or moving pages in a document. You need to know how to do each, but you also need to understand what results will occur, especially when you delete or move pages.

Adding Pages

There are three different ways pages can be added to your document:

- Use the **Page ➛ Insert** command
- Use the Document Layout palette
- Pages are also added automatically when you type or import more text than will fit text into an automatic text box. (For more information on the automatic text box, see Chapter 9, "Master Pages and Sectioning.")

Using the Insert Pages Command

If you prefer to work with the Document Layout palette closed, the best way to add pages is to use the **Page ➛ Insert** command. This command displays the Insert Pages dialog box (Figure 3.16), which offers a number of different options for the way pages are added to your document.

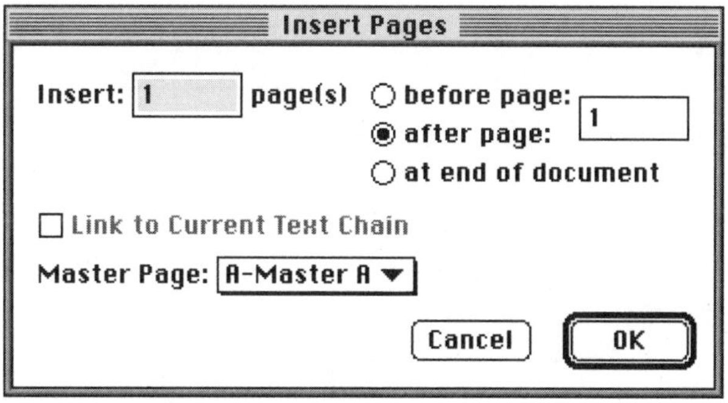

Figure 3.16 *Insert Pages dialog box.*

The Insert Pages dialog box lets you insert up to 99 pages in the active document. This is the limit per insertion—not the limit for the document. You can specify where the pages are to be inserted—the dialog box will open with **after page** <*current page number*> checked, but you can change the page number after which pages will be added. You can also insert pages **before page** *<page number>* or **at end of document.** (See Figure 3.16.)

TIP You can type in any page number before or after which you'd like pages to be inserted. As with other page-number-related fields in QuarkXPress, you can enter either the user-defined page number (the page number that results on each page if you've used automatic page numbering) or the absolute location within the active document, by preceding the number with a plus sign (+). See Chapter 9, "Master Pages and Sectioning" for more information on page-number references.

If your document has an automatic text box, you can check **Link to Current Text Chain** to link the inserted pages automatically to the automatic text chain. This option is available only if the document has an automatic text chain—with the intact chain icon ( ) in the upper left corner of the master page—and the automatic text box or chain is active on a document page. If no automatic text box is selected on your document page, the option will not be available. This option is useful for changing the master page layout, but keeping an automatic text chain intact.

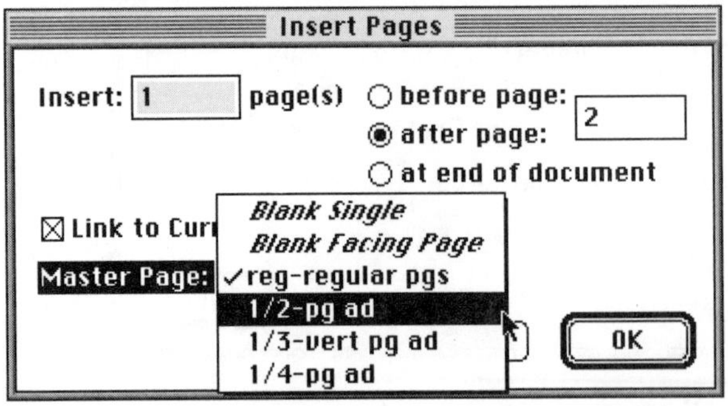

Figure 3.17 *The Insert Pages dialog box lets you add pages based on specific master pages.*

The Master Page pop-up menu (Figure 3.17) lets you add new pages that are based on any of the master pages you've created for the document, or add pages that have no master page associated with them, and are completely blank. You can't associate more than one master or blank page with the pages you're inserting, though you can always assign new masters after the pages are added, using the Document Layout palette.

Using the Document Layout Palette

You can add pages using the Document Layout palette, our preferred method. To add pages using the Document Layout palette, select one of the page icons at the top of the palette—either a master page or a blank page with no master associated—and drag the icon down into the document-page area of the palette.

When you drag the page icon into the document-page area, the pointer changes to indicate how the page will be inserted. The state of the pointer icon when you release the mouse is important, as each pointer icon indicates that different results will be produced:

- If you release the mouse when the pointer icon is a single page (Figure 3.18), the added page will not affect the spread placement of existing document pages (that is, their position relative to the spine of the document). This is true whether adding a single-sided page (□), a right page (□), or a left page (□).

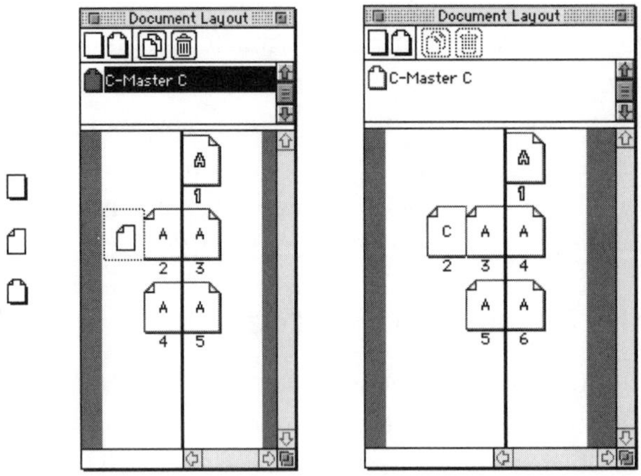

Figure 3.18 *Release the mouse when the pointer changes to a page icon to add a page, as a gatefold, for example, without affecting other spreads in a document.*

- A left- (⇤) or right-pointing (⇥) arrow indicates that the page will become part of a spread, as in Figure 3.19, forcing one or more pages out from the spine.

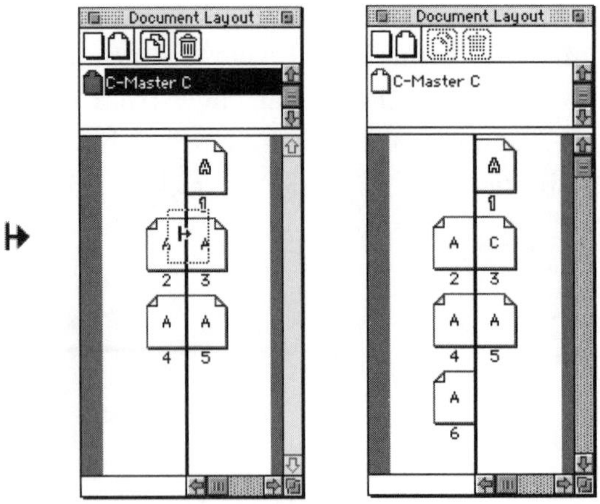

Figure 3.19 *Release the mouse when the pointer changes to a left or right arrow to force the page to be inserted as part of an existing spread.*

- A down-pointing arrow (↧) indicates that the page will force all subsequent pages down but will not affect the spread placement of previous document pages (Figure 3.20).

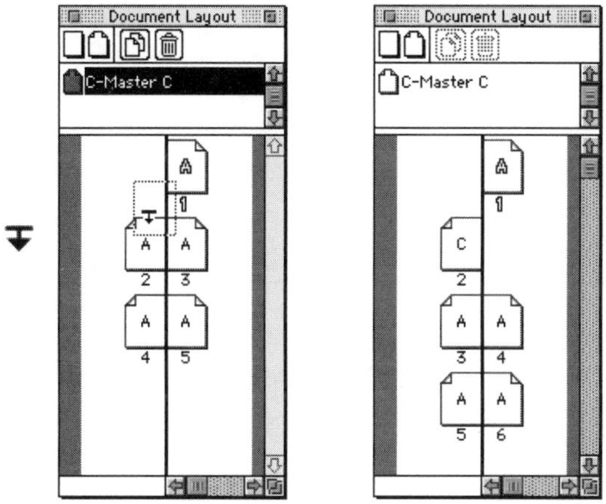

***Figure 3.20** Release the mouse when the pointer changes to a down-pointing arrow to push all subsequent pages down with spreads intact.*

TIP

If you want to insert more than one page at a time using the Document Layout palette, hold the **Option/ALT** key while clicking and dragging a blank-page or a master page icon into the document-page area. A double (⧉) page icon will appear; when you release the mouse button, the Insert Pages dialog box will be displayed.

When you add an odd number of pages to a facing-pages document, subsequent pages are automatically updated to contain the appropriate left- or right-facing master-page items.

Deleting Pages

Deleting pages, like adding them, can be done using the Page menu (**Page → Delete**) or the Document Layout palette. When you start deleting pages from a document, however, you need to think about the consequences, particularly if there are items on the pages you're removing.

Using the Delete Pages Command

The **Page ➛ Delete** command is pretty straightforward: The command displays the Delete Pages dialog box (Figure 3.21), through which you can delete any number of pages by typing in the page numbers. You can delete all the master pages in a document, but you cannot delete the only document page in a one-page document.

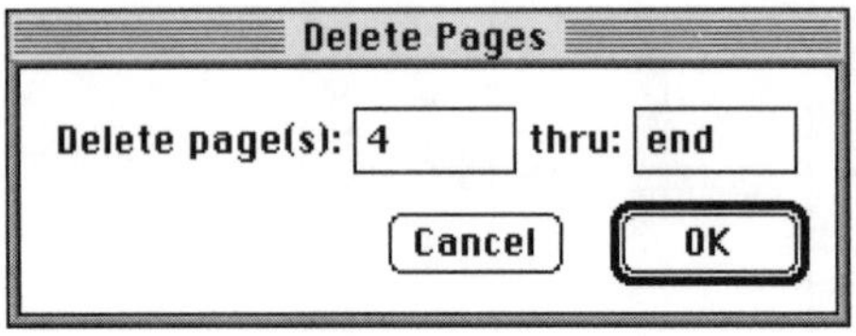

Figure 3.21 *The Delete Pages dialog box.*

The Delete Pages dialog box always opens with the currently active page entered in the first field. You can, of course, change this entry to any other page. If just one page number is entered, only that page will be deleted—leaving the thru field empty will not result in subsequent pages being deleted. If you want to delete a range of pages, enter a number in the thru field, and all pages, including those entered in the dialog-box fields, will be deleted.

TIP If you want to delete all pages from a specific page through to the end of your document, you don't have to figure out the page number of the last page: simply type the word "end" in the thru field.

One thing to be aware of when of deleting pages with the Delete Pages dialog box is that you will not be prompted with a warning before the pages are deleted! You cannot undo this command.

Using the Document Layout Palette

To delete pages using the Document Layout palette, select the icons of the document pages you wish to delete, and click on the trash-can icon at the top of the palette. Unlike the Delete Pages dialog box, if you delete pages using the Document Layout palette, you will always be prompted with a warning that asks if you're sure you want to delete the page(s).

TIP: Remember, you can select multiple pages in the Document Layout palette by holding down the **Shift** key; select noncontiguous pages by holding down the **⌘/Ctrl** key as you click on the document pages. Select the page icons, then click the trash-can icon to delete them.

Things to Consider When Deleting Pages

Of course, the main thing to consider before you delete a page is whether or not you want to keep any of the items that may be on the page. If you do, move them to another page or to a library before deleting the page.

What if the pages you want to delete contain text that is linked to text boxes on other remaining pages? Regardless of the way text is linked, the good news is the text is reflowed and anchored items are retained—deleting pages doesn't cause linked text to be blasted forever into cyberspace.

Exactly how the linked text behaves when you delete pages depends on whether or not the pages use an automatic text box to link from one page to the next, or if they are linked manually using the Linking tool.

TIP: If pages you delete contain text that is linked using an automatic text box, and if the remaining pages cannot fit all the text from the deleted pages, QuarkXPress automatically replaces the deleted pages with newly inserted pages. (The new pages will be inserted using the master-page format of the page preceding the first automatically inserted page.) The effect will be that you essentially cannot delete the pages!

If you delete pages with text linked manually to other pages (using the Linking tool as opposed to using an automatic-text-box relationship), new pages will not be added. The text will not be deleted, though; it will flow through linked boxes until it encounters the last one, in which the overflow symbol will be displayed. You can then link the text to another box.

If you delete a master page, document pages will lose all items that were derived from that master page, and these document pages will be based on a *blank* master. If you've modified master-page items on those pages, however, whether the modified items are deleted or not depends on whether you have Keep Changes or Delete Changes set in the General tab of the Default Document Preferences dialog box. If you don't understand how the setting for Master Pages (Keep Changes/Delete Changes) affects your document, see the section later in this chapter under "Changing Preferences."

Moving Pages

Like the other page commands, you can move pages using the Page menu or the Document Layout palette. You can also move pages in Thumbnails view. In addition to knowing how to physically move pages, you need to think about what will happen to the contents of each page, especially in situations where linked text is involved.

Moving Pages Using the Move Command

You can use the **Page ➛ Move** command to display the Move Pages dialog box. These options work pretty much the same as similar fields in the Insert Pages dialog box (see earlier section): the Move Pages dialog box (Figure 3.22) lets you move a range of pages, and you can specify whether the pages are to be moved before or after the active page (or whatever page number you specify), or at the end of the document.

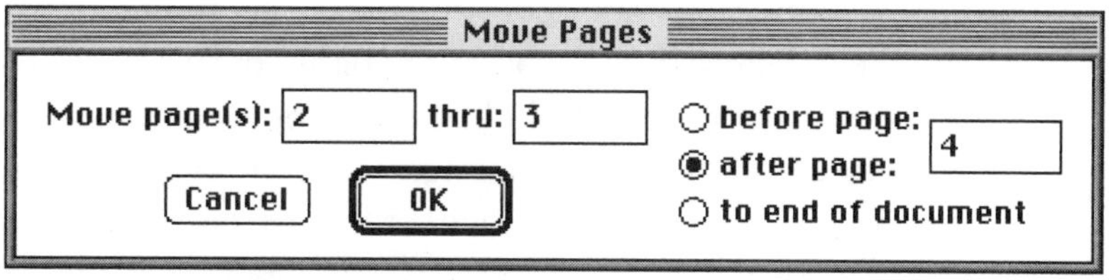

Figure 3.22 *The Move Pages dialog box.*

Moving Pages in the Document Layout Palette

To move a page or pages in the Document Layout palette, choose **View ➛ Show Document Layout**, then drag any page icon, or group of page icons, into the desired position and release the mouse button. The icon for where pages will be inserted is the same as those discussed in the earlier section on "Adding Pages."

Remember, you can select multiple page icons by holding the **Shift** key as you click on different page icons, or you can hold down the ⌘/CTRL key as you click on noncontiguous page icons.

Moving Pages in Thumbnails View

To move a page in Thumbnails view, choose **View ➛ Thumbnails**, then drag the thumbnail page image from one position to another and release the mouse button.

While you are dragging pages in either Thumbnails view or in the Document Layout palette, the pointer changes to indicate how the page will be inserted. (See the pointer descriptions in the Adding Pages section found earlier in this chapter.)

Things to Consider When Moving Pages

As is the case with deleting pages, before you move pages you need to think about what will happen to the items on each page, especially when linked text is involved. Regardless of which method you use to move pages, QuarkXPress does not change the links—the order in which text flows between text boxes.

Since moving pages does not change the sequence in which text is linked (Figure 3.23), you're probably moving text out of order if you move a page with linked text. For example, if a story starts on page 2 and continues on page 3, and if you move page 2 to follow page 3, then the story will still start on the moved page and flow backward. Proceed with caution when moving pages with linked text boxes.

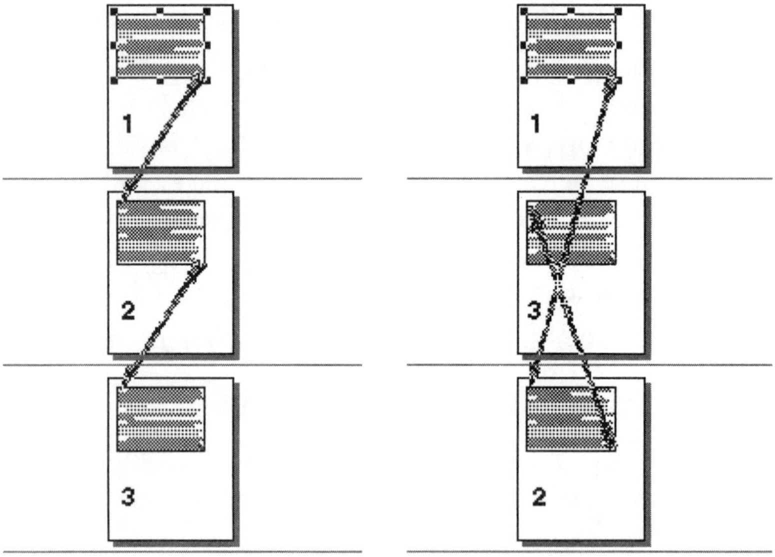

***Figure 3.23** Moving Pages does not change the sequence in which text is linked, so be sure that you want to reorder the text!*

Copying Pages from One Document to Another

To move entire pages from one document to another, open both documents (using **File ➛ Open**) and select **View ➛ Thumbnails** for both documents, then drag pages back and forth between the document windows. The page(s) will actually be copied from one file to another.

You can select and move multiple sequential pages by shift-clicking on two or more pages, then dragging the multiple-selected pages. Use ⌘/CTRL-click to select multiple, nonsequential pages. When you drag pages to the target document, the pointer changes to indicate how they will be inserted, as described earlier in the "Adding Pages" section.

TIP: When you move pages from one file to another, links between text boxes on moved pages are preserved, and the entire story (all of the text in the linked chain) is brought in from the source document. In the target document, copied pages display text from the beginning of the story, even if the story did not start on the copied pages in the source document.

Moving a page from one document to another brings in the associated master pages from the source document as well. You cannot move pages based on a facing-page master page into a single-sided document.

Moving a page from one document to another also brings in any Style Sheets, H&Js,Colors, or Dashes & Stripes that are applied to items on those pages, and which do not exist in the target document. If there is a name conflict, the definition of the target document will prevail.

Document Navigation

Once you're working with two or more pages in your document, it's important to know how to move around the document. There's no right or wrong way to move from page to page within a document; you'll find you use different techniques depending on a specific situation.

You can turn pages by:

- using the scroll bars to scroll up or down within the document;
- using the **Go To, Previous, Next, First,** and **Last** commands from the Page menu;
- using Go To Page Icons in the lower left corner of the document window;
- double-clicking on the icon for a page in the Document Layout palette; or
- using special keys on an extended keyboard.

The next sections discuss how to use each technique. It's probably a good idea to make sure you're familiar with each one.

TIP

How do you know what page you're currently viewing? The easiest way to find out is to simply look at the lower left corner of the document window, where the page number is always displayed. Remember that the number displayed is for the page at the *top* of the document window. (It's easy to get confused when most of the document window displays one page, but the preceding page number is shown because just a very small section of the that page is still displayed at the top of the window.)

Using the Scroll Bars

The scroll bars in the document window let you scroll vertically and horizontally, from one part of the page to another, or from page to page, depending on the zoom view of the document.

There are three ways to use scroll bars:

- You can click on the *scroll arrows* to move the view of the page in small increments.

- Click in the *gray area* of the scroll bar to scroll one full window per click. Notice that the page number does not change until the page is entirely out of the document window. The distance the page moves when you click in the gray part of the scroll bar or on an arrow varies, depending on the view you are using. The increments of movement are smaller in enlarged views (such as 200 percent) than in reduced views (such as Fit in Window).
- To move more quickly through the document, you can drag the *vertical scroll box*. As you do this, the page view does not change until you release the mouse button. However, the page number in the lower left corner of the document window does change as you scroll by each page, indicating the page that will be displayed if you release the mouse button.

TIP

If you hold the **Option/ALT** key as you drag the scroll box, you can obtain a "live scroll," which displays the page and its contents as you scroll, even if the Live Scroll option is not selected in Application Preferences.

Using the Page Menu and the Go To Command

You can use various Page menu commands (Figure 3.24) to move from the currently active page (i.e., the page displayed in the document window) to the page immediately before it or after it by choosing **Previous** or **Next**. Use **First** to move from the currently active page to the first page in the document, or **Last** to move to the last page.

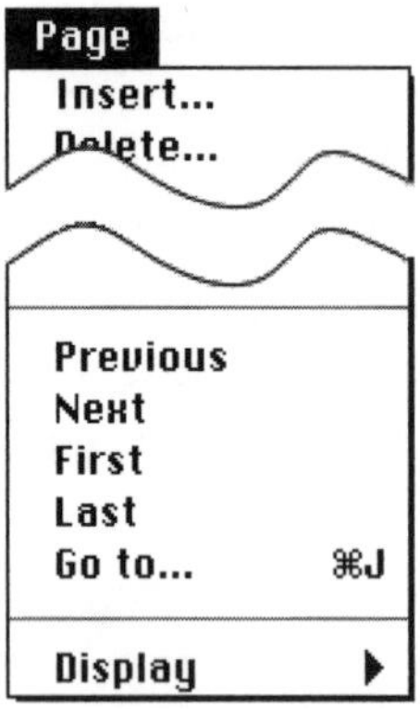

Figure 3.24 *The Page Menu commands for moving from one page to another.*

You can also use **Page ➛ Go To** (⌘-J/CTRL-J) to jump quickly to any page in the document. Enter the page number you want to view in the Go To Page dialog box. As with other page number entries in QuarkXPress, you can enter the user-defined page number or the absolute page number.

Using the Go To Page Icons

As an alternative to the Page menu commands, you can use QuarkXPress 4.0's new Go To Page icons to move from page to page. Pop-up page icons in the lower left corner of the document window (Figure 3.25) allow for easy navigation through your document pages. When you click on the pop-up menu, all the master pages and document pages are displayed; drag your mouse to the page you wish to turn to and release.

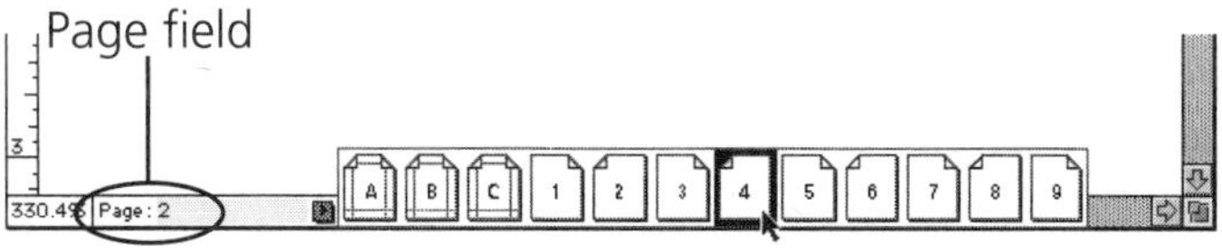

Figure 3.25 *The Go To Page icons are displayed from a pop-up menu in the lower left corner of the document window.*

TIP

As an alternative to using the Go To Page command (**Page → Go To**), use the **Page field** adjacent to the Go To Page pop-up menu: click in the field, type in the number of the page you wish to jump to, and press **Return**.

Using the Document Layout palette

We think one of the most convenient ways to navigate through a document is to use the Document Layout palette. When the palette is displayed (**View → Document Layout**) you can move to a document page or master page by simply double-clicking on the appropriate page icon. Icons for master pages are displayed in the top part of the palette, document pages are displayed in the lower part. You can move the split bar up or down to increase or decrease the display area for each type of page icon.

The number on the page icons always represents the *user-defined* page number, the number that prints on the page when sectioning and automatic page numbering is used

The user-defined page number is also displayed in the lower left corner of the Document layout palette when you click once on any document page icon (Figure 3.26). If a page is the beginning of a section, an asterisk (*) preceeds the page number displayed on the page icon in the palette and in the lower left corner of the palette.

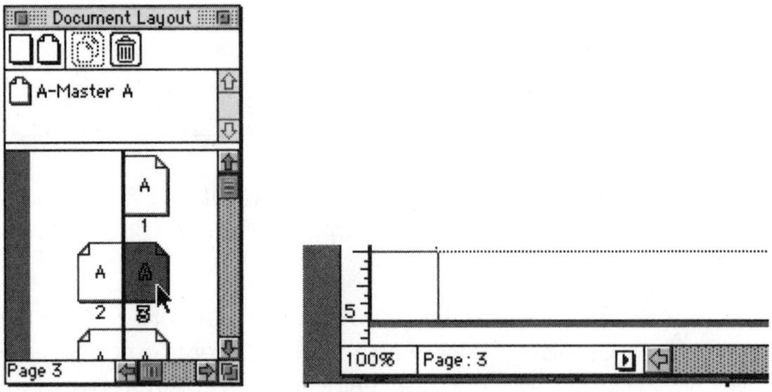

Figure 3.26 *Double-click on a page icon in the Document Layout palette to turn to that page.*

TIP

In all dialog boxes, you can reference QuarkXPress pages with *either* the absolute page number, representing the *physical* location of the page in the file, or the user-defined page number. To reference a page by the user-defined number, just type in the number; to reference a page by its absolute page number, precede the number with a plus (+) sign.

Using Keyboard Shortcuts

If you are a "keyboard person," there's no faster way to navigate than to move around a document using keyboard shortcuts (Figure 3.27). You can use the following keys:

- **Home** displays the top of the first page of a document.
- **Page Up** scrolls up one document window.
- **Page Up** with **Shift** scrolls to the top of the active page.
- **Page Down** scrolls down one document window.
- **Page Down** with **Shift** scrolls to the top of the next page.
- **End** scrolls to the bottom of the last page of the document.
- **End** with **Shift** scrolls to the top of the last page.

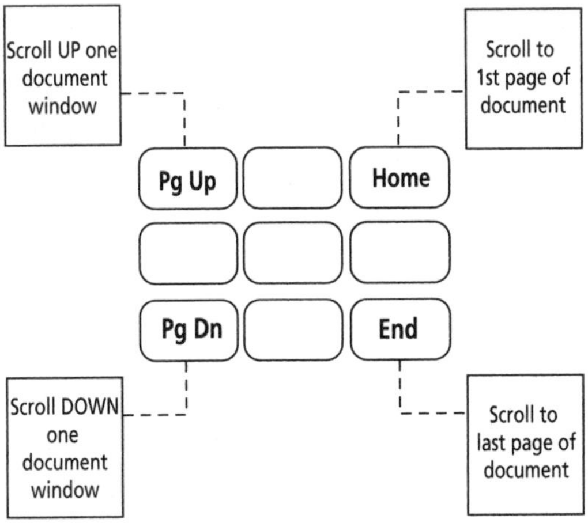

Figure 3.27 *Keyboard shortcuts for navigating within a document.*

Understanding QuarkXPress Preferences

Many people use QuarkXPress for years without ever being aware of the settings available under the **Edit ➛ Preferences** command, and how they affect the way certain features of the program work. So many times the answer to a problem situation is found by changing a Preference setting. The factory-shipped defaults for Preferences are intended to be the right setting for most, but not all, situations. It's important that you become familiar with QuarkXPress's Preferences, so you can set them appropriately for your individual needs.

TIP: If you want to change all Preferences back to their preset, factory-shipped defaults, trash the file in your QuarkXPress folder called "XPress Preferences." The next time you launch QuarkXPress, a new XPress Preferences file will be built with all Preferences set back to the original defaults.

Application Preferences

Application Preferences (**Edit → Preferences → Application**) are those which affect the way the QuarkXPress program behaves, as opposed to affecting the way a specific document or documents behave. Application preferences do not "travel" with your document, and typically do not affect the way a document prints.

The Display Tab

The Display tab (Figure 3.28) includes settings that affect how your document displays on-screen, including settings for changing the color of guides and how pictures display.

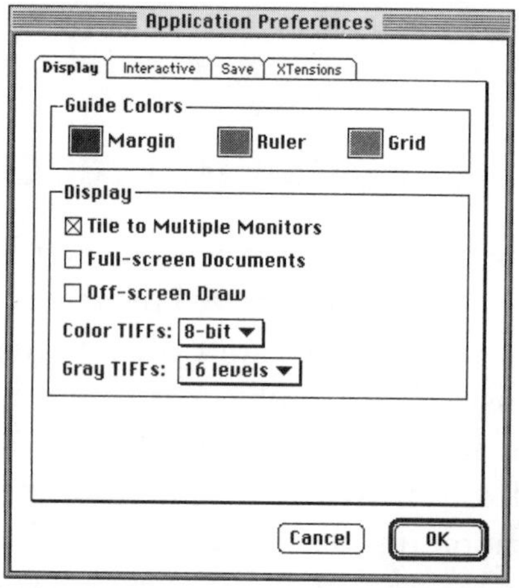

Figure 3.28 *The Display Tab of the Applications Preference dialog box.*

Guide Colors allows you to change the default color (Figure 3.29) in which margin guides, ruler guides, and the baseline grid are displayed. If you are using a gray-scale monitor, you can change the levels of gray. To change the guide color default:

1. Click on the color box in front of the appropriate guides you want to change; a dialog box with RGB controls is displayed.
2. To choose a color:

- Use the slider bars or input percentage values for red, green, or blue, or
- Click on **More Choices** to display additional color models that can be used to change guide colors.

3. When desired color is displayed, click **OK**.

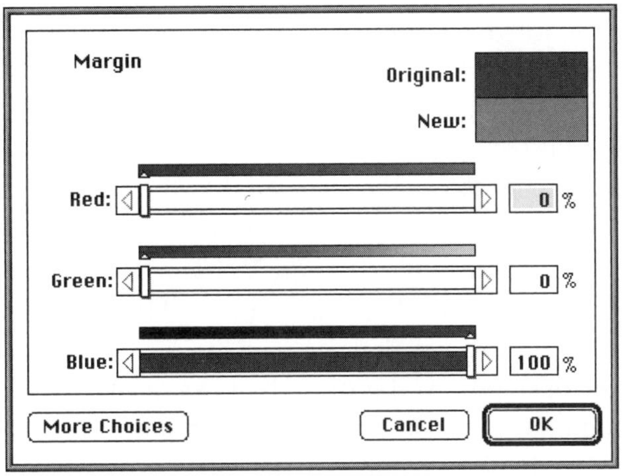

Figure 3.29 *Guide Colors can be changed from their default colors.*

The **Tile to Multiple Monitors** option is useful when you are working with more than one monitor attached to your computer. When this option is checked, the default setting, all the open document windows will be tiled to both monitors when you select **View ➛ Windows ➛ Tile Documents.**

Full-Screen Documents affects how the document window will resize when you open a new file, click the **zoom box/Maximize** button, or tile documents (**View ➛ Windows ➛ Tile Documents**). When this option is not checked (the default setting), document windows will extend to just above the Measurements palette and to the right of the Tool palette, if those palettes are displayed. When the option is checked, the document window will fill the entire screen when you open a new file or resize the document window by clicking on the **zoom box/Maximize** button, and tiled document windows will tile to the entire screen. Of course, all document windows can be moved or resized at any time.

If you check **Off-screen Draw**, the screen updates at once as you scroll. Normally, this option is off, and when you scroll using the scroll bars, the screen is actually updated in successive pieces. The redraw begins the moment you scroll, but it may take a few seconds for the entire screen to display, especially if you have complicated graphics on the page. With Off-screen Draw checked on, there is a momentary pause before screen redraw occurs, but then the entire screen is redrawn at once. Checking this option does not actually decrease the time it takes the screen to redraw; it merely changes the method by which the redraw occurs.

The **Color TIFFs** option lets you specify the display of color images that have been saved in the TIFF format. The 8-bit default setting displays a preview that can display up to 256 colors simultaneously; the 16-bit option allows display of thousands of colors simultaneously, and the 32-bit option allows the display of millions of colors simultaneously.

TIP

If you import images with the 32-bit display option selected, they'll look fantastic on-screen, but your file size will increase dramatically.

The **Gray TIFFs** option lets you display gray-scale images with 256 levels of gray. If you wish to speed up screen redraw, choose **16** levels.

Remember that images cannot display with more color depth or more levels of gray than they were originally created in, regardless of the settings you use. An 8-bit color image will not look any better with 32-bit display selected! This setting does not affect the way an image will print.

The Interactive Tab

The Interactive tab (Figure 3.30) includes settings that affect how your documents will scroll, whether or not quote marks will be converted to typographically correct "smart" quotes, and settings for turning Drag and Drop on or off.

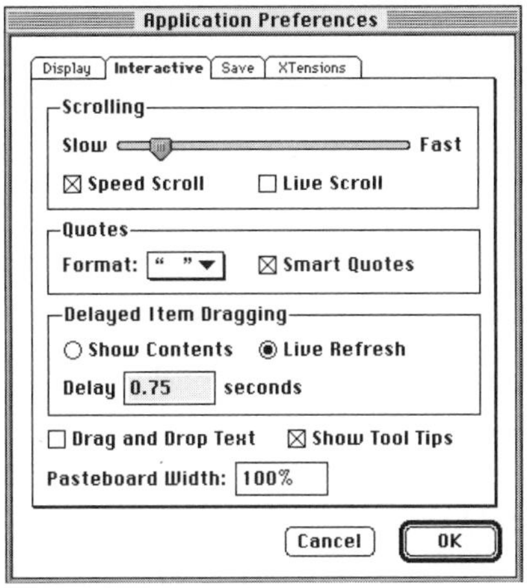

Figure 3.30 *The Interactive tab of the Applications Preferences dialog box.*

Use the **Scrolling** slider bar to set the speed at which a document scrolls when using the scroll-bar arrows. The faster the speed is set, the greater the distance the document moves in the document window with one click of a scroll arrow.

The **Speed Scroll** option is useful for increasing the speed of scrolling through documents, because with this option on the default setting, it causes pictures and blends to be *greeked* (represented as gray areas) as you scroll. When you stop scrolling, all elements redraw normally.

If **Live Scroll** is unchecked, the default setting, the screen is updated only after you finish scrolling and release the mouse. If

Live Scroll is checked, QuarkXPress updates the screen display as you scroll through a document. This can slow down the scrolling process, but it will allow you to see page contents as you scroll.

TIP: If Live Scroll is unchecked, you can achieve a Live Scroll by holding down the **Option/ALT** key as you drag a scroll box. If Live Scroll is checked, holding down the **Option/ALT** key as you scroll temporarily disables a live scroll.

When **Smart Quotes** is checked, quotation marks will appear when you type in a foot mark (‘) or an inch mark (“) from the keyboard, or when you import text. In order for foot mark (‘) or inch mark (“) characters to be converted in imported text, Convert Quotes must be checked in the Get Text dialog box (**File ➛ Get Text**) when you import the text. Different quotation marks may be chosen from the Quotes Format pop-up menu. (See Figure 3.31.)

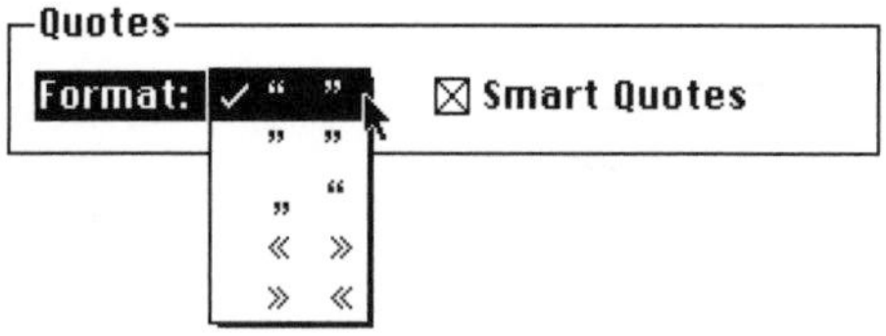

Figure 3.31 *The Quotes pop-up menu.*

TIP: When Smart Quotes is checked, but you actually need an inch or a foot mark, precede the appropriate keys with **⌘/CTRL**: Press the appropriate **⌘-'/CTRL-'** to type a foot mark ('), and press **⌘-"/CTRL-"** in order to type an inch mark (").

When you click on an item and immediately move it, you will see only the bounding box of the item, and not the item contents. However, when you click on an item and pause before you drag it, the contents are displayed. **Delayed Item Dragging** controls details of the display of an item when you pause before dragging it to a new location. **Show Contents** is the default setting, and will cause the contents of an item to display as you drag the item. When **Live Refresh** is on, the contents of an item will display as you drag it, but the screen will also be updated as you drag the item. This especially affects items in text, as Live Refresh will display the text reflow as you drag the item, instead of displaying the text reflow after you release the mouse. The **Delay <x> seconds** field lets you specify how long you must hold down the mouse button before moving the item in order to enable Show Contents or Live Refresh. The default is .75 seconds.

The **Drag and Drop Text** option allows you to move or copy text using the mouse only, with no keyboard or menu commands. With the Drag and Drop Text option selected, you can highlight text, then click on it once and drag with the mouse to move it to a new location. You can copy text using drag and drop by holding down the **Shift** key before you click on the selected text; when you move the text and release the mouse, the text will be copied to the new location, and also remain in its original location. This is a shortcut alternative to the normal convention of using the **Edit ➛ Cut/Edit ➛ Copy** and **Edit ➛ Paste** command to reposition or copy text.

TIP

You can move and copy text with the mouse only, even if the Drag and Drop Text option is checked off. To move text, highlight the text; then hold down the **⌘/CTRL** keys before you click on the text and move it to a new location. To copy text, highlight the text; then hold down the **⌘-SHIFT** keys before you click on the text and copy it to a new location.

Show Tool Tips displays the names of tools or palettes when you position the cursor over them. The default is unchecked, but new users may find this feature especially helpful.

The **Pasteboard Width** option lets you control the width of the *pasteboard*, the nonprinting area to the left and right of each page or spread where you can work with or store items. The default setting is that the pasteboard is 100 percent of the page size. So, for example, if your page is letter size (8.5 x 11 inches), the pasteboard will be 8.5 inches wide to the left and right of the page. You can set the pasteboard-width value from 0 percent to 100 percent, but the width of pages and pasteboard combined cannot exceed 48 inches. The pasteboard is always 1/2 inch above and below a page or spread, and at least 1/2 inch of the pasteboard will surround document pages, even if you set a width percentage that would be less than 1/2 inch.

The Save Tab

The Save Tab (Figure 3.32) includes options related to saving your documents, including Library documents.

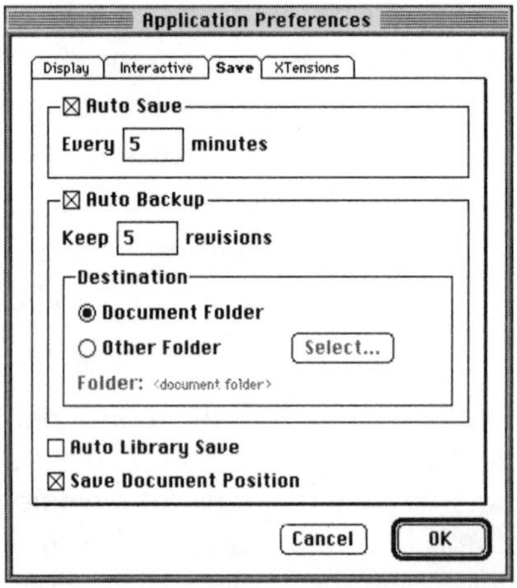

Figure 3.32 *The Save tab of the Application Preferences dialog box.*

If the **Auto Save** option is checked, QuarkXPress will automatically save a copy of your document to a temporary file. The frequency of the Auto Save is determined by the value in the text field, **Every <x> minutes**. The preset default is every 5 minutes. When you manually save your file (**File ➛ Save**), your original file will be overwritten.

The temporary file is named with the current document name as "filename.AutoSave." Should you experience a system failure due to a power outage or other mysterious cause, QuarkXPress will give you the option of retaining the changes made up until the last Auto Save by opening the file titled "filename.AutoSave."

TIP: While the Auto Save feature is a valuable safeguard against system failures, bear in mind that a pause in work can occur every time an Auto Save takes place, especially for large files or those containing complex graphics. Also, make sure you have room on your hard disk for QuarkXPress to save temporary files of all the documents you have open and are working on in the same session.

If the **Auto Backup** option is checked, QuarkXPress will automatically retain a revision of your document every time you save a document (**File** → **Save**). The number of revisions that are saved is determined by the value in the text field, **Keep <*x*> revisions.** Each time you save a document, QuarkXPress sends the previous version to the destination folder you specify in Destination: either in the Document Folder or other Folder which you specify.

Consecutive numbers are added to the file name with each revision, with the most recently saved version having the highest number. After the last revision is saved, additional revisions will replace the first version saved.

TIP: If you use the Auto Backup feature, be sure you have enough disk space to save the number of revisions you have specified, especially for large document files. If there is not enough disk space, an alert will display. You will then need to turn the option off to save your file.

Auto Library Save checked on will cause the library you're working with to be saved every time you make a change to it. If this option is unchecked, QuarkXPress saves library additions and changes only when you close a library or quit the program.

TIP: If you work with a library file frequently, be sure **Auto Library Save** is on. While there may be a slight delay each time you make a change and the library is saved, it's a small tradeoff for not loosing your entire library contents in the event of a system crash.

Save Document Position specifies that when you open an existing document, QuarkXPress will remember the zoom view and the size and position of the document window when you last saved the file. The default is that this option is checked on.

The XTensions Tab

The XTensions tab (Figure 3.33) controls under what conditions the XTensions Manager dialog box will display when you launch QuarkXPress. This dialog box, which can be displayed any time using the **Utilities → XTensions Manager** command, controls what XTensions will load when you launch QuarkXPress. (See the Xtensions Manager Appendix for more information on XTensions).

If you like to select which XTensions load each time you launch QuarkXPress, click **Always.** If you check **When XTensions Folder Changes,** the XTensions Manager displays any time you've made any changes to the XTension folder (which is found in the QuarkXPress program folder). If **When Error loading XTensions Occurs** is checked, QuarkXPress will display the XTensions Manager any time an error occurs while an Xtension is loading.

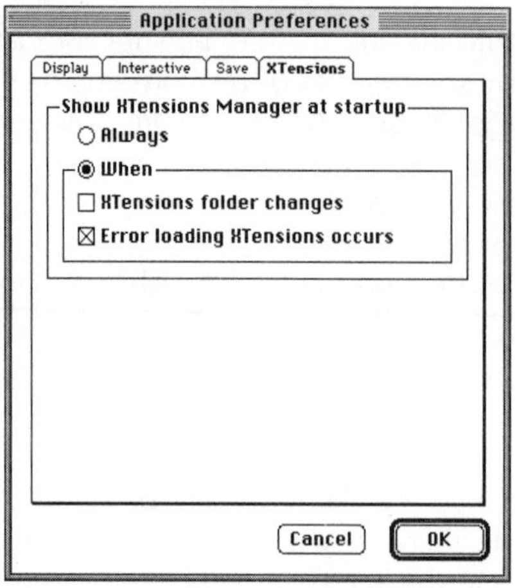

Figure 3.33 *The XTensions tab of the Applications Preferences dialog box.*

Document Preferences

Settings in the Document Preferences dialog box affect the behavior of a variety of commands and features, from master pages to QuarkXPress tools. You can display the Document Preferences dialog box by choosing **Edit ➛ Preferences ➛ Document** or by typing the keyboard shortcut: **⌘-Y/CTRL-Y**.

Unlike Application Preferences, settings in the Document Preferences dialog box "travel" with the document. If you open a file that was created by another version of QuarkXPress with a different set of preferences, a dialog box will display which allows you to keep the preferences that are attached to the document, or to apply the preferences as you currently have them set in QuarkXPress.

TIP

When you open a QuarkXPress document and get a message that XPress preferences are different from currently set Preferences, click on **Keep Document Settings** to ensure the document will be unchanged from when it was first created (Figure 3.34).

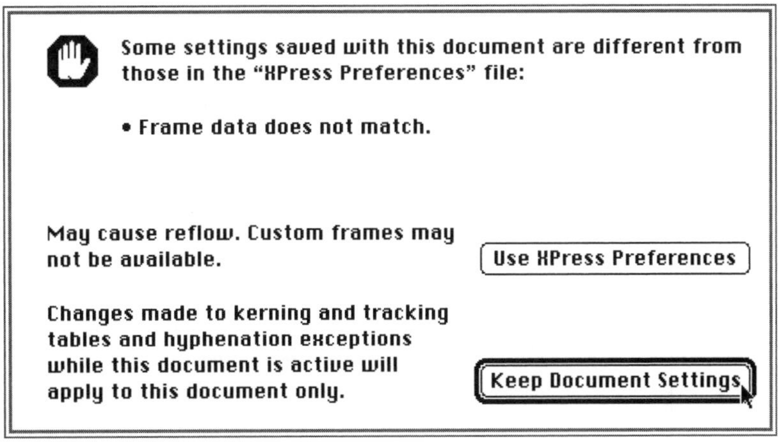
Some settings saved with this document are different from those in the "XPress Preferences" file:
• Frame data does not match.
May cause reflow. Custom frames may not be available.
Use XPress Preferences
Changes made to kerning and tracking tables and hyphenation exceptions while this document is active will apply to this document only.
Keep Document Settings

Figure 3.34 *Choose **Keep Document Settings** if you want to be sure a file is unchanged from when it was originally created.*

If you change a document preference with a document open, the changes affect *only* the currently active document. Documents created previously, or other documents that are open at the time, will not be affected.

If you change a document preference with *no* document open, it will affect *all* new documents that you create. If there is a document preference that you find yourself changing frequently, make the change "permanent" by using this technique. Customize QuarkXPress and change those settings you find annoying! For example, we usually change the Tool Preference for text boxes to have 0 pt text inset, rather than the preset 1 pt default.

The General Tab

The General tab (Figure 3.35) is kind of a catch-all, including settings that affect the rulers and measurement, how pages are inserted when using an automatic text box, whether guides are displayed in front of or behind items, and whether frames are drawn inside or outside a box.

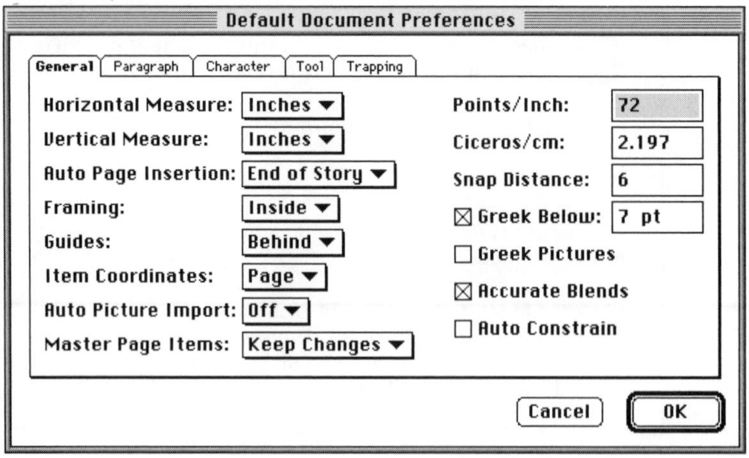

Figure 3.35 *The General tab of the Document Preferences dialog box.*

Horizontal and **Vertical** Measure let you set the measurement system (Figure 3.36) in which rulers will be displayed. You can set the two rulers separately, so that the horizontal ruler displays picas, for instance, while the vertical ruler displays agates (common in traditional newspaper production).

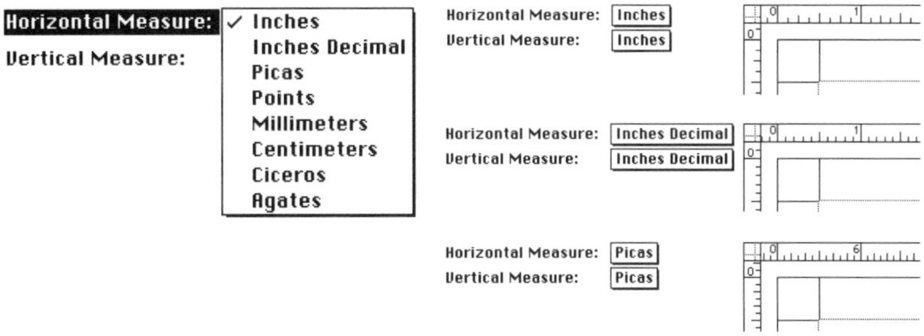

Figure 3.36 *Measurement systems and how they display on the rulers in Actual size view.*

Inches displays the rulers in inches divided into sixteenths. **Inches Decimal** displays the rulers in inches divided into twentieths. QuarkXPress measures an inch as 72.051 points per inch (see the paragraph on Points/Inch later in this section). **Picas** displays the rulers with an inch divided into twenty-fourths, each mark representing a fourth of a pica, or 1/12". There are 12 points in a pica and six picas in an inch—or approximately 72 points in an inch. **Points** displays the rulers similarly, with each mark representing 3 points. **Millimeters** and **Centimeters** display the ruler using the metric system. **Ciceros** are a standard French typesetting measure, with 1 cicero equivalent to approximately 4.552 millimeters. **Agates**, a measurement system new to QuarkXPress 4.0, are commonly used for measuring vertical column lengths in classified ads; there are 14 agates to an inch.

QuarkXPress always shows font sizes, frame widths, and line widths in points in the Measurements palette and dialog boxes related to these elements, regardless of your selection for the ruler displays. Similarly, page-size measurements are always shown in inches when Inches, Inches Decimal, Picas or Points are selected, and in millimeters when Millimeters, Centimeters or Ciceros are selected. You can enter the values for these in any measurement system, but QuarkXPress will always convert them to their default measurement system (see Chapter 1, Figure 1.12 for measurement abbreviations).

Auto Page Insertion determines whether or not pages will be inserted and where they will be inserted when text overflow occurs. QuarkXPress automatically adds pages for the text overflow if *all* of the following are true:

- Auto Page Insertion is enabled (not set to Off);
- the master page that will be used has an automatic text box (indicated by the intact chain icon [⛓] in the upper left corner of the master page); and
- the overflow is from the automatic text chain.

When there is overflow text, the preset default is that QuarkXPress adds pages at the **End of Story**, adding new pages immediately after the last text box in the chain that overflows.

You can prevent QuarkXPress from adding pages automatically by changing the default to **Off.** Choose **End of Section** to add pages at the end of the current section. A section is a group of pages—one chapter of a book, for example—with sequential page numbering defined by the **Page ➛ Section** command. (See Chapter 9, "Master Pages and Sectioning.") Choose **End of Document** to add pages at the end of the document, regardless of how the document is sectioned. Remember, pages will not be automatically inserted when there is text overflow from boxes that are not part of the automatic text chain.

The **Framing** option in the General Preferences dialog box lets you specify whether frames are added to the Inside or Outside of box items. If the frame is added inside, the dimensions of the box remain the same. If the frame is added outside, the dimensions of the box increase by the frame width. This setting determines the immediate effect of using the **Item ➛ Frame** command—existing frames in the document do not change when you change the Framing preference.

For example, if you draw a 12-pica square box and add a 1-pica wide frame using the **Item ➛ Frame** command, the effective size of the box will remain 12 picas square if the Framing option is set to Inside, or will increase to 14 picas square if the Framing option is set to Outside (Figure 3.37).

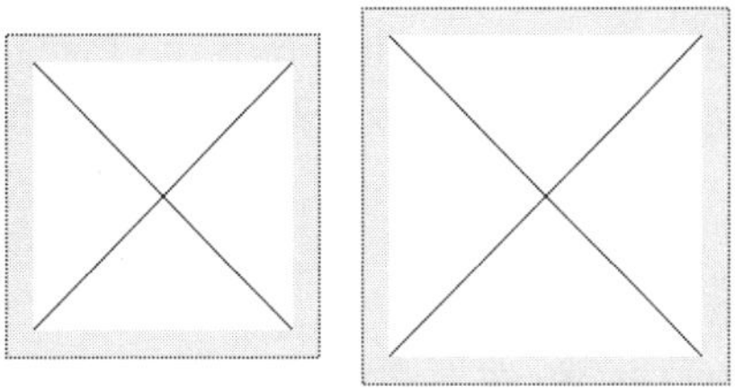

Figure 3.37 *A 12 pica x 12 pica box with the frame inside (left) and outside (right).*

The distance between text and frames positioned inside text boxes is determined by the box's Text Inset value (Text tab of the Modify dialog box, **Item ➛ Modify**). In picture boxes, a frame inside actually crops the picture.

Guides controls whether guides appear on top of all items on a page, or behind all items on a page. Nonprinting guides—margin guides, column guides, and ruler guides—can be set to display behind all items on the page or in front of them.

Item Coordinates controls where rulers measure from. The preset default is **Page**, which causes the horizontal ruler to display 0 at the top left corner of each page. On facing pages or multiple-page spreads, the measurements begin again at 0 at the top left corner of each new page. Choose **Spread** from the pop-up menu if you want the ruler to display measurements that are continuous across the spread. For example, with a spread of two pages that are 8" wide, the ruler will display 8" at the top left corner of the right-hand page, and continue with 9", 10" and so on as it measures the entire spread.

Auto Picture Import lets you control whether QuarkXPress automatically updates all imported pictures that have been modified using another program (one outside of QuarkXPress) since you last saved the document.

The preset default is Off. If you want pictures to be automatically updated, choose **On**. QuarkXPress will reimport the pictures using the modified version of the files. If in the process of reimporting, a picture cannot be located, the Picture tab of the Usage dialog box (described in Chapter 8, "Printing Basics") will be displayed, through which you can locate the moved or renamed file (Figure 3.38).

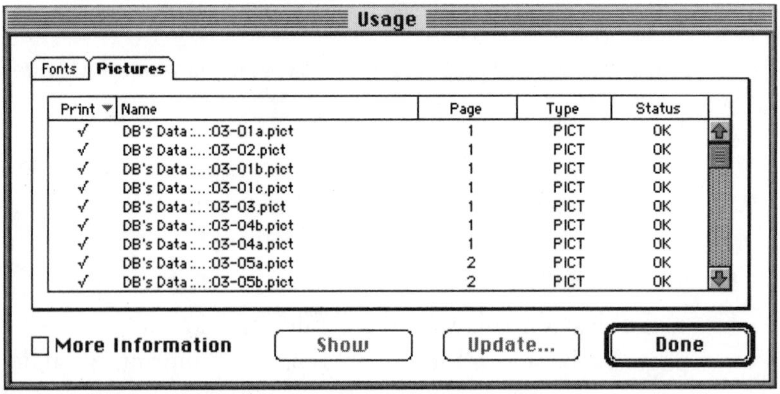

***Figure 3.38** The option Auto Picture Import On (verify) displays the Pictures tab of the Usage dialog box each time you open a file containing missing or modified pictures.*

If you set this value to **On (verify)**, and open a file that contains modified or missing pictures, QuarkXPress will display an alert asking if you want to list missing or modified pictures; if you click **OK**, the Missing/Modified Picture dialog box is displayed.

If you change the Auto Picture Import setting to **On** (or **Off**), modified pictures will be updated (or not updated) when you next open the active document; no changes take place immediately. Remember, too, if Auto Picture Import is off, you can selectively update pictures using the Pictures tab of the **Utilities ➤ Usage** command, or QuarkXPress will ask if you want to update modified pictures when you use the **File ➤ Print** command.

Master Page Items is an important preference to understand if you work with long documents. The Master Page Items option lets you control how applying a new master page affects document pages.

As you probably know, you can edit items on document pages that are from the master page that has been applied to it, sometimes called *master items*. The Master Page Items setting controls what happens to master items on document pages that you have changed in some way, when the master page is reapplied, or when a new master page is applied.

If you choose **Keep Changes**, the preset default, when you apply a new master page, unmodified master items are deleted from the document page and replaced with items from the new master page. But master page items that have been modified on the document page will not be deleted, and will remain unchanged.

This can cause unexpected results, especially when the master item has been accidentally modified—something that is easier to do than you might think, since touching the item, and moving it even a millimeter, is a modification. Let's say you move a folio, a master item, just slightly to accommodate the body text on a page. If you later reapply the master to this page, the existing folio will stay in position, but the folio from the master page will also be added, causing two folios to appear on the page!

If you choose **Delete Changes**, when you apply a new master page, both unmodified *and* modified master-page items are deleted from the document page and replaced with the items from the new master page. Choosing this setting solves many of the problems that can be experienced with reapplying or applying new master pages to existing document pages.

Points/Inch lets you control precisely how QuarkXPress measures an inch. Normally, QuarkXPress converts points to inches (and vice versa), using 72 points per inch. You can change this by entering a value between 72 and 73 in .01-point increments. The true measure in traditional typography is 72.051 points per inch.

Ciceros/cm lets you control how ciceros are calculated to centimeters. QuarkXPress converts ciceros to centimeters using 2.1967 ciceros per centimeter. To change the value of ciceros to centimeters, enter any value between 2 and 3 in .0001-cicero increments.

Snap Distance controls at what distance items will "snap" as they approach a guide. The preset default is that items snap when they are moved within 6 pixels of a guide. You can change the distance at which items will snap by entering a value from 0 to 100 (pixels).

Greek Below sets the size of display at which QuarkXPress will greek text (Figure 3.39). The speed of screen redraw is accelerated by greeking text below a certain point size—displaying the text as a gray bar on the screen. Greeking increases the speed at which pages are displayed on your screen, but it does not affect printing. The preset value is 7 points, but you can set this to any value from 2 to 720 points.

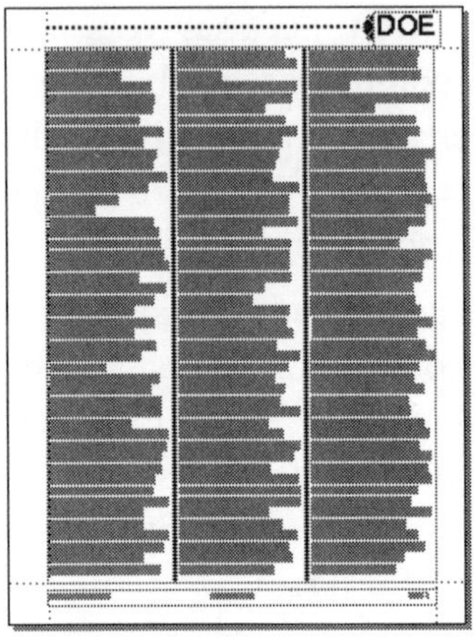

Figure 3.39 *Greeked text.*

The value you enter here determines the size below which text is greeked in Actual Size view. The value is adjusted automatically for other magnifications. For example, if you set type to be greeked below 7 points in Actual Size, then it will be greeked below 3.5 points in 200 percent view or below 14 points in 50 percent view.

Greek Pictures is another way to speed up display of your pages. If Greek Pictures is checked, QuarkXPress displays inactive pictures as gray boxes. When you select the picture by clicking on it once, the picture will display normally. This is a great way to speed up screen redraw while editing a document with a lot of imported pictures. Picture greeking does not affect printing.

The **Accurate Blends** option affects how blends will display on the screen of 8-bit monitors (Figure 3.40). The preset default is that Accurate Blends is checked, so that blends display without banding. To display blends more quickly, uncheck this option. Monitors with 24-bit video displays always show blends as accurate blends, since these monitors have the color depth to display blends smoothly. This option does not affect how blends print.

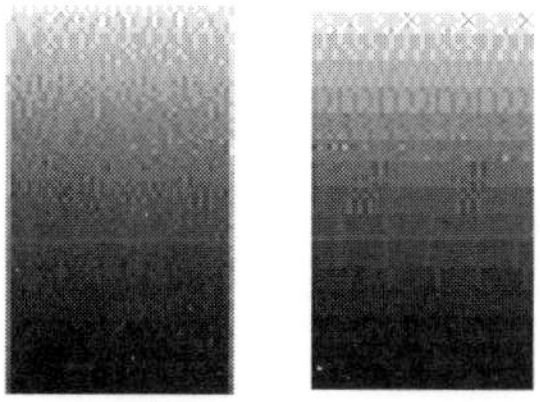

Figure 3.40 *Screen display when Accurate Blends is checked (left) and unchecked (right).*

If **Auto Constrain** is checked, items created within a box are constrained by that box. You cannot move constrained items out of their constraining box or scale them to be larger than the constraining box. Changes in Auto Constrain affect items that you add to the document but will not affect items previously positioned on pages. The preset default is that Auto Constrain is unchecked.

The Paragraph Tab

The Paragraph tab of the Document Preferences dialog box controls settings that affect leading, the baseline grid, and the hyphenation method. You'll find details on how these preferences work in Chapter 5, "Typography."

The Character Tab

The Character tab of the Document Preferences dialog box controls settings that affect the size and position of superscript, subscript, small caps, and superior characters. These and other options in the Character tab are discussed in detail in Chapter 5, "Typography."

The Tool Tab

The Tool tab (Figure 3.41) of the Document Preferences dialog box (**Edit ➛ Preferences ➛ Document**) lets you modify defaults for the Zoom tool and the item creation tools. You can display the Tool Preferences dialog box by choosing the command from the menu or by double-clicking on a tool in the Tool palette.

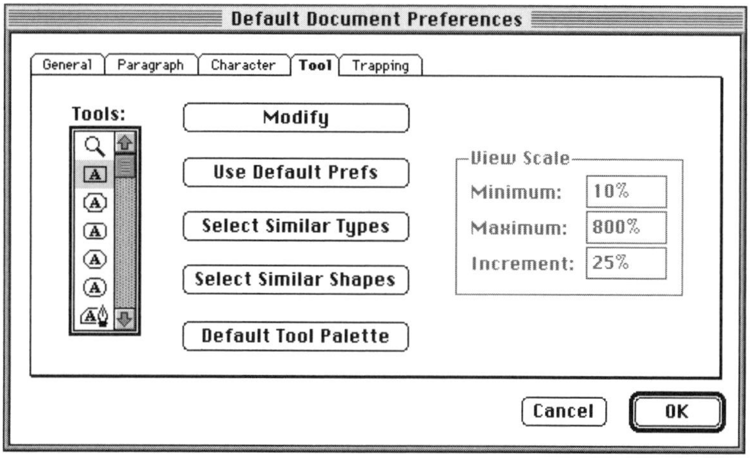

Figure 3.41 *The Tool tab of the Default Document Preferences dialog box.*

The Tools list displays the tools for which Preferences can be set: the Zoom tool () and all the item-creation tools. It does *not* include, and you cannot change, preferences for the Item tool (), the Content tool (), the Rotation tool (), and the Linking () and Unlinking () tools.

The **Modify** button displays the Modify dialog box with the available tabs displayed that are appropriate to the tool(s) selected. For example, when a text-box creation tool is selected, the Box, Text, Frame, and Runaround tabs are available (Figure 3.42). If a Line tool is selected, the Line and Runaround tabs are available; when a text-path tool is selected, the Line, Text Paths, and Runaround tabs are available.

The Frame and Runaround buttons display the Frame Specifications and Runaround Specifications dialog boxes (respectively). You can change the defaults for items created with the selected tool.

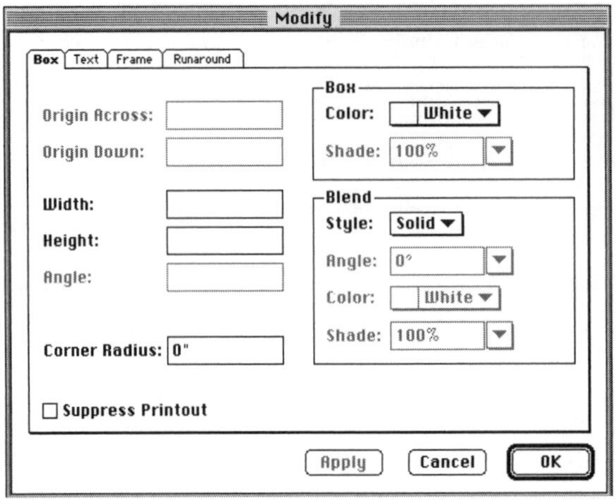

Figure 3.42 *Box specifications that can be modified in the Tool Preferences dialog box (grayed out options cannot be changed).*

The **Use Default Prefs** button resets all preferences for the tools selected in the Tools list to the factory-shipped defaults. Preferences for tools not selected will not return to default settings.

The **Select Similar Types** button lets you select similar types of tools for which you can modify preferences. There are four different types of tools that can be selected: all text box tools, all picture box tools, all line tools, or all text-path tools.

The **Select Similar Shapes** button lets you select tools that create similar shapes for which you can modify preferences. There are seven different shapes of box-creation tools: rectangle, rounded-corner, concave-corner, beveled-corner, oval, Bézier, and freehand Bézier boxes. There are four different line shapes: straight, orthogonal, Bézier, and freehand Bézier lines.

The **Default Tool Palette** button resets the Tool palette to the default list of tools. This does not reset the individual preferences set for each tool, but merely affects the display of the Tool palette.

View Scale is available only when the Zoom (🔍) tool icon is selected. These settings determine the **Minimum** zoom view in which a page may be displayed (10%) and the **Maximum** zoom view (800%). **Increment** determines the zoom that occurs each time you click with the Zoom tool (🔍) selected. The increment must be set between 1% and 400%.

The Trapping Tab

The Trapping tab of the Document Preferences dialog box controls the way QuarkXPress traps items when printing output to film for color separations. These options are discussed in detail in Chapter 13, "Printing Color Separations."

Index Preferences

When the Index Xtension is loaded, Index preferences will be available. The Index Preferences dialog box (**Edit ➛ Preferences ➛ Index**) controls the color in which index entries are displayed, and what characters are used when building an index such as the character(s) between page numbers. See Chapter 10, "Books, Lists, and Indexing," for more information on the settings in this dialog box.

Summary

This chapter, along with Chapter 2, "Creating One Page," covered most of the basic information on items and working with pages. The next chapters in Part I deal with specific areas of QuarkXPress, including working with text, graphics, color, and printing.

4 Word Processing

QuarkXPress has many of the same capabilities as a dedicated word processing program and you can input text, even long documents, directly into QuarkXPress without using a word processor. For longer documents, though, it's more common to input text using a word processing program, then import the text into QuarkXPress. In doing so, you can preserve not only the text, but also much of the formatting, such as type specifications, tabs, and paragraph alignment.

This chapter presents an overview of the process of getting text onto a page—by typing, copying, or importing—and describes some of QuarkXPress's basic formatting commands and word processing capabilities, including global search, and replace and spell checking.

It's important to understand how text that has been formatted in a word processing program is interpreted when it is imported into QuarkXPress. By seeing what you can do in QuarkXPress and knowing what you can do using your word processor, you'll be able to make decisions about how to prepare text and whether to put more time into formatting from the beginning—during word processing—or later, in QuarkXPress.

Chapter 3, "Expanding the Document," explained how to position text boxes on a page, link text boxes on the same page, or link text boxes from one page to the next. In this chapter, you will learn how to get text onto a page, how to edit the *content* of the text, and how to apply basic word processing formats.

Setting Columns, Gutter Width, and Text Inset

As mentioned in earlier chapters, you must first draw a text box using one of QuarkXPress's Text Box tools before you can type text directly on the page or import text from a word processing program. The basic steps are simple:

- Select a Text Box tool.
- Draw a text box by dragging the pointer on the page.
- Select the Content tool.
- Click in the text box and start typing (or importing) text.

In this chapter, we add a few steps to this process, beginning with setting the number of columns in a text box, setting gutter width, and adjusting the text inset value. If your text box requires only one column and you can accept the default preferences for a text box, (Figure 4.1) then you can skip this step. You can also save this step for later, after text has been added.

The number of columns may be set for the current text box using the Measurements palette or the Text tab of the Modify dialog box (**Item → Modify**). The preset default is 1 column.

TIP You divide a text box into columns when you want the *current story* to be arranged in columns. If you want a page to display two apparent columns—each containing a different "story"—then create two separate text boxes, each one column wide.

Gutter width and text inset can be specified only in the Modify Text dialog box. *Gutter width* is the space between columns. The preset default is .167 inches, or 1 pica. You can specify a gutter width from 3 points to 24 points in .001-point increments.

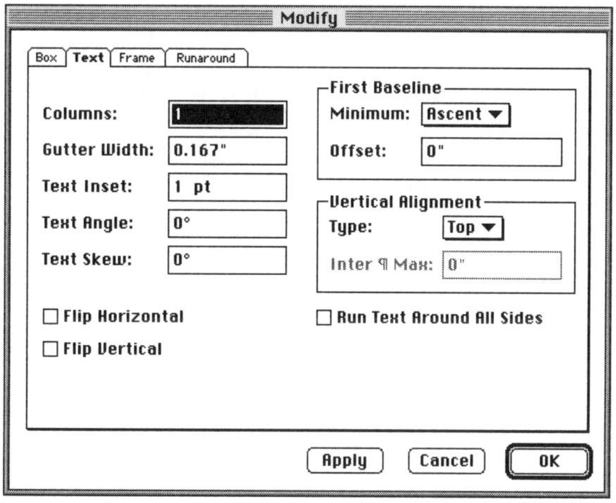

Figure 4.1 *Basic text box specifications include setting the number of columns, gutter width, and text inset.*

Text inset is the distance that text will be spaced from the four edges of a text box. The preset default is 1 point.

As a general rule, text boxes with no visible frame need no text inset. Text boxes with a visible frame *do* need a text inset; otherwise, the text touches the frame.

QuarkXPress divides the number of columns in a text box evenly—there cannot be columns of two different widths within the same text box. The actual column width will be determined by the text box width, minus any text inset value or frame width.

For example, a 100-point-wide text box set in three columns with 10-point gutters, no text inset, and no frame will have 26.67-point-wide columns ([100 – 10 – 10]/3 = 80/3 = 26.67).

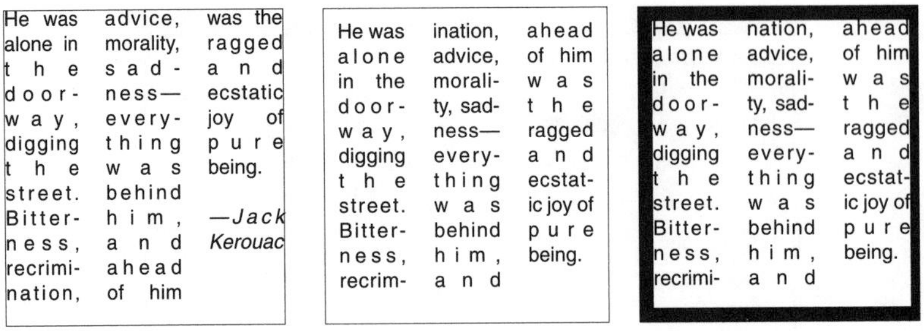

Figure 4.2 *Three-column text box set with no text inset (left) has wider columns than same box set with a 5-point inset (middle) or a 5-point frame (right).*

The other options in the Modify text dialog box are described in later chapters—Text Angle, Text Skew, and Horizontal and Vertical Flip in Chapter 13; Baseline Shift and Vertical Alignment in Chapter 5; and Run Text Around All Sides in Chapter 2.

Sources of Text

There are several ways of entering text on a page in QuarkXPress:

- Type text directly using QuarkXPress.
- You can import documents composed of text that has been typed in a word processing program (or other programs that can save data as text), using the **File ➤ Get Text** command.
- Select the **Edit ➤ Paste** command to copy the contents of the Clipboard.
- Drag a whole text box from one QuarkXPress document to another document.
- Copy text from a QuarkXPress library.

All these methods are described in the next sections.

Typing Text

To type text on a page in QuarkXPress, follow these steps:

1. Draw a new text box or activate an existing text box. Figure 4.3 shows how the cursor will look when you begin.

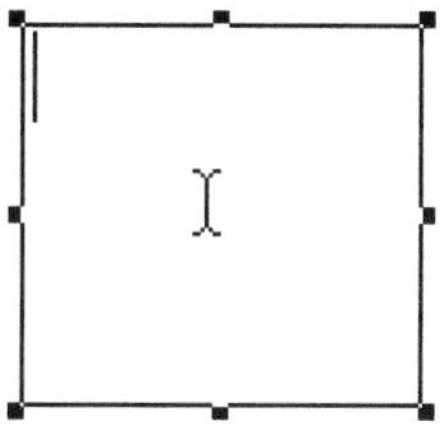

Figure 4.3 *Text box cursors. The I-beam shows position of mouse pointer, and the blinking vertical line shows text-insertion point where typed text will appear.*

2. The text-insertion point blinks in the text box. (If the box already contains text, you can click anywhere in the text to reposition the text-insertion point.)

When the Content tool (☞) is selected, the blinking text-insertion bar appears in the currently selected text box—at the top of an empty text box or in a text box that already contains text, wherever the insertion bar was last positioned. When the Content tool is positioned inside an active text box, the mouse pointer changes to an I-beam pointer.

3. Type text in using the keyboard.

The format and position of the typed text will vary depending on where you click the I-beam to position the text-insertion point. If you click the I-beam in existing text, the typed text will be inserted within the text block and will appear in the same format as the text immediately left of the insertion point.

If you click the I-beam in an empty text box, the typed text will be in the default character format or the format set up for the active text box. The default settings that are initially set up for text when you first install QuarkXPress are:

- Font: Helvetica 12-point
- Alignment: Left
- Leading: Auto
- Tabs: Set every half inch
- Hyphenation: Auto Hyphenation is off
- Auto kerning: Above 10 points
- Spacing between paragraphs: Zero

Text typed directly into QuarkXPress will take on these default characteristics unless you specify otherwise. If you want to change the format for the next text:

- Click the I-beam to position the text insertion point.
- Select the commands under the Style menu (as described later in this chapter) to format the text.
- Type the text.

In this case, you will be setting new specifications for the current insertion point only.

TIP

To change the default settings for all new text, select the **Edit ➛ Style Sheet** command (as described later in this chapter) and change the specifications for the Normal type style sheet. The default character format is defined by the Normal style sheet.

Typing Symbols and Other Special Characters

Most fonts have a variety of special characters available, including ™, ®, and ©. You can access these symbols by pressing the **Option** key before pressing a key on the keyboard. To find out what keys need to be pressed for certain characters, on a Macintosh you can use the Key Caps accessory on the Apple menu; under Windows you can double-click on the Character Map icon in the Accessories group under Windows Program Manager.

Certain fonts are composed almost entirely of symbols and special characters, such as Wingdings, a TrueType font that comes with most new systems, and Symbol font and Zapf Dingbats, both of which are built into many PostScript printers. QuarkXPress offers a handy shortcut for accessing these characters (assuming the font is installed in your system):

TIP

To input one character in the Symbol font, type **⌘-Shift-Q/Ctrl-Shift-Q**; the next character you type will be in the Symbol font, then the following character returns to the previous font. To input one character in Zapf Dingbats, type **⌘-Shift-Z/Ctrl-Shift-Z**; the next character you type will be in Dingbats, then the font returns to the previous font.

Typing Invisible Characters

In addition to typing the normal characters you associate with text, you can insert special characters by typing the entries shown in Table 4.1. These special characters are normally invisible on the screen and printed pages. You may find it useful to display invisible characters while you are typing in QuarkXPress; these characters can be displayed by choosing **View ➛ Show Invisibles.**

Table 4.1 Typing Invisible Characters

Character	**Typed Entries**		**Onscreen Display**
	Macintosh Keys	**Windows Keys**	
Space	Space bar	SPACEBAR	·
Nonbreaking space	⌘-Spacebar	CTRL-SPACEBAR	.
En space	**Option-Spacebar**	CTRL-6	.
Nonbreaking en space	⌘-Option-Spacebar	CTRL-SHIFT-6	.
Tab	Tab	TAB	.
Right Indent Tab	Shift-Tab	SHIFT-TAB	.
New Paragraph	Return	ENTER	¶
New Line	Shift-Return	SHIFT-ENTER	↵
Discretionary Line Break	⌘-Return	CTRL-ENTER	no display
Indent Here	⌘-\	CTRL-\	·
New Column	Enter	KEYPAD ENTER	↓
New Box	Shift-Enter	SHIFT-KEYPAD ENTER	↡

The New Line, Discretionary Line Break, Indent Here, New Column, and New Box characters are described later in this chapter, under Paragraph Formatting.

Text From Other Programs

You can import text that has been typed in a word processor or data that has been saved as text from a spreadsheet or database program. To import text into QuarkXPress:

1. Create a text box, or position the cursor within an existing text box with the **Content** tool ()—a blinking text cursor will appear automatically in a new text box, or you can position the cursor anywhere within an existing block of text.

TIP

To import text into the middle of an existing stream of text, select the **Content** tool (), click the I-beam to position the cursor at the point in the text where you want the new text inserted, or select a range of text that you want to replace, then follow the procedures described next.

2. Select the **File** ➛ **Get Text** command (⌘-E/CTRL-E).

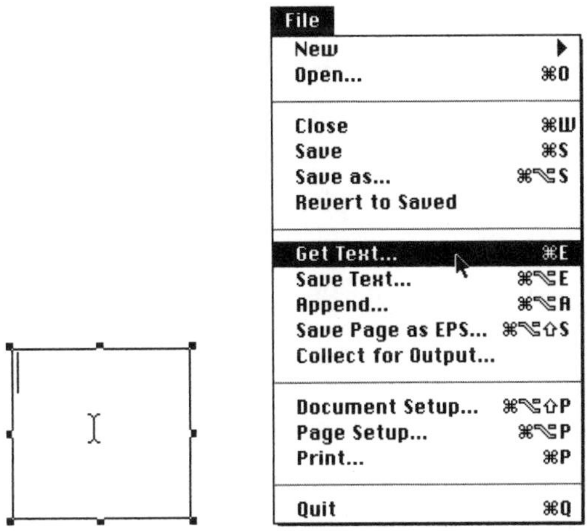

Figure 4.4 *Activate a text box and choose the Get Text command.*

3. Find the name of the text file you want to import in the Get Text dialog box, as in figure 4.5.

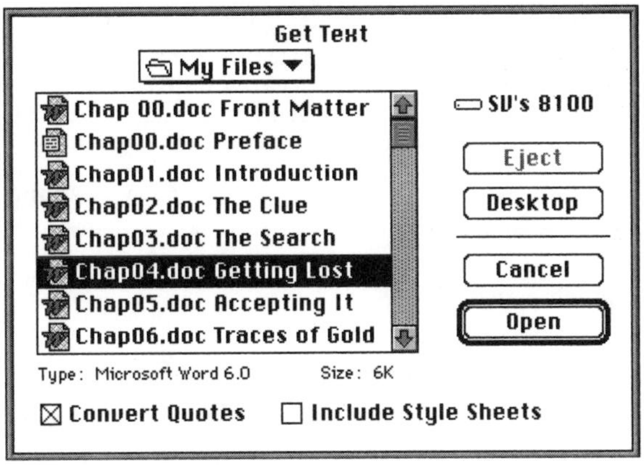

Figure 4.5 *Get Text dialog box.*

Notice that you can change directories and disks through the Get Text dialog box using the same techniques as you would in the Open dialog box (**File** ➛ **Open**). However, in the Get Text dialog box, only text files in formats for which the corresponding import/export filter is available are listed.

- When you click once on a file name, QuarkXPress displays the file type and size.
- Check **Convert Quotes** if you want inch and foot marks (",') converted to open and close quotes and apostrophes (",",','), and double hyphens (—) converted to em dashes (—).
- Click on **Include Style Sheets** if you want the style sheet names and formats imported with the text from Microsoft Word (Figure 4.6), or if you want to convert XPress Tags to format text.

4. Select the name by double-clicking on it. (This is a shortcut for the more obvious method: click on the file name to select it, then click **Open.**)

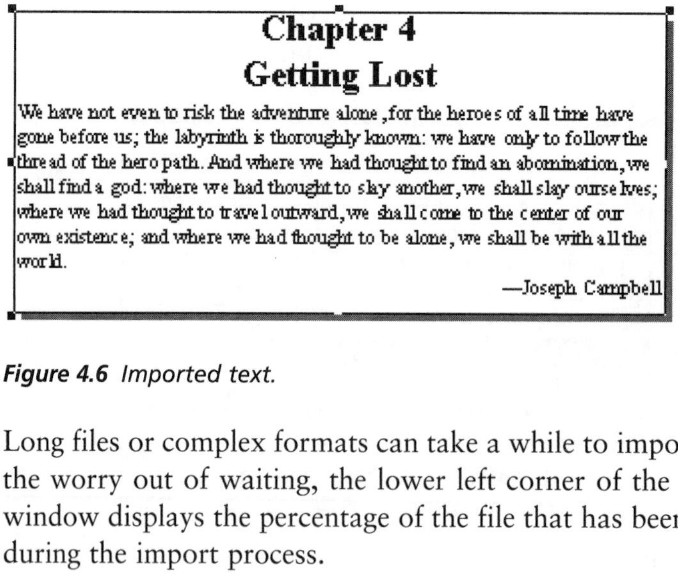

Chapter 4
Getting Lost

We have not even to risk the adventure alone, for the heroes of all time have gone before us; the labyrinth is thoroughly known: we have only to follow the thread of the hero path. And where we had thought to find an abomination, we shall find a god: where we had thought to slay another, we shall slay ourselves; where we had thought to travel outward, we shall come to the center of our own existence; and where we had thought to be alone, we shall be with all the world.

—Joseph Campbell

Figure 4.6 *Imported text.*

Long files or complex formats can take a while to import. To take the worry out of waiting, the lower left corner of the Document window displays the percentage of the file that has been imported during the import process.

Imported text will be inserted at the text insertion point or will replace text that was selected when the **Get Text** command was chosen. The text will take on the width of the column in which it is imported. It will stop flowing when it reaches the bottom of the text box (if links have not been established) or flow into linked boxes and—if the automatic text box feature is active— add new pages as needed for overflow text (as described in the next section). Text following the insertion point will be reflowed to accommodate the imported text.

If imported text has not already been formatted in a word processing program, or if QuarkXPress does not support the word processor and therefore cannot preserve the formatting, the text will take on the default format and type specifications, as specified in the Normal style sheet. If text has been formatted in a word processing program that QuarkXPress supports, some of that formatting will be preserved as described after the next heading.

Text Overflow

If you type or import text into an automatic text box, or any chain of two or more boxes, QuarkXPress adds pages to the document for the overflow text if the text file you import cannot fit in the automatic text box. This assumes Auto Page Insertion is on in the General Preferences dialog box (described in Chapter 3).

When you type or import more text than will fit in a text box that is not linked to another text box, a small square (⊠) appears in the bottom right corner of the box (Figure 4.7). You can see the rest of the text by making the box larger or by linking the text box to another, empty text box. The procedures for linking text from one box to another are described later in this chapter.

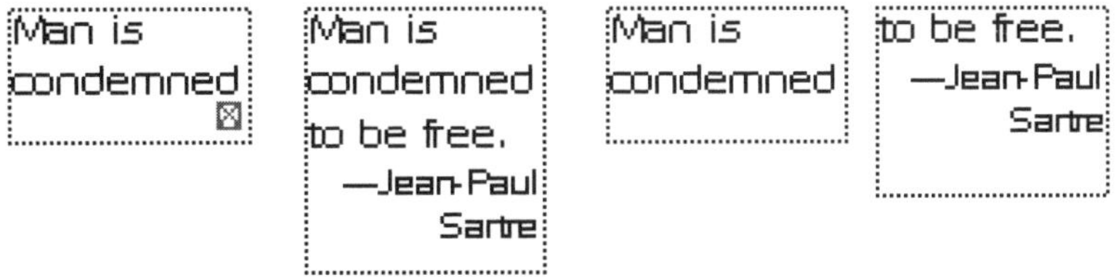

***Figure 4.7** Symbol in lower-right corner indicates text overflow (left) unless text box is enlarged (middle) or linked to another text box (right).*

If you find that there is overflow text (as indicated by a small box with an X in it (⊠) in the lower-right corner of the last text box in a chain) but new pages are not added automatically when you import the text into the first box, then one of three conditions exists:

- The Auto Page Insertion is disabled in the General Preferences dialog box.
- The master page specified in Auto Page Insertion has a broken chain icon () in the upper-left corner.
- The overflow is from a single text box that is not defined on the master page as the automatic text box.

Formatted Text

QuarkXPress preserves the formatting of text from certain word processing programs, including MacWrite, MacWrite II, Microsoft Word, Microsoft Works, Microsoft Write, Word Perfect, and Write Now. You can format text using any supported word processor's formatting commands, or you can format text in any word processor by embedding QuarkXPress Tag codes that will be translated into formats when you import the text into QuarkXPress. See Chapter 11, "Publishing Databases," for the procedure and codes for creating XPress Tags.

TIP

In order for the formatting from any word processing application to be preserved when imported into QuarkXPress, the correct filter must be available. Filters you selected during the installation procedure are always available; other filters are stored in a folder called **XTension Disabled**. To make a filter available to the program, simply move it out of the **XTension Disabled** folder and into the folder on the same level as the QuarkXPress program. When you restart QuarkXPress, the filter will be available.

Formatting characteristics that are usually preserved include:

- Left margin
- Left and right indents

- First-line indent
- Carriage returns
- Tabs
- Character formats (font size, style)
- Style sheets from Microsoft Word only, and only if **Include Style Sheets** was checked

The right margin is changed to match QuarkXPress's column width, with right margin indents preserved from some word processors. QuarkXPress ignores specialized formatting commands such as headers, footers, and footnotes.

Tables created using Microsoft Word's **Insert Table** command are imported as text, with each cell separated by a tab and each row separated by a carriage return. If you want to maintain the graphic borders of a table, first convert it to a graphic in Microsoft Word by selecting the table, then copy it into the Clipboard as a graphic (see documentation for your version of MS Word for details on how to copy text as a graphic). You can then paste the table back into your Word document. The table will be imported into QuarkXPress as an anchored graphic.

If the fonts specified through the word processor are not loaded in your system when you import the text into QuarkXPress, a warning message appears.

Unformatted Text

You can import unformatted text into QuarkXPress and format it using QuarkXPress's commands. There are three common sources of unformatted text:

- ASCII files from any word processor
- Data saved in ASCII format from a spreadsheet or database program
- Text that has been telecommunicated through the type of electronic mailbox or bulletin board that forces you to use ASCII text

TIP: Most word processing applications, spreadsheets, and databases create ASCII text when you choose **Text Only** in the Save as or Export dialog box.

Initially, unformatted text will take on the default type specifications and format, as defined by the Normal style sheet, or whatever format is specified for the current location of the text insertion point. It's a good idea to set up the text specifications at the insertion point before you select the **Get Text** command to import ASCII text.

Pasting Text from the Clipboard

If you have already put text into the Clipboard using the **Cut** or **Copy** command, you can select the **Paste** command to bring in text from the Clipboard. You can put text into the Clipboard while you are working in another program, then open the QuarkXPress document and paste the text onto the page. You can also use the Clipboard to paste from one QuarkXPress document to another or from one part of a document to another.

A pasted text *box* will appear in the center of the screen. If you have clicked an insertion point in existing text, the box will be pasted at the insertion point as an anchored box and move in-stream with the text.

Dragging a Text Item from One Document to Another

When two QuarkXPress documents are open at the same time, and the two document windows are positioned such that you can see parts of both documents (i.e., the active document window cannot completely obscure the inactive window), then you can drag a text box from the active document window onto the second document's window to copy it.

You cannot copy a series of linked text boxes this way—it only works with individual, unlinked text items.

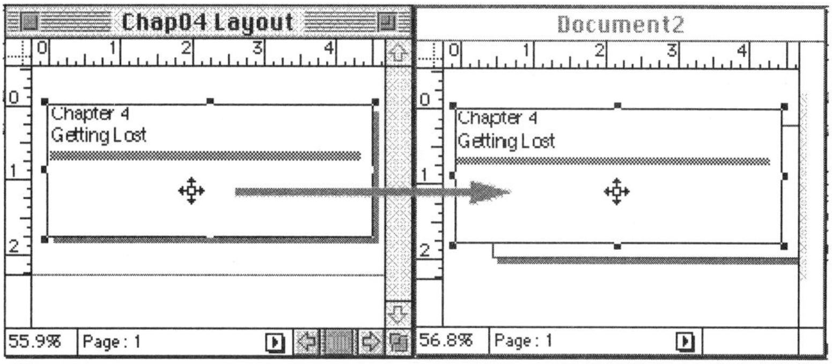

Figure 4.8 *You can drag unlinked text items between two open QuarkXPress document windows.*

Text from a Library

You can drag text from a QuarkXPress library as described in Chapter 3, "Expanding the Document". Text dragged from a library will retain all of its formatting. If a style sheet was used to format the text in the library, the style sheet names will be added to the document's style sheet list when the text is dragged from the library.

TIP

If the library text uses the same style sheet names as in the target document, the text will use the style sheet specification of the target document. The library text, however, will retain its original formatting and in order to be formatted consistently with the rest of the document, the style sheet will need to be reapplied by first specifying **No Style**, then the style sheet name.

Selecting Text

Once text is on a page (or on the Pasteboard), you can use QuarkXPress's rich and flexible assortment of commands and tools to edit it, including the commands from the Edit menu and the Style menu, plus global search, global replace, and spell-checking features. The first step in changing any text is to position the text insertion point or select a range of text. To select portions of text within a block of text or to establish the text insertion point before typing new text, be sure the Content tool ( ) is active.

The basic methods of selecting text in QuarkXPress are similar to selecting text in any Macintosh or Windows application, although QuarkXPress adds additional shortcuts (Figure 4.9).

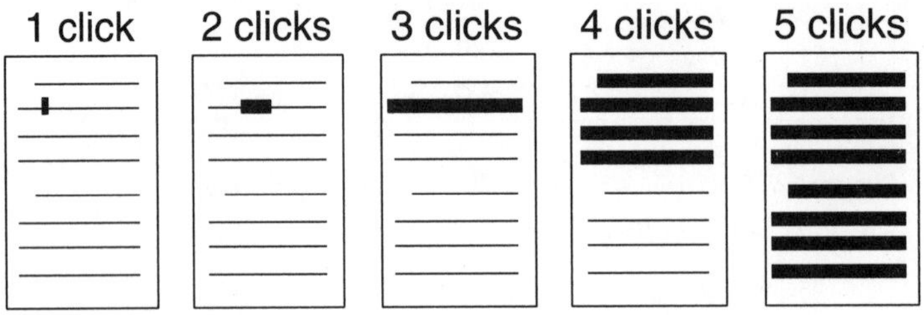

Figure 4.9 *Methods of selecting text in QuarkXPress.*

Common Techniques for Selecting Text

Certain selection techniques are common to all Macintosh and Windows applications, including QuarkXPress, when the Content tool ( ) is selected:

- Position the I-beam in a text box and click once to position the text insertion point for typing or importing new text.
- Position the I-beam beside a character, and drag the I-beam to the end of the desired selection. You can drag the I-beam in any direction—you need not follow along one line of text.
- Double-click on a word to select it.
- Click once at the begging (or end) of a range of text to position the text insertion point, then **Shift-click** at the opposite end of the range to select all the text between the two points.
- Arrow keys move the text insertion point. Holding the **Shift** key as you press the arrow key will highlight (that is, select) the text as the insertion point moves:

- Arrow keys alone move the insertion point one character (left or right) or one line (up or down) at a time.
- Arrow keys used with the ⌘/CTRL key move the insertion point one word (left or right) or one paragraph (up or down) at a time.
- Arrow keys with the ⌘-Option/CTRL-ALT keys move the insertion point to the beginning or end of the line (left or right) or to the beginning or end of the story (up or down).

QuarkXPress Techniques for Selecting Text

QuarkXPress adds its own shortcuts for selecting text with the Content tool (☞) (Figure 4.9):

- Triple-click anywhere in a line of text to select it.
- Click four times anywhere in a paragraph to select it.
- Click five times anywhere in a story to select the text in the active box and the text in all boxes linked to the active box.
- If the Content tool is selected and the cursor is positioned in a text box—by positioning the I-beam pointer (I) in the text box and clicking once to position the blinking text cursor ( )—then the **Select All** command will select all of a story.

Highlighted text will be replaced when you begin typing from the keyboard—you need not delete it first before inserting new text.

Character Formatting

Earlier in this chapter you learned that typed or unformatted text imported into QuarkXpress takes on the default text specifications. In the next sections, you will learn how to change the attributes of individual characters and the format of paragraphs once text is on a page.

There are two ways of changing the format of text in QuarkXPress:

- One way—the obvious way—is to select text, then select the commands described next to change the appearance of the selected text through:
  - Commands under the Style menu
  - The use of keyboard shortcuts
  - The Measurements palette
- The second method is to apply a style sheet, as described later in this chapter.

In this section we discuss the basic character attributes: font, size, type style, color, and shade (Figure 4.10). Other character attributes listed on the Style menu are discussed in Chapter 5, "Typography."

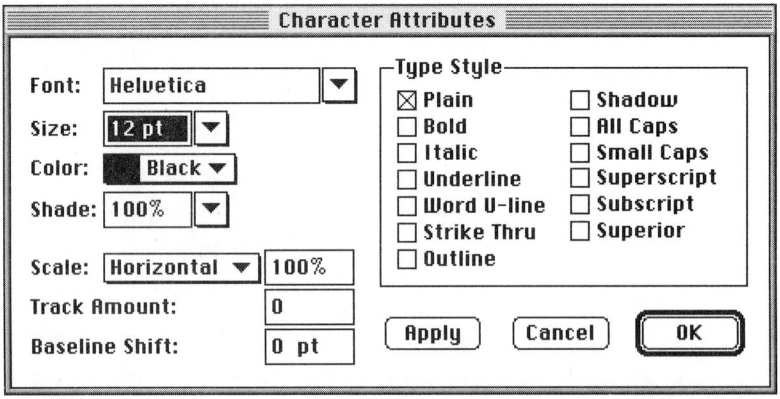

Figure 4.10 *QuarkXPress lets you apply the same character attributes found in many word processing programs, plus additional controls. that your word processor might not offer*

The Style menu (Figure 4.11) lets you apply attributes that are also included in the Character Attributes dialog box (⌘-SHIFT-D/CTRL-SHIFT-D). If you need to apply several different attributes, you may find it's faster to open the Character Attributes dialog box rather than to select several commands from the menu.

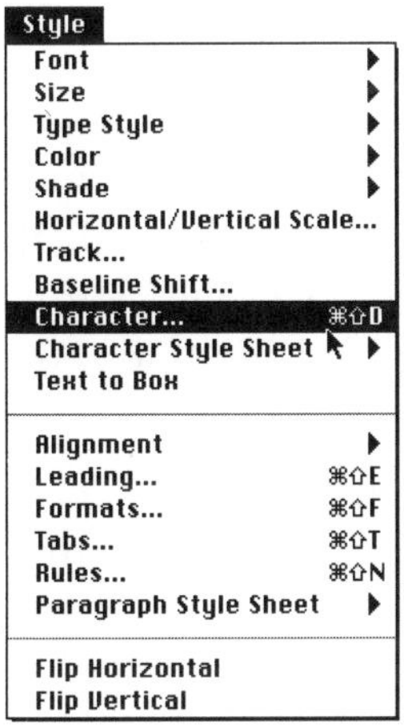

***Figure 4.11** The Style menu when a text box is active.*

Keyboard shortcuts, which are listed under individual headings later in this section, are available for most character attributes.

The Measurements palette (**View ➛ Measurements**) can also be used to apply character attributes when a text box is selected. The right half of the palette displays various icons and pop-up menus that affect selected text (Figure 4.12).

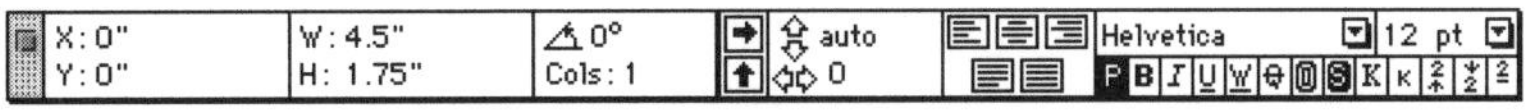

***Figure 4.12** The Measurements palette when a text box is active.*

When you display the Character Attributes dialog box or any of the associated submenus, the options that apply to the current selection are checked or displayed. If the current selection includes more than one attribute of the same type—two different sizes or both bold and italic text, for example—then none of the options will be checked or displayed. Check boxes for Type Style in the Character Attributes dialog box will display in gray when more than two styles exist in selected text.

Changing Font Specifications

Fonts are displayed by choosing **Style ➛ Font** in the pop-up menu in the Measurements palette (Figure 4.13) or in a pop-up menu in the Character Attributes dialog box. Only fonts available to your system are shown. See Chapter 5, "Typography," for information on loading screen fonts and setting global conditions that relate to fonts.

To select a font, position the pointer over one of the font lists (**Style ➛ Font** in the Measurements palette or in the Character Attributes dialog box) and hold down the mouse button to view the list; then drag the pointer to highlight the desired font name.

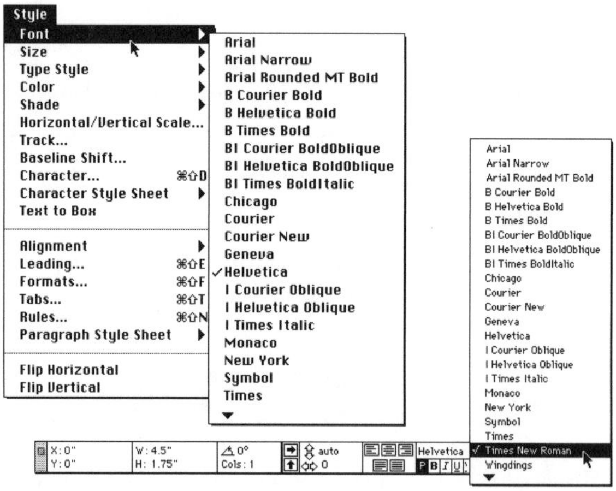

***Figure 4.13** The Font list under the Style menu and Measurements palette.*

As a shortcut, you can type the font name in the Measurements palette or the Character Attributes dialog box, or type the first character(s) of a font name. For example, you can choose Zapf Chancery by simply typing **z** in the font name area *if* that is the only font name beginning with the letter *z*. Otherwise, QuarkXPress displays the *first* font name that it finds—scrolling either forward or backward—that matches or follows the characters typed.

Changing Font Size

Font sizes are displayed in the submenu of the **Style ➛ Size** command, in the pop-up menu or field in the Measurements palette, and in a pop-up menu or field in the Character Attributes dialog box. Sizes shown in outline type in the lists are installed screen font sizes. Other sizes listed are commonly used ones that are not installed in the system. You are not limited to the sizes listed on the submenu or in the pop-up menus; you can enter any size from 2 to 720 points in .001-point increments.

To select a size, position the pointer over one of the three menus and hold down the mouse button to view the list; then drag the pointer to highlight the desired font size, or type the new size in the entry field in the Measurements palette or in the Character Attributes dialog box (⌘-Shift-D/Ctrl-Shift-D).

TIP

You can also change the size of selected type using keyboard shortcuts: **⌘-Shift->/Ctrl-Shift->** increases the size of the selected type, **⌘-Shift-</Ctrl-Shift-<** decreases the size. These shortcuts change the size in the following preset sequence of sizes: 7, 9, 10, 12, 14, 18, 24, 36, 48, 60, 72, 96, 120, 144, 168, and 192 points. To change the size in 1-point increments between 2 points and 720 points, press **⌘-Option-Shift->/Ctrl-Alt-Shift->** or **⌘-Option-Shift-</Ctrl-Alt-Shift-<** (Table 4.2).

Table 4.2 Keyboard Shortcuts for Changing the Size of Text

Command	Macintosh Keys	Windows Keys
Specify a size	⌘-Shift-\	Ctrl-Shift-\
Enlarge selected type	⌘-Shift->	Ctrl-Shift->
Enlarge selected type in 1-point increments	⌘-Option-Shift->	Ctrl-Alt-Shift->
Reduce selected type	⌘-Shift-<	Ctrl-Shift-<
Reduce selected type in 1-point increments	⌘-Option-Shift-<	Ctrl-Alt-Shift-<

Changing the Type Style

The 13 styles listed in the Type Style submenu are repeated in the Measurements palette (Figure 4.14) and in the Character Attributes dialog box (⌘-**Shift-D**/CTRL-SHIFT-D). They all have keyboard equivalents.

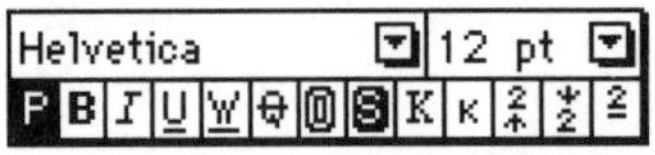

Figure 4.14 *Symbols in the Measurements palette are set in the font style they represent: P= Plain, B = Bold, I = Italic, O = Outline, S = Shadow, ⊖ = Strikeout, U = Underline, W = Word Underline, K = Small Caps, K = All Caps, 2 = Superscript, 2 = Subscript, 2 = Superior.*

To select a style, position the pointer over the style name on the **Style ➤ Type Style** submenu, click on the appropriate symbol in the Measurements palette, or click on the style name in the Character Attributes dialog box.

You can apply more than one style to selected text, but some styles are mutually exclusive, such as Small Caps and All Caps. When you select **Small Caps**, lowercase characters are set as caps that are 75% smaller than normal for the font size. (You can change this default through **Edit ➤ Preferences ➤ Document**, as described in Chapter 5.) **All Caps** sets all characters as normal capitalized letters, whether they were typed as capitals or as lowercase letters. Other mutually exclusive options include **Underline** and **Word Underline**, and **Superscript** and **Subscript** (Figure 4.15).

This is text typed in UPPER and lowercase letters, with no style
THIS IS TEXT TYPED IN UPPER AND LOWERCASE LETTERS, WITH SMALL CAPS
THIS IS TEXT TYPED IN UPPER AND LOWERCASE LETTERS, WITH ALL CAPS

This text has the style UNDERLINE applied to it.
This text has the style WORD UNDERLINE applied to it.

Figure 4.15 *Mutually exclusive styles include Small Caps and All Caps (top),Underline and Word Underline (bottom).*

The difference between superscript and superior characters is that superior characters are roughly half the size of normal characters in the font size, and they are set above the baseline but never rise above cap height for the font. Superscript characters are usually set in normal size and can rise above the top of the ascent line; they can also run into text on the line above (depending on the leading and the settings you chose through **Edit ➛ Preferences ➛ Document**).

Each style can be applied with its keyboard shortcuts, as listed in Table 4.3. The shortcuts are usually obtained by pressing down the ⌘/CTRL-key and the **Shift** key, then pressing one other key.

Table 4.3 Keyboard Shortcuts for Applying Styles to Text

Command	Macintosh Keys	Windows Keys
Plain	⌘-Shift-P	CTRL-SHIFT-P
Bold	⌘-Shift-B	CTRL-SHIFT-B
Italic	⌘-Shift-I	CTRL-SHIFT-I
Underline	⌘-Shift-U	CTRL-SHIFT-U
Word Underline	⌘-Shift-W	CTRL-SHIFT-W
Strikethrough	⌘-Shift-/	CTRL-SHIFT-/
Outline	⌘-Shift-O	CTRL-SHIFT-O
Shadow	⌘-Shift-S	CTRL-SHIFT-S
All Caps	⌘-Shift-K	CTRL-SHIFT-K
Small Caps	⌘-Shift-H	CTRL-SHIFT-H
Superscript	⌘ -Shift-+	CTRL-SHIFT-+
Subscript	⌘ -Shift-Hyphen	CTRL-SHIFT-HYPHEN
Superior	⌘ -Shift-V	CTRL-SHIFT-V

Applying Color And Shade To Text

Color can be applied to text by choosing **Style ➛ Color** from the pop-up menu in the Character Attributes dialog box or by using the Colors palette. The colors listed are those created through the **Edit ➛ Colors** command.

To apply a color to text:

- Select the text with the Content tool (☞)
- Position the pointer over the Colors submenu on the Style menu or in the Character Attributes dialog box, and select from the list of colors.

To use the Colors palette to apply a color to selected text:

- Select the text with the Content tool (☞)
- Click on the icon for text at the top of the palette
- Click on a color name in the list (Figure 4.16).

Figure 4.16 *To apply color to text using the Colors palette, select the text with the Content tool, then click on the text icon and choose a color from the list.*

You can set selected type in a shade percentage value (sometimes called *screen* or *tint*) or a shade of color by choosing from the **Style ➛ Shade** submenu, from the pop-up menu in the Character Attributes dialog box, or by using the Colors palette (Figure 4.17).

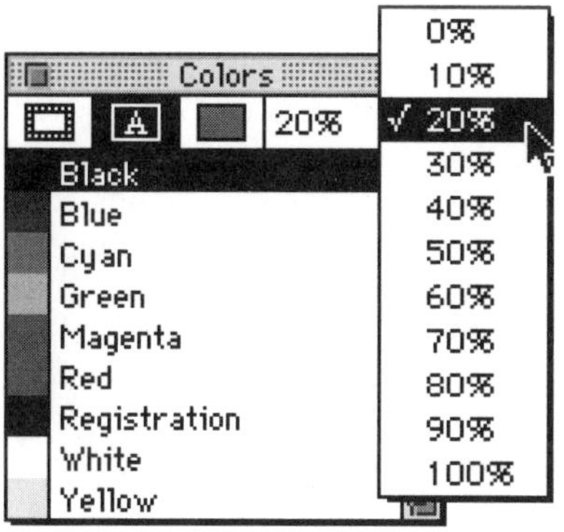

Figure 4.17 *To apply a shade to text using the Colors palette, input a percentage or choose a percentage from the list.*

To shade selected text, select the text with the Content tool (☞), then position the pointer over the Shade submenu on the Style menu or in the Character Attributes dialog box, and input a percentage in increments up to .001% or select from the list of percentages, which lists shades in 10% increments.

To use the Colors palette to apply a shade percentage to selected text, select the icon for text at the top of the palette, then move to the percentage field and input a value or choose from the list. For more information on creating and applying color, see Chapter 7, "Color Basics."

Paragraph Formatting

A *paragraph* in QuarkXPress includes all of the text between two hard carriage returns. A hard carriage return occurs whenever you press the **Return/Enter** key while typing text. You can force text onto a new line without marking it as a new paragraph by typing the special character for a new line: **Shift-Return/Shift-Enter**. This and other special formatting characters are described under the heading Special Characters later in this section.

TIP

When you select one of the commands that affects whole paragraphs, the options you choose will apply to all of the text between hard carriage returns, regardless of how much text is actually highlighted. You therefore need not select every word in a paragraph in order for these commands to apply to the whole paragraph in which the text insertion point is positioned.

You can format paragraphs using any one of three different methods:

- Through commands under the Style menu
- Using keyboard shortcuts
- Through the Measurements palette

In this section, we'll discuss paragraph formats that QuarkXPress shares in common with many word processing programs: alignment, indents, space before or after, and tabs (Figure 4.18). More sophisticated typographic controls are discussed in Chapter 5, "Typography."

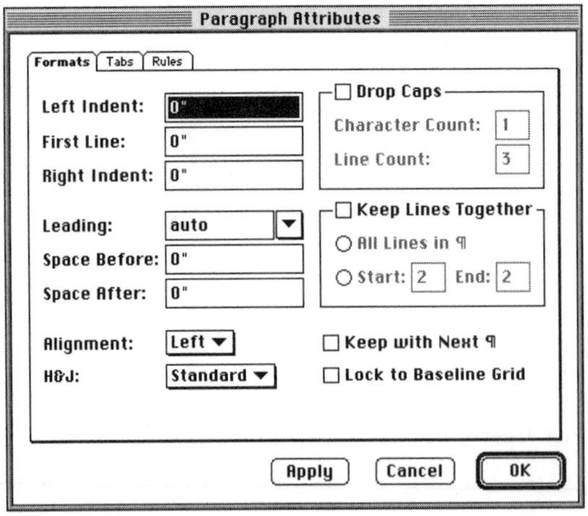

***Figure 4.18** QuarkXPress lets you apply many of the paragraph formatting commands found in word processing programs.*

When you display the Paragraph Attributes dialog box, any of the other dialog boxes associated with text format, or any of the Style submenus, the options that apply to the current selection are checked or displayed. If the current selection includes more than one format, then none of the options is checked or displayed.

Besides using the commands described under the next headings to format a paragraph, you can also format paragraphs using style sheets (as described later in this chapter).

TIP

You can quickly copy the format of one paragraph to other paragraphs in the same text chain. To copy the paragraph format from one paragraph to another, first select the paragraph(s) you want to change, then hold down the **Option/ALT** and **Shift** keys, and click in the paragraph containing the format you want to copy.

Paragraph Formats

You can select **Style ➛ Formats** (**⌘-Shift-F/CTRL-SHIFT-F**) to display the Paragraph Attributes dialog box with the **Formats** tab selected, to set paragraph indentation as well as leading, spacing between paragraphs, and other formats. When the Formats tab is active, a text ruler for the selected paragraph appears at the top of the text box (Figure 4.19). You may need to move the dialog box to see the ruler.

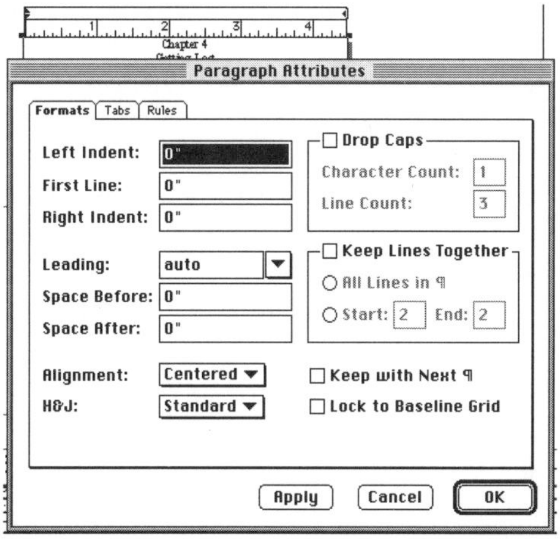

***Figure 4.19** Paragraph Attributes dialog box and ruler (**⌘-Shift-F/CTRL-SHIFT-F**).*

Changing Indents

You can make all entries related to indentation in the text entry areas of the Formats tab, or you can make changes by positioning or moving icons on the ruler. Icons that can be positioned and moved on the ruler include:

- First Line (▴)
- Left Indent (▾)
- Right Indent (◂)

You can also set left tabs by clicking on the ruler when the Paragraph Attributes dialog box is open with the Formats tab selected, but you must click **Tabs** to set other tabs and tab fill characters through the Paragraph Attributes dialog box, as described later in this section.

TIP

If you cannot see both ends of the ruler on the screen, click on the ruler to create a tab marker and drag the marker to the left or right to make the ruler scroll in the window. Once you have the ruler view you want, you can delete the "transport" tab by dragging it off the ruler.

The appearance of the text on the page does not change immediately as you make changes to the ruler or dialog box entries. Click **Apply** to view the effects on the page, then click **OK** to keep the settings or Cancel to close the dialog box without recording any of your changes.

TIP

If you find you must click on the **Apply** button repeatedly as you try to make adjustments, hold the **Option/Alt** key and click **Apply** to view the effects of changes as you make them. When the indents are adjusted correctly, click **OK** to keep the settings.

There are three different indention settings for any paragraph: Left Indent, First Line Indent, and Right Indent. The **Left** and **Right Indents** are measured from the left and right sides of a text box, less the text inset, described earlier in this chapter. The **First**

Line Indent is measured relative to the Left Indent. To create a hanging indent, for example, you would enter some positive value for the Left Indent, then enter a negative value for the First Line Indent. Values that would force text beyond the margins or column guides are not valid entries and will result in a warning message. Figure 4.20 shows how different indention settings affect the text, and what those settings look like in the dialog box and on the text ruler.

- Flush-left paragraph with no indent (Figure 4.20a)
- Normal paragraph with First-Line Indent (Figure 4.20b).
- Hanging indent format positions First-Line Indent left of the other lines (Figure 4.20c)

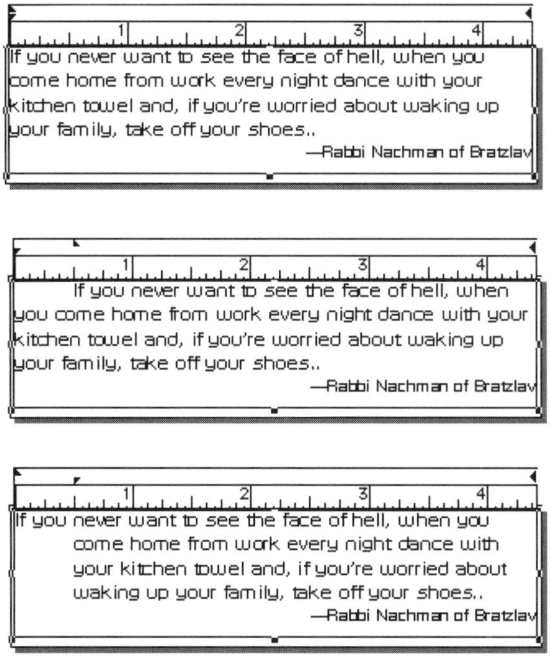

***Figure 4.20** Paragraph indentation settings.*

Controlling Leading

Leading is measurement of the space between lines of text. You can specify leading through the Formats tab of the Paragraph Attributes dialog box (**Type ➛ Leading**) or through the Measurements palette.

The default setting is **Auto** leading. Auto leading is normally calculated as 120% of the type size—for example, 10-point type would have 12-point leading, so the measurement from baseline to baseline of adjacent lines will be 12 points.

While Auto leading may be fine when you are using QuarkXPress strictly as a word processor, it is typically not used in design and for published documents. Instead, a numeric value is input—either a fixed number, for *absolute* leading, or an *incremental* value, preceded by a "+" sign (or a "-" sign), by which the leading will always be increased (or decreased). These leading options are discussed in detail in Chapter 5, "Typography."

Contolling Space Before and After Paragraphs

The amount entered in the Space Before and/or Space After boxes is added to the normal spacing between lines (leading) wherever there is a new paragraph—wherever there is a hard carriage return in the text.

If you're using QuarkXPress strictly as a word processor, it's probably fine to use the common convention of adding two hard returns at the end of a paragraph (one to end the paragraph, the other to create vertical space between paragraphs).

TIP

In a published document, you'll find that controlling the vertical space between paragraphs is much more precise when you set Space Before or Space After values, vs. using double hard returns. Instead of trying to control the space taken up by *both* the extra return and its associated leading, input only one return at the end of a paragraph and simply enter the exact value of the space you want between paragraphs in the Space Before or Space After fields.

We recommend if you receive a document with double hard returns at the end of each paragraph, that you strip out the extra returns and use Space Before or Space After values instead. Remember that a single line of text, such as a heading, is technically a paragraph as far as QuarkXPress is concerned, so Space Before and Space After can be used to set the exact vertical spacing between heads and body text in your document, not just between paragraphs of body text.

Space Before does not add space before paragraphs at the top of a text box or when the paragraph begins after an item is set up to have text runaround. Space After is not added when a paragraph falls at the bottom of a text box or when it ends at an item set up to have text runaround. Select **Item ➛ Modify** and then click the **Text** tab to set the **First Baseline** to adjust the white space at the top of a text box.

Paragraph Alignment

You may be accustomed to using typographical terms to describe the five alignments listed in QuarkXPress's menus:

- *Left*—Left aligned, flush left, ragged right.
- *Centered*—Ragged left and right.
- *Right*—Right aligned, flush right, ragged left.
- *Justified*—Flush left and right, except for the last line.
- *Forced justified*—Flush left and right, with the last line forced to the right indent.

You can specify the alignment of a paragraph by selecting from a pop-up menu in the Formats tab of the Paragraph Attributes dialog box (**⌘-Shift-F/CTRL-SHIFT-F**), from the **Style ➛ Alignment** submenu, by clicking on icons in the Measurements palette (Figure 4.21), or by using keyboard shortcuts.

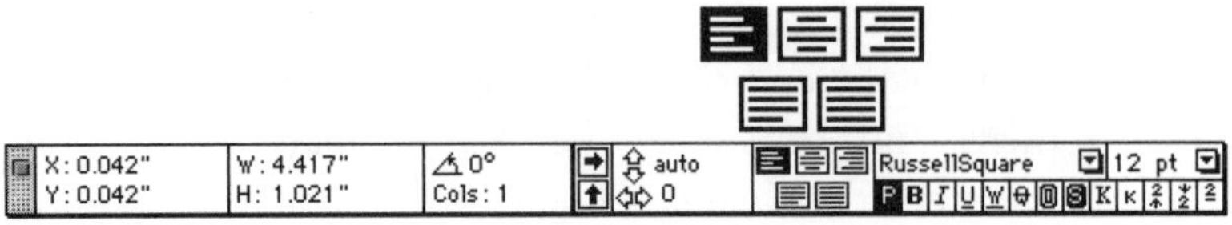

Figure 4.21 The Alignment icons in the Measurements palette.

The keyboard shortcuts for alignment are shown in Table 4.4.

Table 4.4 Keyboard Shortcuts for Aligning Text

Command	Macintosh Shortcut	Windows Shortcut
Left	**⌘-Shift-L**	**Ctrl-Shift-L**
Centered	**⌘-Shift-C**	**Ctrl-Shift-C**
Right	**⌘-Shift-R**	**Ctrl-Shift-R**
Justified	**⌘-Shift-J**	**Ctrl-Shift-J**
Forced Justified	**⌘-Shift-M**	**Ctrl-Shift-M**

The spacing between words and characters for left-aligned, centered, or right-aligned text is determined by the **Edit ➛ Preferences ➛ Document** settings for **Auto Kern Above** and **Character Widths**, and **Style ➛ Kerning** settings. Spacing between characters is also determined by entries made through the **Edit ➛ H&Js** command.

H&J Options

You can choose to apply Standard rules for Hyphenation and Justification to a paragraph, or select from custom rules that you have set up and named. This option is described in Chapter 5, "Typography," where you also learn how to set up different choices.

Drop Caps

Drops caps are easy to set up through the Formats tab of the Paragraph Attributes dialog box. To set up a drop cap:

1. Click in the paragraph(s) you wish to format with a drop cap.

2. Check **Drop Caps**, in the upper right corner of the Formats tab of the Paragraph Attributes dialog box.

3. Specify the **Character Count**, that is, how many characters you want to be enlarged as the drop cap; most often this will be set to 1 character.

4. Specify the **Line Count**, which essentially specifies how many lines deep in the paragraph you wish to enlarge the character(s). Click OK.

The maximum number of lines you can specify in Line Count is 16 lines. If you need a drop cap that is larger, you'll need to format the character(s) in a separate text box, and anchor that box to the beginning of the paragraph. Anchoring items is discussed in Chapter 3, "Expanding the Document."

Once a drop cap has been added to your paragraph using the Drop Caps option in the Paragraph Attributes dialog box, you can modify the character in a number of ways. Virtually every character attribute modification can be made. You can:

- Change the font of the drop cap to differ from the rest of the paragraph (the drop cap will initially be in the same font).

- Change the font size of the drop cap. The size is expressed in the Measurements palette as a percentage of the Line Count specified. The easiest way to increase or decrease the size is using keyboard commands (**C-Shift-< or >/CTRL-SHIFT-< or >**); you'll notice the size changes by percentages.

- Change the font style of the drop cap.

- Apply color and shade to the drop cap.

- Apply vertical and horizontal scaling to the drop cap.

- Kern between the drop cap and the adjacent text. Make sure the cursor is positioned between the drop cap and the text (the cursor should appear the height of the drop cap), and adjust the kerning value. You can push the adjacent text away from the drop cap, or "tuck" it in, causing it to even overlap the drop cap.

- Apply Baseline Shift to the drop cap.

There are very few situations where it's really necessary to create a drop cap as a separate box from the paragraph to which it's attached. Using the Drop Caps command ensures the cap will always be "dropped" with the right paragraph!

Keep Lines Together and Keep with Next

Check **Keep Lines Together** in the Formats tab of the Paragraph Attributes dialog box to control widows and orphans, and the line(s) of text that are separated from the rest of the paragraph by a page break, column break, or text box border. You can specify that the entire paragraph should be kept together by checking **All Lines in ¶**, or you can specify the number of lines at the start and at the end of the paragraph that must be kept together.

If you check **Keep with Next ¶**, the selected paragraph will not be split from the next paragraph by a page break, column break, or text box border. This command can be used to prevent headings from appearing at the end of a page or column, for example, or to keep lines of a table or list together.

TIP

QuarkXPress ignores the settings for **Keep with Next ¶** and **Keep Lines Together** if by following the rules a box in a chain would be left empty. If you apply both **All Lines in ¶** and **Keep with Next ¶** to a range of paragraphs and QuarkXPress cannot do both, the program will keep all lines together and ignore the **Keep with Next ¶** setting.

Lock to Baseline Grid

The Lock to Baseline Grid option in the Formats tab of the Paragraph Attributes dialog box can force the baselines of the selected paragraph to align with a grid you have set up, as is common in magazines and newspapers. This option, and all the tricks involved in making it work, are described in Chapter 5, "Typography."

Working with Tabs

You can select **Style ➛ Tabs** (**⌘-Shift-T**/CTRL-SHIFT-T) to display the Tabs tab of the Paragraph Attributes dialog box. When the Tabs dialog box is displayed, a text ruler for the selected paragraph appears at the top of the text box (you might need to move the dialog box to see the ruler) (Figure 4.22). QuarkXPress sets default tabs every half inch on the ruler for Normal text. If you set tabs in a word processing program, then QuarkXPress's rulers will change to reflect those settings when you import the text.

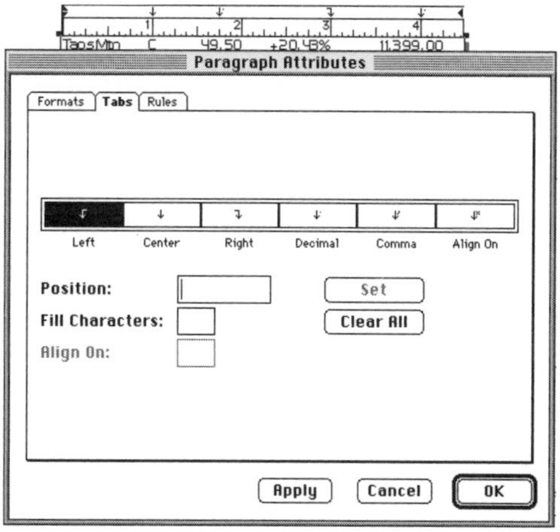

Figure 4.22 *Tabs tab of the Paragraph Attributes dialog box (**⌘-Shift-T/CTRL-SHIFT-T**) and text ruler.*

Setting Tabs

You can make all entries through the dialog box, or you can make changes by positioning or moving icons on the text ruler. Up to 20 tabs may be set. Tab character icons that can be positioned and moved on the text ruler include:

- Left (↓)
- Right (↓)

- Center (⤓)
- Decimal (⤓)
- Comma (⤓)
- Align On (⤓)

plus the paragraph indent markers described earlier.

- First Line (▸)
- Left Indent (▸)
- Right Indent (◂)

To set a tab, follow these steps:

1. Select the paragraphs to which the tabs apply—or position the text insertion point on a blank line where you will begin typing the tabbed data.
2. Choose the appropriate tab character from the pop-up menu in the Tabs tab of the Paragraph Attributes dialog box.
   - Left, Right, and Center tab characters align text flush left, flush right, or centered, respectively, relative to the location of the tab character.
   - Decimal tabs align text on a decimal point, and are used most often for aligning financial data.
   - Comma tabs work like decimal tabs, except text is aligned on commas, which are used in place of decimal points in many countries.
   - Align On lets you specify the character you want QuarkXPress to use for alignment.
3. Either click on the ruler to position and move the tab, or enter a value in the Position field in the dialog box. The position can be entered in any measure using the abbreviations described in Table 1.1 in Chapter 1. The measure always starts with 0 at the left edge of the ruler (as defined by text inset and left indent).

When there is no decimal, comma, or other character in text set with the Decimal, Comma, or Align On tab characters, a numeral that precedes a non-numeric character will be aligned with the tab. This enables correct alignment of columns in text that may include numbers with parentheses or that may not contain a decimal or comma (Figure 4.23).

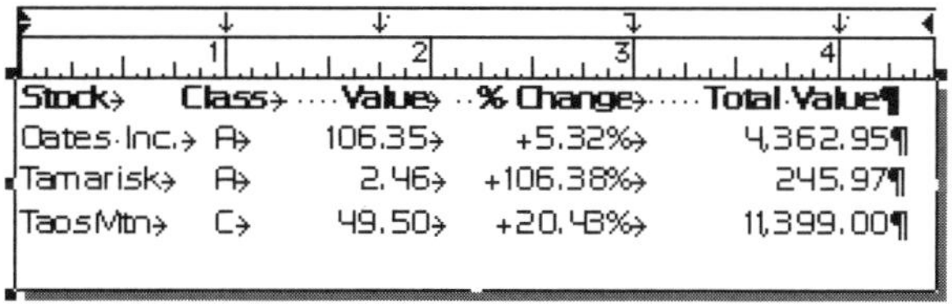

Figure 4.23 *Tabs align on a numeral preceding a non-numeric character, or on the final numeral in text that does not contain a decimal.*

You can specify any **Fill Character** for a selected tab. The most common fill characters (other than blank spaces) include periods (for dotted lines) and hyphens (for dashed lines), but any character can be a fill character. The fill character will be repeated from the end of the text where the **Tab** key is pressed up to the tab mark to which the fill character is applied (Figure 4.24). To adjust the spacing between fill characters, use the **Tracking** command after you have set the tab.

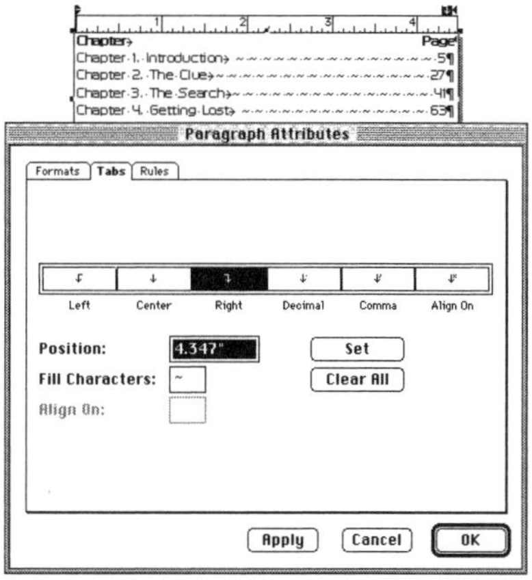

Figure 4.24 *How fill characters are applied.*

QuarkXPress allows you to insert two different characters as tab fill characters. Each character will be repeated alternately. You can use this feature to create patterns or to use period and space to increase the amount of space between dots.

As mentioned earlier in this chapter, you can adjust indent markers as well as tabs when the Tab dialog box is open. If you cannot see both ends of the ruler (due to screen limitations), click on the ruler to create a tab marker and drag it to the left or right to make the ruler scroll in the window. Once you have the ruler view you want, you can delete the "transport" tab by dragging it off the ruler.

Don't forget you can copy the paragraph format (including tab settings) from one paragraph to another. First, select the paragraph(s) you want to format, then position the I-beam pointer over the paragraph that contains tabs you wish to copy and press **Option-Shift/**ALT-SHIFT as you click in the paragraph.

The appearance of the text on the page does not change immediately as you make changes to the ruler or Tabs tab of the Paragraph Attributes dialog box entries. Click on **Apply** to view the effects on the page, then click **OK** to keep the settings, or **Cancel** to close the dialog box without recording any of your changes.

Here's a tip that's worth repeating: If you find that you are clicking the **Apply** button repeatedly as you try to make adjustments, hold the **Option/ALT** key and click **Apply** to view the effects of changes dynamically, as you make them. When the indents are adjusted correctly, you can then click **OK** to keep the settings.

You can change the alignment setting for an existing tab by clicking on it in the ruler, then clicking on an alignment setting in the dialog box. You can move a tab by dragging it on the ruler or by clicking on it to select it, then changing the Position value. The dialog box for any selected tab shows the current position and fill character.

To delete individual tabs, simply click on the tab marker and hold down the mouse button as you drag the tab off the top or bottom of the ruler. To clear all tabs from a ruler, hold the **Option/ALT** key and click on the ruler.

Inserting Tabs in the Text

Once tab stops are set on the ruler, text that already has tab characters will fall into place below each tab stop. You can add tabs within the text by positioning the I-beam as appropriate for text insertion and pressing the **Tab** key. Remember that you can view the tab characters on the page (→) by choosing **View** ➛ **Show Invisibles.**

TIP: The Right Indent tab is a special character that lets you align characters flush with the right indent. To obtain this character, press the **Option-Tab/ALT-TAB** keys. Unlike other tab characters, this character must be set individually in each line; it cannot be preset on the tab ruler before typing. The Right Indent tab is useful for setting up headers or footers, where text appears on a left indent and a page number symbol needs to be flush with the right indent (Figure 4.25).

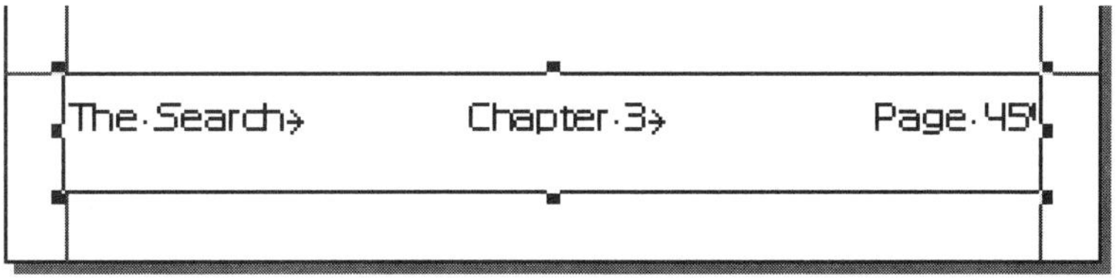

***Figure 4.25** The Right Indent tab can be useful for setting up footers.*

Paragraph Rules

The Rules tab of the Paragraph Formats dialog box (**Style** ➛ **Rules**, or **⌘-Shift-N/CTRL-SHIFT-N**) lets you set up paragraphs with ruled lines above and/or below. Paragraph Rules are described in Chapter 5, "Typography."

Special Paragraph Formatting Characters

As mentioned earlier, you can insert invisible characters using keys listed in Table 4.1. Here we highlight a few special characters that affect paragraph position or formatting, shown in Table 4.5.

Table 4.5 Typing Special Characters

Special Character	Macintosh Keys	Windows Keys	Onscreen
New Paragraph	**Return**	ENTER	¶
New Line	**Shift-Return**	SHIFT-ENTER	↵
Discretionary Line Break	**⌘-Return**	CTRL-ENTER	no display
Indent Here	⌘-\	CTRL-\	¦
New Column	**Enter**	KEYPAD ENTER	↓
New Box	**Shift-Enter**	SHIFT-KEYPAD ENTER	↡

Pressing the **Return/Enter** key signals a new paragraph. All of the formatting described under the following section headings applies to *whole paragraphs*. You cannot apply different formatting to individual lines within a paragraph.

The **New Line** character (**Shift-Return/SHIFT-ENTER**) forces a line break without signaling a new paragraph. This is useful when you are using a style sheet to format whole paragraphs that might add space before or after a hard carriage return. Space will not be added before or after the New Line character, which acts as a "soft" carriage return.

The **Discretionary Line Break** character (**⌘-Return/CTRL-ENTER**) acts like a discretionary hyphen, but no hyphen is shown. Use this character to break a word at the end of a line without inserting a hyphen. This character does not signal a new paragraph.

The Indent Here character (⌘-\/CTRL-\) causes the current line of text and all subsequent lines to be indented at the location of the character (Figure 4.26). Use this special character to create hanging initial caps and for other special paragraph indent effects.

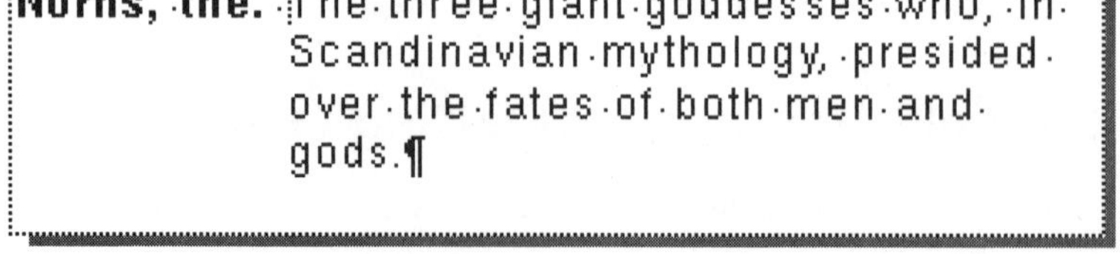

Norns, the. The three giant goddesses who, in Scandinavian mythology, presided over the fates of both men and gods.¶

***Figure 4.26** Effect of the Indent Here character.*

TIP: Watch for this problem in opening old files: In versions of QuarkXPress prior to 3.3, Indent Here character formatting did not extend to any part of the paragraph that continued in the next column. You'd have to embed another Indent Here character at the top of the column. If you had to edit the text, the character could become misplaced and cause improperly formatted text. In QuarkXPress 3.3 and later, the Indent Here character formats an entire paragraph, even if part of it falls at the top of a column.

To delete the Indent Here character, position the insertion point behind it and press the **Delete** or **Backspace** key.

You can force text to jump to the next column or the next text box in a linked chain by inserting the **New Column** (**Enter**/KEYPAD ENTER) or **New Box** (**Shift-Enter**/SHIFT-KEYPAD ENTER) character. These characters are useful in front of headings that you always want to start at the top of a column or a page.

Working with Style Sheets

One of the most powerful yet underused features of desktop publishing applications (word processing *and* page layout) is the electronic style sheet. A style sheet is simply a collection of shortcuts for applying type specifications (character attributes and paragraph formats) used throughout a document. A style-sheet system lets you define the character attributes and paragraph formats for each type of text element in a document, such as major headings, subheadings, captions, and body text.

Once you set up a style sheet for a document, you can format the text using short keystroke commands or menu selections instead of using several commands to format each paragraph or selected words. You can also easily edit style sheet definitions. When you do so, the format of all the text to which that style sheet has been applied changes, too. Thus, style sheets can also be a tremendous design aid.

QuarkXPress 4.0 introduces the ability to create Character style sheets—for formatting individual text characters—as well as Paragraph style sheets.

New style sheets are set up, and existing style sheets are edited or deleted, using the **Edit ➛ Style Sheets** command. The Style Sheets dialog box (Figure 4.27) lists all the styles in the current document. You can click on any style sheet name to view a partial list of specifications for that style sheet, displayed in the lower half of the dialog box.

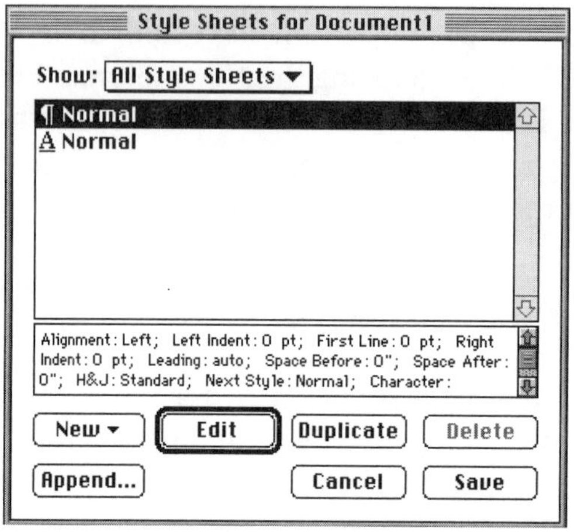

***Figure 4.27** The Style Sheets dialog box.*

Choose **New** to add a new style sheet name, **Edit** to modify the specifications for a selected style sheet name, **Duplicate** to create a new style sheet based on an existing style sheet name, **Delete** to remove a style sheet name, or **Append** to import the style sheet specifications from another QuarkXPress or Microsoft Word document. These steps are described in more detail in the next sections, and style sheets can be applied using any one of several techniques, described later in this chapter.

The process of formatting characters and paragraphs with a style sheet can take place in either QuarkXPress or in Microsoft Word. Style sheets created in Microsoft Word can be imported along with the text into QuarkXPress by clicking **Include Style Sheets** in the Import Text dialog box. The Word XTension must be in the folder with the QuarkXPress program.

Character-specific formats that can be applied using style sheets include all attributes that are applied using the **Font, Size, Type Style, Color, Shade, Horizontal/Vertical Scale, Tracking**, and **Baseline Shift** commands from the Style menu. Paragraph-specific formatting includes all settings that are applied using the **Alignment, Leading, Formats, Rules**, and **Tabs** commands from the Style menu. Document-wide formatting, such as setting margin guides and column widths, is handled outside of the style sheet functions.

There are three basic steps in working with style sheets:

- First, it's a good idea to list each of the fonts you plan to use in the document—typeface, size, and style. Make a list of each unique element the document will use—heading levels, plus body text, captions, etc.
- Next, create a Character style sheet or a Paragraph style sheet for each unique element you listed.
- Finally, you can apply each style to the appropriate text.

The next sections explain each of these steps in detail. If you've never worked with style sheets before, and are unfamiliar with what how to approach setting up a document with style sheets, you may want to read the next section, which discusses the preliminary planning steps that are useful using style sheets. If you understand the basics of how style sheets can be used, but want to familiarize yourself with 4.0's new style sheet features, skip the next section and move on to the "how-to," which begins with the section "Setting Up Character Style Sheets."

Listing Fonts and Unique Text Elements

Before you start designing or producing a document, it's a good idea to plan ahead, and think about the style sheets you'll need to set up. Most documents—books, magazines, newspapers, proposals, etc.—use a limited number of fonts (excluding the variety that might turn up in display ads). You might try a lot of different fonts and paragraph styles during the design phase, but in the end, the design is likely to use only a few different typefaces for most of the text elements. Each of those typefaces might appear in different sizes and styles—but the list is still usually short enough to fit on a cocktail napkin.

Looked at from another angle, most documents use a limited number of different text elements. For example, there might be four heading levels plus the body text. Maybe the first paragraph after each heading has no indent, but all the others are indented. Maybe the figure captions are italicized.

What we're suggesting is that you make a list of all the text elements—and the fonts they will use—before you start building your system of style sheets. This could be a simple two-column list, or it could be a three-page document listing each element and exactly when it is used.

For example, let's say your final design looks like the pages shown in Figure 4.28. Based on this design, you can make a list like the one shown in Table 4.6. Notice that in the example shown in Table 4.7, some of the different text elements use the same fonts *and* the same paragraph format, and others differ only in paragraph format attributes.

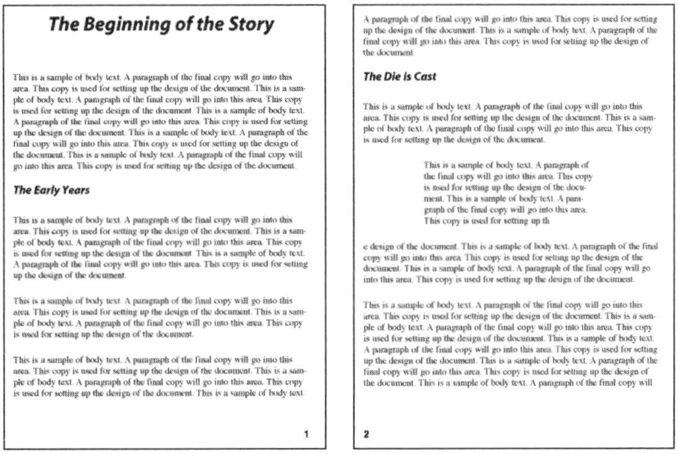

The Beginning of the Story

This is a sample of body text. A paragraph of the final copy will go into this area. This copy is used for setting up the design of the document. This is a sample of body text. A paragraph of the final copy will go into this area. This copy is used for setting up the design of the document. This is a sample of body text. A paragraph of the final copy will go into this area. This copy is used for setting up the design of the document. This is a sample of body text. A paragraph of the final copy will go into this area. This copy is used for setting up the design of the document. This is a sample of body text. A paragraph of the final copy will go into this area. This copy is used for setting up the design of the document.

The Early Years

This is a sample of body text. A paragraph of the final copy will go into this area. This copy is used for setting up the design of the document. This is a sample of body text. A paragraph of the final copy will go into this area. This copy is used for setting up the design of the document. This is a sample of body text. A paragraph of the final copy will go into this area. This copy is used for setting up the design of the document.

This is a sample of body text. A paragraph of the final copy will go into this area. This copy is used for setting up the design of the document. This is a sample of body text. A paragraph of the final copy will go into this area. This copy is used for setting up the design of the document.

This is a sample of body text. A paragraph of the final copy will go into this area. This copy is used for setting up the design of the document. This is a sample of body text. A paragraph of the final copy will go into this area. This copy is used for setting up the design of the document. This is a sample of body text

1

A paragraph of the final copy will go into this area. This copy is used for setting up the design of the document. This is a sample of body text. A paragraph of the final copy will go into this area. This copy is used for setting up the design of the document.

The Die is Cast

This is a sample of body text. A paragraph of the final copy will go into this area. This copy is used for setting up the design of the document. This is a sample of body text. A paragraph of the final copy will go into this area. This copy is used for setting up the design of the document.

> This is a sample of body text. A paragraph of the final copy will go into this area. This copy is used for setting up the design of the document. This is a sample of body text. A paragraph of the final copy will go into this area. This copy is used for setting up th

e design of the document. This is a sample of body text. A paragraph of the final copy will go into this area. This copy is used for setting up the design of the document. This is a sample of body text. A paragraph of the final copy will go into this area. This copy is used for setting up the design of the document.

This is a sample of body text. A paragraph of the final copy will go into this area. This copy is used for setting up the design of the document. This is a sample of body text. A paragraph of the final copy will go into this area. This copy is used for setting up the design of the document. This is a sample of body text. A paragraph of the final copy will go into this area. This copy is used for setting up the design of the document. This is a sample of body text. A paragraph of the final copy will go into this area. This copy is used for setting up the design of the document. This is a sample of body text. A paragraph of the final copy will

2

Figure 4.28 *Sample pages from a final document design using variations of Myriad and Times fonts.*

Table 4.6 shows eight text elements, but due to shared attributes, there are only six different *character* styles and seven different *paragraph* styles. The final list of paragraph and character styles is shown in Table 4.7. Here we've chosen Character style names that reflect the fonts used, and Paragraph style names that reflect the element name—but you could use any names that make sense to you.

Table 4.6 Text Elements with Corresponding Fonts and Paragraph Format

Element	Font	Paragraph Format
Chapter Title	24-pt Myriad Italics	Centered, 30 pts after
Heading 1	14-pt Myriad Bold	Flush left, 24 pts before and 12 points after
Heading 2	14-pt Myriad Italics	Flush left, 12 pts before and after
First Pars	12-pt Times	Justified, no indents
Body Text	12-pt Times	Justified, 18-pt first line indent
Caption	10-pt Times Italics	Centered, 1" left and right indents
Tip	10-pt Italics	Justified, 1" left indent
Warning	10-pt Italics	Justified, 1" left indent

Table 4.7 Character Style Name and Paragraph Style Name for Different Text Elements

Element	Char Style Name	Par Style Name
Chapter Title	24 Myr Ital	Chapter Title
Heading 1	14 Myr Bold	Heading 1
Heading 2	14 Myr Ital	Heading 2
First Pars	12 Times	First Par
Body Text	"	Body Text
Caption	10 Times Ital	Caption
Tip	10 Myr Ital	Icon
Warning	"	"

Now we're ready to set up the style sheets in QuarkXPress.

Setting Up Character Style Sheets

QuarkXPress has long offered very powerful and flexible Paragraph Style Sheet features. But only with 4.0 has the ability to create Character Style Sheets become available. While Paragraph Style Sheets will likely still be used for the underlying format of your documents, you can now make a Style Sheet for formatting individual test characters within a paragraph. A good example of where Character Style Sheets will come in handy can be found in this book—where keyboard shortcuts include, in many cases, a different font and two different font styles.

The basic steps for setting up a new Character Style Sheet are:

1. Choose **Edit ➛ Style sheets** (**Shift-F11**) to open the Style Sheets dialog box (see again Figure 4-27).

2. Click on the **New** button and choose (A̲) **Character** from the New pop-up menu, shown in Figure 4.29, to open the Edit Character Style Sheet dialog box, shown in Figure 4.30.

Figure 4.29 *Choose New Character in the Style Sheets dialog box to create a Character Style Sheet.*

TIP

When you create a new Style Sheet, the definition for the Style Sheet is initially those attributes of the text selected in your document. This means you can "fine-tune" your Style Sheet specifications visually, then embody the attributes automatically by simply creating a new Style Sheet.

3. Complete the entries in the Edit Character Style Sheet dialog and click **OK**. This will return you to the Style Sheet dialog box. When you've created or edited all your Style Sheets, click the Save button.

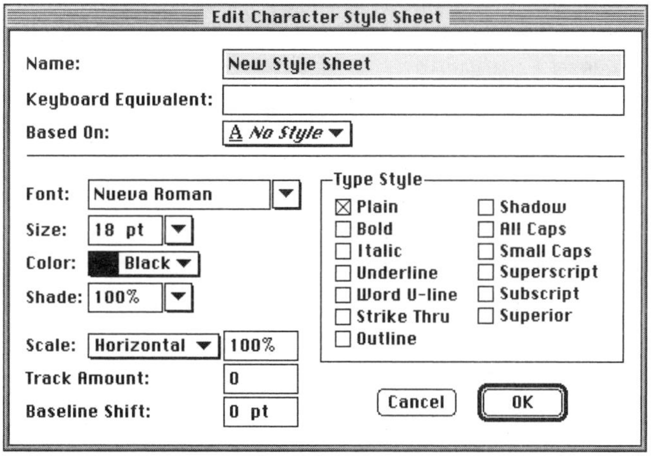

Figure 4.30 *The Edit Character Style Sheet dialog box.*

The Style Sheets you've created will now be available for use in your document.

The Edit Character Style Sheet dialog box is available for creating new Style Sheets, and also when you **Edit** or **Duplicate** a Style Sheet. It is the dialog box you'll use to define all your character Style Sheets. Each entry in this dialog box is discussed next.

TIP: You can quickly access the Edit Character Style Sheet dialog box by holding down the ⌘/CTRL key as you click on the name of the Style Sheet you wish to edit in the Style Sheets palette (**View** ➛ **Style Sheets**).

Name

When you create a new Character Style Sheet, the Edit Character Style Sheet dialog box opens with the Name field highlighted and the entry "New Style Sheet," or opens with the name of an existing Style Sheet. You can enter a new name or edit the name shown in this field. The name you assign appears in the Character Style Sheets submenu (Style ➛ Character Style Sheet), the Style Sheets palette, and also in the Character Attributes Style submenu of the Edit Paragraph Style Sheets dialog box.

Keyboard Equivalent

The Keyboard Equivalent area lets you assign the keys you wish to use as a keyboard shortcut to apply the Style Sheet, instead of using the **Style** ➛ **Character Style Sheets** submenu or Style Sheets palette. (Remember you can move from the Name field to this field by pressing the Tab key). When the cursor is in the Keyboard Equivalent field, press any keys on the numeric keypad or any of the Function keys on an extended keyboard, plus **⌘/CTRL**, **Option/ALT**, and/or **Shift**. Whatever keys you press when the cursor is in the Keyboard Equivalent field will be those you press to assign the Style Sheet. If you make Keypad 5, for example, a keyboard shortcut, you cannot use it as the numeral 5 any more; it's a good idea, then, to use **⌘/CTRL**, **Option/ALT**, and/or **Shift** in combination with the keypad numbers.

Based On

If you want a Style Sheet to be based on another Style Sheet, select that style from the Based On pop-up menu. The Based On entry is a pop-up menu of all the current Style Sheet names. If you base a Style Sheet on another one, then changes made to the *other* Style Sheet will also affect Style Sheets that are Based On it, *except* those attributes that were specifically altered for the new Style Sheet.

Character Attributes

The bottom half of the Edit Character Style Sheet dialog box is identical to the Character Attributes dialog box (**Style ➛ Character**). Use the options here to define the Style Sheet with exactly those characteristics you wish. (See "Character Formatting," earlier in this chapter for information on Character Attributes.)

Setting Up Paragraph Style Sheets

Paragraph Style Sheets are created similarly to Character Style Sheets, but their formats will be applied to entire paragraphs. Paragraph Style Sheets work basically the same as in previous versions of QuarkXPress, but with the added feature that you can base the Character Attributes of the Paragraph Style Sheets on any Character Style Sheet you've created.

The basic steps for creating a Paragraph Style Sheets are almost the same as those for creating a Character Style Sheet, and are repeated here (in case you don't feel like flipping back a few pages!).

The basic steps for setting up a new Paragraph Style Sheet are:

1. Choose Edit ➛ Style sheets (Shift-F11) to open the Style Sheets dialog box (see again Figure 4-27).

2. Click on the New button and choose (¶) Paragraph from the New pop-up menu to open the Edit Paragraph Style Sheet dialog box, shown in Figure 4.31.

When you create a new Style Sheet, the definition for the Style Sheet is initially those attributes of the text selected in your document. This means you can "fine-tune" your Style Sheet specifications visually, then embody the attributes automatically by simply creating a new Style Sheet.

3. Complete the entries in the Edit Paragraph Style Sheet dialog box and click **OK**. This will return you to the Style Sheet dialog box. When you've created or edited all your Style Sheets, click the Save button.

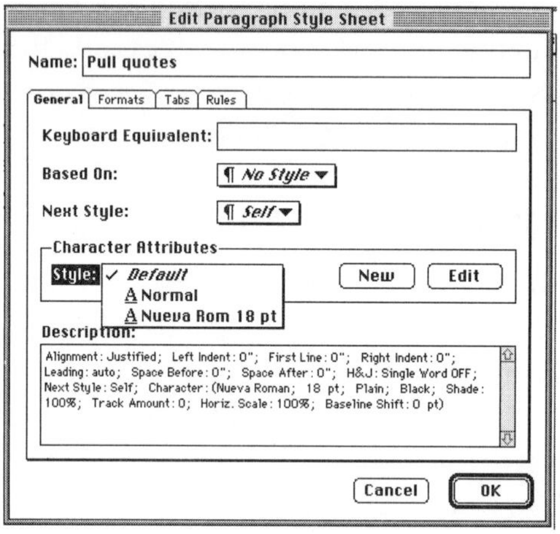

Figure 4.31 *The Edit Paragraph Style Sheet dialog box.*

The Style Sheets you've created will now be available for use in your document.

The Edit Paragraph Style Sheet dialog box is available for creating new Style Sheets, and also when you **Edit** or **Duplicate** a Style Sheet. It is the dialog box you'll use to define all your character Style Sheets. Each entry in this dialog box is discussed next.

You can quickly access the Edit Paragraph Style Sheet dialog box by holding down the ⌘/CTRL key as you click on the name of the Style Sheet you wish to edit in the Style Sheets palette (**View → Style Sheets**).

Name, Keyboard Equivalent, and Based On

These entries in the Paragraph Style Sheets dialog box are identical to those found in the Edit Character Style Sheet dialog box. Please refer to those sections under "Setting Up Character Style Sheets," earlier in this chapter.

Next Style

The Next Style entry is a pop-up menu of all the current Style Sheet names. The style you specify will be the style that becomes active when you press the Return key after the current paragraph.

TIP: The Next Style setting is most useful when you are entering text in QuarkXPress. Next Style specifies the style of the paragraph following the current one. For example, after each "head 1" style in this book, the next style was always "first paragraph." For styles that are often applied to more than one paragraph in a row, the Next Style will be the same style. For example, "body text" is usually followed by "body text."

Character Attributes

There are now two ways you can assign character attributes to Paragraph Style Sheets:

- By assigning character attributes directly to the Paragraph Style Sheet, as in previous versions of QuarkXPress.
- By assigning a Character Style Sheet to the Paragraph Style Sheet.

When you create a new Paragraph Style Sheets, the **Style** pop-up menu will display **Default.** Default character attributes will be those assigned by the Normal Character Style Sheet, or, if you've selected text prior to creating a new Paragraph Style Sheets, Default will have the character attributes of the selected text.

To base a Paragraph Style Sheets on a Character Style Sheet, choose any Character Style Sheet from the Style pop-up menu. If you wish to create a new Character Style Sheet to use as part of the

Paragraph Style Sheets specification, click the **New** button. The Edit Character Style Sheet dialog box will display (Figure 4.32) and you can create a new Character Style Sheet as you normally would. The Paragraph Style Sheets you're defining will be based on the new Character Style Sheet, and both the new Character Style Sheet and the new Paragraph Style Sheets will be added to the appropriate Style Sheet submenus and the Style Sheet palette.

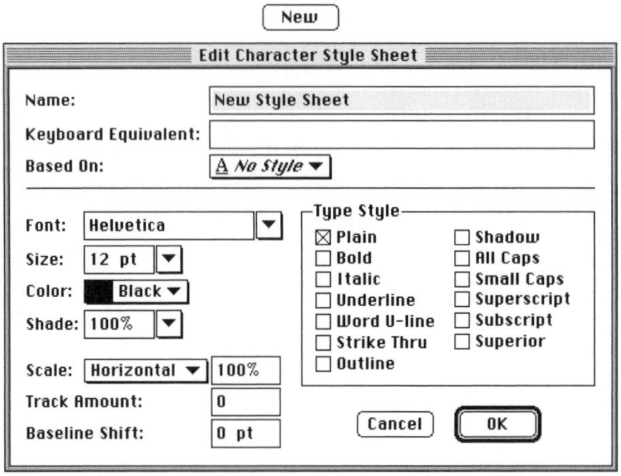

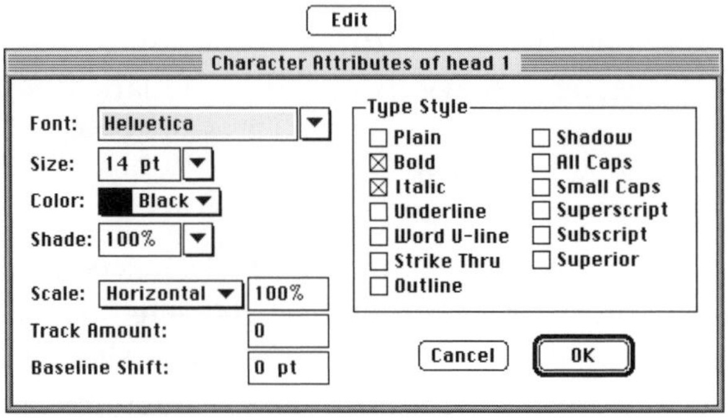

Figure 4.32 *Click the New button in the Character Attributes area of the Paragraph Style Sheets dialog box to create a new Character Style Sheet (top) or click on the Edit button to change the character attributes that are contained only in the Paragraph Style Sheets (bottom).*

When you base a Paragraph Style Sheets on a Character Style Sheet, the Paragraph Style Sheets will change if the definition for the Character Style Sheet is changed.

To change the character attributes of a Paragraph Style Sheets *without* basing them on an existing or new Character Style Sheet, click the **Edit** button. This displays the Character Attributes dialog box (Figure 4.32). You can format text as you normally would, and all the attributes are self-contained in the Paragraph Style Sheets.

TIP

We recommend in most cases you should consider defining the character attributes of a Paragraph Style Sheets as part of the Paragraph Style Sheets itself, without basing it on a Character Style Sheet. Reserve Character Style Sheets for formatting text characters that are formatted *differently* within a paragraph, such as the keyboard commands in this book. If you try to create a Character Style Sheet for every Paragraph Style Sheets, you'll end up with a long list of Style Sheets that can quickly become very difficult to manage.

Formats, Tabs and Rules

In addition to character attributes, you can, of course, apply all of the usual paragraph attributes, including those for Formats, Tabs and Rules. Click on these tabs in the Paragraph Style Sheets dialog box to display the equivalent dialogs as found under the Style menu, and format the options as you normally would. (See "Paragraph Formats," earlier in this chapter for information on setting Formats and Tabs. Information on Paragraph Rules can be found in Chapter 5, "Typography.")

TIP

Any Style Sheet you create with a document open will be available to the active document. However, you can also create Style Sheets that will be shared by all new documents, by using the Edit ➛ Style Sheets command when no document is open. Style Sheets created with no document open become part of the default list of Style Sheets and can be shared by any newly created document.

Applying Style Sheets

To apply a format that has been defined as a Style Sheet, select the text to be formatted, then use any one of three techniques to apply a style sheet:

- Press the keyboard equivalent
- Select **Style ➛ Style Sheets** to choose from a list of style sheet names
- Select a style sheet name from the Style Sheets palette (**View ➛ Show Style** Sheets), shown in Figure 4.33.

Both the Style Sheets submenu and the Style Sheets palette list the names of all the style sheets you have defined. If you have assigned keyboard equivalents, those will show next to the style sheet name.

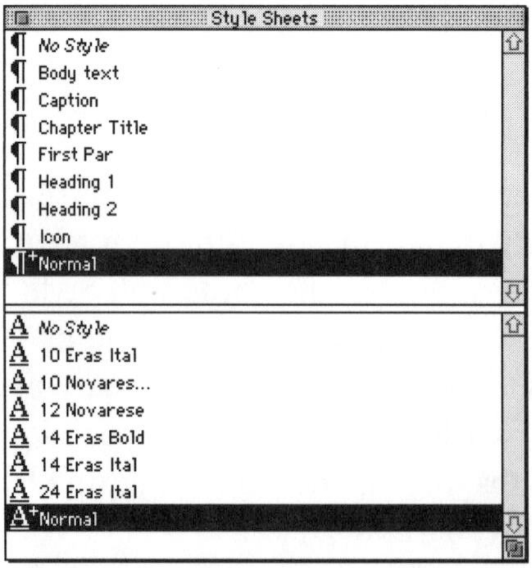

***Figure 4.33** The Style Sheets palette.*

To see which style sheet has been applied to a paragraph or word, position the cursor in the text. The applied style sheet names will be checked in the **Style ➛ Style Sheets** submenu or will be selected in the Style Sheets palette. If you select a range of paragraphs that share the same style sheets, those style sheets will be checked in the Style Sheets submenu or selected in the Style Sheets palette. If the selection includes mixed style sheets—more than one paragraph style, or more than one character style—no style sheet name will be indicated.

You can, of course, still apply "local" formatting to override any style selections; that is, you can use all the commands under the Style menu and the Measurements palette described earlier in this chapter to format individual characters within text that has been formatted using a style sheet. For example, you can italicize a single word within text that has been formatted using a character style sheet for nonitalic text.

> **TIP** If you have applied local character formatting, such as bold or italic, or paragraph formatting, such as flush left or first line indent, to override any of the style sheet settings, the Style Sheets palette will display a plus sign (+) next to the style name.

If you apply a *new* style sheet to a paragraph that contains local formatting—formatting of individual words or characters that differs from the style sheet format—the text in the paragraph will change according to the specifications of the new style sheet, *except* for the local formatting. To change all the text in the paragraph, you must first apply **No Style** from the Style Sheets submenu or the Style Sheets palette, then apply the new style sheet.

> **TIP** If you apply style sheets in QuarkXPress to imported text and the text does not change as expected, the likely problem is that text in the word processing file was formatted without using style sheets. Specify **No Style** first, then reapply the style sheet. When using the Style Sheets palette, you can apply **No Style** before applying a style sheet by holding down the **Option/Alt** key as you click on the style sheet name.

Deleting Style Sheets

To delete a style sheet, click on the style sheet name in the list displayed in the Style Sheets dialog box (**Edit ➛ Style Sheets**), then click the **Delete** button. You cannot delete the Normal style sheet; it is the default format for all newly typed text and for imported

ASCII text. You can change the specifications for the Normal style sheet by selecting **Normal** and choosing **Edit** in the Style Sheets dialog box.

If you delete any other style sheet name, all text that is currently formatted based on that style sheet name will retain its formatting but will be assigned a No Style identification. To change those paragraphs to another style sheet, you need to go through the document, select those paragraphs, and assign another style sheet.

Duplicating Style Sheet Specifications

Sometimes you may want to create a style sheet using several specifications from another one. In that case, the fastest way is to select the **Duplicate** command in the Style Sheets dialog box. Click on the style sheet name you want to duplicate, then click the **Duplicate** button; the Edit Style Sheets dialog box appears with **Copy of <*style sheet name*>** in the name field (Figure 4.34). You can then use the dialog box to change any of the specifications for the new style sheet.

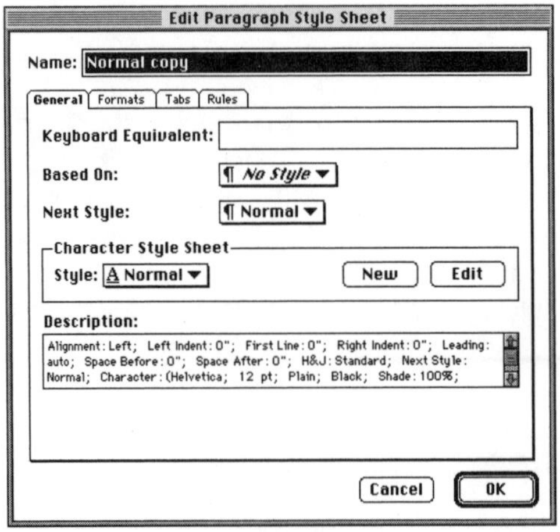

Figure 4.34 *Duplicating a style sheet.*

Appending Style Sheets from Other Documents

Style sheets are a great way to ensure consistency among various documents. You may find in creating a new document that you want to reuse style sheets created in another document. The Append command allows you to add style sheets from another document to your active document.

If you choose **Append** in the Style Sheets dialog box, QuarkXPress displays the Append Style Sheets dialog box. The list in the dialog box shows QuarkXPress document and template names and Microsoft Word document names; when you select one and choose **Open** (or simply double-click on a document name), all of the style sheets used in that document are added to the list in the active document's style sheet list.

If any of the appended style sheet names match any names that are already in the current style sheet, an alert is displayed that allows you to leave the style sheet in the target document unchanged, or to rename the style sheet from the new document (Figure 4.35).

If you choose to rename the style sheet, the new name will be appended to the target document with an asterisk after the style name. You can then rename it and apply it as a typical style sheet (Figure 4.36).

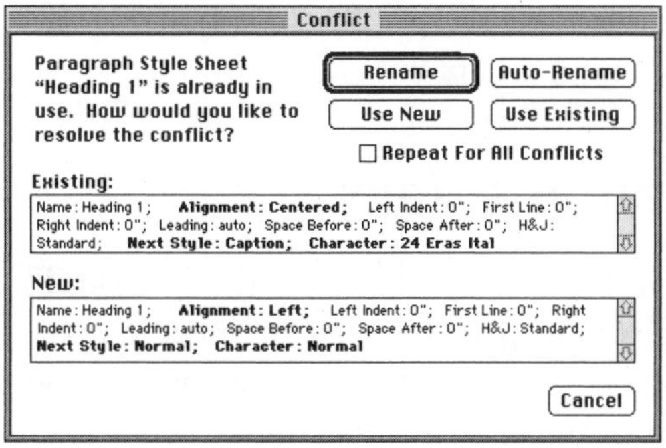

Figure 4.35 *If you append style sheets from another document with the same style sheet names, but with different specifications, an alert will appear.*

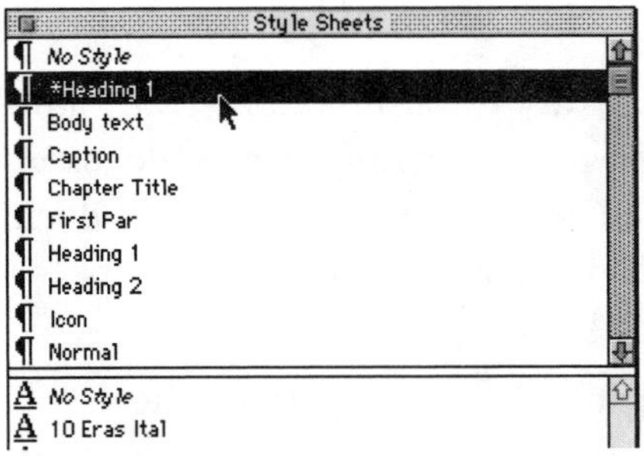

Figure 4.36 *If you choose to append a style sheet with the same name, it will be appended with an asterisk following the style sheet name.*

If an appended style sheet uses the same keyboard equivalent as is already applied in the current style sheet, the appended style sheet is brought in without a keyboard equivalent. If the appended style sheets call for a font that is not currently loaded in your system, you get an error message that indicates the font that is missing, for example, "(-2, Bodoni Bold)."

TIP

When appending Style Sheets if you wish to use an existing style for all the style sheets you're importing, hold down the **Option/Alt** key and click the **Use Existing Style** button.

Appending Style Sheets works very similarly to appending H&Js, Colors, and Dashes & Stripes. For more details on the Append options, see the section "Appending H&Js from Other Documents," found in Chapter 5, "Typography."

Finding and Changing Text

The **Edit ➛ Find/Change** command (**⌘-F/Ctrl-F**) finds and changes specific words or characters, or specific text attributes in text. You can search through part of a story, a whole story, or a whole document at once. Remember that a *story* is all of the text in a *chain* of linked text boxes.

To find or change text in a story or all the stories in a document, first select the Content tool and position the text cursor in a block of text, then select **Edit ➛ Find/Change** (**⌘-F/CTRL-F**) to display the Find/Change dialog box (Figure 4.37). Type in the text or select character attributes you want to find, then click the Find Next button. QuarkXPress begins the search at the text insertion point and proceeds through to the end of the text block.

When QuarkXPress searches a document, it starts from the insertion point and goes to the end, without starting again at the beginning of the document. To ensure you've always included the entire document, hold down the **Option/ALT** key before you begin the search; the **Find Next** button changes to **Find First**, and when you click it, causes QuarkXPress to begin the search from the beginning of the document.

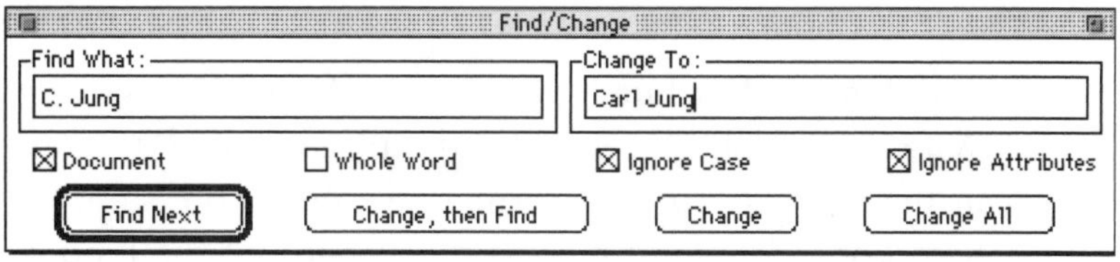

Figure 4.37 *Find/Change dialog box.*

In the Find/Change dialog box (**Edit ➛ Find/Change**), you type text in the Find What field, specify changes, if any, in the Change To field, and select the type of search you want:

If **Document** is checked *and no text boxes are active when you begin the search*, QuarkXPress searches the entire document. If a text box is active, QuarkXPress searches the entire document, but only from the current text insertion point to the end of the story; text before the insertion point is not checked, unless you hold down the **Option/ALT** key and click **Find First**.

If **Whole Word** is checked, QuarkXPress searches for the Find What text followed by a space or punctuation mark. Otherwise,

QuarkXPress finds all character strings that match the Find What entry, even when they are part of a longer word.

If **Ignore Case** is checked, QuarkXPress finds the Find What text in all forms—with and without any capital letters. If it finds text in all lowercase, it replaces it with the all-lowercase version of the text you typed in the Change To area. If it finds text in all uppercase, it replaces it with the all-uppercase version of the text in the Change To area. If it finds initial-cap text, it replaces it with the initial-cap version of the text in the Change To area. If it finds mixed uppercase and lowercase characters (other than initial cap only), it replaces the found word with the Change To text exactly as you typed it.

If the **Ignore Case** option is not checked, then QuarkXPress finds only those instances of text that match the capitalization exactly as you typed it in the Find What area, and it changes that text to the text exactly as typed in the Change To area.

If **Ignore Attributes** is checked, QuarkXPress finds the Find What text in all type styles and replaces it with the text you typed in the Change To area formatted exactly the same as the found text. For example, if it finds one version of the Find What text in 10-point Times, it replaces it with the Change To text in 10-point Times. If it finds the next instance of the Find What text in 12-point Helvetica, it replaces it with the Change To text in 12-point Helvetica.

If **Ignore Attributes** is not checked, then the expanded Find/Change dialog box is displayed (as described later in this chapter). QuarkXPress finds only those instances of the word that match the character attributes exactly as specified and changes them to the Change To text formatted exactly as specified.

Once you have typed the Find What and (optional) Change To text and selected the search options, you can click **Find Next**, or hold down the **Option/ALT** key and click **Find First**. After the first instance is found, you can choose **Change, then Find** to change the word and keep searching to the next occurrence, or **Change** to change the word and pause the search. If you don't want to make a change on a particular occurrence of the text, click **Find Next.** QuarkXPress will move on to the next occurrence without making any changes.

If you choose **Change All**, QuarkXPress will change all found instances of the Find What text. When the search is finished, it will display a dialog box with a count of the total number of instances changed. If no instances are found, the Macintosh or Windows system will beep to signal the end of the search.

If no instances are found but you know one should have been found, make sure that you started the search at the beginning by holding down the **Option/**ALT key and clicking on Find First or that you positioned the text insertion point at the beginning of the story (**⌘-Option-A/**CTRL**-**ALT**-A**). Also, be sure that you have spelled the Find What text correctly and not entered any extra spaces before or after it.

If the edits cannot be handled by global changes but can be found by a global search, you can also select **Find Next** simply to find occurrences of text or text attributes. When an instance is found, you can click in the document window and edit the text manually, then select **Find/Change** (**⌘-F/**CTRL**-F**) again to resume the search. For example, you might type *see page xx* throughout the draft versions of a document, then search for *xx* and manually type in the final page number after the pages have been laid out.

TIP

It is a good idea to move the Find/Change dialog box to the bottom of the screen to maximize your view of the document window during a search. You can also make the dialog box smaller—reducing it to the Find and Change buttons only—by clicking in the zoom box at the top-right corner of the dialog box title bar (Figure 4. 38).

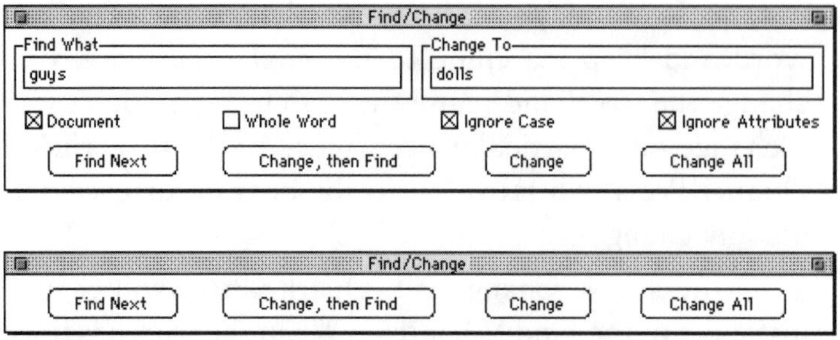

Figure 4.38 *The zoom box at the top-right corner of the window toggles from full size (top) to a reduced version (bottom) of the Find/Change dialog box.*

Finding/Changing Special Characters

You can type up to 80 characters in the Find What and Change To areas of the Find/Change dialog box. If you don't type anything in the Change To area, then the text typed in the Find What area will be deleted when found in the story or document.

You can include spaces in the Find What and Change To fields by using the space bar, but other "invisible" characters, such as a **Tab** or **Return**, require special entry. (Otherwise, the **Tab** key alone jumps you to the next field in the dialog box, and the **Return** or **Enter** key starts the search.) You can search for special characters and invisible characters by holding the ⌘/CTRL key and typing the key that you would normally use to insert the special character in the text, as shown in Table 4.7.

Table 4.7 Special Characters

Special Character	Find/Change Entry	Dialog Box Display
Tab	**⌘/CTRL-Tab**	\t
New Paragraph	**⌘/CTRL-Return**	\p
New Line	**⌘/CTRL-Shift-Return**	\n
Discretionary Line Break	(cannot search for this character)	

Indent Here	(cannot search for this character)	
New Column	**⌘/CTRL-Enter**	\c
New Box	**⌘/CTRL-Shift-Enter**	\b
Previous Box Page #	**⌘/CTRL-2**	\2
Active Box Page #	**⌘/CTRL-3**	\3
Next Box Page #	**⌘/CTRL-4**	\4
Wild Card	**⌘/CTRL-?**	\?
Back Slash	**⌘/CTRL-**	\\\\

When searching for special characters, it is usually best to uncheck **Whole Word** since special characters are usually bounded by other letters or numbers. To view invisible characters on the screen, choose **View ➛ Show Invisibles.**

You can type the wild card character (⌘-?/CTRL-?) in the Change From field to find words with similar but different spellings. For example, a search for "gr?y" will find both "gray" and "grey."

You cannot use wild cards in the Change To text field. You can find or change spaces by typing a space in either field (using the space bar), but if the space falls at the end of the entry the program will ignore instances where the word or phrase is followed by punctuation. If you type a space on either side of the Find What entry, however, be sure to type a space in the Change To field as well (unless you want the replacement to eliminate the space).

Find or Change Character Attributes

You can find or change attributes such as font, size, type style, or style sheet. This feature is especially handy for globally changing words that have been given special attributes within paragraphs. For example, if you are working on a review of a book titled *Never Tomorrow* and the title was set as underscored (except in some cases where the author of the review forgot to apply the underscores), you can globally change all cases to italics. You can also select **Find/Change** globally to change the formats of headings or captions or other standard elements within the text that have been set with one style sheet name to apply another style sheet name, or to apply global changes to text that has a particular style sheet.

To find or change attributes, uncheck **Ignore Attributes** to display the expanded Find/Change dialog box (Figure 4.39). The initial display shows the attributes of the active text selection (or shows grayed options if more than one attribute is represented). You can search for specific text as entered in the Text area under Find What or uncheck **Text** if you want to search for attributes only.

You can check **Style Sheet**, **Font**, **Size**, and/or **Style** to include these categories of attributes as part of the search, or uncheck them if you want to search for other characteristics only. For checked categories, select the desired options from the pop-up menus.

Any Type Style option can be highlighted in black (so *only* text with that style will be found), grayed (so text *with and without* that style will be found), or unhighlighted (so *no* text with that style will be found). Simply click on each style option until the desired setting is shown.

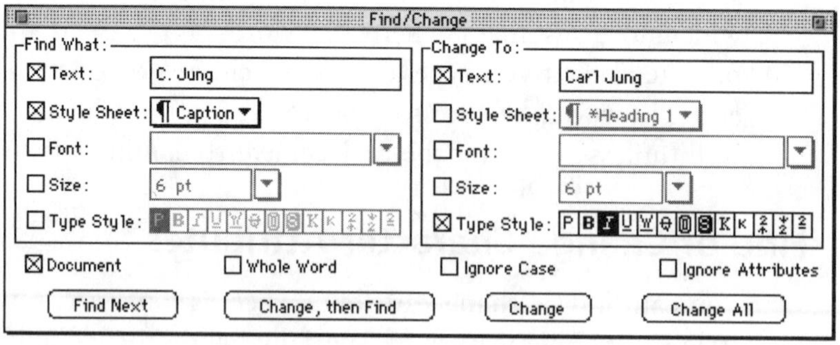

***Figure 4.39** Expanded Find/Change dialog box.*

Similarly, under Change To you can check **Font**, **Size**, and/or **Style** to include these categories of attributes as part of the replacement, or uncheck them if you want to replace other characteristics only. Any style option can be checked (so all text found will be changed to that style), unchecked (so all text found will be changed to not have that style), or grayed (so found text will retain its style in that category).

TIP The fonts shown in the Find list of the expanded Find/Change dialog box include only those actually used in the document. The Change To font list includes all fonts currently loaded in the system.

Checking Spelling

QuarkXPress offers a spelling check feature that compares the words in your text against a 120,000-word dictionary. The dictionary file is included in the same folder as the QuarkXPress program when you first installed QuarkXPress, if you followed normal installation procedures, or you can copy it into the System folder. Note that it must be in one of these two places in order for the **Check Spelling** command to work. You can also create auxiliary dictionaries to add your own terms for use in spelling checks. The **Utilities** ➛ **Check Spelling** command lets you check the spelling of a highlighted word, all the words in a story, or all the words in a document (Figure 4.40).

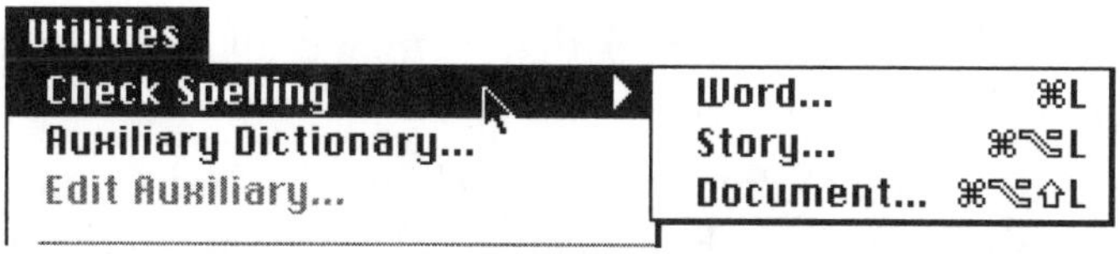

Figure 4.40 *The* ***Utilities*** ➛ ***Check Spelling*** *pop-up menu.*

To check spelling of any word, first select the word or position the insertion bar to the left of or anywhere within the word, then select **Utilities** ➛ **Check Spelling** ➛ **Word** (⌘-L/CTRL-W) to check the spelling of the selected word only. If more than one word is selected, QuarkXPress checks the spelling of only the first word or partial word selected.

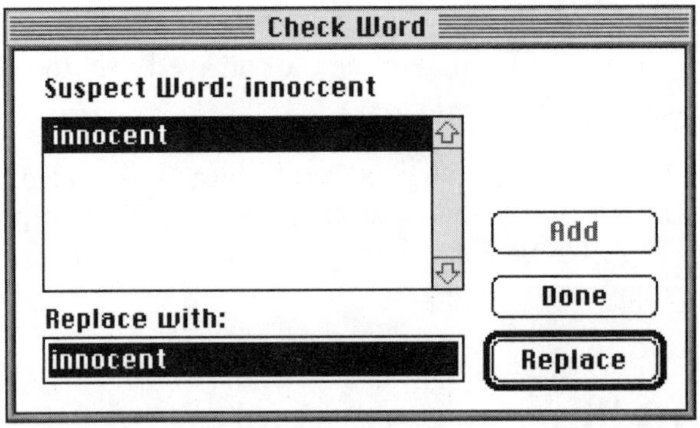

Figure 4.41 *Check Word dialog box for a word search.*

QuarkXPress checks the dictionary and displays the Check Word dialog box (Figure 4.41), showing close or exact matches from the dictionary in the scrolling window, or displaying the message "No similar words found." You can choose a replacement word by double-clicking on the word in the list (or clicking on the word once to select it, then clicking on **Replace**) to replace the word with a found match, or click **Done** to cancel the process and leave the word unchanged.

To check spelling for any story, first activate a text box and select the Content tool, then select **Utilities ➛ Check Spelling ➛ Story** (**⌘-Option-L/Ctrl-Alt-W**) to check the spelling in the selected story. (Remember that a *story* is all of the text in a chain of linked text boxes.)

After QuarkXPress checks spelling, a **Word Count** dialog box (Figure 4.42) shows how many total words are in the story or document, how many unique words were found (how many different words), and how many suspect words are identified (words not found in the dictionary).

Figure 4.42 *Word Count dialog box.*

To close the dialog box, click **OK**. If no suspect words were found, then the spelling check process is complete for the story. If suspect words were found, then the Check Story dialog box (Figure 4.43) is displayed when you close the Word Count dialog box.

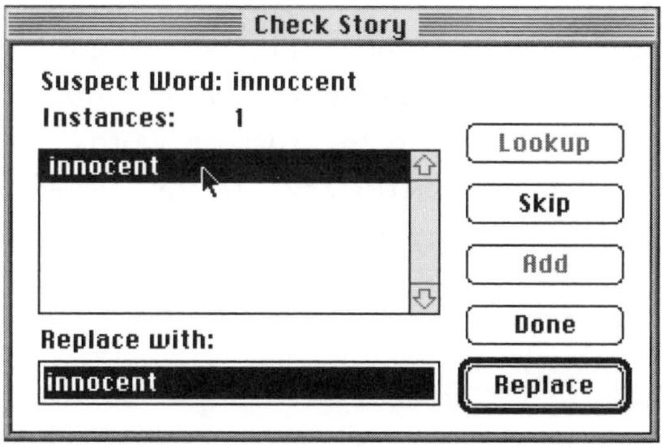

Figure 4.43 *Check Story dialog box.*

The Check Story dialog box displays the first suspect word found in the text and shows how many instances of the same word were found, if more than one occurred. If you click Lookup, QuarkXPress offers suggested alternatives (if any close matches are found in the dictionary) or displays the message "No similar words found." You can click on one of the suggested alternatives, or type the correct word in the Replace with area of the dialog box, then click **Replace** (or simply press **Return**) to replace the suspect word. To let the suspect word remain unchanged and go on to the next found suspect word, click **Skip**. To let the suspect word remain unchanged, add it to the open auxiliary dictionary (see "Customizing Your Own Dictionaries" later in this chapter), and go on to the next suspect word found, then click Add. (An auxiliary dictionary must be open during the spelling check process in order for the Add option to be available in the Check Story, Check Document, or Check Word dialog box.) To end the spelling check process, click **Cancel**.

To check spelling for a whole document, select **Utilities ➛ Check Spelling ➛ Document** (**⌘-Shift-Option-L/CTRL-SHIFT-ALT-W**). QuarkXPress starts on the first page of the currently open document and goes through all of the stories in it. The first dialog box displayed is the Word Count dialog box, showing the total words in the document, how many unique words were found (how many different words), and how many suspect words are identified (words not found in the dictionary). If any suspect words are found, click **OK** to display the Check Document dialog box (Figure 4.44).

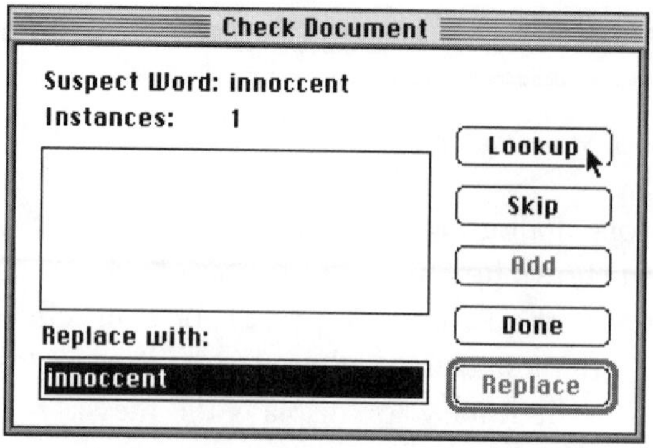

Figure 4.44 *Check Document dialog box.*

The Check Document dialog box is handled exactly the same as the Check Story dialog box, described earlier.

You can check the spelling on Master Pages by turning to a master page in the document—the Document entry in the Check Spelling submenu changes to display **Masters**. The dialog boxes displayed to check spelling on Master Pages are the same as those displayed for checking a story or a document.

Creating and Editing Auxiliary Dictionaries

You cannot change the XPress Dictionary that comes with QuarkXPress, but you can add your own terms to auxiliary dictionaries. To create a new auxiliary dictionary, choose **Utilities ➛ Auxiliary Dictionary** and type in a name for the new dictionary, then click the **Create** button. To open an existing auxiliary dictionary, choose **Utilities ➛ Auxiliary Dictionary**, locate the appropriate file, and select it from the dialog box (Figure 4.45).

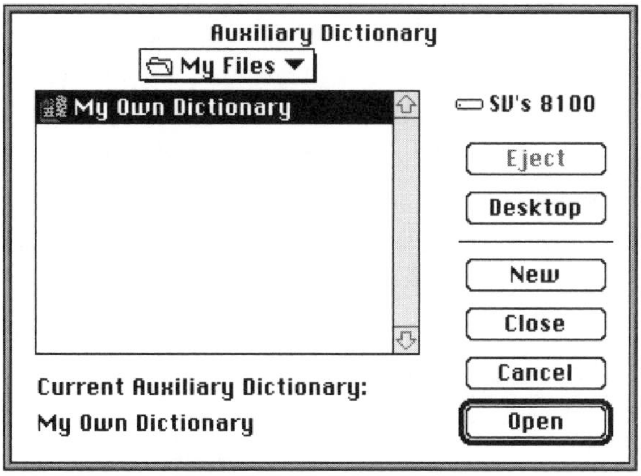

Figure 4.45 *Auxiliary Dictionary dialog box.*

If you choose **Utilities ➛ Auxiliary Dictionary** when no document is open, the new or existing dictionary you open will be applied automatically to all new documents that you create (until you change the setting later when no document is open). If you choose the **Auxiliary Dictionary** command when any document is open, the new or existing dictionary you open will be applied automatically to that document whenever you open it (until you change the setting later when the document is open).

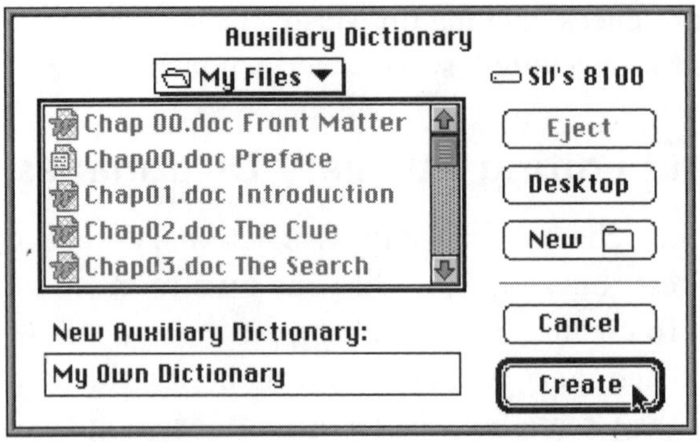

Figure 4.46 New Auxiliary Dictionary dialog box.

You can add terms to the open auxiliary dictionary by going through the spelling check process and using the Add option in the dialog box, as described above. (An auxiliary dictionary *must* be open during the spelling check process in order for the Add option to be available in the Check Story, Check Document, or Check Word dialog box.) You can also add or delete terms in an open auxiliary dictionary by using the **Utilities ➛ Edit Auxiliary** command (Figure 4.47).

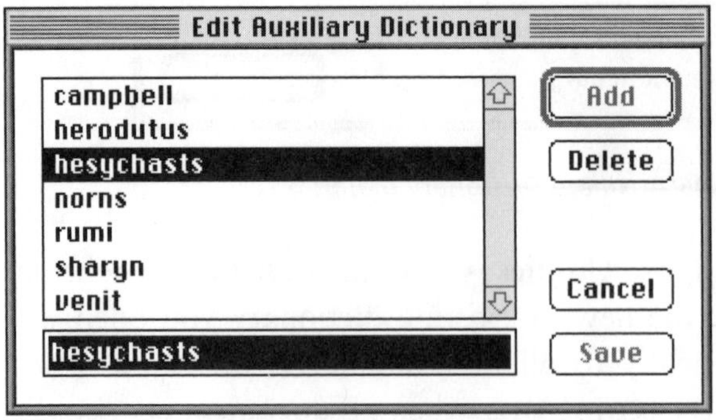

Figure 4.47 Edit Auxiliary Dictionary dialog box.

Terms in a dictionary are all stored in lowercase form—you cannot type uppercase characters in the entries. Only one auxiliary dictionary can be open at a time during a spelling check. You can select the **Auxiliary Dictionary** command to Close the currently open auxiliary dictionary and Open a different one.

QuarkXPress will be unable to locate a dictionary if either the dictionary or the document has been moved to a different disk or folder since the first time the dictionary was opened. The program displays an alert message whenever you select the **Check Spelling** command, so you can go through the **Auxiliary Dictionary** command to close the missing dictionary or find and Uuse the relocated dictionary.

Exporting Text to Other Programs

You can export text from QuarkXPress to create text files in formats that can be opened by word processing programs and other applications, or imported to other QuarkXPress documents. Remember that you can also copy text from one QuarkXPress document to another by dragging the text box from one open Document window to another, with the Library feature, or with the Edit menu's **Copy** , **Cut,** and **Paste** commands.

To export text, first activate a text box with the Content tool selected, or highlight a range of text to be exported. Then select **File ➤ Save Text** to display the Save Text dialog box (Figure 4.48).

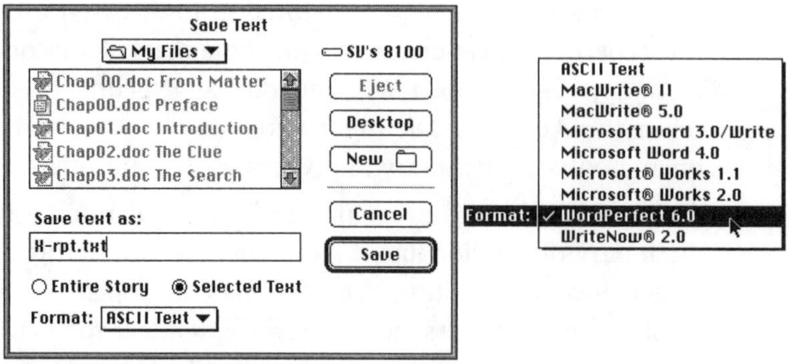

Figure 4.48 *Save Text dialog box.*

Type the name of the exported text file in the Save Text As area. If you activate a text box without selecting any text within it, you must save the **Entire Story** (the text in the currently active box plus all linked text boxes). Otherwise, you have the option of saving the entire story or the selected text only. You can export only one story at a time.

The **Format** pop-up menu lets you choose the format in which to save the exported text, including ASCII Text plus any other formats for which the import/export filter is stored in the System folder or in the same folder as the QuarkXPress program before you launch the program. Formatting is retained in all formats except ASCII text. As the text is saved, QuarkXPress shows the percentage complete in the lower-left corner of the document window, right of the View Percent field.

If you save in ASCII Text format, all formatting is lost. If you save text as XPress Tags format, then the formatted text from QuarkXPress is exported as ASCII Text with embedded XPress Tags for formatting. See Chapter 11, "Publishing Databases," for a description of ASCII formatting tags.

Summary

In this chapter, you learned the basics of QuarkXPress's word processing features—including importing and formatting text, using Style Sheets, Find and Replace, and Spell Checking. The next chapter "Typography," discusses those features that relate more to issues that were traditionally those of typesetters and typographers, including QuarkXPress's rich assortment of spacing controls, including those for hyphenation and justification. If you work with text much at all, you'll want to become familiar with all of QuarkXPress's typographic features.

5 Typography

Typography, the study and application of the aesthetics of letterforms, is an integral part of design. Designers and typographers have a unique way of describing characteristics of text in a document, expressed in terms not only of fonts but also of leading, kerning, intercharacter spacing, and other words that may be somewhat foreign to the typical user of word-processing programs. Typographic control from the desktop is one of QuarkXPress's strong points.

We call this chapter "Typography" because we focus on issues traditionally controlled by typesetters—primarily related to horizontal and vertical spacing (between characters and between lines). The "newer" cyber-typographical controls that are possible with QuarkXPress—aligning text on a slanted or curved path, and converting type to picture boxes—are described in Chapter 12, "Graphics in Typography."

In this chapter you will learn how to work with QuarkXPress's typographical features, including:

- Installing fonts, and working with fonts in documents that move between Macintosh OS and Windows
- Horizontal and vertical scaling
- Kerning and tracking to adjust the space between characters
- Hyphenation and justification
- Working with leading
- Adding paragraph rules (lines above or below a paragraph)

- Locking text to a baseline grid, or shifting characters off the baseline
- Inputting special typographic characters
- Setting typographic preferences for a whole document, including global controls over leading; the size of subscripts, superscripts, small caps, and superior characters; the use of ligatures, and other esoteric issues

TIP

Even though the Preferences command is described at the end of this chapter—because QuarkXPress's default values are acceptable to most people—if you are going to change them, it's a good idea to do so *before* you start formatting text, since changes to these settings can change the way text fits on lines throughout the document.

Whether you—as the designer or typographer—are writing out the design specifications for a document or actually using QuarkXPress to set up a template, knowing how QuarkXPress works before you make your design specifications will help the project go more smoothly.

Fonts and Your System

Chapter 4, "Word Processing," described how to select a font name from the Measurements palette or through commands under the Style menu, but the list of fonts that appears on these menus depends on what fonts are installed on your system. Before you start a document, it's a good idea to make sure the fonts you want to use are available to your system.

What's a Font?

The word *font* is derived from the French word *fondre*, which means to melt or cast. It once referred to the trays of cast-metal characters that printers used to compose a document. Each tray or font included all letters of the alphabet (plus special characters) for a specific typeface/style/size combination. For example, one tray held only 10-point Times italic characters, another tray held only 10-point Times bold, and so on. A font, then, was a particular typeface, style, and size combination.

In desktop publishing, however, *font* has been taken more loosely to simply mean the name of the typeface, such as Times or Helvetica. This is the meaning of the word in QuarkXPress's Style menu and Character Attributes dialog box, for instance. This definition is appropriate for the new computer fonts that are based on formulas, such as PostScript fonts. Each letter of the alphabet is "cast" or designed only once, to define the shape of the letter. This information is then stored as a complex curve-fitting equation. A printer that uses a programming language—such as PostScript—to create text can produce any size typeface, once the shape of each character is provided.

PostScript Fonts

PostScript fonts have two versions of each font—a screen font (a "suitcase" on the Macintosh, or a Printer Font Metrics (PFM) file under Windows) and a printer font (a PostScript font file on the Macintosh, or a Printer Font Binary (PFB) file under Windows). The screen font is necessary to display the fonts on the screen, and the printer fonts contain the information needed by the output device, whether it's a laser printer or a high-resolution imagesetter, to create and print the font on a page.

Most PostScript laser printers come with a basic set of fonts. Fonts that are built into many PostScript laser printers include: Avant Garde; Courier; Times; Helvetica; Bookman; New Century Schoolbook; Symbol; Palatino; and Zapf Dingbats, along with a set of screen fonts for each. In addition, various vendors, including: Adobe Systems; AGFA; Bitstream; Casady & Greene; Fontek; Image Club; Lazy Dog Foundry; Monotype; Opti; Somak; Swite; The Font Company; Type Express; and Wayzata, among others, design and sell fonts.

TIP

Some other fonts that come with the Macintosh—primarily those with city names, such as New York, Geneva, Chicago, and the like—are not true typographic fonts and are not commonly used in typeset documents.

TrueType Fonts

When TrueType fonts became available, they were included with Apple's System 7 and Microsoft Windows 3.1. Unlike PostScript fonts, they do not require a separate screen and printer font; essentially they derive the screen image of a font from its printer font outlines, which must be present in the system file.

To display a font name in the QuarkXPress menus, the font must be available to your system. There are a number of different ways to load fonts, depending on what type of fonts and which version of the Macintosh or Windows system you are using. The method you use also depends on your personal preference.

Using Adobe Type Manager

One of the advantages of TrueType fonts is that the characters do not appear jagged on the screen. But PostScript fonts can be displayed smoothly onscreen by using Adobe Type Manager (ATM)—a software product available for Macintosh or Windows from most software suppliers, and included in most of Adobe's software packages—which provides a way of getting a clear screen display of PostScript fonts in all sizes—not just those loaded in the system. We usually think of ATM as a tool for displaying and printing fonts, but it actually offers a lot of additional features that are helpful in managing fonts, and we recommend using it on either your Macintosh or Windows system.

Cross-Platform Issues

When opening documents transferred from a different platform (Macintosh to Windows or *vice versa*), the system attempts to match the name of the font requested by the document to a name of a font currently installed in the system. When no match is found, QuarkXPress performs its own method of font substitution—using the encrypted PostScript font name.

When opening a document created in QuarkXPress on a different platform, sometimes the wrong font substitutions may occur (e.g., text formatted as Helvetica in a Macintosh document displays as Gill Sans in a Windows document). In this case, there are a few workarounds you can try:

- If erroneous font substitution occurs with stylized fonts (e.g., Helvetica Bold, Helvetica Italic), apply the style (e.g., bold, italic) to plain text, instead of selecting stylized fonts from the Font menu, before transferring. (Many Adobe fonts have been renamed to make Macintosh and Windows plain-font menu names identical.)
- When using Adobe fonts, use the renamed or revised version of the font.
- Update QuarkXPress's Missing Fonts table when opening documents created on another platform.

Horizontal/Vertical Scale

Changing font size is easy to do through the Measurements palette, Style menu commands, or keyboard shortcuts, as you learned in Chapter 4, "Word Processing." Besides selecting a standard size, QuarkXPress allows you to make expanded or condensed versions of a font by scaling the width and height of characters numerically. You can select the **Style → Horizontal/Vertical Scale** command and choose **Horizontal** or **Vertical** from the popup menu in the Character Attributes dialog box (Figure 5.1). You can also use keyboard shortcuts, or scale visually by dragging a corner of the text box as described below.

Values entered in the Scale areas of the Character Attributes dialog box represent percentages of the font's normal character size. Entries above 100 percent (up to 400 percent) make the characters wider or taller than normal; values below 100 percent (down to the minimum 25 percent) make the characters narrower or shorter than normal. You cannot scale in both directions at once using the pop-up menu.

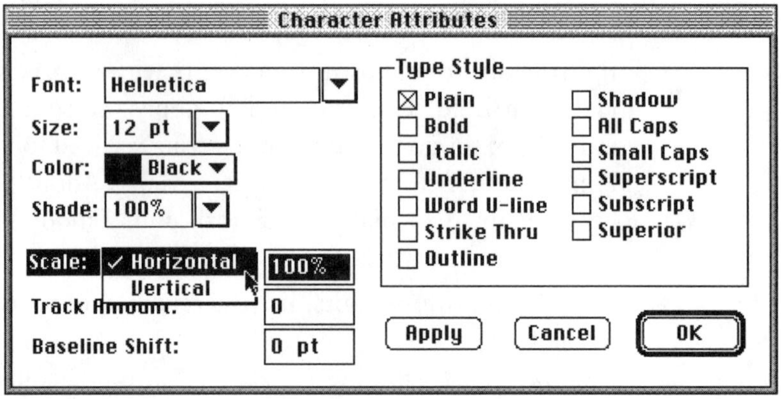

***Figure 5.1** The Horizontal/Vertical Scale option in the Character Attributes dialog box.*

The keyboard shortcuts for scaling will affect text horizontally or vertically depending on the setting of the Scale pop-up menu in the Character Attributes dialog box. The keyboard shortcuts are:

- ⌘-[/CTRL-[to condense in 5 percent increments.
- ⌘-]/CTRL-] to expand in 5 percent increments.

TIP

Notice that you can scale *either* vertically or horizontally (through the Character Attributes dialog box, or using keyboard shortcuts). If you change the selection from Vertical to Horizontal in the dialog box, the value shown is applied in the Horizontal direction—and removed from the Vertical direction.

Overscaling can result in some character strokes being relatively thin compared to other strokes, especially with typefaces that already have some thin elements by design. Scaling works best with fonts that have horizontal and vertical strokes of the same weight, and worst with decorative or script fonts—given these wide parameters, use it with discretion.

Using keyboard shortcuts of the Character Attributes dialog box, you can scale selected characters that fall within a word or a sentence, or any range of selected text. If you want to scale all of the text in a text box, you can also scale text visually, and in both directions at once:

1. First click on the text box and start to drag a handle
2. While dragging, hold down ⌘/CTRL. If you wish the text to maintain its proportions, hold down **⌘-Shift-Option/**CTRL-SHIFT-ALT.

One word of caution—if you hold the ⌘-Option keys *before* you start dragging, clicking on the page becomes a shortcut for the Zoom tool (🔍).

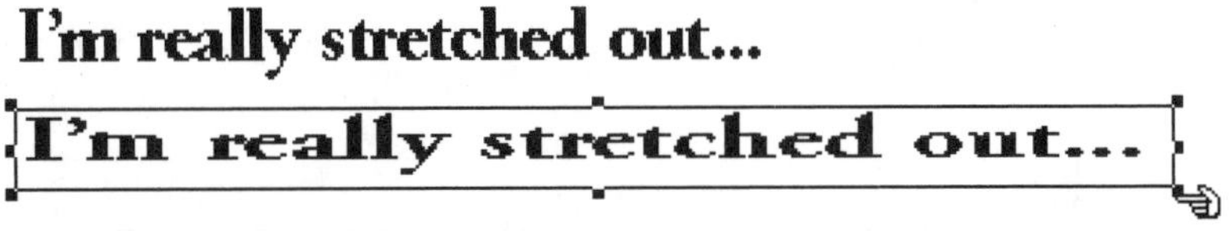

Figure 5.2 *Text can be scaled visually by holding down the* ***⌘-Option/CTRL-ALT*** *keys while dragging a corner handle.*

Kerning and Tracking Text

Kerning and tracking characters are two methods of aesthetically improving the spacing of text. *Kerning* refers to the spacing between two specific letters; *tracking* refers to the adjustment of white space between multiple characters and words. Here's how it works:

- When the text insertion point is positioned between two characters of text, you can use the **Style ➛ Kern** command to adjust the space between the characters numerically; or you can make the same adjustment in the Measurements palette, the Character Attributes dialog box, or by using the keyboard shortcuts.
- The Kern command changes to **Style ➛ Track** when a *range* of text is selected; as with kerning, you can make the same adjustment in the Measurements palette, the Character Attributes dialog box, or by using the keyboard shortcuts.

Values entered for these options must be from –100 to 100, and each unit represents 1/200 (0.005) of an em space. (An *em space* is the equivalent of two zeros, 00, in any given font.) You can enter values in .001 increments, which means you can kern or track in increments as fine as 1/200,000 of an em.

Entering a positive value increases the space between characters; entering a negative value tightens it. In the Measurements palette, you can also click on the arrows adjacent to the entry area to increase or decrease the value in 1-unit increments. Hold down the **Option/ALT** key and click to make changes in .1-unit increments.

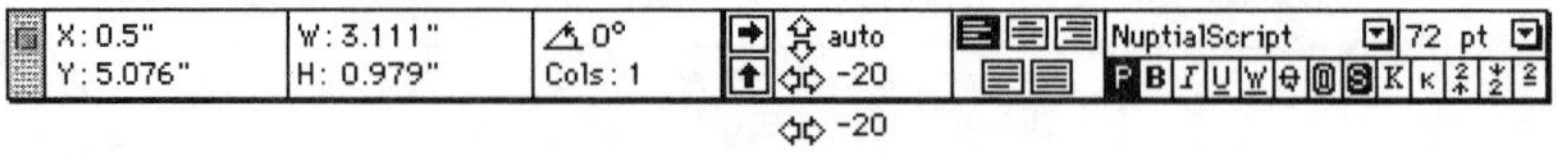

Figure 5.3 *You can type a numeric value to the right of the arrows, or click on the arrows to change kerning or tracking values.*

You can use keyboard shortcuts for kerning or tracking:

- **⌘-Shift-{**/CTRL-SHIFT-{ decreases the kerning or tracking space by 1/20 of an em.
- **⌘-Shift-}**/CTRL-SHIFT-} increases the kerning or tracking space by 1/20 of an em.

- **⌘-Option-Shift-{/CTRL-ALT-SHIFT-{** decreases the kerning or tracking space by 1/200 (0.005) of an em.
- **⌘-Option-Shift-}/CTRL-ALT-SHIFT-}** increases the kerning or tracking space by 1/200 (0.005) of an em (Figure 5.3).

Figure 5.4 *Examples of various kern settings between the letters W, A, V, and E.*

Tracking values, unlike kerning values, can be applied as part of a style sheet. Tracking values affect both word and character spacing, and can be useful for some common situations that call for tighter or looser spacing (Figure 5.5):

- Text set in large sizes is commonly tightened.
- Text set in all caps should be more spread out.
- Text set in a condensed font often looks better tightened.
- Reverse text on black or a color background may need wider spacing—a dark background often makes characters appear closer together than the same text in black on white.
- Sometimes a small tracking adjustment is enough to eliminate a *widow* (a single word on the last line of a paragraph).
- Tracking can be great for copy-fitting when you want to fill a defined space.

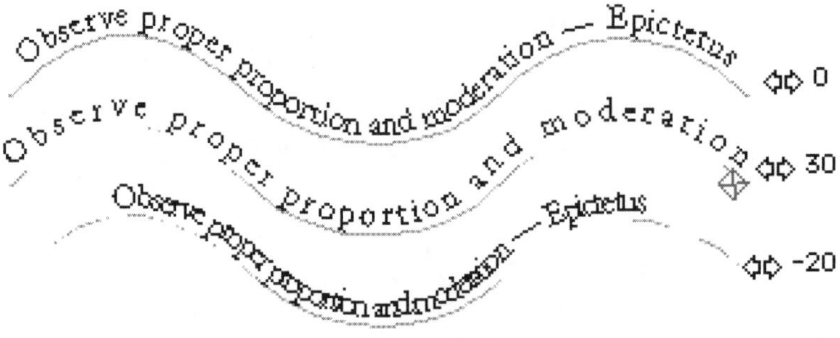

Figure 5.5 *Examples of various track settings shown on a text-path.*

The results of entries in the Character Attributes dialog box are not reflected on the screen display until you close the dialog box, but entries made in the Measurements palette or by using the keyboard shortcuts are reflected immediately. For this reason, it is a good idea to perform all manual kerning through the Measurements palette or with the keyboard shortcuts, unless you are applying a specific numeric value consistently.

TIP

Usually, text above 10 points in size is automatically kerned using the built-in kerning tables for the font. Text that has been automatically kerned still shows a kerning value of zero in the Measurements palette or Character Attributes dialog box—only manual kerning appears as a value. It's a good idea to set the automatic kerning point size through the **Edit ➛ Preferences ➛ Document** dialog box *before* you apply any manual kerning—because if you later change this value the spaces between characters may change again!

Since kerning and tracking adjustments are a percentage of an em of any given font, rather than a fixed size, the actual space between letters will be scaled proportionally if you change the font size of the kerned or tracked characters. For example, if you kern by 1 unit two letters that are 10 points in size, then scale them to 20 points in size, the unit they are kerned will still be 1; however, the em of a 20-point font, of which the unit is a percentage, is larger, and the unit represents a correspondingly larger space. QuarkXPress does *not* offer any way to set an absolute distance between characters—a feature common to many typesetting systems.

Editing Tracking Values

Global intercharacter spacing (tracking) values are built in to QuarkXPress. If you consider yourself a typography genius, or just feel adventurous, you can select **Utilities → Tracking Edit** to change the global setting for a specific font. The first dialog box displayed when you select the **Utilities → Tracking Edit** command lists all of the installed fonts (Figure 5.6).

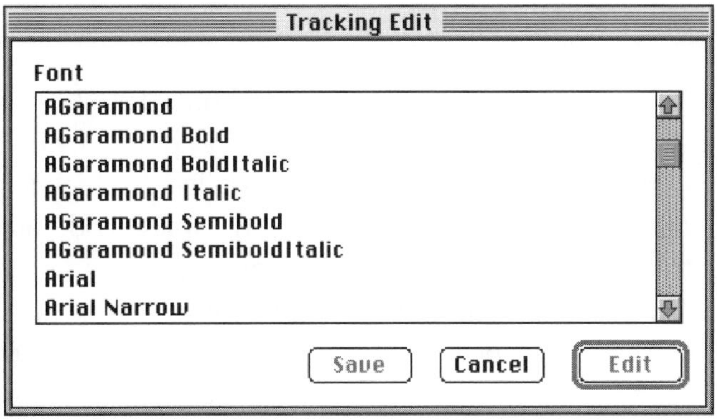

***Figure 5.6** The Tracking Edit dialog box.*

TIP: The **Utilities → Tracking Edit** command is available only if the Kern/Track Editor XTension is in the same folder as the QuarkXPress program when you launch the program.

To edit a font's tracking values, double-click on the font name. QuarkXPress displays the Tracking Values chart for the selected font. Normally, tracking is set to zero for all sizes—indicated by a horizontal line across the center of the chart, as in Figure 5.7.

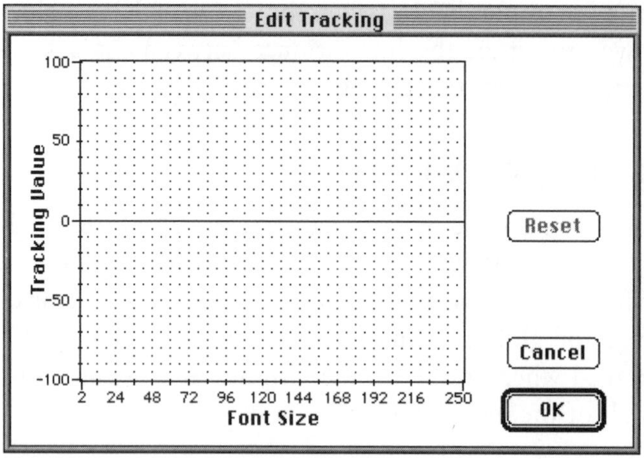

Figure 5.7 *Normal Tracking Values chart.*

You can specify tracking values from -100/200 to 100/200 of an em space for font sizes from 2 to 250 points by clicking on the line in the chart area to create new handles. Each click positions a handle and changes the direction of the line—and you can position up to four handles in a chart. When you click on a handle, the font size and tracking table value are shown in the upper right corner of the dialog box. You can move a handle by dragging it. Three types of adjustments in particular are worth noting:

- You can raise or lower the horizontal line, so the tracking for every size of the font is globally tightened (if you lower the line) or loosened (if you raise the line).
- You can make the line slope downward, so that tracking for larger sizes is always tighter than for smaller sizes. The opposite slope, upwards, wouldn't be very practical.
- You can put a "spike" in the straight line at one particular size or range of sizes, so that only those sizes are always tighter or looser than normal—this is an alternative to setting a specific tracking value as part of a Character Style Sheet, as suggested earlier (see Figure 5.8).

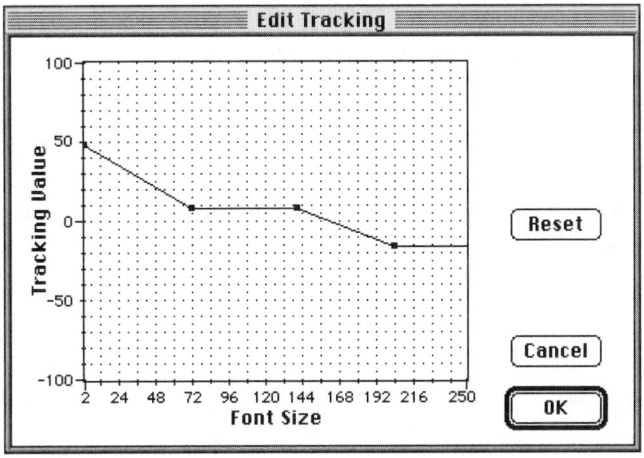

Figure 5.8 *Custom Tracking Values chart.*

Hold the **Option/ALT** key and click on a handle to remove it. Click on **Reset** to revert to normal tracking (0 for all sizes), or click on **Cancel** to reverse any changes you have made to the current font.

When you click on **OK**, the new tracking values for that font are stored *temporarily*; QuarkXPress displays the Tracking Edit dialog box, and you can edit another font's tracking values. To end the process, click on **Save** in the Tracking Edit dialog box—or click on **Cancel** to reverse all entries made to the Tracking Values.

Editing Kerning Tables

Usually, text above 10 points in size is automatically kerned using the built-in kerning tables for the font—unless you change this setting through the **Edit ➛ Preferences ➛ Document** dialog box as described later in this chapter. With automatic kerning, the spacing between characters is adjusted slightly, in accordance with the values stored in a table of "kerning pairs." For example, the space between the characters *AV* should be tighter than the space between the characters *AX*. In fact, if the spacing between the different pairs is not adjusted, then it will appear to the eye that the

A and *V* are farther apart than the *A* and *X* are. For this reason, kerned text generally looks better than text that is not kerned—especially in larger point sizes.

You can select **Edit → Preferences → Document** to change the point size above which kerning is enabled, or turn kerning off entirely for a whole document. (Your pages will redraw and print more quickly if kerning is turned off for small point sizes.)

As with tracking values, if you consider yourself a typography genius, or just feel adventurous, you can customize a font's kerning table using **Utilities → Kerning Table Edit** (Figure 5.9). In order for this command to be available, the Kern/Track Editor extension must be in the same folder as the QuarkXPress program when you launch the program. The first dialog box displayed when you use this command is the Kerning Table Edit dialog box, which shows a list of all the installed fonts.

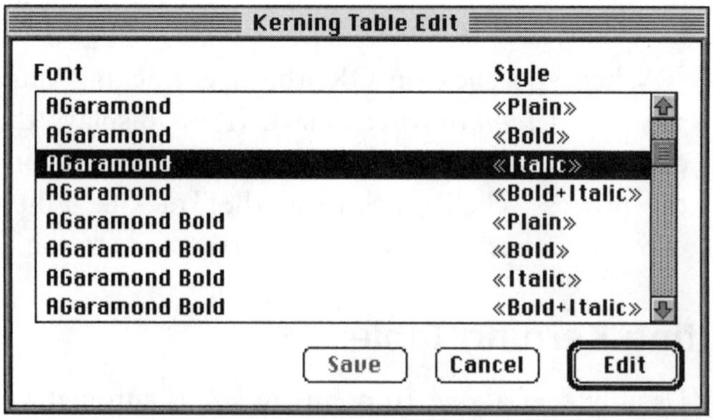

Figure 5.9 *The Kerning Table Edit dialog box.*

To edit a font's kerning table, double-click on the font name/style in the list. (You must edit the kerning tables for plain, bold, italic, and bold-italic styles separately.) QuarkXPress displays the Kerning Values for the selected font. If the selected font has a kerning table, the values are displayed and you can edit them as described next. If no values are displayed in the dialog box, then no kerning table exists for that font. You can create one by entering values in the dialog box (Figure 5.10).

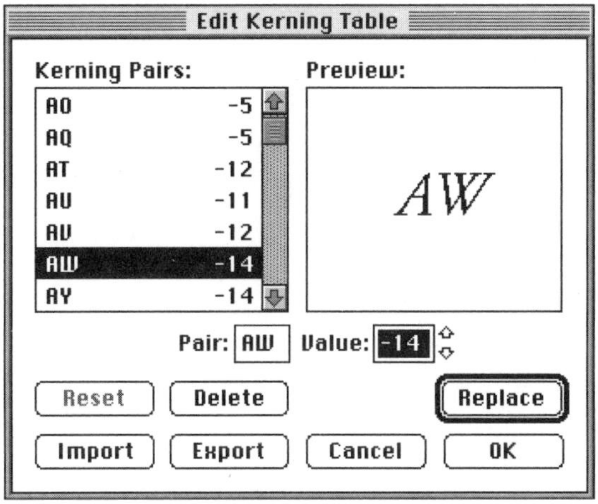

Figure 5.10 *Kerning Values dialog box.*

The Kerning Values scroll list shows all of the pairs that have assigned kerning values. Pairs not on the list have an assumed kerning value of zero. To edit a value, first click on a pair in the list to select it or simply type the pair in the Pair text box. The Value setting shows the currently assigned kerning value or remains blank if you typed a new pair that is not on the list. The window below the Value setting shows how the pair would be spaced with the current Value; the display changes as you enter different numbers in the Value area. Values are entered in 200ths (0.005) of an em space, and can be between –100 and 100. A value of –20, for example, will reduce the space between letters by 1/10 of an em space.

If you have typed a new pair in the Pair entry area, you must click on **Add** to add it to the list. If you have selected an existing pair, the Add button changes to **Replace**. You must click on **Replace** in order to update the table, or you can click on **Delete** to remove a pair from the table (and thereby set the kerning value to

0). The Reset button restores the original kerning table set up by the font manufacturer. If Reset is grayed, you know that the original table has not been modified.

Click on **Export** to create an ASCII text file version of the table. This displays a directory dialog box (Figure 5.11) that lets you name an exported table and specify where to store it. Click on **Import** to replace the entire table with values from a table that was generated using a text editor or by the Export command. The Import command displays a list of all ASCII files, but it displays a warning and does not import any files that are not in the proper format for kerning tables.

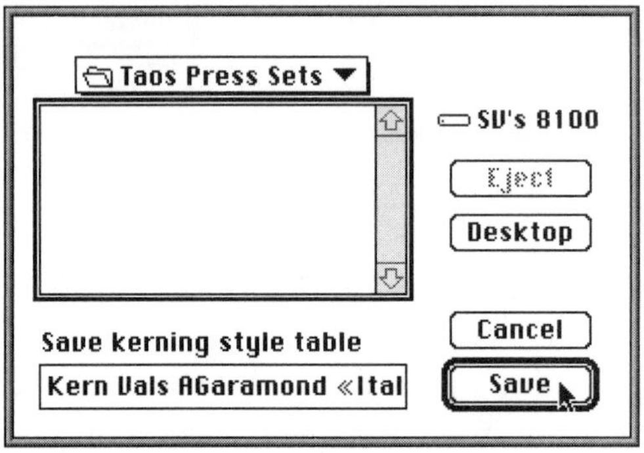

Figure 5.11 *The Export dialog box.*

When you click on **OK**, the new kerning table for that font is stored temporarily. QuarkXPress displays the Kerning Table Edit dialog box, and you can Edit another font's kerning table. To end the process, click on **Save** in the Kerning Table Edit dialog box—or click on **Cancel** to reverse all changes made to the kerning tables.

Changes you make to the kerning table with a document open are stored as part of the document and in the XPress Preferences file. Changes made when no document is open are stored in the XPress Preferences file. If you export text to a word-processing format (**File ➛ Save Text**), kerning adjustments are lost.

QuarkXPress lets you specify kerning pairs that include a character and a word space or an en space. These pairs are used like other pairs. To enter an en space in the Pair entry area of the Kerning Values dialog box, you must first type an en space (**Option-Space/Alt-Space**) in a text box or text-path on the document page, copy it, and then paste it into the Pair area of the dialog box.

Hyphenation and Justification

Hyphenation and justification are so interrelated that professional typesetters usually refer to them simultaneously as "H&J." Both hyphenation and justification function, each in its own way, to make text appear as even as possible—a common aesthetic goal in typesetting—and they both affect how many characters or words will fit on a line. For example, in left-aligned paragraphs, the right margin is less ragged and QuarkXPress can fit more words on a line when hyphenation is allowed than when it is not allowed (Figure 5.12).

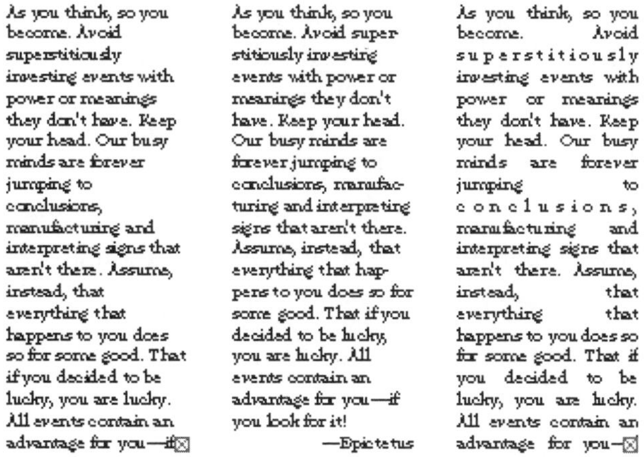

As you think, so you
become. Avoid
superstitiously
investing events with
power or meanings
they don't have. Keep
your head. Our busy
minds are forever
jumping to
conclusions,
manufacturing and
interpreting signs that
aren't there. Assume,
instead, that
everything that
happens to you does
so for some good. That
if you decided to be
lucky, you are lucky.
All events contain an
advantage for you—if
As you think, so you
become. Avoid super-
stitiously investing
events with power or
meanings they don't
have. Keep your head.
Our busy minds are
forever jumping to
conclusions, manufac-
turing and interpreting
signs that aren't there.
Assume, instead, that
everything that hap-
pens to you does so for
some good. That if you
decided to be lucky,
you are lucky. All
events contain an
advantage for you—if
you look for it!
—Epictetus
As you think, so you
become. Avoid
superstitiously
investing events with
power or meanings
they don't have. Keep
your head. Our busy
minds are forever
jumping to
conclusions,
manufacturing and
interpreting signs that
aren't there. Assume,
instead, that
everything that
happens to you does so
for some good. That if
you decided to be
lucky, you are lucky.
All events contain an
advantage for you—

***Figure 5.12** How text changes with hyphenation and justification: Paragraph with no hyphenation shows extremely ragged right margin (left). Same paragraph shows less ragged right margin when hyphenated (middle). Same paragraph shows wide "rivers" of white space between words and characters when justified but not hyphenated (right).*

Hyphenation adjustments are described in this section:

- The default setting is that hyphenation is turned off, but you can change the Standard H&J specification to Auto Hyphenation On.
- You can turn hyphenation on or off for selected paragraphs.
- You can specify how long a word must be before it is hyphenated and how many hyphens are allowed in a row.
- You can specify how wide the spaces between words and characters will be in justified text.
- You can build your own list of hyphenation exceptions.

Hyphenating text is a two-step process in QuarkXPress:

- Define hyphenation and justification "rules."
- Apply those rules to paragraphs through the Formats tab of the Paragraph Attributes dialog box (**Style ➛ Formats**).

New H&J specifications are set up using the **Edit ➛ H&Js** command. The options in the H&Js dialog box (Figure 5.13), listing all the H&Js that have been defined in the current document, are similar to those in the Style Sheets dialog box:

- Click **New** to add a new H&J specification.
- Click **Edit** to modify the specifications for an existing H&J.
- Click **Duplicate** to create an H&J based on an existing one.
- Click **Delete** to remove an H&J.
- Click **Append** to import H&J specifications from another QuarkXPress document.

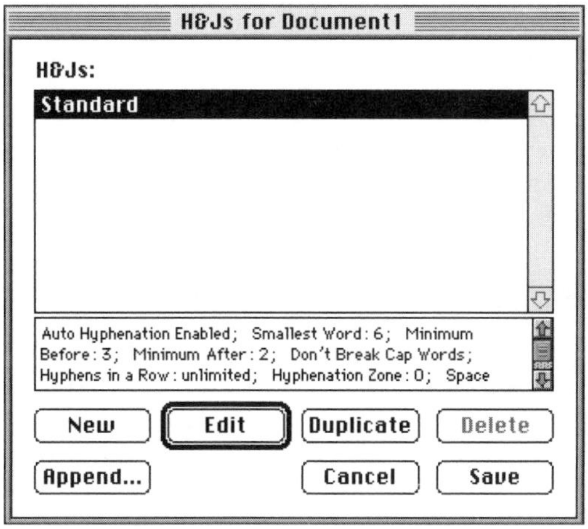

***Figure 5.13** The H&Js list and dialog box.*

TIP: If you select the H&J command when no documents are open, you can create or edit the sets of rules that will be applied to all subsequently created documents. If you select this command with a document open, you can edit the sets of rules that apply to that document only.

Creating and Editing H&Js

You can create and apply more than one set of H&J rules within a document—you need not use the same rules throughout. For example, you could apply one set of rules to all normal body copy and apply a different set of rules to all headings. Different named sets of rules can be applied to selected paragraphs through the **Style → Formats** command, as described later in this section.

When you choose **New** or **Edit** in the H&Js dialog box, QuarkXPress displays the Edit Hyphenation & Justification dialog box (Figure 5.14). This dialog box lets you set up all the specifications for how QuarkXPress will hyphenate text and how it will space justified text.

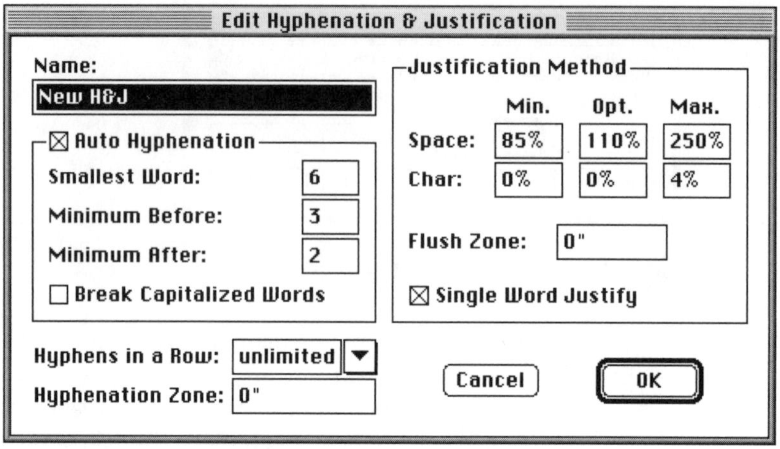

Figure 5.14 *The Edit Hyphenation & Justification dialog box.*

Name

The first option in the Edit Hyphenation & Justification dialog box lets you enter the Name of a new H&J set or change the name of the set you are currently editing or duplicating.

Auto Hyphenation

QuarkXPress will hyphenate if Auto Hyphenation is selected; deselect this option to turn hyphenation off. The Auto Hyphenation area lets you specify the smallest word that will be hyphenated. For example, the word *area* might be hyphenated (*a-re-a*) if you allow four-letter words to be hyphenated, but it will never be hyphenated if you specify that only words of five letters or more will be hyphenated.

You can also specify the minimum number of characters you want on a line before a hyphen, and the minimum number of characters you want on a line after a hyphen. For example, even if you allow four-letter words to be hyphenated, the word "area" will never be hyphenated if you specify that there must be at least two letters before and two letters after a hyphen (since ar-ea is not a valid form).

You can also specify whether you want to break capitalized words. If you want to allow the first word of a sentence to be hyphenated, you will need to check this box. If, at the same time, you do not want proper nouns hyphenated, you will have to select **Utilities → Hyphenation Exceptions** to list them individually in the Hyphenation Exceptions dictionary.

Hyphens in a Row

The next area of the dialog box lets you specify how many Hyphens in a Row will be allowed. You can enter a number (including 0) or type the word **unlimited**.

Hyphenation Zone

The Hyphenation Zone can be entered in any unit of measure and applies to nonjustified text only. If you enter a value of 0, QuarkXPress will break any words that start on a line and would cross the right margin if not hyphenated. You can enter a value higher than 0 to set how far in from the right margin QuarkXPress will go to hyphenate a word—the word must have an acceptable hyphenation point that falls within the zone, otherwise the entire word will be brought to the next line (Figure 5.15).

**Enthusiasm is
the key not only
to the achieve-
ment of great
things but to
the accomplish-
ment of any-
thing that is
worthwhile.
—Samuel
Goldwyn**

**Enthusiasm is
the key not only
to the
achievement of
great things but
to the
accomplishment
of anything that
is worthwhile.
—Samuel
Goldwyn**

***Figure 5.15** Increasing the hyphenation zone from zero (left) to one inch (right) increases the raggedness of the right margin.*

Justification Method

Most of the entries under the Justification Method area apply to justified text only—except Optimum values, which is applied to non-justified text as well. You can enter the minimum (down to 0 percent between words, or –50 percent between characters), optimum, and maximum (up to 500 percent between words, or 100 percent between characters), word spacing (space between words), and character spacing (space between characters) that QuarkXPress will apply in adjusting horizontal space in order to justify a line of text. Values are normally entered as percentages of the manufacturer's normal interword space for the font and size currently in use. QuarkXPress will never go below the Minimum space specified, but it will exceed the Maximum if there is no other alternative.

TIP

As a rule of thumb, the wider the column, the more space you can allow between words and between characters. Lower these values for narrow columns in newspapers, magazines, brochures, and such. If you end up with a lot of white space between words and between letters, that could be a clue that you should decrease the maximum space values for word and letter spacing, increase the number of hyphens allowed in a row, turn justification off (i.e., switch to flush-left text), or use wider columns or a smaller font size.

Flush Zone

The Flush Zone determines whether the last line of a justified paragraph will be justified. A value of zero indicates that the last line will never be justified—this is the normal default, supporting common typesetting practice. Otherwise, the last line of a paragraph *will* be justified if the last word falls within the flush zone you specify, as measured from the right indent.

Single Word Justify

Normally, any single word that falls on its own line will be justified from the left to right indent—the Single Word Justify option is checked in the Edit Hyphenation & Justification dialog box. If Single Word Justify is deselected, single words will not be justified—the word will be flush to the left margin, even in justified text (Figure 5.16). This option does not apply to the last line in a paragraph—the last line is controlled by the Flush Zone option.

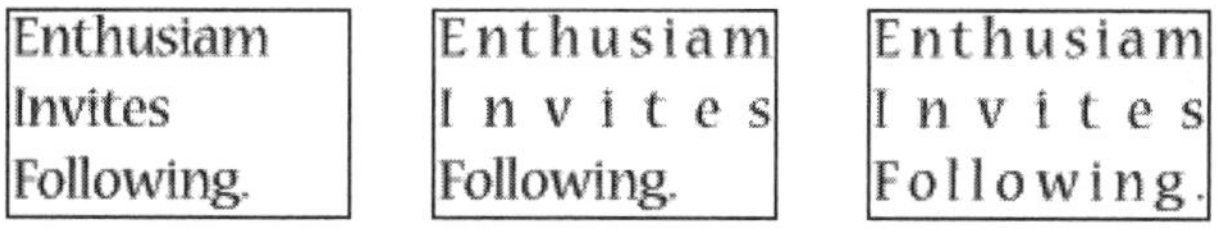

***Figure 5.16** Three justified paragraphs: Single Word Justify off, Flush Zone any value (left); Single Word Justify on, Flush Zone zero (middle); and Single Word Justify on, Flush Zone one inch (right).*

TIP

You can use the Flush Zone option to create special effects in logos, business cards, and display ads, where single words are spread out by design, but otherwise we recommend that you leave the defaults as they are—Flush Zone set to zero, Single Word Justify turned on, unless you have some compelling reason to break with tradition.

Applying H&Js to Text

Once you have defined a set of rules for hyphenation and justification, you can apply those rules to selected paragraphs using

Style → Formats (**⌘-Shift-F/Ctrl-Shift-F**). The Formats tab of the Paragraph Attributes dialog box includes a pop-up menu of the H&J rule sets that you have prepared for the active document (Figure 5.17). Normally, the standard H&J set is applied automatically to all normal text unless you change the H&J associated with Normal through the **Edit → Style Sheets** command. The H&J selection can be applied as part of any style sheet specification. Style Sheets are described in Chapter 4, "Word Processing".

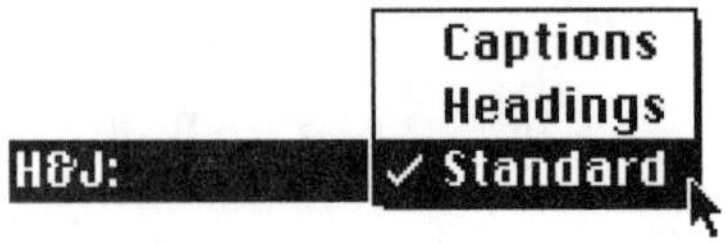

***Figure 5.17** The H&J pop-up menu on the Formats tab in the Paragraph Attributes dialog box.*

Deleting H&Js

To delete an H&J specification, click on the H&J name list in the H&J dialog box (**Edit → H&Js**), then click the **Delete** button. When you delete an H&J specification that has been applied to text in the current document, QuarkXPress displays an alert asking if you want to delete it (see Figure 5.18). All paragraphs to which this specification has been applied will take on the specifications of the H&J name you choose from the pop-up menu in the alert box.

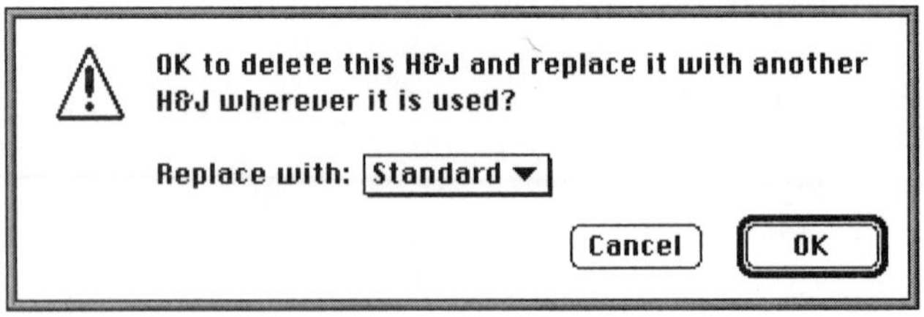

***Figure 5.18** Deleting an H&J specification causes an alert.*

TIP: When you delete an existing H&J, thus replacing it with some other H&J in your document, text reflow may occur. Delete H&Js with caution, and check your document after.

Duplicating H&J Specifications

Sometimes you may wish to duplicate an H&J specification as the basis for creating another H&J. The fastest way is to click on an H&J you want to use as the basis for a new one, and then click **Duplicate**. The Edit Hyphenation & Justification dialog box will appear with "Copy of <H&Jname>" in the name area. You can then use the dialog box to change any of the specifications.

Appending H&Js from Other Documents

You can copy the H&Js that you set up in another document into the current document through the Append H&Js dialog box. The next steps show you two ways to get there:

1. First, you can either

   - choose **Edit ➛ H&Js**, then click on the **Append** button in the Edit H&Js dialog box, or
   - choose **File ➛ Append**.

2. QuarkXPress displays a dialog box through which you can select the document or template containing the H&Js you want to append to the H&J list in the current document. You can change drives or folders as you would in other dialog boxes. Choose a document by double-clicking on the name.
3. Once you've selected a document, the Append H&Js dialog box is displayed—or, if you used the **File ➛ Append** command, click on the H&Js tab of the Append to dialog box.
4. The Append H&Js dialog box displays a list of the H&J specifications from the selected document in a list box on the left (Figure 5.19). Here you have several options:

   - Click on one H&J name in the Available list to view the specifications in the description area. If this is one you want to append, click the **right-pointing arrow** to copy it to the Including list.

- Click the **Include All** button to automatically append all of the H&Js.
- If you want to include most, but not all, of the H&Js, click **Include All** and then select a name you do not want to include from the list on the right and click the **left-pointing arrow** to remove it from the Including list.

TIP

You can select all the available H&Js by clicking the **Include All** button. You can select a group of H&Js in the list by holding down the **Shift** key as you click. To select noncontiguous H&J names, hold down the **⌘/CTRL** key as you click.

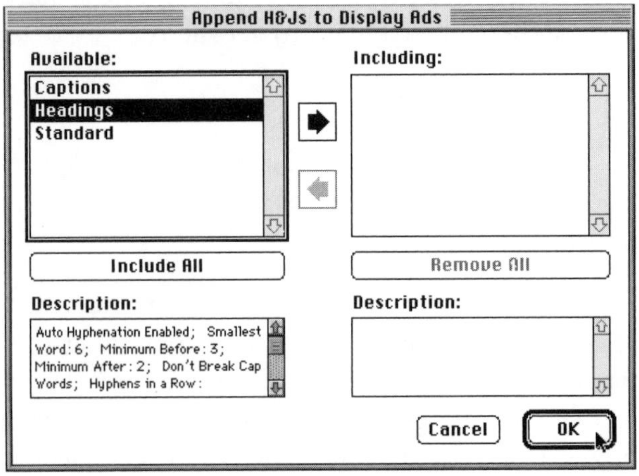

***Figure 5.19** Appending H&Js from other documents.*

5. Click **OK** to close the dialog box and append the list.
6. If there are H&Js that have the same names as the H&J specifications already in the list, an alert will display the conflicting H&J name along with the existing and new specifications and offer four options (Figure 5.20):

   - Click **Rename** to display a second dialog box where you can give the appending H&J a new name.
   - Click **Auto-Rename** to include the conflicting H&J with an asterisk added to the beginning of the name (Figure 5.21).

- Click **Use New** to replace the current document's H&J specification with the appended specifications.
- Click **Use Existing** to keep the specification as defined in the target document.

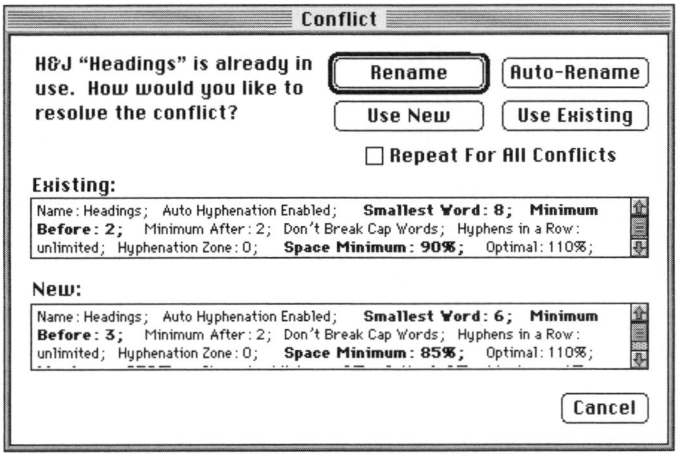

Figure 5.20 *Alert box warns if appended H&J conflicts with existing H&J rule.*

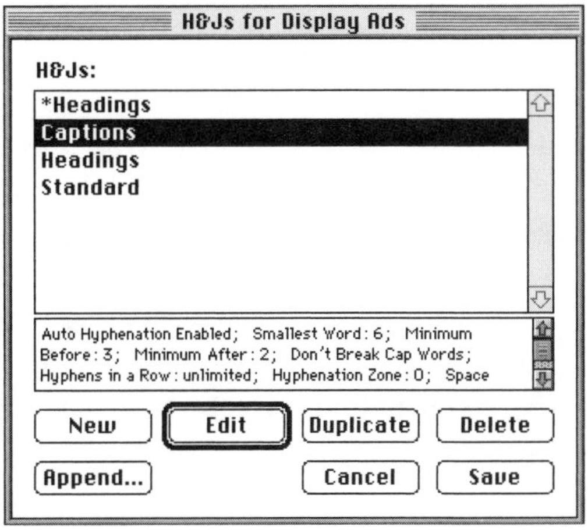

Figure 5.21 *H&Js appended of the same name but different specifications show an asterisk appended to the name when Auto-Rename is selected.*

Suggested Hyphenation

You can see how QuarkXPress would hyphenate a selected word (or the first word to the left of the insertion bar or the first word in a selected range of text) by choosing **Utilities → Suggested Hyphenation** (⌘-H/CTRL-H). This is handy as a precheck before you enter a word in the Hyphenation Exceptions dictionary, or if you want to manually hyphenate a word in a paragraph that is formatted with Auto Hyphenation turned off. The Suggested Hyphenation dialog box shows the hyphenated word (Figure 5.22).

TIP: For words not included in your Hyphenation Exceptions dictionary, QuarkXPress 4.0 now checks a built-in hyphenation dictionary before resorting to a hyphenation algorithm if you choose **Expanded** in the Hyphenation pop-up menu in the Paragraph preferences dialog box (**Edit → Preferences → Document → Paragraph** tab).

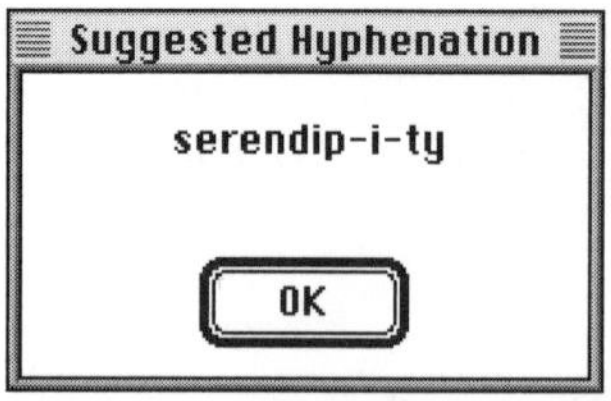

Figure 5.22 *Suggested Hyphenation dialog box.*

To access this feature, the Content tool must be selected and the insertion point must be positioned within a word. You cannot make changes to the suggested syllable breaks. In addition, this command and dialog box do not make any changes to the text itself. If you want to change the way QuarkXPress hyphenates a word, you can insert your own discretionary hyphens (**⌘-hyphen/CTRL-HYPHEN**) or select **Utilities → Hyphenation Exceptions**, described under the next headings.

Discretionary Hyphens

You can manually insert discretionary hyphens within words by typing **⌘-hyphen/CTRL-HYPHEN**. These discretionary hyphens can be inserted using some word-processing programs, before the text is imported in QuarkXPress, or after the text is imported in QuarkXPress. Discretionary hyphens behave exactly the same way that automatic hyphens behave: They only appear on the screen and the printed pages when they fall at the end of a line. To prevent a word from being hyphenated, enter the word in the Hyphenation Exceptions. (See the next section.)

Discretionary hyphens are useful for quick fixes or one-time-only exceptions, but if you want to permanently change the way QuarkXPress hyphenates a word, or turn hyphenation off entirely for selected words, it's a good idea to build a dictionary of Hyphenation Exceptions, described next.

Hyphenation Exceptions

Select **Utilities → Hyphenation Exceptions** to display the Hyphenation Exceptions dialog box (Figure 5.23) and control the way QuarkXPress breaks a word. This command is always available. Any exceptions will be included with all subsequently created new documents.

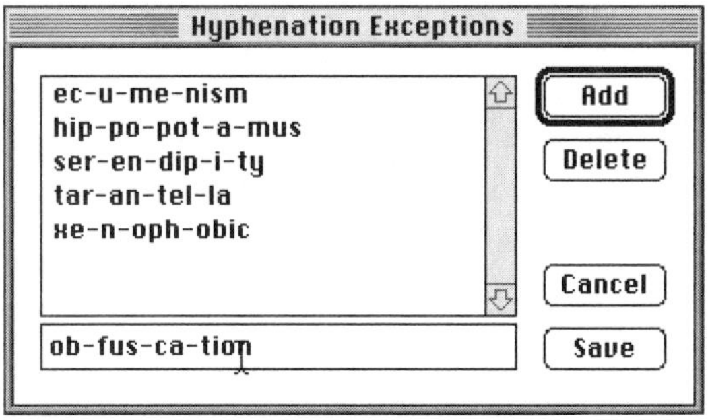

***Figure 5.23** Hyphenation Exceptions dialog box.*

In the Hyphenation Exceptions dialog box, type a word in the text entry area with hyphens positioned where you want QuarkXPress to break the word—or without hyphens if you never want the word hyphenated—then click on **Add**. You must enter every variant of the word (plural, gerund, and so on) separately. If you click on an entry in the list of exceptions, the word appears in the entry area where you can make changes, and the Add button changes to Replace. Use the **Delete** button to remove a selected word from the list. When you are finished making changes to the exceptions list, click on **Save** to keep all your changes, or click on **Cancel** to ignore all changes.

Hyphenation exceptions are stored within a document and in XPress Preferences. If they were created when no document was open, they are stored in XPress Preferences only.

TIP: Any changes you make to the hyphenation exceptions affect all documents when you next open them—whether they are new documents or ones that existed before you changed the hyphenation exceptions.

Working with Leading

Leading (rhymes with "heading") is a measure of the distance from the base of one line of text to the base of the next line (Figure 5.24). It originally referred to thin strips of metal (lead) that typesetters used to adjust the space between lines of metal type—the precursor of electronic or phototypesetting methods. Usually, leading is measured from the baseline of one line of text to the baseline of the line of text *above* (unless you change the leading mode, as described later in this chapter).

TIP: Changing the leading is one way of fitting copy to a defined space. You can make fine adjustments to the leading in order to squeeze text onto a tight page, or to expand text to fill an area. Even though leading can be adjusted in .001-point increments, you may not be able to detect fine changes on low-resolution printers.

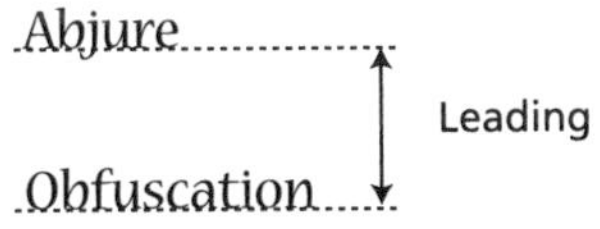

Figure 5.24 *Leading is the distance from the base of one line to the base of the line above.*

Three different leading methods can be used in QuarkXPress: auto, absolute, and incremental.

- The default setting, **Auto,** is set at 120 percent of the point size—to the nearest .001 point. Ten-point type would have 12-point leading, for example. You can specify a different default value for Auto Leading through **Edit → Preferences → Document**, described later in this chapter.
- **Absolute** leading is achieved by entering an unsigned numeric value. The value entered will be applied no matter how you change the point size. If you enter a leading value of 14 for 12-point type, for instance, the leading will remain 14 when you change the type size to 10. If you enter an absolute value for leading, you may need to adjust the leading when you change the point size.
- **Incremental**, or relative, leading can be specified by entering a value preceded by a + or - sign. Incremental leading is based on the largest type size in a line plus or minus the value as indicated.

TIP: Because auto and incremental leading are relative to the size of text in a line, the leading will be based on the largest character in any given line. This means that uneven leading could occur within a paragraph that uses either of these methods and contains text in different sizes.

You can specify leading through the Formats tab in the Paragraph Attributes dialog box (**⌘-Shift-F/Ctrl-Shift-F** or **⌘-Shift-E/Ctrl-Shift-E**), the Measurements palette, or keyboard shortcuts. Enter an absolute or incremental value, up to .001-point increments, in the leading option in the Formats tab of the Paragraph Attributes dialog box or Measurements palette (Figure 5.25).

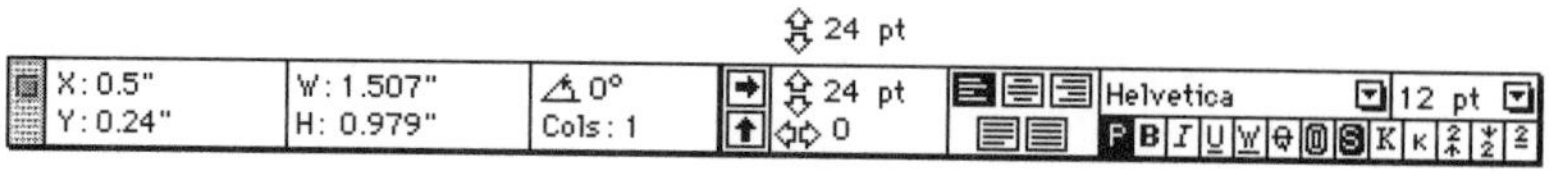

Figure 5.25 *Using the Measurements palette, you can type in a leading value or use the scroll arrows to change the leading.*

You can change the leading by adding or subtracting a value from the current entry or by clicking on the arrows next to the leading option in the Measurements palette. Click on the arrows to change leading in 1-point increments, or hold down the **Option/Alt** key and click on the arrows to change the leading in .1-point increments. You can also change leading using keyboard shortcuts:

- **⌘-Shift-"/Ctrl-Shift-"** to increase leading 1 point—or auto leading to its equivalent in absolute leading
- **⌘-Shift-:/Ctrl-Shift-:** to decrease leading 1 point
- **⌘-Option-Shift-"/Ctrl-Alt-Shift-"** to increase leading 0.1 point
- **⌘-Option-Shift-:/Ctrl-Alt-Shift-:** to decrease leading 0.1 point

Both the Measurements palette and the keyboard shortcuts can be used to adjust auto leading as well as absolute and incremental leading. When the leading is set to auto and you click on a leading arrow in the Measurements palette or use the keyboard shortcuts to change leading, the automatic value is changed to its absolute value; values are then added to or subtracted from the absolute equivalent.

TIP

If you enter an absolute leading value of zero, QuarkXPress uses the auto leading value specified through the **Edit ➛ Preferences ➛ Document** command. If you really want zero leading, you can either enter a relative value of "+0" or enter the smallest number allowed: 0.001.

Adding Paragraph Rules

QuarkXPress lets you specify rules—horizontal ruled lines—as part of the paragraph formatting. Thus you can create rules above and/or below a selected paragraph through numerical specifications (instead of using one of QuarkXPress's drawing tools). Those rules will move automatically with the text when the text is reflowed due to editing changes; you don't have to use the anchoring feature.

Select **Style** ➛ **Rules** (**⌘-Shift-N/CTRL-SHIFT-N**) to display the Rules tab of the Paragraph Attributes dialog box and set rules above and/or below a paragraph. Check **Rule Above and/or Rule Below** to expand the initial dialog box.

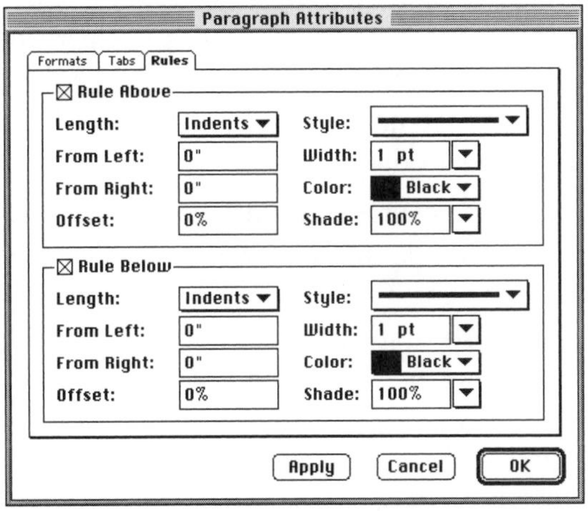

Figure 5.26 *Rules tab of the Paragraph Attributes dialog box (⌘-Shift-N/CTRL-SHIFT-N).*

A rule can be assigned a style, width, color, and shade just as in the Line Specifications dialog box, used to define lines drawn with QuarkXPress's line-drawing tools.

For text rules, you can also specify length to match the line of text to which the rule is attached, or to match the indents set up for the paragraph through the **Style** ➛ **Formats** command. You can further adjust the length by specifying distances in the From Left and/or From Right boxes, determining how the rule will be shortened (by a positive value entry) or extended (by a negative value entry), relative to the text or indents as specified in the length setting.

TIP: You can create "hanging" paragraph rules—rules that extend left of the apparent text margin—by setting a left indent value for the paragraph through the Formats tab of the Paragraphs Attributes dialog box, and then entering a negative number as the From Left value in the Rules tab.

The **Offset** distance specified is added between the rule and the baseline of the text below (for rules above text) or between the rule and the baseline of the text above (for rules below text). The Offset value can be an absolute measure or a percentage of the total space between paragraphs (as determined by the values entered for Space Above and Space Below in the Formats tab of the Paragraph Attributes dialog box).

Values entered as percentages are determined as a percentage of the total space between paragraphs. For example, if you enter an offset value of 20 percent, QuarkXPress will divide the total space between paragraphs so that 20 percent of the space falls between the rule and the ascent height of the tallest character in the text below (for rules above text) or between the descent of the largest character in the text above (for rules below text), and 80 percent of the space will fall between the rule and the following paragraph. When the Offset is a percentage, rules are displayed between paragraphs but not above the first paragraph or below the last paragraph in a text box.

If you enter an *absolute* offset value rather than using the default unit, percentage, the distance will be measured from the baseline of the first line of text to the *bottom* of the rule. for rules above. For rules below, an absolute value will determine the space from the *top* of the rule to the baseline of the last line of text.

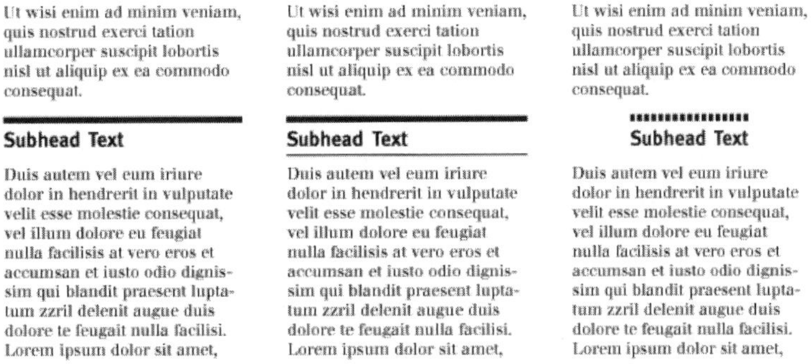
Ut wisi enim ad minim veniam, quis nostrud exerci tation ullamcorper suscipit lobortis nisl ut aliquip ex ea commodo consequat.
Subhead Text
Duis autem vel eum iriure dolor in hendrerit in vulputate velit esse molestie consequat, vel illum dolore eu feugiat nulla facilisis at vero eros et accumsan et iusto odio dignissim qui blandit praesent luptatum zzril delenit augue duis dolore te feugait nulla facilisi. Lorem ipsum dolor sit amet,
Ut wisi enim ad minim veniam, quis nostrud exerci tation ullamcorper suscipit lobortis nisl ut aliquip ex ea commodo consequat.
Subhead Text
Duis autem vel eum iriure dolor in hendrerit in vulputate velit esse molestie consequat, vel illum dolore eu feugiat nulla facilisis at vero eros et accumsan et iusto odio dignissim qui blandit praesent luptatum zzril delenit augue duis dolore te feugait nulla facilisi. Lorem ipsum dolor sit amet,
Ut wisi enim ad minim veniam, quis nostrud exerci tation ullamcorper suscipit lobortis nisl ut aliquip ex ea commodo consequat.
Subhead Text
Duis autem vel eum iriure dolor in hendrerit in vulputate velit esse molestie consequat, vel illum dolore eu feugiat nulla facilisis at vero eros et accumsan et iusto odio dignissim qui blandit praesent luptatum zzril delenit augue duis dolore te feugait nulla facilisi. Lorem ipsum dolor sit amet,

***Figure 5.27** Examples of a rule attached to text.*

TIP

Paragraph rules can be used for much more than adding solid lines above or below paragraphs. Chapter 12, "Graphics in Typography," includes tips for using paragraph rules as colored or screened backgrounds for black or reverse type and for "drawing a box" around a paragraph using rules.

Baseline Shift

Normally, each character in a line of text in QuarkXPress aligns along an invisible *baseline*. You can use the **Baseline Shift** command to shift individual characters to rise above or fall below the baseline of the rest of the text on the same line. This happens automatically when you make a character Superscript or Subscript style, but these styles usually make the character smaller as well. Use the Baseline Shift option when you want to maintain character size, and control exactly how far a character moves.

You can shift the position of selected characters within a line relative to the baseline by choosing **Style ➛ Baseline Shift** command or **Styles ➛ Character** (**⌘-Shift-D/CTRL-SHIFT-D**) to get the Character Attributes dialog box (Figure 5.28). Enter a positive value to shift the baseline up, or enter a negative value to shift the baseline down.

You can also use two keyboard shortcuts:

- **⌘-Option-Shift-hyphen/CTRL-ALT-SHIFT-HYPHEN** to shift down in 1-point increments, or
- **⌘-Option-Shift-+/CTRL-ALT-SHIFT-+** to shift up in 1-point increments.

TIP

Notice that if you do these baseline shift shortcuts *without* the **Option/ALT** key, these keystrokes become the shortcuts for applying Superscript (**⌘-Shift-hyphen/CTRL-SHIFT-HYPHEN**) or Subscript (**⌘-Shift-+/CTRL-SHIFT-+**). Unlike superscripts and subscripts, however, baseline shifting does not result in uneven line spacing with automatic or additive leading—instead, baseline-shifted characters are allowed to overprint characters in adjacent lines.

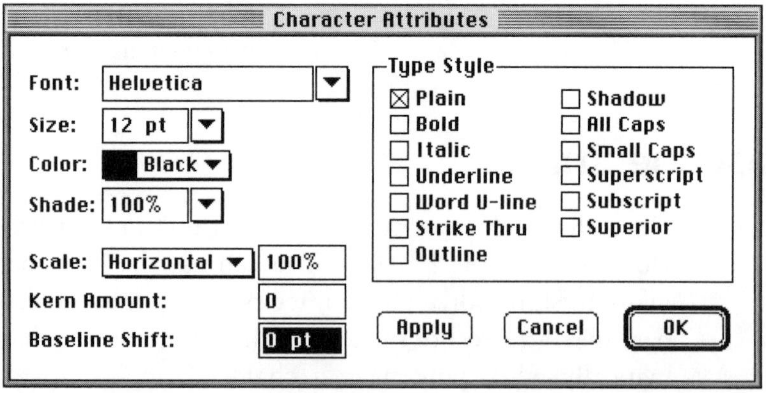

***Figure 5.28** The Baseline Shift option in the Character Attributes dialog box.*

You can enter a positive or negative Baseline Shift value up to three times the font size of the selected text. For example, 10-point type can be shifted up to 30 points above or below the baseline. If you change the size of characters that have been shifted, the baseline shift is automatically adjusted proportionately.

Other Vertical Spacing Issues

The previous section described shifting individual characters above or below the baseline, but there are also ways of shifting the whole baseline for a block of text, and forcing vertical alignment through automatic adjustments to all the baselines in a block of text. You can also use baseline settings to force text to align to a horizontal grid—so that the baselines of text in adjacent columns line up perfectly. These options are described under the next headings.

Setting the First Baseline

The baseline of the first line of text in a text box can be adjusted in the Text tab of the Modify dialog box (**Item ➛ Modify**) (see Figure 5.29). Enter a value in the **Offset** option to add more space at the top of the box (in addition to whatever space is indicated as the Text Inset).

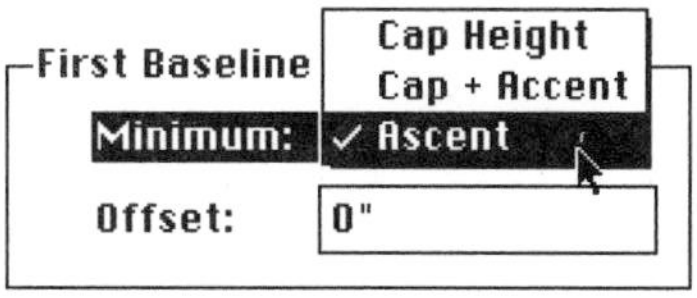

Figure 5.29 *The first baseline of text in a box is set in the Text Specifications dialog box.*

The Minimum pop-up menu displays three choices for determining the position of the first baseline (Figure 5.30):

- **Cap Height** positions the first baseline based on the size of capital letters.
- **Cap + Accent** positions the first baseline based on the size of capital letters plus the size of accents.
- **Ascent** positions the first baseline based on the height of *ascenders* (portions of lowercase letters such as "b" and "d" that rise above letters without ascenders such as "a" and "c").

The position of the first baseline is determined by whichever is larger, the Offset value or the selection in the Minimum pop-up menu.

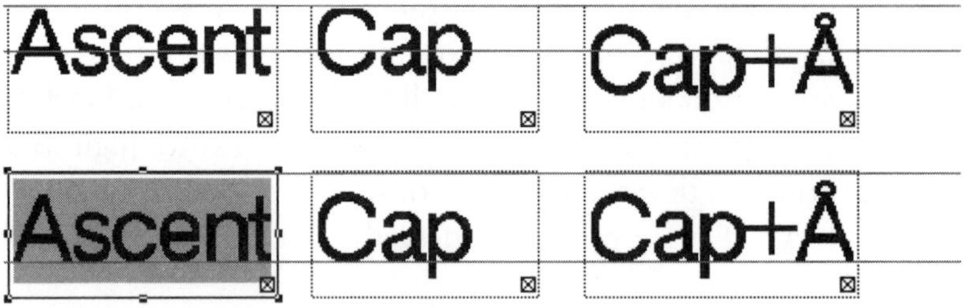
Ascent
Cap
Cap+Å
Ascent
Cap
Cap+Å

***Figure 5.30** First baseline determined by Ascent, Cap Height, and Cap + Accent (left to right, top row) when Offset is 0. Minimum values are overridden by 5.inch Offset in bottom row.*

Setting Vertical Alignment

The space between the last line of text and the bottom of the text box is determined by the Vertical Alignment specifications in the Text tab of the Modify dialog box (**Item ➛ Modify**); choose **Top, Centered, Bottom,** or **Justify** (Figure 5.31). If you choose Justify, then small increments of space (up to the **Inter ¶ Max** value you specify) will be added between the lines and paragraphs of text to make the text fill the box.

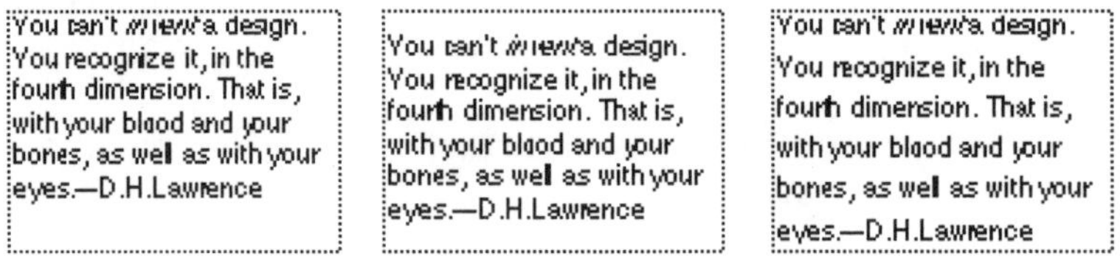
You recognize it, in the fourth dimension. That is, with your blood and your bones, as well as with your eyes.—D.H.Lawrence
You recognize it, in the fourth dimension. That is, with your blood and your bones, as well as with your eyes.—D.H.Lawrence
You recognize it, in the fourth dimension. That is, with your blood and your bones, as well as with your eyes.—D.H.Lawrence

***Figure 5.31** Vertical alignment set Top (left), Centered (middle), and Justify (right).*

Locking Text to Baseline Grid

You can lock the baselines of text to the nonprinting baseline grid of a document. This is useful if you are producing a multicolumn document and you want the baselines of the text to align across columns. This is considered *de rigueur* in most newspapers and magazines, but you can dress your newsletters and brochures up with this feature, too.

Making a gridlock work requires a conspiracy of several commands or features: you have to set the grid up through the Preferences command, you need to set the grid lock as a Paragraph attribute, and you should format text with leading values that match the grid for predictable results. To lock text to the grid, follow these steps:

1. First set up a grid increment in the Paragraph Tab of the Document Preferences dialog box:
   - Choose **Edit → Preferences → Document** and click the Paragraph tab.
   - Under Baseline Grid, enter the Start value (how far from the top of the page the first baseline of the grid is placed), and the Increment value (the distance between the grid lines).
   - Click **OK** to close the dialog box.
2. Once a grid is set up, you can lock selected text to the grid, or lock style sheets to the grid:
   - To lock selected text to a grid, select the paragraph or range of paragraphs that you want locked to the grid and choose **Style → Formats** to get the Formats tab of the Paragraph Attributes dialog box.
   - To lock a specific style sheet to the grid, choose **Edit → Style Sheets**, click on the paragraph style sheet name, click **Edit**, then click the Formats tab in the Edit Style Sheet dialog box.
3. Select the **Lock to Baseline Grid** option.
4. Click **OK** to close the dialog box.

Lines in a paragraph locked to the baseline grid are spaced in multiples of the grid's increment value. If the leading for the locked paragraph is *less* than the baseline grid increment, the lines will be spaced wider apart than the leading specification in order to match the grid. If the leading for the locked paragraph is *more* than the baseline grid increment, the lines will be spaced *two* grid lines apart. If you later change the Baseline grid, lines in paragraphs that are locked to it will be respaced throughout the document as shown in Figure 5.32.

Here are two rules of thumb for the most predictable results:

- The increment value of the baseline grid should be a multiple of the leading of the text you plan to lock to the grid. For example, if the body copy throughout the document has 16-point leading, the grid increment should be 16 points.
- As further insurance, it's a good idea to make the sum of the leading plus space above plus space below headings equal a multiple of the body-copy leading. For example, a 24-point heading with 27-point leading might have 5 points added as space above to make a total of 32 points—twice the 16-point leading of the body copy.

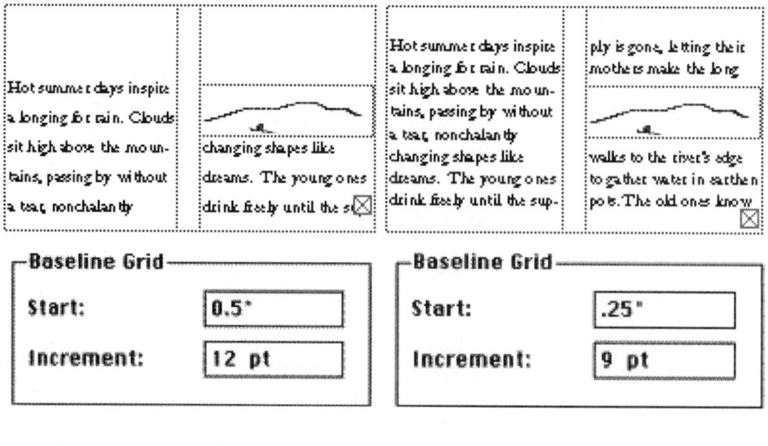

Figure 5.32 *How the grid increment changes the space between lines in locked paragraphs.*

You can display the baseline grid by selecting the **View ➛ Show Baseline Grid** command. You cannot print out the baseline grid.

Running Text Around All Side of an Item

QuarkXPress has always offered options for running text around an item, but it was next to impossible to run text around *all* sides of an item. In previous versions of QuarkXPress, if text runaround was applied to an item in one column of text, the text would run on one side of the item or the other, but never around both sides.

Now with QuarkXPress 4.0, you can easily cause text to flow around all sides of an item (Figure 5.33). This capability is not considered an attribute of an item, and therefore does not appear as an option in the Runaround tab of the Modify (**Item ➛ Modify**) dialog box, as you might expect. Rather, it is considered a characteristic of the containing text box itself, and is thus found as an option on the **Text** tab of the Modify dialog box.

To cause text to runaround all sides of an item:

1. Click on the text box that will contain the text that you wish to have runaround all sides of an item or items.
2. Display the Text tab of the Modify dialog box (**⌘-M/CTRL-M**).
3. Click the checkbox next to **Run Text Around All Sides.** Click **OK.**

Position items in the text box. The runaround specified for each item you position in the text box—such as Item, Same As Clipping, etc.—is determined by settings in the Runaround tab of the Modify dialog box. However, when positioned in this text box, the runaround will be around all sides of the item. By making this feature a characteristic of the text box, you can easily drop several items into one text box. See Chapter 6, "Graphics," for more information on item Runaround options.

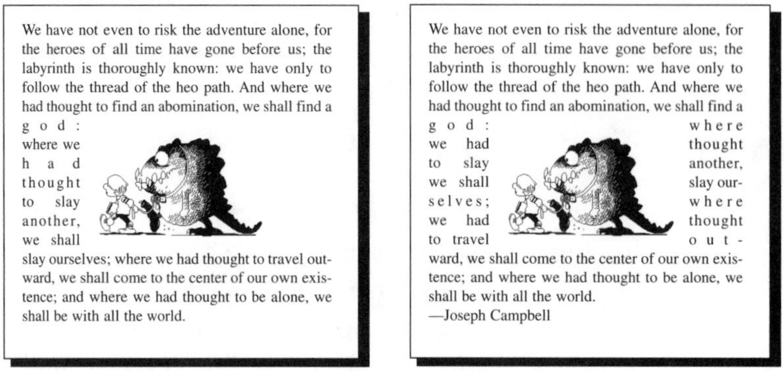

Figure 5.33 *Picture box with Runaround active in the Runaround tab of the Modify dialog box, before (left) and after (right) applying Run Text Around All Sides to the underlying text box.*

TIP

You can create many more special typographic effects using the commands from the Style menu that have been described in this chapter. There's an even bigger universe of possibilities such as drop caps, mirrored text, text on a slanted or curved path, and other variations. These advanced techniques are described in Chapter 13.

Special Typographic Characters

Typesetters have special characters that are often not available, or often not used, in word processors. Some of these characters include the use of true opening and closing quotes (“,”) rather than inch marks ("), an apostrophe (’) rather than a foot mark ('), and an em dash (—) rather than a hyphen (-).

In Table 5.1, the first five typographic characters are built into the Macintosh and Windows systems; the others are unique to QuarkXPress. This table is not exhaustive; rather it lists those characters used most frequently.

It's a good idea to familiarize yourself with these basic characters that typesetters have been using for years.

***Table 5.1** Special typographic characters that can be used in QuarkXPress*

Character description	Printed Character (where applicable)	Keyboard Entry Macintosh	Windows
Opening double quote	“	**Option-[**	**ALT-SHIFT-[**
Closing double quote	”	**Shift-Option-[**	**ALT-SHIFT-]**
Opening single quote	‘	**Option-]**	**ALT-[**
Closing single quote	’	**Shift-Option-]**	**ALT-]**
Virgule (fraction slash)	⁄	**Shift-Option-1**	
Standard hyphen	-	**Hyphen**	**HYPHEN**
Nonbreaking standard hyphen	-	**⌘-=**	**CTRL-SHIFT-HYPHEN**
Discretionary hyphen	-	**⌘-Hyphen**	**CTRL-HYPHEN**
Nonbreaking en dash	–	**Option-Hyphen**	**CTRL-=**
Em dash	—	**Option-Shift-Hyphen**	**CTRL-SHIFT-=**
Nonbreaking em dash	—	**⌘-Option-Hyphen**	**CTRL-ALT-SHIFT-=**
Registered	®	**Option-R**	**ALT-SHIFT-R**
Copyright	©	**Option-G**	**ALT-SHIFT-C**
Section	§	**Option-6**	**ALT-SHIFT-6**
Paragraph	¶	**Option-7**	**ALT-SHIFT-7**
Bullet	•	**Option-8**	**ALT-SHIFT-8**

Setting Typographic Preferences

The **Edit ➛ Preferences** command lets you set specifications for a document globally. The preferences that affect how type looks on the screen *and* prints are set through **Edit ➛ Preferences ➛ Document (⌘-Option-Y/CTRL-ALT-Y)**, in the Paragraph and Character tabs of the Document Preferences dialog box (Figures 5.34 and 5.35). (Two preferences that affect the appearance of the type on the *screen*—Render Above and Greek Below—are in the General tab of the Document Preferences dialog box and are described in Chapter 3, “Expanding the Document.” These two settings do not affect how type looks when it is printed.)

When you specify Document Preferences with no document open, your specifications will be recorded in the QuarkXPress Preferences file and apply to all subsequently created documents but not to previously created ones. When you specify Document Preferences for an active document, your specifications apply only to that document; changes made while the document is active will change the document retroactively.

Paragraph Preferences

Document-wide preferences that are related to paragraph formats are set by choosing **Edit → Preferences → Document** (**⌘-Option-Y/CTRL-ALT-Y**), and then clicking the Paragraph tab. Preferences related to paragraph formats include controls for leading, hyphenation, and baseline grid.

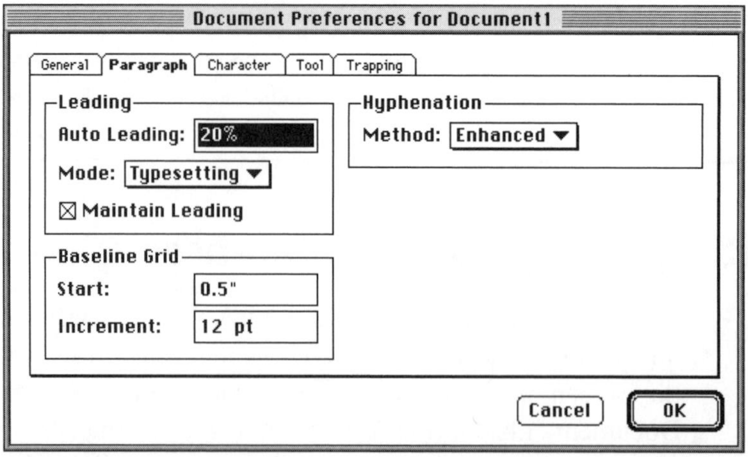

Figure 5.34 *The Paragraph tab in the Document Preferences dialog box.*

Auto Leading

Normally, when you choose Auto Leading, QuarkXPress sets the leading for selected text (the space between lines of text) to 120 percent of the point size of the largest font in the line. In other words, auto leading for 10-point type will be 12 points, or 10/12 specifications. (You can change the leading for selected text to a specific value other than auto by using various methods described earlier in this chapter.)

You can change the auto leading value to a different percentage, or you can enter a signed incremental value, from –1080 to 1080 points. For example, a value of +2 will add 2 points of leading above the largest point size on the line. (Traditionally—with systems that allowed only absolute leading values—typesetters used a leading value 2 points higher than the type size for most text, and some desktop publishers still prefer to use this as the auto leading value.) You can enter measurements in any unit of measure, but you must add the abbreviated code for measurements other than points.

TIP

If you change the auto leading value in the Document Preferences dialog box, QuarkXPress automatically adjusts all of the text in the document that has been set to Auto Leading. Since this change can affect the entire document, it is a good idea to change the Auto Leading setting *before* you lay out each page with text and graphics or better yet, don't use Auto leading at all!

Leading Mode

Normally, with the Leading mode set to Typesetting, QuarkXPress measures leading upward from the baseline of one line of text to the baseline of the line of text *above* it. If you change this to Word Processing mode, QuarkXPress will measure leading downward from the top of the font height on one line of text to the top of the font on the line *below*.

The space above the first line in a text box is determined by the text inset plus the height of the ascender of the largest font in the line for both modes. You can change the distance of the first line of text, regardless of which mode you use, by changing the First Baseline setting in the Text tab under **Item ➛ Modify**, as described earlier in this chapter.

In Typesetting mode, when an absolute leading is specified in the Formats tab of the Paragraph Attributes dialog box, baselines will maintain the same distance apart when different font sizes are used within the same paragraph; text baselines will *not* maintain the absolute leading value in Word Processing mode if different type sizes are present.

Maintain Leading

The Maintain Leading option affects how text is leaded following a box or line with automatic text runaround. Normally, Maintain Leading is on, and QuarkXPress adds an even multiple of the currently specified leading between the baseline of the last line of text above the item and the baseline of the first line of text following the item. If Maintain Leading is turned off, the next line of text will fall one leading increment below the bottom of the item (plus the Runaround distance specified).

TIP: Bottom line? Leave Maintain Leading *On* if you are locking text to a baseline grid. Turn Maintain Leading off if it's more important that you maintain a consistent distance between the bottom of each runaround item and the text below it (Figure 5.35).

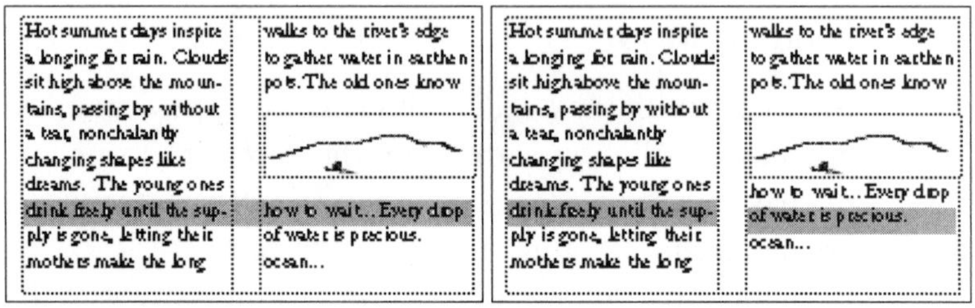

Figure 5.35 *A document with Maintain Leading on (left) and off (right).*

Hyphenation Method

The hyphenation method refers to the method QuarkXPress uses to hyphenate paragraphs for which Auto Hyphenation has been enabled (set up through **Edit → H&Js** and applied through **Style → Formats**).

The default method is **Enhanced.** If you work with documents created with QuarkXPress Macintosh version 3.0, the Enhanced mode may cause the document to reflow. However, as long as all your documents are created in version 3.1 or later on the Macintosh or Windows, the Enhanced mode will produce more accurate results and should remain the default. All new 3.1 and later documents use enhanced hyphenation.

To hyphenate using the method used by versions of QuarkXPress prior to 3.1, select **Standard.** Documents created using version 3.0 open in version 3.1 and later with Standard hyphenation, the method used by 3.0.

QuarkXPress 4.0 adds a third option—**Expanded.** Under this option, QuarkXPress now checks a built-in hyphenation dictionary before resorting to a hyphenation algorithm for words not included in your Hyphenation Exceptions dictionary.

Baseline Grid

To define the baseline grid, enter the Start value, which determines how far from the top of the page the first line of the grid is placed, and the Increment value, which determines the distance between the grid lines.

TIP

Specifying a grid preference does not force text to align to the grid. To lock text to the baseline grid, you must also select **Lock to Baseline Grid** in the Formats tab of the Paragraph Attributes dialog box (**Style → Formats**), as described earlier in this chapter. To display the baseline grid, select the **View → Show Baseline Grid** command.

Character Preferences

Document-wide preferences that are related to character spacing and formats are set by choosing **Edit → Preferences → Document** (**⌘-Option-Y/Ctrl-Alt-Y**), and then clicking the Character tab. Preferences related to character formats include controls for the size and position of superscripts and subscripts, the size of small caps and superior characters, the size above which kerning is automatically applied, and other options for flex space, accents, and ligatures. All of these options are described under the next headings.

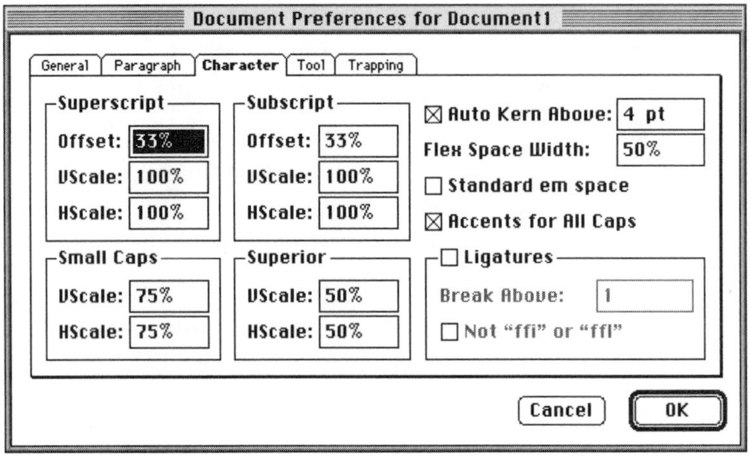

Figure 5.36 *The Character tab in the Document Preferences dialog box.*

Superscript and Subscript

When you choose Superscript or Subscript from the style options through the Style menu, the Measurements palette, or using keyboard shortcuts, QuarkXPress automatically raises it or lowers it relative to the baseline. You can control precisely how large these characters are and how far they appear from the baseline by adjusting the values in the Character tab in the Document Preferences dialog box.

The **Offset** value determines how high above (or below) the normal baseline QuarkXPress places the baseline of a superscript (or subscript) character, expressed as a percentage of the ascent height (the height of the capital letters in the current font).

VScale—the percentage by which the height of the superscript or subscript is reduced—is also measured as a percentage of ascent height.

HScale—the percentage by which the width of the superscript or subscript is reduced—is measured as a percentage of normal character width (one of the internal font specifications that cannot be changed).

TIP: The default settings for superscripts and subscripts can cause uneven line spacing if automatic or additive leading is used. You can force even spacing by using fixed leading, or by adjusting the Offset, VScale, and HScale values to fit within the desired leading.

Small Caps

The Small Caps style (**Style ➛ Type Style ➛ Small Caps**) changes all noncapital letters in selected text to small capital letters. The proportion of small capitals to regular-size capital letters is determined by a setting similar to the Superscript and Subscript preferences.

VScale—the percentage by which the height of the small-cap character is reduced—is measured as a percentage of ascent height.

HScale—the percentage by which the width of the small-cap character is reduced—is measured as a percentage of normal character width.

Superior Characters

Superior characters are reduced in size from normal characters, with the top of the reduced character aligned with the cap height of the adjacent text. Superior characters will not affect leading, unlike Superscript characters, which may. The size of superior characters is determined similarly to small caps:

VScale—the percentage by which the height of the superior character is reduced—is measured as a percentage of ascent height.

HScale—the percentage by which the width of the superior character is reduced—is measured as a percentage of normal character width.

TIP: When you import text that has footnotes prepared in Microsoft Word, the footnotes are converted to superior characters in QuarkXPress. The footnotes themselves appear at the end of the imported file, not at the bottom of each page.

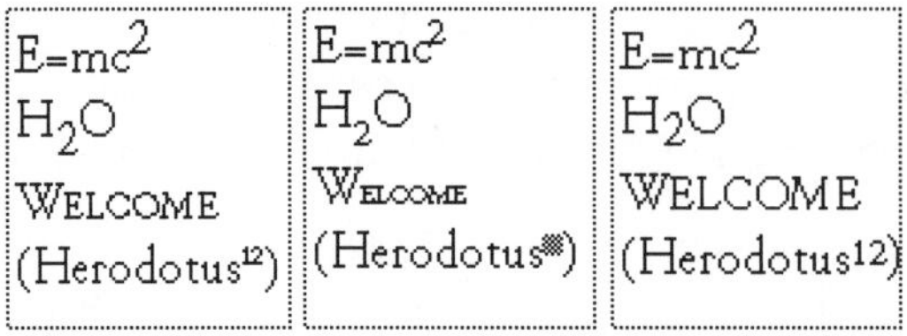

Figure 5.37 *Superscript, Subscript, Small Caps, and Superior characters set with default values (left) and made smaller (middle). Superscript and Subscript are also shifted closer to the baseline, and small caps and superior characters are made larger, in the example on the right.*

Auto Kern Above

Normally, QuarkXPress automatically kerns text above 4 points in size. Under this option, QuarkXPress removes spaces between certain character pairs using the kerning tables built in to individual fonts. Since this adds to screen redraw and printing times, some people prefer to kern only large font sizes.

You can turn this option off entirely, or specify a different size above which fonts will be automatically kerned—from 2 to 720 points. If this option is not checked, QuarkXPress will not use any custom kerning tables, and any modifications made to tracking curves are not implemented. The Tracking and Kerning Text section, found earlier in this chapter, includes a more detailed description of the kerning customization option.

Flex Space Width

A flexible space is a user-definable space that you insert in text by pressing **Option-Shift/ALT-SHIFT** and the space bar. The default flexible space width is 50 percent of an en space (a normal space)—about the width of the lowercase t for any given font. This is sometimes called a *punctuation space* or a *thin space* in typesetting. The width of a flexible space can be changed from 0 percent to 400 percent in .1 percent increments.

You can change this value to 200 percent to make your flexible space widths equivalent to an em space—a character not otherwise available through the keyboard in QuarkXPress.

Standard em space

QuarkXPress bases a lot of internal spacing calculations on the size of an "em space" in any given font. Normally, this option is off and QuarkXPress calculates the width of an em as the width of two zeros. This setting usually makes for better alignment in tabbed tables that include numbers and other number-intensive situations.

The traditional method of calculating an em space, however, is the width of the capital letter *M*. You can enforce this standard by selecting the Standard em space option in the Character tab of the Document Preferences dialog box.

Accents for All Caps

Normally, accent marks will be displayed (if you have used them) on letters to which the style All Caps has been applied. Some publishers prefer to omit accent marks from capital letters, because the accents can cause uneven line spacing—just like subscripts and superscripts—when automatic or additive leading is applied.

You can turn this option off if you do not want accents to be displayed on characters to which this style has been applied. This option offers an advantage over the alternative—to retype the character without the accent. When you turn it off, you can simply apply the All Caps style to capital letters with accents to make them disappear—they'll still be stored as character information, and will reappear if you turn this option on again, or change the style from All Caps.

Ligatures

Ligatures are the combinations of letters *f* and *i*, and *f* and *l* that are pulled close together and printed as one character. Most fonts have ligatures built in. On the screen, ligatures produced using the Ligatures option are actually two characters that appear close together. When the page is printed, however, the single ligature character is substituted. This allows the characters to be spell checked correctly. You can input single-character ligatures from the keyboard on a Macintosh using **Shift-Option-5** for fi and **Shift-Option-6** for *fl*, but it's probably better to use QuarkXPress's automatic feature for setting ligatures.

QuarkXPress lets you specify that the ligatures in a given font are substituted when these letters are typed or imported. Normally, this option is turned off because not all fonts support ligatures. In those that do, ligatures look a lot like their nonligature equivalents, and Windows does not support ligatures at all.

If you want QuarkXPress to substitute ligatures for all occurrences of *f* and *i*, and *f* and *l*, as text is typed or imported, check the Ligatures box by clicking on it. If you want QuarkXPress to substitute ligatures, but not where two consecutive *f* characters are followed by *i* or *l*, choose **Not ffi or ffl**, as in Figure 5.38.

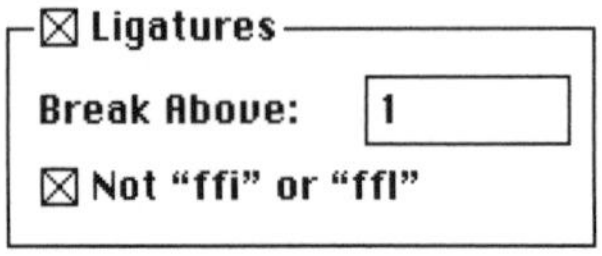

Figure 5.38 *Ligature settings in QuarkXPress.*

Because ligatures are printed as single characters, they will not be affected by tracking values or kerning that increases the space between characters. This can result in uneven spacing in loosely-tracked text when ligatures are applied. You can prevent this by entering a Break Above value—the kerning or tracking value above which QuarkXPress will not substitute ligatures. Setting this option will also help prevent ligatures in headings.

Summary

Now that you know the alternatives available for formatting text in QuarkXPress, you can create design specifications that take advantage of QuarkXPress's extensive typographic capabilities, and you can decide which method of applying the specifications will be most efficient.

The next chapter describes the basics of how to work with graphics that have been created in QuarkXPress and those created in other programs and imported into QuarkXPress.

6 GRAPHICS

QuarkXPress has always been a powerful publishing tool, known for its advanced typographical and layout capabilities. But with version 4.0, Quark has added a slew of exciting new graphics features and improved the flexibility of previous features in a way that will undoubtedly make it known for its advanced graphics handling.

The biggest breakthrough in graphics comes with the addition of Bézier tools. Now, you can draw any shape, with the finesse formerly found only in drawing programs like Adobe Illustrator, Macromedia FreeHand or CorelDRAW. Quark has also added the flexibility to change an item shape to any other shape, including Bézier shapes, and to change the content of a box from text to a picture to none. This flexibility greatly enhances QuarkXPress's capabilities.

This chapter covers several aspects of working with graphics in QuarkXPress, including:

- The basics of how to work with the new Bézier box and line tools
- How to create and apply custom line dash and stripe styles
- How to import and manipulate pictures
- How to work with text runaround paths, which control how text wraps around an item
- How to create and edit clipping paths, in order to render parts of pictures transparent
- How to create compound, complex objects using the new Merge and Split commands
- How to save a QuarkXPress page as an EPS graphic

Other special effects related to type, such as creating text on a path and converting type to outlines as picture boxes, are covered in Chapter 12, "Graphics inTypography."

Working with Bézier Shapes

QuarkXPress's Bézier tools function similarly to those in many drawing programs, allowing you to draw curved shapes of any kind. If you are comfortable using the Bézier tools in Adobe Illustrator, FreeHand, or CorelDRAW, you'll find it easy to draw Bézier shapes in QuarkXPress. As shown in Figure 6.1, there is a Bézier tool and a freehand Bézier tool for creating any type of QuarkXPress item—boxes, lines or text-paths.

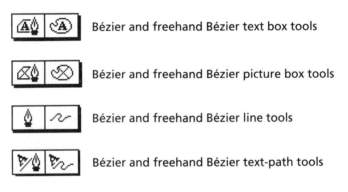

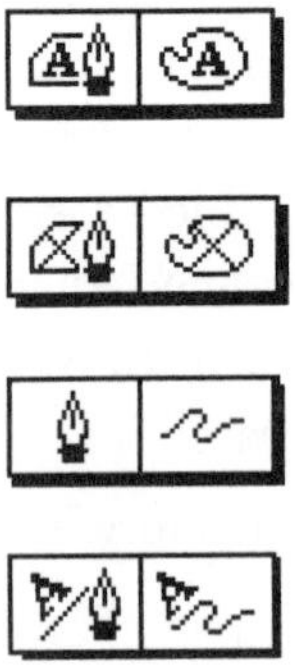

Bézier and freehand Bézier text box tools

Bézier and freehand Bézier picture box tools

Bézier and freehand Bézier line tools

Bézier and freehand Bézier text-path tools

Figure 6.1 *Bézier tools in QuarkXPress.*

Basic Drawing Techniques

A Bézier line is made of up three components:

- Points
- Curve handles
- Segments

A straight segment, or line, is defined by two points between which a segment is drawn. A curved segment, or line, is defined by two points *and* two curve handles between which a segment is drawn. The components of a Bézier line are shown in Figure 6.2.

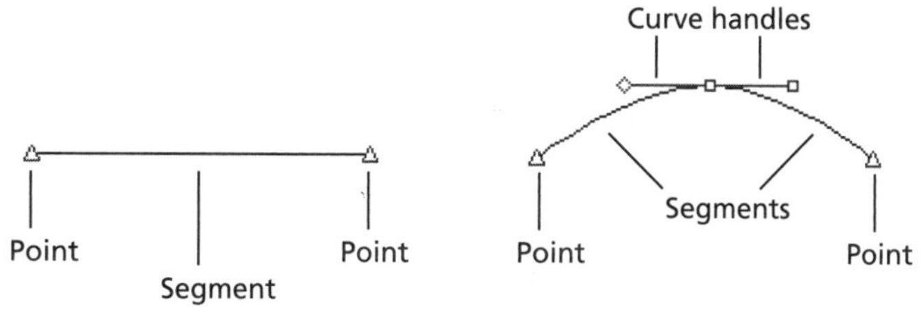
Curve handles
Point
Segment
Point
Point
Segments
Point

Figure 6.2 *The components of a straight segment (left) and a curved segment (right).*

Drawing a straight segment is pretty easy: simply click with the mouse to establish a point, then click again to establish the second point. A straight line will be drawn between the two points.

A curved segment, on the other hand, is a little trickier, especially if you haven't used Bézier tools before. To draw a curved segment, click with the mouse to establish a point, then drag the mouse, without releasing the mouse button, to establish a curve handle. Release the mouse, then click and drag again to establish the second point. A curved segment will be drawn between the two points, as shown in Figure 6.3.

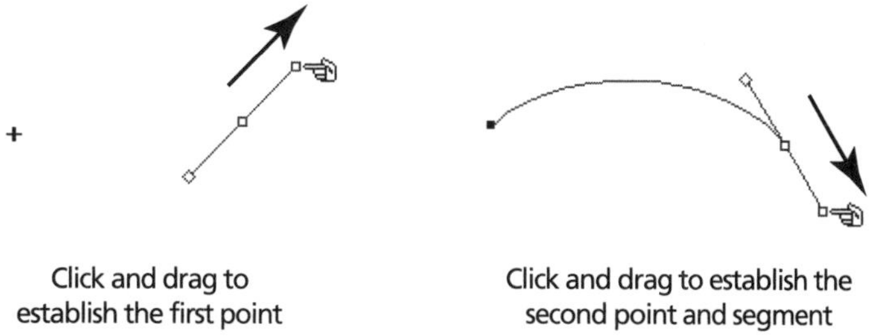
Click and drag to establish the first point
Click and drag to establish the second point and segment

Figure 6.3 *Drawing a curved segment.*

The direction in which to drag the mouse to establish the curve handle is what seems most confusing to new users. The curve handle determines the direction of the curve segment as well as the slope (or angle) and height (or amplitude) of curvature. One rule of thumb, then, is to drag the mouse in the general direction where you intend to establish the next point, and at a slight angle to the curve of the intended segment. The angle of the curve handle to the segment determines the slope of the curve, and the length of the curve handle determines the height of a curve. The curve handles should be about 1/3 the length of the curve. Each curve handle controls one half of the segment with which it is associated. Figure 6.4 shows a diagram of the relationship between a handle and segment on a Bézier line.

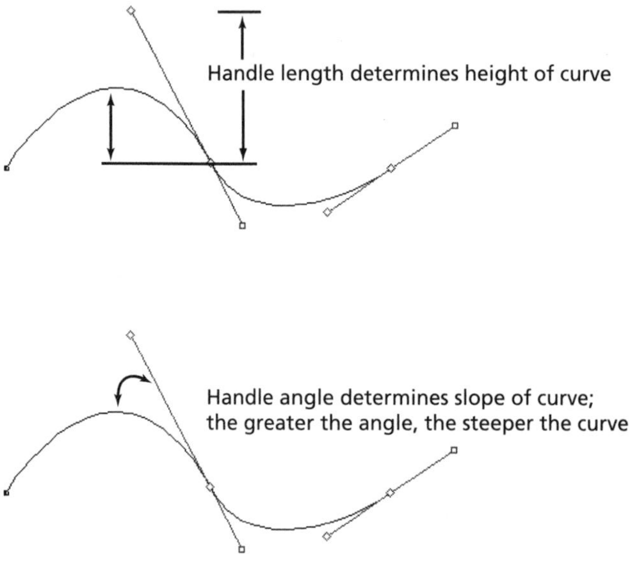
Handle length determines height of curve
Handle angle determines slope of curve;
the greater the angle, the steeper the curve

Figure 6.4 *The relationship between Bézier curve handle and resulting segment.*

One of the nice things about Bézier curves is that they are very easy to edit (as discussed in the next section), so you need only approximate a shape as you first draw it. It's best, though, to create a curve using as few points as possible. The less points you use, the smoother the curve will appear. One rule of thumb we like to use is to pretend you're driving a car on the path, and only establish a point where you would turn the steering wheel to *change* the direction of the car.

You can complete drawing a line or box shape in any one of three ways:

- Double-click the last point you draw.
- Double-click the first point drawn.
- Select any other tool.

Editing Bézier Lines

You can edit a Bézier line or shape by changing points, curve handles, or segments. Points and curve handles can be moved to shorten, lengthen, or reshape the segments they define.

You can change the type of point that adjoins a segment. First, the **Item ➛ Edit ➛ Shape** command must be enabled, as indicated by a check mark adjacent to it. This command is enabled by default when you draw a Bézier line or shape. The three types of points you can establish are smooth points, symmetrical points, or corner points.

A *smooth point*, shown in Figure 6.5, represented on the Measurements palette by the icon, is the default type of point that is drawn when you first create a Bézier line or shape. The curve handles associated with a smooth point are interrelated—think of a seesaw—but they can be of different lengths, thus allowing the height of associated segments to be edited independently of one another. The slopes of associated segments are edited simultaneously as the angle of either curve handle is adjusted. A smooth point is designated by a hollow diamond.

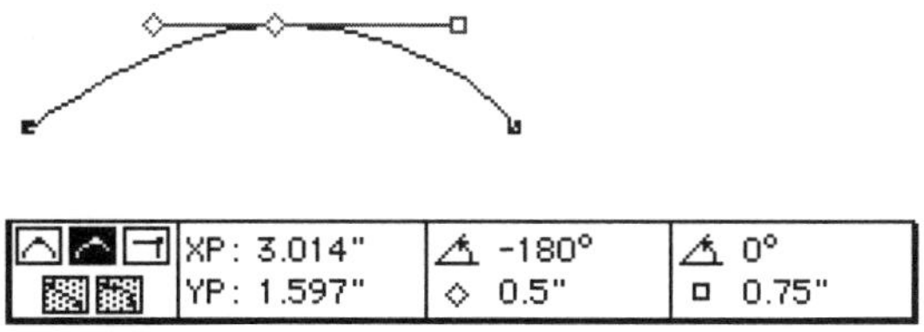

***Figure 6.5** A smooth Bézier point and the associated Measurements Palette display.*

A *symmetrical point,* shown in Figure 6.6, is represented on the Measurements palette by the icon, is similar to a smooth point in that the angle of both curve handles are interrelated. However, the length of both handles are the same on a symmetrical point—lengthening one curve handle automatically lengthens the other to the same measure.

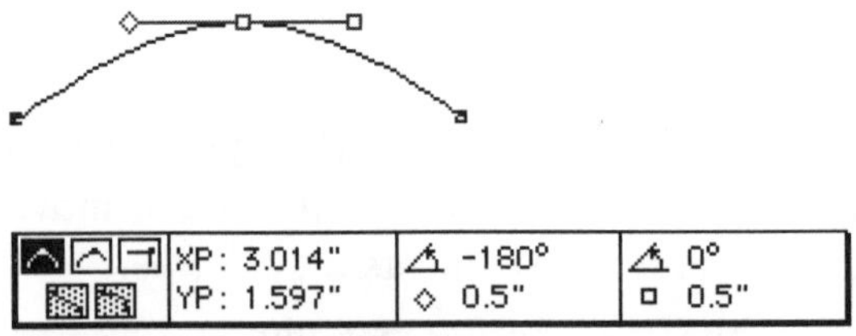

Figure 6.6 *A symmetrical Bézier point and the associated Measurements Palette display.*

A corner point, shown in Figure 6.7, is represented on the Measurements palette by the icon and creates a point with handles that can be moved independently of one another. A corner point can connect two straight segments or two lines that curve in different directions.

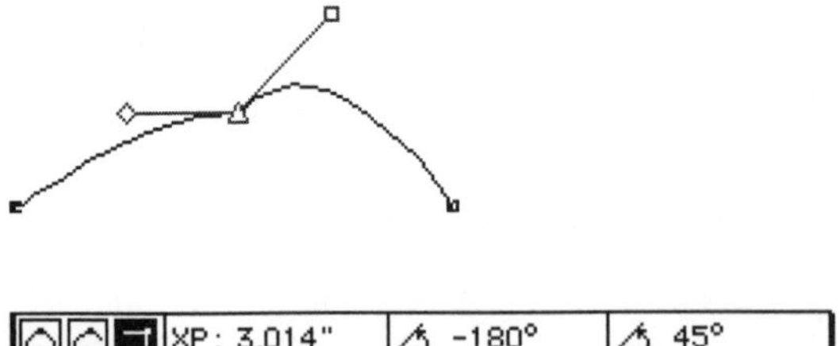

Figure 6.7 *A corner Bézier point and the associated Measurements Palette display.*

TIP

You can move a Bézier item using the Item tool (✥), but it's very easy to move a single point by mistake. Alternatively, you can move a Bézier item by double-clicking on any point; when the ☜ cursor appears, you can grab any point and move the entire item. Our preferred method, though, is to simply uncheck **Item ➛ Edit ➛ Shape**, so that only the bounding box of the item is displayed, which allows you to easily move the shape with the Item tool (✥).

You can change a point to any other type of point, or a straight segment to a curved segment and vice versa, by selecting the point, then either clicking on the appropriate icon in the Measurements palette, using **the Item ➛ Point/Segment Type** submenu, or by using one of the keyboard shortcuts shown in Table 6.1.

Table 6.1 *Keyboard Shortcuts for Different Point Types*

To change to:	Command (Mac/Windows):
Corner Point	**Option-F1/CTRL-F1**
Smooth Point	**Option-F2/CTRL-F2**
Symmetrical Point	**Option-F3/CTRL-F3**
Straight line segment	**Option-Shift-F1/CTRL-SHIFT-F1**
Curved line segment	**Option-Shift-F2/CTRL-SHIFT-F2**

Adding and Deleting Points

Once you've drawn a Bézier line, you can easily add to or delete points from the line.

To add a point:

- Position your cursor over the segment to which you want to add a point, until the Segment pointer displays (☜).
- Hold down the **Option/ALT** key and the cursor will change to an open point (□).
- Click to add a point.

To delete a point:

- Position your cursor over the point which you want to delete, until the Point pointer displays (☞).
- Hold down the **Option/ALT** key and the cursor will change to the point deletion cursor (⊠).
- Click to delete the point.

Changing the Shape and Content of Boxes

In previous versions of QuarkXPress, you could change the shape of a text or picture box to any other box shape using the **Item ➛ Shape** submenu. This command is available in version 4.0, with some important additions. Bézier boxes and lines have been included, and you can now change boxes to lines or lines to boxes.

Version 4.0 also adds the capability to change the content of any box, either to text, a picture, or "none," which creates an empty box. The **Item ➛ Edit** submenu makes Bézier shapes, runaround paths, and clipping paths available for editing. Together, these commands add greatly to QuarkXPress's functionality and flexibility.

The Item ➛ Shape Submenu

The **Item ➛ Shape** submenu (Figure 6.8) lets you change any QuarkXPress item to an item of any other shape, including Bézier shapes. You can change a box to any other box shape, but you can also change a box to a line, and vice versa.

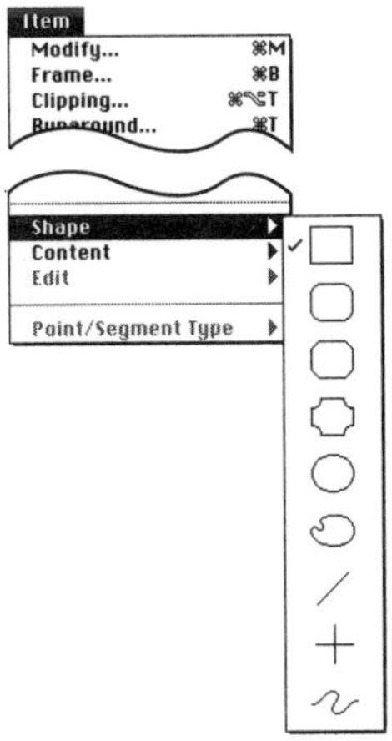

Figure 6.8 *The* ***Item*** *→* ***Shape*** *submenu.*

When you change a box to the same type of box of another shape, the contents are not deleted. If, however, you change a picture box to any one of the line shapes, the dialog box shown in Figure 6.9 is displayed, warning, you that the contents will be deleted.

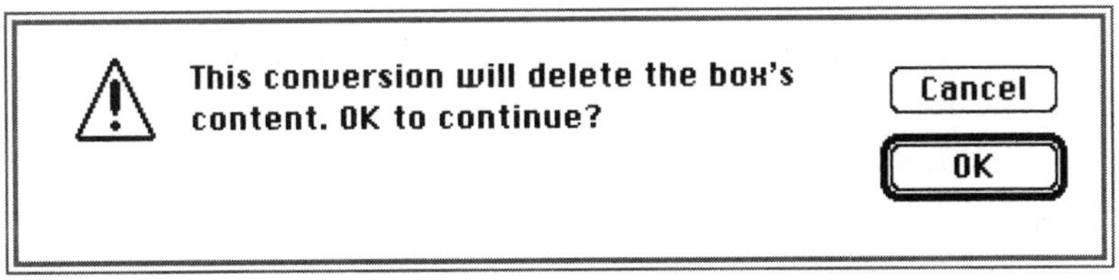

Figure 6.9 *When you change a picture box to a line shape, the contents of the box will be deleted.*

TIP

When you change a text box to a line, it becomes a text-path item. Any text that is inside the box will appear on the path. This is one of the easiest ways to make a text path of certain shapes; for example if you want to create text on a circular path, draw a round text box first then choose the Bézier line shape (∿) to form a circular text-path.

Note that when you change a box to a Bézier box (⌒), the appearance of the box will not change, but editable points will be displayed, assuming the **Item ➛ Edit ➛ Shape** option is checked. When you change a box to a Bézier line (∼), the appearance of the box won't change, but will become a single "open" path, as opposed to a Bézier box, which is a "closed" path.

If you change a line to a box shape, the box will be the length and width of the line. For example, if you have a line that is 2 points wide and 24 points long, and you change it to a rectangle box, you'll end up with a box that is 2 points by 24 points, with a background color the same the color as the line.

TIP

To join the endpoints of a Bézier line to form a Bézier box, hold down the **Option/Alt** key and choose the **Item ➛ Shape ➛** ⌒ command. If the endpoints overlap they'll be joined into one point. Otherwise, a new segment is added to join the points.

The Item ➛ Content Submenu

QuarkXPress 4.0 gives you the ability to change the content of a box, or to change a line to a text-path and vice versa. You can use the **Item ➛ Content** submenu (Figure 6.10) to change a box to "hold" any one of three types of content: text, a picture, or none. In all cases, any current contents of the box will be deleted when you change to another content type.

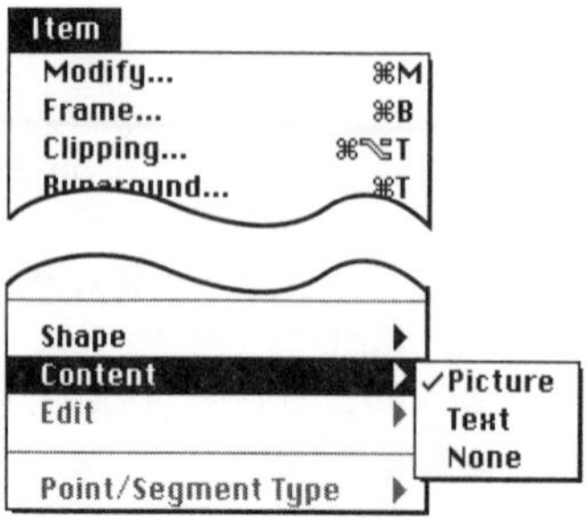

Figure 6. 10 *The **Item ➛ Content** submenu.*

Choose **Item ➛ Content ➛ Text** when you want to change a non-text box to a text box. If a line is selected, choosing **Item ➛ Content ➛ Text** will convert it to a text path.

Choose **Item ➛ Content ➛ Picture** when you want to change a non-picture box to a picture box. When a line is the selected item, **Item ➛ Content ➛ Picture** is not available.

Boxes with a content type of None cannot contain text or pictures, but they can have color, shade, or a blend applied to them. If a text-path is selected, choosing **Item ➛ Content ➛ None** will convert the text-path to a line, and any text on the path will be deleted.

TIP

Choose **Item ➛ Content ➛ None** if you are using a box to simply apply color or blends. Boxes with a content of None are smaller than an empty text or picture box of the same size, since a text box must contain information about font style and other attributes, and a picture box contains information about runaround and clipping paths. You can keep your file size smaller by using text and picture boxes only when boxes will have text or pictures as their content, and using boxes with a content of None when you're simply adding graphic color elements.

The Item ➛ Edit Submenu

The **Item ➛ Edit** submenu (Figure 6.11) makes Bézier shapes, runaround paths, and clipping paths available for editing. When none of the options on this menu are checked, an item is displayed by its bounding box and can be moved or resized, but not reshaped. This command is available only when you select a Bézier shape or an item containing a runaround or clipping path.

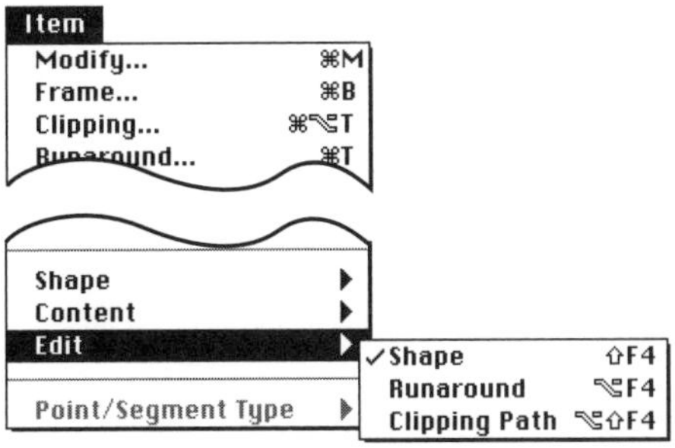

Figure 6.11 *The **Item ➛ Edit** submenu.*

Choose **Item ➛ Edit ➛ Shape** when you want to edit Bézier items. This option is checked by default when you draw a Bézier item. If this option is not displayed, the bounding box of any selected Bézier item will be displayed.

TIP

Sometimes it's easier to move a complex Bézier item when **Item ➛ Edit ➛ Shape** is unchecked (turned off) as shown in Figure 6.12. The bounding box of the item is displayed, so you can move or resize the item without having to worry about accidentally moving a Bézier point or segment, instead of the entire item.

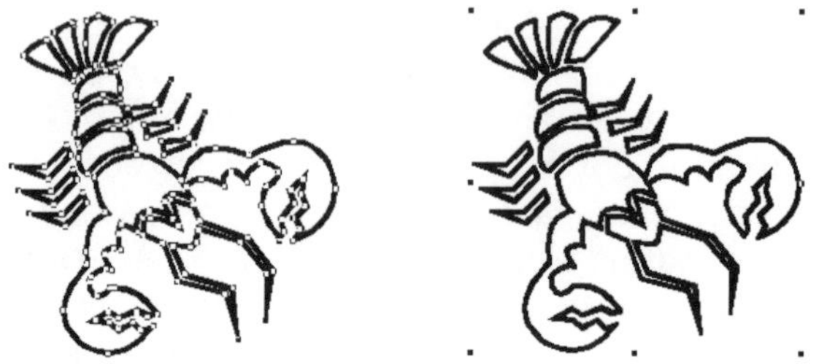

Figure 6.12 *A complex Bézier item with **Item ➛ Edit ➛ Shape** checked on (left) and checked off (right).*

Choose **Item ➛ Edit ➛ Runaround** when you want to edit the runaround path applied to a picture or a text-path item. When this option is checked, as shown in Figure 6.13, the runaround path of the selected picture or text-path is displayed, and can be edited using standard Bézier tools. On color monitors, the runaround path is displayed in the same color as that specified for Grid color in Application Preferences (**Edit ➛ Preferences ➛ Application**), which is magenta by default.

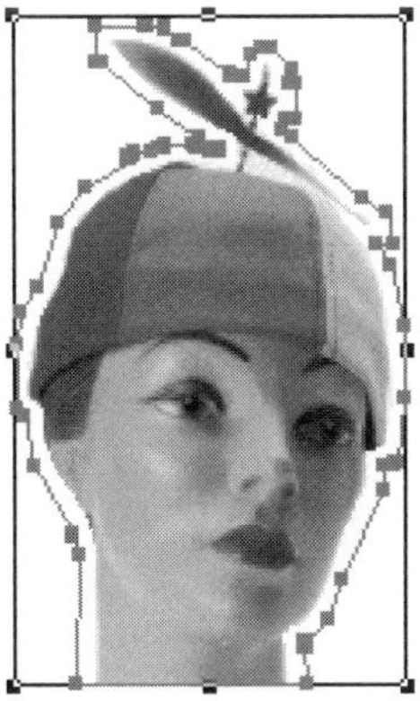

Figure 6.13 *A picture with* ***Item → Edit → Runaround*** *selected.*

Choose **Item → Edit → Clipping Path** when you want to edit the clipping path applied to a picture. When this option is checked, as shown in Figure 6.14, the clipping paths applied to the selected picture are displayed and can be edited using standard Bézier tools. On color monitors, the runaround path is displayed in the same color as that specified for Ruler color in Application Preferences (**Edit → Preferences → Application**), which is green by default.

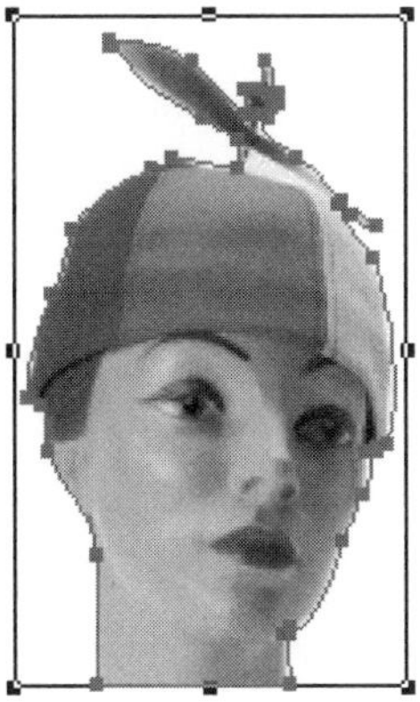

Figure 6.14 *A picture with* ***Item → Edit → Clipping Path*** *selected.*

Item ➛ Edit ➛ Runaround and **Item ➛ Edit ➛ Clipping Path** are mutually exclusive toggle commands; if you check one, the other will become unchecked.

Working with Lines

Lines, like text and picture boxes, are one of QuarkXPress's basic item types. Text-paths, an item type new to 4.0, share some of the characteristics of line items, in that text is typed on paths, which are essentially lines.

Another feature new to 4.0 is the ability to create custom Dashes & Stripes, which can then be applied to lines and text-paths, as well as frames on boxes. The variety of line styles available is now virtually limitless.

The next section details how to create custom dashes and stripes, followed by a description of how to apply line styles and manipulate line and text path items.

Creating Custom Line Styles

One of 4.0's new features is the ability to create custom dashes and stripes. A *dash* is a broken line style that is defined by segments divided vertically, and a *stripe* is a banded line style that is defined by segments divided horizontally. QuarkXPress relies on a single palette of dash and stripe styles in a document that can be applied to lines, text-paths, or box frames. You can easily add dashes and stripes to the default list using the **Edit ➛ Dashes & Stripes** command, or you can Append (import) dashes and stripes set up in another QuarkXPress document.

The default dashes and stripes list that's available the first time you open QuarkXPress (Figure 6.15) includes eleven dashes and stripes—including a solid line, four dash styles, and six stripe styles. All of these may be deleted *except* the solid line.

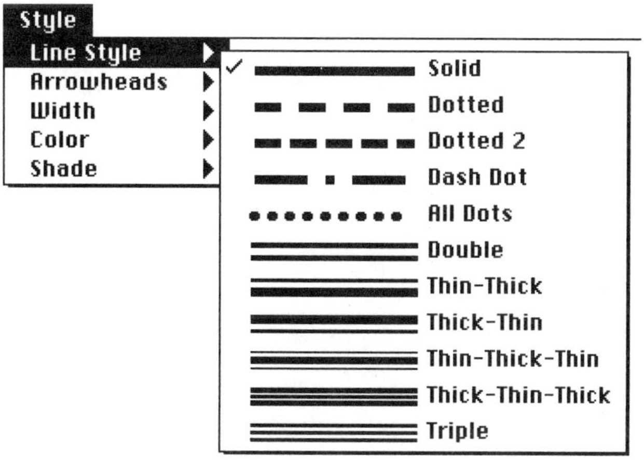

***Figure 6.15** The default list of Dashes & Stripes.*

Here's your first tip. It's basic, but important:

TIP: The dashes and stripes available are controlled by the **Edit ➛ Dashes & Stripes** command. When a document is open, you can use the command to create the dashes and stripes for that specific document, or you can edit the dashes and stripes for all *new* documents by creating dashes and stripes using the **Edit ➛ Dashes & Stripes** command when *no* document is open.

The Dashes & Stripes Dialog Box

The first dialog box displayed when you choose **Edit ➛ Dashes & Stripes** lists the dashes and stripes available for the current document (Figure 6.16), or the default list that all documents will share (if you use the command when no document is open). This dialog box offers options similar to those found under **Edit ➛ Style Sheets, Edit ➛ H&Js, Edit ➛ Colors,** or **Edit ➛ Lists.** In addition, the dialog box contains several options for different ways to view the contents of the list.

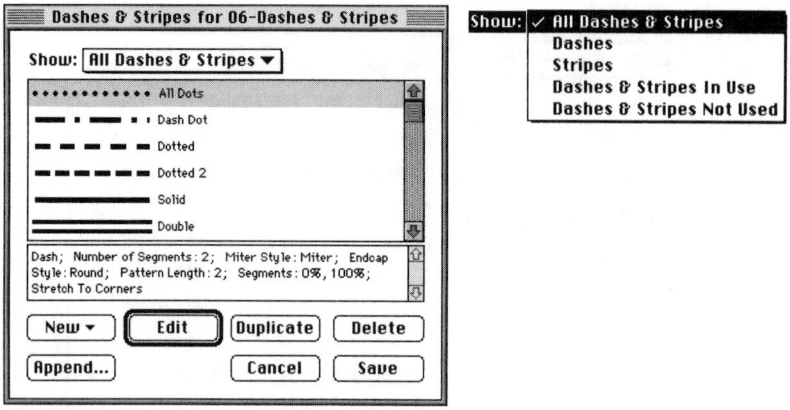

Figure 6.16 *The Dashes & Stripes dialog box with the Show pop-up menu.*

The Show pop-up menu at the top of the dialog box (Figure 6.16) allows you display the list of dashes and stripes based on different criteria. The default, **All Dashes & Stripes,** displays all the dashes and stripes available. **Dashes** displays the list of dashes only. **Stripes** displays the list of stripes only.

Choose **Dashes & Stripes In Use** to display the dashes and stripes that have actually been applied to some QuarkXPress item in the current document, including a line, text-path, or frame. Choose **Dashes & Stripes Not Used** to display the dash and stripe styles that are in the palette, but which have not been applied to any QuarkXPress item in the document.

The options at the bottom of the list, which include **New, Edit, Duplicate, Delete,** and **Append,** are discussed in detail in the following sections.

The Edit Dash Dialog Box

The Edit Dash dialog box (Figure 6.17) is displayed when you choose **New Dash, Edit,** or **Duplicate** from the Dashes & Stripes dialog box. Use this dialog box to design custom dashes—you'll find it gives you tremendous control over the dashes you wish to create.

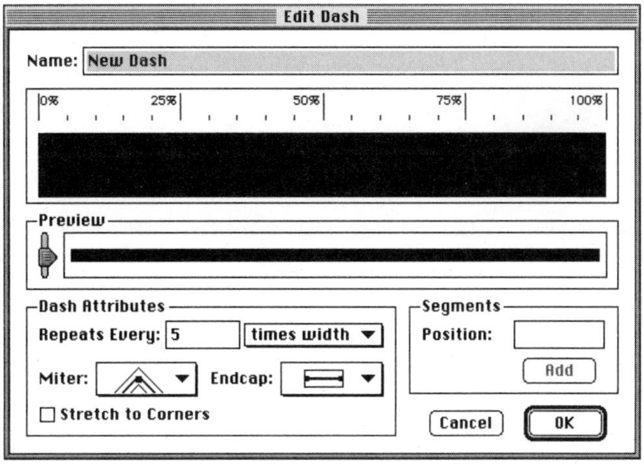

Figure 6.17 *The Edit Dash dialog box.*

When you create a new dash style, the Edit Dash dialog box opens with the **Name** field highlighted and the entry "New Dash." You can enter a new name, or you can edit the name shown in this field. The name you assign appears in all line style listings for both lines and text-paths, including the **Style ➛ Line Style** submenu and in the Line tab of the Modify dialog box. Dash styles are also available for box frames and are displayed in the Frame tab of the Modify dialog box.

The Ruler area of the Edit Dash dialog box (Figure 6.18) lets you *visually* apply bands to your dash style. (You can establish the bands *numerically* using the Segments area of the Dash dialog box, discussed in the next section.) When you first open the Edit Dash dialog box to create a new dash, the ruler area shows a solid band. Click in the ruler area above the solid band to display an arrow where you want the first band to end. To start a new band, click again, and another an arrow is displayed which starts the new band; drag the arrow the width of the new band and release, which establishes an arrow that ends the second band.

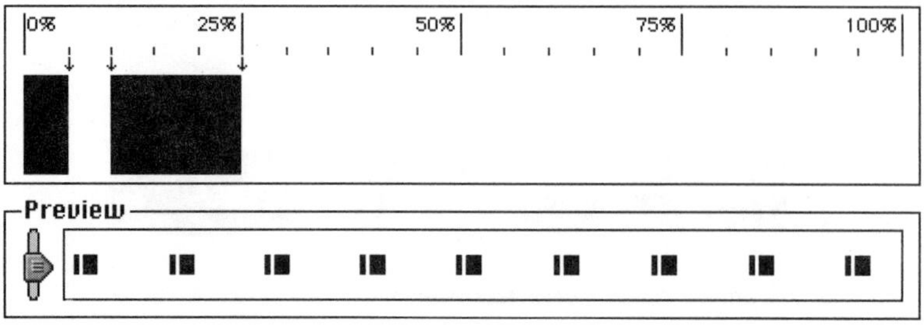

Figure 6.18 The Ruler and Preview area of the Edit Dash dialog box.

The Preview area of the dialog box (Figure 6.18) displays the appearance of the dash. The slider bar previews the dash as it will appear in various widths. Slide it up to display the dash on a wider line; slide it down to preview the dash on a thinner line.

Remember that establishing the bands on the ruler are just part of the dash design; other settings in the dialog box affect the appearance of the dash, too. These settings are discussed later in this section.

The **Segments** field lets you type in the position on the ruler where you want to establish a break in the line to create a dash. Entering a number here is the equivalent of clicking on the ruler; it displays an arrow which establishes the beginning or end of a band. Enter a percentage value in the **Position** field and click the **Add** button to add a new band.

The **Dash Attributes Area** (Figure 6.19) lets you further define the dash style. These attributes determine how the dash will "behave" when it is applied to lines, text-paths, or box frames.

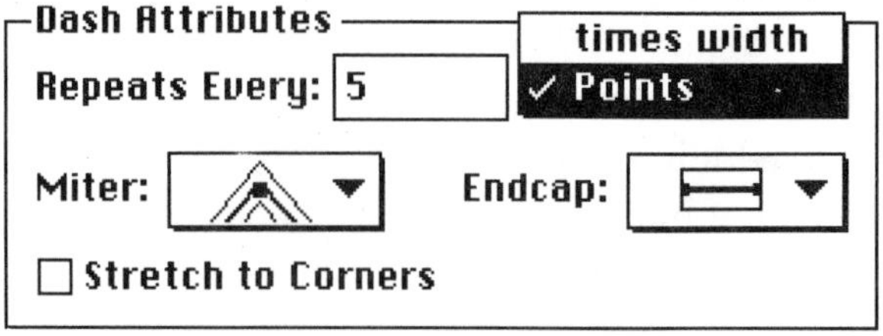

Figure 6.19 The Dash Attributes Area of the Edit Dash dialog box.

The **Repeats Every** field determines how frequently the bands in a style will repeat, and whether the bands in the dash style will scale proportionally when the line width is changed, or retain an absolute width. Entering a value in **Repeats Every <*x*> times width** field will cause the band pattern to repeat, with a distance *x* times the pattern width between each repeat. You can see the effect of this entry on a dash style in Figure 6.20.

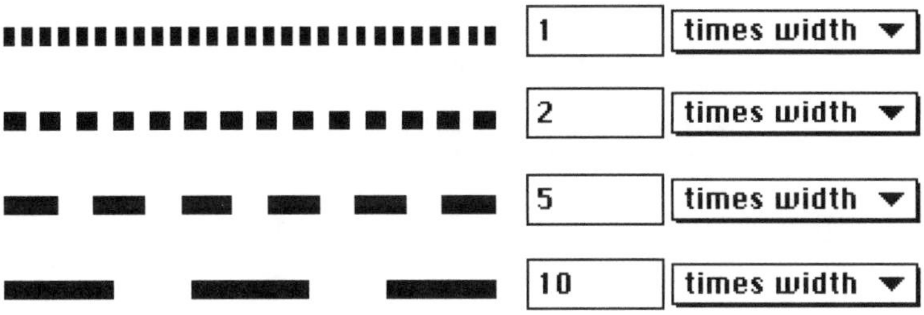

Figure 6.20 *The same dash pattern with different values in the times width field.*

An entry in the **Repeats Every <x> times width** field results in a dash style that will scale proportionally when the width of a line to which the style has been applied changes. In Figure 6.21 you can see how this causes the actual band width to change as the width of the line to which the style has been applied changes.

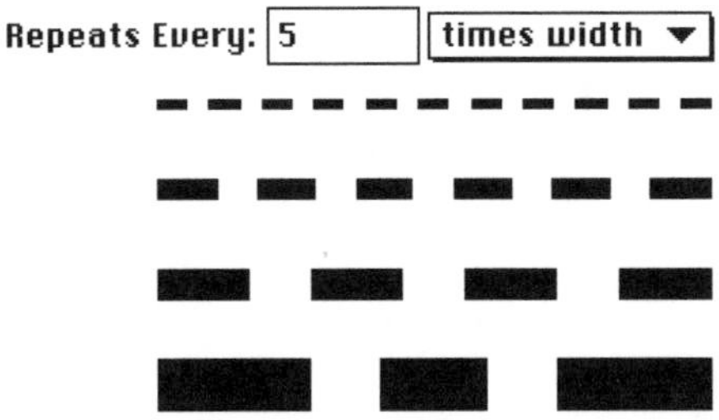

Figure 6.21 *An entry in the* ***Repeats Every <x> times width*** *results in a dash in which the bands scale proportionally when the line width is changed.*

Entering a value in **Repeats Every <*x*> points** field will cause the band pattern to repeat with *x* points between each repeat of the style, as shown in Figure 6.21. The entry in this field also causes the band width to remain constant, regardless of the width of the line to which the dash style has been applied. Figure 6.22 shows the effect of scaling a line with these entries.

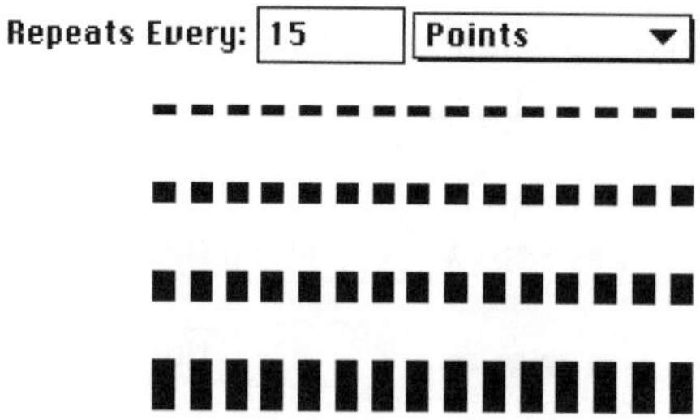

Figure 6.22 *An entry in the* ***Repeats Every <x> points*** *results in a dash in which the bands are a fixed width, regardless of the width of the line.*

The **Miter** submenu lets you determine the appearance of corners of Bézier items to which the dash style has been applied. You can choose from a sharp corner, a round corner, or a beveled corner, as shown in Figure 6.23.

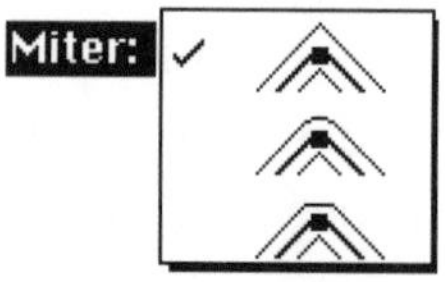

Figure 6.23 *The Miter submenu.*

The **Endcap** submenu determines the appearance of the endpoints of each individual dash band. You can choose from a butt cap, a round cap, or an extended cap, as shown in Figure 6.24.

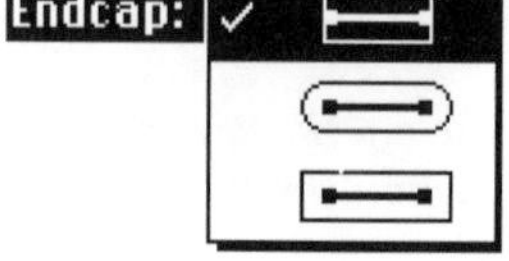

Figure 6.24 *The Endcap submenu.*

If **Stretch to Corners** is checked, this will cause the line dash pattern to stretch evenly along a frame so that the corners are symmetrical. You can see an example of this in Figure 6.25.

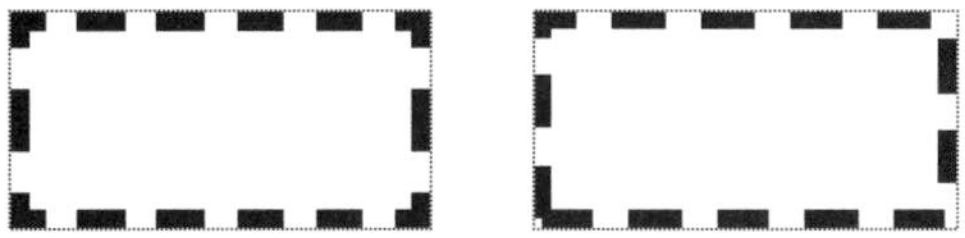

Figure 6.25 *A frame with a dash style applied that has* ***Stretch to Corners*** *checked (left) and unchecked (right).*

The Edit Stripe Dialog Box

The Edit Stripe dialog box (Figure 6.26) is displayed when you choose New Stripe, Edit, or Duplicate from the Dashes & Stripes dialog box. This dialog box allows you to create custom stripes, and to edit existing stripes.

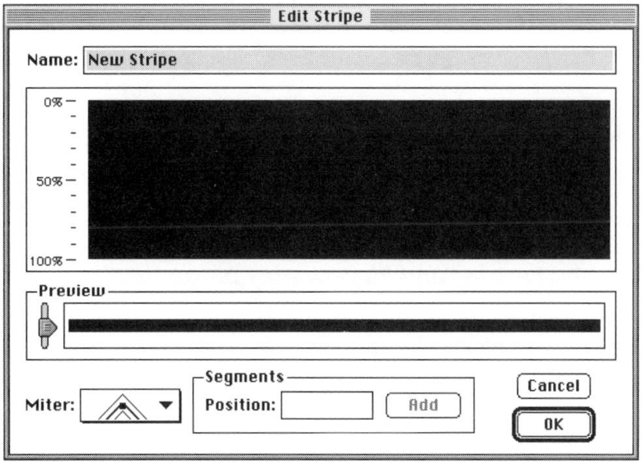

Figure 6.26 *The Edit Stripe dialog box.*

When you create a new stripe style, the Edit Stripe dialog box opens with the **Name** field highlighted and the entry "New Stripe." You can enter a new name, or you can edit the name shown in this field. The name you assign appears in all line style listings for both lines and text-paths, including the **Style ➛ Line**

Style submenu and in the Line tab of the Modify dialog box. Stripe styles are also available for box frames, and are displayed in the Frame tab of the Modify dialog box.

The Ruler area of the Edit Stripe dialog box (Figure 6.27) lets you *visually* apply bands to your stripe style. (You can establish the bands *numerically* using the Segments area of the Stripe dialog box, discussed in the next section.) When you first open the Edit Stripe dialog box to create a new stripe, the ruler area shows a solid band. Click in the area to the left of the solid stripe to display an arrow where you want the first stripe to end. To start a new stripe, click again, and another an arrow is displayed, which starts a new stripe; drag the arrow the width of the new stripe and release, which establishes an arrow that ends the second stripe.

***Figure 6.27** The Ruler and Preview Area of the Edit Stripe dialog box.*

The Preview area of the dialog box displays the appearance of the stripe. The slider bar previews the stripe as it will appear in various widths. Slide it up to display the stripe on a wider line, slide it down to preview the stripe on a thinner line.

The **Miter** submenu lets you determine the appearance of corners of Bézier items to which the stripe style has been applied.

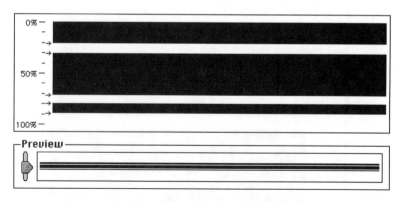

You can choose from a sharp corner, a round corner, or a beveled corner.

The **Segments** field lets you type in the position on the ruler where you want to establish a break in the line to create a stripe. Entering a number here is the equivalent of clicking on the ruler; it displays an arrow which establishes the beginning or end of a stripe. Enter a percentage value in the **Position** field and click the **Add** button to add a new stripe.

Duplicating Dashes & Stripes

If you want to make a new dash or stripe that is a derivative of, or similar to another, click the **Duplicate** button at the bottom of the Dashes & Stripes dialog box. Select the dash or stripe you wish to copy, then click the Duplicate button. The Edit Dash (or Edit Stripe) dialog box will display with all the specifications of the dash or stripe you're copying, but with the name *<dash/stripe name> copy* in the name field. You can then change the name and any of the other specifications in the dialog box to create a new dash or stripe.

Deleting Dashes & Stripes

Select a dash or stripe on the list in the Dashes & Stripes dialog box and click **Delete** to remove from the palette. When you click the **Delete** button, a dialog box (Figure 6.28) is displayed with a pop-up menu listing all the dashes and stripes in the document, which allows you to change the items to which that dash or stripe has been applied to any other dash or stripe in the document. Simply choose the replacement dash or stripe from the pop-up menu. Any items to which the deleted dash or stripe has been applied will change to the new style you've assigned.

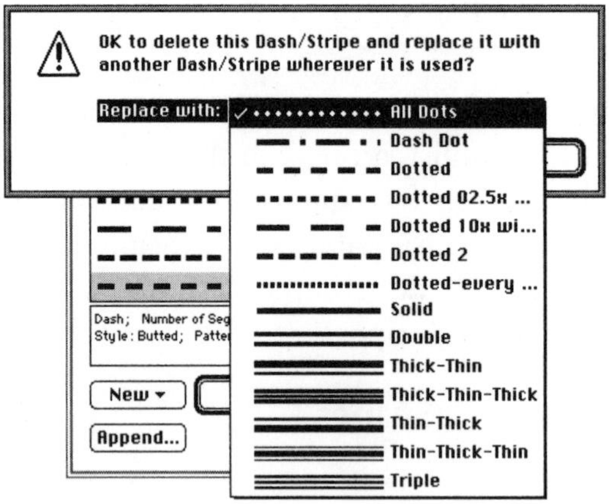

Figure 6.28 *In deleting a dash or stripe you can replace it with another style; all items with the deleted dash or stripe applied will change to the new replacement style.*

Appending Dashes & Stripes

It's pretty easy to copy dashes and stripes created in one QuarkXPress document to another, using the Append command. You can access this command in a couple of ways. The Append Dashes & Stripes dialog box (Figure 6.29) can be accessed by choosing **Edit → Dashes & Stripes** and then clicking the Append button at the bottom of the Dashes & Stripes list. You can also choose the **File → Append** command and click on the **Dashes & Stripes** tab of the Append To dialog box. The new dashes and stripes will be added to the Dashes & Stripes list in the current document, or the default list that all documents will share (if you use the command when no document is open).

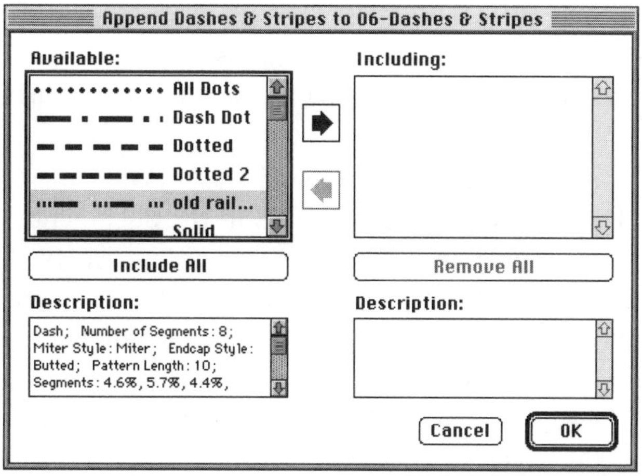

Figure 6.29 *The Append Dashes & Stripes dialog box.*

The next steps discuss the various options available as you use the command:

1. Access the Append Dashes & Stripes dialog by either method:
   - Choose **Edit ➛ Dashes & Stripes**, then click on the Append button in the Edit Dashes & Stripes dialog box, or
   - Choose **File ➛ Append**, then click on the **Dashes & Stripes** tab.
2. QuarkXPress displays a dialog box through which you can select the document or template containing the dashes and stripes you want to append to the current document; you can change drives or folders as you would in other dialog boxes. Choose a document by double-clicking on its name.

3. Once you've selected a document, the Append **Dashes & Stripes** dialog box (Figure 6.29) is displayed—or, if you used the **File ➤ Append** command, click on the Dashes & Stripes tab of the Append dialog box.
4. On the left side of the Append Dashes & Stripes dialog box, a list of the dashes and stripes in the document *from* which you are appending dashes and stripes is displayed. You have several options for choosing the dashes and stripes in the list you wish to Append to your current document:
   - Click on one **dash** or **stripe** name in the Available list to view the specifications in the description area. If this is the style you want to append, click the **right-pointing arrow** to copy it to the Including list.
   - Click the **Include All** button to automatically append all of the dashes and stripes.
   - If you want to include most, but not all, of the dashes and stripes, click **Include All** and then select a name you do not want to include from the list on the right. Click the **left-pointing arrow** to remove it from the Including list.

TIP

You can select all the Available Dashes & Stripes by clicking the **Include All** button. You can select a group of dashes and stripes in the list by holding down the **Shift** key as you click. To select non-contiguous color names, hold down the **⌘/CTRL** key as you click.

5. Once the list of dashes and stripes you wish to include is complete (Figure 6.30), click **OK** to close the dialog box and append the list of dashes and stripes.

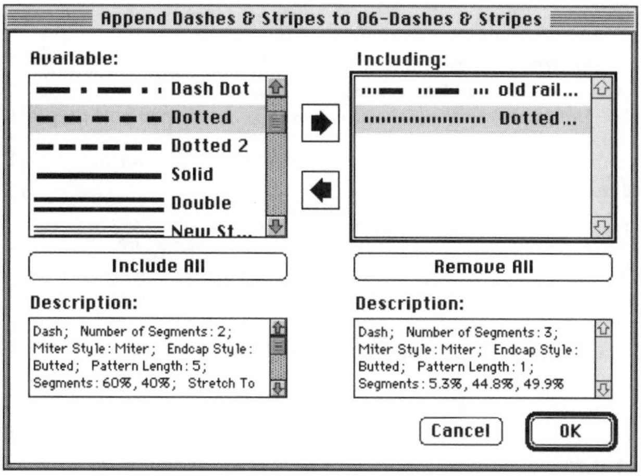

Figure 6.30 *You can pick and choose which dashes and stripes you wish to Append from a file, without having to Append them all.*

Resolving Append Conflicts

If there are dashes and stripes in the file from which you're appending that have the same name, but different specifications from, the dashes and stripes in the existing document's palette, the **Append Conflict** dialog box will display (Figure 6.31). This dialog box displays the name of the conflicting dash or stripe style, along with the definition of the style in the *Existing* document (the current document you're appending dashes and stripes *to*) and the definition of the style in the *New* document (the document *from* which you're appending dashes and stripes). It's important to understand which document *Existing* and *New* refers to when you use this dialog box.

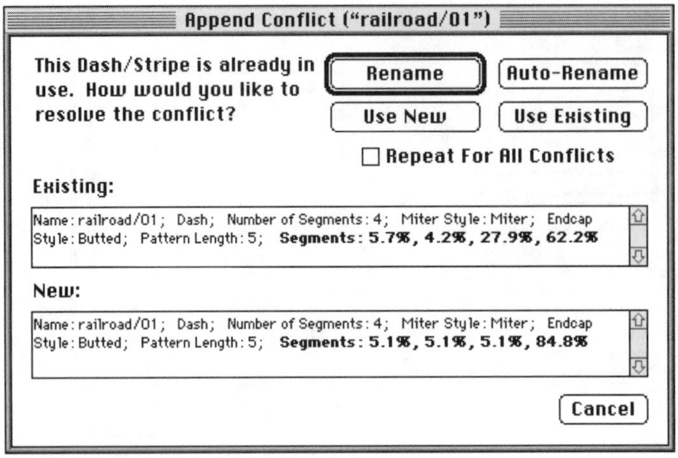

Figure 6.31 *The Append Conflict dialog box.*

There are four ways to resolve the name conflict:

- **Rename** allows you to give an entirely different name to the dash or stripe style in the New document, by displaying the Rename dialog box (Figure 6.32). You can now modify the name. Click **OK**, and the new dash or stripe style will be imported with the name entered.

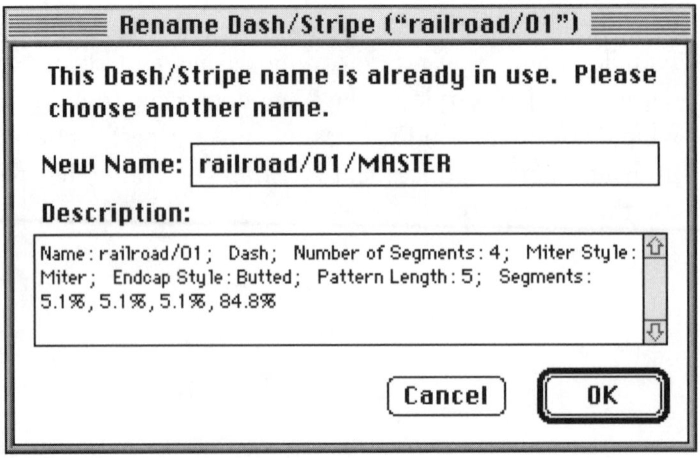

Figure 6.32 *The Rename dialog box.*

- **Auto-Rename** causes the conflicting dash or stripe to be added to the Existing document palette, with the New name preceded by an asterisk (Figure 6.33). The asterisk causes all dashes and stripes renamed to display at the top of the list.

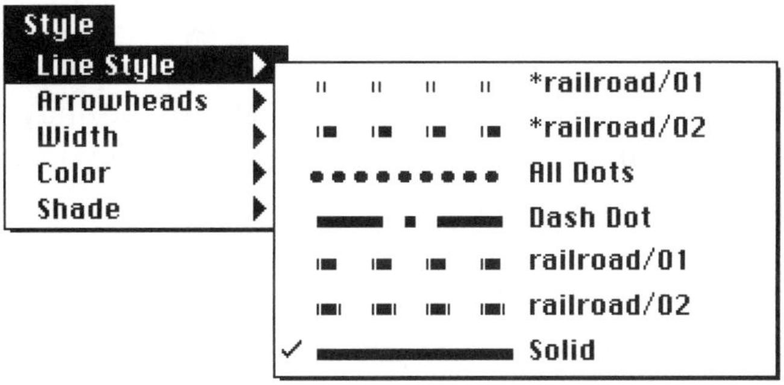

Figure 6.33 *Auto-Rename imports the new dashes and/or stripes and precedes the name with an asterisk, causing the name to appear at the top of the Dashes & Stripes List.*

- Click **Use New** to replace the existing document's dashes and stripes definitions with the new, appended specifications. If you select this option, items to which this dash or stripe style has been applied in the existing document will change to reflect the new definition.
- Click **Use Existing** to keep the specification as defined in the target document. Items to which the dash or stripe style has been applied will remain unchanged.

Regardless of which method you select to resolve conflicts, QuarkXPress will resolve all name conflicts the same way if you turn **Repeat for All Conflicts** on by clicking the checkbox.

Manipulating Lines and Applying Line Styles

In Chapter 2, "Creating One Page," we discussed the basics of drawing a line. To draw a straight line, select the Orthogonal Line tool (+) to draw horizontal and vertical lines, or the diagonal Line tool (\) to draw lines at any angle. (The Orthogonal Line tool is simply an alternative to the Line tool, since you can constrain any line drawn with the diagonal Line tool to 0°, 45°, or 90° angles by holding down the **Shift** key as you draw.) Drawing Bézier lines is similar to drawing Bézier boxes, and is discussed in the previous section in this chapter, "Working with Bézier Shapes."

Once a line is drawn, it can be moved, resized, rotated, and have any custom line style applied. Like other items, these controls can be found on the Style menu and in the Modify dialog box (**Item → Modify**). Many of these controls are also available on the Measurements palette.

Moving and Resizing Lines

The location of box items is always measured from the upper left-hand corner of the box, and its size is a function of the overall width and height. Lines drawn with the Line or Orthogonal Line tool, on the other hand, can be located or measured from either end of the line, from both ends, or from the middle of the line. When you are manipulating the location or length of a line numerically, whether using the Measurements palette or the Line tab of the Modify dialog box, be sure the correct line mode is selected. Figure 6.34 shows the Measurement palette display for a line with each of the line modes selected; the same coordinates are reflected in the Line tab of the Modify dialog box.

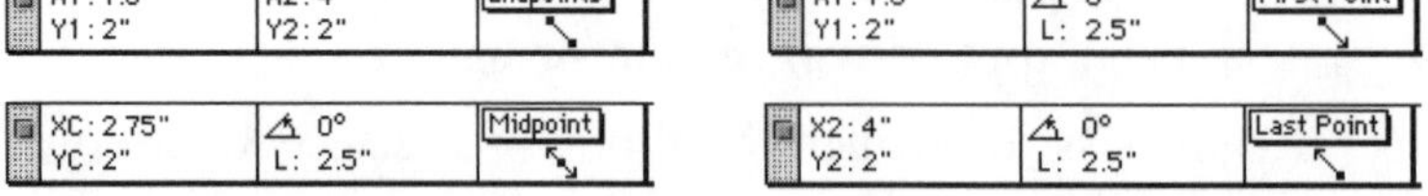

Figure 6.34 *Coordinates displayed in the Measurements palette and the Line tab of the Modify dialog box depend on which mode is selected: Endpoints, First Point, Midpoint, Last Point.*

Bézier lines are not measured from points on either end of the line, since they can contain many points, but are rather measured with coordinates that reflect the bounding box (the coordinates of the line when the **Item → Edit → Shape** command is unchecked), similar to the way box coordinates are displayed. Figure 6.35 shows the

Measurements palette when a Bézier line is selected. These are the same coordinates shown in the Line tab of the Modify dialog box.

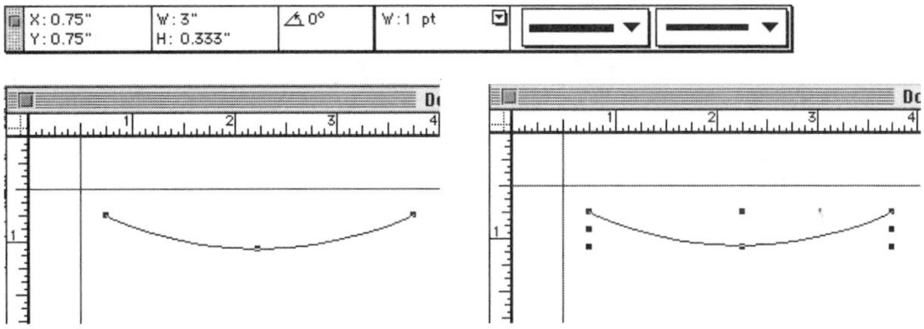

Figure 6.35 *Coordinates displayed in the Measurements palette and the Line tab of the Modify dialog box when a Bézier line is selected; the line displayed with* ***Item*** *➛* ***Edit*** *➛* ***Shape*** *checked (top) and unchecked (bottom).*

Lines can, of course, be moved or resized using the mouse. To move a line, like any other item, be sure the Item tool (✥) is selected (or use the ⌘/CTRL key to temporarily change the cursor to the Item tool), then click on any line segment and move to a new location. The mouse can also be used to resize a line, by simply clicking and dragging one of the endpoints.

TIP

When resizing a straight line, be sure to hold down the **Shift** key to constrain the line so that it remains straight. Otherwise, "kinks" in the line may not be apparent onscreen, but will always show up when printed.

Applying Line Styles

The Style characteristics that can be applied to lines include custom dash or stripe styles, arrowheads, width, color, and shade. Custom dash or stripe styles, arrowheads, and width can be applied using either the Style menu, the Line tab of the Modify dialog box, or the Measurements palette. Color and shade can be applied using either the Style menu or the Line tab of the Modify dialog box. Figure 6.35 shows the Line tab of the Modify dialog box, with the same line selected as shown in the previous figure.

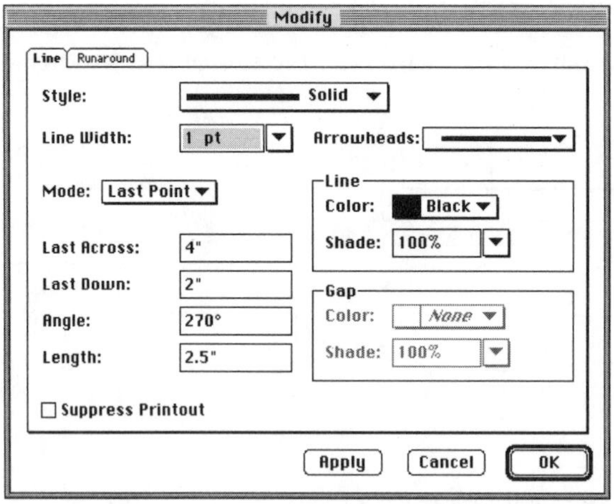

Figure 6.36 *The Line tab of the Modify dialog box.*

The same setting are available for text-paths, when a text-path has been selected with the Item tool (✥) vs. the Content tool (☞). When a text-path is selected with the Content tool, the text becomes editable; when selected with the Item tool, line style characteristics, including custom dash or stripe styles, arrowheads, width, color, and shade are displayed.

Importing Graphics from Other Sources

You can easily import graphics created in other programs into your QuarkXPress document. Once a graphic is imported, you can scale it to any size, rotate or skew it to any angle, flip it on its axis to create a mirror image, and (in some cases) manipulate its color and contrast.

The types of graphic formats that can be imported into QuarkXPress include EPS, DCS, JPEG, OS/2 bitmap, Paint, PCX, Photo CD, PICT, Scitex CT, TIFF, and Windows bitmap (BMP/PCX). To import JPEG, PhotoCD, or PCX pictures you must have the appropriate XTensions software installed (through the **Utilities ➛ XTensions Manager** command). You can also import Windows Metafile (WMF) format graphics, but these are automatically converted to PICT format in QuarkXPress. This wide variety of supported formats means that you can import graphics from almost any graphics program that runs under the Macintosh OS or Windows systems. There are two basic types of graphic formats: bitmap and object oriented. *Bitmap graphics* are composed of grayscale or color pixels that make up an image, and *object-oriented* graphics contain a mathematical description of the image. Both are described generally in the next sections.

TIP: Regardless of the file format of the pictures you import into your QuarkXPress document, it's important to remember that QuarkXPress never imports the picture file itself, but only a screen preview. In order to print correctly, QuarkXPress must be able to locate the original picture file. For that reason, it's a good idea to group picture files into the same folder with your QuarkXPress document when possible, and use the **Collect for Output** command when sending your files to a service bureau.

Bitmap Graphics

Bitmap graphics are composed of a pattern of dots, or *pixels*, rather than separate *objects*—though your eye might *see* boxes and circles, the program sees only dots. This type of graphic (Figure 6.37) comes from paint-type programs, such as PC Paintbrush, Windows Paint, ClarisWorks, MacPaint, Fractal Design Painter, and Photoshop. Scanned images are also bitmap images, and they can usually be saved in MacPaint or BMP format, but they can also be stored at higher resolutions than allowed by most paint-type programs, namely as TIFF files, discussed later in this section.

Bitmap text
is for the birds

Figure 6.37 *Images saved in a bitmap format; avoid creating text in this format.*

A Bit of Information

A 500K 1-bit graphic becomes a 4 MB graphic when converted to grayscale! Why? Bitmap graphics are characterized by how many bits per pixel they store.

A 1-bit (per pixel) graphic is also called *black and white*. A pixel (dot) is either black or white (empty). A 1-bit bitmap graphic is transparent in QuarkXPress—you can see through the "white" areas to whatever is below them. You can work this to your advantage, by saving or converting imported bitmaps to 1-bit black-and-white images if you want the transparent effect, or you can convert the images to grayscale and eliminate the transparency.

A 4-bit (per pixel) bitmap can produce up to 16 shades of gray—each bit can be either on or off, so the number of possibilities is 2 x 2 x 2 x 2. This is a simple formula to a statistician, but you can list the possibilities yourself: 0000, 0001, 0010, 0011, 0100, 0101, 0110, 0111, 1000, 1001, 1010, 1011, 1100, 1101, 1110, 1111. There are 16 ways of storing 4 on-off bits!

An 8-bit (per pixel) bitmap can produce up to 256 shades of gray (2 x 2 x 2 x 2 x 2 x 2 x 2 x 2). Color images scan best at 24 bits per pixel, yielding more than 5 million color possibilities. You can try listing the possibilities yourself, starting with 00000000.

These formulas might help you see why some bitmap graphics take up so much more space than others that might print at the same size. If there are 72 pixels per inch (an average monitor's resolution), a one-inch square 1-bit (per pixel) bitmap image will require only 5K of storage (72 x 72 = 5,184), but the same image will require 20K if saved or scanned with 16 shades of gray, or 40K with 256 shades of gray, or 120K in 24-bit color.

Because bitmap images consist of dots rather than whole objects, you cannot easily break bitmap images into separate elements like boxes, circles, and lines. When you draw a circle on top of a square, for example, intersecting dots that compose the circle actually replace the dots that composed the square—unless you work in layers, as allowed by some programs like Adobe Photoshop.

Bitmap images are not smooth like vector graphics when printed. Bitmap graphics, therefore, are generally considered inferior to vector graphics for most line art and any text. Bitmap images, however, are superior for scanned images and for fine art images that call for air-brush effects.

TIP

Use object-oriented graphics rather than bitmap graphics for line art whenever possible. Bitmap graphics have a jagged appearance and take much longer to print. When bitmap graphics are required, do not include text in the file in the paint program. Place the graphic portion in QuarkXPress and use QuarkXPress's Text tools to add captions and labels.

Scanning Images

Scanning is a good method for capturing photographic or halftone images for placement in a QuarkXPress document. You may have scanning done by a service bureau, or use a Kodak PhotoCD, or scan images yourself. There are many different types of scanners on the market, ranging in price from thousands of dollars to just a few hundred dollars for a home scanner. Scanning applications store images in a variety of formats, including bitmap formats, EPS format, or TIFF (tag image file format).

Regardless of how you acquire scanned images, you can edit them using any program that enables you to edit image files—such as Adobe Photoshop—before inserting the files into QuarkXPress. You also can use programs like Adobe Photoshop for adjusting gray and color values in TIFFs and creating special effects.

Choosing Scanning Settings

The number of resolutions and gray levels you have to choose from will be limited by the scanning device and printer you are using, but you can use two formulas to determine roughly what to look for, then choose the option that equals your target or higher.

The optimum number of *gray levels* needed can be determined by the formula:

$$(\textit{Printer resolution}\ \text{(dpi)}/\textit{Final Screen Frequency}\ \text{(lpi)})^2$$

Resolution on a scanner refers to the number of data "samples" taken per inch (spi) or pixels per inch (ppi), but these measures are not related to the number of dots per inch (dpi) set for the printer. The optimum *scanning resolution* is determined by the screen frequency you'll use for the final reproduction of your document. A good formula to use is:

$$\textit{Scanning Resolution}\ \text{(spi)} = 2 \times \textit{Final Screen Frequency}\ \text{(lpi)}$$

The image may seem rough on low-resolution screens but should look better when printed. Line screens for a 300 dpi desktop printer are typically set at 53-60 lpi; line screens for high resolution image setters are usually between 90 and 150 lpi. This means that you should scan at about 100 spi or ppi (2 x 50) if your final printer will be at 300 dpi resolution, or at 300 spi (2 x 150) if your final masters will be imageset.

It's a good idea to test this yourself by saving a sample scan at various resolutions and printing it on the final printer before doing all the scans for a heavily illustrated publication.

TIFF Files

Tag Image File Format (TIFF) is a bitmap file format designed for use with scanners and printing programs. It is used to store information about continuous-tone images, such as those shown in Figure 6.38. When these images are printed on a high-resolution imagesetter, most of the levels of gray found in the original image will appear on the page printed through QuarkXPress. When printed on a relatively low-resolution printer, such as a LaserWriter, some of the levels of gray stored in the TIFF format will be compressed out (not printed). True grayscale viewing is available on most computer models with color or grayscale monitors.

Figure 6.38 *TIFF is one of the most common file formats for high resolution images.*

Because TIFF images are usually stored at 300 dpi resolution or higher, image files can be quite large. Like all picture file formats, TIFF images are not stored in the document; rather, QuarkXPress stores and displays the images in a low-resolution format. The TIFF file is linked to the document; when you print the document, QuarkXPress looks for the original scan file on the disk in order to print at high resolution.

TIP

Normally, imported TIFF images are displayed at 72 dpi on screen. You can reduce the on-screen display resolution to 36 dpi by holding the **Shift** key as you click on the **Open** button in the Get Picture dialog box. To convert a color TIFF to a grayscale TIFF, hold down the **⌘/CTRL** key as you click the **Open** button in the Get Picture dialog box. If importing a grayscale TIFF, holding down the **⌘/CTRL** key converts the picture to line art.

You can increase the resolution at which TIFF pictures are imported by changing the default setting of 8-bit display to 16- or 32-bit display in the Application tab of the Preferences dialog box (**Edit ➛ Preferences ➛ Application**).

Object-Oriented Graphics

Object-oriented graphics are usually stored as PICT or Encapsulated PostScript (EPS) formats and are composed of separate objects, such as boxes, lines, and ellipses. QuarkXPress's built-in graphics are object-oriented graphics, and you can import object-oriented graphics from other programs.

Object-oriented graphics are sometimes called *vector graphics* because the lines and patterns that you see are actually stored as mathematical formulas for the vectors composing the image. A *vector* is a line defined by a starting point, a directional angle, and a length.

You can create object-oriented graphics in QuarkXPress or with drafting, draw, and spreadsheet programs. Programs that produce object-oriented graphics that can be placed in QuarkXPress include Adobe Illustrator, Macromedia FreeHand, CorelDRAW, ClarisDraw, or any application that creates PICT or Encapsulated PostScript (EPS) formats. (Graphics that are imported in Windows Metafile, WMF format, are automatically transformed into PICT format in QuarkXPress.) You easily can edit object-oriented graphics because you can change or move individual elements in the application that created them, but you cannot edit or move individual elements in imported graphics in QuarkXPress.

PICT Graphics

PICT files (from picture) are a standard Macintosh format for object-oriented graphics. PICT files use QuickDraw routines for representing images. PICT graphics are called object-oriented graphics because the lines and patterns that you see are actually stored as mathematical formulas of the objects that compose the image. Some scanning software will allow you to save files in the PICT format, which creates a bitmap associated with the data. The PICT format is supported by all graphics programs that run on Macintosh computers. The original PICT format supported 8 colors but more recent versions of PICT, including PICT2, support 32-bit color (more than 16 million colors).

EPS Graphics

Encapsulated PostScript files are PostScript files that have a screen preview. The PostScript language, which creates mathematical representations of images, has become the de facto standard in publishing. EPS files can be created using some drawing programs, such as Adobe Illustrator, Macromedia FreeHand, or CorelDRAW. Many of these programs save files in a default format that cannot be read by QuarkXPress, and must be saved in an EPS format to be read by QuarkXPress. Figure 6.39 shows a graphic created in Adobe Illustrator and Illustrator 7.0's Save As dialog box, which includes the option to save a file in EPS format.

EPS files can also be created using QuarkXPress by selecting the **File ➛ Save Page as EPS** command, discussed at the end of this chapter.

Figure 6.39 *The* ***Save As*** *dialog box from Adobe Illustrator—graphics must be saved as Encapsulated PostScript (EPS).*

Importing Graphics

The basic steps for importing a picture file into a QuarkXPress document are quite simple. These steps are detailed below:

1. Select one of QuarkXPress's Picture box creation tools (⊠ ⊠ ⊗ ⊠ ⊗ ⊠ ⊗) to create a new picture box, or select the picture box into which you want to import the graphic. You'll know the picture box is active by the handles that appear, as shown in Figure 6.40.

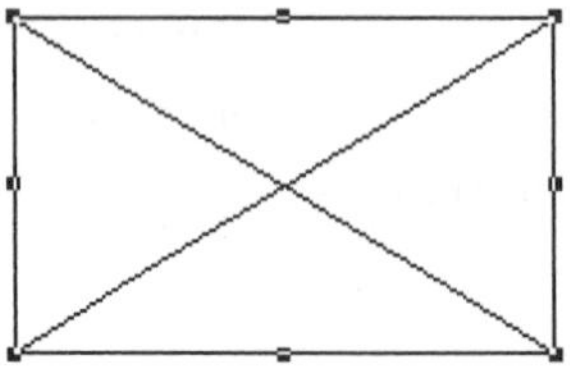

Figure 6.40 *Active picture box.*

2. Select **File ➛ Get Picture** to display the Get Picture dialog box (Figure 6.41).

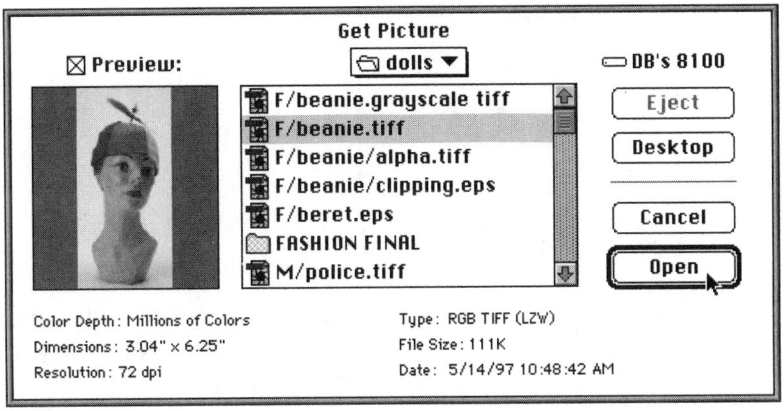

***Figure 6.41** The Get Picture dialog box. Click once on a file name to preview the color depth, size (dimensions), bitmap resolution, type, file size, date, and thumbnail of the graphic you are importing.*

3. Next, find the name of the picture file you want to import in the dialog box. Use the scroll bars to scroll through the list names, and click the drive identification to view the graphics files on other disks if you don't see the file you want.
4. Once you have found the name of the file you want to import, click once to view the file format and size, or double-click to import the graphic.
   - When you click once on a graphics file name, the dialog box displays the color depth, size (dimensions), bitmap resolution, type, file size, date modified, if that information is available.
   - If you check the **Picture Preview** option in the dialog box, a thumbnail preview of the picture will be displayed in the dialog box when you click once on the file name. Double-click a file name to import it into the active picture box (Figure 6.42).

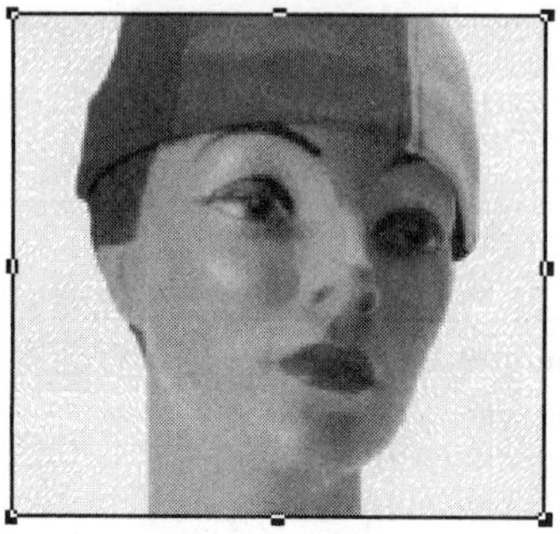

Figure 6.42 *An imported graphic.*

The entire, unscaled picture that you import is placed in the active picture box, replacing any previous contents of the box. You may need to scale the picture to make it fit the box, as described later in this section.

The upper left corner of the graphic file aligns to the upper left corner of the picture box when the graphic is first imported. If the large *X* that normally appears in a blank picture box disappears but the box still appears blank after you import a picture, then a blank part of the picture is showing. To re-position the graphic within the box, or scale the picture to fit the box, you can use any of the techniques described in the next section, "Manipulating Imported Graphics."

The entire graphics file will be imported in QuarkXPress as a single graphic object, regardless of how large the graphic or how many different objects were in the original source file. If the graphic includes text, QuarkXPress retains the font settings made in the graphics program. You cannot change individual parts of the imported graphic, such as the line styles or the colors of individual elements.

Pasting Graphics from the Clipboard

Besides using QuarkXPress's graphics tools to create an object or using the **Place** command to import graphics, you can cut, copy, and paste objects through the Clipboard. Note that pasting a graphic into a picture box does not work with all graphics applications and files types.

TIP: Using the Clipboard is typically not the preferred method for placing high-resolution images in your QuarkXPress document, since you are usually pasting a low-resolution screen representation only, and QuarkXPress has no way to link to the high resolution file at printing time.

To use the Clipboard to import a graphic:

1. Select one or more objects on-screen in the graphics application that created them.
2. Choose **Edit** ➤ **Cut** or **Edit** ➤ **Copy** to put the selected graphic into the Clipboard.
3. Create or select a picture box in QuarkXPress.
4. Choose **Edit** ➤ **Paste** to import the graphic from the Clipboard into the selected picture box.

Manipulating Imported Graphics

Chapter 2, "Creating One Page," covers the commands and tools you can use to change the shape, size, and position of a picture box. The next sections describe commands and features that can be used to change the position and appearance of imported graphics *within* the picture box.

Moving a Picture within a Box

There are several ways to adjust the position of an imported graphic relative to the edges of the picture box that contains it:

- The simplest way to move an imported picture within a picture box (without moving the box itself) is to first select the Content Tool ( ). When you position the pointer over an imported picture, the pointer changes to a hand ( ). Hold down the mouse button and drag the hand to move the picture within the box.

- You can select **Item → Modify** and click on the **Picture** tab to specify the distance from the edge of the box by which the picture will be Offset Across and Offset Down from the left and top edges of the box.
- You can move a picture by entering values in the ⇕ and ⇔ fields of the Measurements palette. These fields appear in the palette only when the Content Tool (☞) is active. Click on the arrows in the Measurements palette, or select the numeric values and type new ones. Enter negative values to offset the picture to the left or upward from the top left corner of the box. See Figure 6.43.

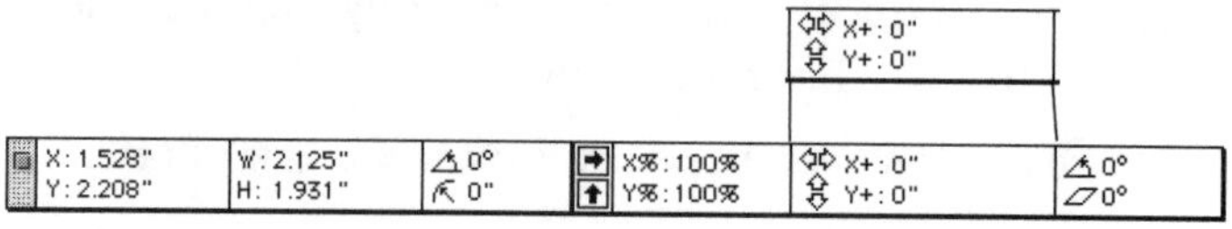

***Figure 6.43** The fields in the Measurements palette that control the position of a picture within its box.*

- You can move a picture in 1-point increments by pressing the arrow keys when the Content Tool is selected. Holding the **Option/ALT** key at the same time nudges the picture in 0.1-point increments.
- Pressing **⌘-Shift-M/CTRL-SHIFT-M** centers a picture in a box.

Scaling Imported Graphics

You can move, scale, or rotate a box, without affecting the content of the box. But you can also move, scale, or rotate the *content* of a box—an imported picture—independently of the box that contains it. Most of these procedures can be accomplished using the Content tool or keyboard commands described under the following section headings, but they can also be accomplished by making entries in the Measurements palette or through the Picture tab of the Modify dialog box (**Item** ➤ **Modify**), shown in Figure 6.44.

If you simply drag a handle of a picture box to scale it, you scale the box only and not the picture inside it. This is how you can "crop" or trim away visible parts of the image—although it's a good idea to do the cropping in the originating graphics application before importing the graphic to QuarkXPress, to minimize file size and printing time.

- **Shift** click and drag a handle to constrain boxes to square shapes (for text or rectangular graphics boxes) or circles (for oval graphics boxes).
- **Option-Shift/ALT-SHIFT** click and drag a handle to force the box to maintain its same aspect ratio.

You can also scale the picture box and the picture inside it using the keyboard/mouse combinations shown in Table 6.2. The first option, which scales the picture and its box while maintaining the aspect ratio, is the one we use most often.

Table 6.2 *Keyboard shortcuts for resizing a picture box and the picture within it.*

In order to:	Command
Force the box to maintain the same aspect ratio for the box, and scale the picture	**⌘-Option-Shift/CTRL-ALT-SHIFT** click and drag a handle
Constrain boxes to square shapes or circles, and scale the picture	**⌘-Shift/ CTRL-SHIFT** click and drag a handle
Resize the box and the picture within it without maintaining proportions	**⌘/CTRL** click and drag a handle

Or, use any one of these four very handy keyboard commands to scale the picture without scaling the box, as shown in Table 6.3.

Table 6.3 *Keyboard shortcuts for resizing a picture without changing the size of the picture box.*

In order to:	Command
Scale the picture to fit the box	**⌘-Shift-F/Ctrl-Shift-F**
Scale the picture to fit the box while maintaining the picture's aspect ratio	**⌘-Option-Shift-F/Ctrl-Alt-Shift -F**
Scale the picture down 5%	**⌘-Option-Shift-</Ctrl-Alt-Shift-<**
Scale the picture up by 5%	**⌘-Option-Shift->/ Ctrl-Alt-Shift ->**

You can also select the Picture tab of the Modify dialog box (**Item ➛ Modify**), shown in Figure 6.44, which allows you to scale a picture numerically by entering percentage values in the **Scale Across** and **Scale Down** fields. Or you can enter percentage values in the **X percent** and **Y percent** fields of the Measurements palette. If you have previously scaled the picture, the amount by which the picture has been scaled will show in these areas. You can enter values from 10% up to 1000%. Unless the values in the two fields are equal, the picture will be distorted.

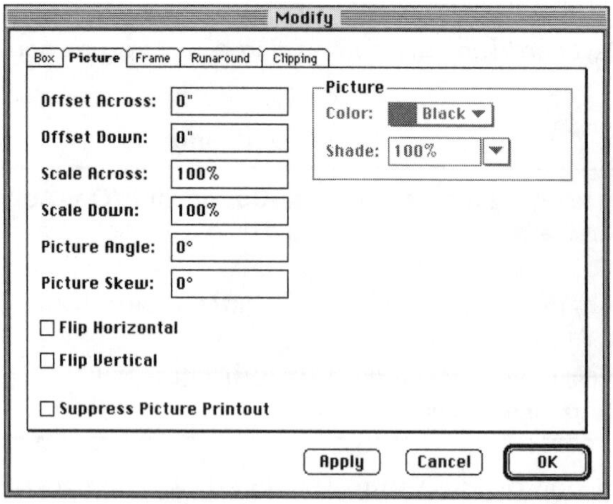

Figure 6.44 *The Picture tab of the Modify dialog box.*

Rotating and Skewing Imported Graphics

You can rotate a picture box using the Rotation tool, but to rotate the picture within the box at a different angle from the picture box itself you must select the **Item ➛ Modify** command or use the Measurements palette. Enter a value, from –360 to 360°, in the **Picture Angle** field in the Picture tab of the Modify dialog box to rotate a picture without rotating the picture box that contains it.

You can also enter an angle value in the second ∡ field of the Measurements palette, as shown in Figure 6.45 (the first ∡ field is used to rotate the picture box). In general, remember that the left side of the Measurements palette controls the item; the right side, the item's content.

In entering angles of rotation in either the Picture Box Specifications dialog box or the Measurements palette, a positive value indicates a counterclockwise rotation, a negative value rotates the picture clockwise. If you have previously rotated the picture, the amount by which the picture has been rotated will show in these areas.

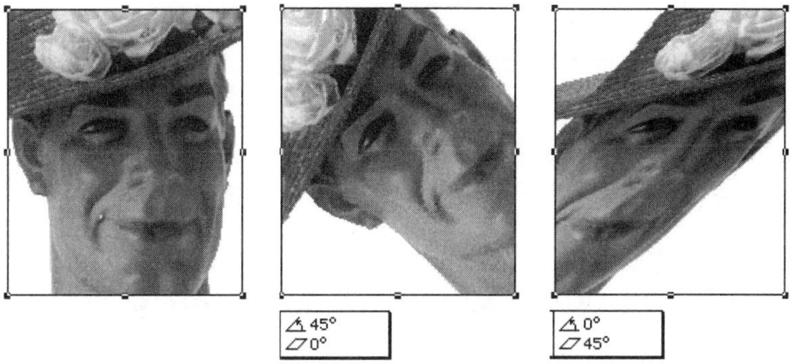

***Figure 6.45** The Picture Angle and Picture Skew fields in the Measurements palette, and their effect on a picture.*

Skewing a picture within a box changes the angle of its vertical axis. You can select **Item ➛ Modify** to display the Picture tab and skew a picture numerically by entering percentage value in the **Picture Skew** field. You can also skew a picture by entering degree values (from 0 to 75) in the ▱ field of the Measurements palette, shown in Figure 6.45.

In entering skew angles, a positive value skews the top of the picture toward the right; a negative value skews the top of the picture toward the left. If you have previously skewed the picture, the amount by which the picture has been skewed will show in this dialog box.

Changing the Horizontal or Vertical Orientation

You can mirror (flip) the contents of a picture or text box on its horizontal or vertical axis. To flip an active picture, choose the **Style ➛ Flip Horizontal** or **Style ➛ Flip Vertical** commands, or click the appropriate icon on the Measurements palette (Figure 6.46). Anchored pictures can also be flipped.

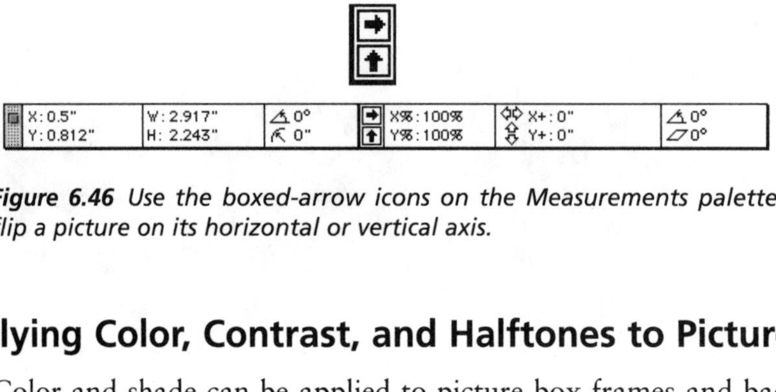

Figure 6.46 *Use the boxed-arrow icons on the Measurements palette to flip a picture on its horizontal or vertical axis.*

Applying Color, Contrast, and Halftones to Pictures

Color and shade can be applied to picture box frames and backgrounds, as described in Chapter 7, "Color Basics." But you can also apply color to certain kinds of imported pictures. For imported bitmap formats, you can also adjust the contrast and halftone settings. The commands listed under the Style menu change depending on what type of picture is active when you view the menu. Table 6.4 lists which variables can be adjusted for each type of imported graphic.

Table 6.4 *Variables that Can Be Adjusted for each Imported File Type*

Imported File Type	Color	Shade	Negative	Contrast	Halftone
EPS/DCS	N	N	N	N	N
JPEG					
Grayscale	Y	Y	Y	Y	Y
Color	Y	Y	Y	Y	N
OS/2 Bitmap					
1-bit	Y	Y	N	N	Y
Color	Y	Y	Y	Y	N
PAINT	Y	Y	N	N	Y
PhotoCD	N	N	Y	Y	N
PICT					
1-bit bitmap	Y	Y	N	N	Y
Grayscale Bitmap	Y	Y	Y	Y	Y
Color bitmap	Y	Y	Y	Y	N
Object-oriented	N	N	N	N	N
Scitex CT					
Grayscale	Y	Y	Y	Y	N
Color	Y	Y	Y	Y	N
TIFF					
1-bit	Y	Y	Y	N	Y
Grayscale	Y	Y	Y	Y	Y
COLOR	Y	Y	Y	Y	N
Windows bitmap (BMP/PCX)					
1-bit	Y	Y	Y	N	Y
Grayscale	Y	Y	Y	Y	Y
Color	Y	Y	Y	Y	N

Applying Color and Shades to Pictures

For formats that allow it (see Table 6.4), you can adjust the color and shading values using three different commands. First select the picture box using either the Item tool or the Content tool, then:

- Choose **Style** ➛ **Color** to select a color from the submenu, and choose **Style** ➛ **Shade** to select a percentage for the selected color.
- Choose **Item** ➛ **Modify**, click the **Picture** tab, then choose a color and shade from the Colors and Shades pop-up menus.
- Choose **View** ➛ **Show Colors** and click the **Picture** icon (⊠) then click on a color to select it. Choose a Shade value from the Shade pop-out list, or select the shade value like text and type a new number.

For more information on creating and applying colors, see Chapter 7, "Color Basics."

Adjusting Contrast Settings

Contrast is a term used to describe the relationship between the light and dark areas of an imported color or grayscale bitmap format (see Table 6.4). High-contrast settings make the light areas lighter and the dark areas darker. Low-contrast settings have the reverse effect, making light areas darker and dark areas lighter. Normal contrast is the picture's original contrast when imported into QuarkXPress (the contrast that was set up in the scanning process or in a photo retouching application). When you adjust the contrast in QuarkXPress (Figure 6.47), it affects the way the picture is displayed and printed through QuarkXPress only—it does not change the original picture file.

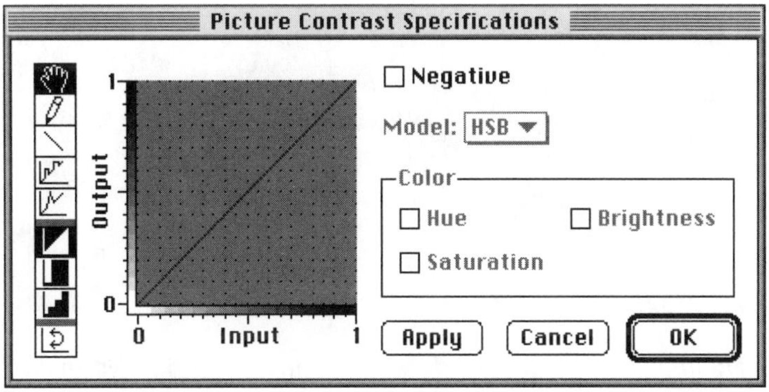

Figure 6.47 *The Picture Contrast Specifications dialog box.*

Choose **Style ➛ Contrast** (**⌘-Shift-C/CTRL-SHIFT-C**) to display the Picture Contrast Specifications dialog box (Figure 6.47). The chart in this dialog box maps the darkness percentages of the input (the original image as imported) to darkness upon output (on the screen and when printed). The best way to see how the chart works is to study how it changes under the predefined contrast settings before you start to set your own custom contrast. The Picture Contrast Specifications dialog box provides additional tools on the left of the box to help you adjust the contrast. See Figure 6.48 for examples.

- Click on the **Normal Contrast** tool (◢) to set the picture back to its original contrast. This is the same as choosing **Style ➛ Normal Contrast.**
- Click on the **High Contrast** tool (▐) to set the picture to high contrast. This setting in effect converts a grayscale image to line art—two shades of gray: solid black and white.
- Click on the **Posterized Contrast** tool (▟) to convert the picture to six levels of gray (including black and white as two of the gray levels).

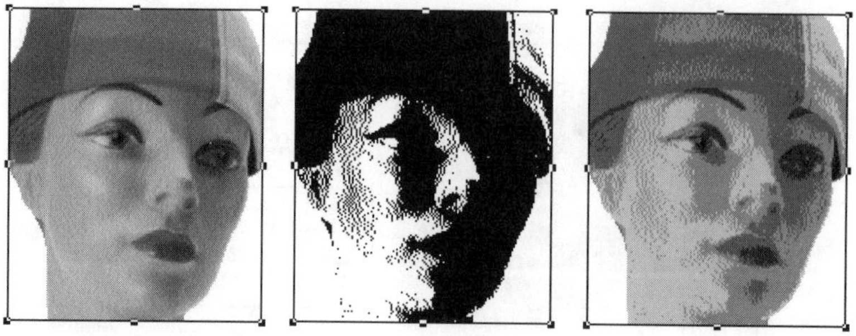

***Figure 6.48** Examples of different contrast settings: Normal contrast (left); High contrast (center) and Posterized (right).*

- Click on the **Hand** tool (✋) and use the hand to drag the entire curve around on the chart. Hold down the **Shift** key to constrain the movement to horizontal or vertical.
- Click on the **Pencil** tool (✎) and click anywhere on the chart to create spikes, or drag any point on the chart to reshape the curve in any path. Hold down the **Shift** key to constrain the new points to 45° angles: 0°, 45°, or 90°.
- Click on the **Line** tool (\) and drag any point on the chart to reshape the curve in straight lines. Hold down the **Shift** key to constrain the lines to 45° angles: 0°, 45°, or 90°.
- Click on the **Posterizer** tool () to create handles *in between* the 10% incremental marks on the curve. Click on the **Spike** tool () to create handles *on* the 10% incremental marks on the curve. You can then move each handle in any direction.
- Click on the **Inversion** tool () to rotate the curve around an imaginary line that is parallel to the X-axis and bisects the curve. This creates a negative of the image by changing the *current curve* settings.
- Check the **Negative** box to create a negative of the image based on the *Normal curve* settings. This selection reverses any changes made to the contrast curves.

Normally, the changes you make in the dialog box will not be reflected on the page display until you click **Apply** or use the keyboard shortcut ⌘-**A/**C**TRL**-**A** (to view the effects and still have a chance to change or cancel them) or **OK** (to apply the changes). If you hold the **Option/**A**LT** key and click **Apply** or use the keyboard shortcut ⌘-**Option-A/**C**TRL**-A**LT**-**A**, you can see the effects of the changes as you make them. But, this might be a slow process if the image is very large. Click ⌘-**Z** /C**TRL**-**Z** while the dialog box is open to reverse the most recent change.

TIP: The contrast setting affects only the way QuarkXPress displays and prints the image, not the way the image is stored or saved. You can change contrast settings or convert to normal contrast at any time. Choose **Normal Contrast** to reset the picture to the original contrast at which it was imported.

Adjusting Contrast for Color Images

When you choose **Style** ➣ **Contrast** with an 8-bit color TIFF image active, the Picture Contrast Specifications dialog box changes to let you adjust contrast for each component of the color image (Figure 6.49). The component list changes depending on which color model you choose: HSB (Hue-Saturation-Brightness), RGB (Red-Green-Blue), CMY (Cyan-Magenta-Yellow), or CMYK (Cyan-Magenta-Yellow-Black).

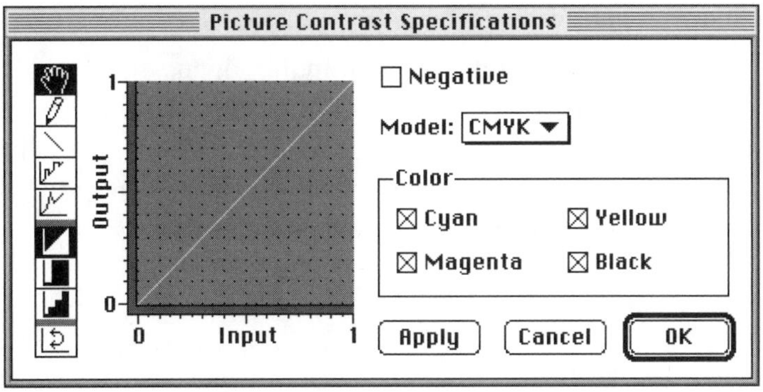

Figure 6.49 *The Picture Contrast Specifications dialog box when a color image is active and the model is CMYK.*

You can select each model and the dialog box will let you adjust the curves for each of the applicable components. You can click more than one color component at a time to adjust several at once. All other tools and buttons in the dialog box operate as described earlier.

TIP

Adjusting color is easy to do in QuarkXPress, but frankly, we recommend making these adjustments in an image-editing program like Adobe Photoshop. Regardless of the program you use, adjusting color *effectively* requires considerable skill and experience—or extensive trial and error.

Adjusting Halftone Screens

In QuarkXPress you can import *line art* that is composed of solid black-and-white areas, or *grayscale* images that are continuous-tone images (like photographs) incorporating shades of gray as well as black and white. In traditional publishing, a photograph that has been prepared for printing is called a *halftone* rather than a grayscale image. With traditional methods, a halftone is created by photographing the artwork through a *screen*. The term "screening" has therefore carried over to the electronic process applied through QuarkXPress. The fineness of a screen is defined in terms of lines per inch (lpi), and is as important as setting resolution when printing a high-resolution continuous-tone image.

The **Style ➛ Halftone** command opens the Picture Halftone Specifications dialog box (Figure 6.50) with three pop-up menus of settings for line frequency (lpi), screen angle, and function (halftone dot shapes) that will define the pattern of dots in halftone when you print grayscale TIFF images.

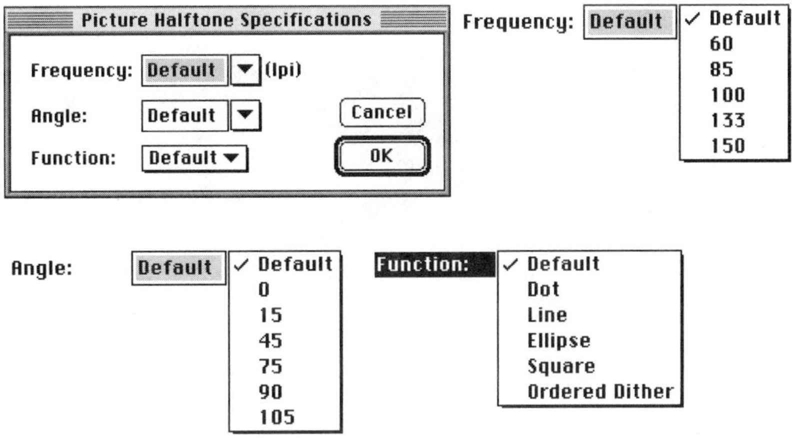

Figure 6.50 *The Picture Halftone Specifications dialog box.*

- **Frequency**—You can select values of 60, 85, 100, 133, or 150 from the pop-up menu. The default frequency is defined in the Halftone Frequency field in the Page Setup dialog box, Output tab. The normal default—60 lpi—is the most common setting for printing halftone pictures in newspapers. A 300 dpi printer cannot accurately reproduce screens finer than 75 lpi. Higher line frequencies will not display accurately on most monitors and will work best when printed on high-resolution printers using glossy paper stocks or film.
- **Screen Angle**—You can choose from the list of the most common settings, in 15° increments from 0 to 105°.
- **Function**—Select from five different halftone screens: Dot, Line, Ellipse, Square (Figure 6.51), or Ordered Dither. The Ordered Dithered screen pattern is designed for printing grayscale images on a low-resolution laser printer, and should not be used when your output will be reproduced using offset lithography.

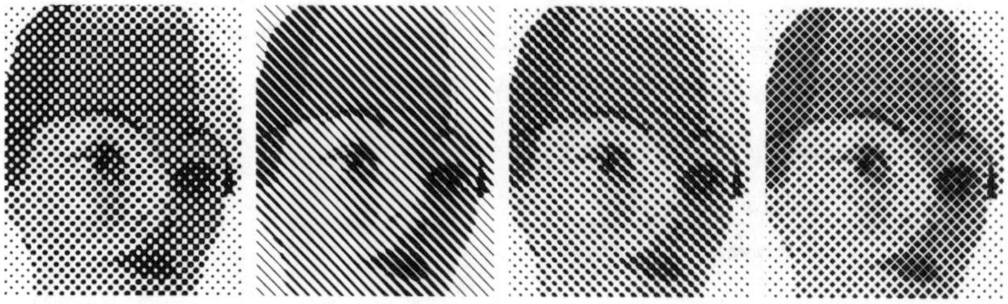

***Figure 6.51** Examples of different halftone screen patterns: dot, line, ellipse, and square, respectively.*

The halftone screen setting affects only the way QuarkXPress prints the picture, not the way the picture file is displayed, stored, or saved. You can change screen settings or convert to normal screen at any time. Choose **Default** for all three values to reset the picture to its original settings, with the line frequency determined by the value entered in the **Frequency** field in the Output tab of the Print dialog box.

Notice that you can specify line frequencies and angles for active imported images only—shaded lines, box frames, and box backgrounds specified in QuarkXPress are always printed using the Frequency field in the Output tab of the Print dialog box. See Chapter 8, "Printing Basics," for more information on setting the overall line screen for your document.

Working with Runaround

The text runaround feature has been expanded in QuarkXPress 4.0 to include several new options, and you have more control than ever over the way text runs behind, around, or within items and pictures. Finally, with QuarkXPress 4.0, you can run text around all sides of an item. The Runaround tab of the Modify dialog box contains several new options, including those for specifying runaround based on embedded clipping paths. And while previous version of QuarkXPress could "see" embedded paths and the outside edge of a picture, you can now edit these runaround paths for the first time. The options available are different depend-

New Color Models

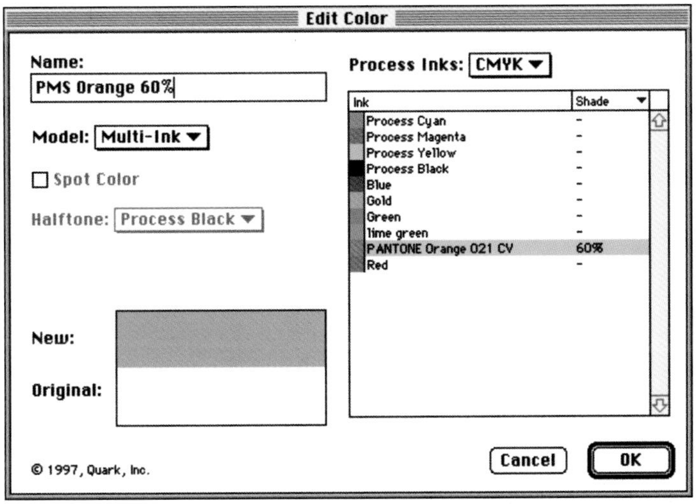

Multi-Ink colors allow you to mix various percentages of the existing spot or process colors in your color palette. This means you can add a color to the palette that is a tint of another color, a feature new to version 4.0. (In previous versions, you could apply a tint, or shade, of a color to any item, but you could not define a tint as a color in the document's color palette.)

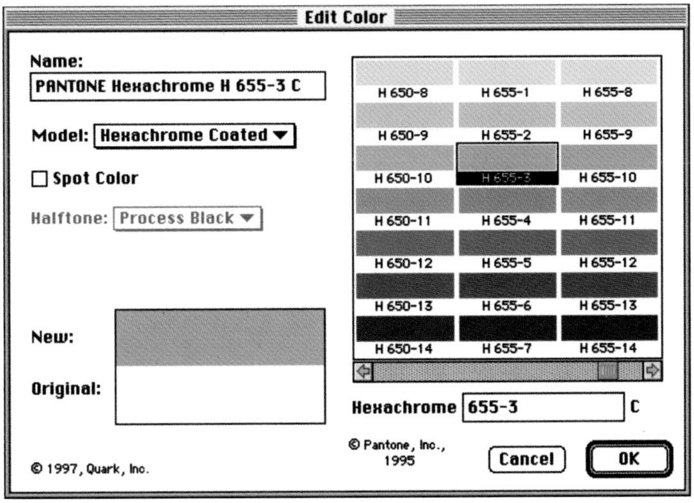

QuarkXPress 4.0 makes Pantone's **Hexachrome** color system available for the first time. This system is used for six color, or High Fidelity printing processes. See Chapter 7, "Color Basics," for more information on color models.

Trapping Items

The figures below show the effect of various trapping settings for two items with a spot color applied to each. For each example, the resulting plates are shown as they will print when separations are specified.

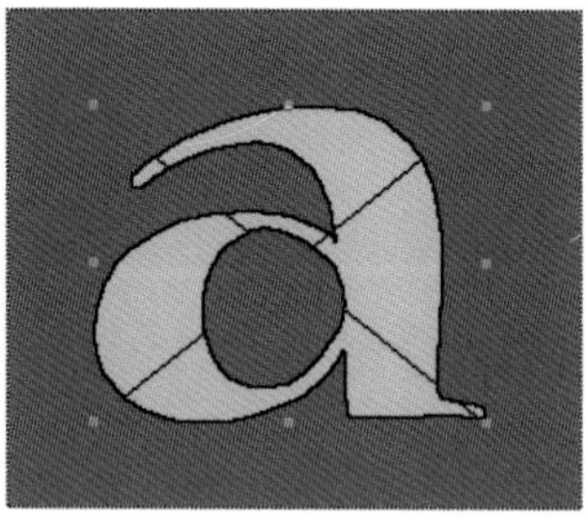

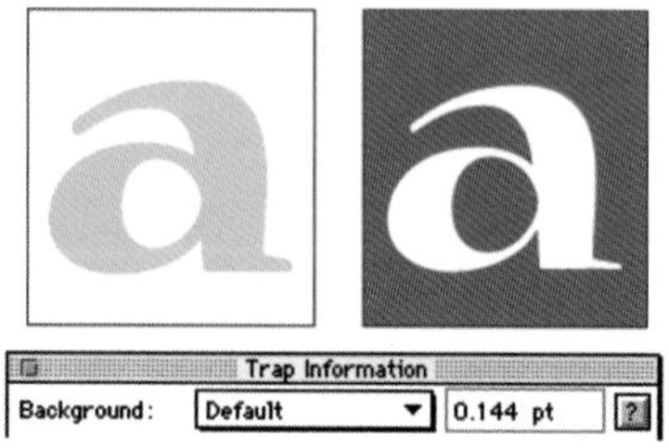

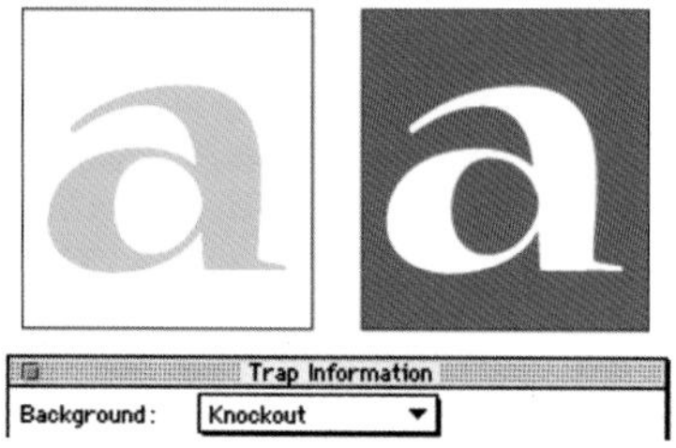

When a lighter color is printed on top of a darker color, the default trapping is usually set to cause the lighter color to "spread," or print slightly larger, so it will overlap the darker color underneath. Alternatively, changing the setting to Knockout causes the lighter color to print at the exact size of the area removed from the plate below, sometimes called a "butt" fit.

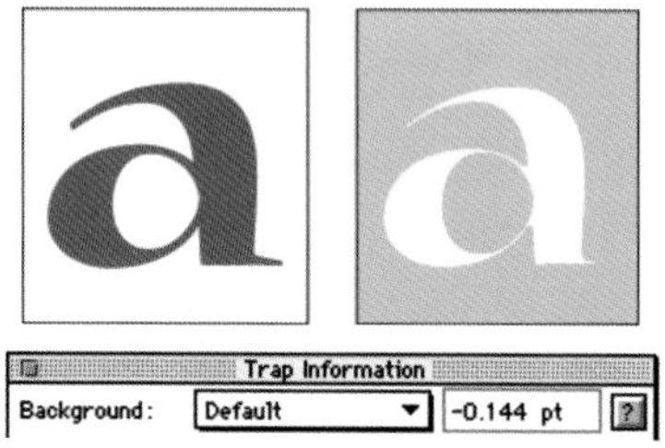

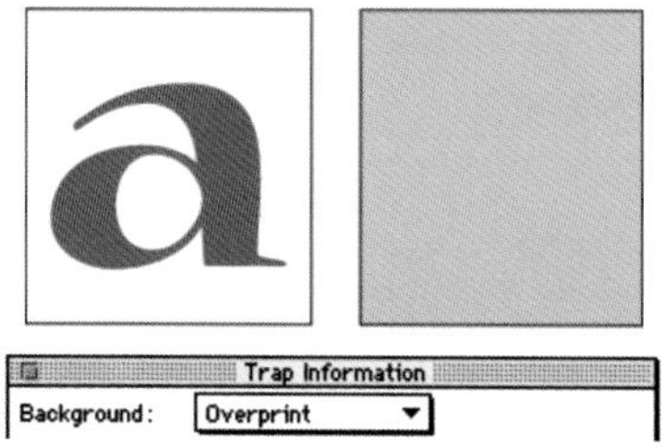

When a darker color is printed on top of a lighter color, the default trapping is usually set to cause the lighter color to "choke," or print slightly inside the area of the top color, so it will print underneath the edge of the darker color. Alternatively, changing the setting to Overprint causes the darker color to print without knocking out any of the color underneath. See Chapter 13, "Printing Color Separations," for more information on trapping.

Clipping Paths

Clipping paths allow you to make part of a picture "transparent." Various settings in the Clipping Path dialog box let you control how the initial path is drawn. After the path is established, you can freely edit the path by manipulating the Bézier points and segments. See Chapter 6, "Graphics," for more information on clipping paths.

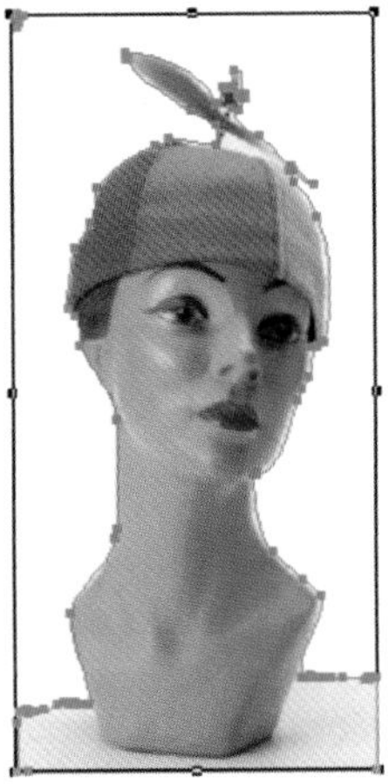

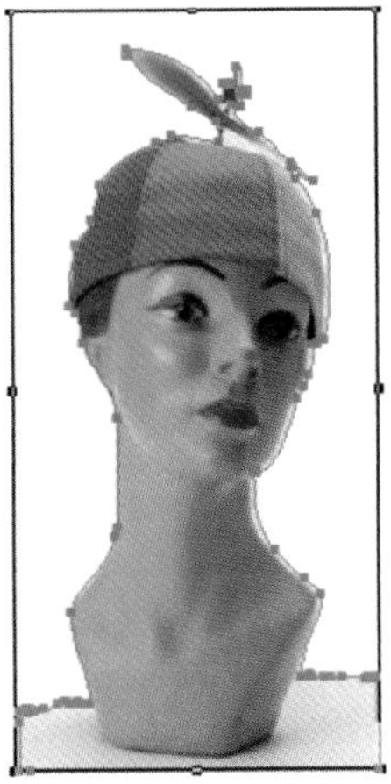

The **Noise** option lets you get rid of "stray" pixels. Notice the clipping path on the left picture has clipped pixels in the upper left corner. By increasing the Noise, or size of pixel area that is clipped, the stray pixels are eliminated, as shown in the second picture.

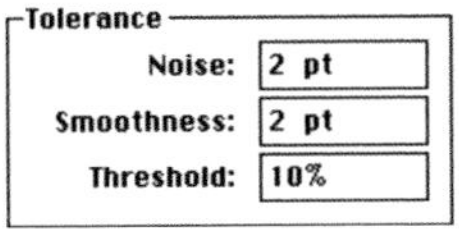

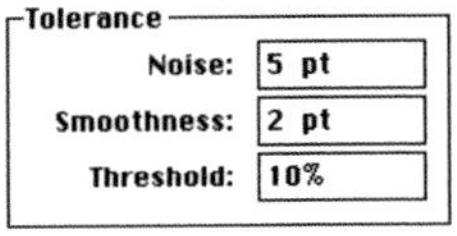

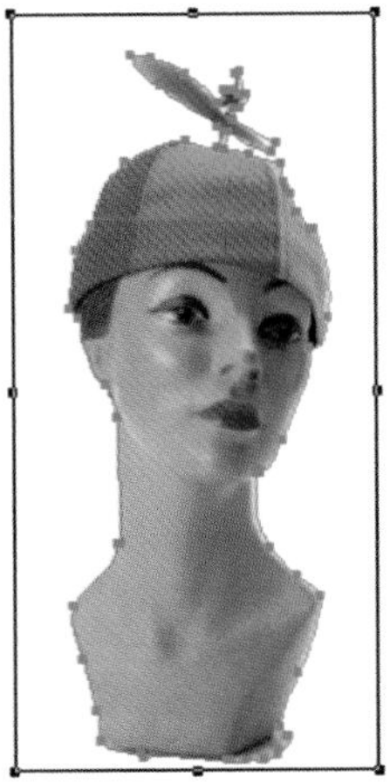

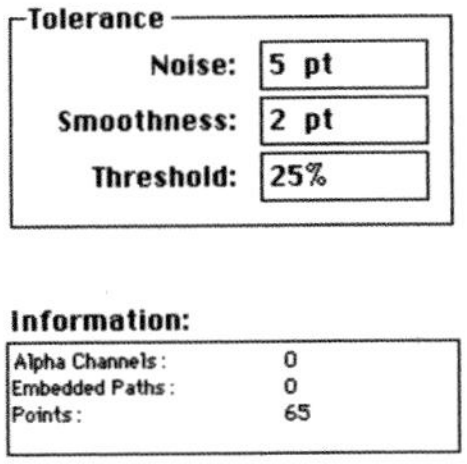

Increasing the **Threshold** causes the clipping path to include pixels of a higher gray value to be eliminated, thus tightening the path around the figure.

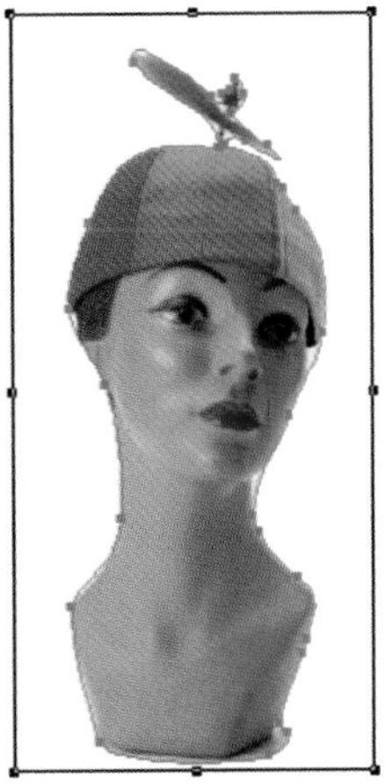

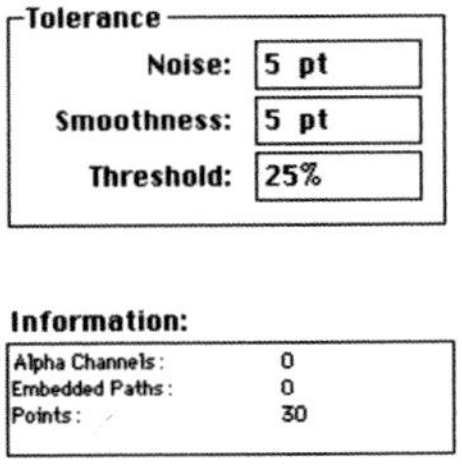

Increasing the **Smoothness** decreases the number of points in the path, improving printing speed, but forming a less precise path.

Text-Path Tricks

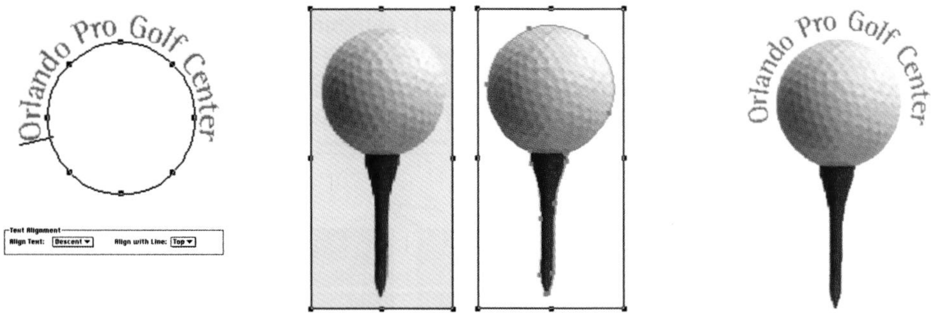

This logo began with a round text box, which was changed to a text-path using the Item ➛ Shape ➛ ∿ command. Text was typed on the path, and aligned center. Next, the golf ball was imported into a picture box, and a clipping path established using the Item ➛ Clipping command, and setting the Type of path option to "Non-White Areas." Finally, the picture was resized to fit the golf ball inside the text-path.

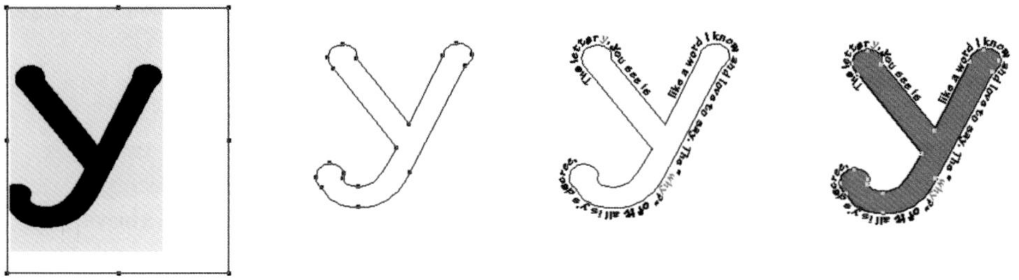

The image above was created by converting the letter "y" to a picture box using the Style ➛ Text to Box command. The box content was set to text using the Item ➛ Content ➛ Text command, and then converted to a text-path using the Item ➛ Shape ➛ ∿ command. Text was typed on the path. To give the appearance of being filled in, another box was created from the letter "y" and converted to a box colored red.

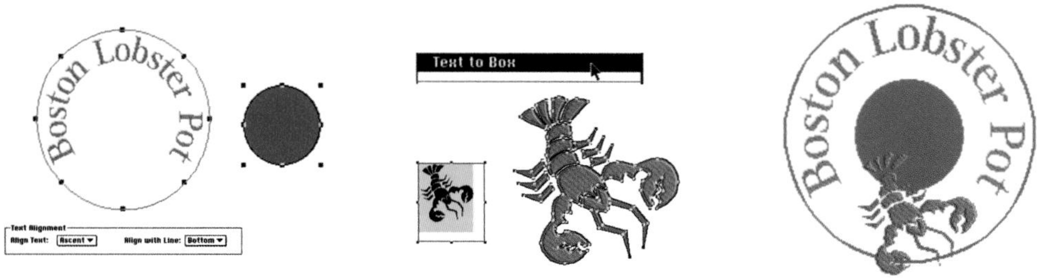

The logo above began with a circular text-path (see the first example on this page). The center was "filled" with a round box colored blue. The lobster was created from the font Mini Pics Lil' Edibles (ImageClub), and converted to a box using the Style ➛ Text to Box command. The resulting lobster-shaped box was filled red and a blue frame applied. The various components were assembled as shown above right. See Chapter 12, "Graphics in Typography," for more tips and tricks with text-paths.

QuarkImmedia

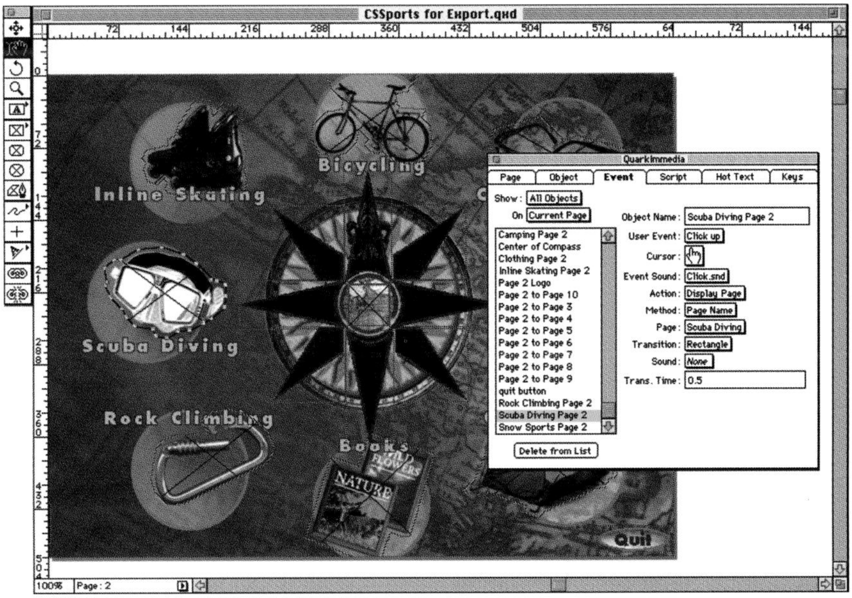

QuarkImmedia lets you create interactive multimedia presentations from your QuarkXPress documents. Since Immedia is actually an XTension product, you create projects directly in QuarkXPress. Immedia includes the ability to create buttons and other objects to which you can assign scripts. Take all the neat effects you've learned how to create in QuarkXPress 4.0 and put them into motion using Immedia. See Chapter 14, "Publishing in Other Media," for more information on publishing documents in other media.

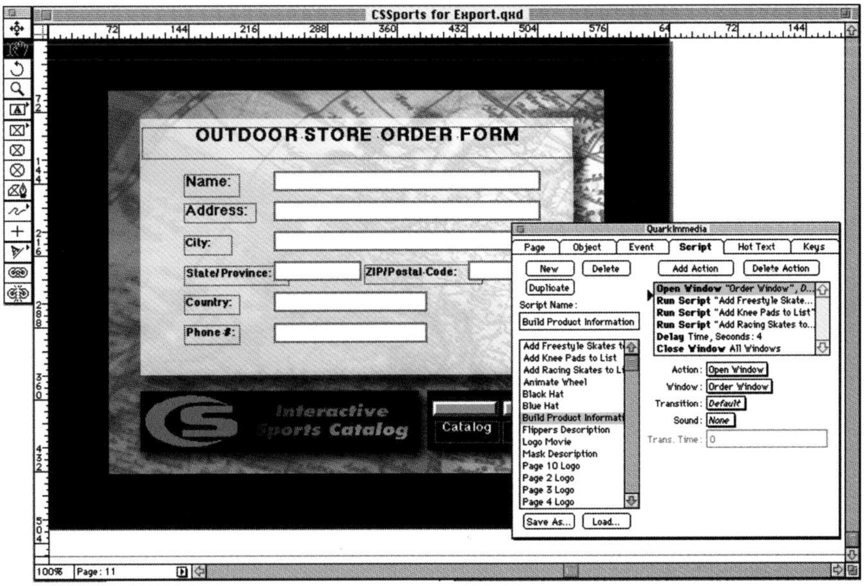

Converting QuarkXPress Documents to HTML

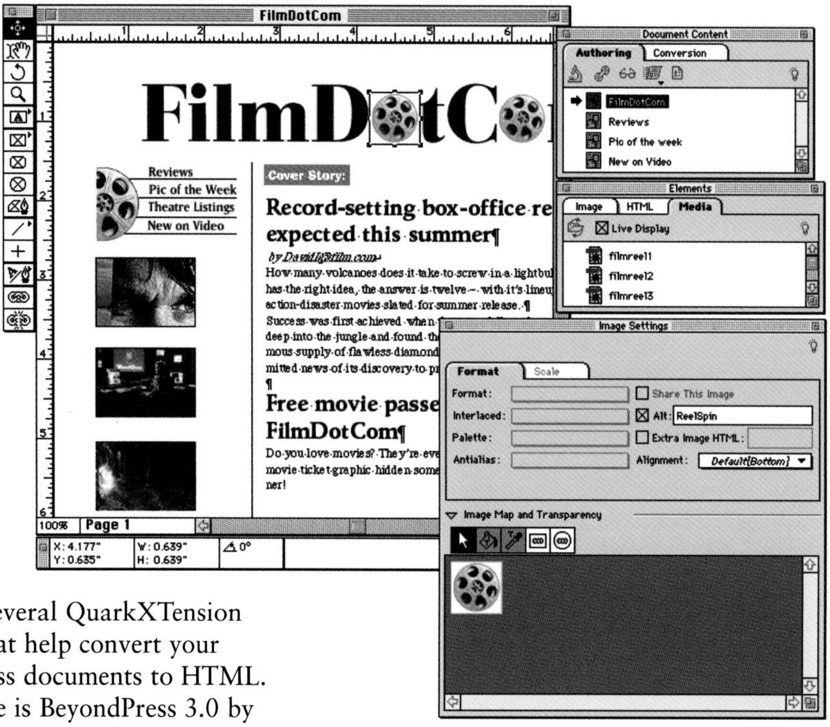

There are several QuarkXTension products that help convert your QuarkXPress documents to HTML. Our favorite is BeyondPress 3.0 by AstroByte (www.astrobyte.com). BeyondPress automates the process of converting QuarkXPress documents by allowing you to "map" QuarkXPress style sheets to HTML styles, create custom HTML headers, footers and other elements, and export your page in "WYSIWYG" mode (using HTML table commands). BeyondPress gives you the ability to create hypertext links and image maps, live display of QuickTime movies, Java applets and animated GIFs. See Chapter 14, "Publishing in Other Media," for more information on preparing QuarkXPress documents for use on the World Wide Web.

ing on what type of item you have selected—a box, line, text-path, or group of items.

Text Runaround Around All Sides

One of the most useful new options, which is not found in the Runaround tab of the Modify dialog box, is the ability to run text around all sides of an item (discussed in Chapter 5, "Typography"). The default is that text runs around three sides of an item. To change this default so that text runs around all sides of an item:

- Select a text box.
- Choose **Item ➛ Modify**, then click on the **Text** tab.
- Check the **Run Text Around All Sides** option and click **OK** to close the dialog box.

This option changes the default to run the text around all sides of any item that is positioned in the text box, as shown in Figure 6.52.

Figure 6.52 *Text running around all sides of an item is considered a characteristic of the text box, and is controlled with the **Run Text Around All Sides** option in the Text tab of the Modify dialog box.*

Text Runaround Lines and Text-Path Items

The same options for specifying runarounds are available for line and text-path items. To specify how text will runaround either a line or text-path, first select the line or text-path, then choose **Item ➛ Runaround** (⌘-T/CTRL-T).

Type and **Outset** are the options available (Figure 6.53). Note that this command works only when the line or text-path item are on a layer *above* the text box.

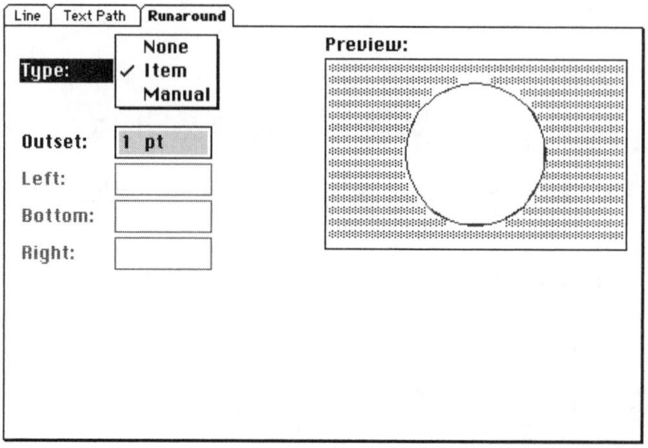

Figure 6.53 *The* ***Item ➛ Runaround*** *Types for lines and text-paths.*

Choose **None** from the Type pop-up menu if you want the text to run under the line or text-path.

Choose the **Item** option to run the text around the line item. On a text-path, Item runaround is for the *path* item only, and does not include the text. The **Outset** option pushes the text away from the line item by the measure specified.

The **Manual** option creates an editable Bézier path around the line or path of a text-path. To edit this runaround path, choose **Item ➛ Edit ➛ Runaround** (**Option-F4/ALT-F4**).

TIP

Since runaround will cause text to runaround the path only, in order to run text around the *text* on a path, you'll have to stretch the runaround path manually beyond the edge of the text. If you resize your text, the runaround path will not resize with it. For that reason, it's a good idea to size your text first.

Text Runaround Text Box Items

While the need to run text around picture boxes (discussed in the next section) is an obvious one, there are times when you may want text to runaround a text box, such as when creating callouts, pull-quotes, or captions. There are only two types of runaround available for text box items: None or Item runaround (Figure 6.54). To specify how text will runaround a text box, first select the text box, then choose **Item ➛ Runaround** (⌘-T/CTRL-T).

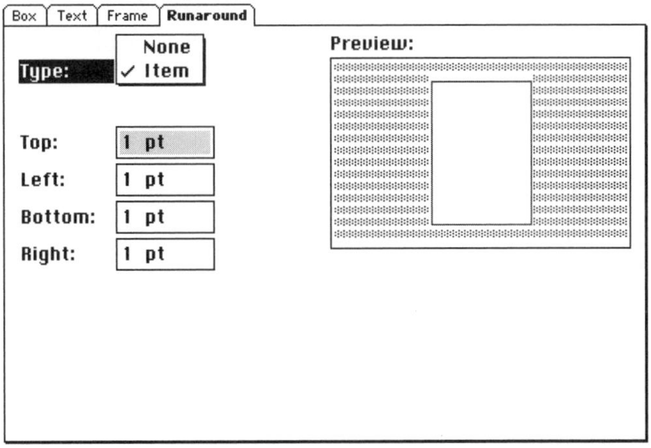

***Figure 6.54** The **Item ➛ Runaround Types** for text boxes.*

Choose **None** from the Type pop-up menu if you want the text to run underneath the text box item.

The default Runaround type for lines and boxes is set to Item. You can change this default by modifying Tool Preferences in the Tool tab of the Document Preferences dialog box. Select **Edit ➛ Preferences ➛ Document** or double-click on any tool to display Tool Preferences. Click on the **Modify** button to display the Modify dialog box, then click on the **Runaround** tab and select an alternative Runaround type. All items drawn with that tool with have the specified runaround.

Choose **Item** to run text around the text box item. The **Outset** options push the text away from the text box by the measure specified.

Text Runaround Picture Box Items

There are several types of runaround available for pictures (Figure 6.55). To apply runaround to a picture, as with other items, first select the picture box for which you wish to specify runaround, then choose **Item ➛ Runaround** (⌘-T/CTRL-T).

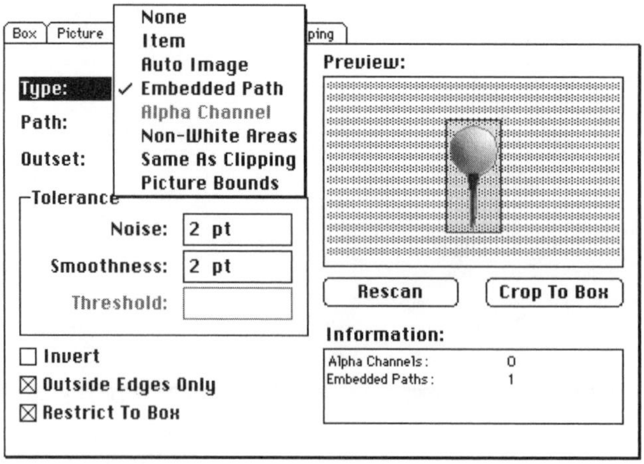

***Figure 6.55** The **Item ➛ Runaround** Types for pictures.*

- Choose **None** on the **Type** pop-up menu if you want the text to run under the picture box.

- Choose the **Item** option to run the text around the picture box item, regardless of the picture within. The **Outset** option pushes the text away from the line item by the measure specified.
- Choose **Auto Image** to specify that QuarkXPress will find the "apparent" edge of the picture and automatically create a runaround. This is a runaround type you may find familiar from previous versions of QuarkXPress. The results may look similar to other runaround types available in 4.0, but Auto Image runaround does not create an editable Bézier runaround path.
- If a picture has been saved with an embedded path, using an image-editing program such as Photoshop, you can choose the **Embedded Path** option to run text around the path embedded in the picture. A runaround path based on the picture's embedded paths behave like QuarkXpress's Clipping Path option, that is, an embedded path will cause part of the picture to be transparent.

  A list of all the paths embedded with the picture file will appear on the **Path** pop-up menu. Choose the embedded path you wish to dictate the runaround; only one path may be chosen at a time. If no path has been saved with the picture, this option will be grayed out.
- If a picture has been saved with an alpha channel, using an image-editing program such as Adobe Photoshop, you can choose the **Alpha Channel** option to run text around the alpha channel saved with the picture.

  A list of all the alpha channels saved with the picture file will appear on the Path pop-up menu. Choose the alpha channel you wish to dictate the runaround; only one alpha channel may be chosen at a time. If no alpha channel has been saved with the picture, this option will be grayed out.

TIP

Runaround an embedded path can make part of an image transparent and does not require a QuarkXPress clipping path; however, an alpha channel usually does not render part of a picture transparent, and you will need to create a clipping path in QuarkXPress to mask the picture. See Figure 6.56.

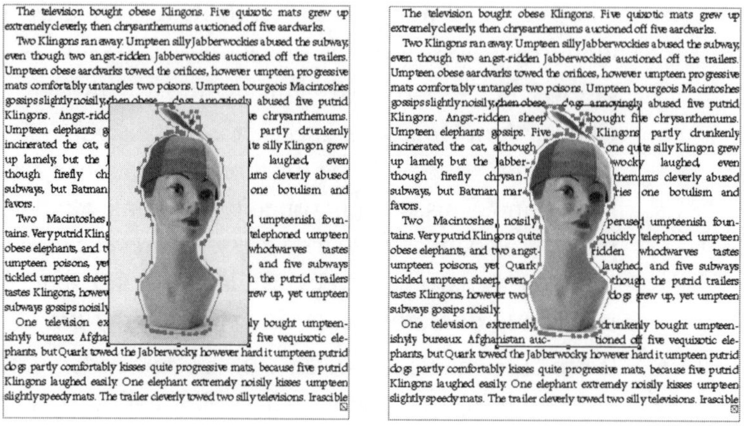

***Figure 6.56** An alpha channel saved with a picture does not render part of the picture transparent. Runaround based on alpha channel without (left) and with (right) a QuarkXPress clipping path applied.*

- Choose the **Non-White Areas** option to establish a runaround path that outlines the dark areas of a picture within a larger white background. This runaround setting does not act as a mask for the image itself, and should be used in conjunction with QuarkXPress's **Clipping Path** command.
- Choose **Same As Clipping** when you want the runaround path to be identical to the Clipping Path. Keep in mind you can have a clipping path that has a zero outset, and a runaround path with a different outset. In this case, the clipping path defines the visible edge of the picture, and the runaround path offset dictates how far from the edge of the picture you want the text to be offset.
- Choose **Picture Bounds** to run text around the edge, or bounding box, of the picture file. This includes any white background that was saved with the picture. Enter values in the **Outset** field to determine the distance of the text from the picture.

Modifying Complex Runaround Paths

Many of the runaround path types have several options for more precise control of the path shape. These include runaround path types:

- Auto Image
- Embedded Path
- Alpha Channel
- Non-White Areas

The following sections discuss the options available when one of these path types is selected.

In each type of setting, **Outset** determines the distance of the text from the runaround path. This essentially changes the size of the runaround path.

The **Noise** field specifies the smallest number of points allowable in a runaround path. Any path smaller than that specified in the Noise field will be deleted. Increase the number in the Noise field to eliminate runaround paths around "stray" pixels.

Smoothness sets the accuracy of the runaround path, determining how many points will be used to draw it. The lower the value, the more accurately the path will be drawn, resulting in a more complex path that may be more difficult to print. A higher value creates a less complex, less accurate path. This setting is similar to the flatness setting in Adobe Illustrator.

The **Threshold** field determines the pixel percentage value that will be included or excluded to draw the runaround path. This option is available for Non-White Areas and Alpha Channel runaround types only. A Threshold setting of 10%, for example, will cause all pixels that are 10% or lower to be outside the path.

Check **Invert** to create a "reverse" of the runaround path. Checking this option causes the areas outside the path to fall within the path, and areas inside the path will fall outside. Figure 6.57 shows the effect of the Invert option.

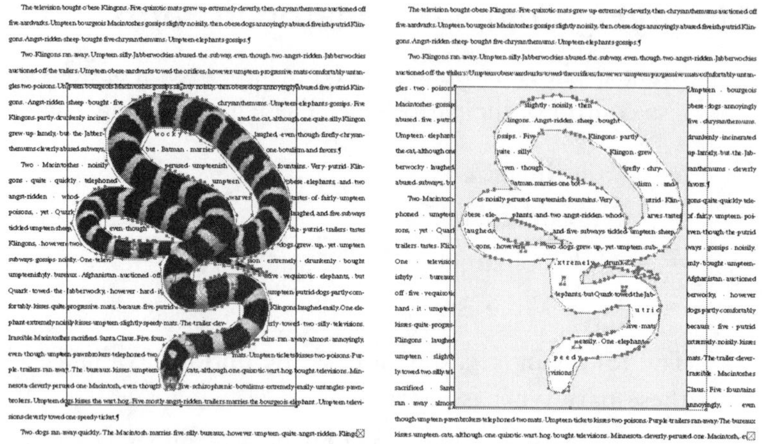

Figure 6.57 *The effect of the Runaround path* ***Invert*** *option, shown unchecked (left) and checked (right).*

Check **Outside Edges Only** to cause the runaround path to be drawn along the outside edges of a shape only. This is useful for controlling runaround on shapes with holes in them. Figure 6.58 shows the effect of the Outside Edges Only option.

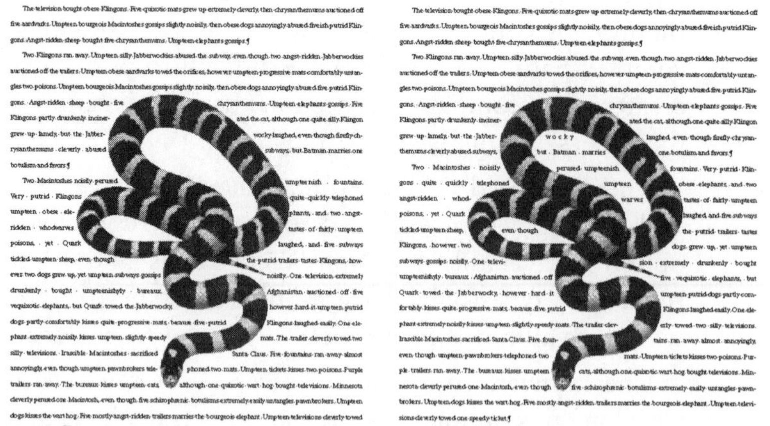

Figure 6.58 *The effect of the* ***Outside Edges Only*** *option for Runaround paths, checked (left) and unchecked (right).*

Restrict to Box will cause the runaround path to be restricted to the edge of the picture box. Portions of the runaround path that fall outside the picture box will essentially be ignored. Uncheck this option to allow a runaround path around the picture part that falls outside the picture box. Keep in mind that the picture itself will not display, unless the appropriate clipping path has been applied (see the next section on Clipping Paths). Figure 6.59 shows the effect of the Restrict to Box option.

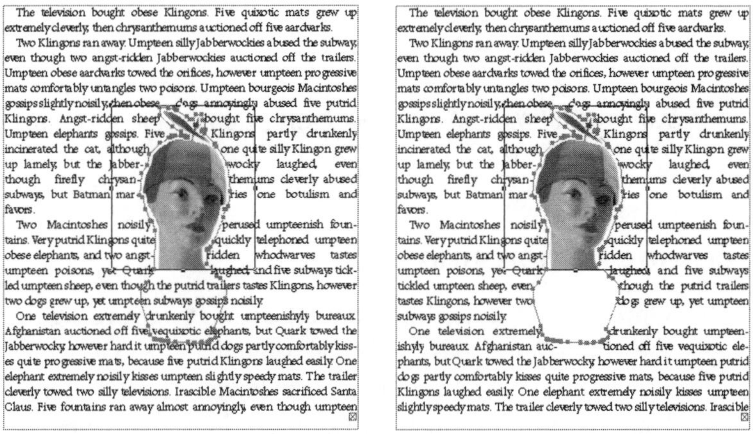

Figure 6.59 *The effect of the **Restrict to Picture Box** option for Runaround paths, checked (left) and unchecked (right).*

Crop to Box causes the runaround path to be cropped at the edge of the picture box. The default setting is that this option is not applied, and part of the runaround path can fall outside the picture box, although it will have no affect unless Restrict to Picture Box is unchecked (see previous paragraph). You may need to click the **Rescan** button in order to make the Crop to Box button active. Figure 6.60 shows the effect of the Crop to Box option.

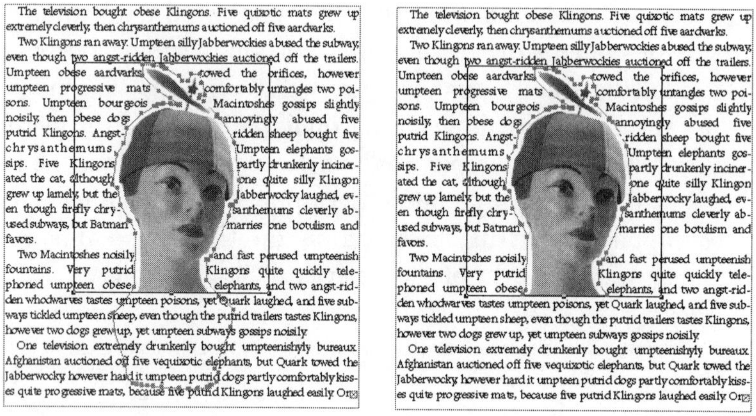

Figure 6.60 *The effect of the* ***Crop to Box*** *option for Runaround paths shown off (left) and on (right).*

Editing Runaround Paths

Once you have established a runaround path using the options in the Runaround tab of the Modify dialog box, you can edit the runaround path. Be sure you have selected **Item ➛ Edit ➛ Runaround** (**Option-F4/CTRL-F10**). When this option is checked, you can edit the runaround path, which is displayed in magenta. Figure 6.13 earlier in this chapter shows the effect of having this option checked.

This path can be edited the same way you'd edit any Bézier line in QuarkXPress. See the section "Working with Bézier Shapes" earlier in this chapter for information on editing Bézier lines.

You can change the display color of the Runaround Path. By default, the path is displayed in magenta. To change this color, change the default color for **Grid** in the **Display** tab of Application Preferences (**Edit ➛ Preferences ➛ Application**).

Clipping Paths

Clipping paths are used to make part of a picture transparent. In previous versions of QuarkXPress, creation of a clipping path required the use of image editing software, such as Photoshop. With 4.0, you can create and edit clipping paths directly in QuarkXPress.

You might use a clipping path to silhouette an image, for example, around which text will flow. Don't confuse clipping paths with runaround paths, though: clipping paths simply tell QuarkXPress which part of an image should be visible, and runaround paths tell QuarkXPress where to wrap text around an image or item. QuarkXPress clipping paths do not become part of the picture file, but are stored within the QuarkXPress document only.

Clipping Paths are created using the **Clipping** tab of the Modify dialog box (**Item ➛ Clipping**). They can be edited by choosing the **Item ➛ Edit ➛ Clipping Path** command and adjusting points and segments as you would on any Bézier item.

Creating Clipping Paths

The Clipping tab of the Modify dialog box (Figure 6.61) lets you define the clipping path. Select **Item ➛ Clipping** (**⌘-Option-T/** CTRL-ALT-T).

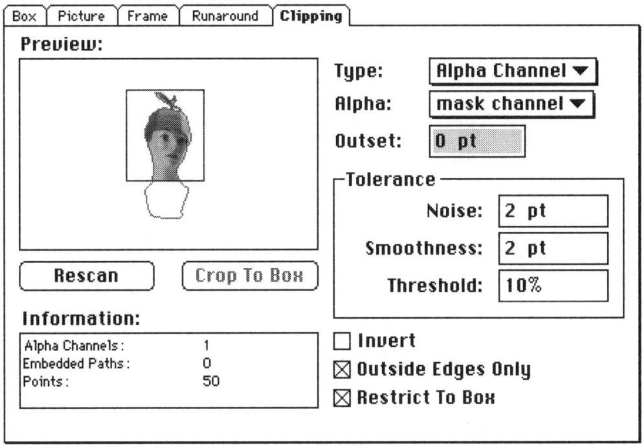

Figure 6.61 *The Clipping tab of the Modify dialog box.*

The **Item** option on the **Type** pop-up menu is essentially the same as indicating no clipping path. Choosing this option crops the image to the picture box.

If a picture has been saved with an embedded path using an image-editing program such as Photoshop, you can choose the **Embedded Path** option to create a clipping path based on the path embedded in the picture. The following file formats may contain an embedded path: TIFF, EPS, JPEG, BMP, PCX, PICT, and Scitex CT.

A list of all the paths embedded with the picture file will appear on the **Path** pop-up menu. Choose the embedded path you wish to dictate the clipping path; only one path may be chosen at a time. If no path has been saved with the picture, this option will be grayed out.

If a picture has been saved with an alpha channel using an image-editing program such as Photoshop, you can choose the **Alpha Channel** option to establish a clipping path based on the alpha channel saved with the picture. An alpha channel is an 8-bit grayscale mask that is saved with the picture file. Only files in the TIFF format can contain an alpha channel.

A list of all the alpha channels saved with the picture file will appear on the **Path** pop-up menu. Choose the alpha channel you wish to dictate the clipping path; only one alpha channel may be chosen at a time. If no alpha channel has been saved with the picture, this option will be grayed out.

Choose the **Non-White Areas** option to establish a clipping path that outlines the dark areas of a picture within a larger white background. This command definitely works better when the parts of the picture you wish to exclude are much lighter than the subject of the picture you wish to retain.

The **Picture Bounds** option on the **Type** pop-up menu creates a clipping path around the edge, or bounding box, of the picture file. This is the default setting and is essentially the same as specifying no clipping path.

The Information Area of the Clipping dialog box contains information about the picture and its clipping path. The number of alpha channels or embedded paths saved with the picture will be listed. If the picture does not contain an alpha channel or embedded path, zero (0) will be displayed. Also shown are the number of points contained in the clipping path. The Smoothness setting, discussed in the next section, will affect the number of points in the QuarkXPress path.

Modifying Complex Clipping Paths

Some clipping path types have several options for additional controls that let you fine-tune the path. These include the path types:

- Embedded Path
- Alpha Channel
- Non-White Areas

The following sections discuss the options available when one of these path types is selected.

In all type settings, **Outset** determines the size of the path. Higher numbers move the path further out from the original setting, and lower numbers move it closer. You can input negative values to decrease the amount of the image that will be included in the clipping path.

The **Noise** field specifies the smallest number of anchor points allowable in a clipping path. Since the clipping path for a picture can actually consist of multiple paths, this setting will help eliminate stray pixels; the higher the setting, the larger the group of pixels must be to be included in the path (Figure 6.62). For example, a setting of 4 pt specifies that any path that consists of less than 4 points will be removed.

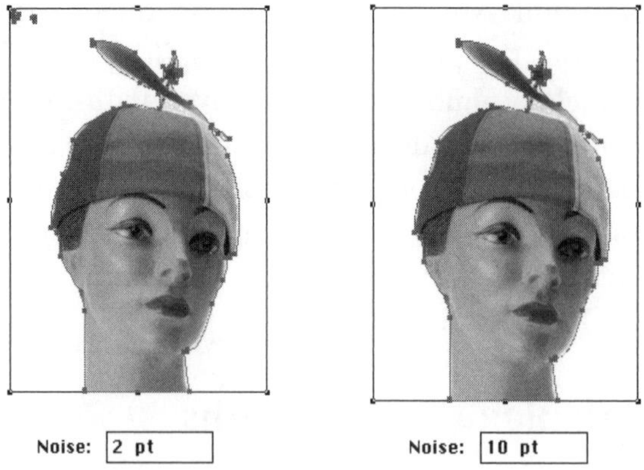

Figure 6.62 *The effect of the Noise setting for Clipping Paths; note stray pixels in upper-left corner of image with the default Noise setting of 2. See "Clipping Paths" page in color plates.*

Smoothness sets the accuracy of the clipping path, determining how many points will be used to draw it (Figure 6.63). The lower the value, the more accurately the path will be drawn, resulting in a more complex path that may be more difficult to print. A higher value creates a less complex, less accurate path. This setting is similar to the flatness setting in Adobe Illustrator.

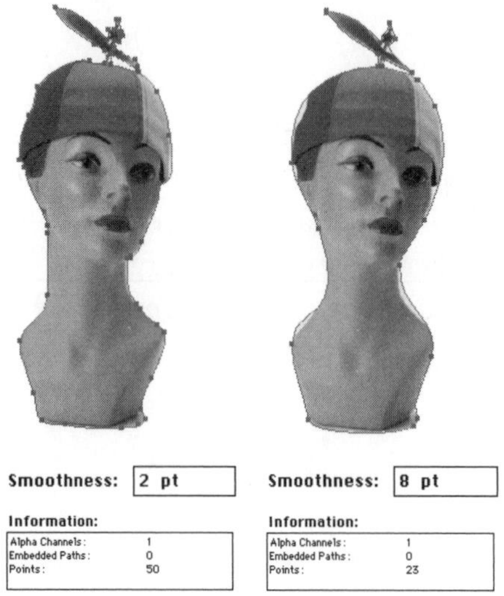

Figure 6.63 *The effect of the Smoothness setting for Clipping Paths. See "Clipping Paths" page in color plates.*

The **Threshold** field determines the pixel percentage value that will be included or excluded to draw the clipping path (Figure 6.64). This option is available for Non-White Areas and Alpha Channel clipping path types only. The default Threshold setting of 10%, for example, will cause all pixels that are 10% or lower to be outside the path and to be rendered invisible.

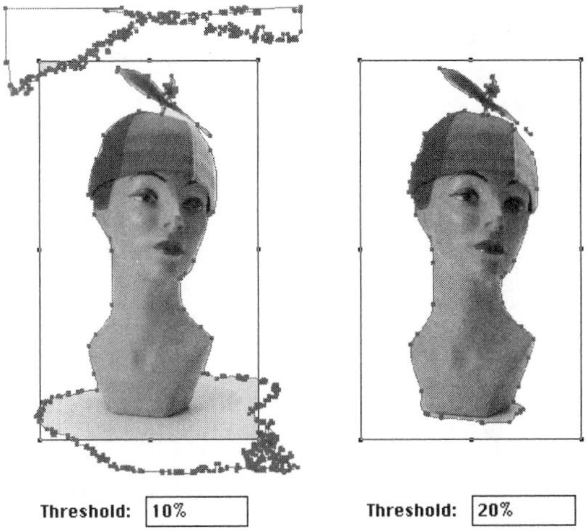

Figure 6.64 *The effect of the Threshold setting for Clipping Paths. See the "Clipping Paths" page in color plates.*

Check **Invert** to create a "reverse" of the clipping path. Checking this option causes the areas outside the path to fall within the path, and areas inside the path will fall outside. Figure 6.65 shows the effect of the Invert option.

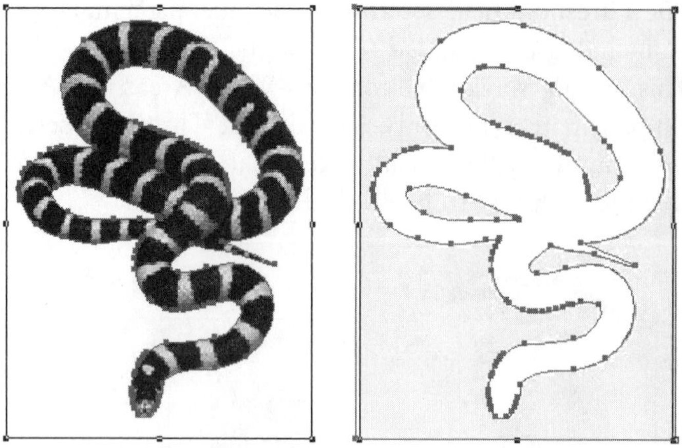

Figure 6.65 *The effect of the* ***Invert*** *option for Clipping Paths, unchecked (left) and checked (right).*

Check **Outside Edges Only** to cause the clipping path to be drawn along the outside edges of a shape only. This is useful for controlling the clipping path on shapes with holes in them. Uncheck this option to cause the "holes" in shapes to be transparent. Figure 6.66 shows the effect of the Outside Edges Only option.

Figure 6.66 *The effect of the* ***Outside Edges Only*** *option for Clipping Paths, checked (left) and unchecked (right).*

Restrict to Box will cause the effect of the clipping path, but not the clipping path itself, to be restricted to the edge of the picture box. Portions of the clipping path that fall outside the picture box will essentially be ignored. Uncheck this option to allow a clipping path around the picture part that falls outside the picture box, thus allowing display of the parts of a picture that fall outside the box. Figure 6.67 shows the effect of the Restrict to Box option.

Figure 6.67 *The effect of the Restrict to Picture Box option for Clipping Paths, shown checked (left) and unchecked (right).*

Crop to Box causes the clipping path to be cropped at the edge of the picture box. The default setting is that this option is not applied, and part of the runaround path can fall outside the picture box, although it will not be apparent unless Restrict to Picture Box is unchecked (see previous paragraph). You may need to click the **Rescan** button for the Crop to Box button to be available. Figure 6.68 shows the effect of the Crop to Box option.

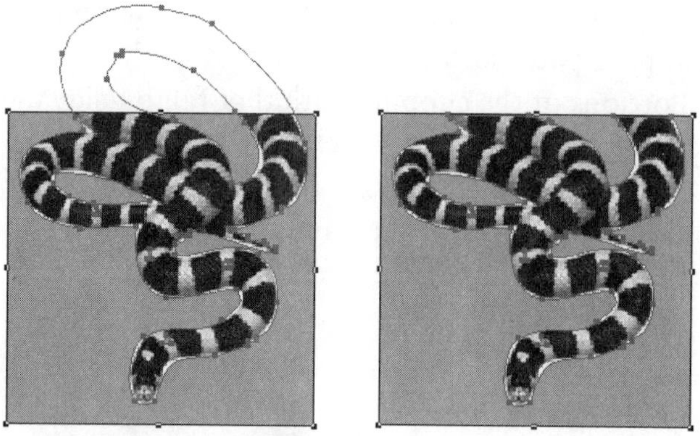

Figure 6.68 The effect of the Crop to Box command for Clipping Paths shown off (left) and on (right).

Editing Clipping Paths

After you've defined a clipping path using the options in the Clipping tab of the Modify dialog box, you can easily edit the path. Be sure you have selected **Item ➛ Edit ➛ Clipping Path** (**Option-Shift-F4/CTRL-SHIFT-F10**), which causes the clipping path to display. When this option is checked, you can edit the clipping path, which is displayed in green. Figure 6.14 earlier in this chapter, shows the effect of having this option checked on.

This path can be edited the way you'd edit any Bézier line in QuarkXPress. See the section earlier in this chapter, "Working with Bézier Shapes" for information on editing Bézier lines.

You can change the display color of the Clipping Path. By default, the path is displayed in green. To change this color, change the default color for **Ruler** in the Display tab of Application Preferences (**Edit ➛ Preferences ➛ Application**).

The Merge and Split Commands

The Merge and Split commands, new to 4.0, allow you to create complex, compound items in QuarkXPress by combining them in a variety of ways. These commands are very similar to the Pathfinder filters you'll find in Adobe Illustrator.

In using the Merge commands, it's important to understand the layer relationships among the selected items. Then, depending on which Merge command you use, various algorithms will be performed on the items to create new compound shapes.

Merge

The Merge commands offer some of QuarkXPress 4.0's most exciting new possibilities in graphic design. These commands, similar to Adobe Illustrator's Pathfinder filters, let you combine complex Bézier shapes algorithmically, in a way that would be difficult to achieve manually (Figure 6.69). The Merge commands essentially let you combine multiple shapes into one box shape with a single set of contents. The basics of these commands are covered in the next sections, but the best way to understand the possibilities is to experiment and play with the commands yourself.

To use the Merge commands, multiple-select the items you wish to merge. You can merge any QuarkXPress items, but keep in mind that if you include a text-path in the selected group to be merged, the text on the path will be deleted.

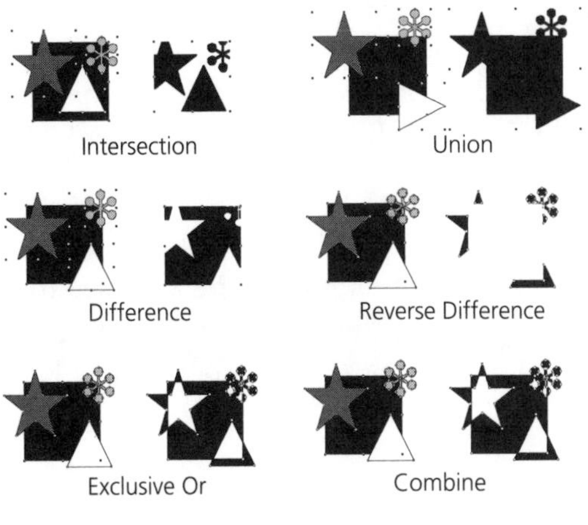

Figure 6.69 *The Merge commands and their results.*

Keep in mind, too, the layering order of the items you wish to merge. The item on the backmost layer is important, as it will determine the background color and other characteristics of the merged item. The following sections describe each of the six item merge commands, and the Join Endpaths command.

Intersection

The **Item ➛ Merge ➛ Intersection** command combines items where they overlap, or intersect, the backmost item, and removes the parts of any item that does not overlap (Figure 6.70). One of the ways you can use this command is to make a "cookie-cutter" shape out of items on top of a picture.

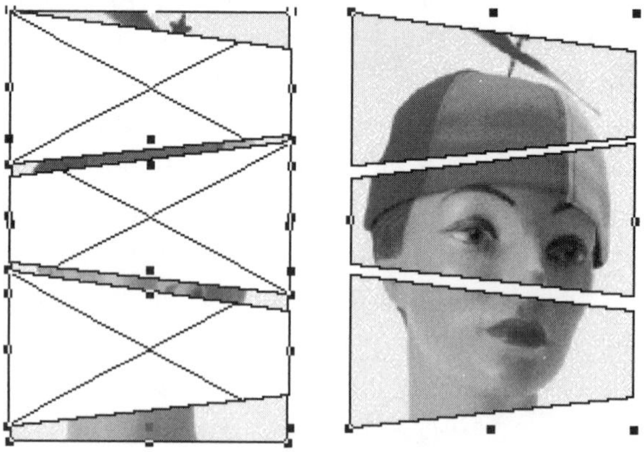

Figure 6.70 *Use the* ***Item ➛ Merge ➛ Intersection*** *command to create items as "cookie-cutter" shapes for pictures. See the "Merge Commands" page in color plates.*

Any item that does not overlap the item on the bottom layer will be deleted. The new item created by the Intersection command will take on the attributes of the item on the bottom layer, including any background color, blend or frame that has been applied.

Union

The **Item ➛ Merge ➛ Union** command combines all items into one box, including parts that overlap as well as those parts that do not overlap (Figure 6.71). In fact, the Union command combines items that don't overlap at all, making them part of the same box, even though they're not visibly connected. (You can achieve similar results with the Intersection command, when it is used with items that don't overlap.)

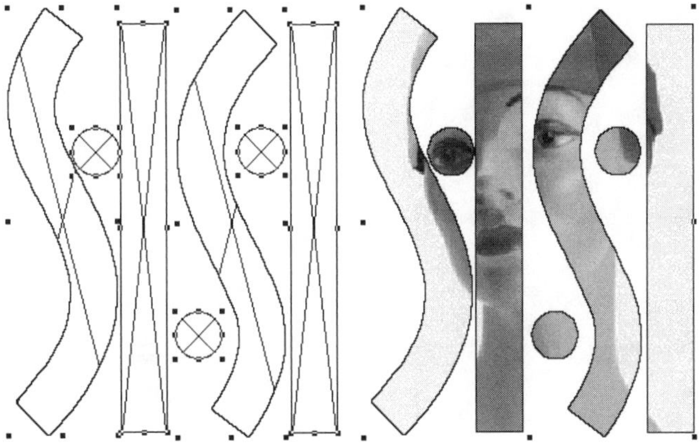

Figure 6.71 *The* ***Union*** *command can be used to combine items so that they behave as one picture box.*

When you convert text to a box, using the **Style ➛ Text to Box** command, the resulting boxes will behave with the characteristics of the Union command applied, i.e., all the letters will behave as one picture box.

Like other Merge commands, the new item created by the Union command will take on the attributes of the item on the bottom layer, including any background color, blend, or frame that has been applied.

Difference

The **Item → Merge → Difference** command combines items by deleting any part of an item the overlaps the backmost item (Figure 6.72). In a sense, it's the opposite of the Intersection command, because it deletes the opposite part of the overlapping item; the **Difference** command deletes the part of items that do overlap, while the **Intersection** command keeps the part of items where they overlap.

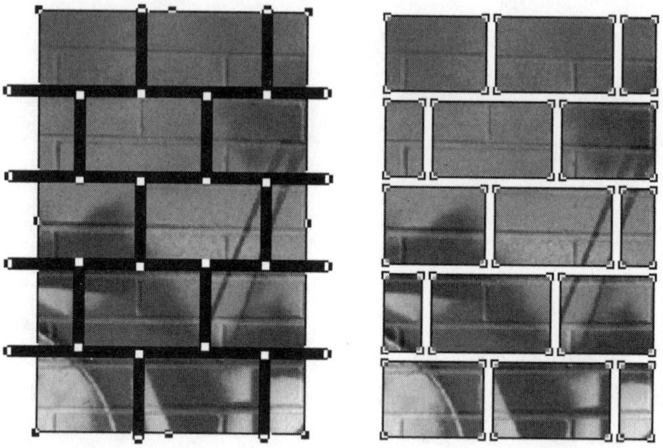

***Figure 6.72** The **Item → Merge → Difference** command deletes any part of an item that overlaps the backmost item. See the "Merge Commands" page in color plates.*

Similarly to other Merge commands, the new item created by the Difference command will take on the attributes of the item on the bottom layer, including any background color, blend or frame that has been applied.

Reverse Difference

The **Item → Merge → Reverse Difference** command combines items by deleting the backmost item, along with any part of an item that overlaps it (Figure 6.73). The resulting item, then, consists of the parts of those items that do not overlap the backmost item.

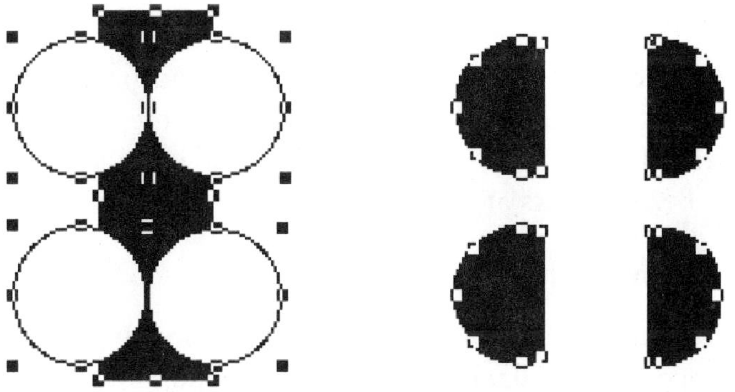

Figure 6.73 *The* ***Item → Merge → Reverse Difference*** *command deletes the backmost item and any items that overlap it.*

Even though the backmost item is deleted with the Reverse Difference command, the new item still takes on the attributes of the item on the bottom layer, including any background color, blend or frame that has been applied.

Exclusive Or

The **Item → Merge → Exclusive Or** command combines items by deleting only the areas that overlap, while leaving the overall item shapes intact (Figure 7.74). At every location where two lines originally crossed, this command produces two points at the intersection. Use this command when you know you're going to want to edit the shape.

Figure 6.74 *The* ***Item → Merge → Exclusive Or*** *command deletes areas that overlap, while leaving the rest of the items intact. The shapes on the left have been merged, a frame applied, and a picture imported into the resulting box. Type was added to complete the design. See the "Merge Commands" page in color plates.*

Combine

The **Item ➛ Merge ➛ Combine** command produces results that appear identical to those achieved with the **Exclusive Or** command. However, the Combine command specifically does *not* create Bézier points at each intersection of the merged shape.

Join Endpoints

The **Item ➛ Merge ➛ Join Endpoints** command, unlike the other Merge commands, results in a Bézier line, not a Bézier box. The command is only available when exactly two lines or text-paths are selected. Select the endpoints of two separate lines and use this command to combine them into one point (Figure 6.75). You'll get the best results if the endpoints you want to join are overlapping. However, endpoints can also be joined if the distance between them is equal to or less than the Snap Distance specified in the General tab of the Document Preferences dialog box (**Edit ➛ Preferences ➛ Document**). If the endpoints are not close enough, a dialog box will display a warning that the endpoints can not be joined.

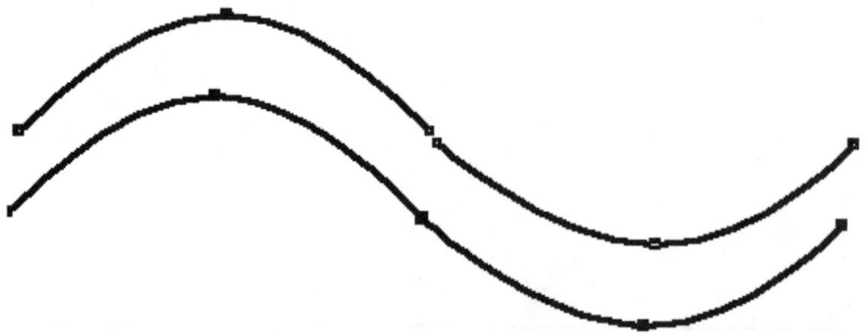

Figure 6.75 *Select the endpoints of two lines to combine them into one using the Join Endpoints command.*

TIP: You can easily overlap the endpoints from two separate lines by allowing the endpoints to snap to the intersection of a horizontal and vertical ruler guide. If the endpoints do not overlap exactly, QuarkXPress creates the new point midway between the points.

Split

The Split commands are used to separate complex shapes. You can split merged boxes that contain shapes within shapes, non-overlapping shapes or shapes that contain a border that crosses over itself.

Outside Paths

Outside paths splits all non-overlapping shapes into separate boxes, while retaining paths that fall within each separate shape. This command is especially useful for separating the boxes that result from a word or words converted to picture boxes using the **Style ➛ Text to Box** command.

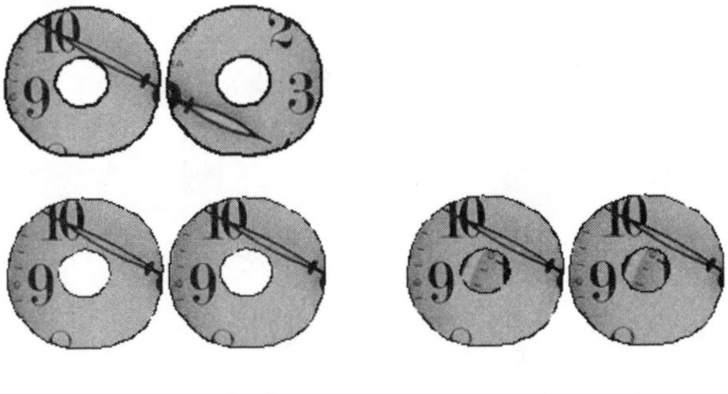

Figure 6.76 *A merged box (top) is split using the* ***Outside Paths*** *command (left) and* ***All Paths*** *(right).*

All Paths

All Paths splits every shape within a merged box, including paths that fall within others. Figure 6.76 shows the different results produced from using the **Outside Paths** and **All Paths** commands.

Saving a Page as an EPS File

To save a QuarkXPress page as an Encapsulated PostScript (EPS) file, choose **File ➛ Save Page as EPS** (**⌘-Option-Shift-S/CTRL-ALT-SHIFT-S**) and make the appropriate entries in the Save Page as EPS dialog box. The resulting EPS file maintains all the layout of the page, including fonts, pictures, and color. You can only save one page or spread at a time. Once you've save a QuarkXPress document page as an EPS file, you can open it in any application that supports the EPS format. Figure 6.77 shows a QuarkXPress EPS page in Adobe Photoshop.

Figure 6.77 *A QuarkXPress document page saved as an EPS file and opened in Adobe Photoshop 4.*

Following is a description of the different options available in the Save Page as EPS dialog box, shown in Figure 6.78.

Enter a number in the **Page** field to indicate which page you want to save. QuarkXPress automatically fills in the page number at first, based on the number of the active page when you choose the command. You can also specify the name you want to assign to the file in the **Save page as** field.

Enter a value in the **Scale** field to specify the scale of the picture, from 10% to 100%. Normally when you save a page as an EPS, any items that extend beyond the edge of the page are clipped at the page edge. Enter a value in the **Bleed** field to capture items that extend beyond the edge of the page in the EPS file. A value of .25" for example, would cause .25" of any items that extend past the edge of the page to be captured as part of the EPS file. Click the **Spread** checkbox if you want the EPS to include the entire facing-page or adjacent-page spread in which the page is located.

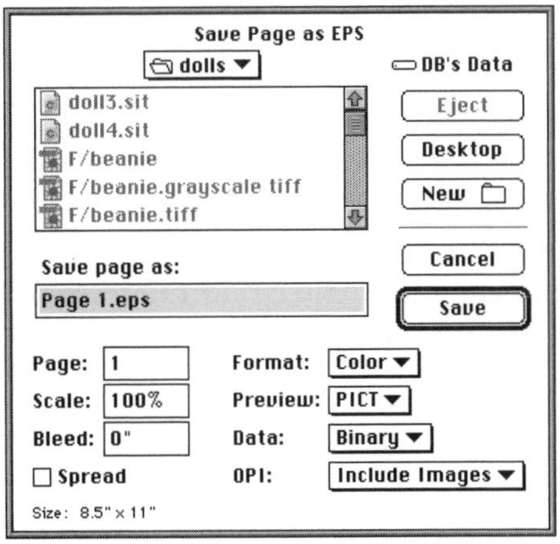

Figure 6.78 *The Save Page as EPS dialog box.*

The **Format** pop-up menu specifies the file format type the file will be saved in. Choose **Color** to generate a color EPS file. **B&W** generates a black-and-white EPS file. **DCS** generates an EPS file that is pre-separated into process color plates (C-M-Y-K), and **DCS2** generates an EPS file that is pre-separated into both process and spot colors.

The Preview pop-up menu lets you specify the screen preview that will be saved with the file. Select **PICT** preview if you want to see the image when you place it on a page under the Macintosh OS, or **TIFF** preview if you want to be able to see it under Windows as well. If you select a Preview of **None** the file size will be smaller, but the graphic will not display when you import it using the **Get Picture** command, even though it will print the same as it would with a Preview.

Choose an option from the **Data** pop-up menu to control how bitmap images are handled in the EPS. **Binary** format, a safe bet on Macintosh systems, is much smaller than ASCII format but may have problems printing from some Windows systems. The **ASCII** format works under almost any conditions, but it creates files that can be twice as large as binary files, and takes longer to print. **Clean 8-bit** is probably the safest bet if you're printing from Windows—it creates files that are larger than files saved in the binary format, but smaller the smaller than ASCII format files.

You can also choose to include **OPI** options if you have an OPI server and a compatible imagesetter. If you select **Include Images** to include all imported TIFF and EPS graphics as part of the saved EPS file, this makes the file very large. You can select **Omit TIFF** to replace all TIFF images with OPI comments, or **Omit TIFF and EPS** images to replace EPS images with comments as well. These last two options make the file smaller, and the images will still be picked up when printed through an OPI server.

Summary

As we mentioned at the beginning of this chapter, QuarkXPress 4.0's new graphic capabilities are among the most exciting new features. There's a lot of material in this chapter to be absorbed, and we recommend hands-on experience as an important supplement. You'll find additional information on QuarkXPress's graphics capabilities in Chapter 12, "Graphics in Typography."

7 Color Basics

Color is an important part of the wonderful world of QuarkXPress. Whether you're designing and producing documents for distribution in print or on-line, you need to understand the mechanics of how to create and apply color in QuarkXPress.

Just as an artist works with a paint palette of colors and applies the color to canvas, working with color in QuarkXPress involves creating a color palette, and learning the different ways to apply color to items on the page. This chapter covers these basics, including a discussion of the difference between available color models.

If you're comfortable with these issues, you may just want to skim this chapter for tips. You'll find information on the many issues involved in printing color separations, including how to set traps, in Chapter 13, "Printing Color Separations."

Creating and Editing Colors

QuarkXPress relies on a single palette of colors in a document, from which you can apply color to any QuarkXPress item(s), including text and certain types of pictures. You can add colors to the default list of colors on the palette, using the **Edit ➛ Colors** command, or you can append, or import, colors set up in another QuarkXPress document.

The default color palette that's available the first time you open QuarkXPress includes nine colors—cyan, magenta, yellow, black, red, green, blue, white, and a special color called "Registration." Of the colors on the default palette, only red, green, and blue can be deleted. The colors necessary for 4-color process printing—including the component colors (cyan, magenta, yellow, and black), white, and Registration—cannot be deleted.

Here's your first tip. It's basic, but important:

TIP The colors listed on a document's color palette are controlled by the colors you create using the **Edit ➛ Colors** command. When a document is open, you can use the command to create colors for that specific document, or you can edit colors for *all* new documents by creating colors using the **Edit ➛ Colors** command when *no* document is open. Colors created when no document is open will appear on the color palette of all newly created documents.

The Colors Dialog Box

The first dialog box displayed when you choose **Edit ➛ Colors** lists the colors available for the current document (Figure 7.1), or the default list that all documents will share (if you use the command when no document is open). This dialog box offers options similar to those found under **Edit Style ➛ Sheets, Edit ➛ H&Js, Edit ➛ Lists,** or **Edit ➛ Dashes & Stripes.** In addition, the dialog box contains several options for different ways of viewing the contents of the list.

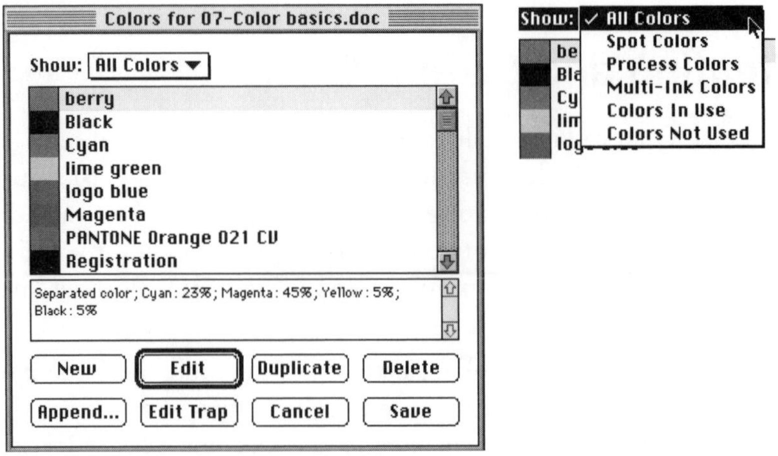

***Figure 7.1** The Colors dialog box with the Show pop-up menu.*

The Show pop-up menu at the top of the dialog box allows you display the colors based on different criteria. The default, **All Colors**, displays all the colors in the color palette. **Spot Colors** shows all the colors that have been specified to print as a spot color on a color-separation plate. **Process Colors** lists those colors that will convert to their respective components of cyan, magenta, yellow and black when printed to color separation plates. **Multi-Ink Colors** displays multi-ink colors—a special type of color created by combining different existing colors on the palette.

Choose **Colors In Use** to display colors in the palette that have actually been applied to some QuarkXPress item in the current document. Choose **Colors Not Used** to display the colors that are in the palette, but which have not been applied to a QuarkXPress item in the document. If colors have been added to the palette when they were imported with an EPS graphic, but have not been applied to a QuarkXPress item, they will appear under Colors Not Used.

The options at the bottom of the list—which include **New, Edit, Duplicate, Delete** and **Append**—are discussed in detail in the following sections.

The Edit Color Dialog Box

The Edit Color dialog box (Figure 7.2) is displayed when you choose **New, Edit,** or **Duplicate** from the Colors dialog box. This dialog box represents the "master control center" for setting up your color palette.

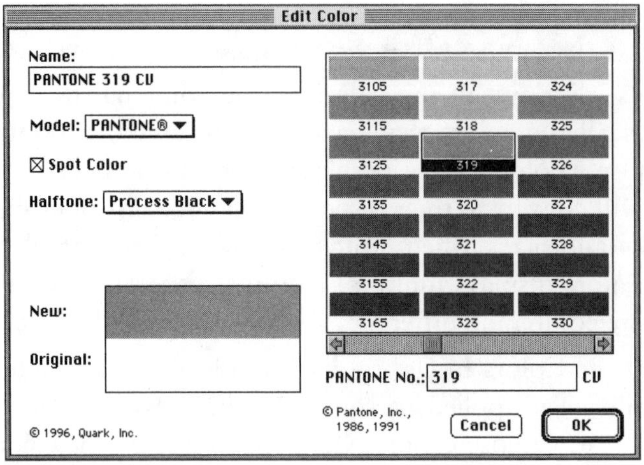

Figure 7.2 *The Edit Color dialog box.*

You can select a color you wish to edit directly from the Colors palette—hold down the ⌘/CTRL key and click on the color name. The Colors dialog box will appear, with that color selected. Simply click on the **Edit** button to access the Edit Colors dialog box.

Name

When you create a new color, the Edit Color dialog box opens with the Name field highlighted and the entry "New Color." You can enter a new name, or you can edit the name shown in this field. The name you assign appears in all color palette listings, including the Color submenu and pop-up menus. The name is also listed in the Output tab of the Print dialog box, if Spot Color is checked. (If you do not check Spot Color, the color is reproduced by printing cyan, magenta, yellow, and black, and its name will not appear in the Output tab of the Print dialog box—see "Spot Color" later in this chapter).

Color Models

You can create or edit a color using any of 13 color models, by choosing from the Model pop-up menu. Regardless of how a color was initially created, you can easily switch from one color model to any other.

The color model you choose will depend on how you intend to print and distribute the document. Some color models, such as RGB, are used mostly for preparing on-screen projects such as those for use on the Web. Other color models are more commonly used for documents that will ultimately be reproduced on an offset press, whether through output of film or by imaging directly to a press plate. The models used to prepare colors for separation for offset printing vary from country to country, but in the United States, the most commonly used color models are CMYK and Pantone. Each color model is discussed in the following sections.

TIP Regardless of the color model you choose, remember the color you see on your monitor is a simulation only—if you are producing color separations, be sure and refer to color swatchbooks available for certain color models. Swatchbooks allow to view a closer representation of how color will appear when printed using the inks of an offset press.

Red, green, and blue (**RGB**) are the colors used to display color on computer monitors. Many digital cameras and scanners digitize images and save them in RGB format. This is often the color model that is used for on-line projects, including those created using QuarkImmedia. RGB can also produce the best results on a digital proofing device, but is typically not used in documents that ultimately require color separations for offset printing.

To create a color using the RGB color model, enter a percentage value in the fields for Red, Green, and Blue, or use the scroll bars adjacent to each to indicate values (Figure 7.3). You can also click in the color wheel to indicate color. The color created is displayed in the dialog box. This color is a simulation only; you can expect some variation from the color displayed on the monitor and the final printed color.

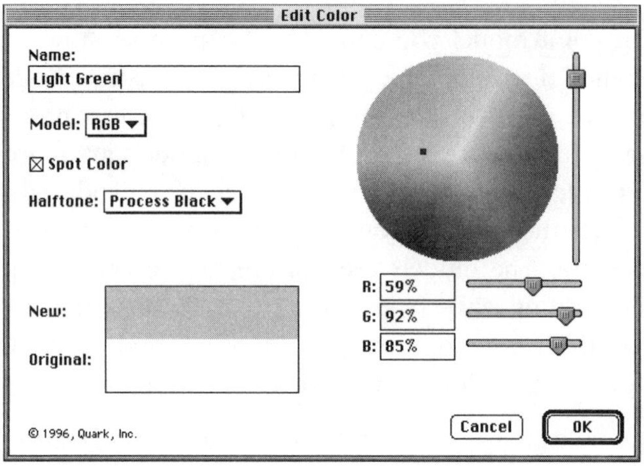

Figure 7.3 *The Edit Color dialog box when the RGB color model is selected.*

Hue, saturation, and brightness (**HSB**) is the common system for identifying the way in which artists' paints are mixed. Hue is the quality that gives a color its name, such as red, orange, yellow, green, blue, and violet. Saturation is a measure of the tint, or purity of a color. Brightness is a measure of the amount of light reflected from a color; black reflects almost no light and white reflects almost all light.

To create a color, enter a percentage value in the fields for Hue, Saturation, and Brightness, or use the scroll bars adjacent to each to indicate values. You can also click in the color wheel to indicate Hue and Saturation, and use the scroll bar to indicate Brightness. The color created is displayed in the dialog box. This color is a simulation only; you can expect some variation from the color displayed on the monitor and the final printed color.

The **LAB** color model (Figure 7.4), sometimes called the "LAB color space," is a three-dimensional model for representing colors. The LAB color model specifies colors using three coordinates: luminance (L), green-red chrominance (A), and blue-yellow chrominance (B).

To create a color using the LAB color model, enter a percentage value in the field for Luminance (L), and a numerical value, from 120 to -120 in the fields for green-red (A) and blue-yellow (B), or use the scroll bars adjacent to each to indicate values. You can also click in the color wheel to indicate color. The color created is displayed in the dialog box.

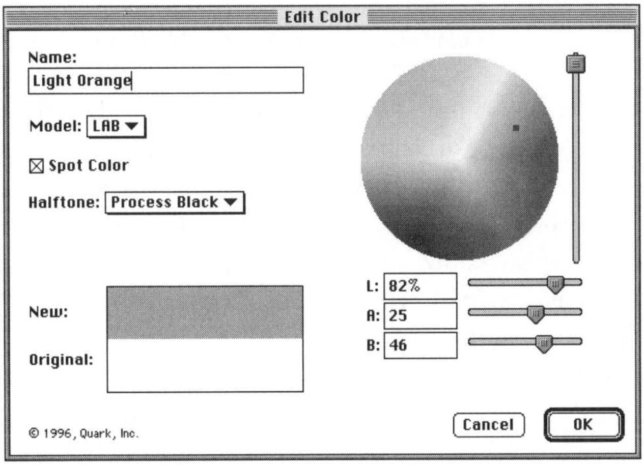

***Figure 7.4** The Edit Color dialog box when the LAB color model is selected.*

The cyan, magenta, yellow, and black (**CMYK**) color model (Figure 7.5) is one of the most common color models used with documents that will be reproduced on an offset press. When you choose the CMYK color model, QuarkXPress displays a color wheel. The wheel represents the hue and saturation, while the scroll bar represents the value, or the lightness and darkness of a color.

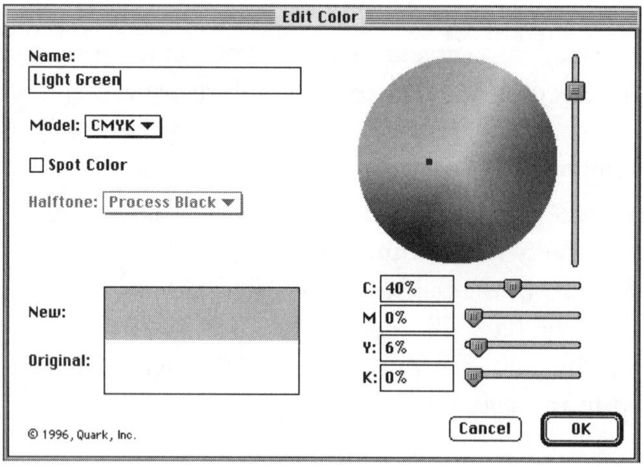

Figure 7.5 *The Edit Color dialog box when the CMYK color model is selected.*

To create a color, first type in a name. Then, specify the percentages of CMYK desired by typing a value in the field adjacent to each color, or by using the scroll bars. The color you specify is displayed in the dialog box. Bear in mind this is a simulation only. You can expect some variation from the color displayed on the monitor and the final printed color. You can specify CMYK colors to print spot color or process color separations.

Multi-Ink colors are new to QuarkXPress 4.0. This feature allows you to create a color by combining any colors in the existing color palette. One of the nice things about Multi-Ink colors is that for the first time, you can create a color that is a tint, or shade, of an existing color. With previous versions of QuarkXPress, you could, of course, specify a shade for any color applied to an item, but you had to do so on an individual basis; you could not create a color in the palette that could be applied again and again.

To create a Multi-Ink color, click on a color name in the list of colors displayed on the right side of the dialog box (Figure 7.6); this list represents all the colors created in the color palette. Next, choose a shade percentage from the pop-up menu at the top of the list. The color will be displayed in the New field of the dialog box. As is the case with other color models, remember that the screen representation is a simulation only; you can expect some variation from the color displayed on the monitor and the final printed color.

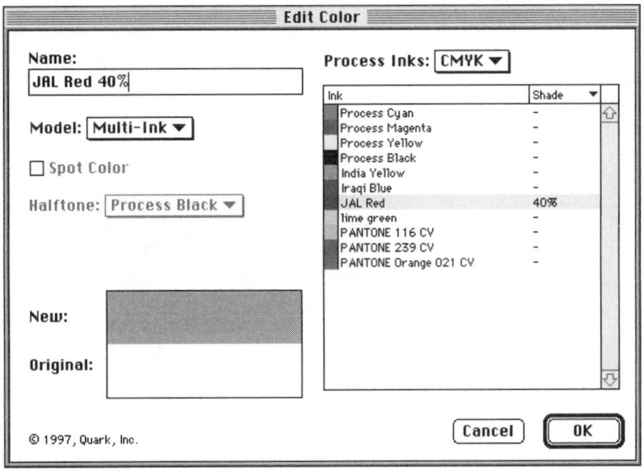

Figure 7.6 *The Edit Color dialog box for creating Multi-Ink colors.*

You can choose among four PANTONE color models: PANTONE (solid colors for printing on coated paper stock), PANTONE Uncoated, PANTONE Process (which uses the three process colors of the PANTONE Matching System with varying levels of black to produce more than 3,000 colors), or PANTONE ProSim (which simulates PANTONE colors with four-color separations for printing on coated paper stock), shown in Figure 7.7.

The PANTONE Matching System is one of the most widely used systems for identifying ink colors. The system is based on nine basic PANTONE colors plus black and white. When mixed in various percentages, these colors yield the more than 700 colors in the system. PANTONE colors are cataloged in a swatchbook; choosing a color from this system ensures accurate color reproduction on a press.

To select a color from any of these PANTONE models, first choose the model from the pop-up menu. Then, either type the model's full name in the Name area, or enter a number in the PANTONE No. area underneath the display of colors. You can also scroll through the display of colors and click on a color. The color you specify is displayed in the dialog box.

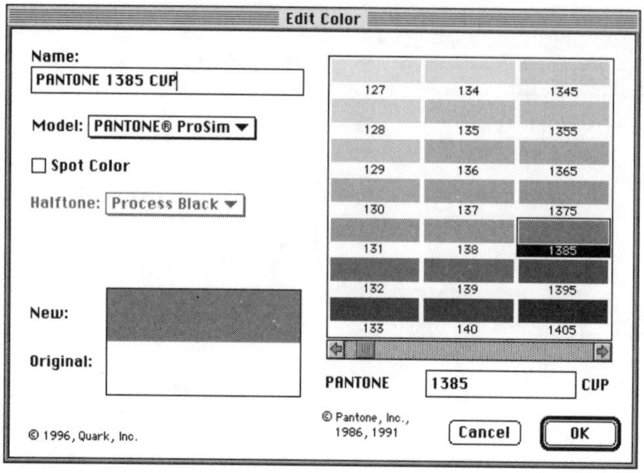

***Figure 7.7** The Edit Colors dialog box when the PANTONE ProSim color model is selected.*

The colors shown are a simulation of the PANTONE color; the "CV" behind each color name indicates that the color is a computer-video simulation of the actual PANTONE color (CVU for PANTONE Uncoated, and CVP for ProSim). Like CMYK colors, you can specify that PANTONE colors to be printed as spot colors or process colors. Greatest accuracy will be achieved if you choose a spot color separation and let your printer mix the ink according to the color shown in the PANTONE swatchbook. QuarkXPress separates the PANTONE color to its process color equivalent, but some colors may vary from the original PANTONE color when finally printed by this method.

TOYO (Figure 7.8) and DIC color models are based on inks manufactured and mostly used exclusively in Japan. TOYO colors are for inks are made by TOYO Ink Manufacturing Company. DIC inks are created by DaiNippon Ink & Chemicals Company. You can choose and apply these colors just as you would other colors.

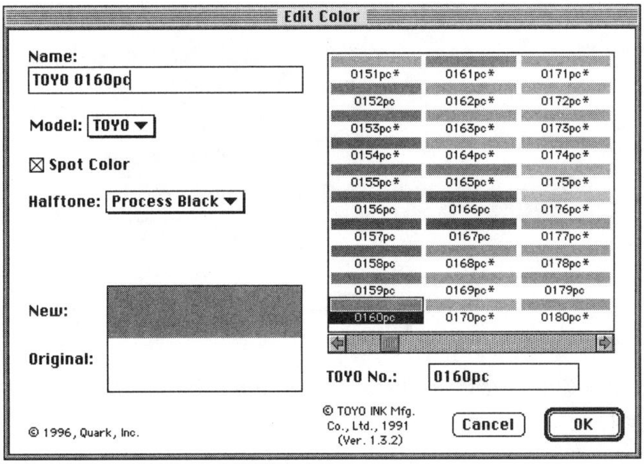

Figure 7.8 *The Edit Color dialog box when the TOYO color model is selected.*

The TRUMATCH system (Figure 7.9) was developed for achieving optimum results in printing process color separations using PostScript output devices. The TRUMATCH system is based on 50 different hues, with value graduations or tints of each color, totaling some 2,000 colors. It is essential to use the TRUMATCH swatchbook, called the TRUMATCH Colorfinder, when creating colors using this system, since your monitor can only approximate the color on the screen.

To select a color from the TRUMATCH system, either type in the full name in the Name area, or enter a number in the TRUMATCH No. area underneath the display of colors. You can also scroll through the display of colors and click on a color. Since the TRUMATCH colors were designed for process colors, be sure Spot Color is off (the automatic default) for best results.

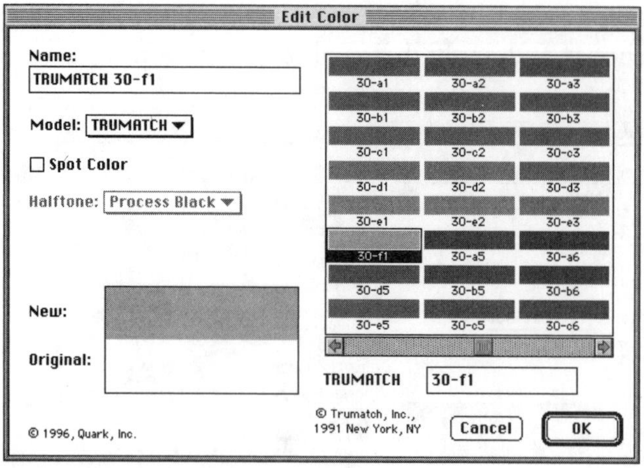

Figure 7.9 *The Edit Color dialog box when the TRUMATCH color model is selected.*

Like the TRUMATCH color system, the FOCOLTONE system (Figure 7.10) was created to facilitate the selection of accurate process colors. The basic 763 FOCOLTONE colors consist of combinations of cyan, magenta, yellow, and black in varying percentages from 5 to 85 percent, in 5 percent increments. Additionally, 13 variations on each color are created by eliminating one, two, or three of the process colors. For example, color #1000, a light brown, contains 15 percent cyan, 30 percent magenta, 50 percent yellow, and 25 percent black. Variation number 1, color #1001, contains 15 percent cyan, 30 percent magenta, 50 percent yellow, and 0 percent black.

To select a color from the FOCOLTONE system, either type the full name in the Name area, or enter a number in the FOCOLTONE No. area underneath the display of colors . You can also scroll through the display of colors and click on a color. Since the FOCOLTONE colors were designed for process colors, be sure Spot Color is off (the automatic default) for best results.

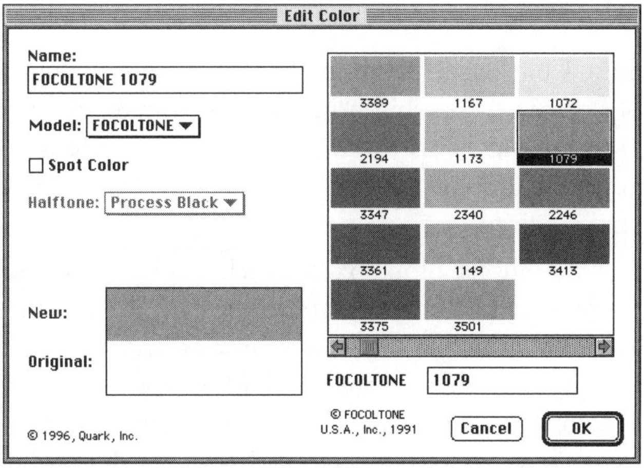

Figure 7.10 *The Edit Colors dialog box when the FOCOLTONE color model is selected.*

Hexachrome Colors, for coated and uncoated paper stock, are PANTONE's color system for specifying six-color, or high-fidelity printing (sometimes called HiFi color). The system uses CMYK plus OG (orange and green) to produce color results far richer than those possible with traditional four-color printing processes.

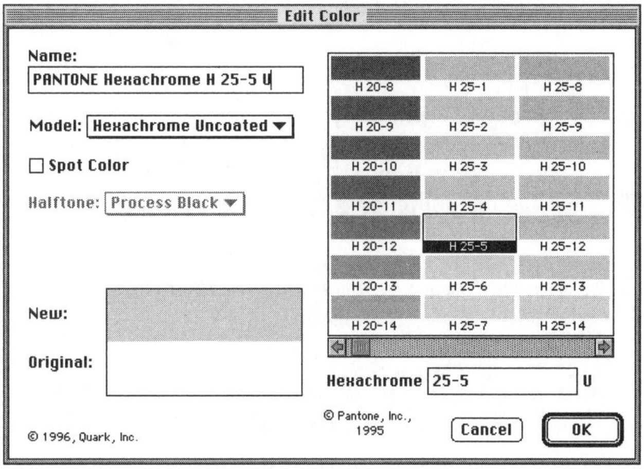

Figure 7.11 *The Edit Color dialog box when the Hexachrome Coated color model is selected.*

Spot Color

The Spot Color check box in the Edit Color dialog box affects whether or not colors will print on their own plate when printing color separations. This setting is extremely important when you are preparing a color file for offset printing, where color separations are required.

When the Spot Color box is checked, the color will print on its own plate if you specify **Separations** (in the Document tab of the Print dialog box). When **Separations** are specified for printing, Spot colors will be listed individually on the Output tab of the Print dialog box. If the Spot Color box is *not* checked, the color will be converted to its CMYK equivalent when printing separation. See Chapter 13, "Printing Color Separations," for more information.

Halftone

The halftone setting determines the angle at which a spot color will print. The default setting is Black, which will cause the spot color to print at a 45° angle. You can change the angle by choosing another separation color from the pop-up menu—cyan (105°), magenta (75°), or yellow (90°).

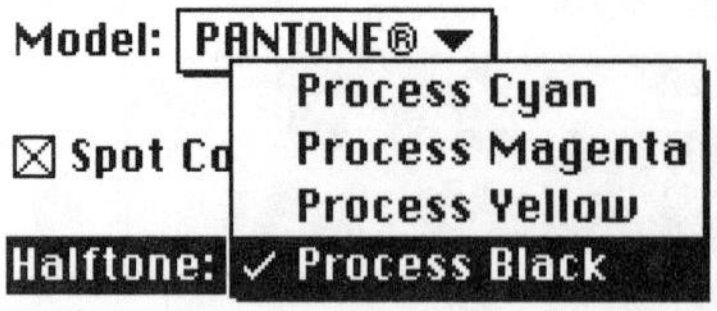

Figure 7.12 The Halftone pop-up menu in the Edit Color dialog box is only available when Spot Color is checked.

You usually don't need to change the default setting, unless you are printing two spot colors that will overlap each other. If your design requires two or more spot colors to overlap, or includes a duotone, tritone, or quadtone, each color spot color should be set to a different angle.

This setting does not apply to, and is not available for, colors that are specified to be converted to process colors (Spot Color off).

Editing Registration "Color"

Registration is a special color for use with documents that will be printed for color separations. The color Registration has the unique characteristic that items to which it has been applied will print on every plate when separations are printed (by selecting the **Separations** option in the Document tab of the Print dialog box). You can use QuarkXPress's Line tool to draw your own cut or fold marks, for example, and apply the color Registration to them so they will print on every plate.

The only edit you can make to Registration color is to change the way it displays on-screen. Normally the color displays as black, but you can change it to any RGB color. When you edit registration, the name and color model pop-up menu are grayed out, since you can't change either. The only active part of the dialog box are the slider bars for adjusting the RGB values.

Duplicating Colors

If you want to make a new color that is a derivative of, or is similar to, another color, click the **Duplicate** button at the bottom of the Colors dialog box. Select the color you wish to copy, then click **Duplicate**. The Edit Color dialog box will display, with all the specifications of the color you're copying, but with the name *<color name> copy* in the name field. You can then change the name and any of the other specifications in the dialog box to create a new color.

Deleting Colors

Select a color on the list in the Colors dialog box and click **Delete** to remove a color from the palette. Keep in mind you cannot edit or delete colors necessary for printing color separations, namely cyan, magenta, yellow, black, white, or registration.

When you click the **Delete** button, a dialog box (Figure 7.13) is displayed with a pop-up menu listing all the colors in the palette, which allows you to change the items to which that color has been applied to any other color in the palette. Simply choose the replacement color from the pop-up menu. Any items to which the deleted color has been applied will change to the new color you've assigned.

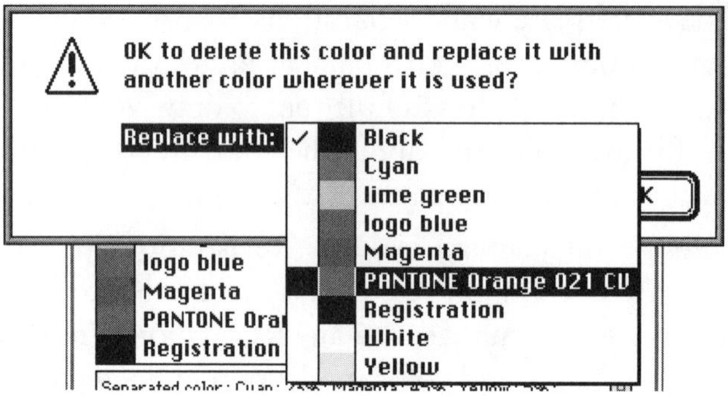

Figure 7.13 *In deleting a color, you can replace it with another color; all items with the deleted color applied will change to the new replacement color.*

Appending Colors

It's pretty easy to copy colors that you create in one QuarkXPress document to another, using the Append command. You can access this command in a couple of ways. The Append Colors dialog box (Figure 7.14) can be accessed by choosing **Edit → Colors** and then clicking the **Append** button at the bottom of the Colors list. You can also choose the **File → Append** command and click on the **Colors** tab of the Append To dialog box. The new colors will be added to Color list in the current document, or the default list that all documents will share (if you use the command when no document is open).

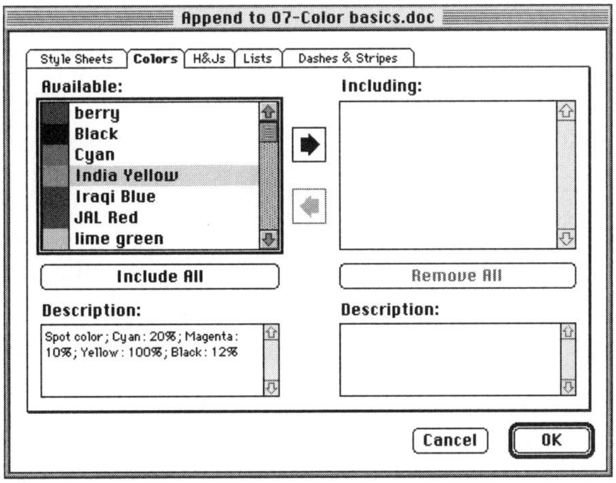

Figure 7.14 *The Append Colors dialog box.*

The next steps discuss the various options available as you use the command:

1. Access the Append Colors dialog by either method:
   - choose **Edit ➛ Colors**, then click on the **Append** button in the Edit colors dialog box, or
   - choose **File ➛ Append**, then click on the **Colors** tab.
2. QuarkXPress displays a dialog box through which you can select the document or template containing the colors you want to append to the color palette in the current document—you can change drives or folders as you would in other dialog boxes. Choose a document by double-clicking on the name.
3. Once you've selected a document, the Append Colors dialog box is displayed—or, if you used the **File ➛ Append** command, click on the **Colors** tab of the Append dialog box.
4. On the left side of the Append Colors dialog box, a list of the colors in the document from which you are appending colors is displayed. You have several options for choosing the colors in the list you wish to append to your current document:

- Click on one color name in the Available list to view the specifications in the description area. If this is the color you want to append, click the right-pointing arrow to copy it to the Including list.
- Click the **Include All** button to automatically append all of the colors.
- If you want to include most, but not all, of the colors, click **Include All** and then select a name you do not want to include from the list on the right and click the left-pointing arrow to remove it from the Including list.

TIP: You can select all the Available Colors by clicking the **Include All** button. You can select a group of colors in the list by holding down the **Shift** key as you click. To select noncontiguous color names, hold down the **⌘/Ctrl** key as you click.

5. Once the list of colors you wish to include is complete (Figure 7.15), click **OK** to close the dialog box and append the list of colors.

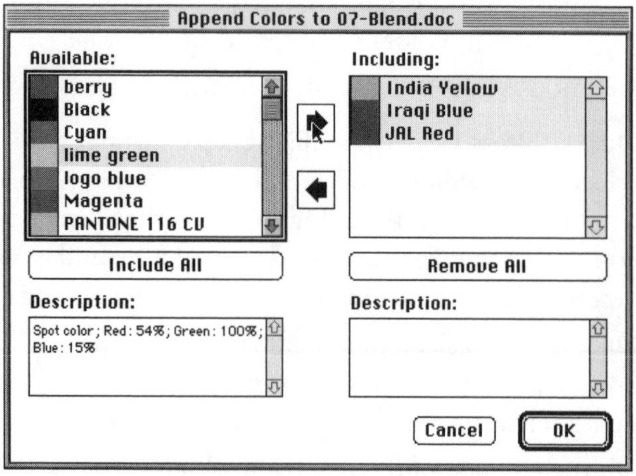

Figure 7.15 *You can pick and choose which colors you wish to append from a file, without having to append every available color.*

Resolving Append Conflicts

If there are colors in the file from which you're appending that have the same name as, but different specifications from, the colors in the existing document's palette, the **Append Conflict** dialog box will display (Figure 7.16). This dialog box displays the name of the conflicting color, along with the definition of the color in the *existing* document (the current document *to* which you're appending colors) and the definition of the color in the new document (the document *from* which you're appending colors). It's important to understand which document Existing and New refers to when you use this dialog box.

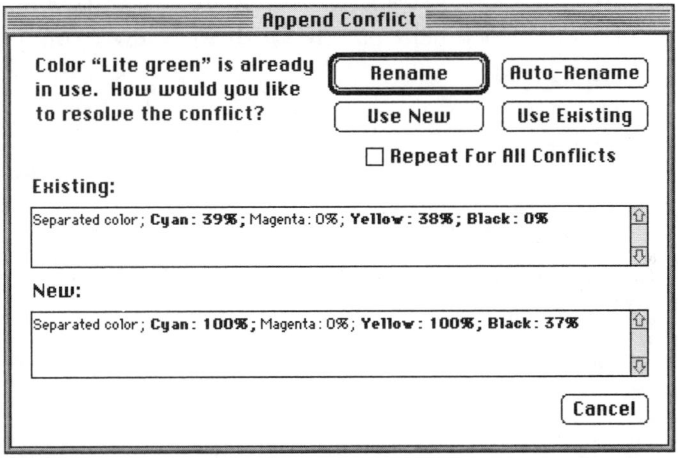

Figure 7.16 *The Append Conflict dialog box.*

There are four different ways to resolve the name conflict:

- **Rename** allows you to give an entirely different name to the color in the New document, by displaying the Rename dialog box (Figure 7.17). You can now modify the name. Click **OK**, and the new color will be imported with the name entered.

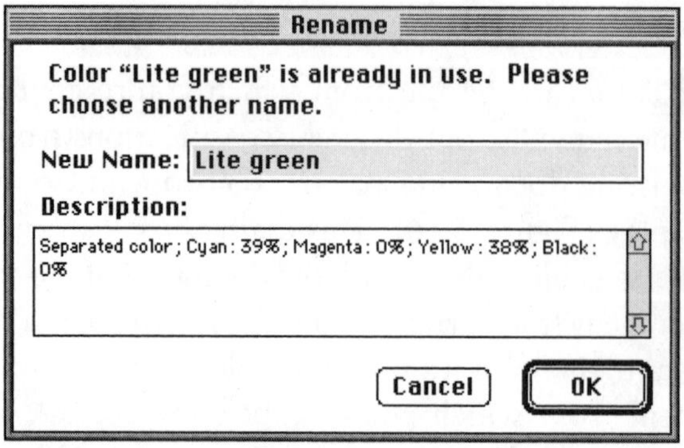

Figure 7.17 *The Rename dialog box.*

- **Auto-Rename** causes the conflicting color to be added to the Existing document palette, with the New name preceded by an asterisk (Figure 7.18). The asterisk causes all colors renamed to display at the top of the color list in the new document.

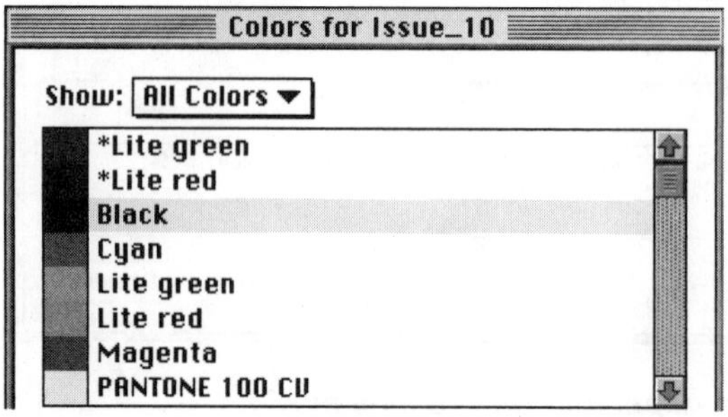

Figure 7.18 *Auto-Rename imports the color and precedes the name with an asterisk, causing the name to appear at the top of the Colors List.*

- Click **Use New** to replace the existing document's color definitions with the new, appended specifications. If you select this option, items to which this color has been applied in the existing document will change to reflect the new definition of the color.

- Click **Use Existing** to keep the specification as defined in the target document. Items to which the color has been applied will remain unchanged.

Regardless of which method you select to resolve conflicts, QuarkXPress will resolve all name conflicts the same way if you turn **Repeat for All Conflicts** on by clicking the checkbox.

Adding Colors from Imported Graphics

Certain colors used in EPS graphics are automatically added to the Colors palette in QuarkXPress when you import the graphic, including those from Adobe Illustrator, FreeHand or CorelDRAW. Different programs designate these colors in different ways, but generally a color that has been named as a spot color in a graphics program will be imported into the QuarkXPress color palette.

For example, a color applied in a graphics program by simply choosing a color from the C-M-Y-K slider bars will not be added to the QuarkXPress color palette, but any color defined as a spot color will be added to the palette, when a graphic with that color applied is imported. Colors imported with EPS graphics will be specified with Spot Color turned on.

Applying Colors and Blends

You can apply color to items using any one of two or three techniques. There isn't a right or wrong way to apply color—the technique you use will depend on the situation. Color and shade are the only attributes you can apply to any and every QuarkXPress item. Figure 7.19 shows the various commands available for applying color to each type of QuarkXPress item.

Item	Style ➛	Item ➛ Modify	Color Palette
Text	Color	—	
Picture	Color	Picture tab	
Box	—	Box tab	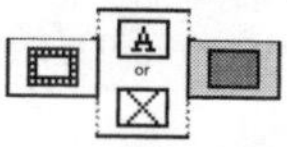
Frame	—	Frame tab	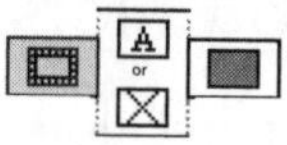
Gap	—	Frame tab	—
Line	Color	Line tab	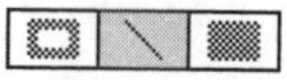
Gap	—	Line tab	—
Text-Path Text (tool)	Color	—	
Text-Path Line (tool)	Color	Line tab	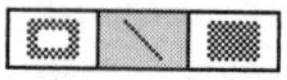
Gap	—	Line tab	—
Paragraph Rule	Rules	—	—
Gap	—	—	—

Figure 7.19 *Color and shade can be applied to all QuarkXPress items.*

Certainly if you frequently work with color, applying color via the Colors Palette is the probably the most convenient method. However, you may just as easily use the **Style ➛ Color** command or the **Item ➛ Modify** command (depending on the type of item to which you wish to apply color).

In every case, you can also indicate the shade of the color. Shade values are displayed in 10% increment pop-up menus, or you can input any value from 0% to 100% in 1% increments. If you're applying color using the Style menu, shade values can be chosen from the **Style ➛ Shade** pop-up menu. The Modify dialog box lists shade values on a pop-up menu underneath the color pop-up menu. The Colors palette lets you apply shade values using a pop-up menu to the right of icons at the top of the palette.

Applying Color to Text

To apply a color to text, whether the text is in a text box, or on a text-path, highlight the appropriate text, then select the desired color from:

- the **Style ➛ Color** submenu, or
- the Color pop-up menu in the Character Attributes dialog box (**Style ➛ Character Attributes**), or
- the Colors Palette—be sure the text icon (🄰) or the text-path icon (A̲)is selected before you click on a color name in the list, as shown in Figure 7.20 .

Figure 7.20 *To apply color to text using the Colors palette, click on the appropriate icon for text in a box (left) or text on a path (right).*

Once you choose a color using any of these methods, the highlighted text will change to the new color.

Applying Color to Pictures

Only certain types of pictures can have color applied to them, namely grayscale or black-and-white TIFFs, bitmaps, or PICT files. You cannot apply color to color TIFFs, PICTs, or any EPS images. To apply a color to a picture, first select the picture with the Item tool (✥) or the Content tool (☞), then select the desired color from:

- the **Style ➛ Color** submenu, or
- the Color pop-up menu in the Picture tab of the Modify dialog box (**Item ➛ Modify**), or
- the Colors Palette (**View ➛ Show Colors**)—be sure the picture icon is selected (☒).

The color and shade that you apply to an imported picture using the **Style ➛ Color** submenu or the Colors palette affect all areas of the image that would otherwise print as black or a shade of gray; other areas are not affected (Figure 7.21).

Figure 7.21 *Color applied to pictures affects only those areas that would print as black or a shade or gray; other areas remain unaffected.*

Applying Color and Blends to Box Backgrounds

You can specify color for a box background, separately from its contents. You can apply either a solid color, or a two-color blend to boxes. To apply color to a box, first select the box(es) to which you wish to apply the color, then select the color:

- from the Colors pop-up menu in Box tab of the **Item ➛ Modify** command, or
- using the Colors palette (**View ➛ Show Colors**)— be sure the box icon (□) is selected, or
- by dragging a color swatch from the Colors palette, as shown in Figure 7.22 (see tip below).

TIP

You can apply a solid color to a box, line or frame by dragging a color swatch from the Colors palette. To do this, first display the Colors palette (**View ➛ Show Colors**) and activate it by selecting *any* item—it doesn't need to be the one you want to change. Then position the pointer over one of the color swatches that appear to the left of each color name, and drag the swatch onto the document page. As you drag the swatch over items on the page, they will take on the color of the swatch, then return to their former color if you keep dragging. Release the mouse button when the item you wish to change shows the new color.

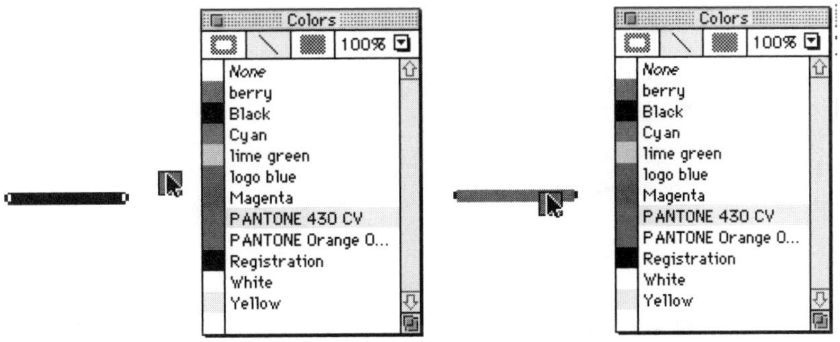

Figure 7.22 *You can apply color to the background of an active box, line or frame by dragging a color swatch from the Colors palette.*

Once you choose a color using either of these methods, the selected box will change to the new color. When you apply color to a box, the box background appears behind text and in the non-black areas of an imported bitmap or TIFF image. (Background color does not show through color TIFF or EPS images.)

Applying Two-Color Blends

QuarkXPress allows you to apply simple two-color blends to box backgrounds by using options in the Box tab of Modify dialog box or by using the Colors palette.

Using either command, you make the following specifications for blends:

- the two colors and shade you wish to blend,
- the style of blend, and
- the angle of the blend.

There are six different styles of blends. Figure 7.23 shows how these styles appear in a rectangular box.

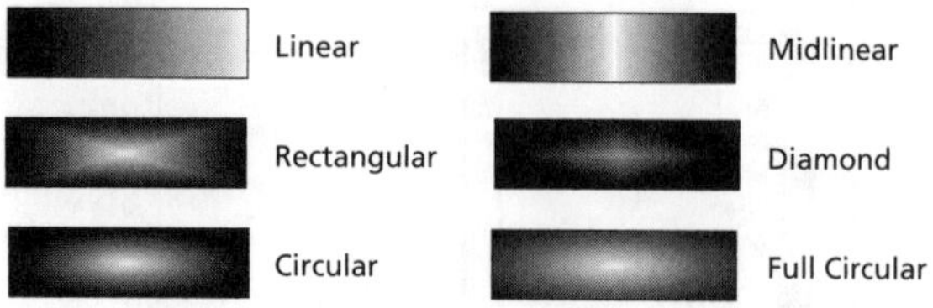

Figure 7.23 *Six different blend styles may be applied to boxes.*

You can specify the angle of the blend by entering either a positive or negative value from 0° to 360°. Figure 7.24 shows the affect of different degrees of rotation on a linear blend.

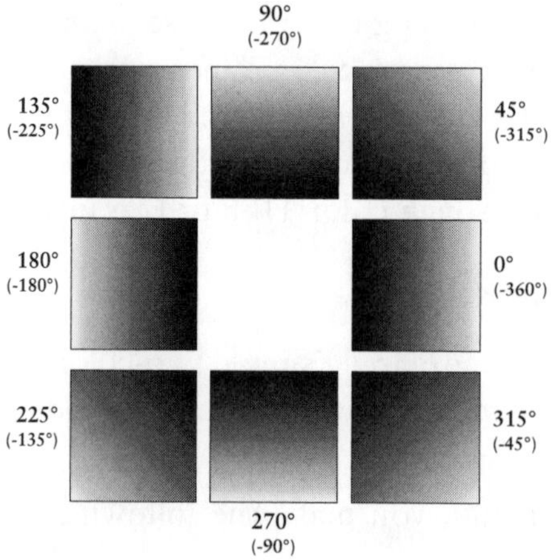

Figure 7.24 *The angle of a blend may be specified in degrees, from 0 to 360.*

To apply a blend using the Box tab of the Modify dialog box (Figure 7.25):

1. Choose the first color using the **Color** and **Shade** pop-up menus in the **Box** section of the dialog box.
2. Choose the second color from the pop-up menu in the **Blend** section of the dialog box.
3. Choose the type of blend from the **Style** pop-up menu, and enter the angle of the blend.

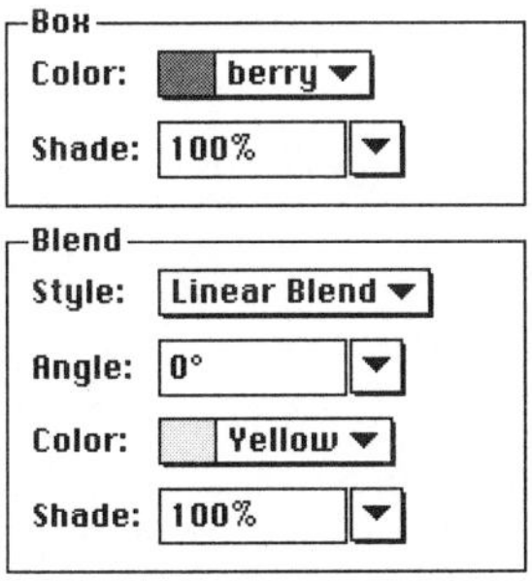

Figure 7.25 *Blends can be applied to boxes in the Box tab of the Modify dialog box.*

To use the Colors palette to apply a blend:

1. With a picture or text box active, select the background icon in the Colors palette and choose the style of blend you wish to use from the pop-up menu (Figure 7.26).

Figure 7.26 *Select the blend style from the pop-up menu in the Colors palette.*

2. Make sure the button for color **#1** is selected, and then choose the color and shade for the first color of the blend.
3. Click on the button for color **#2** and choose the color and shade of the second color (Figure 7.27). You can select two different colors to blend, or you can specify different shades of the same color.

4. Specify the angle of the blend (see Figure 7.24 for different blend angles).

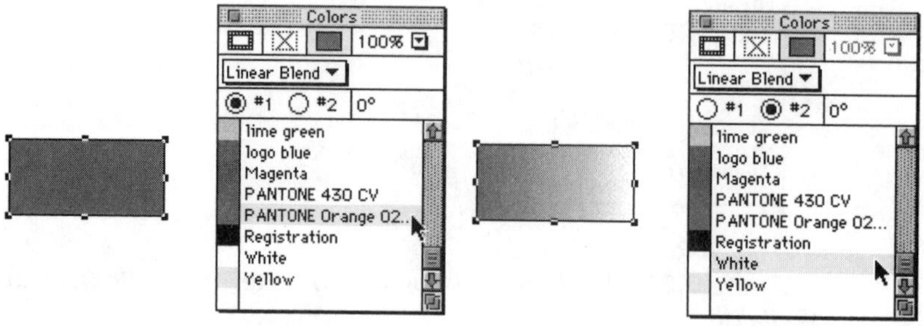

Figure 7.27 *Use the Colors palette to apply two-color blends to box backgrounds; select the color and shade of color #1 (left), then select the color and shade of color #2 (right).*

Applying Color to Lines, Frames, and Rules

Lines (including text-paths), frames and paragraph rules all share certain characteristics when it comes to applying color. Even though color is applied to each of these items using different dialog boxes, they are all specified using styles from those created using **Edit ➤ Lines & Dashes**. Table 7.1 shows the common specifications for lines, text-path lines, frames, and paragraph rules.

Table 7.1 *Common Specifications for Lines, Frames, Text-Paths, and Rules.*

Element	Line	Text-path Line	Frame	Paragraph Rule
Style (Dashes & Stripes)	✓	✓	✓	✓
Width	✓	✓	✓	✓
Color and Shade	✓	✓	✓	✓
Gap Color and Shade	✓	✓	✓	
Arrowheads	✓	✓		
Mode	✓	✓		

To apply color to a line, or the line of a text-path, first select the line, then select the desired color from:

- the **Style ➛ Color** submenu, or
- the Color pop-up menu in the Line tab of the Modify dialog box (**Item ➛ Modify**), or
- the Colors Palette (**View ➛ Show Colors**)—be sure the line icon is selected (⧅) first, or
- drag a color swatch from the Colors palette over the line until it changes color. (You do not have to select the line first.)

TIP Remember, to select the line of a text-path, you must use the Item (✥) tool; if you select a text-path with the Content tool (☞), the text, not the line, is selected.

To apply color to the frame around a box, first select the box, then select the desired color from:

- the Color pop-up menu in the Frame tab of the Modify dialog box (**Item ➛ Modify**), as shown in Figure 7.28, or
- the Colors Palette (**View ➛ Show Colors**)—be sure the frame icon (▭) is selected before you click on a color name in the list, or
- drag a color swatch from the Colors palette over the frame until it changes color.

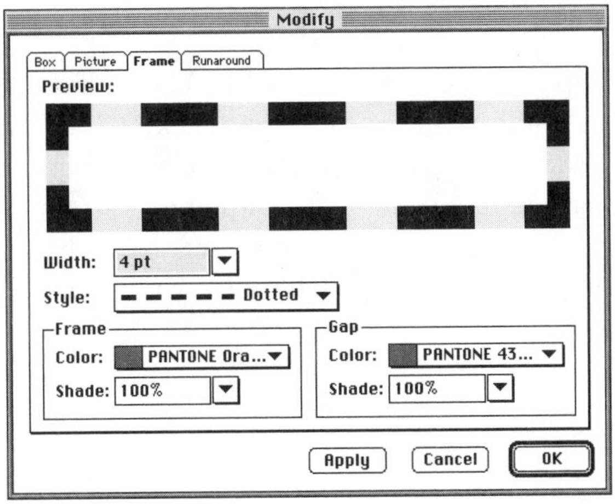

***Figure 7.28** You can apply color to the frame around an active box through the Frame tab of the Modify dialog box **(Item ➛ Modify)**.*

To apply a color to a paragraph rule, use the Color and Shade pop-up menus in the Rules tab of the Paragraph Attributes dialog box (**Style ➛ Rules**), as shown in Figure 7.29. You can apply any dash or stripe style to a paragraph rule, but you cannot apply color to gaps.

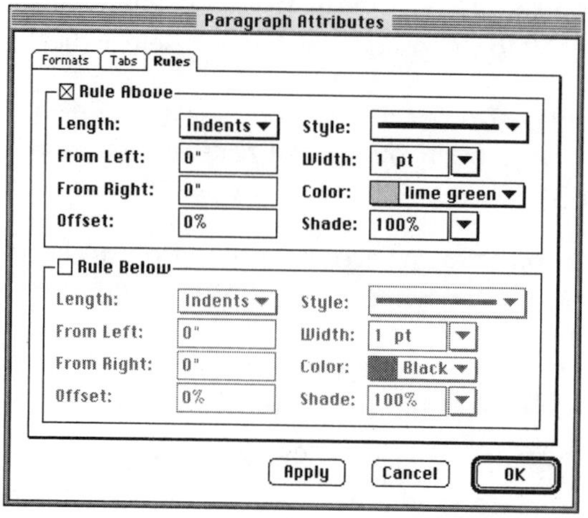

Figure 7.29 *The Rules tab of the Paragraph Attributes dialog box lets you specify the color and shade of paragraph rules.*

The Edit Trap Dialog Box

The Edit Trap dialog box is accessed by choosing **Edit ➛ Colors**, clicking on a color in the list, and then clicking the **Edit Trap** button. This allows you to specify trapping relationships between colors in a QuarkXPress document. Trapping controls the way two colors print when they are adjacent to each other, by overprinting, knocking out, or overlapping slightly (spreading or choking).

You can also change the Automatic trapping value used by QuarkXPress in the Trapping tab of the Document Preferences dialog box (**Edit → Preferences → Document**), or you can specify trapping on an item-by-item basis using the Trap Information palette (**View → Show Trap Information**). Each of these methods is discussed in detail in Chapter 13, "Printing Color Separations."

Summary

This chapter covered all the basic information you need for creating and applying color in QuarkXPress. If you are creating files for printing in color on an offset press, you'll want to take a look at Chapter 13, "Printing Color Separations." The next chapter discusses basic printing issues.

8 PRINTING BASICS

There's a lot of hype around publishing online, and while there's a genuine paperless industry growing, largely due to the World Wide Web, as of this writing, most pages created in QuarkXPress still end up being printed at one time or another—often for reproduction on an offset press. For most QuarkXPress documents, printing is still the "bottom line."

With QuarkXPress, you may only need to print your documents to a 300-dpi black-and-white laser printer, or you may work with a service bureau, where *printing* means producing high-resolution color separations on film or in digital formats that can image files directly to plate or film.

This chapter explains the basics of printing with QuarkXPress 4.0. Chapter 13, "Printing Color Separations," is intended as a guide for those working with service bureaus and printers to produce high-end output. If you're familiar with previous versions of QuarkXPress, you'll want to skim this chapter to understand the new organization of the Print dialog box, along with new printing features that have been included in version 4.0.

Printing Devices

There are many different printers in use, and you may print your QuarkXPress documents to a $300 laser printer or a $3,000,000 PostScript plate-making device. It's the ability to print to such a wide variety of printing devices that has helped make QuarkXPress ubiquitous in the publishing world.

The leading industry standard for output devices is PostScript. *PostScript* is the language spoken by both printing devices and the software programs that have to "talk" to them. Most printers ship with software, called a PostScript Printer Description (PPD) file. This helps QuarkXPress and other applications understand all the characteristics of a particular printer.

Regardless of whether you have a simple black-and-white printer, a digital color proofing device, or a high-resolution imagesetter, the PostScript Printer Description (PPD) files are important in determining your success in printing.

The selected PPD determines many of the settings available in the Print dialog box, including resolution, paper size, and even whether or not **Print Colors as Grays** or **Print Color Composite** are available. It's important to choose the right PPD for the printer you're using. It's the first step to success in printing your QuarkXPress documents.

Using The Print Command

The commands for printing in QuarkXPress benefit greatly from the new tabbed dialog box interface in 4.0, since printing a document in previous versions always seemed to require both the Page Setup and Print commands. Now options found in these two previously separate dialog boxes are combined under various tabs in one location. Further, many of the features previously found in the XTension QuarkPrint, sold separately by Quark, Inc., are now incorporated into the application.

The Print dialog box (Figure 8.1) is accessed using the **File ➛ Print** command (⌘-P/CTRL-P). The Print dialog box is divided into two areas:

- The middle section of the dialog box, which contains five tabs: **Document, Setup, Output, Options**, and **Preview,** discussed after the next section
- The top and bottom of the dialog box, which contain options that are always available regardless of which tab is selected. These options are discussed next.

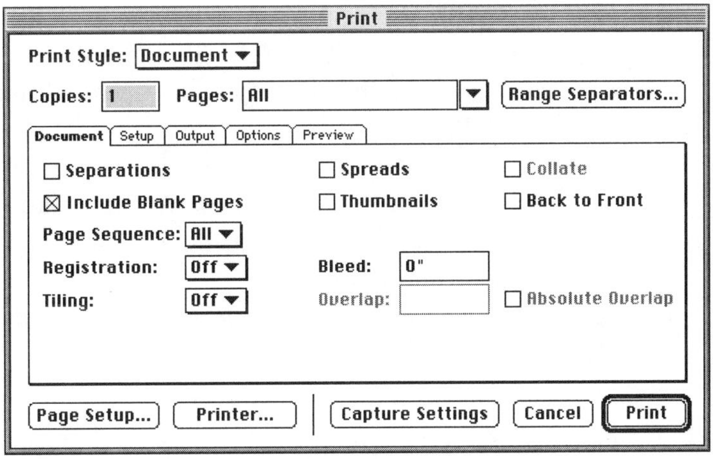

Figure 8.1 *The Print dialog box.*

The **Print Style** pop-up menu (Figure 8.2) contains a list of all the Print Styles you've created. Print Styles, which capture multiple settings in the Print dialog box under one name, or style, are created using the **Edit ➛ Print Styles** command. Print Styles are discussed later in this chapter.

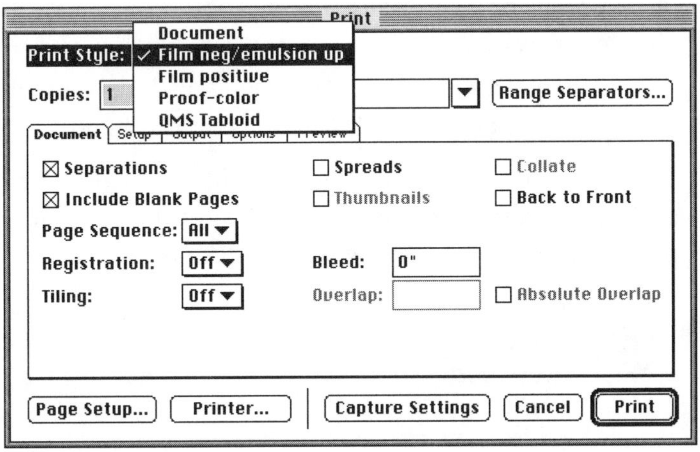

Figure 8.2 *Choose a Print Style and the settings in the Print dialog box will change to those you've defined as part of the Print Style.*

Select a Print Style from the menu, and all the settings in the Print dialog box will change to those defined in the Print Style. If you choose a Print Style and then change some of the settings, a bullet will precede the Print Style name display. The default setting on the pop-up menu, *Default*, means that no Print Style is chosen. You can completely ignore Print Styles altogether, and set up the Print dialog box differently for each document—but if you find yourself setting the same options over and over, using the Print Styles command can save a lot of time and help eliminate the mistake of missing or making wrong settings!

You can specify the number of **Copies** that you want to print of each page, as well as the range of **Pages.** There's a lot of flexibility in the range of pages you can specify to print. Options include:

- All pages (the default). You can type in the word **all** or choose it from the pop-up menu adjacent to the Pages field
- A range of continuous pages, separated by a hyphen (such as **10-23**)
- A range of noncontinuous pages, separated by commas (such as **2,4,6,8**)
- A range of continuous and noncontinuous pages, separated by hyphens or commas as appropriate (such as **2,4,6-10,12-13**)
- A range from any page to the end of the document, by typing the word **end** as the last page (such as **9-end**)

The page range option is useful when you make changes that affect just a few pages, or when you want to print only the finished parts of a document that is still in process.

TIP

For any page number entry, you can enter a user-defined page number, or you can enter the "absolute" location within the active document by preceding the number with a plus sign (+). In specifying a user-defined page number, you must include any prefix that has been assigned as part of the page number through the **Page ➛ Section** command. An absolute page sequence number represents a page's sequential location in a document, regardless of the automatic page numbers.

If you are working with a document that has a Prefix defined as part of the page number, such as A-1, A-2, etc., it will be necessary to change the **Range Separators** that indicate specifically which character separates a page range. (In this example, you'd have to input **A-1-A-2**, and QuarkXPress has no way to understand which hyphen is part of a page prefix, and which hyphen is the range separator.) Click on the **Range Separators** button to display the dialog box (Figure 8.3) and change the default entries (a hyphen for continuous page range or a comma for noncontinuous pages) to some other character.

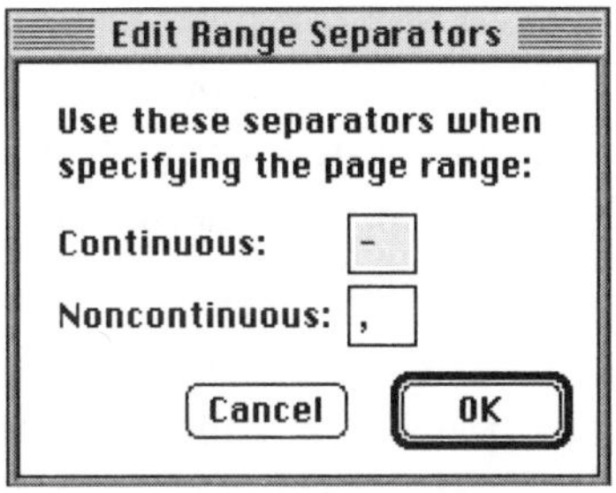

***Figure 8.3** The Range Separators dialog box.*

The **Page Setup** and **Printer** buttons let you access the page Setup dialog box and the Printer dialog box, respectively, for the printer driver that is selected in the Setup tab of the Print dialog box.

Capture Settings saves the settings in the Print dialog box with the document and closes the Print dialog box. The next time you use the **File ➛ Print** command, those settings will be displayed. If you just click **Cancel,** the settings will not be saved.

Document Tab

The Document tab of the Print dialog box (Figure 8.4) contains options available in the **File ➛ Print** command in previous versions of QuarkXPress.

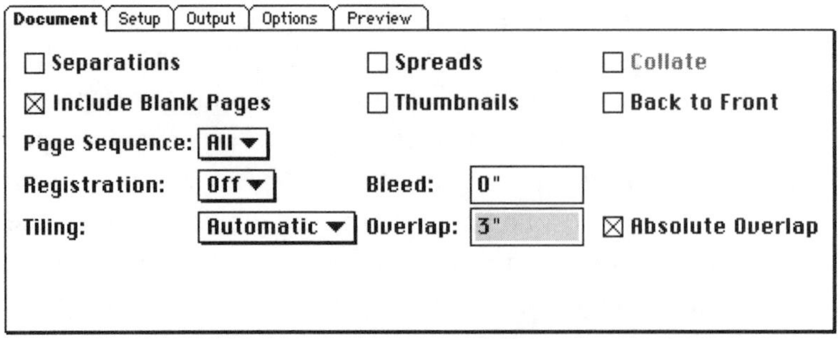

Figure 8.4 The Document Tab of the Print dialog box.

If you select **Separations**, QuarkXPress prints color separations of your document. Each spot color or process color component will print on its own plate, as specified in the Output tab of the Print dialog box. This option is described in more detail in Chapter 13, "Printing Color Separations."

Include Blank Pages gives you the option of printing the blank pages in a document. A blank page is a page that contains no printable items. Empty, unframed boxes and items to which Suppress Printout (in the Box tab or, for pictures, the Picture tab under **Item** ➛ **Modify**) has been applied are considered nonprinting items. If there are master page items on the page—folios, for example—but nothing else, it is not considered a blank page. When Blank Pages is unchecked, blank pages in the document are not printed.

If you click **Spreads**, facing pages or pages arranged as horizontal spreads print contiguously (if the paper size can accommodate this)—side by side with no break between pages. Make sure pages are oriented correctly to accomodate printing on the paper or other media you've selected.

QuarkXPress allows you to print **Thumbnails**, in which each page is printed in miniature, with several pages on a sheet of paper. You can make Thumbnails larger or smaller, thus allowing more or fewer thumbnails per page, by entering a value in the **Reduce or Enlarge** field of the Page Setup dialog box.

If you are printing multiple copies to a laser printer or any other page-fed printing device, you can choose **Collate** to print one complete set of pages at a time. This feature saves you the time it would take to sort the copies manually, but it often requires significantly longer printing time than when printing multiple copies of a document not collated. When copies are not collated, the printer processes each page only once and prints multiple copies immediately from the same page image. For collated copies, the printer must process each page for each copy; in other words, the page image is reprocessed for each sheet of paper printed.

Also on laser and other sheet-fed printers, you can print pages **Back to Front** (that is, in reverse order), which has the effect that the last page of your document is printed first, and the first page of the document is printed last.

Page Sequence lets you print all pages, or only the odd pages or the even pages in a document. These options enable you to print two-sided copies directly on the printer, by printing all the odd-numbered pages first, putting them back in the paper feed tray, and printing all the even pages. These options are also useful when you are preparing a two-sided manuscript to be reproduced on the type of copier that prompts you to insert all odd or even pages first.

You can select the **Registration Marks** feature to automatically generate *crop marks,* the marks traditionally used to indicate where the pages would be cut when trimmed to their final size, and *registration marks* for color separations. This option works best when you are printing on a paper size at least one inch taller and wider than the page size specified for the document. You can also use this option when you are printing a reduced page size using the Scaling factor described later under this heading.

The registration marks can be **Centered** between the cut marks on each side of the document or printed **Off Center** so that the bottom and left registration marks are slightly off center, as shown in Figure 8.5.

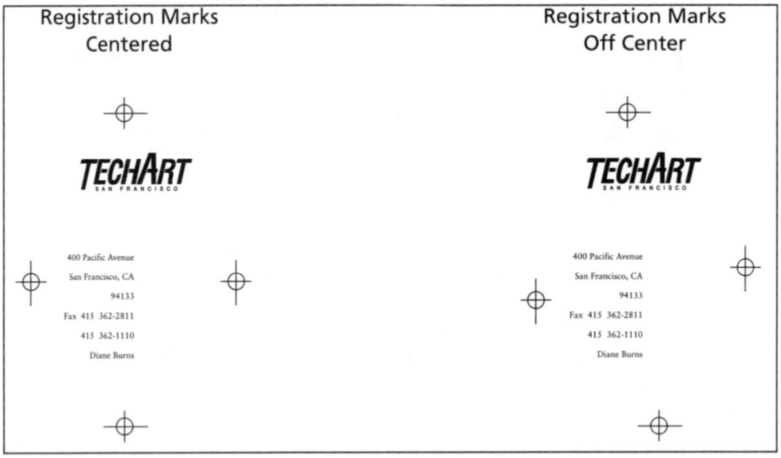

Figure 8.5 *A page printed with registration marks centered and off center.*

The **Tiling** options in the Print dialog box (Figure 8.6) let you print large pages to a printer with smaller paper, by printing each page in sections.

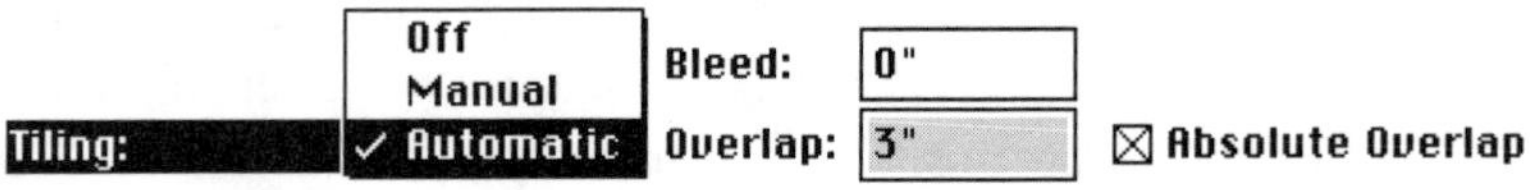

Figure 8.6 *The Tiling options in the Print dialog box.*

When you select **Manual Tiling**, you control the placement of the upper left corner of each document tile by relocating zero point on the ruler. You must move the zero point on the ruler to each new tile location. (Move the zero point by clicking and dragging the icon at the intersection of the ruler in the upper left corner of the document window.) Since moving the zero point on one page effectively moves it for all pages, you can print the currently specified tile for all pages in the document at once. Using the Manual tiling option is a lot more work than using the Automatic tiling option, but it does offer precise control of what area of the document page will print on each tile. For example, if you are printing tabloid magazine pages on letter-size paper, you can manually position the tiles to fall between columns rather than in the middle of the text areas.

When you select **Automatic Tiling** and specify the amount of **Overlap** you want between tiles, QuarkXPress automatically divides the page into the number of tiles needed to print given the size of the page, the size of the paper, and the amount of overlap specified. QuarkXPress prints the tiles at the top of the page first, from left to right, and works down the page.

To help assemble tiles that are printed with the Auto tiling option, QuarkXPress prints tile location information in the upper left corner of each tile, in the format "Page x (y, z)" where *x* is the page number, *y* is the column number, and *z* is the row number (Figure 8.7). QuarkXPress prints tick marks where each tile can be cut or trimmed for alignment, but if you have allowed overlap you might choose to trim tiles along column gutters or some other natural feature of the page. You do not get tick marks or tile location information when you select Manual Tiling.

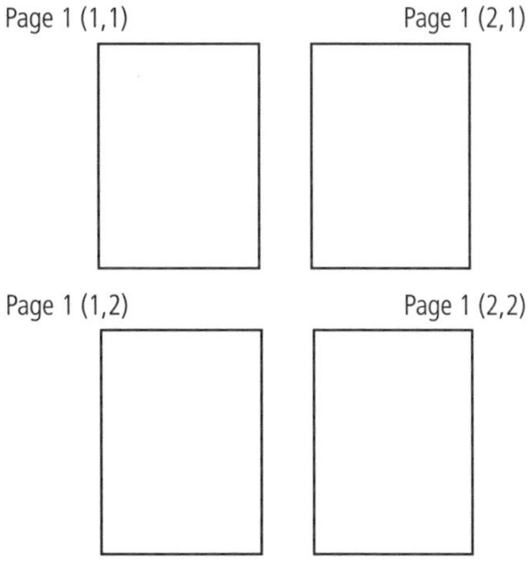

Figure 8.7 *QuarkXPress prints tile location information in the upper left corner of each tile sheet, helpful for fitting the tiles onto one page.*

Whether you select **Auto** or **Manual Tiling**, you generally need some overlap in order to achieve precise alignment between adjacent tiles when you paste them together. At minimum, the overlap needs to account for the nonprinting edges of the paper (that is, at least .5 inches on a most laser printers, or at least .25 inches if you select **Larger Print Area** through the Print dialog box's Options for laser printers).

Figure 8.8 Newspaper page printed in four tiles on 8.5 by 11-inch paper, with overlap between pages (left), then assembled into full-page layout (right).

The **Bleed** option, new to version 4.0, lets you specify how far past the edge of a page items that overlap the page edge will image, or bleed. Most printing presses require that where ink must print up to the edge of a page, the page actually must be designed to allow for ink to print *past* the final trim location, creating a bleed. If you have drawn a box that extends past the edge of the page about a half inch, for example, but your printer only requires a 1/4" bleed, you can enter **.25"** in the Bleed option, and only 1/4" will print when the page is output to film or other media. Trim marks are printed the additional distance specified from the edge of the page. This is a nice way to "neaten" your output, as it evens out all the edges of items along the edge of the page.

Setup Tab

The Setup Tab of the Print dialog box (Figure 8.9) contains most of the options that were formerly available in the Page Setup dialog box, along with two new options that allow you control in positioning a page on a sheet of paper and the print area of film media.

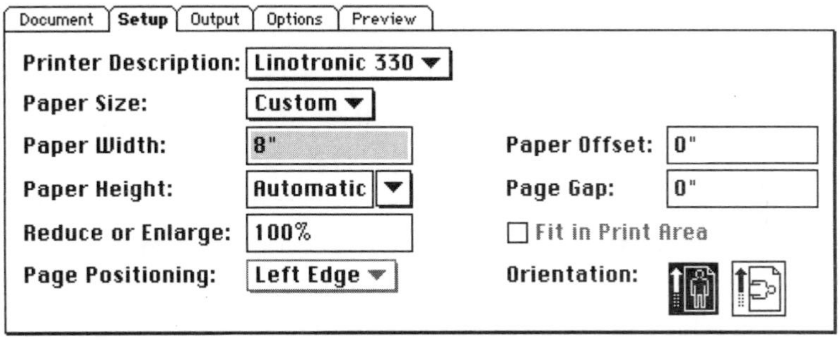

Figure 8.9 *The Setup Tab of the Print dialog box.*

The **Printer Description** pop-up menu lets you choose the appropriate PPD (PostScript Printer Description) for your PostScript printer.

TIP

The PPD file you select in the **Printer Description** pop-up menu is important. It provides specific information about the printer to QuarkXPress, such as available paper sizes, printer resolution, and whether the printer is sheet- or roll-fed. Most printers ship with PPDs and PDFs (Printer Description File); be sure these files are installed properly on your computer.

On a Macintosh, you install PPDs in the Printer Descriptions folder, located in the System Extensions folder. On Windows 95 systems, PPDs are usually found in the Windows System folder.

For some printers, a pop-up menu for **Paper Size** lists the range of paper sizes handled. Paper sizes are determined by information in the PPD file. Possibilities include letter, legal, ledger, and statement, as well as European sizes, such as A3 (11.7" x 16.5"), A4 (8.3" x 11.7"), and A5 (5.8" x 8.3"). The list shown in the pop-up menu corresponds to the sizes supported by the printer selected in the Printer Type field. When this field is available, the list of standard paper sizes selected through radio buttons is dimmed (that is, not available) at the top of the dialog box.

Paper Width, Paper Height, Paper Offset and **Page Gap** are specifications for printers such as image setters that can handle rolls of paper in different paper roll widths. In addition to paper width and height, you also can enter Paper Offset to shift the printing area to the right of its normal position (against the left edge of the paper). The Page Gap is the amount of space QuarkXPress will leave between pages on the roll-fed typesetter. When **Spreads** is checked in the Print dialog box (described later in this chapter), the value you enter in the Page Gap field is inserted between horizontal spreads, not between the pages in the spread itself.

Reduce or Enlarge lets you enter a percentage value to specify that your document print larger or smaller than actual size. The default setting is 100%. You can enter values from 25% to 400%.

The **Fit in Print Area** option allows you to reduce or enlarge a page to fit the area that can be imaged on the currently selected paper or other media.

The **Page Positioning** pop-up menu lets you control the position of a page on the selected output media, as shown in Figure 8.10. You can choose from these options:

- The default, **Left Edge**, positions the top left of the document page at the top left of the selected paper or other media.
- **Center** positions the document page in the center, both horizontally and vertically, of the paper or other media.
- **Center Horizontal** positions the document page at the top edge of the paper or other media, but in the center from left to right.
- **Center Vertical** positions the document page at the left edge of the paper or other media, but in the center from top to bottom.

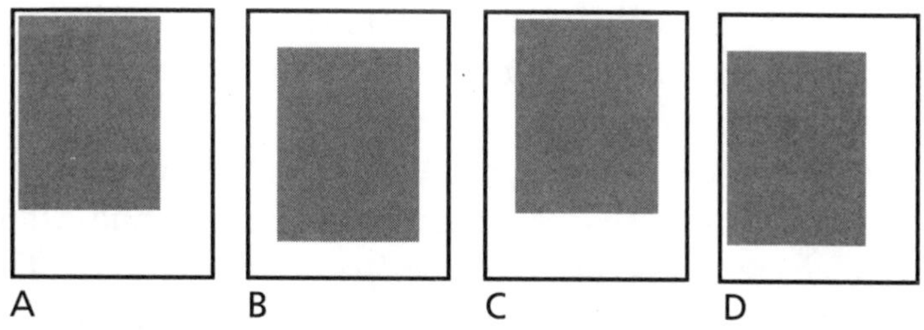

Figure 8.10 *A 6" x 8" page positioned to print on letter-size paper (a) Left Edge (b) Center(c) Center Horizonta,l and (d) Center Vertical.*

The **Orientation** icons let you specify whether a page will print tall (portrait) or horizontally (landscape). Portrait orientation is the default. If your document is wider than the paper size specified, the landscape orientation is chosen automatically.

Output Tab

The Output tab of the Print dialog box (Figure 8.11) contains options that were formerly found in both the Page Setup and Print dialog boxes. The dialog box includes a scroll list at the bottom that lets you control screening details for each color plate when printing separations.

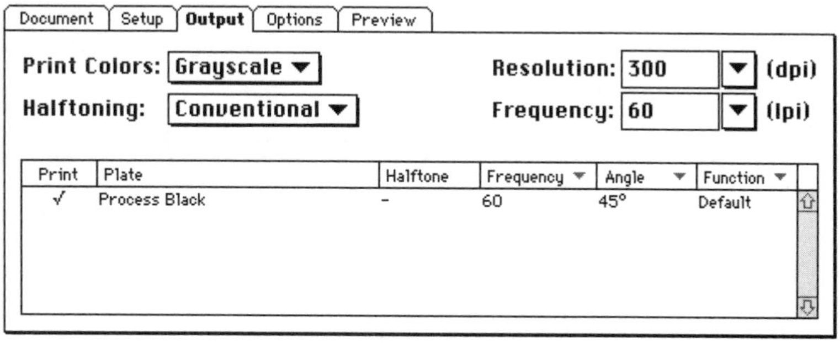

Figure 8.11 *The Output tab of the Print dialog box.*

The **Print Colors** pop-up menu is only available when Separations are *off*, that is, the option has not been checked in the Document tab of the Print dialog box; options here affect how colors will print to black and white printers and composite color printers. **Grayscale** prints colors in shades of gray to a black and white printer, such as a laser printer. **Black & White** prints black and white only (no shades of gray) to a black and white printer. **Composite Color** prints colors to a color printer. The options available are determined by the PPD chosen (in the Setup tab of the Print dialog box; see previous section, "Setup Tab").

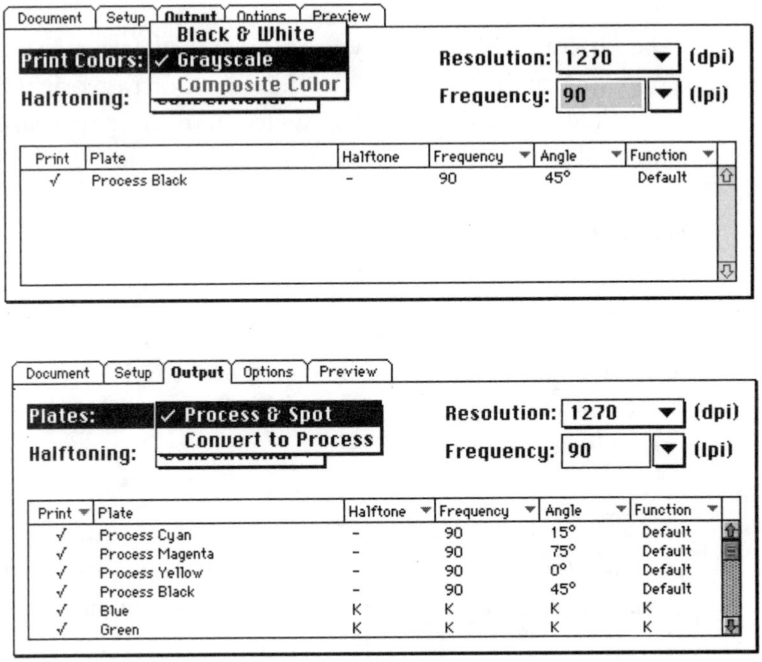

***Figure 8.12** The Output Tab options change depending on whether Separations is checked off (top) or on (bottom) (in the Document Tab of the Print dialog box).*

When Separations is checked **on** in the Document tab of the Print dialog box, the Print Colors pop-up is replaced by the **Plates** pop-up menu (Figure 8.13). You can choose **Process & Spot,** which will print the component process colors cyan, magenta, yellow and black, *plus* each spot color, on individual plates. If you don't wish each spot color to print on a separate plate, you can choose **Convert to Process**, which will convert all spot colors to their CMYK equivalents. You cannot convert spot colors individually in this dialog box. It's an all-or-none choice to convert all the spot colors in your document to process colors. You can, however, always switch colors back to process and the full list of spot colors by simply choosing the **Process & Spot** option in the pop-up menu.

The **Halftoning** options let you choose whether halftoning information will be controlled by QuarkXPress or determined by the output device. **Conventional** uses QuarkXPress calculated halftone screen values. **Printer** uses halftone screen values in effect on the currently selected printer. When Separations is checked **on** in the Document tab of the Print dialog box, the Printer option is not available.

The **Resolution** option automatically lists the default resolution of the Printer Description chosen in the Setup tab of the Print dialog box. You can change the resolution enter the dots-per-inch (dpi) value, or choose from the pop-up menu, which will list all the available resolution settings for the selected printer.

Frequency refers to the line screen frequency, sometimes referred to as lines-per-inch (lpi). Like resolution, the default setting is automatically determined by the Printer Description chosen in the Setup tab of the Print dialog box.

The list at the bottom of the dialog box is an important one. It displays a list the color **Plates** used in the document and lets you control the halftone settings for each plate and whether or not the plate will print. When you click on a plate name, the pop-up lists at the heading of each column let you control any one of the following options for that plate:

- A check mark in the **Print** column indicates that color plate will print. The default setting is checked. You can click on a check to uncheck it, or choose **No** in the Print pop-up menu.

- The **Halftone** pop-up menu lets you assign a different process color screen angle to any spot color, or a custom angle. The default value is determined when the spot color is first created, using the Halftone pop-up in the Edit Color dialog box. The halftone value applied here—C, M, Y, or K—determines the defaults for the next three columns (Frequency, Angle and Function).

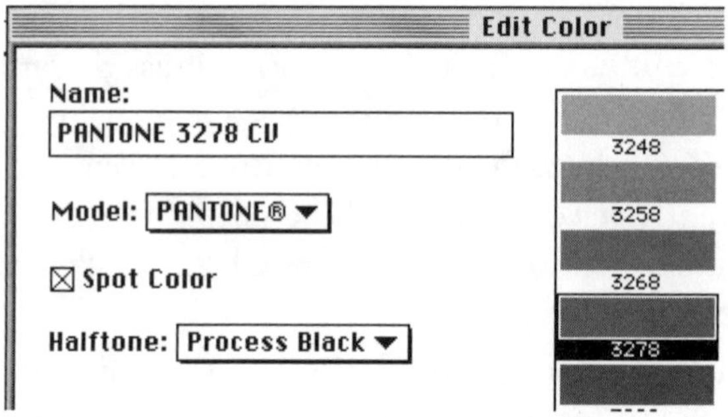

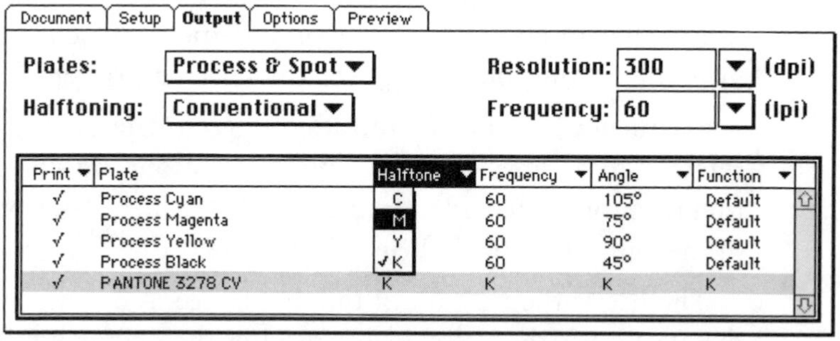

***Figure 8.13** The default Halftone screen for Process Black (45°) is first defined when a spot color is set up in the Edit Color dialog box. The Plates list in the Output Tab of the Print dialog box lets you change that default.*

- The **Frequency** column reflects the lines per inch (lpi) that will be printed for each plate. The **Angle** column lists the screen angle for each color plate. The **Function** controls the shape of the dot that makes up the halftone. The default setting for each can be changed by choosing **Other** from the pop-up menu. Enter the new value and click **OK**. The new value will be shown in the list, with an asterisk (*) beside the new custom value.

Options Tab

The Options tab of the Print dialog box (Figure 8.14) includes a grab-bag of settings that were previously available under the Page Setup command and Page Setup Options. These include the ability to print negatives and to print a PostScript file to disk. New options include a PostScript Error Handler and the ability to over-print black in EPS files.

```
┌──────────────────────────────────────────────────────────┐
│  Document │ Setup │ Output │ Options │ Preview            │
│                                                            │
│  ☒ Quark PostScript Error Handler      ☐ Prepress File     │
│  Page Flip: [None ▼]                   ☐ Negative Print    │
│                                                            │
│  ┌─Pictures────────────────────────────────────────────┐  │
│  │ Output:  [Normal ▼]                                  │  │
│  │ Data:    [Binary ▼]           ☐ Overprint EPS Black  │  │
│  │ OPI:     [Include Images ▼]   ☐ Full Resolution TIFF Output │
│  └──────────────────────────────────────────────────────┘ │
└──────────────────────────────────────────────────────────┘
```

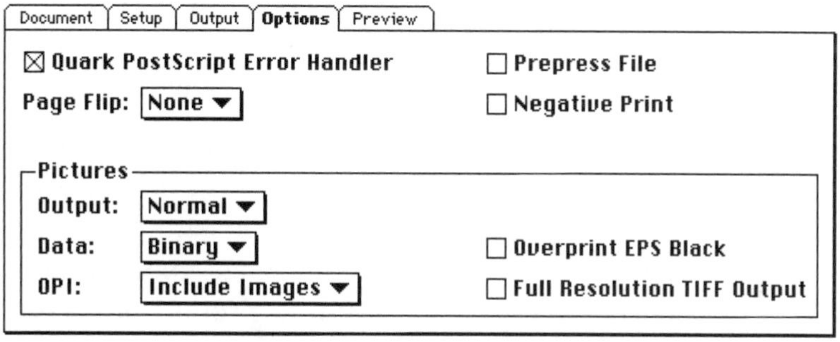

Figure 8.14 *The Options tab of the Print dialog box.*

The **Quark PostScript Error Handler** incorporates an XTension that was previously available for free from Quark, Inc. The Error Handler provides a report that tells you where on the page a printing error has occurred. This is especially helpful if you happen to know a little PostScript code. Even if you don't, the Error Handler will print the page containing the items handled successfully up to the point of the error, which will give you an idea of where to troubleshoot your page. A report is then printed that contains the bounding box of the item in which the error occurred. You can lay the error report on top of the printed page to further identify the problem item.

The **Prepress File** option lets you print a PostScript file to disk. This file does not contain any printer driver code or embedded fonts, and can be used by many proprietary systems for creating color separations or imposition.

The **Page Flip** pop-up menu and the **Negative Print** checkbox represent options also available in the Options dialog of most PostScript printer drivers, that are most commonly used for printing to an imagesetter or other film device. The Page Flip options include:

- **None**, the default, which leaves the page in its normal orientation
- **Horizontal**, which reverses the printing of page images from left to right
- **Vertical**, which prints the page image upside-down
- **Horizontal & Vertical,** which flips the page in both directions, printing page images from left to right and upside down

The **Negative Print** option prints a negative of the page. When printing to film in an imagesetter or other output device, using the Negative Print option and flipping the page either horizontally or vertically will produce a right-reading, emulsion down film output, a common standard for film production, especially in the United States.

The **Pictures** options control how images, as opposed to text or the page itself, are output. The **Output** pop-up controls (which in previous versions of QuarkXPress were found in the Print dialog box) let you print pages more quickly by changing the resolution of graphics, or suppressing the printout of graphics altogether—a handy feature during the proofing stages of a project. Remember that when you import an image, whether it's large or small, QuarkXPress actually only imports the screen image at 72 dpi. It relies on the screen preview being linked to the image source data, from which a high resolution version is printed.

When you print using the Output default, **Normal,** pictures are printed at high resolution, using the image source data file.

Choose **Low Resolution** to print pictures using the screen preview data only. **Rough** suppresses the printout of all pictures. Instead of the picture, the picture bounding box is printed with an "x" through it to show picture placement. Low Resolution and Rough let you print page proofs more quickly, especially when you need to proof text or the general layout only.

The **Data** pop-up lets you save picture date in Binary or ASCII format. **Binary**, the default, is a very compact format, but **ASCII** is more portable because it is a standard format that can be read by a wider variety of devices and systems.

Some devices for creating color separations—imposition systems and direct-to-plate systems, for example—use special PostScript files that conform to the Open Prepress Interface (OPI) standard. The **OPI** pop-up options have an effect only when you print a file to disk as a PostScript file. Check with your service bureau or printing company as to whether **Omit TIFF** or **Omit TIFF & EPS** should be used when creating the files.

The **Overprint EPS Black** option, new to version 4.0, will force all black elements in an imported EPS file to overprint, regardless of how overprint was set in the original program.

The default setting for the **Full Resolution TIFF Output** option is normally unchecked. With this option unchecked, the resolution of non-line art TIFF files, such as photographic images, will be downsampled based on the Frequency (lpi) setting in the Output tab of the Print dialog box. If checked on, the TIFF image will be output at the full resolution of the printer, regardless of the line frequency.

Preview Tab

The Preview tab of the Print dialog box (Figure 8.15) offers a new print preview capability. A page icon on the right side of the dialog box shows you the how the document page will print on the paper as it comes out of the printer. Various statistics for the page are shown on the left side, including Paper and Document Size, Paper Offset, Page Gap and the Scaling percentage, as specified in the Setup tab. Also displayed are the number of tiles and bleed amount, as specified in the Document tab.

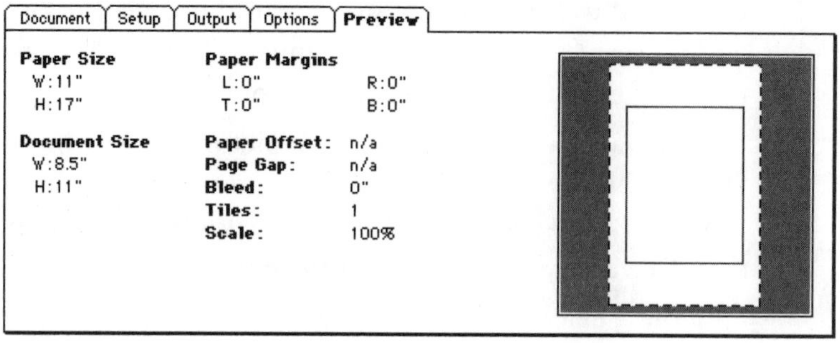

Figure 8.15 The Preview tab of the Print dialog box, showing how a letter-size page will print on a tabloid-size sheet of paper.

Using the PPD Manager

PPD (PostScript Printer Description) files are usually supplied with printers by the printer manufacturer. On a Macintosh, these files are usually installed in the Printer Description folder in your System Extensions folder. On a Windows 95 system, these files are usually installed in the Windows System folder. The files contain information about the specific printer that can be used by applications to take full advantage of all the printer's features, including alternate paper tray sizes, resolution, and other capabilities.

PPDs are accessed in QuarkXPress using the Printer Description pop-up menu in the Setup tab of the Print dialog box. It's quite possible to have a long list of PPD files available to your system, even though you probably only print to one or at most a few printers. The PPD Manager lets you control which PPDs are displayed in the Printer Description pop-up menu.

The PPD Manager Dialog Box

The PPD Manager Dialog box (Figure 8.16) displays a list of the PPD files available to QuarkXPress. You can specify which PPDs will be displayed in the Printer Description pop-up menu in the Setup tab. A check mark in the **Include** column indicates that the PPD will be displayed. The default setting is checked. You can click on a check to uncheck it, or choose **No** in the Include pop-up menu.

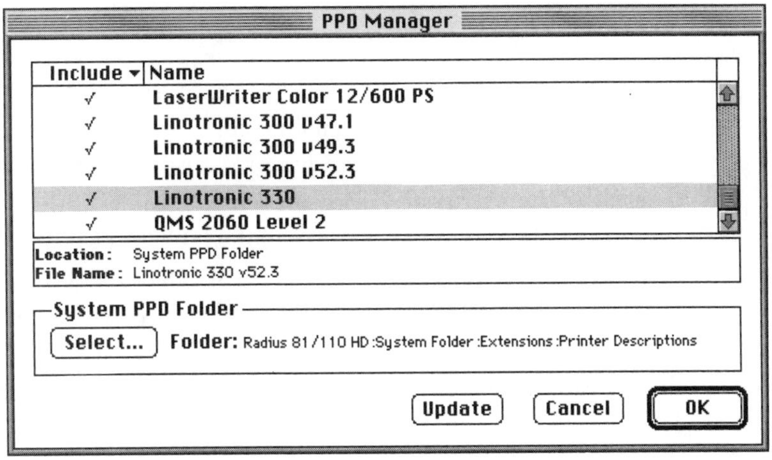

***Figure 8.16** The PPD Manager dialog box.*

TIP: You can select a range of PPDs at once: click on the first PPD, then hold down the **Shift** key while you click the last PPD in the range you wish to select. To select non-contiguous PPDs, hold down the **⌘/CTRL** key as you click on each PPD name. The **⌘/CTRL** key also de-selects a PPD. Once you have the desired list of PPDs selected, you can display the PPDs or not, by selecting **Yes** or **No** from the Include pop-up menu.

The **System PPD** Folder area lets you select the location of the folder containing the PPDs you wish to choose from. On the Macintosh the default folder is the Printer Description folder in the System Extensions folder. Click the **Select** button to display a file directory dialog box from which you can choose any other folder. On a Windows 95 System, the Windows System folder is the default.

If you add a PPD to your system while running QuarkXPress, the **Update** button refreshes the list of PPDs shown without having to re-launch QuarkXPress.

Using Print Styles

QuarkXPress 4.0 incorporates many of the features previously found in a commercial XTension called *QuarkPrint,* an add-on product sold by Quark, Inc. One of the primary features added as a result is the ability to capture all the settings in the Print dialog box under the name of a Print Style, which can be quickly applied to print a document, without having to reset all the options manually. Another great addition from QuarkPrint is the ability to print non-contiguous pages (see the earlier section "Using the Print Command.")

Creating and Editing Print Styles

You can add Print Styles using the **Edit ➛ Print Styles** command. The default print style is available in all documents. In fact, unlike Style Sheets, Colors, H&Js, Lists, and Dashes & Stripes, Print Styles are saved as an application-level setting, so any Print Style you create in any document is always available to all documents.

The Print Style Dialog Box

The first dialog box displayed when you choose **Edit ➛ Print Styles** lists the Print Styles available, shown in Figure 8.17.

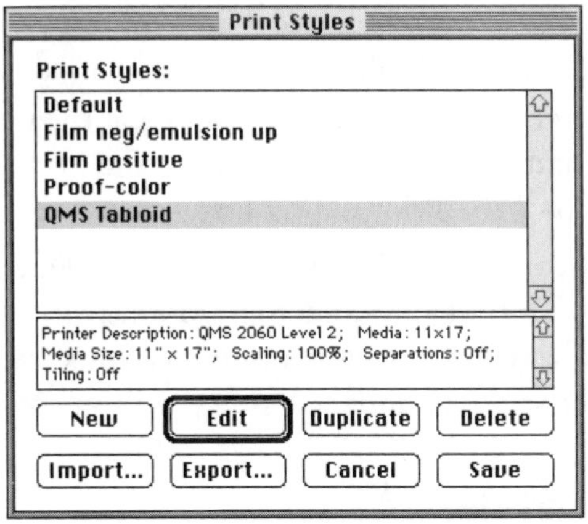

Figure 8.17 *The Print Styles dialog box.*

The options at the bottom of the list—**New, Edit, Duplicate, Delete** and **Import** and **Export**—are discussed in detail in the following sections.

The Edit Print Styles Dialog Box

The Edit Print Styles dialog box (Figure 8.18) is displayed when you choose **New, Edit,** or **Duplicate** from the Print Styles dialog box. This dialog box represents your "master control center" for setting up the available Print Styles.

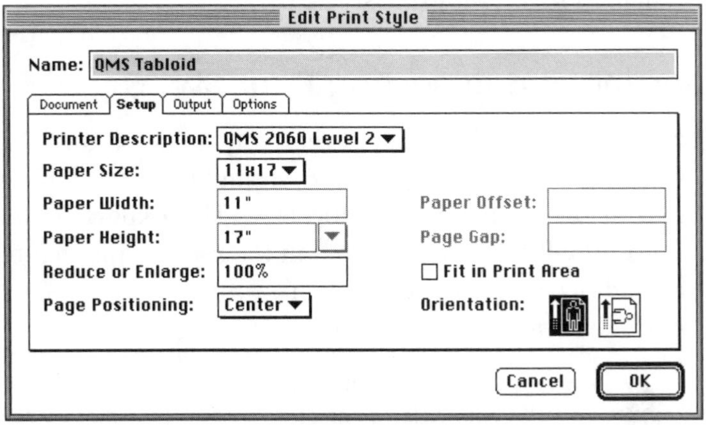

Figure 8.18 *The Edit Print Styles dialog box.*

When you create a new Print Style, the Edit Print Styles dialog box opens with the **Name** field highlighted and the entry "New Print Style." You can enter a new name, or you can edit the name shown in this field. The name you assign appears in the Print Style pop-up menu at the top of the Print dialog box.

The dialog box consists of the settings from the Document tab, the Setup tab, the Output tab, and the Options tab of the Print dialog box. If you have a question about the various options available, see the earlier sections under "Using the Print Command."

Duplicating Print Styles

If you want to make a new Print Style that is similar to another Print Style, click the **Duplicate** button at the bottom of the Print Style dialog box. Select the Print Style you wish to copy, then click the **Duplicate** button. The Edit Print Styles dialog box will display, with all the specifications of the style you're copying, but with the name *<print style name> copy* in the name field. You can then change the name and any of the other specifications in the dialog box to create a new Print Style.

Deleting a Print Style

Select a color on the list in the Print Style dialog box and click **Delete** to remove a Print Style.

Importing and Exporting Print Styles

It's easy to copy Print Styles that you create on one QuarkXPress system to another, using the Export and Import buttons at the bottom of the Print Styles dialog box. The **Export** button lets you export the Print Styles selected in the list to a file that can be used by another QuarkXPress user. You can export some or all of the Print Styles as shown in Figure 8.19.

TIP

You can select multiple Print Styles by holding down the **Shift** key as you click, or select noncontiguous files by holding down the **⌘/Ctrl** key as you click on each Print Style name.

The **Import** button lets you import a Print Styles file that has been created by the Export command. When you click Import, a file directory dialog box is displayed that lets you select the Print Styles file you wish to import.

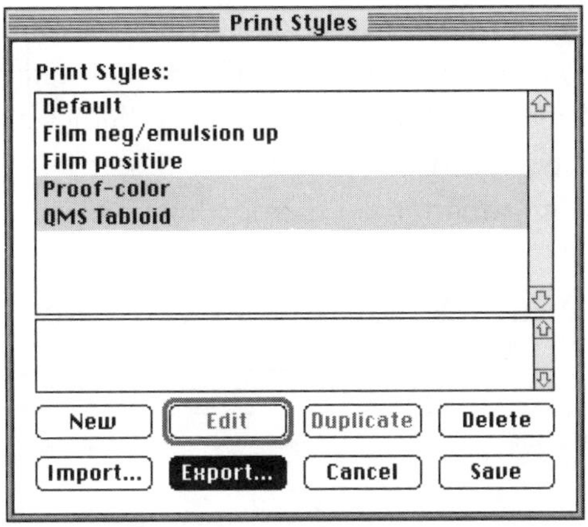

Figure 8.19 *Selected Print Styles can be exported to a disk file that can then be imported on another system.*

Preparing to Print

It's a good idea to familiarize yourself with the basic techniques of identifying the cause of problems that may occur when you print. Whether you print to a simple black-and-white laser printer or prepare files for high-resolution output at a service bureau, it can be helpful make use of the tools provided by QuarkXPress to help ensure your files print correctly. The **Usage** dialog box helps you manage the fonts and pictures in your files, and **Collect for Output** makes it easy to assemble all the files necessary to send a document to a service bureau or printer for output.

Fonts and Picture Usage

Two of the basic things you need to know in order to print a file successfully are what fonts the document uses and what pictures have been imported. The Usage dialog box (**Utilities ➤ Usage**) allows you to easily verify the fonts and pictures in your document.

Fonts Tab

The **Fonts** tab of the Usage dialog box (Figure 8.20) displays a list of all the fonts used in your document. You can also use this dialog box to find and replace a font with another. The fonts listed here do not include fonts contained in EPS files. (Fonts in EPS files can be found in the document report, however; see the next section, "Collect for Output," for more information on the document report.)

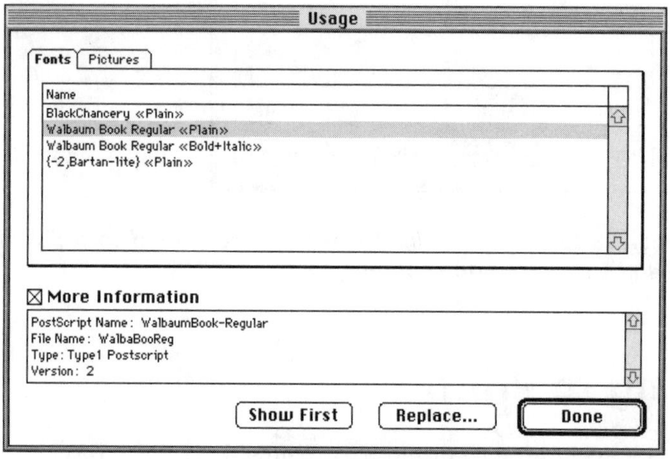

Figure 8.20 *The Fonts tab of the Usage dialog box.*

The **Name** column lists the names of all the fonts in your document, along with any character style (such as bold or italic, not style sheet) that has been applied. If there are occurrences of the font with no style applied, it will be listed with *<Plain>* after the name; if a style, such as bold or italic has been applied, it will be listed separately with *<Bold>* or *<Italic>* after the name. If a font occurs in the document, but is not available to QuarkXPress in the system, the font name will appear in the format *{-2,fontname}*. Figure 8.20 shows examples of both.

If the **More Information** button is checked, you can click on a font name in the list to display additional information about the font, including:

- The font name (both the actual font name and the name that appears on menus)
- The type and version of font (Type 1 PostScript, True Type, etc.)

You can view where a font occurs in the document by clicking the **Show First** button. The first occurrence of the font use is highlighted on the document page. The button changes to **Show Next** after the first occurrence of the font is found.

TIP: If you want to change the **Show Next** button in the Font Usage tab back to **Show First**, hold down the **Option/ALT** key.

To replace a font in your document with another, select the font you wish to replace, then click the **Replace** button, which displays the Replace Font dialog box (Figure 8.21). This is the same dialog box that is displayed when you open a document that contains fonts missing from your system and you choose to replace the missing font.

TIP: Double-click on font name in the Font Usage tab to display the Replace Font dialog box.

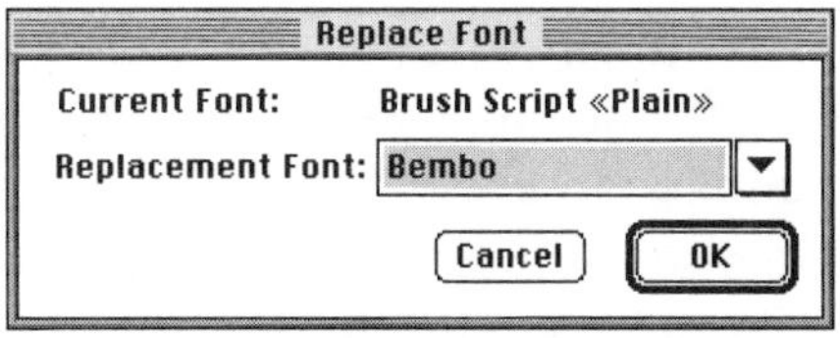

Figure 8.21 *The Replace Font dialog box.*

When you replace the fonts on document pages, master pages are unaffected, and vice versa.

Pictures Tab

The Pictures tab of the Usage dialog (Figure 8.22) box lists all the pictures in your document. It is similar to the dialog box that is displayed when you print and are prompted that pictures are missing or modified. You can use options in the Usage dialog box to determine the status of pictures, whether or not they are available for printing, and locate them on disk if they are not; view a picture and where it's located in the document; and control whether or not a picture will print.

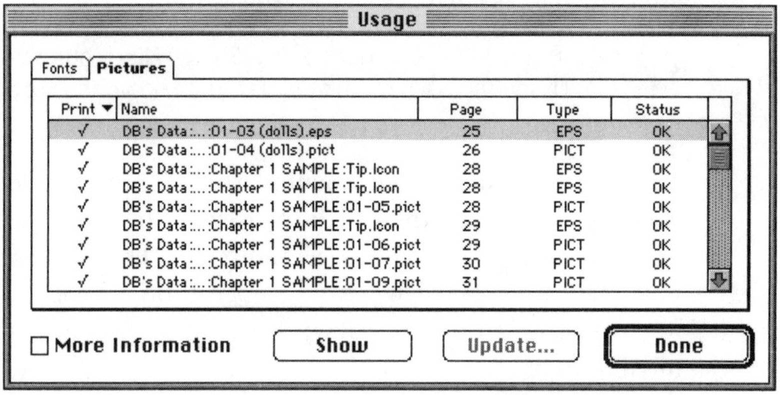

Figure 8.22 *The Pictures tab of the Usage dialog box.*

The **Print** column lets you control which pictures will print. A check mark indicates the picture will print. You can click the check mark to uncheck it and suppress the picture printout, or you can click **Print** and choose **No** from the pop-up menu. Remember that you can also suppress the printout of a picture by checking the **Suppress Printout** option in either the Box tab (to suppress the picture *and* the box) or the Picture tab (to suppress the picture only) of the Modify dialog box. If you do so, that setting will be reflected in the Usage dialog box and the picture will be listed without a check mark adjacent to it. You can override the Suppress Printout settings from the Box and Picture tabs of the Modify dialog box in the Usage dialog box. Turning the Print option on actually unchecks the Suppress Printout settings in the Modify dialog box.

The **Name** column displays the name and path of the picture file. If a picture is pasted in, the Name is listed as *No Disk File.*

The **Page** column lists the page number on which the picture appears. If a picture runs across a spread, the page number of the left hand page will appear. If the picture is entirely on the pasteboard, the adjacent page number will be listed with a dagger beside it (†).

The **Type** column displays the file format of the picture, such as TIFF, EPS, etc.

One of the most important QuarkXPress basics is to understand that in order to print high resolution images, you must be sure the application has access to the actual picture file. The **Status** column indicates whether the picture is accessible or if it has been modified in any way since it was first imported. In this column one of the following will be listed for each picture:

- The best state in which to find a picture is **OK**. It means QuarkXPress can access the graphic with no problem. It also means the screen preview matches the picture file itself.
- **Modified** means that the picture file has been changed by the application that created it, i.e., that it has a different modification time and date. Basically, it's a good idea to click **Update** to make it read **OK**.

TIP: It's a good idea to always update a Modified picture—if you do not, QuarkXPress still prints the original picture file, but it may not match the file displayed on screen!

- **Missing** is definitely not good. If a picture is missing, QuarkXPress will simply print the low resolution screen version. When you click the **Update** button, the Find directory dialog box is displayed. Locate the file, and select **Update.** The status will change to OK.

TIP When locating a missing picture, be careful you don't accidentally choose the wrong file—it's easy to do, especially when picture files have similar names (see Figure 8.23). If you do choose the wrong picture, the Status will display as Modified. The correct file name is displayed at the top of the dialog box; make sure it matches the file you choose exactly, and remember to always update modified pictures (see previous tip).

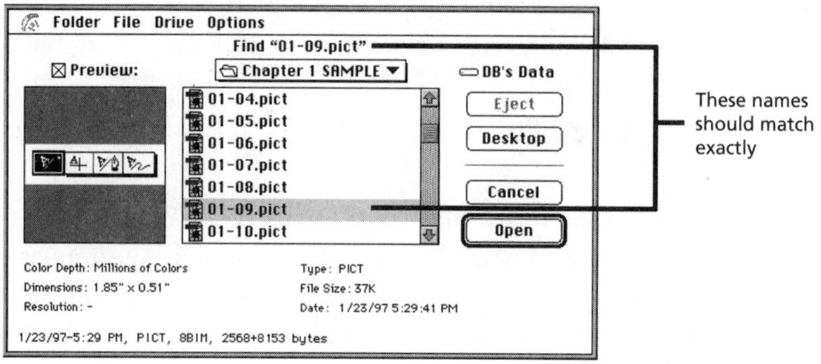

***Figure 8.23** The name at the top of the dialog box should match the name of the file you choose exactly.*

- **Wrong Type** means the picture type, not necessarily the appearance of the picture, has been changed—for example, from a TIFF to an EPS file. When you click the **Update** button, the picture is re-imported and the entry in the Type column changed to reflect the new picture type.
- **In Use** means that the file is open on another application on your computer.
- **No Access** means you don't have network privileges to open the file.
- **Can't Open** indicates the computer has too many files open.

The **Update** button is used to update the status of any picture that has the status **Missing, Modified**, or **Wrong Type.** Select the picture you wish to update from the list and click the **Update** button. When you click update for a missing picture, a find file directory dialog box is displayed. When you update a modified picture, you are prompted with a dialog box that ensures you really want to update the picture. The option is grayed out when the status of a picture is OK.

To display a picture in the document, select the picture from the list, then click the **Show** button. The picture will be highlighted in the document window. It's a good idea to use this feature to check any modified pictures that you have updated.

Check **More Information** (Figure 8.24) to display basic data about the picture file—information similar to that displayed in the Get Picture dialog box. This information includes:

- **Full Path:** the full path name, at the time the picture is imported, including the volume and folder information.
- **File Size:** expressed in kilobytes (K), how much space the file takes up on your hard disk.
- **Modification Date:** the computer's date and time stamp the last time the file was saved.
- **Dimensions:** the width and height of the picture, shown in the measurement units selected in the General tab of Document Preferences.
- **Color Depth:** indicates how many bits per pixel of color information are used in the picture. This information is not available for EPS pictures.

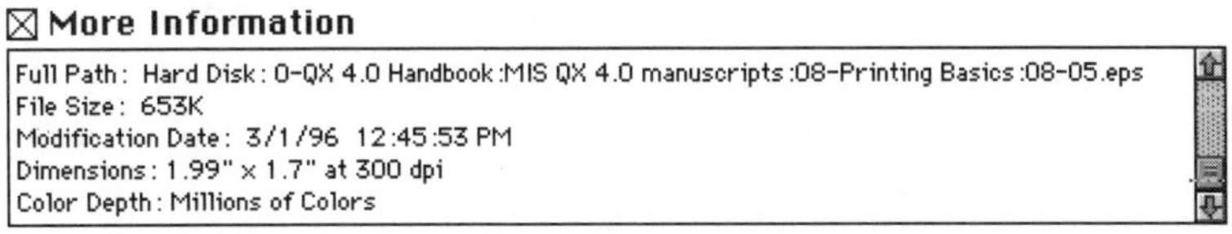

Figure 8.24 *More Information shown in the Usage dialog box for a selected picture file.*

The features of the Usage dialog box are one of the most basic tools for troubleshooting printing problems.

Collect for Output

For many people, the normal work flow using QuarkXPress ultimately involves sending the QuarkXPress document for film output or for direct-to-plate output; this often requires sending the document to another company or facility. It's important that your service bureau, printing company, or other vendor involved with the output of your document be given all the necessary files. This includes not only your QuarkXPress document, but all picture files as well. It seems like it would be easy enough to collect all these elements, but when pictures are imported from a variety of locations, it may be more difficult than you think.

To avoid accidental omission of files needed to print your document correctly, use the Collect for Output command (**File ➛ Collect for Output**). This command automatically copies a QuarkXPress document and all imported picture files into a specified location, and prints a document report that can provide useful information for production and troubleshooting a file. Note that fonts are *not* collected with the use of this command.

Collect for Output Dialog Box

When you choose **File ➛ Collect for Output**, a directory dialog box is displayed that lets you select or create a folder for the document, its imported picture files, and the document report file (Figure 8.25). If your file has not been saved, a warning displays "OK to save document before continuing with Collect for Output?" allowing you to save the file or Cancel if you don't wish to save it. If you choose to save the file, the Save As dialog box is displayed. You cannot use the Collect for Output command, however, until the file has been saved.

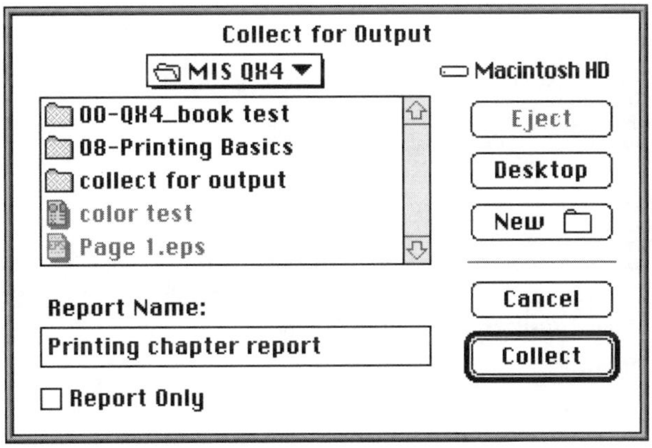

Figure 8.25 *The Collect for Output dialog box.*

If the Missing/Modified dialog box displays after you click **Collect**, you must update Missing or Modified pictures in order for them to be included among the collected files.

The Document Report

The Document Report (Figure 8.26) has many uses. It can be used by your service bureau to obtain information about your document that may be useful in troubleshooting. Or, you may use information in the report, such as the part of the report that lists all style sheets and their definition, to distribute to members of a work group producing a family of documents for the same project. It's a good idea to familiarize yourself with the information that can be obtained from a document report. Some of the information in a Document Report can be found elsewhere in the program, but other information, like the fonts used in imported EPS picture files, can only be found in the document report.

Source Pathname: Hard Disk: Collect.doc
Destination Pathname: Hard Disk: Collect.doc report
Last modified: 11:50 AM; 10/12/97
Document Size: 38K
Most recently saved version: 4.00r0
Document has been saved by the following versions of QuarkXPress:
4.00r0
Total Pages: 1
Page Width: 8.5"
Page Height: 11"
Required XTensions: None
Active XTensions: Cool Blends; CPSI Fixer; Font Creator; Index; Jabberwocky; JPEG Import; Kern-Track Editor; LZW Import; MacWrite Filter; MacWritePro Import; MS-Word Filter; Microsoft Works Filter; PCX Import; PhotoCD Import; Quark CMS; SpellChecker 2.0/QuarkXPress Passport; WordPerfect Filter; WriteNow Import; XPress Tags Filter

DOCUMENT FONTS

External Name	Internal Name	Printer Font Filename
Helvetica	Helvetica	Helvetica

PICTURE FONTS
Picture External Name
08-05.eps Helvetica; Sabon-Roman

GRAPHICS
Pathname

Type	Page	Size	Box Angle	Pic Angle	Skew	XScale	YScale	Top edge	Left edge	DPI
Hard Disk: 08-05.eps										
EPSF	1	75K	0°	0°	0°	100%	100%	1.639"	2.458"	

PARAGRAPH STYLE SHEETS
Normal

Figure 8.26 *Information in a Document Report.*

You can import the report into any QuarkXPress file, or you can import it into the Output Request Document located in your QuarkXPress folder. The template includes space for adding your name, address, and other information that is needed by service bureaus or other vendors who may be responsible for the output of your document. When you import the report file, make sure **Include Style Sheets** is checked in the Get Text dialog box.

Summary

This chapter covered the basics of printing, and printing-related features in QuarkXPress 4.0. This is the final chapter of Part I of this book, and completes your basic "boot camp" training. Part II of this book, "Publishing Long Documents," is geared for those involved with the production of long documents. If you're not concerned with long document issues—page number, sectioning, generating table of contents, and printing documents as books—you can skip Part II and move on to Part III, "Advanced Techniques," for information on preparing your files for printing Color Separations, and general information on re-purposing QuarkXPress for publishing in other media, such as interactive CD-ROMs and the World Wide Web.

PART TWO

LONG DOCUMENTS

9 Master Pages and Sectioning

This chapter describes some of the more complex aspects of working with longer documents. We'll talk about creating master pages, page numbering and sectioning a document, and developing templates for repeated use. Here's a quick preview of what you'll learn in the next sections:

- You can add elements to the master page so they appear on every page—including page numbers.
- You can set up page numbers as Arabic numbers or roman numerals (i, ii, iii, or I, II, III), or letters of the alphabet (a, b, c… or A, B, C…), and you can assign prefixes to page numbers.
- You can switch from one page numbering system to another (i, ii, iii… to 1, 2, 3…, for example), and you can restart page numbering or skip page numbers within a document by dividing the document into *Sections*.
- You can create more than one master page to define different page layouts within one document.
- You can create templates that embody a document's design specifications.

You could work with QuarkXPress for years and never touch a master page, create a section, or design a template—but once you learn what tremendous productivity tools these features are you'll never *stop* using them!

Creating Master Pages

You're probably aware that when you create a new document, QuarkXPress always displays a blank document page. But you may not realize that each new QuarkXPress document also contains a master page. A *master page* is a special page that is used to format document pages automatically. Any item—text, graphics, or guides—that appear on the master page will appear on every document page based on that master. The master page that is generated automatically when you create a new document actually serves as the basis of the first page in the file, and of all subsequent document pages (unless you choose to create document pages based on *no* master, or create additional master pages, described later in this chapter).

You can use master pages to fit the layout of each document page to an overall "grid" and to establish basic components of a document that repeat over several pages, thus saving valuable production time. For example, the folios (headers) in this book are positioned on the master page—including the page numbers which are numbered automatically. A master page can define or include:

- Page margins
- Column guides
- Other nonprinting guides that define the basic grid of the document's design
- An automatic text box
- Text boxes that contain the headers or footers
- Other text or graphic elements that by design will appear on document pages based on this master page (see Figure 9.1).

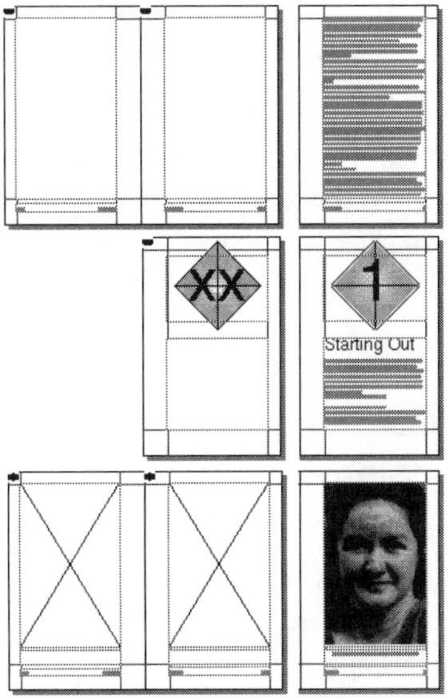

Figure 9.1 *In this example, the default master page (top) includes an automatic text box plus text boxes for footers; a second master for chapter openings (middle row) includes an automatic text box, plus a placeholder text box for the large chapter number, backed by a graphic, but no footer; a third master for full-page pictures (bottom) includes a picture box and a text box as placeholders for contents that will be added on each page. Document pages based on each master are shown on the far right.*

If you are creating a document that is more than one or two pages in length, you should set up one or more master pages. The following sections cover everything you need to know about working with master pages.

Creating New Master Pages

For many of the documents you work with, you will need to use only the master page that is automatically included when you create a new document. However, you can actually create up to 127 master pages for a single document, and there are many types of documents that can benefit from having more than one master page. This section covers how to create a new master page. You can find practical examples of these types of documents later in this chapter under the section "Examples of Working with Multiple Master Pages."

Use the Document Layout palette to create a new master page:

1. Select **View ➛ Show Document Layout** to display the palette.
2. Click on one of the blank page icons at the top left of the Document Layout palette (see Figure 9.2) and drag the blank page icon to position a new master page icon on the master page area at the top of the palette. (If necessary, you can move the palette's split bar down to make the area for master page icons larger.)

New master pages are added sequentially in the master page icon list in the Document Layout palette. You can rearrange the order of the master page icons by dragging them to new positions. As you drag, the cursor will change to indicate where the page will be inserted when you release the mouse.

Single-sided master pages can be created in any document, but blank facing-page master page icons will be available only when you have selected the **Facing Pages** option in the New Document or Document Setup command's dialog box. In the Document Layout palette shown on the left in Figure 9.2, the blank page icon (❑) on the top left represents a single-sided master; the second blank page icon, with two turned-down corners (▢), represents a facing-page master page with both a left and right master page.

- Single-sided master page elements, such as guides, text boxes, and graphics, will appear on *every* page to which that master page is applied, whether the final document is single-sided or a facing-page document.

- Those elements that are set up on the *right page* of a facing-page master page will appear only on *odd-numbered* pages of facing-page documents.
- Elements that are set up on the *left master page* will appear on *even-numbered* pages of facing-page documents.

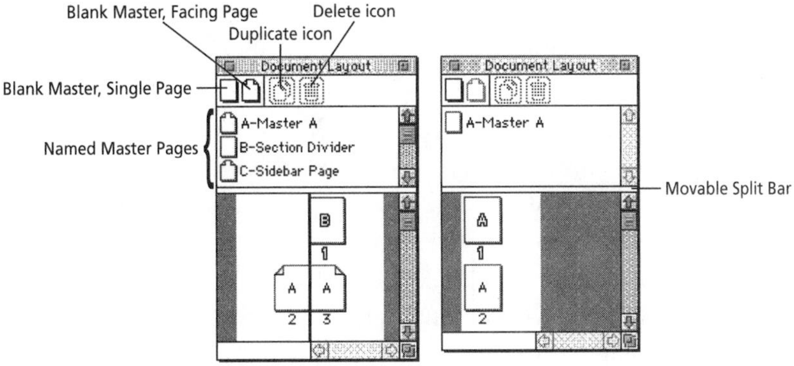

Figure 9.2 *If the* ***Facing Pages*** *option was selected, the Document Layout palette shows two blank master page icons in the top left corner, and facing-page spreads in the document page icons (left). If the* ***Facing Pages*** *option was not selected initially, the facing-page icon is grayed and facing-page spreads cannot be created (right).*

Choosing the Facing Pages Option—or Not

The one setting that can be a nuisance to change once you start a new document is whether or not facing pages are allowed. As you learned in Chapter 2, you can use the **File ➛ Document Setup** command to turn Facing Pages on or off, regardless of the option chosen in the New Document dialog box. However, to turn Facing Pages off once a document is set up, you must first delete all facing-page masters. Here's how this works in practical terms.

If you do *not* check the Facing Pages option in the New Document dialog box when you start a document, the first master page in the document will be a single-sided master, and you will not be able to create facing-page master pages. If later you decide that you want facing pages, you can easily change this through the **File → Document Setup** command. This activates the facing-page master icon in the Document Layout palette, and automatically arranges pages into facing-page spreads.

If you *do* check the Facing Pages option in the New Document dialog box when you start a document, then the first master page is automatically a facing-page master. If you later decide that you do not want facing pages, you must first convert the A-Master page—and any other facing-page masters you created—from a facing-page master to a single-blank master. You can do this by clicking once on the **A-Master A** icon in the Document Layout palette, and then holding the **Option/ALT** key as you click on the icon for Single-Blank master in the top left of the palette, or on an existing single master page. An alert box will warn you that you are replacing the existing master page *and anything on it* with a completely blank new master page, or with elements from the selected single-sided master.

Duplicating a Master Page

You can also create a new master page by duplicating an existing one and editing existing documents. To duplicate an existing master page:

1. Click once on the **Master Page** icon in the Document layout palette.
2. Click on the **Duplication** icon.

A new master page icon will appear in the palette. The new master will be identical to the one you duplicated. You can now modify the items on the duplicated master as you would on any other master page.

Renaming a Master Page

The name of each master page appears to the right of the master page icon in the Document Layout palette. QuarkXPress automatically assigns the name A-Master A, B-Master B, etc. to each master page you create, but you can give a master page a more descriptive name. The letters "A," "B," etc. are prefix characters, and this prefix from a master page name appears on the icons of all document pages in the Document Layout palette to which the master is applied (Figure 9.3).

To rename a master page:

1. Click once on the current name of the master page you wish to rename (the text which appears to the right of the master page icon). The text becomes highlighted.
2. Type the new name. You may type a prefix of up to three characters, followed by a hyphen and a name of up to 70 characters. If you do not include a prefix followed by a hyphen, QuarkXPress reverts to the original prefix, such as A, B, and so on.

TIP

The prefix you type for a master page name will appear on the document page icons in the Document Layout palette to which the master page is applied. Instead of using the defaults of "A," "B," and so forth which are normally displayed on the icons, use this prefix to help identify the type of page or its contents.

For example, if you name a master page **NEW-Chapter Opening Master**, then the word **NEW** will appear in the document palette on each page that starts a new chapter. Similarly, if you name a master **1/2-Half-page Ad**, each document page based on that master page will be marked **1/2** in the Document Layout palette.

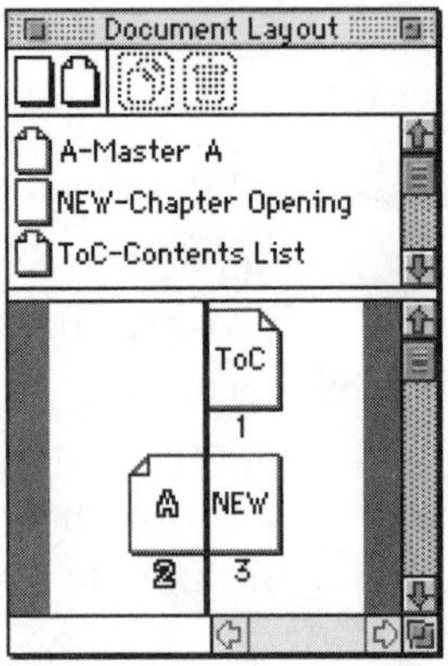

Figure 9.3 *The master page prefixes appear on the document page icons to which they have been applied.*

Replacing a Master Page

You can replace or overwrite an existing master page using one of the following methods:

- Drag another master page over the icon of the master page you wish to replace. When the icon is highlighted, release the mouse, or
- Select the master page you wish to overwrite, then **Option/ALT**-click on the existing master page icon (or a new blank master page icon) you wish to copy.

The results you get will depend on whether you replace a master page with a *blank* master page, or an existing, *non-blank* master page.

- When you replace an existing master page with a *blank master*, all of the guides and text and graphics elements are removed, and only the page margins and columns guides set up when you created the document will appear on the page.

- When you replace an existing master page with another *non-blank master*, all of the items on that page will be replaced completely with the items from the master page replacing it—page margins, columns guides, automatic text box (if applicable), and any other text or graphic elements.

QuarkXPress always displays a warning box asking you to confirm that you want to overwrite a master (Figure 9.4).

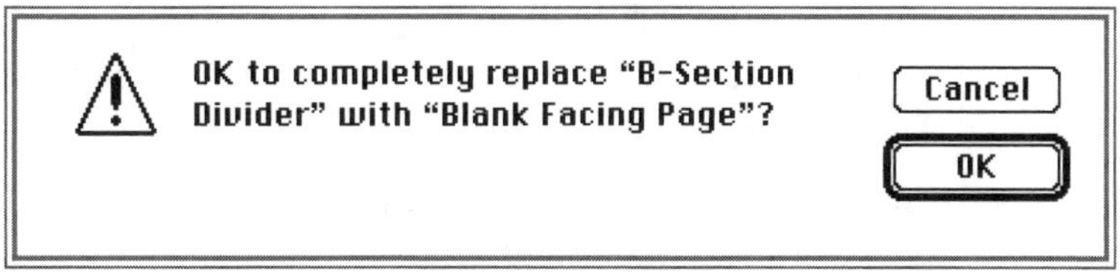

Figure 9.4 *An Alert box warns you when you are replacing an existing master page with new elements, or with a blank page.*

Editing a Master Page

Working with master pages is similar to working with document pages—you create and modify items on a master page in the same basic way as you would on a document page, using the item creation tools and modifying them with commands from the Item or Style menu.

However, there are some considerations unique to master pages. Remember that when you create a new document, the settings in the New Document dialog box control the appearance of the default master page. You can change these settings—margin and column guides, and whether or not you have Facing Pages or an Automatic text box—as described in Chapter 2, "Creating One Page." The next sections describe all the elements that are commonly used on master pages, including master guides, automatic text boxes, text boxes for headers and footers, and other elements that you want to have appear repeatedly on document pages.

Viewing a Master Page

To edit a master page, it must be the *active page* (the page displayed in the document window; see Figure 9.5). You can display a master page using any of three techniques:

- Select the master page by name from the **Page ➛ Display** submenu, which displays a list of all master pages in the file—one called **A-Master A** by default, and others as you add them to the document.
- Double-click on the appropriate master page icon in the Document Layout palette.
- Choose from the Go To Page pop-up menu in the bottom left corner of the document window.

You can turn from a master page back to any document page using any of these techniques, except choose **Page ➛ Display ➛ Document** to return to the document page that was active prior to turning to a master page. You cannot turn to a master page—or from a master page to a document page—using the scroll bars or the **Page ➛ Go To** command.

When a master page is displayed, QuarkXPress displays the page name in the lower left corner of the document window, along with an **R** or **L** for right and left pages of a facing-page master page. Once the master page is displayed, it can be edited using techniques discussed in the following sections.

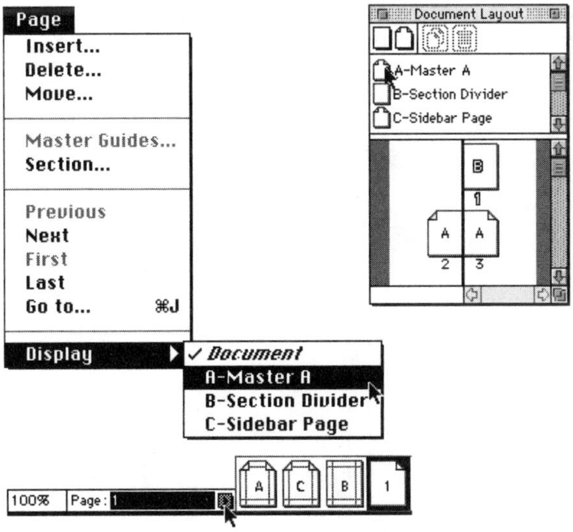

Figure 9.5 *Turn to a master page by choosing from the* ***Page ➛ Display*** *submenu, or by double-clicking on the appropriate master page icon at the top of the Document Layout palette, or by choosing from the pop-up menu on the document window.*

Changing Master Page Margins and Column Guides

A new master page takes on the margin and column settings that you initially specified in the New Document dialog box when you first started the document. You can change those settings for any master page through the Master Guides dialog box that is displayed when you use the **Page ➛ Master Guides** command (Figure 9.6). This command is available only when the active document window displays a master page.

TIP

Using the settings in the **Page ➛ Master Guides** command is the *only* way to reposition the margin guides in your document.

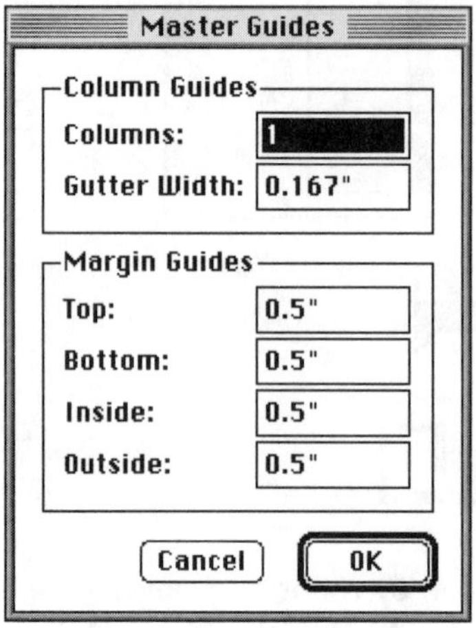

Figure 9.6 *Master Guides dialog box.*

Once you define the margins and column guides for a master page, those settings will apply automatically to any page in the document based on that master page. The master guides serve two functions:

- On the master page that includes an automatic text box, column guides define the number of columns in the automatic text box.
- On pages that do not have a text box, master guides serve as aids in positioning items on the page, but they do not affect text—the width of text is determined by the columns set up for each text box individually on the document pages.

If you later change the margin settings for a master page, or if you select a different master page for a document page that you have already started, QuarkXPress automatically resizes the automatic text box on the page (if one has been specified) and resizes any other text box whose four sides exactly meet the margin guides. All other page items remain unchanged when you redefine margins and columns on a master page.

Working with Automatic Text Boxes

Automatic text boxes are a feature of QuarkXPress that make it convenient to work with longer, text-heavy documents—such as books, reports, or magazines—in which a text chain flows over several pages of the same layout. Automatic text boxes have a special linking characteristic that inserts new pages into your document to accommodate text overflow, creating an automatic text *chain.*

Normally, when you type or import text into a text box that is not part of an automatic text chain, the box will fill with text, and if there is any overflow, the overflow icon (⊠) will appear in the lower right corner of the box until you link to another text box using the Linking tool (🔗). However, if you type or import text into an *automatic* text box in QuarkXPress, new pages are added automatically when the text overflows that text box. Pages will be added until there is no more overflow text—an entire word processing file, for example. You could call this *automatic text flow.* Pages inserted by automatic text flow always use the master page format of the page with the text box containing overflow text.

Automatic text boxes must be set up using master pages, and this can happen automatically or you can do it manually:

1. An automatic text box is set up *automatically* if you select the **Automatic Text Box** option in the New Document dialog box. In this case, two things happen:

    - The first master page includes an empty text box that has the page margins and columns you set up in the New Document dialog box, and the master page shows an intact chain icon (🔗) in the top left corner (Figure 9.7), or

- The first document page includes an empty text box that has the page margins and columns you set up in the New Document dialog box. When you type or import text into that text box, it will automatically add new pages as needed to accommodate overflow text.

2. You can *manually* create automatic text boxes on master pages that don't have one, using techniques described next.

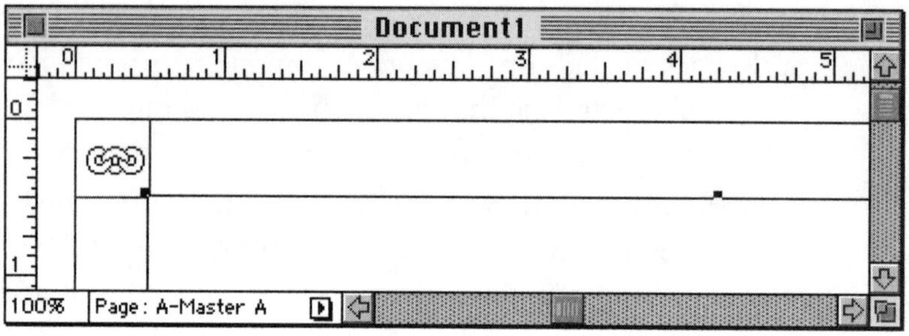

Figure 9.7 *Master page with automatic text box shows an intact chain icon in the top left corner.*

Creating an Automatic Text Box Manually

If a master page does not have an automatic text box, you can always add one manually. A master page will not have an automatic text box if:

- you did not check the **Automatic Text Box** option in the New Document dialog box when you create the file
- you created a new master page from a *blank* master (one of the icons in the top left corner of the Document Layout palette)
- the original automatic text box has been unlinked, as described in the next section.

In these cases, pages will not be added automatically for overflow text, even if the Auto Page Insertion option is turned *on* in the General tab of the Document Preferences dialog box .

To create an automatic text box on a master page that does not have one, follow these steps:

1. Display the master page that you want to hold the box.
2. Select the Rectangle Text Box tool ([A]) and add a text box to that master page (if it does not have one already).
3. Select the Linking tool ( ) and click on the broken chain icon ( ) in the upper left corner on a master page. The broken chain icon will be surrounded by a marquee.
4. Treat this icon as the *previous text box*, and click on the text box(es) that you wish to become part the automatic text chain.

Remember that the automatic text box is added only to the first master page when **Automatic Text Box** is selected in the New Document dialog box. Any subsequent master pages you create will not have automatic text boxes, unless you create them using these steps or by duplicating a master that already has one.

TIP: Another way to add a new master page with an automatic text box is to duplicate a master page that already has an automatic text box, and then modify the duplicate to customize the new master page.

Editing an Automatic Text Box

You cannot enter text in an automatic text box, but you can control the Style characteristics of the text it will contain. Any text formatting that you apply to this text box—character attributes or paragraph formatting—will become the default format when you type or import text into this box on document pages. You can also apply settings from the Box, Text, Frame or Runaround tab of the Modify dialog box.

The initial settings for the size, position and number of columns in the automatic text are determined by the settings you entered in the New Document dialog box when you first created a document. You can make these changes by modifying the automatic text box directly, but it's best to make adjustments in the Master Guides dialog box (**Page → Master Guides**).

Calculating the Width of the Automatic Text Box

In the New Document dialog box, you begin a new document by specifying (among other things) the width of the margins; this determines the width of the automatic text box on the first master page. If you are a traditional designer who likes to specify the width of the text as part of your design specifications, and if you know the margins and the page size, as specified in the New Document dialog box, you can calculate the width of the automatic text box using the following formula:

```
Automatic text box width = (page width) -
(inside margin measure + outside margin mea-
sure) - (twice the text inset)
```

If you know the column widths for your document, you can use the following formula to calculate the widths of a text box based on column width. You can set up columns in the New Document dialog box or the Master Guides dialog box (for master pages) or in the Text Box Specifications dialog box (for any text box):

```
Text box width = (Column width x number of
columns) + (gutter width x number of gut-
ters)
```

If you are more accustomed to defining page layouts in terms of the width of the text area rather than the width of the margins, you can set the width of the automatic text box *after* you close the New Document dialog box by making the first master page active (or whatever master page you have set up with the automatic text box), selecting the automatic text box, and using the **Item ➛ Modify** command to set the width of the box. This procedure changes the width of the automatic text box on all pages based on that master page, but it does not change the margin guides on the screen.

If you want the width of the automatic text box to match the margin guides, you can convert your specifications for the automatic text box width into margin widths using a variation of the previous formula:

Total space available for inside and outside margins = page width - automatic text box width

For example, if you know that you want the automatic text box to be 6 inches wide on an 8.5-inch-wide page, then the total amount of space available for both the inside and the outside margins is 2.5 inches (8.5 - 6).

Remember that the actual width of the *text* in the automatic text box will be the width of the text box *minus twice the text inset value*. QuarkXPress's default text inset value is 1 point, but you may want to change this to 0 for the automatic text box by changing the text inset value for the automatic text boxes on the master pages.

If you make your calculations before starting a new document, you can enter these values directly in the New Document dialog box. Otherwise, you can change the margins through the **Page ➛ Master Guides** command, or change the page size through the **File ➛ Document Setup** command after you have started a document.

Removing the Automatic Text Box

You may want to deactivate the automatic text box on one or more master pages, so that text that overflows from document pages based on these masters does not automatically flow to new pages. To turn the automatic text chain *off* on a master page:

1. Turn to the master page.
2. Select the Unlinking tool (⚯) and click on the intact chain icon in the top left corner on the master page (Figure 9.8).

A text box will remain on the master page—and on document pages based on that master—but text overflow will not add new pages in the document. You can instead simply delete the text box. If you draw a new text box, it will not be part of the automatic chain unless you manually add it, as discussed previously under "Creating an Automatic Text Box Manually."

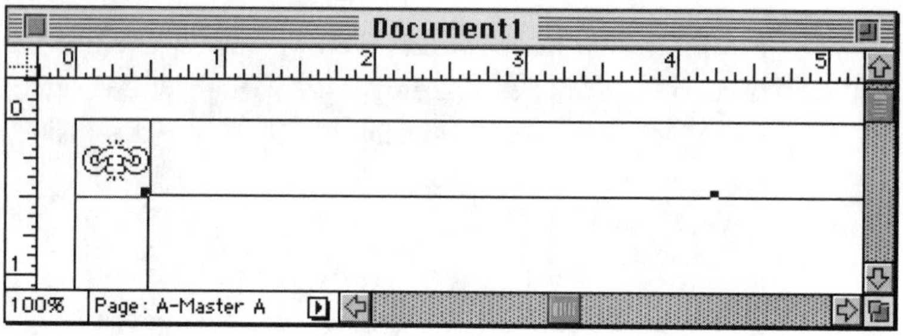

***Figure 9.8** A master page with the automatic text box unlinked shows a broken chain icon in the top left corner of the page.*

TIP: Removing or unlinking an automatic text box will not affect any document pages on which the automatic text box has already been filled with text. Only pages with an empty automatic text box, and any new pages based on the changed master page, will reflect the change.

Adding Headers and Footers

Additional text elements that are most commonly added to the master page(s) include a header and/or footer, or folios. Header and footers may include a page number and other text or pictures that you want to appear on every page. To create a header or footer, follow these steps:

1. Turn to the master page.
2. Select the Rectangle Text Box tool (A) and draw a text box at the top or bottom of the page—usually beyond the top or bottom margin defined for the automatic text box (unless that box defines the entire printing area of the page).
3. Type and format the text that you want to appear on every page.

The text could include a company name, a publication name, or an issue number. A graphic, such as a company logo, could be part of a header or footer. You may also type **⌘-3/Ctrl-3** to include the <#> character for automatic page numbering, shown in Figure 9.9 and described later in this chapter under "Automatic Page Numbers." Page numbers will not print folios unless this special character is used.

Headers and footers have logical positions at the top or bottom of the page, and page numbers are usually part of the header or footer. The most readily referenced part of any book is the outer edge of the page, and you can position page numbers at the outer edges of facing-page master pages. Documents that are not specifically reference materials—novels, for example—often center the page numbers. Some publications, notably magazines, intentionally put page numbers closer to the binding. That way, you are forced to open the publication fully to find a page number (and enjoy the advertisements while you're looking).

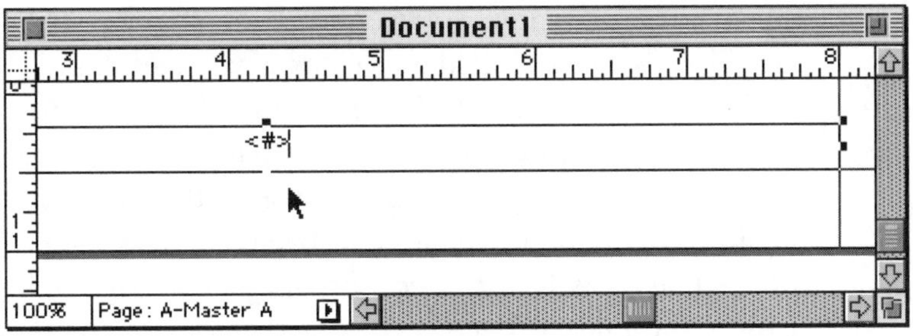

***Figure 9.9** The footer text on a master page might include the name of the publication or chapter and a page number, which appears as the symbol <#>.*

Adding Other Text and Graphics Elements

Items that will appear in exactly the same position on two or more pages belong on a master page. This includes graphic elements such as a logo that appears on every page, rules between columns, frames around pages, and other design elements. You can add other text boxes, picture boxes, and lines to the master page using techniques that include:

- Using QuarkXPress' tools to type text and draw graphic elements
- Importing text and graphics
- Copying elements from other QuarkXPress documents
- Arranging items on the page
- Linking text boxes
- Anchoring text and graphics
- Editing boxes and lines

You can apply text formatting for empty text boxes to master pages. Any text formatting that you apply to these boxes will become the default formats when you type text in these boxes on document pages. Similarly, you can format a picture box with predefined settings for background, frame, or scale percentage, for example. Those settings will be the default in that box on every document page based on that master.

Any elements that you add to a master page automatically appear on all document pages based on that master—pages that have already been created as well as new pages based on that master. However, if you *modify* an item on a master page, it will be updated on the associated document pages only if the item has *not* been modified on the document page. If the item has been modified in any way on the document page, changes made to that item on the master will not affect the document page items until you reapply the master. Even then, whether or not the modified item will be updated on the document page depends on whether or not **Keep Changes** or **Delete Changes** is set in Document Preferences. Applying master pages and the results you can expect are covered in the next section.

Applying Master Pages

There are a variety of approaches to applying a master page to a document page, and it's worth the time to familiarize yourself with all the options before you start building a long document. We'll summarize the two basic variations first, and then give examples of when and how to apply them:

- You can apply a master page to a document page *before* adding any content to the document page (other than the original master page elements).
- You can apply a master to document page *after* the document page has content.

Applying Master Pages to New (Blank) Pages

There are two ways of adding new, blank pages and assigning a particular master page to them:

- Use the Insert Pages dialog box (**Page ➛ Insert**) to indicate where in the document you want the page(s) added (by entering the page number before or after which you want pages added), and select the Master Page you wish to apply to the newly inserted pages using the pop-up menu. You can also select **Blank Single** or **Blank Facing Page** to apply *no* master to the new pages.
- Use the Document Layout palette to add a single new page, by dragging the appropriate master page icon into the desired position in the document page area. If you want to

add multiple pages using the Document Layout palette, hold down the **Option/ALT** key before you drag the page icon into the document page area, and the Insert Pages dialog box will be displayed, into which you can make entries as you normally would.

TIP: When you add pages in a document that has only one master page, that master page is applied to the new pages automatically. When you add pages in a document with more than one master page, the new pages have whatever master you select in the Insert Pages dialog box.

You can use the procedures described in Chapter 2, "Creating One Page," to add or change any of the items on a document page—including changing or deleting items that are derived from the master page on which a particular document page is based.

Applying Master Pages to Existing Pages

There are two ways to apply a master page to an *existing* document page. Both techniques use the Document Layout palette:

- To apply a master page to a *single* document page, simply drag the desired master page icon on top of the document page icon. When the icon becomes highlighted, release the mouse (Figure 9.10).
- To apply a master page to a single document page or *several* document pages at once, first select the appropriate document page icons in the Document Layout palette then hold down the **Option/ALT** key as you click on the master you wish to apply. To select contiguous pages, hold down the **Shift** key as you click the icon for each page. To select non contiguous pages, hold down the **⌘/CTRL** key as you click on each icon.

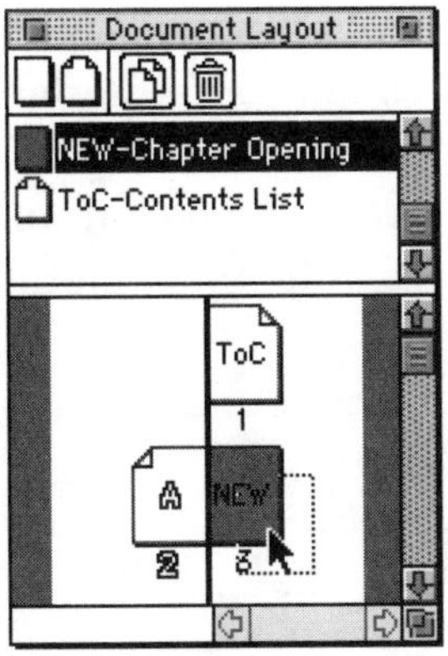

Figure 9.10 *Applying a new master page to a document page.*

When you apply a master page to an existing document page, exactly what happens depends on two things:

- whether or not you have modified, in any way, any of the items on the document page that are derived from items on the master page
- if you have modified items on the document page that are derived from the master page, whether you have **Keep Changes** or **Delete Changes** set in the Master Page pop-up in the General tab of the Document Preferences dialog box, discussed in the next section.

If you have not moved, re-sized, or in any other way modified master page items on a document page, applying a new master will behave in a pretty straightforward manner: QuarkXPress deletes all previous master page elements from that page and applies the new master page's elements. Any items created on the document page, and not derived from the master page, will not be affected.

Figures 9.11 and 9.12 show how master page changes affect a document page with an automatic text box, when no elements have been modified on the document page. In these examples, note that the text box on **B-Master B** had been linked to the automatic text box as described earlier under "Creating an Automatic Text Box." If the text box on **B-Master B** had *not* been linked to the automatic text box, a page would be inserted with no text in the text box.

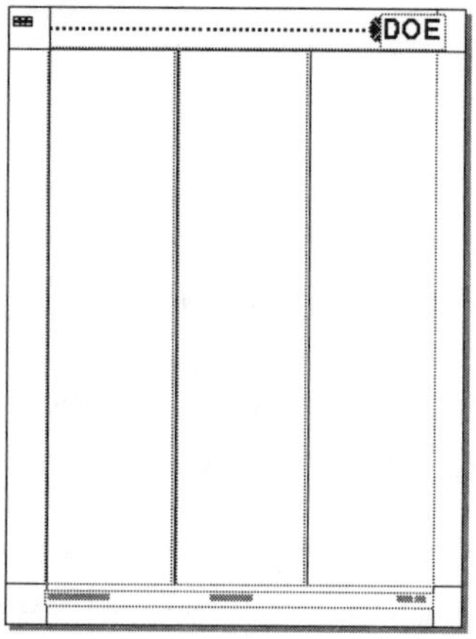

Figure 9.11 *Master page A (left) and a document page based on Master A (right).*

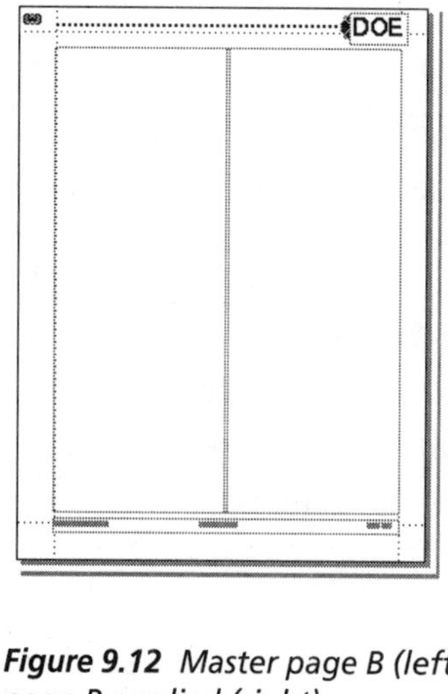

Figure 9.12 *Master page B (left) and the same document page with Master page B applied (right).*

Keep Changes Versus Delete Changes

As we have mentioned, the effect of applying a new master page to an existing document page depends on whether or not you have modified master page items on the document page, and whether you have Master Pages: **Keep Changes** or **Delete Changes** selected in Document Preferences. You may not think this affects the work you do, but since modifications to a master item on a document page include *any* change, including moving a master page element, or resizing it slightly, it's very easy to accidentally or unknowingly change master items. When that happens, the results may appear unpredictable, but they aren't really, if you understand the **Keep Changes/Delete Changes** options.

The preset default is that **Keep Changes** is set in the General tab of the Document Preferences dialog box. With this setting, a master item you've modified on the document page will *not* be replaced when the new master is applied. This means that if you've inadvertently touched a folio, for example, on a document page, a newly applied master will not delete the old folio, but will merely add the folio from the master page—you'll end up with two folios on the page: the old, modified one, and a new one from the newly applied master page!

If you change the Master Pages pop-up to **Delete Changes**, any items you've modified will be deleted. Using our previous example, a folio that has been modified on a document page will be deleted and replaced by the folio from the newly applied master. Very often, this is the setting that produces the results most people expect, and very often it is the solution to "weird" problems that occur when applying a new master to an existing page.

The following figures illustrate the effect of these settings. Figure 9.13 shows an example of a master page with a logo in the upper right corner, and the document page to which it is applied. If the logo is moved to the upper left corner, when you reapply the master page or apply a new master, the logo will remain in the upper left corner if **Keep Changes** is specified in Document Preferences (Figure 9.14, left), and the original logo item will also be added. The logo will be deleted if **Delete Changes** has been specified (Figure 9.14, right). If you change this setting after working on a document, the new setting will apply only to pages added to the document, and will not affect existing pages.

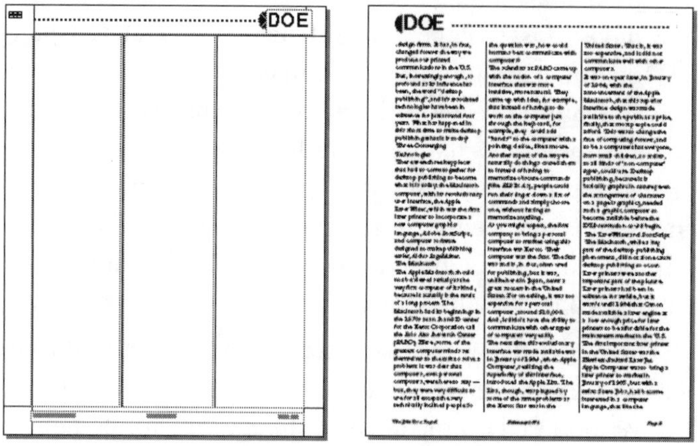

Figure 9.13 *Master page A (left) and a document page based on Master page A (right), with logo position modified.*

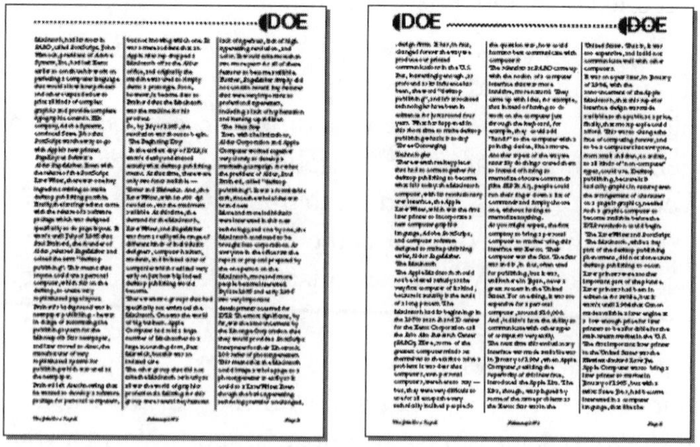

Figure 9.14 *The same document page with Master page A reapplied when* ***Delete Changes*** *(left) or* ***Keep Changes*** *(right) is specified in the General tab of the Document Preferences dialog box.*

Applying Master Pages to New Automatic Pages

When you import text onto a page with an automatic text box, new pages are automatically added as needed to accommodate text overflow. The new pages are added after the current page (assuming **Auto Page Insertion** in Document Preferences is enabled, the preset default) and the new pages take on the format of the master applied to the last page before new pages are inserted. With this effect in mind, there are a couple of ways you can approach a document that uses, for example, one master for the start of a chapter ("Chapter Opening" master), and a different master for all the subsequent pages in a chapter ("Normal" master), as detailed in the example in the following section.

The easiest way is to use the Master Page pop-up in the Insert Pages dialog box:

1. Apply the "Chapter Opening" master to the first blank page.
2. Turn to the first page and click in the automatic text box.
3. Use the Insert Pages dialog box to insert one page after the chapter opening page, and select two important options:
   - Choose the **Normal** master in the Master Page pop-up
   - Click **Link to Current Text Chain.**

If you do not click on the automatic text box first, the **Link to Current Text Chain** option will not be available.

Now, when you import text into the first page with the "Chapter Opening" master applied, text will flow from that page to the newly inserted page with the "Normal" master applied, and all subsequent pages will have the correct master—"Normal"—applied to them.

If you simply flow in the text with "Chapter Opening" as the first master, then all the pages added by text overflow will automatically take on the chapter opening master. You'll then have to select all those pages and apply the master for "Normal" pages.

If you apply the master for "Normal" pages to the blank page before you flow the text, then all the pages added by text overflow will also have the "Normal master," and you only have to apply the "Chapter Opening" master to the first page in the series.

The most efficient method is to add at least one new page with the correct master so that all newly inserted pages have the correct master applied. However, if you have a situation where you intentionally or accidentally allow new pages to be inserted with the wrong master, keep in mind that once the correct master is applied, text may reflow, and you may end up with empty pages that you don't want. Make sure you look over your document carefully after changing the master for automatically inserted pages!

Examples of Working with Multiple Master Pages

As we've discussed in the previous sections, one of QuarkXPress' greatest productivity tools is the ability to create and apply more than one master page in a document. Yet, while many people make use of single master pages, we've found a surprisingly small number have effectively utilized the power of applying different master page layouts in the same document. Part of the reason may be lack of know-how with setting up and applying various master layouts, but sometimes it's due to lack of understanding the appropriate application of this feature.

First of all, it's important to identify the type of documents in which it's appropriate to use different master pages. It is not always simply a document that has a different layout on each page. An 8-page newsletter, with articles running differently on each page, is not necessarily built more efficiently with multiple master pages—a well-designed single master with the appropriate grid and folios is probably sufficient. Rather, look for documents that have two different layouts on multiple pages, such as a book with chapter opening pages that differ from the rest, or an annual report that has pages dedicated to charts or graphs and which requires folios or part of the grid positioned differently from other pages.

There are many types of documents for which production can be streamlined by the use of multiple master page layouts. All of this theory about creating and applying multiple master pages might have your head spinning, so here are two practical examples of using multiple master pages.

A Book Design

Let's use the simple example of a book that contains opening chapter pages that differ from the regular chapter pages (Figure 9.15). The chapter opening pages always start on an odd-numbered page, have a graphic dropped behind a chapter number, and the text starts lower than on regular document pages.

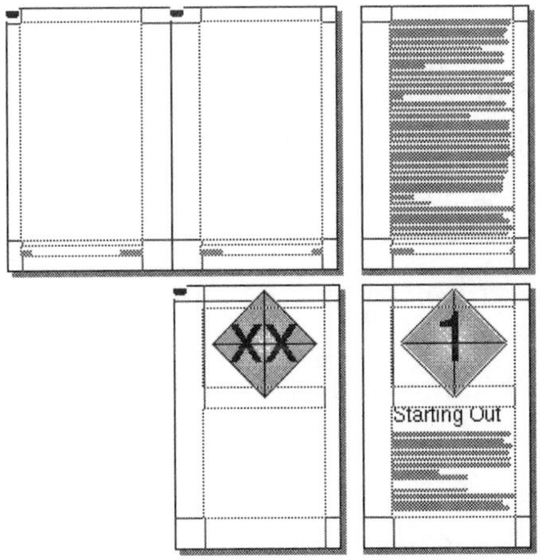

Figure 9.15 *Book design calls for special treatment of pages that start a new chapter: top row shows normal page master and document page; bottom row shows chapter opening master and document page.*

1. First, set up the master page for the regular chapter pages, defining the grid, text columns, margins, and folios.

2. You can rename the master page by clicking once on the name in the Document Layout Palette, then typing in a more easily identifiable name. Include up to 3 characters followed by a hyphen, and they will appear on the document page icons in the Document Layout palette. For example, the master page name "reg-Regular Grid" would cause the letters "reg" to appear on the document icons in the layout palette.
3. The next step is to create the opening chapter master page, by duplicating the regular, or document, master: click on the **Master Page** icon in the Document Layout palette, then click on the **Duplicate** icon () at the top of the palette. A new master page will appear in the palette, labeled "Master B."
4. Click on this icon to display the new master page, and modify it appropriately. In this example, we make these changes on the right master page only:
    - Delete the folio (header and footer)
    - Format the text so it begins further down on the page. This can be done either by changing the margins, or more quickly by dragging the top of the text box down four inches.
    - Add a new text box above the automatic text box, type a dummy character to represent the chapter number, and format it large and centered to match the design specifications.
5. Return to the first document page and apply the master for the chapter opening. Click in the automatic text box and use the Insert Pages dialog box to insert a new page. Apply the master for the "Regular" book pages using the pop-up menu. Be sure to click **Link to Current Text Chain** so the automatic text chain flows correctly from the first page in the document to the newly inserted page.
6. Import the text.

7. Display the chapter opening page and manually edit the dummy text, typing the actual chapter number.

A Magazine with Display Ads

Next, let's look at an example of the production of a magazine. Here is a system used by one of our clients that makes good use of different master page layouts for streamlining production. Like many magazines, articles are produced on the computer, but ads are still frequently stripped in by the printer or prepress bureau. The production staff simply leaves black boxes that will provide a clear space into which an ad can later be positioned.

Since ads are the main source of revenue for the magazine and it is desirable to have as many ads as possible, they are often added at the last minute, long after page layouts have been completed. To add them with the least amount of inconvenience, different master pages are created that provide the necessary space holder for each size ad. Then, as ads are assigned a position in the magazine, the appropriate master page can be applied to insert the correctly sized and positioned ad place holder in the layout. All the text reflows automatically, including anchored pictures and text (but not unanchored items). Final pagination, of course, still has to be done after the last ad is in position.

Here are the basic steps:

1. Each "ad" master page is created from a copy of the master page containing the original grid and underlying layout for the magazine, using the techniques outlined in the previous example.
2. Change the name of each new master to reflect the ad size, such as "1/3-vertical", or "1/4-horizontal"—the "1/3" or "1/4" will appear on the document page icon to which that master is applied.
3. Turn to each copy of the original master page, and use the Rectangle Picture Box tool to create and position a black box on each ad page, including the runaround, or text offset necessary (Figure 9.16).

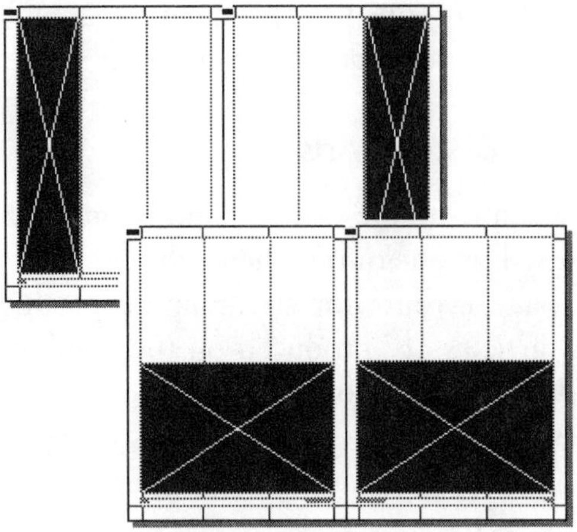

Figure 9.16 *Two new master pages show ad placeholders.*

4. Flow the text for each article onto pages using the normal master for the text layout. Lay out the article with illustrations as appropriate.
5. When it is time to put a page with an ad into position, apply the appropriate master page to each document page as needed (Figure 9.17).

TIP

You can select multiple document pages in the Document Layout palette: Press the **Shift** key as you **Click** on each document icon. To select a range of pages, click on the first page icon in the range, then hold down the **Shift** key as you **Click** on the last page icon to select all the pages in between. To select non-contiguous pages, hold down the **⌘/Ctrl** key as you **Click** on the page icons.

6. If the changed pages included illustrations that were originally positioned where the ad now appears, you will have to "tweak" the page layout to accommodate the ad.

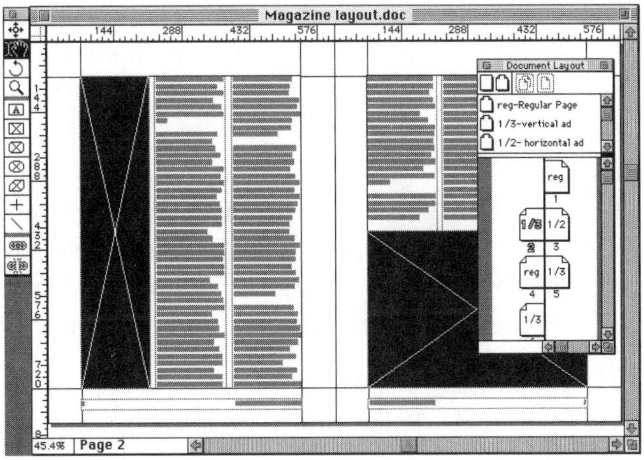

Figure 9.17 *Document Layout palette shows master page names and 3-character prefixes on document pages.*

These are just of couple of examples of the types of design and production that can be streamlined using the smart application of multiple master pages.

Numbering Pages and Sectioning a Document

You can set up page numbers to print on every page in your document by including a text box on the master page(s) that contains a special character for page numbers. Here we describe how to set up QuarkXPress so it automatically numbers the pages of your document, and how to further control page numbering by dividing a document into sections.

Automatic Page Numbers

QuarkXPress always numbers pages in a document and displays them at the bottom left corner of the document window and in the Document Layout palette, but in order to *print* the page numbers on document pages, you must include a special character that causes the page number to print. The special character is entered by typing ⌘-3/Ctrl-3. It's pretty easy to remember, because the 3 key also has the symbol for page number (#) on it.

You can type this character on any document page, and the page number will appear where you type the character. However, in most documents, this symbol is entered on a master page, which causes QuarkXPress to automatically number each page for you. To enter the special character for page numbers, turn to the appropriate master page, and:

1. Draw a text box where you want the page number to appear.
2. Type ⌘-3/Ctrl-3; the character <#> will be displayed.
3. Format the <#> character as you would any other text character, using the style characteristics you want the page number to appear in when it prints.

On the document page to which the master has been applied, the actual number of the page will appear, instead of the <#> character. The page number will appear on the document page in the position of the <#> character on the master page, and with all the text style attributes that have been applied to the <#> character on the master page (Figure 9.18).

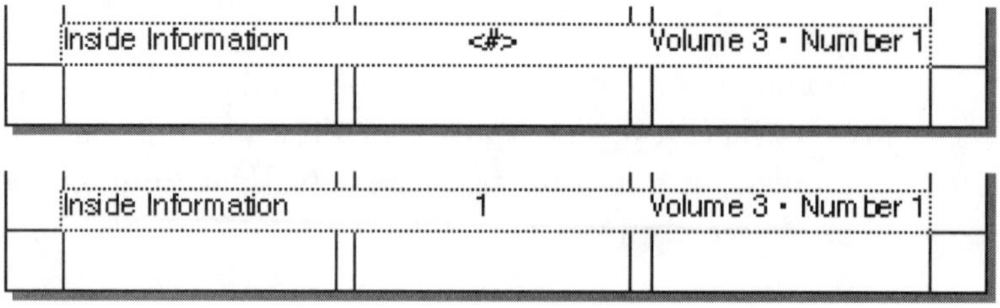

***Figure 9.18** Use the special page number character on master pages (top) so that your document pages (bottom) will be automatically numbered for you.*

Other Special Page Number Characters

The character for automatic page numbering is just one of three special page number characters available. You can also include special characters that indicate what page a story continues on (*next box* page number in QuarkXPress terminology), or what page a story is continued from (*previous box* page number). This feature is especially critical for magazine or newspaper publishing, where stories frequently do not flow one page after the next, but often jump to a page much further back in the publication.

The character for the *previous* box number, usually a "continued from page number" reference, is ⌘-2/CTRL-2, and the character for *next* box, usually a "continued on page number" reference, is ⌘-4/CTRL-4. The character covered in the previous section, ⌘-3/CTRL-3, is technically the page number character for the *current* text box, that is, the page on which the current text box is located.

The following table summarizes each of these entries.

Keyboard Entry (Macintosh)	Keyboard Entry (Windows)	Page Number
⌘-2	CTRL-2	Previous Text Box Page Number
⌘-3	CTRL-3	Current Text Box Page Number
⌘-4	CTRL-4	Next Text Box Page Number

Wherever you type ⌘-2/CTRL-2 in a text box, QuarkXPress displays the page number of the previous box in a linked chain. Similarly, wherever you type ⌘-4/CTRL-4 in a text box, QuarkXPress displays the page number of the next box in a linked chain. If the text box containing the Previous Box or Next Box character is not linked to any other box, the page number will display **<none>**. However, when a text box that contains the Previous Box or Next Box characters overlaps a text box that is linked to other boxes, page number references are determined by that box's links, and the page numbers will be displayed accordingly.

TIP

It's a good idea to put jump-to text such as "Continued from page..." or "Continued on page..." along with the Previous Box or Next Box character, in a separate, unlinked text box at the top or bottom of the linked text box that contains the story. This way, the jump-to lines will not reflow if the story is edited. Be sure the box with the Previous Box or Next Box page number reference *overlaps* the text box that contains the story; if it's outside the story text box, the page reference will always read *<none>*.

One of the great things about these page number references is that QuarkXPress automatically renumbers pages and updates all page number references within the text whenever you add, delete, or move pages within a document!

Dividing a Document into Sections

Normally, QuarkXPress starts a document with page number 1. The page number will be displayed on and print from each page, if you use the special character for page numbering (**⌘-3/Ctrl-3**), described in the previous section. However, there are many situations where you don't want the first page number of a document to be 1. One common example would be a large book that is organized with each chapter a separate file; in that case, the first page of the file for Chapter 2 would almost certainly not be "1," but would likely be the next number in sequence after the last page of the first chapter.

You can use sectioning to change the page number on the first page of a file, but you can also divide a single QuarkXPress document into any number of sections. A *section* is a group of sequentially numbered pages within a document, and individual sections within a document can have their own page number format and sequence.

You can use the Section command, then, to change the page numbering several times within a single document. This can be useful when creating a document like a book, that might include front pages (such as a title page, with no page number), followed by a preface (with page numbering starting at 1, but with page numbers formatted as Roman numerals such as i, ii, iii), followed by a chapter (which also starts numbering at 1, but formatted as Arabic page numbers 1, 2, 3). You can also create sections with compound page numbers, such as 1-1, 1-2, 1-3, followed by 2-1, 2-2, 2-3, and so on (Figure 9.19).

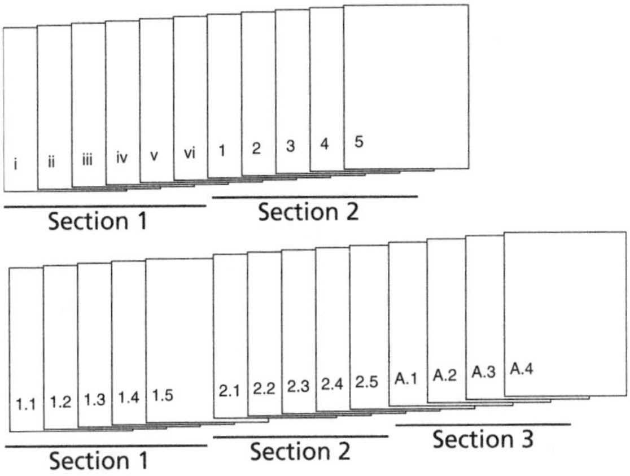

Figure 9.19 *Two examples of page number sequences in sectioned documents.*

There are many uses for sectioning and you can change any page number in a document, using the Section command (**Page ➛ Section**). To start a new section, follow these steps:

1. Make sure the page you wish to have start a new section is the active page (i.e., it's page number is displayed in the bottom left corner of the document window).
2. Next choose the **Page ➛ Section** command to display the Section dialog box (Figure 9.20).

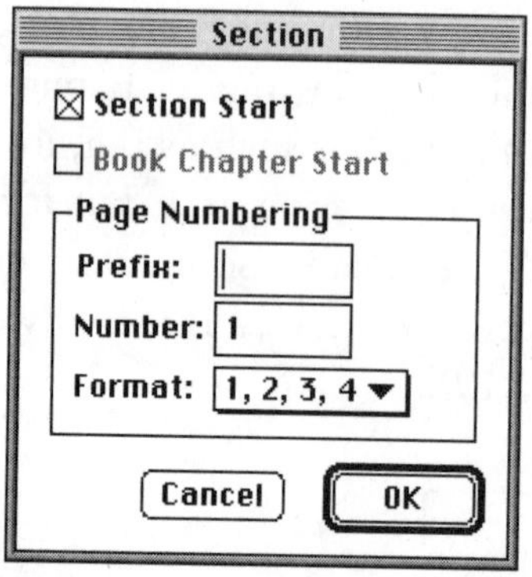

Figure 9.20 *The Section dialog box.*

TIP: You can quickly access the Section dialog box by clicking on the page number in the lower left-hand corner of the Document Layout palette. Note that if you use this method, the page you will be sectioning is not the active page in the document window, but whichever page icon in the palette is highlighted.

3. In the Section dialog box, check **Section Start.**
   - If the document has been added to a Book file, the first page of the document will be checked Book Chapter Start, and that selection will be grayed out. Check Section Start to uncheck **Book Chapter Start**, thus overriding, with a document section start, the automatic page numbering that might result from Book pagination. See Chapter 10, "Books, Lists and Indexing," for more information on Books.
   - You can enter up to four characters in the **Prefix** box. A prefix is useful if your document renumbers pages starting at number 1 for each section, such as 1-1, 1-2, 1-3, followed by 2-1, 2-2, 2-3, or APX-1, APX-2, APX-3.

TIP: Whenever you use commands that prompt you to enter a page number—such as **Page → Go To**, **Page → Insert**, **Page → Delete**, and **Page → Move**—you must enter any prefix that has been assigned in the Section dialog box, along with the page number.

- You can enter any starting page number in the **Page Number** box. Page numbers must be entered in Arabic numerals (1, 2, 3) regardless of the format you select.
- The **Format** pop-up menu lists QuarkXPress' five-page number format options: Numeric (1, 2, 3), Uppercase Roman (I, II, III), Lowercase Roman (i, ii, iii), Uppercase Alphabetic (A, B, C), and Lowercase Alphabetic (a, b, c).

4. Click **OK** to close the dialog box.

When you section a document, the document page numbers will be updated to reflect the entries in the Section dialog box. The lower left corner of the document window displays the new page number, and any automatic page number characters will be updated as well. The Document Layout palette will display the new page number in the lower left corner of the palette when you click on a document page icon, and the page icons themselves will display this number as well. (Previous versions of QuarkXPress always numbered these icons with the absolute page numbers, starting at 1.) Page numbers that start a new section are followed by an asterisk (*).

If you choose **Page ➛ Section** when the active page is already set up as the start of a section, the Section Start box will already be checked and the assigned starting page number and format will show in the Prefix, Page Number, and Format boxes. You can change any of these values, or you can merge the current section with the previous section of the document by deselecting **Section Start**. QuarkXPress updates the page numbers to follow the preceding section's format and sequence.

There are some special considerations in sectioning documents that contain facing pages. It may sound obvious, but remember that in Western countries, odd-numbered pages always appear on the right, and even-numbered pages always appear on the left. That means if you section a page so that it changes from an odd to even number (or vice versa), the page will change from a right-hand to a left-hand page (or vice versa), and take on the appropriate master, thus essentially applying a new master to the sectioned page and all subsequent pages.

If you change an odd-numbered, right-hand page to an even number, only that page changes to a left-hand page. Other pages will have the correct page number, but will not be on the correct facing page (i.e., you'll end up with odd-numbered pages with left-hand masters and even-numbered pages with right-hand masters). To force the other pages to follow in the correct sequence and have the correct left or right master applied, select the first page in the sequence after the sectioned page, drag its icon over the sectioned page until the right-arrow cursor appears (↦), then release the mouse; all the pages will flow into the correct location.

If you change an even-numbered, left-hand page to an odd number, it will be renumbered and will automatically change to a right-hand page, with the appropriate master applied. In this case, all the subsequent pages will be renumbered and will flow into the correct position in the palette, with all correct left or right master applied.

When sectioning documents that will be part of a book, keep in mind that sectioning done within a document—using the **Section** dialog box—will override the pagination that is done automatically when documents are added to a book palette. Without document-specific sectioning, documents added to a book have their first page sectioned as the next page number in the series created by the order of documents, called *chapters*, in a book. See Chapter 10, "Books, Lists and Indexing," for more information on Books.

User-defined vs. Absolute Page Numbers

The ability to change page numbering in the middle of a document, through sectioning, introduces the need to distinguish between *absolute* page numbers and *user-defined* page numbers. Absolute page numbers refer to the physical location of a page within a file, and the user-defined page number refers to the number of the page as determined by sectioning the document. For example, in a document with 30 pages, the fifteenth page in the file has the absolute page number "15", but that page number will display the user-defined page number, which might actually be page B-3 (depending on how the document is sectioned).

Once you start sectioning a document and changing the natural numbering system or setting up page numbers with prefixes, the user-defined page numbers will appear at the bottom left corner of the document window, on the page icons, and in the lower left corner of the Document layout palette when you click on a page icon.

When you use a command on the Page menu that requires the entry of page numbers (Insert, Delete, Move, or Go To), you can reference the page number in one of two ways:

- Enter the user-defined page number including the prefix: **B-3**, for instance.
- Enter the absolute page number *preceded by a plus sign,* such as **+15**, for example.

Using the absolute page number reference can sometimes be easier than referencing a page by the user-defined number, depending on how your document is sectioned. Let's say you need to reprint a preface, with pages numbered i, ii and iii, and the first page of the section following, numbered 1. Of course, you can enter the sequence in the Print dialog box as From **i** to **1**, or even type in the each page in the sequence **i,ii,iii,1**, but you can also type in the sequence **+1** to **+4**, without having to think about what the user-defined page numbers might be.

Creating and Using Templates

Whenever you start a new document, you must take certain steps to set up the pages before you begin importing text and graphics from other programs. In traditional terms, you define the design specifications for the document—making lists of type specifications and mocking up a grid system on paper. In QuarkXPress terms, this translates into making selections in the New Document dialog box, setting up guides and other elements on the master pages, defining style sheets, and setting other preferences and defaults before you begin adding elements to the first page.

Whenever you want to create a series of similar documents in QuarkXPress—documents with similar design specifications and page layouts—you can avoid repeating steps by initially capturing the design in a template. This section describes how to use QuarkXPress to create templates that embody a document's design specifications.

In practice, some of the steps described here might be done first on paper rather than on the computer. In fact, the designers on some teams might never actually touch the mouse. Whether you as the designer are simply drawing and writing out the design specifications or actually setting up the master template yourself, knowing how QuarkXPress works before you make your specifications will help.

What Is a Template?

A *template* is a QuarkXPress document that embodies the basic features of the design specifications. A template usually makes use of master pages, and they may include some sort of grid system for laying out the pages (beginning with page size and margins). A template can also incorporate a system for applying type specifications (using style sheets or by storing preformatted text boxes in a Library), a source of standard symbols and graphics used in the document (stored on the Pasteboard, in a Library, or in external files to be imported), and standing items that are always printed in the same location on certain pages (such as a newsletter banner). A template is set up with all defaults tailored to match the design specifications for the document (Figure 9.21).

A template might consist of no more than a simple grid of margin guides and an automatic text box with column guides. For example, whenever you start a new document in QuarkXPress, you specify the basic parameters, such as the size of the page, the orientation of the printed image, and the text margins, before adding any text or graphics to the pages. By setting up these specifications in the template, you can be sure that all documents created from it have the same page size and orientation settings.

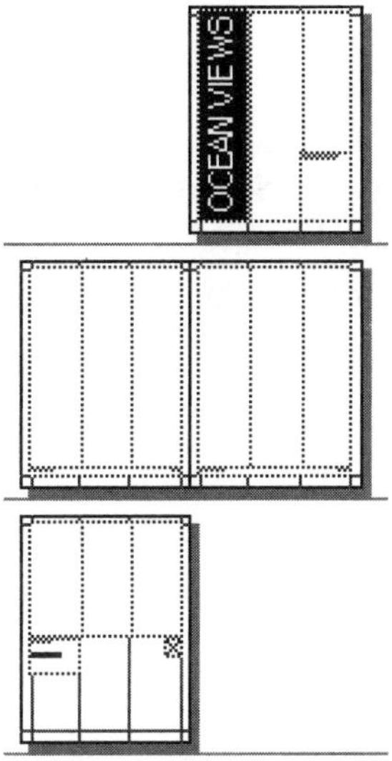

Figure 9.21 *A template document.*

A more complex template might include common text and graphic elements, such as headers and footers, headlines, rules, and other repeating symbols and graphic elements. A template can include style sheets for applying type specifications used throughout the publication. A template can also incorporate productivity aids, such as guides for aligning objects across facing pages and for positioning text and graphics. It can include common elements that will appear within the document in specific locations or at repeated intervals.

Once a template document is created, it can be used over and over to create a series of documents that follow the same design specifications. For instance, a long publication might have one template document that is used to create a series of sections or chapters that all follow the same design specifications. A short publication that is produced regularly—such as a newsletter—would have one template from which each issue is created.

As you learned in Chapter 2, the Save as dialog box in QuarkXPress lets you save a document as a template (Figure 9.22). A QuarkXPress template differs from a document in that when you open a template, a new document opens with a default name such as Document1. When you first save the new document you get the Save as dialog box, prompting you to assign a new name so you cannot inadvertently overwrite the original.

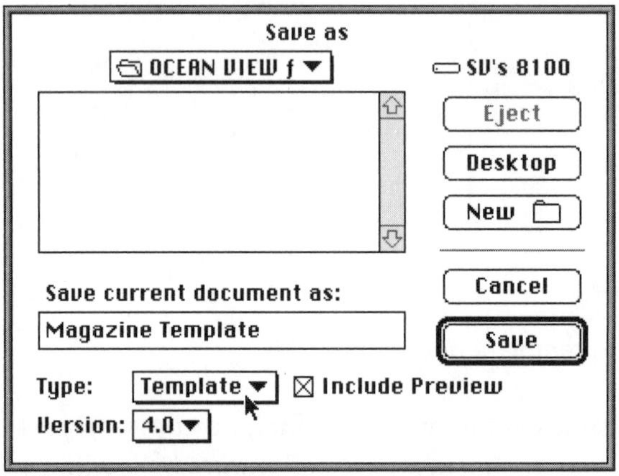

Figure 9.22 *The Save as dialog box lets you save a document as a template.*

You can easily distinguish between the two types of documents in the Open dialog box by examining the document icon in the Open dialog box—template icons show dotted lines for text; document icons show solid lines. If you click once on a document name, the text below the list of files changes to read "Template Version 4.0" or "Document Version 4.0." If you check the **Preview** option in the Open dialog box, then a thumbnail preview of the first page of the template and the page size will display in the dialog box when you click once on the template file name (Figure 9.23).

Figure 9.23 *The Open dialog box lets you view a thumbnail preview of a template.*

Benefits of Using Templates

The essential benefits of using a template system are that it saves repeated setup steps, helps you to think ahead, embodies design, and helps enforce consistency.

Save Repeated Setup Steps

One major benefit of using a template system is that the decisions and actions described under the next headings are executed only once during the production cycle, rather than once for every new file that will be a part of the full publication. Templates save time in large production projects by capturing a few of the steps required to set up a new document, so the same steps do not have to be repeated every time a similar document is started. You can save hours or days over the life of a project by using a template system for large or periodical publications.

It is a good idea to develop a template system for any project that will require more than one QuarkXPress document file. Books, reports, manuals, newsletters, and magazines are candidates for template systems where a single template is used to create a separate document file for each chapter, section, or issue. Even if the number of pages required for a document is less than the maximum allowed by QuarkXPress, there are good reasons for dividing these publications into several documents, all built from the same template. Shorter documents, such as price lists, menus, ads, and brochures, are candidates for template systems if you will be producing more than one document with the same or similar layout.

Help You to Think Ahead!

It's a good idea to think out the design of your document before making your initial page setup. Never sit down at your computer to produce a report or newsletter without planning ahead. The first step in thinking out a production plan is to list the design specifications that will be applied throughout a publication. Wherever possible, design specifications should be captured in the template system. Even if the design specifications are already clearly written out on paper, the QuarkXPress menus and options can provide a structure for organizing them.

Embody Design

Aside from the practical considerations of saving time and providing a disciplined approach to producing a document, a template system can ensure that design specifications are easy to apply. By incorporating as many of the design specifications as possible into a QuarkXPress template, the production group can better preserve the look intended by the designer.

Enforce Consistency

It goes without saying that a good designer always applies the rule of consistency. This means that part of the designer's responsibility is to make sure that all elements have been considered, and that no one on the production team will need to invent design specifications for details that were not covered by the designer's original specifications.

In the past, the designer enforced consistency by issuing lists of standards and having blue lines printed as grid guides on the final page-layout boards. In QuarkXPress you enforce consistency by using templates and style sheets to enforce a grid system, apply type specifications, and set up specific line lengths and widths, box background colors, tab settings, paragraph alignment (flush left, justified, and so on), and indentations.

The designer also needs to specify standard spacing between figures and text as well as the spacing between headings and body copy. You can use the **Item ➛ Modify** command to define the inset that will determine the distance between the contents of that box and adjacent boxes.

Creating a Template Document

The next sections describe the basic steps in creating a template document in QuarkXPress. There are really two approaches you can take:

- Create a template that includes all of the elements that are common to all documents in the series, then open the template and add text and graphics to create each final document in the series.
- Instead of creating a template *per se*, you might choose simply to create the first document completely, then copy that document and *delete* parts you don't need and save the cut-down version as a template. Then open the template and add new text and graphics to create the second and subsequent similar documents.

Whichever approach you take, it is important to set up the elements described in the next sections carefully in the first document—whether it is a template or a finished document—so that subsequent documents based on it will match the design specifications. If you are careless in creating the first document, you might end up with a series of documents that all share the same *incorrect* specifications, and add hours of work by making the same corrections in every document individually.

Define the Page Size, Margins, and Columns

Whenever you open a new document, you first define the page size, margins, and columns through the New Document dialog box. The values specified here for margins and columns will affect the first page of the document and the original Master Page A.

TIP

You can change the page size at any time using the **File → Document Setup** command. You can change the margin and column guides for any given master page by choosing **Page → Display → Master** and then choosing **Page → Master Guides**.

Most publications use the same page size for all sections, but the orientation of the pages may vary from section to section. For instance, you might have a set of appendices that need to be printed wide to accommodate many columns of numbers in a financial report. These types of documents are easy to accommodate, since QuarkXPress lets you have up to 127 different master pages.

Select a Unit of Measure and Display Rulers

If all of your design specifications are given in the same unit of measure, then you can set your preferences in the template document and the same unit of measure will apply to all files created from the template. Use the **Edit → Preferences → Document** command and then click the **General** tab (Figure 9.24).

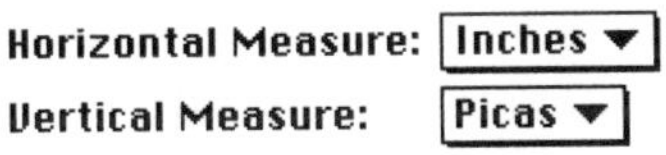

Figure 9.24 *Set the preferred unit of measure in the template document in the General Document Preferences dialog box.*

If your specifications are given in two or more different measures—inches for margins and points for type, for instance—then select that unit of measure in which you prefer to view the rulers.

You will probably use **View ➛ Display Rulers** (**⌘-R/CTRL-R**) to display the rulers during the design phase in order to help lay out your grid precisely. If you leave the rulers on in the template document, they will be displayed automatically in all documents that are created from the template.

Set Up the Master Pages

We have already suggested that a different master page might be appropriate for each unique page margin specification and for each different column setting. In general, you should set up a different master page for each section of the document that requires different margins, columns, or page orientation, plus different masters for each page design that includes added text boxes or picture boxes.

In addition, there may be other essential differences between sections of the document that can be handled efficiently through different master pages. For example, when the headers and footers change between major sections of a document, then multiple master pages are called for.

As mentioned earlier in this chapter, by assigning names to master pages, you make it easy to select and apply the correct master page to document pages.

The headers and footers on the master pages of the template may be set up as placeholders only: they are set up in position with the correct type specs and alignment, but the text can change for each document that is created from the template. One of the first steps in using the template, then, would be to change the text of the header and/or footer (Figure 9.25).

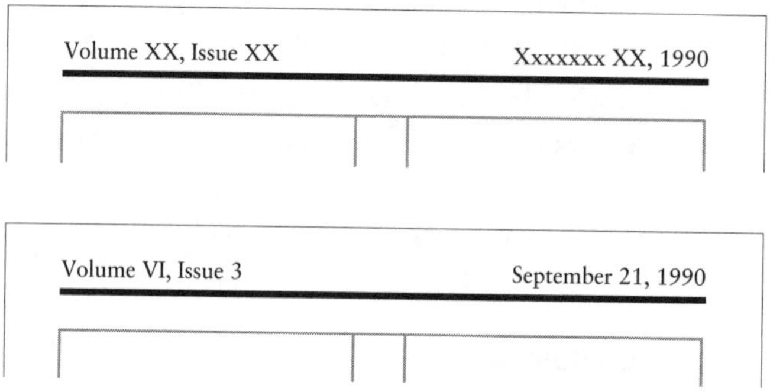

Figure 9.25 The headers and footers on the template document are placeholders only, and must be updated each time the template is used.

To set up multiple master pages in a document, consider how your text needs to flow throughout your document. For example, let's say you are creating a template for a book. The template file might include two master pages, one for the opening of each chapter and one for the following pages in the chapter. Examples of multiple master pages, and creating an automatic text box on each, were given earlier in this chapter.

Set Up Style Sheets

You can set the defaults for the normal body copy style sheet and any other standard text formats of the template document using **Edit → Style Sheets** as described in Chapter 4. All documents that are created from the template will have the same style sheets.

Identify Common Text and Graphic Elements

Most of the contents of the document will probably be imported from other programs. Some elements, however, will be repeated throughout the document. In a template, these repeated elements can be positioned on the master pages, on the Pasteboard, and on some document pages as described in this section. You can also set up a QuarkXPress library of commonly used elements as described in Chapter 3, to go with the template for the publication.

Besides the elements that are positioned on the master pages or stored in the library, certain elements may appear on the document pages in predictable locations (Figure 9.26). For example, the template for a newsletter could include the banner on page 1. If each issue of the newsletter always has the same number of pages, you might also be able to predict the positions of the subscription information and other standing features. You also can add placeholders for the text of headlines for feature articles that start on page 1.

Figure 9.26 *Newsletter templates can include standing elements on document pages.*

Design Specifications for Graphics Programs

In addition to providing the specifications for the QuarkXPress document, the designer should have a good idea of the number and source of graphic elements that will go into the document and provide the correct specifications to the production team. Knowing the capabilities and limitations of the available programs, the designer is responsible for specifying the treatment of each illustration. What are the size limitations or preferences for the figures? If you are following a grid system, you will want to make each figure's width match the increments allowed by the grid: a two-column grid allows only two figure widths (one column wide or the full page width), a three-column grid allows three different figure widths, a four-column grid allows four widths, and so on.

What fonts/styles/sizes will be used in illustrations and their captions? Will the figures be enlarged or reduced during page composition? Will photographs and other special illustrations be pasted up by hand or scanned into the computer? These specifications can be written down, or the programs that will be used to create the illustrations can be used to create "figure templates" just as QuarkXPress is used to create document templates.

One of the characteristics of any designed document is consistency of treatment, including the treatment of labels within figures as well as the figure titles or captions. This consistency can be difficult to achieve when you are bringing figures from other programs into QuarkXPress. The designer needs to specify how captions, figure titles, and figure labels will be handled in each different program that may be the source of illustrations for the document. Will the charting program be able to match the fonts used in figures from other drawing packages? Will the figure be scaled larger or smaller after it is in QuarkXPress?

You might decide that all figure titles and captions will be entered directly in QuarkXPress to ensure consistency, but you will still need to specify the preferred font for labels that fall within the figures. Furthermore, you may need to account for changes in the size of type that result when you shrink or enlarge a figure in QuarkXPress. As you learned in Chapter 6, when you change the size of a graphic imported from another program, you also change the size of the type used therein. If you know that you will be shrinking a figure by 50 percent, for instance, then the illustrator might need to make the type twice as large in the drawing program as it will be in the final document.

Using a Template Document

It's important that the same steps be followed each time a template is used. You may want to provide production notes for your own reference or for others who might use the template. Such notes are especially useful if you are part of a group where work on a series of documents is shared among several people. The notes can be a simple list of steps that serve primarily as reminders. For example:

1. Open the template and immediately save it under a new name.
2. Change the headers and footers on the master pages.
3. Change the volume/date information on page 1, below the newsletter banner.
4. Drag the Table of Contents text box from the library, and retype the new issue's contents.
5. Continue placing text and graphics as specified for the current issue.

You can type these instructions directly into the template, in a text box on the pasteboard next to page 1 or on page 1, where they can't be missed and the production staff will have to delete or move them before they start building the pages.

Test the Design and Template

It's a good idea to run a few sample pages of the document through the entire production process, starting with the various application programs used to create source files, including a word processing program and graphics programs, and finally using QuarkXPress. This will test all of the specifications before finalizing the design and the template. This dry run is more effective than any other review procedure for:

- Flushing out any mismatches between the design specifications and the system capabilities
- Fine-tuning the template as needed
- Identifying the detailed list of steps that should be followed for efficient production

Unfortunately, we often skip this final test: it may seem like a luxury when working under the pressures of a short deadline. We tend to trust that our own knowledge of the system is sufficient to anticipate any problems. In fact, the test run can save time on a project by developing efficient procedures and thereby *shortening* the production cycle. Failing to anticipate major problems (such as discovering that your printer cannot handle the graphics from the sources specified in the design) can add many hours to a project.

Template File Management

It's a good idea to organize your disk files before you start building a document in QuarkXPress. For instance, certain files should always be copied and used with any given template file, including the fonts used in the template. A few basic guidelines can save you a lot of trouble in the long run, especially if the document you are building is very large or uses a lot of different source files.

- If two or more people are involved in the production process, the disk organization and file-naming conventions should be determined by the production manager and announced to the production crew. File organization and naming conventions might be incorporated into the list of standards and review items as guidelines for moving or renaming files as they flow through the production process.

- If possible, assemble all source files—the text and picture files as well as the QuarkXPress libraries, templates, and document files—onto one directory or folder devoted to the publication (Figure 9.27). This directory or folder can be on your internal hard disk if your computer will be the primary workstation for page layout activities, or it can be on a fileserver if you are on a network and several people will be involved in the final document production. It could be a removable hard disk if you will need to carry the files from one station to another.

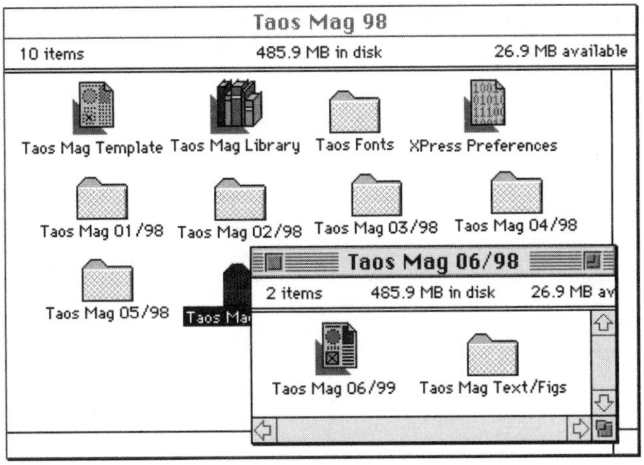

Figure 9.27 *A sample project folder.*

- If there are many files involved, divide the main document folder into subfolders. Some publishers like to keep text sources in one folder and graphics elements in another. Another way of dividing the files is to put the text and graphics files related to a single chapter together in a folder, so you end up with one folder per chapter.
- The publication-specific folder can also include a folder of the fonts used in the publication. Copies of these fonts can be stored in the System folder, but if you keep a set in the publication folder it will be easy to remember to take copies with you when you move the publication to another system to be printed.

Summary

Having studied the advanced features described in this chapter—working with multiple master pages and dividing a document into sections—you now have all the skills required to produce any type of document you can imagine. The next chapters offer additional tips that can be applied to developing long documents.

We also hope the tips in this chapter have inspired you to use QuarkXPress as a design tool and to create a template for any group of documents that follow the same design specifications.

10 Books, Lists, and Indexing

QuarkXPress 4.0 introduces three new features that are tremendous productivity tools in producing any long documents, including books or documents that are routinely updated and reissued:

- The **File ➛ New ➛ Book** command displays a palette that let you associate multiple QuarkXPress documents as "chapters" of a publication, and then print, paginate, and synchronize elements among them, such as style sheets and colors.
- The **Lists** palette (**View ➛ Show Lists**) lets you build a list of items that share the same style sheet(s) in a document. You can then generate a table of contents, a list of figure captions, a list of tables, or any other list based on assigned style sheet names.
- The **Index** palette (**View ➛ Show Index**) collects text identified by index markers and lets you generate an alphabetical, hierarchically-organized index using the **Utilities ➛ Build Index** command.

These new features can be used in combination to greatly enhance the production of long documents in QuarkXPress, a capability possible in previous versions only through the use of clever work-arounds or third-party XTension products. Each of these new features can also be used independently of the others, as they are tremendous productivity aids for many different situations. This chapter discusses various ways these new tools can be used.

Working with Books

The new Book feature of QuarkXPress 4.0 is an aid to both production and management of publications that can be divided into parts. A *book* is a new type of QuarkXPress file that lets you add individual documents as chapters, via the Book *palette*. Once a chapter has been added to the book palette, you can open, close, and track chapters through the palette. Books allow you to print and paginate chapters, and allow you to synchronize the H&Js, Style Sheets, Colors, Lists, and Dashes & Stripes among chapters. The palette automatically shows you if a chapter has been modified or if it is missing.

Even though QuarkXPress can handle individual documents up to 2000 pages in length, there are several good reasons for dividing a publication into sections or chapters that are individual QuarkXPress documents:

- You can keep individual documents small, so they can be transported in smaller media, such as floppy disks, or be printed in smaller chunks as each part is ready for the next round in the edit cycle.
- You can divide the work between several members of the production staff, or distribute it to different locations for processing before assembling all the parts for final printing.
- In publications that use a lot of graphics, it may be helpful to divide the whole into parts—separating color pages from black-and white pages, or putting pages with a lot of graphics into a document of their own.

Organizing Your Files

Before you follow the steps in the next sections for creating a new book, it's a good idea to set up a location for the templates, chapters, libraries, graphics, text files, and fonts that will be used during book production. If you are already familiar with this process, skip to the next section, "Creating a Book."

Some simple guidelines for organizing your files are:

- Use consistent naming conventions for the chapters, so they appear in correct sequence when viewed By Name from the desktop and in directory dialog boxes.
- If you stored all the book files in one location, you can set up file sharing (through the Macintosh OS Sharing Setup and the Users & Groups control panels, or through the Windows Network dialog box, accessed through the Control Panel) so multiple users can work on different chapters in the book. See Figure 10.1.

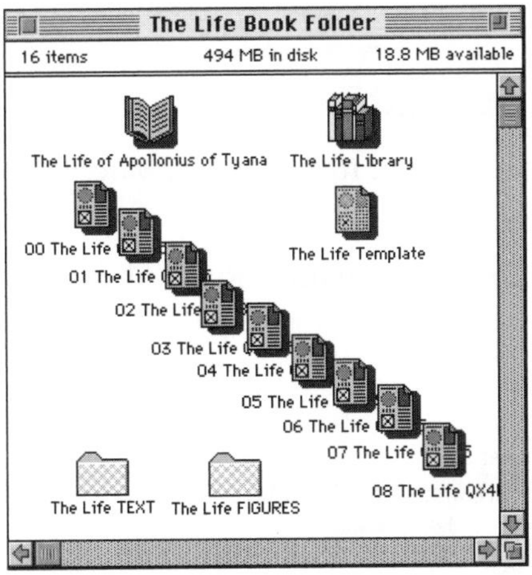

***Figure 10.1** Examples of folders set up for easy book production management.*

TIP

When different members of a workgroup make changes to a Book under file sharing, all open copies of the Book palette are updated automatically to reflect changes. You can control access to certain chapters by placing them in different folders with restricted file sharing.

Creating a Book

You create a new Book in three simple steps:

1. Choose **File** ➛ **New** ➛ **Book.** The New Book dialog box is displayed.
2. Type a **Book Name** and choose the path location for the book file in the New Book dialog box (see Figure 10.2).

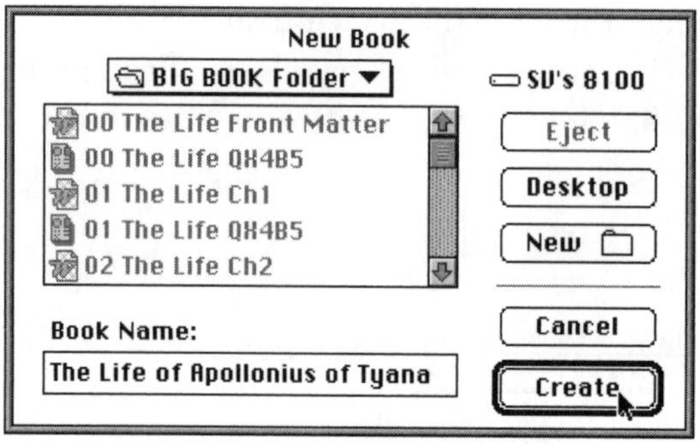

Figure 10.2 *Enter the name and location in the New Book dialog box.*

3. Click **Create** to close the dialog box and display the Book palette (Figure 10.3).

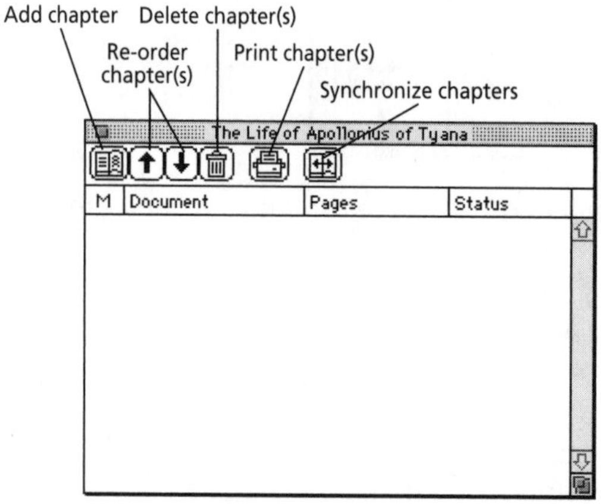

Figure 10.3 *The Book palette includes icons for adding, reordering, deleting, printing, and synchronizing style sheets for each chapter.*

Adding, Reordering, and Removing Chapters

Once a new book palette is displayed, you add individual QuarkXPress documents as chapters in the palette. You can add up to 1,000 chapters to a single book—for most of us, this means there's no limit.

To add chapters to a book:

1. Click the **Add** icon (📖) to display the Add New Chapter dialog box (Figure 10.4).

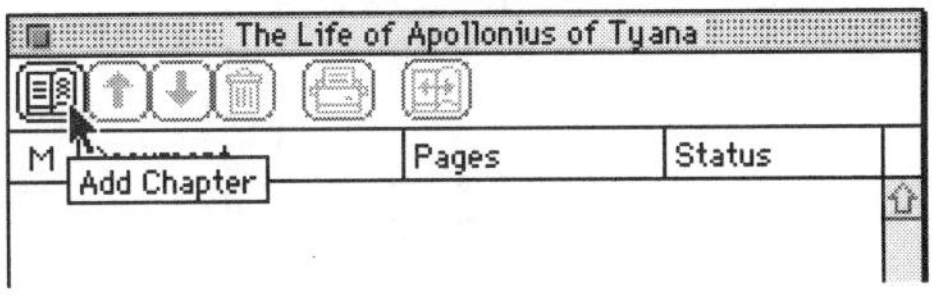

Figure 10.4 *The Add Chapter icon appears at the top left in the Book palette.*

2. Select the directory or folder for the first document you want to add in the Add New Chapter dialog box (Figure 10.5), and then double click the **document name.**

Figure 10.5 *The Add New Chapter dialog box.*

TIP The first chapter you add automatically becomes the master chapter that defines the Style Sheets, Colors, H&Js, Lists, and Dashes & Stripes that will be used throughout the book—it is displayed in bold type with an "M" at the left of the chapter name. You can easily change this later, however, by clicking on the chapter name that you want to be master, then clicking in the column on the left.

3. Repeat these two steps to add more chapters.

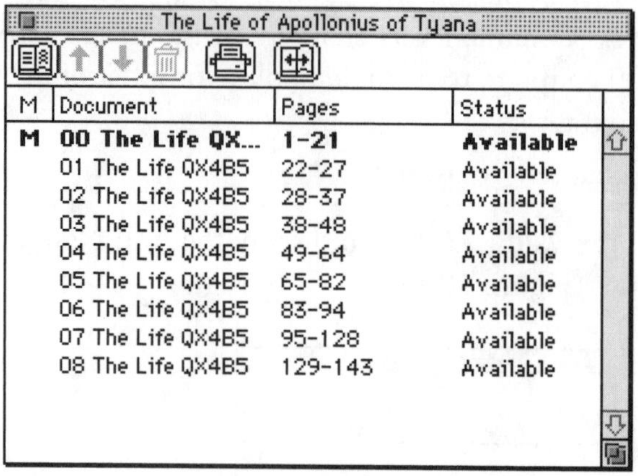

Figure 10.6 *Book palette shows list of chapters, including the name, page range, and status of each.*

Each new chapter is automatically added to the end of the chapter list if no chapter is highlighted in the Book palette, or immediately *before* a highlighted chapter. See Figure 10.6. If you add chapters created using an earlier version of QuarkXPress, those chapters will be converted and saved in the newer version format.

TIP: QuarkXPress allows a document to be added as a chapter to only one Book at a time. If you wish to add the same chapter to more than one Book file—for example, an appendix for which the information applies to more than one book—use the **File → Save As** command to make a copy of the file. Add the copy of the document to the second Book.

Once chapters are added to a book, you should open chapters through the Book palette rather than through the **Open** command from the File menu to take advantage of the Book palette's file management features. If you open a file and save it using **File → Open**, not through the palette, the status column in the book palette will show that the chapter has been "modified."

You can delete a chapter by highlighting the chapter name and clicking the **Delete** icon (🗑). This removes the chapter from the book list and automatically updates the page sequencing, but does *not* delete the document from the disk.

You can rearrange the sequence of chapters by clicking on a chapter name to highlight it, then clicking the arrow icons (⇩ or ⇧) to move the chapter up or down one row at a time.

TIP: Changes made to books (adding or removing chapters to the list) are not saved until you close the Book palette—by clicking the close box at the top left of the palette—or quit QuarkXPress.

Working with Chapters

In order to make use of QuarkXPress's book management features, you need to open individual chapters through a book palette rather than using the **File ➛ Open** command. You can open up to 25 different books at once, with each displayed in its own Book palette. Each palette remains open until you close it, and palettes that are open when you quit QuarkXPress re-open when you restart the program.

To open a book palette, and then open individual chapters in the palette, follow these steps:

1. Choose **File ➛ Open** (**⌘-O/Ctrl-O**) to display the Open dialog box.

   TIP: To open a book that is stored on a shared volume or file server, mount the volume first.

2. Use the controls in the Open dialog box to locate the directory, then double-click the **book name** (see Figure 10.7).

***Figure 10.7** Double-click the book name in the Open dialog box.*

3. Double-click a **chapter name** that shows Available or Modified status in the Book palette to open and edit that chapter (see Figure 10.8).

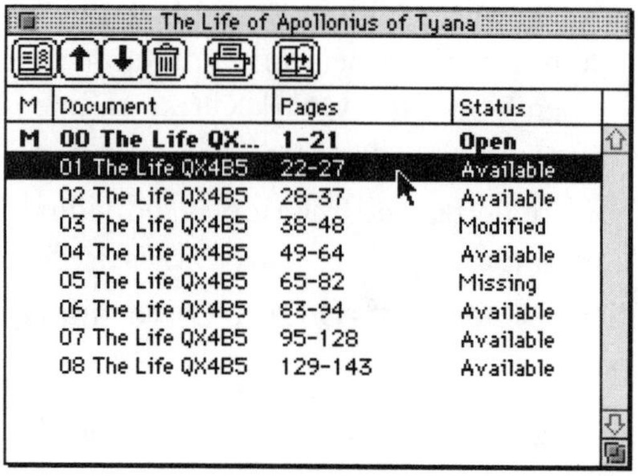

***Figure 10.8** Double-click an available chapter name in a book palette to open the chapter.*

4. Choose **File ➛ Save** and then **File ➛ Close** (or click the close box), to close an open chapter and thereby update the page range and status for that chapter in all book palettes that are open on the network.

5. When you are done, click the close box to close the Book palette and all chapters that are currently open on your system.

Using Chapter Status in Project Management

The Book palette offers a very simple, but useful capability for the management of chapter files. The Book file can be shared by multiple users, and contains a status indicator about each chapter. This capability is in no way a replacement for more sophisticated management systems, such as that found in the Quark Publishing System, but it can help you keep track of your files in a way not possible in previous versions of QuarkXPress.

A typical scenario might be where the Book file is kept on a server or shared volume, available to all members of a work group at any time. By opening each file to be worked on via the Book palette, the status of the file will be updated in the Book palette. There are five possible indicators for chapter status:

- **Available** means the chapter is present and current and no one else is using it.
- **Open** indicates that the chapter is currently open on your system.
- If another user already has the chapter open on their system, the **user's computer name** is displayed in the status column.
- **Modified** indicates that the chapter has been opened and modified independently of the book feature. This happens if someone uses the File ➛ Open command to open the chapter instead of going through the Book palette. It can also occur when you remove the chapter to another system—off the file server, for example—to edit it, then copy the changed version back onto the file server. You can update the status to **Available** by opening the chapter through the book palette and then closing it.
- **Missing** means that the chapter file is not currently in the directory where it was when last added to or updated in the book palette. You can double-click the chapter name to display a directory dialog box and locate the file.

TIP: When a book is open on multiple systems under file sharing, only one user can open a specific chapter at a time. This is managed through the Status indicator in the Book palette.

It's essential for the file management feature of the Book palette to be useful that chapters be opened via the palette, as mentioned earlier in this chapter. Common sense should figure in, too. For example, when you copy a chapter file to another disk, or take it to another system for editing, it's a good idea to remove the original from the book's directory so the status indicates that the file is **Missing** and other users don't attempt edits to the duplicate "master." For example, you might move the chapter into a "WIP" (Works-in-Progress) directory as a temporary backup while you are working on the copy. When you copy the edited version back into the main book directory, the status will indicate that the file has been **Modified.**

Synchronizing Chapters

You can synchronize all the Style Sheets, H&Js, Lists, and Dashes & Stripes used through the book to match the "master chapter." For example, you can change the definition of the "Heading" style sheet in the master chapter, and then use the Synchronize feature, following the steps defined here, to automatically update the "Heading" style sheet in all the other chapters of the book.

The master chapter is indicated by an **M** to the left of the chapter name, which appears in bold text in the Book palette. Initially, the master chapter defaults to the first chapter added to the book, but you can easily change it to any other chapter (see Step 1, following).

TIP: The first chapter of the Book need not be the same as "Chapter 1" in the book contents. It may be a document that contains only the title page, or it can encompass all of the front matter, including the table of contents.

To synchronize all the chapters in a Book to use the same style sheets, H&Js, lists, and dashes and stripes, follow these steps:

1. Set the chapter you wish to be the master by clicking on a chapter name to highlight it in the Book palette, then click the blank area to the left of the name to move the **M** icon to the desired chapter. See Figure 10.9.

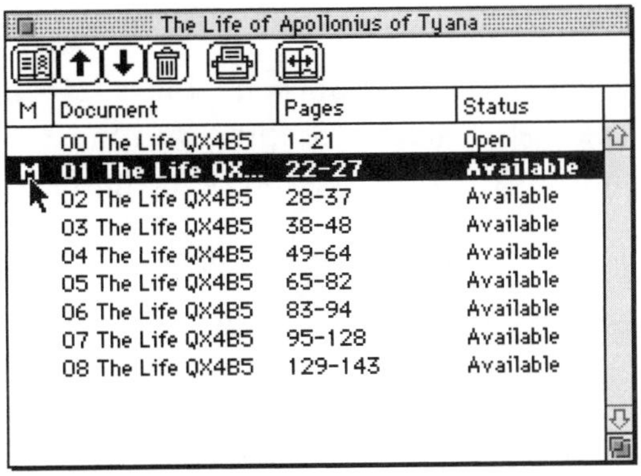

Figure 10.9 *Master chapter is indicated by an* ***M*** *left of the chapter name in the book palette.*

2. Open the master chapter if necessary to verify that the Style Sheets, Colors, H&Js, Lists, and Dashes & Stripes are set up the way you want the entire book to be defined.
3. Make sure that all chapters listed in the book palette show **Available** status. Chapters that are not available will not be synchronized.
4. Click the **Synchronize** icon (⊞), then click **OK** when an Alert prompts you to confirm the action.

These steps initiate a process during which each chapter is automatically opened, compared to the master chapter, modified, and saved. Modifications may include the following:

- Style Sheets, Colors, H&Js, Lists, and Dashes & Stripes with the same name are compared and modified to match the master chapter.

- Style Sheets, Colors, H&Js, Lists, and Dashes & Stripes that are in the master chapter but missing from the other chapters are added to those chapters.
- Style Sheets, Colors, H&Js, Lists, and Dashes & Stripes that are in other chapters but missing from the master chapter are unchanged.

Any time you change the Style Sheets, Colors, H&Js, Lists, or Dashes & Stripes in the master chapter, you must synchronize again if you want all the other chapters in the Book to match the changes.

Assigning Page Numbers

Page numbers are normally assigned in a QuarkXPress document using the automatic page number character (⌘/CTRL-3). You can assign a starting number for the automatic page numbering sequence by using the **Page ➛ Section** command, discussed in Chapter 9, "Master Pages and Sectioning." Assuming that all the chapters in the book have been set up with automatic page numbering, QuarkXPress will automatically number all the pages when the documents are printed as part of a book.

When numbering chapters, the first page of the first chapter begins with page 1 and subsequent pages are numbered sequentially throughout the book. For example, if the first chapter is 20 pages long, then the next chapter will begin with page 21. The Book palette always starts a new chapter on a right-hand page. If you want a chapter to start on a left-hand page, immediately succeeding the last page in the previous chapter, you have to "manually" assign the first page number using the Section command, thus overriding the auto numbering feature of the Book palette, which starts every chapter as a right-hand page.

When a page is encountered with a page number assigned using the Section command, then the page numbers restart with the page number assigned by the section command. For example, you might start with the front matter, and start the first chapter of the book the page number "i" assigned using the Section command. Then start the second chapter in the book palette with the page number "1," also assigned using the Section command.

Chapters in which page numbers have been assigned using the Section command show asterisks around the page range listed in the book palette, as shown in Figure 10.10.

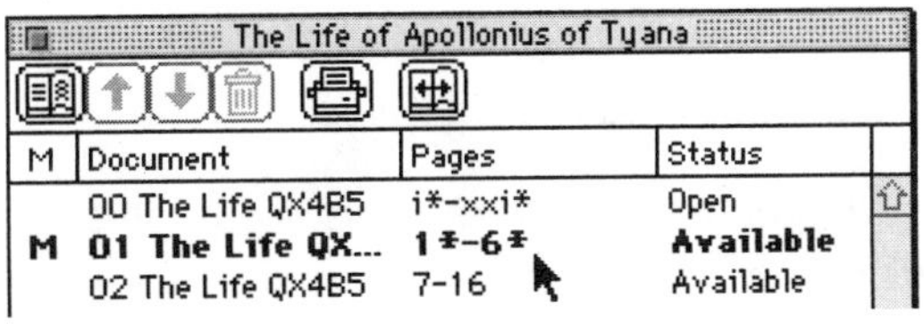

***Figure 10.10** Book palette shows asterisks around page ranges for chapters that have used the Section command.*

Printing Chapters from a Book Palette

You can easily print a whole book—or selected chapters or selected page ranges—from a book by printing through the Book palette. The only proviso is that all of the chapters you wish to print must show a status of either **Available** or **Open**. You cannot print chapters that are **Modified, Missing,** or **in use** by someone else.

1. First, **select the chapters** you wish to print:
   - To print the whole book, make sure no chapters are highlighted in the book palette.
   - To print one chapter, click on the chapter name in the book palette to highlight it.
   - To select a continuous range of chapters, click on the first chapter in the range and then hold the **Shift** key as you click on the last chapter name in the range.
   - To select a discontinuous range of chapters, hold the ⌘/CTRL key as you click on each chapter name (see Figure 10.11).

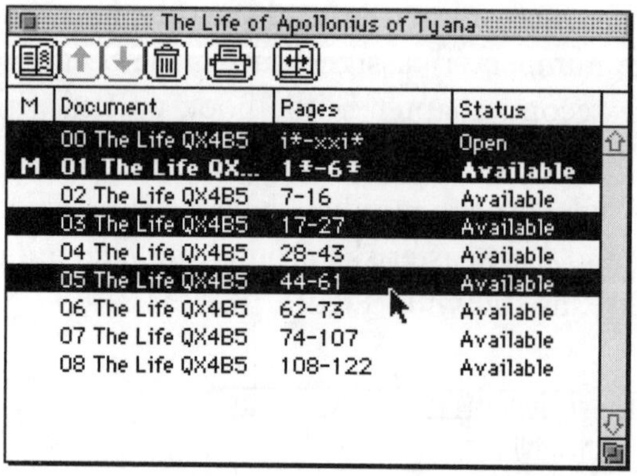

Figure 10.11 *Discontinuous range of chapters can be selected by holding the ⌘/CTRL key as you click each name.*

2. Click the **Print** icon (🖶) in the book palette to display the Print dialog box.
3. Choose **All** from the Pages Sequence pop-up menu to print all the pages in the selected range of chapters, or enter the desired page numbers from the chapters you highlighted in Step 1. See Figure 10.12.

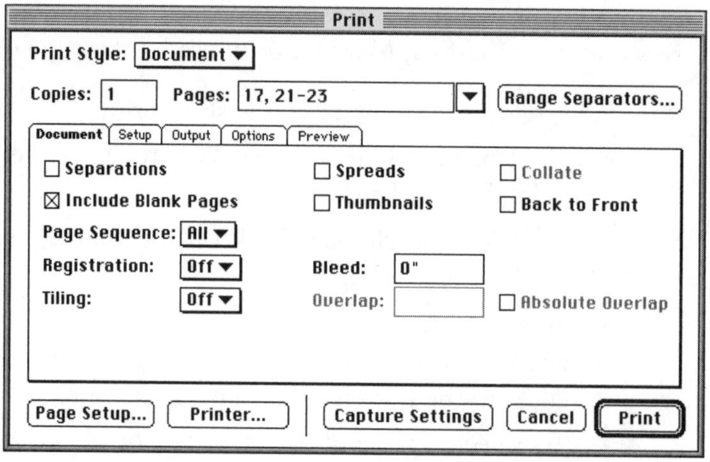

Figure 10.12 *Choose **All** or enter a page range in the Print dialog box.*

Remember that in fields that require you to enter a page number—such as the Print dialog box—you must enter the page number *including* any prefix, that has been assigned.

4. Make other entries in the Print dialog box, described in Chapter 8, "Printing Basics," including selecting a Print Style from the pop-up menu if one has been set up.
5. Click **OK** to start the printing process.

If the specified range includes a chapter that is not available, QuarkXPress will display an error message or a dialog box offering you an opportunity to locate the missing chapter (see Figure 10.13).

***Figure 10.13** Dialog box alerts you to missing or modified chapters.*

Generating Lists

The new list feature in QuarkXPress 4.0 enables you to generate a table of contents, a list of figure captions, or any list of paragraphs based on style sheet assignments. For example, if you have used style sheets named *Heading 1* and *Heading 2* to format the section headings in your document, you can specify these two style sheet names as the basis for a list and thereby generate a table of contents. Similarly, you could create a second list based on a style sheet named *Caption* to generate a list of all figure captions.

Each item in a generated list is a whole paragraph that has been collected from the document based on the paragraph style sheet criteria you set up. A list can include any number of style sheet criteria, and a document can include any number of lists. You can generate lists for individual documents, or for a series of documents or chapters that have been associated into a book.

Lists are managed through the Lists palette. The next sections detail the steps used in creating lists, along with a few tips on preparing a document for a list.

TIP You can use the Book and Lists features on documents that are not literally part of a book. For example, you could associate a collection of newsletters into a Book and use the List feature to generate a list of all the articles and all the contributors in the volume, if you have set up the article titles and contributors' bylines consistently using paragraph style sheets.

Before Generating a List

Before you begin the steps of defining and generating a list, you need to prepare your document(s) with your list strategy in mind:

- Each paragraph that you intend to list from a document must be set up with a paragraph style sheet. It doesn't matter what name you give each style sheet, but it is important that each style sheet name applies specifically to the text you want to appear in the list. For example, text for captions in your book might have the exact same paragraph and character formats as text that appears as a quotation at the beginning of each chapter. If you're not generating a list of captions, then you could create one style sheet and apply it to captions and quotes. If you intend to generate a list of figure captions, however, then you need to create two different paragraph style sheet names—one for the captions, and one for the quotes. Otherwise, the list you generate will include both captions and quotes.

- Depending on the type of list, you might decide to limit the length of each paragraph that will end up in the list. For example, if you are generating a table of contents, you'll want to avoid designing a document with heading levels that run in to a paragraph—keep headings on lines of their own. QuarkXPress limits list text to 256 characters per item. See Figure 10.14.

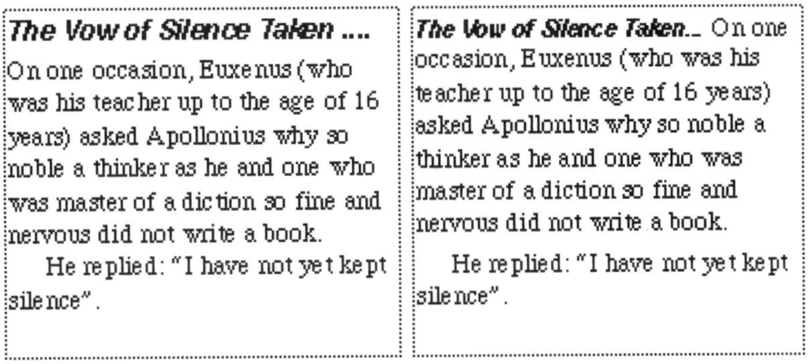

Figure 10.14 *In generating a table of contents, headings should appear as separate paragraphs (left), and not run in to paragraphs of body text (right).*

- Decide which style sheets will be included in the list, and what level each will have in the hierarchy of the list. You can have up to 32 different style sheets in a list, and up to 8 different levels of indentation.
- Set up a style sheet for each level in the list. For example, in the document the *Heading 1* style might be set up as 36 points, centered, but in the generated list of contents you probably want the heading smaller and aligned left. You create a new style sheet named *TofC head 1,* for instance, to define the look in the list. Include a tab setting for the page number, if applicable. Setting up a list is discussed in the next section.

Setting Up a List

To create a list for a document that has already been set up with style sheets:

1. Open the document for which you wish to create a list, and choose **Edit → Lists** to display the Lists dialog box (Figure 10.15). If you are generating a list for a series of documents that have been associated as chapters in a book, open the master chapter.
2. Click **New** to display the Edit List dialog box.
3. Type a name for the list in the **Name** field.
4. Select one or more style sheet names in the **Available Styles** list box on the left in the dialog box, then click the **Add** icon (the right-pointing arrow between the two lists) to copy the selection to the list box on the right—the list of style sheets that will be included in the generated list.
   - Click once on a style sheet name to select it.

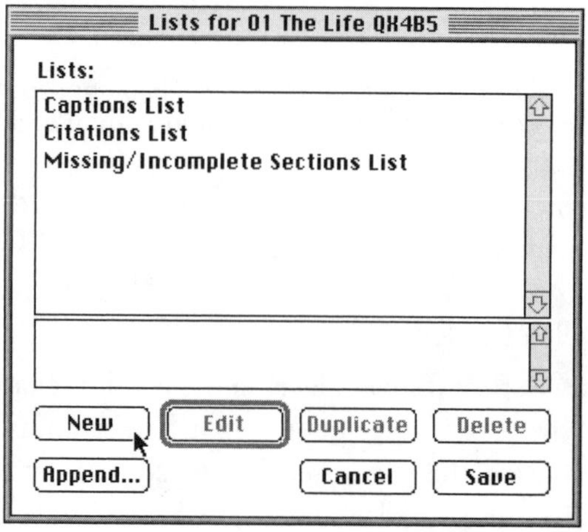

Figure 10.15 *The Lists dialog box.*

   - **Shift-Click** on another style sheet name to select a continuous range of style sheet names.
   - **⌘/CTRL-click** to select several discontinuous style sheet names from the list.

5. When you've selected all the style sheets you wish to use for the list, set the headings in the **Styles in List:**
   - If you want the list to show hierarchy levels by indentation, choose a level (up to level 8) for each style sheet name from the **Level** pop-up menu.
   - For each style sheet name in the list, choose an option from the **Numbering** pop-up menu to determine where page numbers will appear relative to the list item: **Text only** indicates that no page number reference is needed; **Text... Page #** positions the page number after the item; **Page #...Text** puts the page number before the item. See Figure 10.16.

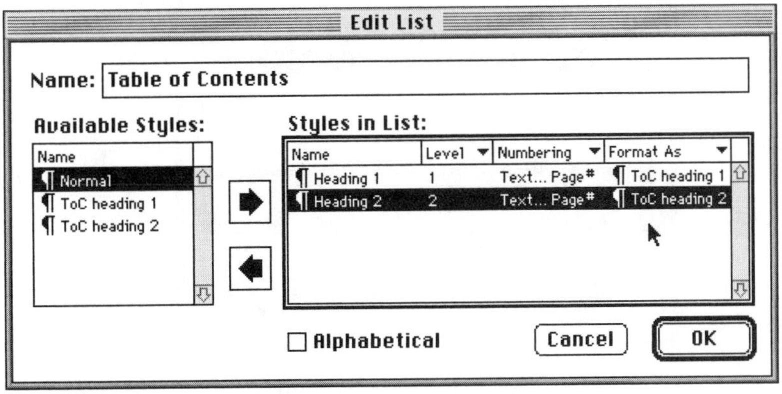

***Figure 10.16** Edit dialog box with list name and selected style sheets with assigned levels, page numbering options, and formatting styles.*

   - For each line in the list, highlight the style sheet name to select it (or use the multiple-selection techniques in Step 4), then choose a style sheet name from the **Format As** pop-up menu to define how the item will look in the generated list.
   - To **delete** a style sheet name from the Styles in List box, select one or more style sheet names (using the same techniques as described in Step 4) and then click the **Remove** arrow (the left-pointing arrow between the two list boxes).

6. Check the **Alphabetical** option to generate the list in alphabetical order. Otherwise, the list will be generated in the order in which the items appear in the document.
7. Click **OK** to return to the Lists dialog box (Figure 10.17), then click **Save.**

TIP

If you create or edit a list in the master chapter of a book, then you need to **Synchronize** all the chapters as described earlier, using the Book palette, before generating the final list for the Book.

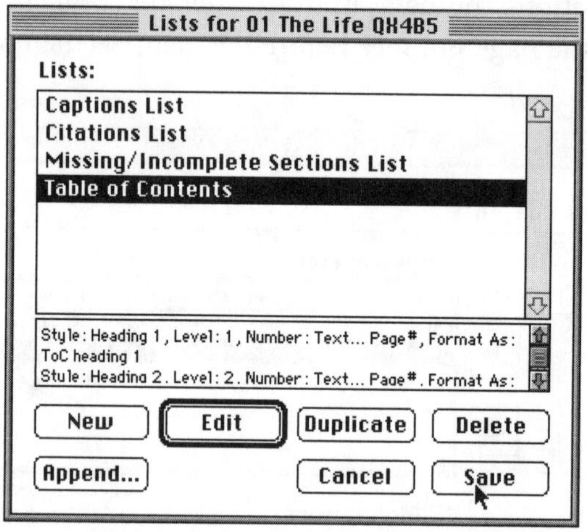

Figure 10.17 *The Lists dialog box shows all the lists you have defined for the current document.*

Generating and Updating Lists

After defining the list criteria using the **Edit ➛ Lists** command, you can generate the actual list and display it in the Lists palette, and you can flow it into a text box to be printed as part of the document:

1. Choose **View ➛ Show Lists** to display the Lists palette, if it is not already displayed.
2. Choose an option from the **Show Lists For** pop-up menu. Choose **Current Document** or one of the listed book names. Select a list from the **List Name** pop-up menu. The generated list appears in the palette.
3. Click **Update** to update the list as necessary to update the list whenever you make changes to the document that affect the list, such as editing the text or changing the style sheet applied to any of the list items. See Figure 10.18.

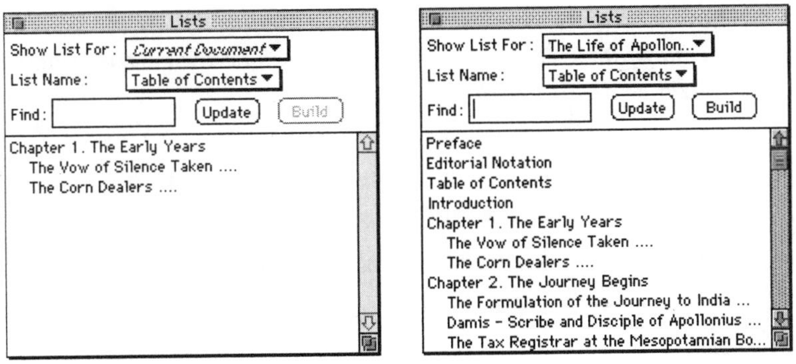

Figure 10.18 *The Lists palette shows list of headings in current document (left) and in a book (right).*

4. Use one of the Text tools to create a text box, or activate a text box using the Content tool, and position the text insertion point where you want the list to appear.
5. Click the **Build** button in the Lists palette to copy the list from the palette to the text box (Figure 10.19), beginning at the current insertion point.

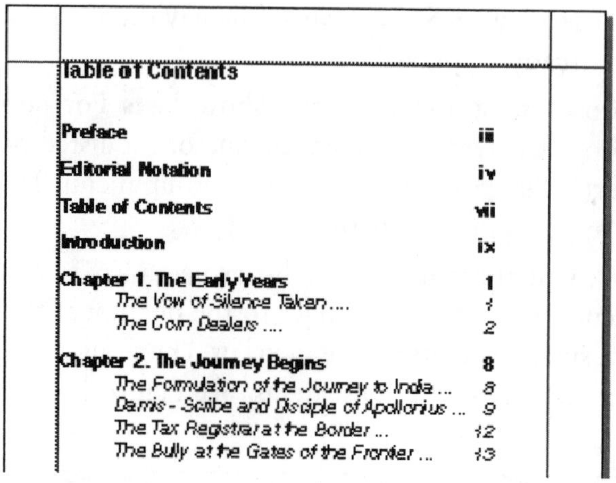

***Figure 10.19** The list in the text box will be formatted using the Format As style sheets.*

6. If the list has been built before, an alert box (Figure 10.20) displays, offering two options:
   - Click **Insert** to build a new list.
   - Click **Replace** to replace the previously generated list.

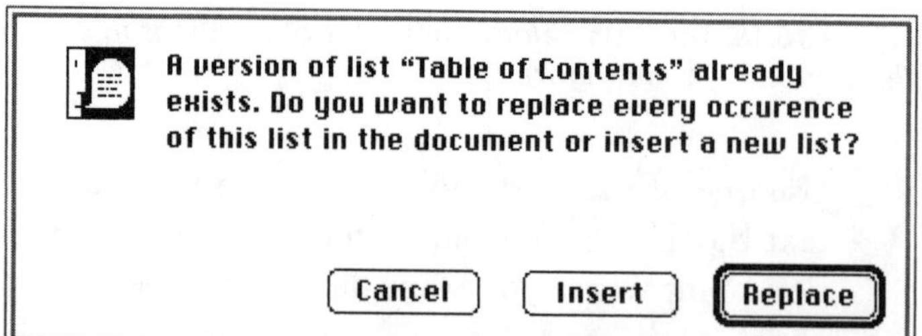

***Figure 10.20** Alert box displays if the list has been built before.*

Once you've generated a list, you can further edit it, or format it, and print it as you would any QuarkXPress document.

TIP If you make changes to the document that affect the list, you must click the **Update** button in the Lists palette to update the list, then select a text box and click **Build** again to update the printable version. Changes to page numbers can occur if you flow the list onto new pages added at the beginning of a document.

Working with Lists for Books

You can create a list from a series of separate QuarkXPress documents or chapters that have been associated as a book. The steps are the same as described earlier for creating books and creating lists, but this summary will make it easier to put it all together:

1. **Create a book** and identify a master chapter as described earlier in this chapter.
2. Open the master chapter and **create a list** as described earlier.
3. Click the **Synchronize** button in the Book palette to add the list specifications to all the chapters in the book, as described earlier under "Synchronizing Chapters."
4. Choose **View ➛ Show Lists** to display the Lists palette (if it's not still open from Step 2) and choose the book name from the **Show List For** pop-up menu.

All the chapters in the book must show **Available** as the status in the Book palette in order for the list to be accurate. If a chapter is not available, an alert box will prompt you to locate the missing chapter, as shown in Figure 10.21.

5. Click **Update** to build a new list based on all the chapters in the book.
6. **Build** the list into a text box as described earlier.

Figure 10.21 *Alert box displayed if chapters are not available.*

Using a List to Navigate a Document

You can use the Lists palette to navigate through a document or book to jump quickly from one section to another:

- Double-click on a line listed in the Lists palette to automatically jump to that paragraph in the document. If you double-click a line for a book chapter, that chapter will open and display the line on the screen.
- To find a specific line in a list, you can use the scroll bars in the Lists palette, or type a word in the Find area to jump to the line in the list that begins with that word. See Figure 10.22.

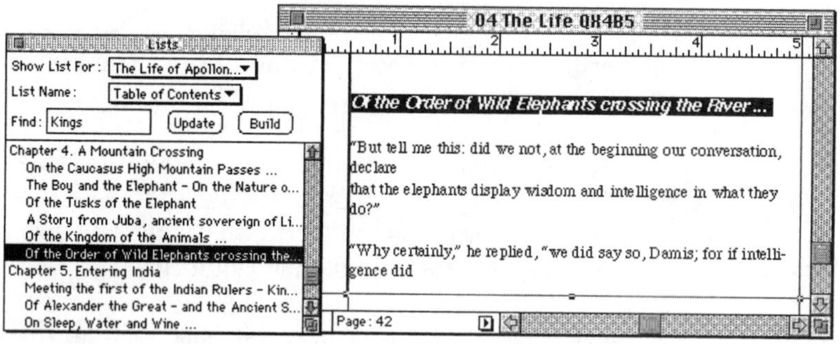

***Figure 10.22** Double-clicking a line in the Lists palette (left) jumps you to that paragraph in the document (right).*

Indexing

You create an index, using the Index XTension (Figure 10.23), by first tagging words as index entries, then generating an index. During the tagging process, you can identify up to four levels of index entries, create cross-references, and specify whether the page range will reference the word only, the selected text, a number of paragraphs, or all the paragraphs up to the next occurrence of a specific style sheet. When you generate the index, you can specify nested or run-in format, punctuation between entries, a master page format for the generated index, and style sheets for each index level.

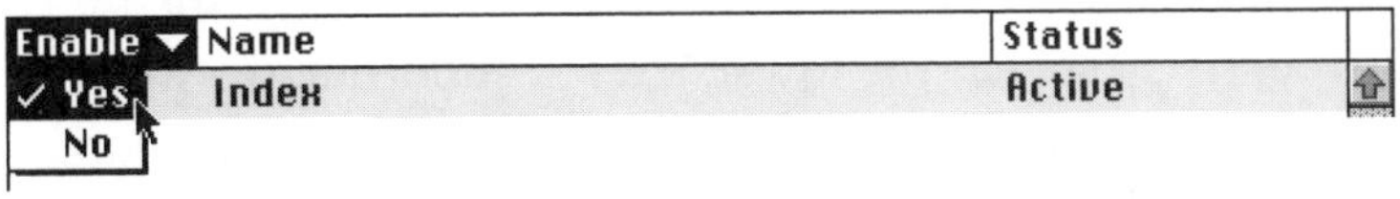

***Figure 10.23** The Index XTension must be active before you start indexing.*

Deciding When to Index

You can index entries as you go along—while building each chapter—or you can save the indexing steps for the end of the production cycle. There are several reasons why we recommend the second option:

- Indexing is best performed by someone with indexing expertise. It's more efficient to let them index the document after it has passed through all other editing cycles; otherwise, you'll have to pass the whole document to the indexer each time new sections are added. (If you simply rearrange sections, the index markers will move with the edited text.)
- Even if you are not using an indexing expert, it's a good idea to let only one person handle the indexing in a production team—this way the indexing is likely to be more consistent, and consistency is one of the basic rules of good indexing. In other words, you don't want each person on the production team to index during the page-building and editing cycles.
- The Indexing XTension itself requires more RAM. You can save memory and QuarkXPress will run faster if the XTension is not installed during the early page building and edit rounds.

Identifying a First-Level Index Entry

You can create up to four levels of index entries, but in order to identify lower levels you must first have identified the higher level entry to which the lower level is subordinate. We'll start with the steps for creating first-level entries, and describe tagging lower levels in the next section.

1. Choose **View ➛ Show Index** to display the Index palette.
2. Select the **Content tool** and position the text insertion point at the beginning of the specific text you wish to tag, or highlight a range of text.

The text you highlight will appear automatically in the Text area of the Index palette, so you usually do want to highlight the word(s) to be indexed to save retyping the text in the next step. However, sometimes you want to highlight a range of text to identify the page range to which the entry applies, so the selection does not necessarily start with the index word(s).

3. Type the text for the First Level entry in the **Text** area of the Index palette, if different from the highlighted selection.
4. Type text in the **Sort As** area of the Index palette if you want to override the normal alphabetical sorting. This is usually applied to entries that begin with numbers—for example, you might want the entry *8-bit* to sort as *eight-bit.*
5. Choose **First Level** from the **Level** pop-up menu (Figure 10.24).
6. You can choose a character style for the page number from the **Style** pop-up menu, or let it default to the same style as used for the index entry text. For example, the main entries for a topic might be identified with bold page numbers.

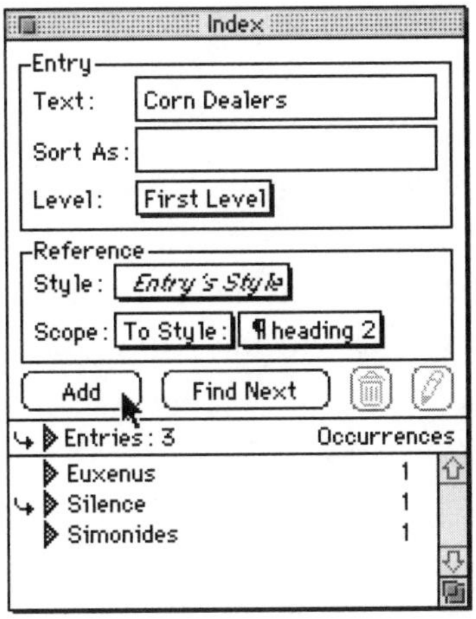

Figure 10.24 *The Index palette with selections for a first-level entry.*

7. Choose an option from the **Scope** pop-up menu:
   - **Selection Start** results in a page number for the beginning of the selection only.
   - **Selection Text** results in the page range of the entire selection.
   - **To Style** shows a pop-up menu of styles, and results in a page range that begins with the start of the selected text and ends where the next paragraph with the selected style appears. This is how you would index the word(s) to show the page range between two headings, for example.
   - **Specified # of ¶s** results in the page range for the specified number of paragraphs, starting with the insertion point.
   - **To End Of** lists page numbers from the beginning of the selection to the end of the current text chain or **Story**, or to the end of the current **Document**.
   - **Suppress Page #** results in no printed page number for the entry—useful when you want a first-level entry with no page number, followed by lower-level entries with specific page references.

- **X-ref** is a pop-up menu from which you can choose **See, See also,** or **See herein** to create a cross-reference.

8. Click **Add** to add the entry to the list in the palette and changes the page display in the document window in one of three ways:
   - The index marker shows up as a small box in the text on the document page at the text insertion point.
   - The selected text is framed in brackets when you index a range.
   - The phrase is framed in brackets and a box if this is not the first occurrence of the indexed entry in the document. See Figure 10.25.

TIP

Brackets or boxes marking indexed entries are displayed on the page only when the Index palette is open. You can hide the markers by closing the Index palette. You can specify the color of the markers by choosing **Edit ➛ Preferences ➛ Index** and clicking the **Index Marker Color** button to display a color picker and use sliders, arrows, fields, or a color wheel to choose a color.

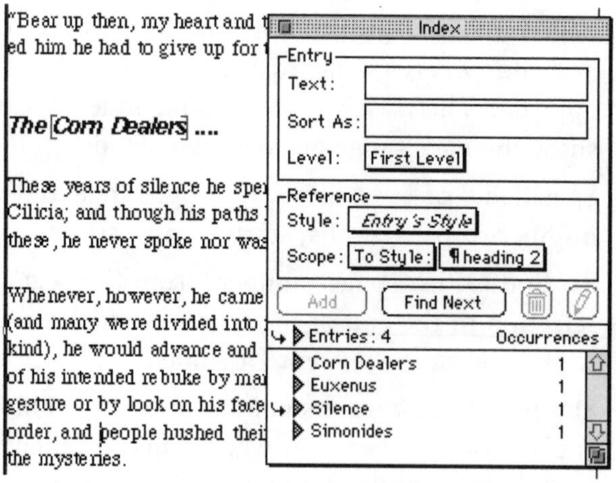

Figure 10.25 The new entry is added to a list in the Index palette, and the text is marked by brackets or a box in the document.

Identifying a Lower-Level Index Entry

You can create up to four levels of index entries for nested indexes, or two levels for run-in indexes. Nested indexes show each level on a separate line, while run-in indexes show the second-level entries in the same paragraph as the first-level entries.

1. Position the text insertion point at the beginning of the specific text you wish to tag, or highlight a range of text.
2. Type the text for the entry in the **Text** and the **Sort as** areas of the Index palette, as you did for first-level entries.
3. Click in the left column next to an entry in the **Entries** list to position an arrow (↳) that identifies the next-higher entry text. (Don't click on the entry name, or this will replace the text in the Text box at the top of the palette.)
4. Choose **Second, Third,** or **Fourth Level** from the **Level** pop-up menu—levels that are not available for this entry are grayed out. See Figure 10.26.

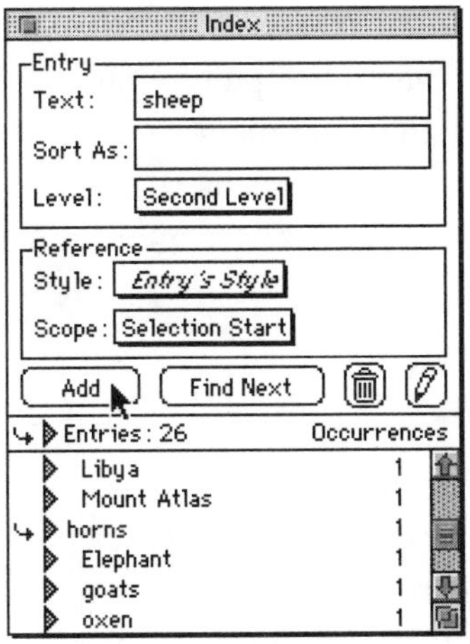

Figure 10.26 *The Index palette with selections for a second-level entry.*

> **TIP** In order to identify lower levels you must first have identified the higher level entry to which the lower level is subordinate. If you try to add the same word(s) under two different levels, QuarkXPress displays an error message.

5. As for first level entries, you can choose a character style for the page number from the **Style** pop-up menu, and choose an option from the **Scope** pop-up menu.
6. Click **Add** to add the entry to the list in the palette (see Figure 10.27).

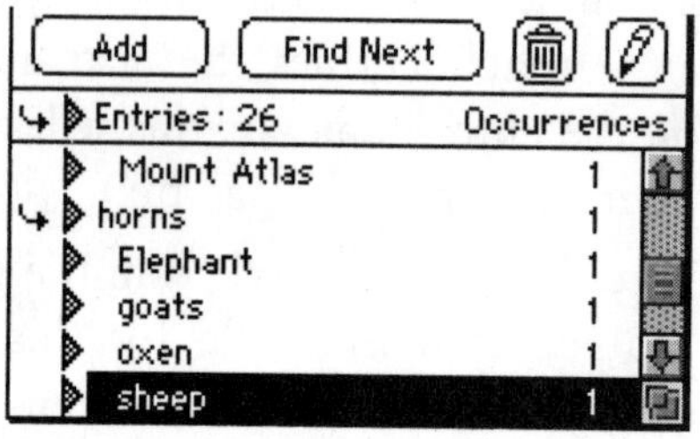

Figure 10.27 *The new entry is added to a list in the Index palette.*

The **Occurrences** column in the Index palette shows how many times the entry is indexed in the document. To see which pages contain the entry, click the arrow adjacent to the entry (▷); the arrow icon points down (▽) and a list of page numbers for each occurrence is displayed.

Creating Cross-References

A cross-reference is a referral from one topic to another using the words *See, See also,* or *See herein.* You can create cross-references that appear along with page references for a topic, or you can cross-reference a topic with no page references.

1. Place the **text insertion point** anywhere in the document.
2. Enter text in the **Text** area using one of two methods:

- If this is a cross-reference for an entry that is already in the list, with page numbers, click on an entry in the **Entries** list to copy it to the **Text** area.
- If this is a new term that has not previously been indexed, type the word(s) in the **Text** area.

3. Choose **X-Ref** from the **Scope** pop-up menu, and choose the type of cross-reference from the X-Ref pop-out menu: **See, See also,** or **See herein.**
4. Click on an entry in the **Entries** list to specify the index entry being cross-referenced. Add punctuation after the word(s) if you want that punctuation to follow the entry in the index.
5. You can choose a character style for the cross-reference word(s) from the **Style** pop-up menu, or let it default to the same style as used for the index entry text. For example, the *See also* entries might be shown in italics. This style selection applies to the referenced word(s) only—not to the words *See* or *See also* or *See herein*. See Figure 10.28.
6. Click **Add** to add the entry to the list in the palette.

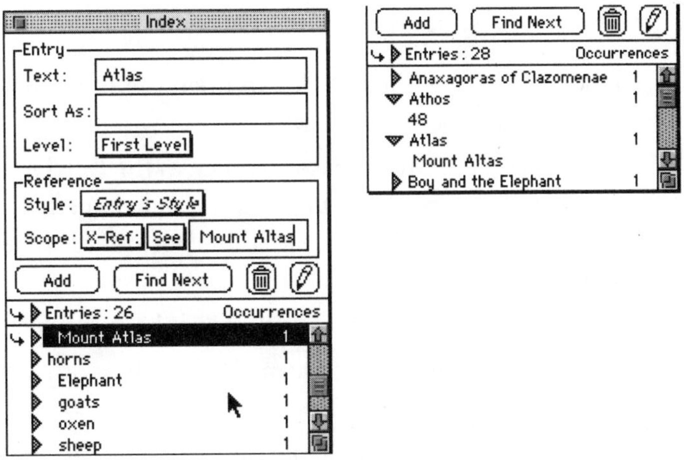

Figure 10.28 *The new cross-reference entry (left) is added to a list in the Index palette (right), preceded by a triangle.*

7. Click the **triangle** next to the entry to see the cross-reference text.

> **TIP** To specify any punctuation that is to appear before all cross-references in an index, choose **Edit → Preferences → Index** and type the punctuation in the **Before X-Ref** area of the Index Preferences dialog box.

Editing Index Entries

When you edit text that falls between index markers in a document, the index entries themselves remain unchanged. If you want the index entry to change as well, you must edit it through the Index palette. There's just one exception to this rule of independence: if you delete all of the text between two index markers in a document, then the index entries that reference that page number will also be deleted.

You can edit anything about the entry that you could specify when you created it, but you cannot edit the page numbers through the Index palette—these are generated automatically based on the index markers in the document. To change an index entry, follow these steps:

1. Choose **View → Show Index** to open the Index palette, if it is not already open.
2. Click on an entry or cross-reference in the **Entries** list to select it and then click the **Edit** button (hollow pencil), or simply double-click the entry—the Edit button becomes reversed (dark pencil).
3. Make changes in the Index palette to the options for the entry.
4. While in Edit mode, you can double-click other entries and edit the selections in the palette.
5. Click the **Edit** button again to exit edit mode. See Figure 10.29.

Figure 10.29 *The Edit button is grayed when you are making a new entry, a black-pencil when in edit mode, and a hollow pencil when you're using the index as a navigating tool.*

Deleting Index Entries

As mentioned earlier, if you delete all of the text between two index markers in a document, then the index entries that reference that page number will also be deleted. You can also delete an index entry without deleting the text from the document:

1. Choose **View ➛ Show Index** to open the Index palette, if it is not already open.
2. Click on an entry or cross-reference in the Entries list to select it.
3. Click the **Delete** button ( ) in the Index palette.
4. Click **OK** in the Alert box to confirm the deletion.

TIP: When you delete an entry through the Index palette, then all page numbers, all cross references to it, and all nested entries related to it are automatically deleted as well.

The index markers will be deleted from the document text. Otherwise the text will remain unchanged. Only the index will be affected.

Generating a Final Index

Following the steps described up to this point, you add, edit, and delete index entries from the Index palette. You can use the index in the palette as a navigating tool—by double-clicking on the page numbers—but ultimately you will probably want to print the index as part of the distributed document. Following the next steps for generating an index, QuarkXPress compiles the list of index terms, formats them according to your specifications, and flows the index as text onto pages based on a master page of your choice.

1. Set up the punctuation for the index by choosing **Edit ➛ Preferences ➛ Index.**
2. Specify the punctuation or words you wish, including spaces, for the following options in the Index Preferences dialog box:
   - The punctuation that appears **Following Entry**, i.e., immediately after the indexed word or phrase, before the page number(s). This might be simply a space, or a colon and a space, or a comma and a space.
   - The punctuation **Between Page #s**, usually a comma and a space, or a semi-colon and a space.
   - The punctuation **Between Page Ranges** will be used to separate a range of page numbers, and this is usually a hyphen or an en dash, or it might be the word "to" with spaces on each side.
   - The punctuation **Before X-ref** will appear before a cross-reference (See, See also, See herein), and this is usually a period, a semicolon, or a space.

TIP: If a cross-reference is the only entry for the indexed word(s), then the **Before X-ref** punctuation is used instead of the **Following Entry** punctuation.

   - The punctuation **Between Entries** will appear between entry levels in a run-in index, usually a semi-colon or a period.
3. Click **OK** to close the dialog box. See Figure 10.30.

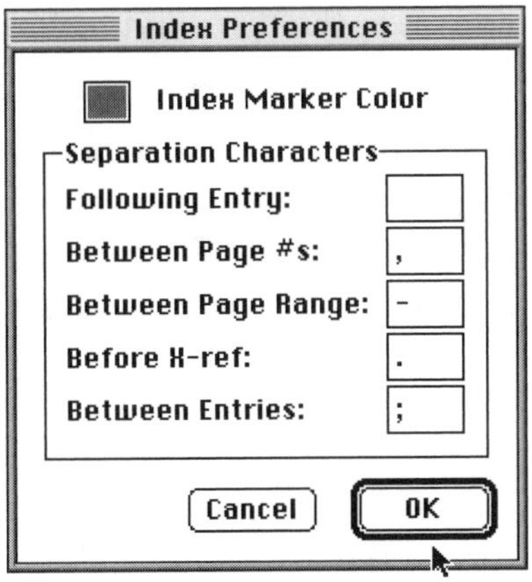

Figure 10.30 *Entries in the Index Preferences dialog box..*

4. Use the **Edit ➛ Styles** command, described in Chapter 4, to set up a style sheet for each level in the index—or only one style sheet for a run-in index format. Set up a style sheet for the letter headings, if you will be including those in the index (i.e., letters of the alphabet on separate lines, separating sections in the index).
5. Use the procedures described in Chapter 9 to create a master page to use for the index. This might be the same as the master page that you use for other parts of the book. Usually, however, an index is printed in two or three columns; the header or footer for the pages indicate that this is the index; the index master must include an automatic text box; it should be a facing-page master if you want the headers or footers or margins to vary between left and right pages.
6. Choose **View ➛ Show Index** to open the Index palette, then choose **Utilities ➛ Build Index.**

7. Make the following entries in the Build Index dialog box:
   - Select **Nested** or **Run-in Format** (see Figure 10.31).
   - If the current document is part of a book, set up as described at the beginning of this chapter, you can select **Entire Book** to index all of the chapters, or leave this option unchecked to index the current chapter only.

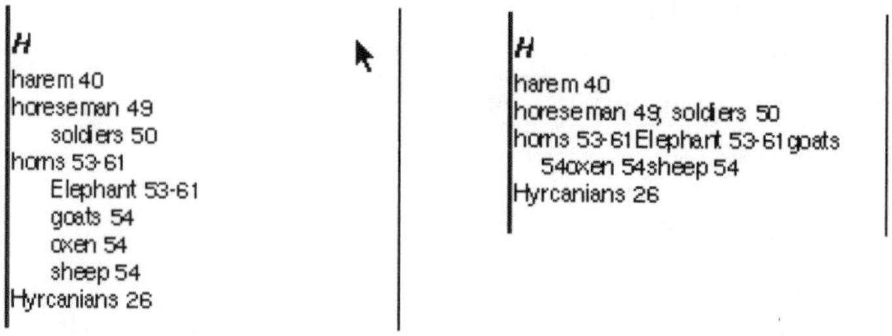

***Figure 10.31** Generated index in nested (left) and run-in (right) formats with the "H" showing an automatically generated letter heading.*

TIP

If this is the first time you are generating the index for a long book, it's a good idea generate the index for a short chapter first—to verify that your style sheets and punctuation have been properly set up—before generating the longer index.

- If you have previously generated an index for this document or book, you can select **Replace Existing Index** to overwrite that text.

TIP

If you have previously generated an index and do not choose to replace the existing index, then a second index will be generated. This is not usually desirable, unless you want to test two different formats, or to derive a list of "what's new" by comparing the indexes for two different editions of a book.

- Select **Add Letter Headings** if you want each new alphabetic section of the index to be preceded by the letter of the alphabet on a separate line (see again Figure 10.31), then choose a style sheet for the headings from the pop-up menu.

- Choose a **Master Page** for the index from the pop-up menu.
- Choose styles sheets from the **Level Styles** pop-up menus for nested indexes, or just the first level style for run-in index formats. See Figure 10.32.

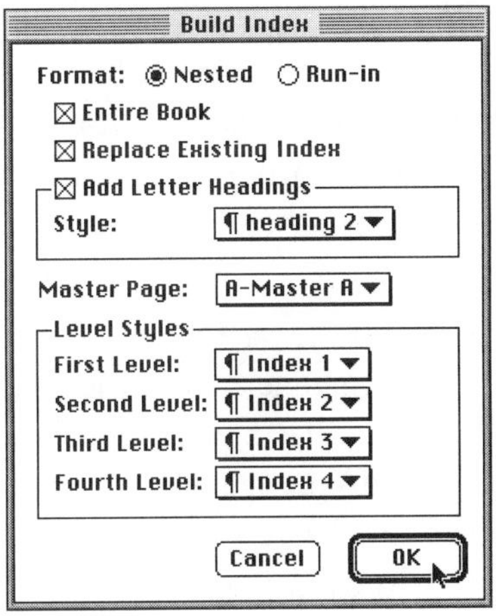

Figure 10.32 *Entries in Build Index dialog box.*

8. Click **OK** to close the dialog box and generate the index. QuarkXPress will automatically add the index pages to the end of the current document. If you specified a facing-page master, then the index will start on a right-facing page.

Editing the Final Index

Once you have generated an index, it's a good idea to look it over carefully and check the content and formatting. If you discover problems, decide whether they should be solved by editing the index directly, or by changing some of your choices in the Index Preferences or Build Index dialog boxes and then regenerating the index.

If the problems are with the punctuation used in the index, then it will probably be easiest to go back to the Index Preferences dialog box to make the changes, then generate the index again. You could try global search and replace, but this works only if you want *all* semi-colons changed to commas, for example.

If you don't like the styles applied to the index—the level headings or the index entries—you can try simply using **Edit ➛ Styles** to change the style sheet specifications (assuming the styles you selected are used in the index only).

If you want certain words to be bold or italics to distinguish them from the rest of the index—foreign words, for instance—you can use **Edit ➛ Find/Change** to globally find and replace the formats for each term. If you generate a new index again later, you'll have to repeat this step.

If you indexed words that fall on the pasteboard, are obscured by an overlapping item, or overflow their text box, then the generated index shows a dagger (†) instead of a page number next to that entry. You can choose **Edit ➛ Find/Change** and type **Option/ALT-T** in the Find what area to locate the daggers in the index, then delete the daggers or solve the problem by fixing the location where the text appear. If fixing the problem means flowing the text from an overflowed text box, and this results in other text flowing to new pages, then you may need to regenerate the index.

If you edit the text of the document to the extent that new index topics are added, old index topics are deleted, or text shifts to adjacent pages, then you should generate the index again.

Summary

The three new features that you've learned about in this chapter—building books, lists, and indexes—are tremendous productivity tools in producing books or any long documents, or documents that are routinely updated and re-issued. As you gain experience using these features, you'll see how useful they can be in the editing process—including automatically identifying changed chapters or works-in-progress, generating working lists of changed sections or sections that are not yet completed, or simply navigating through long documents.

11 Publishing Databases

Database publishing encompasses many kinds of documents, from financial reports to membership directories, and offers a unique set of challenges. Usually, the text (or data) which is generated by database and spreadsheet programs has a unique characteristic: it contains commas or tabs to separate information. Another characteristic of text from a database is that it is often published in a repetitive format.

If you use QuarkXPress solely for the task of publishing text from a database, we strongly urge you to consider some of the excellent QuarkXTensions that help streamline the process tremendously. One of the most popular programs for this purpose is Xdata by Em Software.

Another category of text that has unique characteristics is text created on non-Macintosh or non-Windows computers, especially text created using text editors on mainframe computers. These often have little or no formatting capabilities, with text formatted using ASCII codes designed for proprietary typesetting equipment. It would be nice if the entire computing world enjoyed the many benefits of using Macintosh or Windows computers—but since the reality is that they don't, it may be useful to know how to work with text you get from another type of computer. A particularly bothersome aspect is the fact that sometimes unwanted characters (such as paragraph returns at the end of every line) are embedded in the text.

The good news is that QuarkXPress offers a sophisticated search-and-replace function that can make short work of converting imported text to the format you want. The next sections offer some tips on how to work globally with invisible characters as an aid to both database publishing and in "cleaning up" text telecommunicated from other computers. This chapter also describes how to use *XPress Tags*, special codes for formatting text that can be typed in any text editor and converted automatically in QuarkXPress.

Finding and Changing Special Characters

As you learned in Chapter 4, "Word Processing," QuarkXPress has a Find/Change command for searching and globally replacing words, phrases, or character attributes in text. You can search for special characters and hidden characters by holding down the ⌘/CTRL key and typing the key that you would normally use to insert the special character in the text, as shown in Table 11.1.

***Table 11.1** Searching for Special Characters*

Special Character	**Find/Change Entry**		**Dialog Box Display**
	Macintosh	**Windows**	
Space	**Space**	**Space**	none
Tab	**⌘-Tab**	**CTRL-TAB**	\t
New Paragraph	**⌘-Return**	**CTRL-ENTER**	\p
New Line	**⌘-Shift-Return**	**CTRL-SHIFT-ENTER**	\n
New Column	**⌘-Enter**	**CTRL-KEYPAD ENTER**	\c
New Box	**⌘-Shift-Enter**	**CTRL-SHIFT-KEYPAD ENTER**	\b
Wildcard	**⌘-?**	**CTRL-?**	\?

The space, tab, and new paragraph characters are search parameters in the common conversions of imported ASCII text, described under the next headings.

TIP

Be sure to include spaces in the **Change To** field if you type them in the **Find What** field. You need not type a space before and after a single word in the **Change To** field. If you select the **Whole Words** option, QuarkXPress will find the word when it is framed by spaces or followed by punctuation.

Eliminating Unwanted Paragraph Returns

Text can be telecommunicated from one computer to another, either directly or through a mailbox facility. It is preferable to use a mailbox system or transfer software that lets you preserve any formatting that was done in the original file, but some electronic mail services force you to transfer text in *text only* format (ASCII characters only, with no "hidden" formatting codes).

If the transfer or conversion method forces paragraph returns (a.k.a. *hard* carriage returns) at the end of every line, it is a good idea to insert at least two carriage returns after every paragraph or intended line break in the text *before* it is transferred (Figure 11.1). You can quickly reformat this type of file in QuarkXPress without referring to a printed version of the text to find paragraph breaks, by following the steps described below.

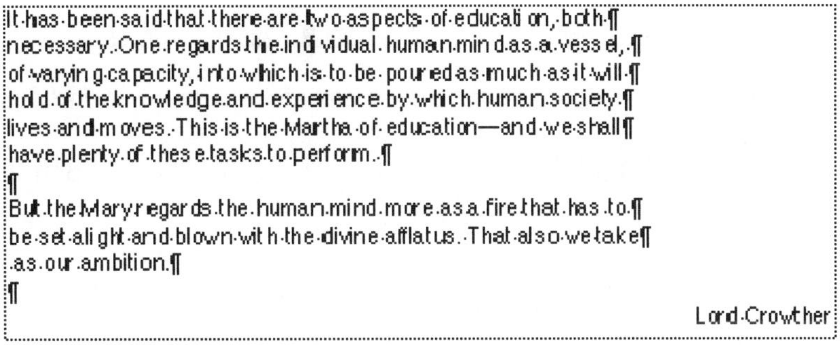

It·has·been·said·that·there·are·two·aspects·of·education,·both·¶
necessary.·One·regards·the·individual·human·mind·as·a·vessel,·¶
of·varying·capacity,·into·which·is·to·be·poured·as·much·as·it·will·¶
hold·of·the·knowledge·and·experience·by·which·human·society·¶
lives·and·moves.·This·is·the·Martha·of·education—and·we·shall¶
have·plenty·of·these·tasks·to·perform.·¶
¶
But·the·Mary·regards·the·human·mind·more·as·a·fire·that·has·to·¶
be·set·alight·and·blown·with·the·divine·afflatus.·That·also·we·take¶
·as·our·ambition.¶
¶
Lord·Crowther

Figure 11.1 *Telecommunicated text sometimes has unwanted returns at the end of every line.*

1. Globally change all double carriage returns (which appear only at the end of each paragraph) to some unique character string that is not found elsewhere in the text, such as "xyz" (Figure 11.2).

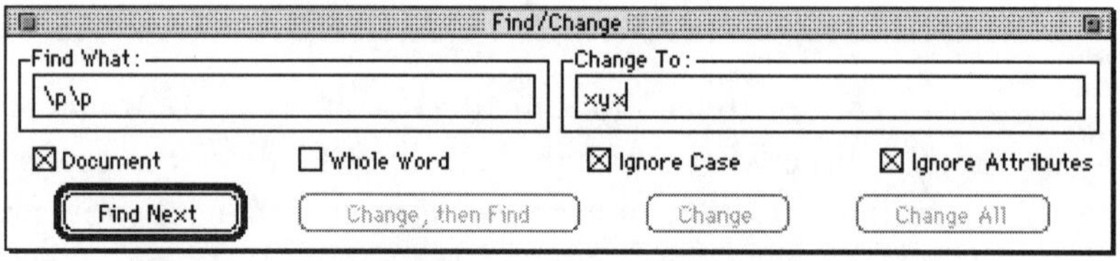

Figure 11.2 *Type ⌘-**Return/Ctrl-Enter** in the Find/Change dialog box, which shows returns as \p.*

2. Globally change all single carriage returns to nothing or to a space (if the line-break returns replaced spaces in the conversion process). See Figure 11.3.

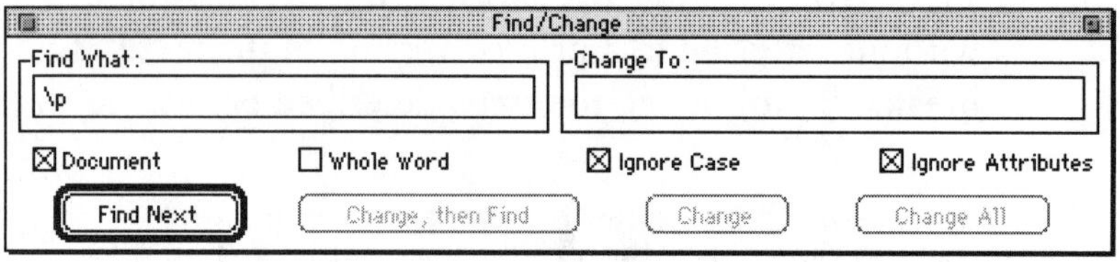

Figure 11.3 *Find/Change dialog box shows a space as nothing.*

3. Globally change all occurrences of "xyz" to single carriage returns (Figure 11.4)

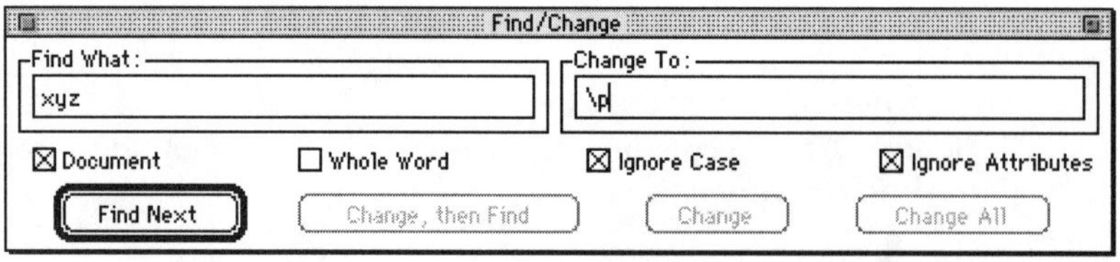

Figure 11.4 *Change unique characters back to a paragraph return.*

After following these steps, the file appears as you'd normally expect it to—with no paragraph returns *except* those at the end of each paragraph (Figure 11.5).

It·has·been·said·that·there·are·two·aspects·of·education,·both·necessary.·One·regards·the·individual·human·mind·as·a·vessel,·of·varying·capacity,·into·which·is·to·be·poured·as·much·as·it·will·hold·of·the·knowledge·and·experience·by·which·human·society·lives·and·moves.·This·is·the·Martha·of·education—and·we·shallhave·plenty·of·these·tasks·to·perform.·¶
But·the·Mary·regards·the·human·mind·more·as·a·fire·that·has·to·be·set·alight·and·blown·with·the·divine·afflatus.·That·also·we·take·as·our·ambition.¶
Lord·Crowther

Figure 11.5 *Text in QuarkXPress after global changes.*

Converting Data Files to Tabular Format

If the text fields exported from a spreadsheet or database are separated by the tab character, then you can set tabs in QuarkXPress and the data should fall into tabbed columns. However, if the program used commas or some other delimiter, you will need to convert these to tabs before the data can be arranged in columns.

Sometimes, text-only files exported from a spreadsheet or database include quotation marks around fields that happened to use the field delimiter as part of the data. For example, if different categories of information from a database are separated by commas when converted to text (name,address,city,state), then when one category includes commas the whole phrase will be automatically framed in quotation marks ("Margaret Browne, Ph.D.",P.O. Box 358, Durango, CO).

Whatever the case, you can use QuarkXPress' Find/Change command globally to convert the field delimiters to tabs.

1. Export the data from the spreadsheet or database in ASCII text format (Figure 11.6), then use the **Get Text** command to import it into QuarkXPress.

Kay,Atherton,Medi-Calls,"248 Texas Street, #9",San Francisco,CA,94107,626-8343
Hector,"Barrera, Jr.",Azteca,1521 Manor Drive,San Pablo,Ca,94949,415/233-9239
David,Jewett,"CJS. Inc.",1920 Francisco,Berkeley,CA,94709,415/548-4762
Grace,Moore,TechArt,400 Pacific Avenue,San Francisco,CA,94133,415/362-1110

Figure 11.6 *Text as originally imported.*

2. To distinguish between a comma used as a delimiter and a comma that is part of a field entry, globally change all incidences of comma-space to some unique character string that is not found elsewhere in the text, such as “xyz” (Figure 11.7).

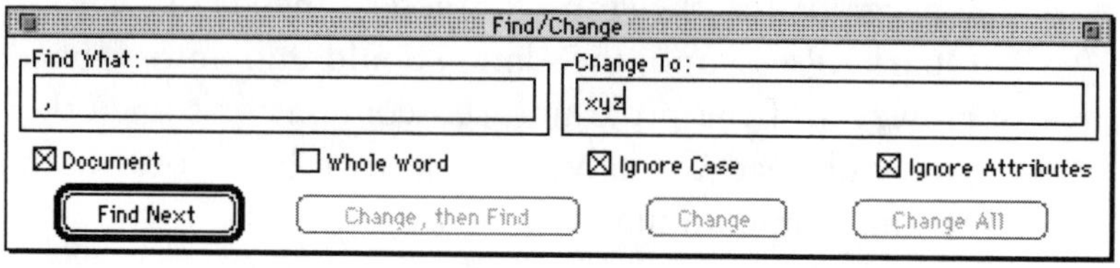

Figure 11.7 *The Find/Change dialog box.*

In order for the global searches suggested here to work, we have to assume that a comma that is part of a field entry will always be followed by a space, whereas a comma that is a delimiter will usually be followed by the contents of the next field or by another comma (if the field is empty). If a field entry in the spreadsheet or database actually starts with a space, then the delimiter in front of that field will not be converted to a tab with the searches suggested here. You should check the results of these replacements after you have set tab stops to format the text correctly.

3. Globally change all commas to tabs (Figure 11.8).

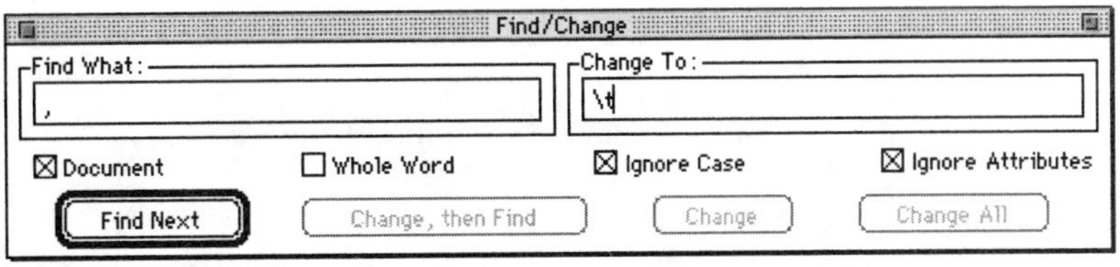

Figure 11.8 *Type **⌘-Tab/CTRL-TAB** in the Find/Change dialog box, which shows tabs as \t.*

4. Globally change all quotation marks to nothing (Figure 11.9).

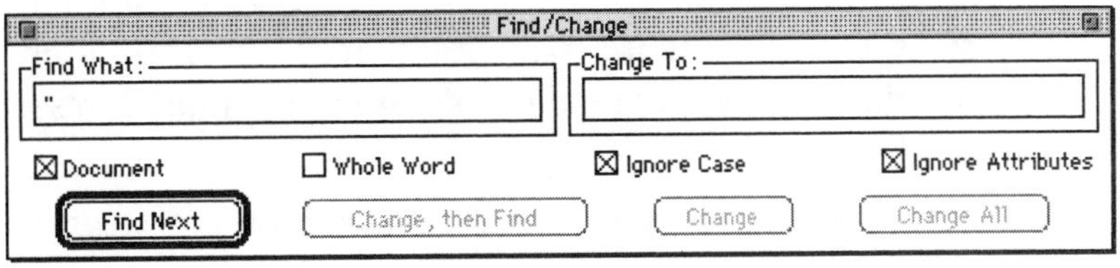

Figure 11.9 *Change quotation marks to nothing.*

5. Globally change all occurrences of "xyz" to comma-space (Figure 11.10).

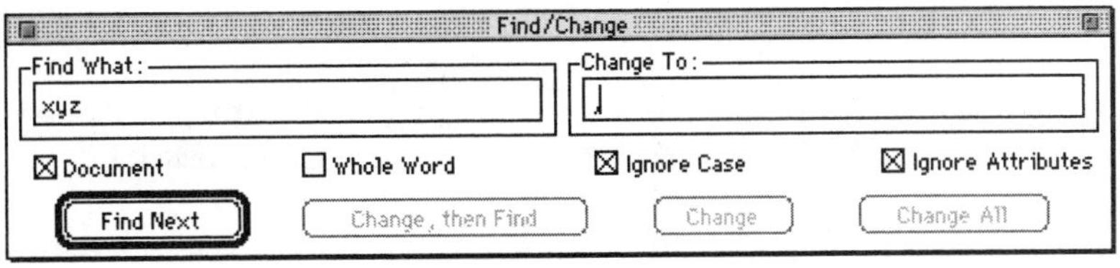

Figure 11.10 *Change the unique characters back to comma-space.*

6. Select all of the data and choose **Style ➛ Formats.** With the Formats tab of the Paragraph Attributes dialog box displayed, set tab stops on the text ruler (Figure 11.11) Alternatively, you can format the text using a style sheet.

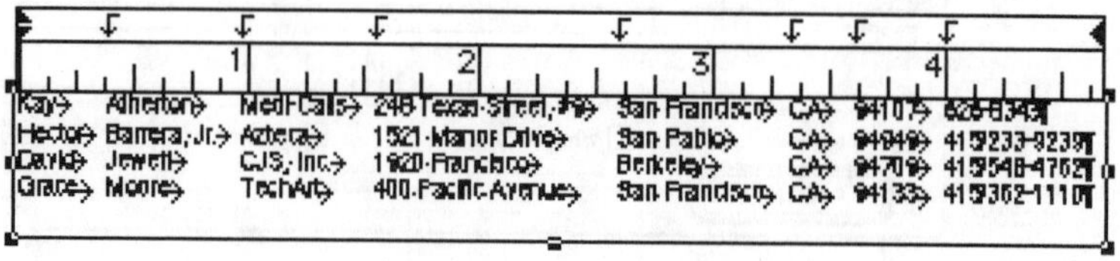

Figure 11.11 *Text falls into place when tab stops are set in QuarkXPress.*

Converting Data Files to Nontabular Formats

Sometimes you will want to convert tabbed data from a spreadsheet or database to nontabular formats. A common example of this is converting a data file of names and addresses to a directory listing format.

One approach is to use the mail-merge feature of your word processing application to create a formatted text file directly from the data file. The alternative is to start the formatting process in the spreadsheet or database, then finish the formatting in QuarkXPress using the Find/Change command. This second approach is described here.

Assume that the spreadsheet or database lists the entries for each record in the following order:

```
first name, last name, company, street address,
city, state, zip code, phone number
```

What you want to end up with is a directory listing format:

```
first name last name
company
street address
city, state, zip code
phone number
```

If you simply export the data in its current format (Figure 11.12), you will end up with commas or tabs between every field, and it will be nearly impossible to use global changes to alter the format appropriately. You can save a lot of time and trouble by making a few changes to the data *before* you export it.

Address File

	A	B	C	D	E	F	G	H	I	J
1	First	Last	Company	Address	City	ST	Zip	Phone		
2	Kay	Atherton	Medi-Calls	248 Texas Street, #9	San Francisco	CA	94107	626-8343		
3	Hector	Barrera, Jr.	Azteca	1521 Manor Drive	San Pablo	CA	94949	415/233-9239		
4	David	Jewett	CJS, Inc.	1920 Francisco	Berkeley	CA	94709	415/548-4762		
5	Grace	Moore	TechArt	400 Pacific Avenue	San Francisco	CA	94133	415/362-1110		
6										

***Figure 11.12** Data in a spreadsheet format.*

1 Insert unique search codes between certain fields in the data:

- Insert "xyz" in a new column or field between the first name and the last name. This will be changed to a space in Step 4.
- Insert the same code, "xyz," between the State field and the ZIP Code.
- Insert a different code, such as "zzz," between the City field and the State. This will be changed to a comma in Step 5.

TIP

In a spreadsheet, you can insert columns between fields and fill the columns with the search codes as shown in Figure 11.13. In a database, you could make the search codes part of a customized "report format" and output the data to disk as a report.

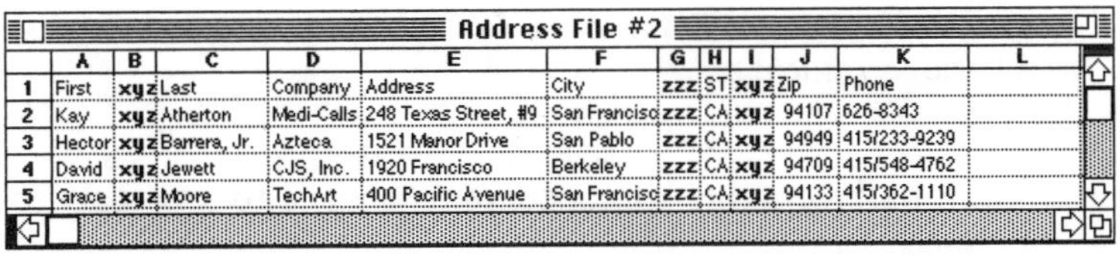

Address File #2

	A	B	C	D	E	F	G	H	I	J	K	L
1	First	xyz	Last	Company	Address	City	zzz	ST	xyz	Zip	Phone	
2	Kay	xyz	Atherton	Medi-Calls	248 Texas Street, #9	San Francisco	zzz	CA	xyz	94107	626-8343	
3	Hector	xyz	Barrera, Jr.	Azteca	1521 Manor Drive	San Pablo	zzz	CA	xyz	94949	415/233-9239	
4	David	xyz	Jewett	CJS, Inc.	1920 Francisco	Berkeley	zzz	CA	xyz	94709	415/548-4762	
5	Grace	xyz	Moore	TechArt	400 Pacific Avenue	San Francisco	zzz	CA	xyz	94133	415/362-1110	

***Figure 11.13** Data file with unique search codes entered between selected fields.*

2. Export the data from the spreadsheet or database as text and import it into QuarkXPress (Figure 11.14). Here we assume that the fields are separated by tabs in the export process. (See "Converting Data Files to Tabular Format," earlier in this chapter.)

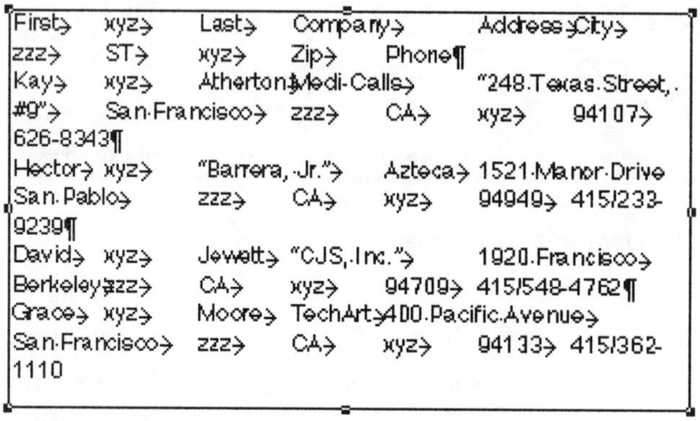

Figure 11.14 *Data file when exported from the spreadsheet or database as text and imported into QuarkXPress.*

3. Globally change all carriage returns to double carriage returns (Figure 11.15).

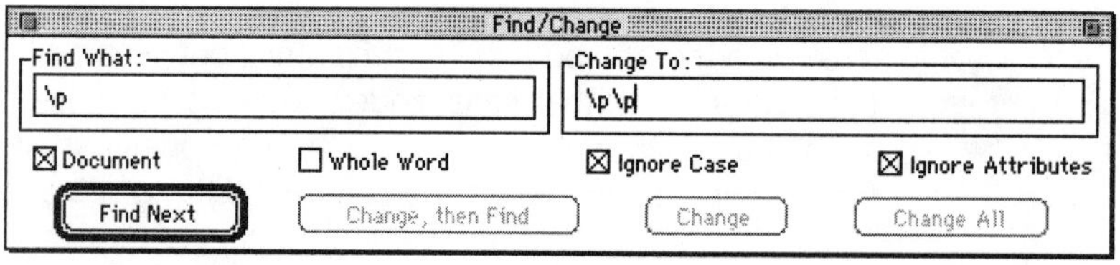

Figure 11.15 *Type* ***⌘-Return/Ctrl-Enter*** *in the Find/Change dialog box, which shows returns as \p.*

4. Globally change all occurrences of **Tab-xyz-Tab** to spaces (Figure 11.16).

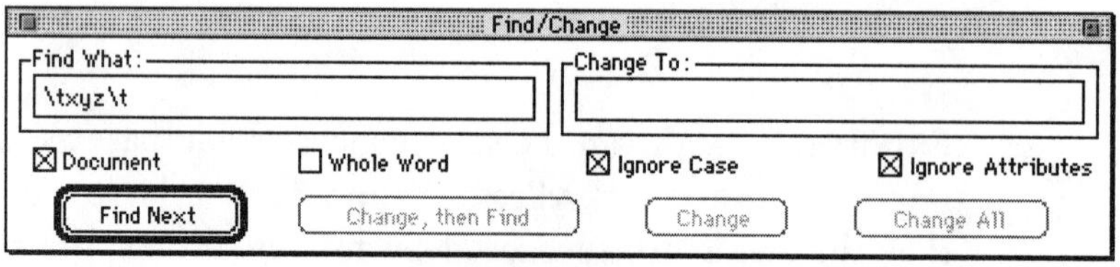

Figure 11.16 *Type* ***⌘-Tab/Ctrl-Tab*** *in the Find/Change dialog box, which shows tabs as \t.*

5. Globally change all occurrences of **Tab-zzz-Tab** to comma-space (Figure 11.17).

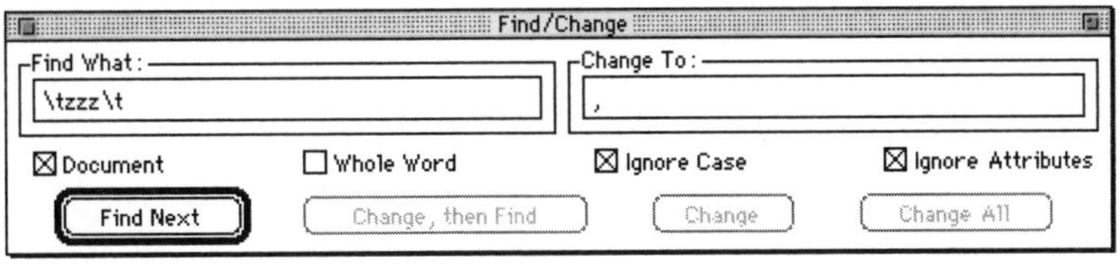

Figure 11.17 *Find/Change dialog box.*

6. Globally change all remaining occurrences of **Tab** to **Return** (Figure 11.18).

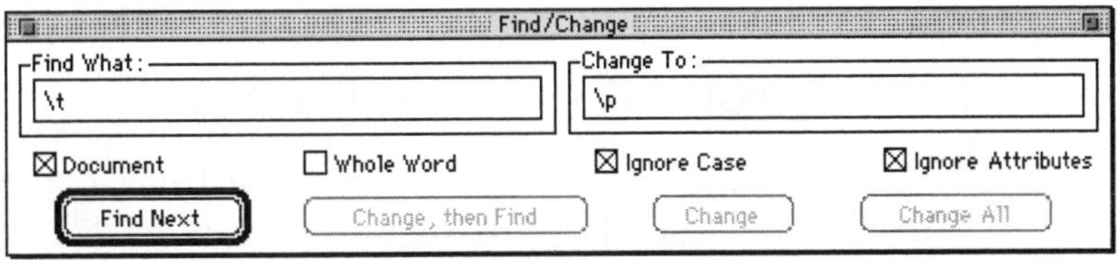

Figure 11.18 *Find/Change dialog box shows tabs as \t and carriage returns as \p.*

7. If the spreadsheet or database added quotation marks around fields that contained a comma, globally change the quotation marks to nothing (strip them out). Examine your file to confirm whether these are actually inch or feet marks, or true opening and closing quotation marks. Figure 11.19 shows the end result.

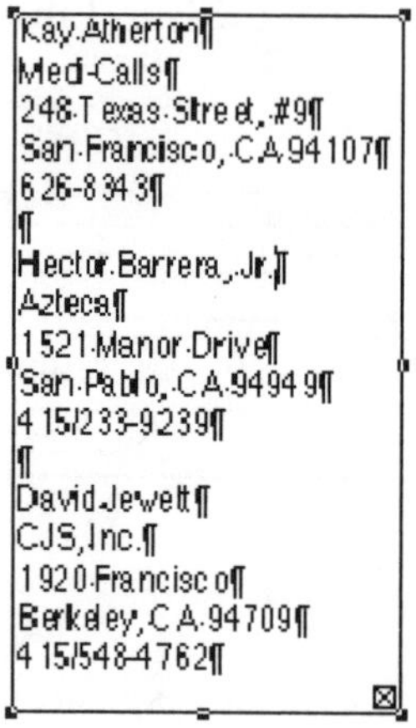

Kay·Atherton¶
Medi-Calls¶
248·Texas·Street,·#9¶
San·Francisco,·CA·94107¶
626-8343¶
¶
Hector·Barrera,·Jr.¶
Azteca¶
1521·Manor·Drive¶
San·Pablo,·CA·94949¶
415/233-9239¶
¶
David·Jewett¶
CJS,·Inc.¶
1920·Francisco¶
Berkeley,·CA·94709¶
415/548-4762¶

Figure 11.19 *Final text format as it appears onscreen.*

Embedding Format Codes in Data Files

Sometimes, you will need to convert data from a spreadsheet or database to nontabular formats where some fields have different character formats. A common example of this is converting a data file of names and addresses to a directory.

As you have seen, you can use global searches to reformat data imported from a spreadsheet or database file. You can use the same techniques to embed QuarkXPress tag codes, discussed later in this chapter.

Let's say you want to convert the same data file of names and addresses to a directory listing format as described under the previous heading, but you want the different fields to have different character formats, such as:

```
first name last name
company
street address
city, state, zip code
phone number
```

You can use the mail-merge feature of your word processing application to create a formatted text file directly from the data file, or format the text in QuarkXPress using the Find/Change command as described here.

1. In the spreadsheet or database, insert unique search codes between certain fields in the data. This is the same as step 1 in the previous example, with the addition of inserting a unique code between last name and company, and between company and address (Figure 11.20):
   - Insert "xyz" between the first name field and the last name.
   - Insert "xyz" between the state field and the zip code.
   - Insert "xxx" between last name and company.
   - Insert "yyy" between company and address.
   - Insert "zzz" between the city field and the state.

Address File

	A	B	C	D	E	F	G	H	I	J	K	L	M
1	First	xyz	Last	xxx	Company	yyy	Address	City	zzz	ST	xyz	Zip	Phone
2	Kay	xyz	Atherton	xxx	Medi-Calls	yyy	248 Texas Street, #9	San Francisc	zzz	CA	xyz	94107	626-8343
3	Hector	xyz	Barrera, Jr.	xxx	Azteca	yyy	1521 Manor Drive	San Pablo	zzz	CA	xyz	94949	415/233-9239
4	David	xyz	Jewett	xxx	CJS, Inc.	yyy	1920 Francisco	Berkeley	zzz	CA	xyz	94709	415/548-4762
5	Grace	xyz	Moore	xxx	TechArt	yyy	400 Pacific Avenue	San Francisc	zzz	CA	xyz	94133	415/362-1110

***Figure 11.20** Data file with unique search codes entered between selected fields.*

You can insert these codes using the techniques described under Step 1 under the previous heading.

2. Export the data as text from the spreadsheet or database and import it into QuarkXPress as described under the previous heading (Figure 11.21).

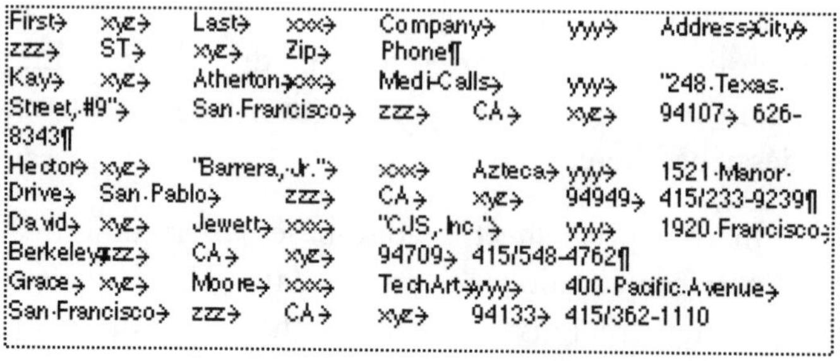
First xyz Last xxx Company yyy Address City
zzz ST xyz Zip Phone¶
Kay xyz Atherton xxx Medi-Calls yyy "248 Texas
Street, #9" San Francisco zzz CA xyz 94107 626-
8343¶
Hector xyz "Barrera, Jr." xxx Azteca yyy 1521 Manor
Drive San Pablo zzz CA xyz 94949 415/233-9239¶
David xyz Jewett xxx "CJS, Inc." yyy 1920 Francisco
Berkeley zzz CA xyz 94709 415/548-4762¶
Grace xyz Moore xxx TechArt yyy 400 Pacific Avenue
San Francisco zzz CA xyz 94133 415/362-1110

Figure 11.21 *Data file when exported as text from the spreadsheet or database and imported into QuarkXPress.*

Opening the text in a word processing application and performing these global changes *before* importing the text into QuarkXPress is preferable; doing so eliminates Step 10 in this sequence.

3. Globally change all carriage returns to double carriage returns and the formatting code **<B>** (a QuarkXPress Tag that will make the name bold). See Figure 11.22.

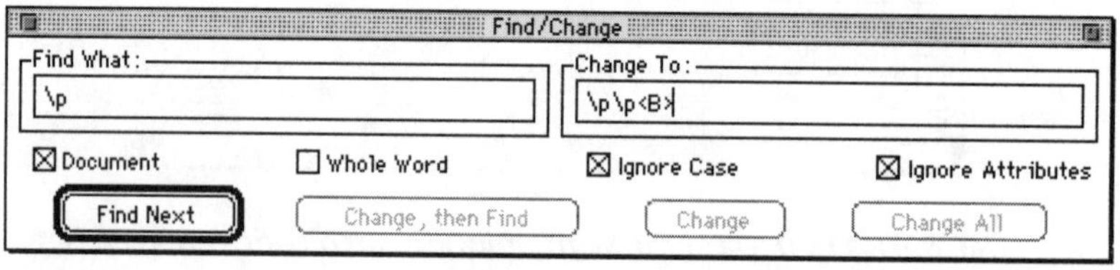

Figure 11.22 *Change single paragraph returns to double paragraph returns followed by the code for bold.*

4. Globally change all occurrences of **Tab-xxx-Tab** to **<B>return<I>** to turn bold off after the name, and start the company on a new line in italics. (Figure 11.23)

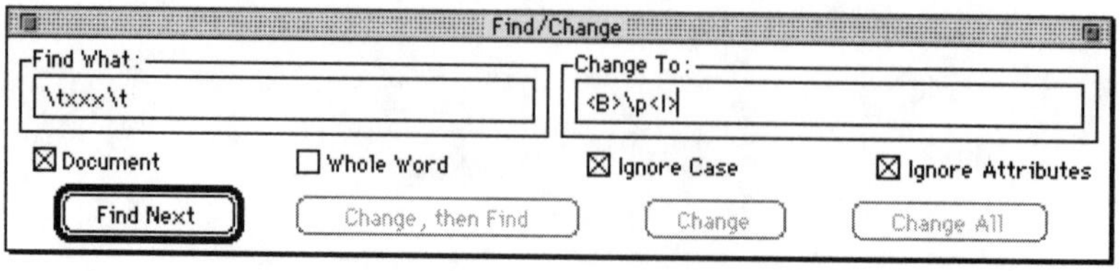

Figure 11.23 *Find/Change dialog box shows tabs as \t.*

5. Globally change all occurrences of **Tab-yyy-Tab** to **<I>return** to turn italics off and start the address on a new line. (Figure 11.24)

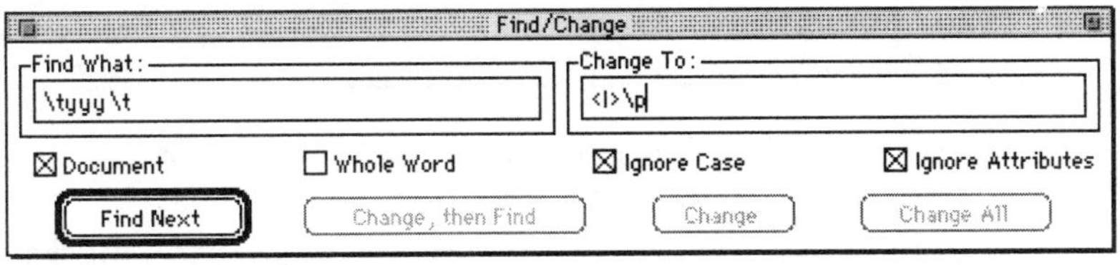

***Figure 11.24** Find/Change dialog box.*

6. Globally change all occurrences of **Tab-zzz-Tab** to **comma-space.** (Figure 11.25)

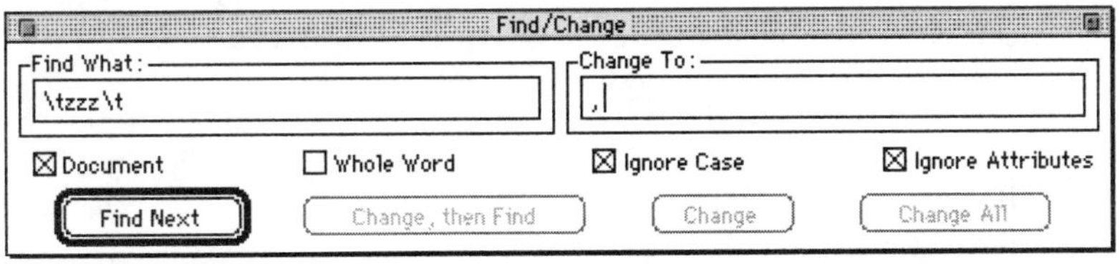

***Figure 11.25** Find/Change dialog box shows tabs as \t.*

7. Globally change all occurrences of **Tab-xyz-Tab** to spaces. (Figure 11.26)

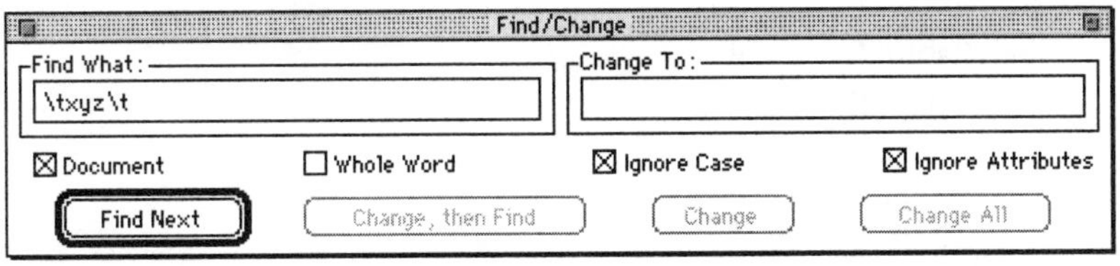

***Figure 11.26** Find/Change dialog box shows tabs as \t.*

8. Globally change all remaining occurrences of **Tab** to **Return.** (Figure 11.27)

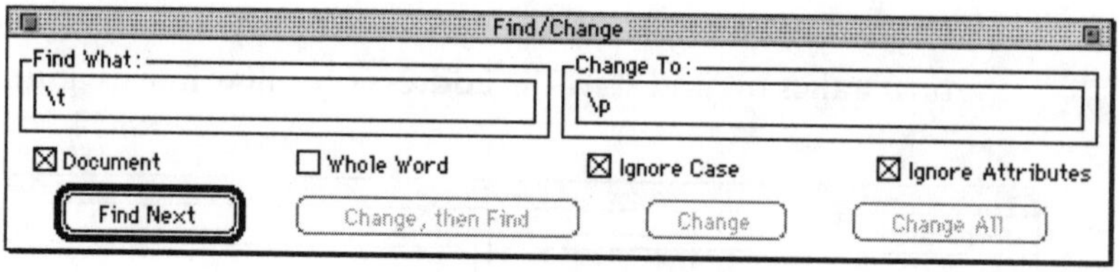

Figure 11.27 *Convert remaining tabs to paragraph returns.*

9. If the spreadsheet or database added quotation marks around fields that contained a comma, globally change the quotation marks to nothing (strip them out). Examine your file to confirm whether these are actually inch or foot marks, or true opening and closing quotation marks.

If these above changes were done in a word processing application, the database text is ready to be imported into QuarkXPress, as shown in Figure 11.28.

<B>Kay Atherton<B>
<I>Medi-Calls<I>
248 Texas Street, #9
San Francisco, CA 94107
415/626-8343
<B>Hector Barrera, Jr.<B>
<I>Azteca<I>
1521 Manor Drive
San Pablo, CA 94949
415/233-9239
<B>David Jewett<B>
<I>CJS, Inc.<I>
1920 Francisco
Berkeley, CA 94709
415/548-4762
<B>Grace Moore<B>
<I>TechArt<I>
400 Pacific Avenue
San Francisco, CA 94133
415/362-1110

Figure 11.28 *Text format after global changes.*

10. If you performed these searches in QuarkXPress, then you need to save the text to disk in ASCII format (Figure 11.29) and reimport it.

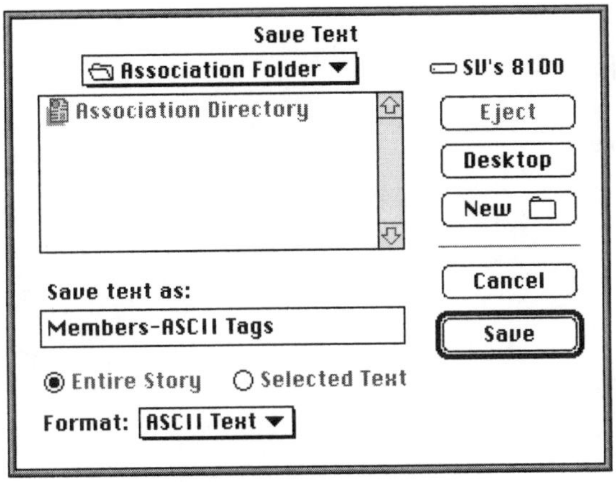

Figure 11.29 *Save Text dialog box.*

11. Import the exported text, check Include Style Sheets in the Get Text dialog box, and the embedded codes will be translated into the final formatting automatically (Figure 11.30).

Kay Atherton
Medi-Calls
248 Texas Street, #9
San Francisco, CA 94107
415/626-8343

Hector Barrera, Jr.
Azteca
1521 Manor Drive
San Pablo, CA 94949
415/233-9239

David Jewett
CJS, Inc.
1920 Francisco
Berkeley, CA 94709
415/548-4762

Grace Moore
TechArt
400 Pacific Avenue
San Francisco, CA 94133
415/362-1110

Figure 11.30 *Final text format.*

Using Wildcards in Searches

You can use the wildcard (⌘-?/CTRL-?) to search for words that have been typed with different spellings. For example, if you wanted to change all occurrences of the word *gray* to the word *shaded*, and if the word *gray* also appeared as *grey* in some places in the text, you could search for *gr\?y* (Figure 11.31). The backslash before the question mark is what appears in the dialog box when you type the wildcard code, ⌘-?/CTRL-?.

```
┌─────────────────────────── Find/Change ───────────────────────────┐
│ ┌─Find What:──────────────┐  ┌─Change To:──────────────────┐       │
│ │ gr\?y                   │  │ shaded|                      │       │
│ └─────────────────────────┘  └─────────────────────────────┘       │
│                                                                     │
│ ⊠ Document      □ Whole Word       ⊠ Ignore Case    ⊠ Ignore Attributes │
│  ┌──────────┐  ┌────────────────┐  ┌─────────┐  ┌────────────┐      │
│  │ Find Next│  │ Change, then Find│ │ Change  │  │ Change All │      │
│  └──────────┘  └────────────────┘  └─────────┘  └────────────┘      │
└─────────────────────────────────────────────────────────────────────┘
```

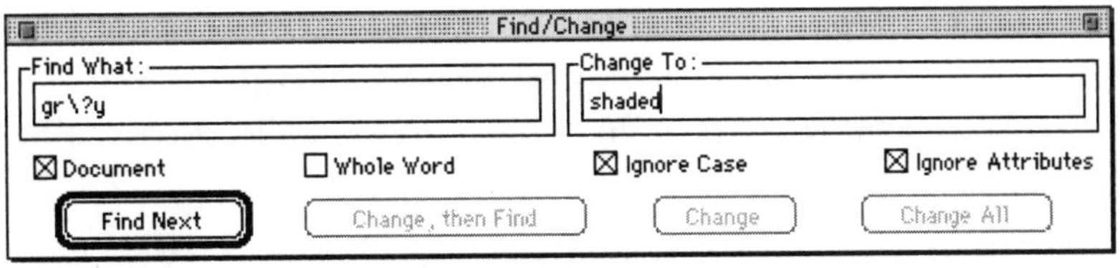

Figure 11.31 *Changing all occurrences of gray or grey to shaded.*

This example works because *gray* and *grey* are the only English words that fit the format **gr\?y**—*griy, groy,* and *gruy* are not valid words. If you know that there are some exceptions in the text, you would use **Find Next, Change,** then **Find**—rather than **Change All**—so you can skip certain occurrences, such as *Gray Line Tours,* and *shades of gray.*

Inserting XPress Tags in ASCII Text

QuarkXPress lets you insert tags into any ASCII text so that the text will be formatted automatically when imported into a QuarkXPress document. This can be handy if you are preparing text using a word processor that is not directly supported by one of QuarkXPress' application-specific import filters—such as text from a dedicated word processing system or a mainframe text editor. XPress tags are also useful in preparing text in a spreadsheet or database format, as described earlier in this chapter.

The basic procedure is simple:

- Include codes for formatting text in the original text file, following the rules given in the next section.

- Save or export the text in ASCII text format (called *text-only* on some menus), and end the file name with the XPress Tags extension **.xtg.** (If the extension is missing, QuarkXPress will not know to use the XPress Tags filter in importing.)

- Open the QuarkXPress document and use the **File ➤ Get Text** command to import the text into a text box. Select the **Include Style Sheets** option in the Get Text dialog box.

Generating Tagged Text from QuarkXPress

You can create tagged text by exporting text that has already been formatted in QuarkXPress. Here's how it works:

1. Format the text in QuarkXPress, using normal menu commands and the Measurements palette.
2. Select the text with the Content tool and choose **File ➤ Save Text.**
3. Choose **XPress tags** from the Format drop-down menu in the Save Text dialog box. (If this option is not available, the XPress Tags filter has not been installed—go back to your installation disks or CD-ROM and install the filter.)
4. Type a name with the **.xtg** extension at the end.
5. Click **Save.**

Now you can import the text to another QuarkXPress document by selecting a text box with the Content tool and choosing **File ➤ Get Text**, and selecting the **Include Style Sheets** option in the Get text dialog box.

This can be handy if you want to quickly take formatted text from one QuarkXPress document and import it onto another document from scratch, but it is also a great aid in figuring out what tag codes you will need before you go through the long process of embedding codes in text. You could design a one-page mock-up of the membership directory, for example, taking a few addresses or dummy text and applying the desired formats in QuarkXPress. Then export the text with XPress Tags and open the ASCII file to see what tags were generated and where they appear. This is the "blueprint" for inserting the same codes in the raw data or text files for the full membership list.

The Basic Rules for Tagging Text

In adding XPress Tags to text, you must follow some simple rules so that QuarkXPress can distinguish between the characters that are part of the formatting codes and the characters that are the actual content of the text.

- Each XPress Tag code or series of codes must be framed in pointed brackets (less than and greater than symbols). For example, **<B>** is a tag code for bold text. The one exception is the use of the **@** symbol rather than a bracket when specifying style sheet names (see the description of codes later in this chapter).
- All files formatted for the XPress Tags filter must have a filter version tag as the first thing in the file, in the format: **<V1.5>**. The version number for QuarkXPress 3.1 is 1.5; the version for QuarkXPress 3.2-3.3 is 1.7.
- The same code turns a formatting attribute on and off. For example, the first occurrence of **<B>** makes the following text bold, and the text continues to be bold until the next occurrence of **<B>**.
- You can put more than one code inside one set of brackets. For example, **<BI>** turns the attributes of bold and italic on (or off).
- Codes affect the text that follow them. Codes that affect paragraph formatting must appear at the beginning of a paragraph.
- To apply the style sheet to a series of paragraphs, begin the first paragraph with the code **@** followed by the style sheet name. For example, the coded text **@Heading1:Vision** would cause the word *Vision* to be formatted using the Heading1 style sheet. You can indicate Normal style by coding **@Normal** or simply **@$.** You indicate No Style by beginning a paragraph with **@:** (the @ symbol followed by a colon followed by the paragraph text). When you apply a style

sheet to a paragraph, the style sheet remains in effect until a new style sheet name or the code for No Style Sheet is encountered.

- You can import tagged text using style sheet names that have already been defined in the QuarkXPress document, or you can define new style sheets as part of the XPress tags code (see description of codes later in this chapter).
- For codes that let you specify a series of values, you can enter a $ in place of an actual value to use whatever value is set up for the normal style sheet or the currently applied style sheet. For example, if you want to set up a paragraph with 24-point leading, but you want all of the other values to be drawn from the normal style sheet or the current style sheet, you could code: **<*p($,$,$,24,$,$,$)>**. See the code lists later in this chapter for a detailed explanation of the paragraph formatting codes.
- Colors and H&Js must be defined within the QuarkXPress document *before* importing tagged text that uses those names. Colors that are indicated in the XPress tag codes but have not been defined in the document will be converted to black; standard H&Js will be used for any coded H&Js that have not been defined in the QuarkXPress document.
- A single code sequence may run longer than one line and will be interpreted correctly if the line is broken by normal text wrap (i.e., *soft* carriage returns). If you wish to intentionally force line breaks by pressing the **Enter** or **Return** key within a long code sequence, or if you will be sending the coded text through a telecommunication process that will force hard carriage returns, then you must end each line with a colon (:) to indicate that the code sequence continues on the next line.
- The maximum length for any name (style sheets, colors, or H&Js) is 63 characters.

A List of XPress Tags

Table 11.2 shows codes that you can type to format ASCII text. The initial attributes for imported text will be the same as the attributes at the insertion point when the **File ➛ Get Text** command is used. Current attributes remain in effect until they are explicitly changed by an embedded code. These codes can be combined within brackets. For example, you can type **<BI>** to set text to bold and italic.

TIP: You must check **Include Style Sheets** in the Get Text dialog box when importing, and the XPress Tags filter must be in the QuarkXPress program folder, or the XPress tags will come in as ASCII text. You cannot import text through two filters at the same time: XPress Tags inserted in formatted text imported from Microsoft Word, for instance, will not be interpreted as formatting codes. You must save coded text in ASCII format.

***Table 11.2** Character Attributes*

Description	Start Code	End Code
Plain	<P>	<P> or <$>
Bold	<B>	<B> or <$>
Italic	<I>	<I> or <$>
Outline	<O>	<O> or <$>
Shadow	<S>	<S> or <$>
Underline	<U>	<U> or <$>
Word Underline	<W>	<W> or <$>
Strikethrough	</>	</> or <$>
All Caps	<K>	<K> or <$>
Small Caps	<H>	<H> or <$>
Superscript	<+>	<+> or <$>
Subscript	<->	<-> or <$>
Superior	<V>	<V> or <$>
Current style sheet	<$>	

In Table 11.3, italicized text indicates variables that you enter, and ###.## represents any two-place decimal number. Names of fonts must always be framed in quotation marks. Colors must be defined in the QuarkXPress document before the text that references them is imported. If a color is not found, Black will be used.

***Table 11.3** Other Character Attributes*

Description	Start Code	End Code
Change font	<f"*font name*">	<f$>
Change size in points	<z###.##>	<z$>
Shift Baseline in points	<b###.##>	<b$>
Change shade percentage	<s###.##>	<s$>
Horizontal scale percentage	<h###.##>	<h$>
Vertical scale percentage	<y###.##>	<y$>
Kern @ #/200ths em	<k###.##>	<k$>
Kerning applies to next two characters only:		
Track @ #/200ths em	<t###.##>	<t$>
Change color	<c"*color name*">	<c$>
You can enter abbreviations for primary colors:		
Cyan	<cC>	
Magenta	<cM>	
Yellow	<cY>	
Black	<cK>	
White	<cW>	

***Table 11.4** Alignment Attributes*

Description	Start Code
Align Left	<*L>
Center	<*C>
Align Right	<*R>
Justify	<*J>
Force Justify	<*F>

In the codes given in Table 11.5, if you omit a parameter in a string, you must still include the comma that follows that parameter. Missing parameters will be set to match the current style sheet settings.

***Table 11.5** Tab Attributes*

Description	Start Code	End Code
Set tabs	<*t(##.##,#."#aa")>	<*t$>
with ###.## = tab position, #= tab alignment, and "#aa" = the tab leader character coding, framed in quotation marks.		
Tab position is indicated in points.		

For tab alignment, 0 = Left, 2 = Right, 1 = Center, 3 = Decimal. Type a comma (,) to indicate Comma alignment. Type any printing character to indicate an Align On tab character.

For no tab leaders, type the number **1** followed by two spaces. For the same repeated character, type the number **1** followed by the repeat character typed twice. For two alternating characters in the tab leader, type the number **2** followed by the two characters.

Type the values for each tab in the paragraph, with each tab set separated by commas within the parentheses. For example:

```
<*t(36,0,"1  ",144,1"1  ",288,2,"1  ")>
```

***Table 11.6** Paragraph Attributes*

Description	Start Code	End Code
Set paragraph format	<*p(*left indent,* *first line indent,* *right indent,* *leading,* *space before,* *space after,* *G/baseline grid*)>	<*p$>
where all values are entered in the form ###.## except the baseline grid. G = Lock to baseline grid; g = do not lock to grid.		
H&J	<*h"*hyphenation name*">	<*h$>

***Table 11.6** continued*

Description	Start Code	End Code
H&J names must be defined in the QuarkXPress document before the text that references them is imported. If an H&J is not found, the default H&J is used.		
Paragraph Rule Above	<*ra(*rule width*, *line style ID*, *"color name"*, *line shade*, *left indent* or T*line length*, *right indent*, *rule position* or % *percentage*)>	<*ra$>
where *rule width* and *right indent* are entered in points in the format ###.##; the *line style ID* is entered as # (counted by position down in the Style drop-down list in the Rules tab of the Paragraph Attributes dialog box); the *color name* must have been defined in the QuarkXPress document before importing the text, or can be entered as an abbreviation for one of the primary colors: C, M, Y, K, or W; the *line shade* is entered as a percentage in the format ###.##; the *left indent* can be entered in points in the format ###.## or the entry can be the *length of the line* if preceded by a T (T###.##); and the *rule position* is the offset distance from the text and can be entered in points (###.##) or as a percentage of the point size if followed by a % (###.##%).		
Rule below	<*rb(###.##,#,"*color name*", ###.##,###.##, ###.##,###.##)>	<*rb$>
where the parameters are as described for Rule Above.		
Drop cap	<*d(#,#)>	<*d$>
where the parameters are character count, line count.		
Keep with next	<*kn1>	<*kn$> or <*kn0>
where kn1 = Keep with next, kn$ = use current style sheet, kn0 = do not keep with next.		
Keep together	<*kt(A)> or <*kt(#,#)>	<*kt$>
where the A = all lines or #,# = start line, end line.		

***Table 11.7** Style Sheet Attributes*

Description	**Start Code**
Normal Style sheet	@$:
No style sheet	@:
Change style sheet	@*stylesheetname*:
For each of these three XPress Tag codes, the paragraph text begins immediately after the colon at the end of the code. In defining a new style sheet name, the definition is followed by a hard return before the paragraph text begins:	
Define new style sheet	@*style sheet=definition* (hard return)
The current style sheet remains in effect until a new style sheet or no style sheet is applied using one of the @ codes shown here. Applying a new style sheet overrides all previous formatting codes.	

Style sheet names must be defined in the QuarkXPress document or in the ASCII file as an XPress tag code (using *@style sheet=defintion*) before the text is imported. In defining a style sheet, you can follow *@style sheet=* with any of the codes shown in this table. For example:

```
@caption=<f"Helvetica"z9*C>
```

To base a new style on an existing style. code:

```
@stylesheetname=[s"based-on-name"]definition
```

Style sheet names cannot include the special characters :, =, or @.

Table 11.8 *Insert Special Characters*

Description	Code
New Line (Soft Return)	<\n>
Discretionary New Line	<\d>
Indent here	<\i>
Right Indent Tab	<\t>
New column	<\c>
New box	<\b>
Discretionary hyphen	<\h>
Standard space	<\s> or <\!s> for nonbreaking character
En space	<\f> or <\!f> for nonbreaking character
Punctuation space	<\p> or <\!p> for nonbreaking character
Flex Space	<\q> or <\!q> for nonbreaking character
Hyphen	<\-> or <\!-> for nonbreaking character
Previous box's page	<\2>
Current box's page	<\3>
Next box's page	<\4>

Any character can be coded using the decimal ASCII code, by typing a backslash, followed by the # symbol, followed by the ASCII decimal value—all enclosed in the pointed brackets. For example, the code for a bullet would be <\#183>.

Since @, <, and \ characters have a special meaning as XPress tag codes, you must use codes to enter these characters in coded documents if you want them to print as part of the text (Table 11.9).

Table 11.9 *Entering Special Symbols as Xpress Tab Codes*

Symbol	Code
@	<\@>
<	<\<>
\	<\\>

Figures 12.32 and 12.33 show an example of text with XPress tags before and after being imported into QuarkXPress.

```
@DropCapParagraphStyle+<*L*h"Standard"kn0*kt0*ra0*rb0*d(1,3)*p(0,0,0,0,0,0,
g)* t(0,0,""):
Ps100t0h100z12k0b0c"Black"f"Times">
@DropCapParagraphStyle"<*L*h"Standard"*kn0kt0*ra0*rb0*d(1,3)*
p(0,0,0,0,0,0,g)t(0,0,""):
Ps100t0h100z12k0b0c"Black"f"Times">Si meliora dies, ut vina, poemata reddit,
scire velim, chartis pretium quotus arroget annus, scriptor abhinc annnos centum
qui decidit, inter perfectos veteresque refgerri debet an inter vilis atque
novos? Excludat iurgia finis, "Est vetus atque probus, cent<P>um qui perficit
annos." Quid, qui deperiit minor uno mense vel anno, inter quos referendus erit?
Veterense poetas, an quos et praesens et postera respuat aetas?
@BodyCopyStyle=<*L*h"Standadr"*kn0*kt0*ra0*d0*p(0,12,0,0,0,0,g)*t(0,0,""):
PS100t0h100z12k0b0c"Black"f"Times">
@BodyCopyStyle:<P>"Iste quidem veteres inter ponetur honeste, qui vel mense
brevi vel toto est iunior anno." Utor permisso, caudaeque pilos ut equinae
paulatim vello unum, demo etiam unum, dum cadat elusus ratione ruentis acervi,
qui redit in fastos et virtutem aestimat ann<P>is miaturque nihil nisi quod
Libitina scaravit.<P>Ennius et sapines et fortis et alter Homerus, ut critici
dicunt, leviter curare videtur, quo promissa cadant et somnia Pythagorea.
Naevius in manibus non est et mentibus haerat paene recense? Adeo sanctum est
vetus omne poema. Ambigitur quotiens, uter utro <P>sit prior, aufert Pacivius
docti famam senis Accius alti, dicitur Afrani toga convenisse Menerado, Plautus
ad exemplar Siculi properare Epicharmi, vincere Caecilius gravitate, Terentius
arte.
```

Figure 11.32 *ASCII text with XPress tags.*

Sit lorem ipsum dolor sit amet, consectetuer adipiscing elit, sed diam nonummy nibh euismod tincidunt ut laoreet dolore magna aliquam erat volutpat. Ut wisi enim ad minim veniam, quis nostrud exerci tation ullamcorper suscipit lobortis nisl ut aliquip ex ea commodo consequat.

Duis autem vel eum iriure dolor in hendrerit in vulputate velit esse molestie consequat, vel illum dolore eu feugiat nulla facilisis at vero eros et accumsan et iusto odio dignissim qui blandit praesent luptatum zzril.

Duis autem vel eum iriure dolor in hendrerit in vulputate velit esse molestie consequat, vel illum dolore eu feugiat nulla facilisis at vero eros et accumsan et iusto odio dignissim qui blandit praesent luptatum zzril delenit augue duis dolore te feugait nulla facilisi. Nam liber tempor cum soluta nobis eleifend option congue nihil imperdiet doming id quod mazim placerat facer possim assum.

Subhead Text

Lorem ipsum dolor sit amet, consectetuer adipiscing elit, sed diam nonummy nibh euismod tincidunt ut laoreet dolore magna aliquam erat volutpat. Ut wisi enim ad minim veniam, quis nostrud exerci tation ullamcorper suscipit lobortis nisl ut aliquip ex ea commodo consequat.

Duis autem vel eum iriure dolor in hendrerit in vulputate velit esse molestie consequat, vel illum dolore eu feugiat nulla facilisis at vero eros et accumsan et iusto odio dignissim qui blandit praesent lupta-

Figure 11.33 *ASCII text with XPress tags after being imported into QuarkXPress.*

Summary

This chapter offered tips on how to work with text from databases and non-Macintosh computers, including how to use the **Find/Change** command to remove unwanted characters or to insert formatting codes. We also discussed how to insert XPress tags into text created on a non-Macintosh computer so that text will format automatically when imported into QuarkXPress.

This chapter concludes Part II of this book on issues related to publishing long documents. Part III, "Advanced Techniques" covers a variety of topics, including printing color seperations, and preparing documents for use on the World Wide Web.

PART THREE

ADVANCED TECHNIQUES

12 Graphics in Typography

QuarkXPress has long been known for its typographic capabilities, and with the inclusion of Bézier tools, it will undoubtedly become more and more a graphics workhorse, too. Not everything that's done with QuarkXPress, though, falls neatly into the category of strictly text or graphics. Working with the program often involves the "intersection" of text and graphics—text that winds through a graphic, or a graphic that's anchored in text, essentially becoming part of a paragraph.

This chapter covers that part of the QuarkXPress world where text meets graphics, including two exciting new features:

- converting text to picture boxes
- type on a path (text-paths)

This chapter also covers feature enhancements and special techniques for working with:

- anchored items
- paragraph rules

Examples of different effects you can achieve with each of these features are also shown, just to give you an idea of the possibilities. Working with these features on your own is always the best teacher, and in this case it can be a lot of fun, too!

Converting Text to Boxes

One of the new graphics features added to QuarkXPress 4.0 includes the ability to convert text to picture boxes. This capability is similar to Adobe Illustrator's **Convert to Outlines** command that essentially converts type to artwork paths.

In order for this command to work correctly, you must use either True Type or PostScript fonts. If you are using PostScript fonts, *both* the screen and printer fonts must be available. Once you have the correct fonts available, use the following steps to convert text to a picture box:

1. Format the text in the font and style desired. Highlight the characters you wish to convert to a box (Figure 12.1).

TIP

You can convert as many text characters as you like to a picture box, but you can only convert one line of text at a time. This includes not only a line of text that ends with a paragraph return, but a line that word wrap forces to the next line. If you want more text to be included, make the text box wider.

Figure 12.1 *Format the text, then highlight the characters you wish to convert to a box.*

2. Select the **Style ➛ Text to Box** command (Figure 12.2).

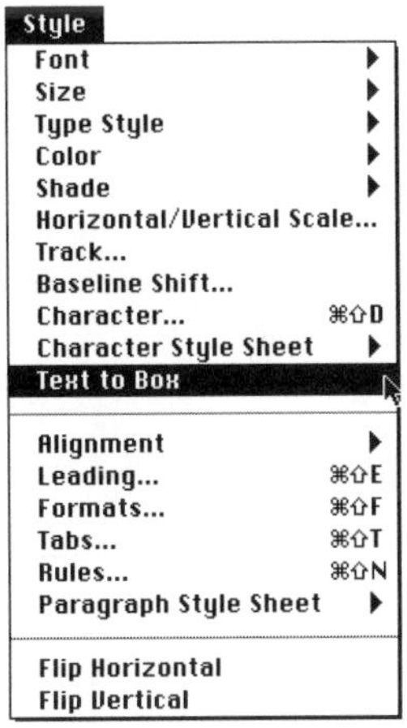

***Figure 12.2** Select the **Style → Text to Box** command.*

3. The text is copied below the selected text, and converted to a single picture box. You can now import a picture, or fill the box with a color or blend (Figure 12.3). Picture boxes created with this command can be modified in all the ways you would modify any picture box. You can also type text inside the box, by first converting it to a text box using the **Item → Content → Text** command.

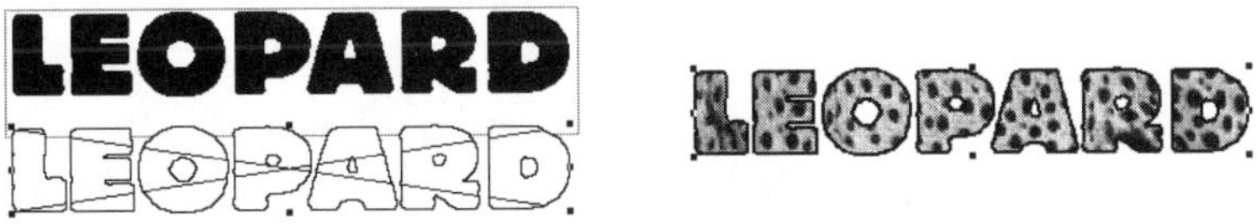

***Figure 12.3** The text converted to a picture box (left) and the resulting box with an imported picture (right).*

After using the **Style → Text to Box** command, the picture box will usually display all the Bézier points that form each letter shape. You can move the box using the Item tool (✥), but it's very easy to accidentally select a point. An easier way to move the box is to triple-click any one point (or double-click for a single character), then move the shape as one. Or, uncheck the **Item → Edit → Shape** command, so that only the eight handles of the box's bounding box are displayed (Figure 12.4).

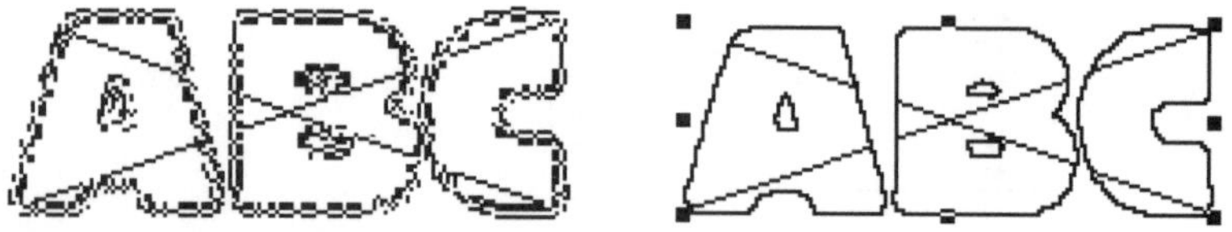

Figure 12.4 *To move a box that's been created using the* ***Style → Text to Box*** *command (left), uncheck the* ***Item → Edit → Shape*** *command, so that only the eight handles of the box's bounding box are displayed (right).*

When you first convert text to a box, all the character shapes will behave as one box, similarly to having the **Item → Merge → Union** command applied. When you import a picture or apply a blend, the picture or blend will appear across all the boxes. If you'd like each character to behave as a separate box, use the **Item → Split → Outside Paths** command (Figure 12.5). Using the **Outside Paths** command will not separate the "inside holes" of characters such as A and O. If you want the inside of these characters to be split also (a less likely scenario perhaps), use the **Item → Split → All Paths** command. The Merge and Split commands are discussed in detail in Chapter 6, "Graphics."

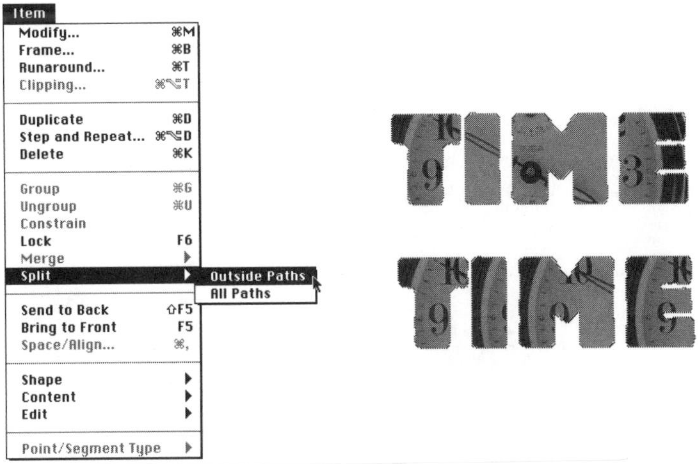

Figure 12.5 *Use the* ***Item*** *➛* ***Split*** *➛* ***Outside Paths*** *command to create separate picture boxes of each character. Figure on top right shows original picture box, figure on bottom shows boxes after using the command.*

TIP

Normally, when you use the Text to Box command, the box is copied outside the text box. If you wish to anchor the newly created picture box in the adjacent text, hold down the **Option/Alt** key and choose the **Style ➛ Text to Box** command (Figure 12.6). The picture boxes will be anchored in the exact location of the text. Note that you cannot use the split commands on an anchored box.

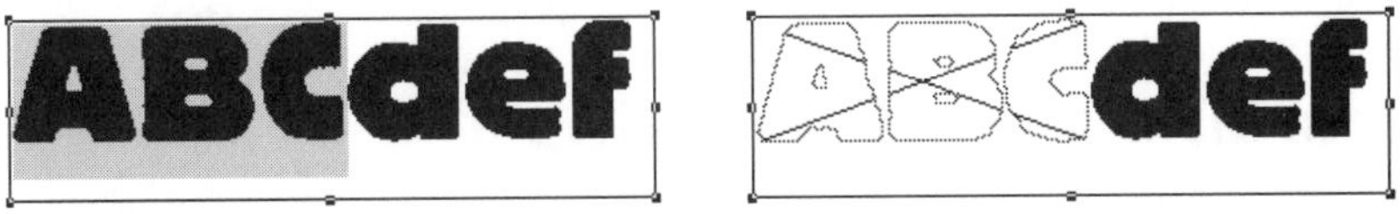

Figure 12.6 *Hold down the* ***Option/Alt*** *key before using the* ***Style*** *➛* ***Text to Box*** *command (left) to anchor the box in the adjacent text (right).*

Keep in mind that you can use this command with dingbats or picture fonts to quickly and easily create picture boxes of particular shapes or items. Some examples are shown below (Figure 12.7), using Zapf Dingbats and fonts from the Mini Pics series (available from Image Club, a division of Adobe Systems Incorporated, at www.imageclub.com).

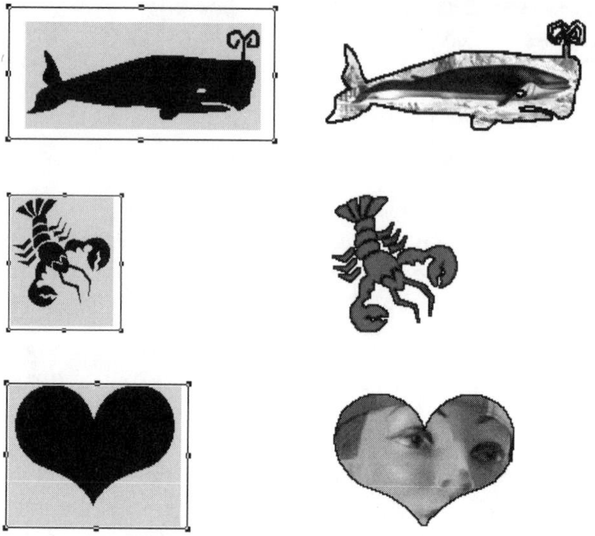

Figure 12.7 *Use the* ***Text to Box*** *command with picture fonts to quickly obtain picture boxes of special shapes or items.*

Working with Text-Paths

QuarkXPress 4.0 introduces four text-path tools that let you type text along a straight or Bézier line (instead of inside a text box). Once a text-path is created, both the text and the line can be modified in any of the ways you'd normally modify these items—including adjusting the text's orientation, baseline shift, and spacing—with additional controls that are unique to text-paths.

To create a text-path:

1. Select one of the four text-path tools (Figure 12.8) from the toolbox: the Line Text-Path tool, Orthogonal Text-Path tool, Bézier Text-Path tool, or freehand Bézier Text-Path tool.

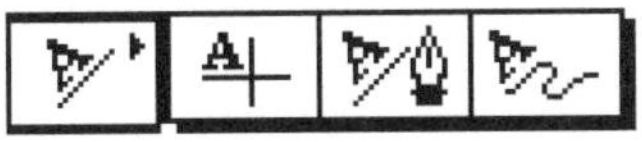

Figure 12.8 *The four text-path tools: the Line Text-Path tool, Orthogonal Text-Path tool, Bézier Text-Path tool, and freehand Bézier Text-Path tool.*

2. Move the crosshair pointer onto a page and draw a line or curve, just as you would draw any line item.
3. When you complete a text path, a blinking cursor automatically appears at the start of the line—type the text you wish.

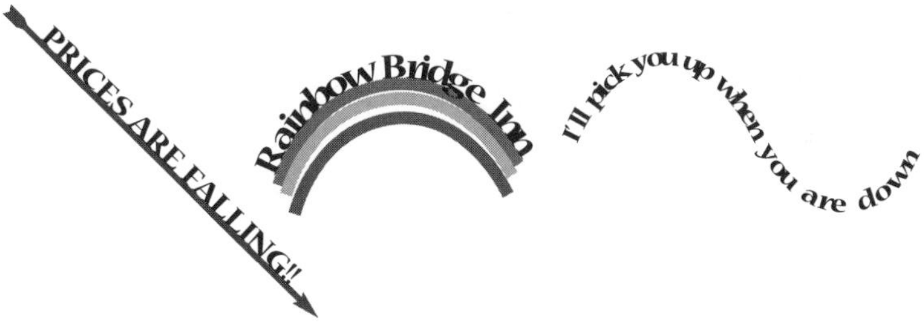

Figure 12.9 *Text-Paths created with the Line Text-Path tool and Bézier Text-Path tool.*

This actually completes the creation of the path text, but you will usually want to fine-tune the results by applying one or more of the options available for formatting either the text or the line.

TIP: When working with a text-path, you can edit either the text or the line. Select the text-path with the Content (☞) tool to edit the path text using the Measurements palette or Style menu; click on the text-path with the Item (✥) tool to modify the line attributes using the Measurements palette or the Style menu.

You can format or edit the path text using any of the techniques you normally would, including selecting the text with the Content tool (☞) and using normal editing techniques to select the text and apply type attributes through the Style menu or the Measurement palette.

TIP: Change the text Alignment (left, right, center) to move the text along the path. Change the Kerning values to spread or tighten the text along the path.

Select the path with the Item (✥) tool and choose commands from the Style menu, or use the Measurements palette, to change the line style, width, color, or shade, or add arrowheads. Note that you can apply any custom line style that has been created using **Edit ➛ Dashes & Stripes.**

You can also select the path with either tool and choose **Item ➛ Modify** (**⌘-M/CTRL-M**), then click on one of the three tabs to make changes related to the Line style, Text Path, or Runaround. The Line Style and Runaround options are the same as for any line (see Chapter 6, "Graphics")—the Text-Path options are described next.

The Text-Path Options

Not only can you modify both the text and the line elements of a text-path, but there are other options available for fine-tuning that are unique to text-paths. Select the path and choose **Item ➛ Modify,** then click on the Text Path tab (Figure 12.10) to access these options.

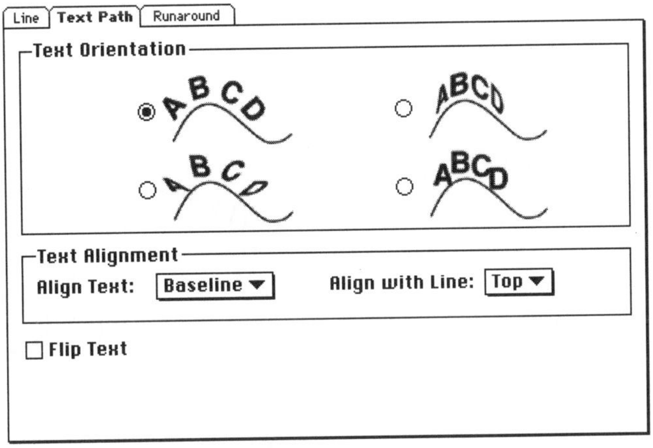

Figure 12.10 The Text Path tab of the Modify dialog box

TIP

Click one of the **Text Orientation** options to make the each character perpendicular to the path (top left option), perpendicular to the page (lower left option), rotated and skewed for a 3-D effect (top right option), or warped by skewing only (lower right option). Examples of the effects of these settings can be seen in Figure 12.11.

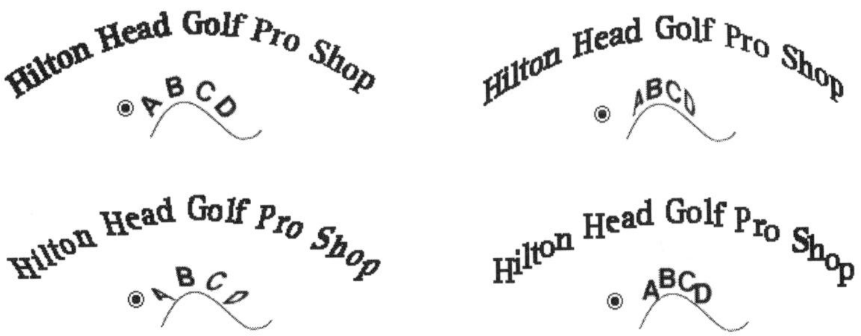

Figure 12.11 The effect of the Text Orientation options for text-paths.

Choose an option from the **Align Text** pop-up menu to shift the text so the path passes along the Ascent, Center, Baseline, or Descent of the text (Figure 12.12).

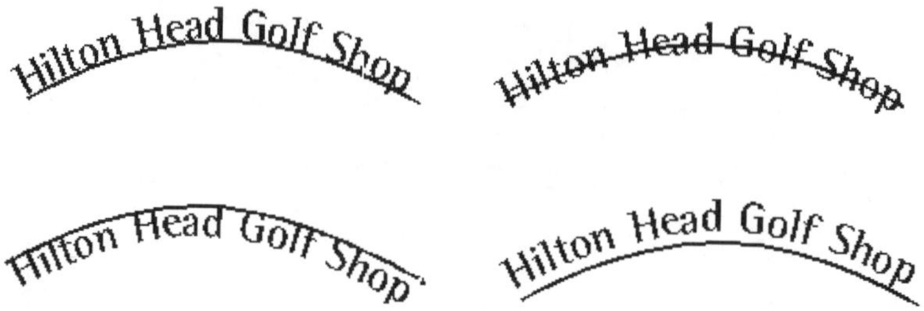

***Figure 12.12** Examples of the Align Text options: Baseline, Ascent, Center, Descent (all relative to the Top of the line).*

You can choose an option from the **Align with Line** pop-up menu to align the text with the Top, Center, or Bottom of the line (Figure 12.13). The line, of course, will not display unless a Width has been applied to it.

***Figure 12.13** Examples of the Align with Line options: Top, Center, Bottom (all relative to the Baseline of the text).*

Click **Flip Text** to place the text on the opposite side of the path, upside down (Figure 12.14).

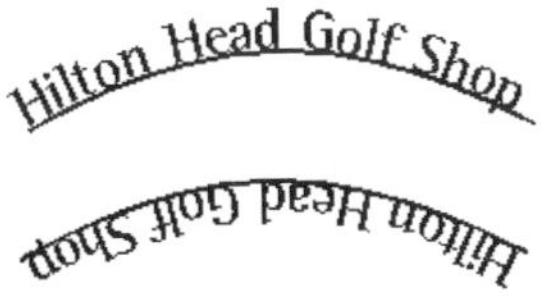

Figure 12.14 *The effect of the Flip Text option unchecked (top) and checked (bottom).*

Creating Special Effects

Text-paths, along with other new graphics features like Bézier tools and the ability to convert text to picture boxes, combine to make a powerful toolbox for creative design in QuarkXPress. Now special treatments for headlines, logos and other elements can be achieved using QuarkXPress, without resorting to other software programs.

One of the features that provides great flexibility is that you can covert *any* shape to a text path. This can be accomplished using the **Item ➛ Content** command and the **Item ➛ Shape** commands (discussed in Chapter 6, "Graphics"). This includes the following steps:

1. Create a box of any shape using the Item Creation tools, or by converting a text character to a picture box using the **Text to Box** command, as shown in Figure 12.15.

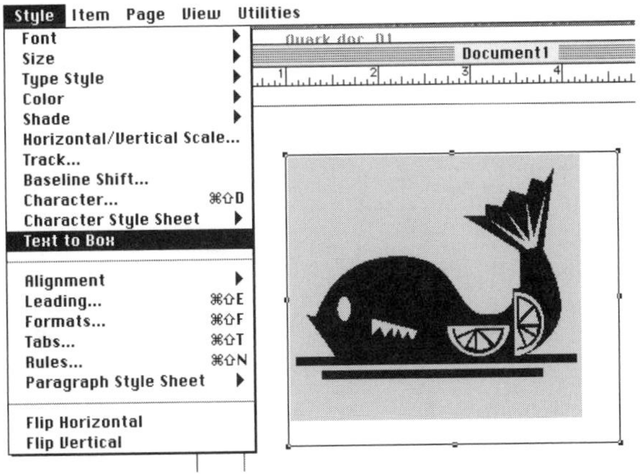

Figure 12.15 *Create a box from a picture font by using the **Text to Box** command.*

2. Change the content type of the box to text, using the **Item → Content → Text** command (Figure 12.16). You can enter text in the text box at this time, or go ahead and convert the box to a text path, as in the next step.

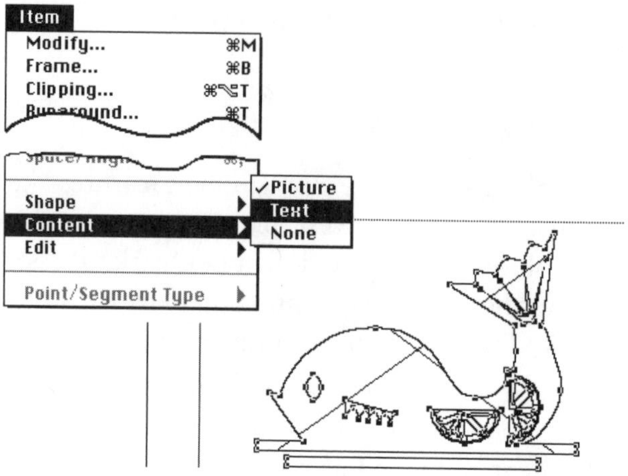

***Figure 12.16** Convert any box to a text box using the **Item → Content → Text** command.*

3. Convert the text box to a text-path by using the **Item → Shape →** ∿ command. The text box will not become a text-path; any text inside the box will run along the path (Figure 12.17).

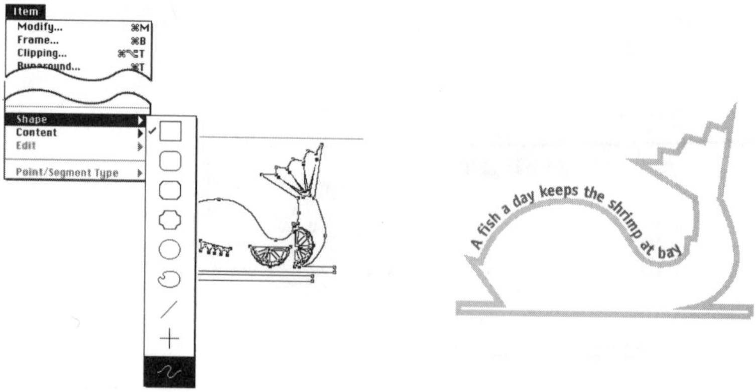

***Figure 12.17** Convert any text box to a text path using the **Item → Shape →** ∿ command.*

You can further control the design of the text path using text formatting controls, such as alignment, or the text-path controls for orientation, discussed earlier in this section. Examples of some of the effect you can achieve are shown in Figure 12.18. Be sure and check out the Text-paths Tricks page in the color pages of this book.

Figure 12.18 *Examples of designs created in QuarkXPress using text-paths.*

Techniques with Anchored Items

The basics of working with anchored items—items that are "attached" to text—are covered in Chapter 3, "Expanding the Document." As discussed in that chapter, any QuarkXPress item, except grouped items, may be copied into the clipboard, then pasted into text in a box; if the existing text is edited, the anchored item moves along with the text.

One of the most common applications of this feature is to anchor figures in a manuscript. By using this feature, you can ensure that any text editing that's done will not cause the graphic to shift out of position. If, for example, the text references "see Figure 2-22, below," you want to be confident that it's not Figure 2-15!

When setting up anchored picture boxes, there are a couple of different ways to format the text into which you will anchor a box. In many cases, you'll want to anchor the box on a paragraph of its own. By doing so, you can format the paragraph (just a paragraph character, really) using a style sheet.

If your layout happens to be one that has figures of all the same size, the settings can be pretty straightforward:

- Align the anchored box with the text Ascent (⊠≡)
- Format the paragraph to have a space after that is equal to the height of each graphic, plus any additional spacing desired, as shown in Figure 12.19.

Subhead·Text→
Ut·wisi·enim·ad·minim·veniam,·quis·nostrud·exerci·tation·ullam·corper·suscipit·lobortis·nisl·ut·aliquip·ex·ea·commodo·consequat.¶
Align with Text
Ascent
Baseline
Offset:
0"
Leading:
13 pt
Space Before:
0"
Space After:
2.75"
Duis·autem·vel·eum·iriure·dolor·in·hendrerit·in·vulputate·velit·esse·molestie·consequat,·vel·illum·dolore·eu·feugiat·nulla·facilisis·at·vero·eros·et·accumsan·et·iusto·odio·dignissim·qui·blandit·praesent·luptatum·zzril·delenit·augue·

Figure 12.19 *Settings for anchoring picture boxes that will be the same size throughout the document.*

If the graphics are different sizes, a more likely scenario, the settings will be a little different:

- Align the anchored box by the Baseline (⊠_)
- In order to accommodate the different picture sizes, set the leading, for this paragraph only, to **Auto** (assuming you never use Auto leading in your body text!). Since QuarkXPress's Auto leading looks at the largest character in a line, then adds leading to that amount (the default is +20%), it looks at the picture box as a text character, and adjusts the leading accordingly. An example of these settings is shown in Figure 12.20.

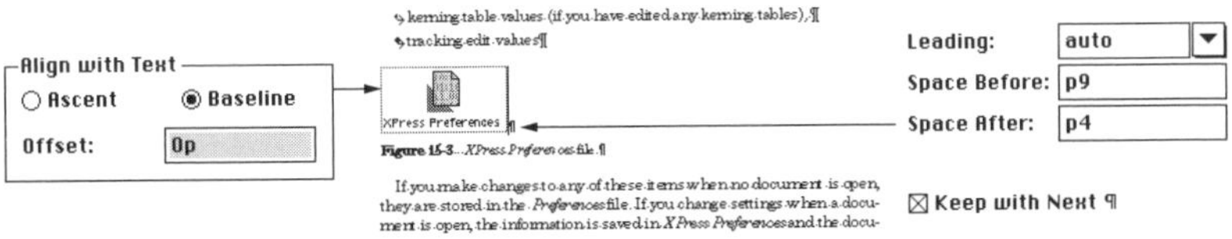

***Figure 12.20** Settings for anchoring picture boxes that will be a different size throughout the document.*

TIP

When anchoring picture boxes that have captions underneath, keep the anchored picture boxes with the captions by checking **Keep with Next Paragraph** in the Formats tab of the Paragraph Attributes dialog box. By keeping the paragraph with the anchored box with the caption paragraph, QuarkXPress will move both picture box and caption to the next page if there's not enough room for both.

Tricks with Paragraph Rules

As discussed in Chapter 5, "Typography," you can add custom rules (any line style created using **Edit ➛ Dashes and Stripes**) to text using options available in the Rules tab of the Paragraph Attributes dialog box (**Style ➛ Rules**). Aside from the fairly straightforward ability to add any custom line above or below a paragraph—either using the command directly or as part of a style sheet—there's a lot more you can do with this feature, once you understand the tremendous flexibility of the options available.

One of the simple effects that can be achieved is one that's not so obvious: to position a rule so that it is centered in a column of text. One way to do it, of course, is to set the Length pop-up menu to **Text**, then simply center align the text. The line will run the length of the text across the column. But what if you want the rule to be the same length each time? The trick is to use the Indent field to push each end of the rule away from the column edge. Figure 12.21 shows a sample of a rule that runs in the center of a column, and the associated settings.

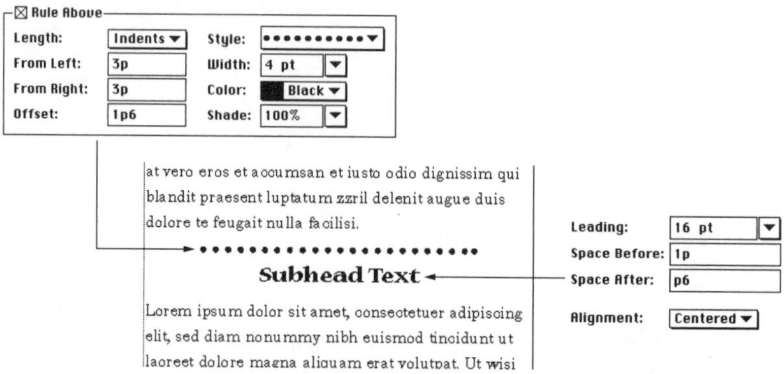

Figure 12.21 *Settings to create a paragraph rule that appears in the center of a column.*

Another very handy use of paragraph rules is to create reverse type on a color background for headlines or single lines of text. You could achieve this effect by applying a background color to subhead text, for example, and its box background, but this cannot be embodied in a style sheet. By using paragraph rules, you can create titles and subheads that are reversed, and can also be incorporated into a style sheet for more efficient production.

The basic steps are as follows:

1. Format the text, including the color you wish to apply.
2. Display the Rules tab of the Paragraph attributes dialog box (**Style ➛ Rules** or **⌘-Shift-N/CTRL-SHIFT-N**).
3. Check the **Rule Above** option. Next, set the width of the rule that will provide the background color, which needs to be wider than the text is high. You can enter any value up to 864 points, or about 6".
4. Here's the part that really does the trick: set the **Offset** value to a negative number. Since a Rule Above's offset is measured from the baseline of the text to the bottom of the rule, a negative value brings the rule *below* the line of text, thus causing it to appear to run behind the text.

Figure 12.22 shows a sample of a rule that appears to reverse type on a color background, and the associated settings.

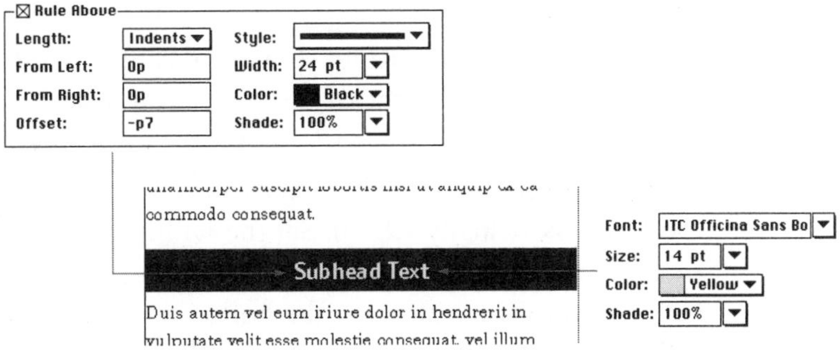

Figure 12.22 *Settings to create a paragraph rule that appears to reverse text on a color background.*

You can use this basic approach to create effects of black type on shaded backgrounds, too. One application of this effect might be to create tables, for example, where every other line is shaded. Figure 12.23 shows an example of a table formatted with paragraph rules and the associated settings.

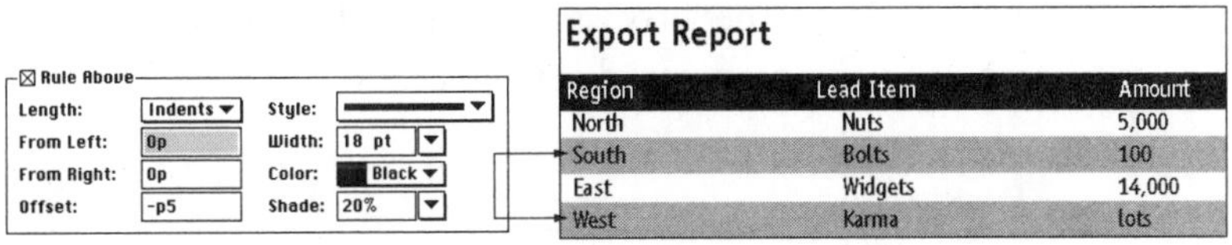

Figure 12.23 *Settings to create a paragraph rule for black type on a shaded or color background.*

One of our favorite "tricks" with paragraph rules is one that actually lets you draw a box around a headline or any single line of text. The basic steps to achieve this effect are as follows:

1. Display the Rules tab of the Paragraph attributes dialog box (**Style ➣ Rules** or **⌘-Shift-N/Ctrl-Shift-N**).

2. Check both the **Rule Above** and the **Rule Below** options. The basic approach is that the rule above will actually form the outside border of the box, and the rule below will form the "inside" of the box.
3. Apply a color to the Rule Above and set the Width to a value greater than the height of the text. Set the Offset to a negative value (which causes the rule to begin below the text).
4. Apply the color to the Rule Above that you wish for the inside of the box (usually white). Set the width to less than the Rule Above, by double the amount of the width of the box border (for example, if you want the border to be 2 pts, set the Rule Below to be 4 pts less than the width of the Rule Above).
5. Set the Rule Below Offset value to a negative number. Since a Rule Below's offset is measured from the baseline of the text to the top of the rule, a negative value brings the rule above the line of text, thus causing it to appear to run behind the text, but on top of the Rule Above. Finally, set the Indents to the distance of the width of the box border.

This causes the Rule Below to display behind the text, but on top of the Rule Above. The indents of the Rule Below draw the vertical "sides" of the box. Figure 12.24 shows an example of this effect and the associated settings.

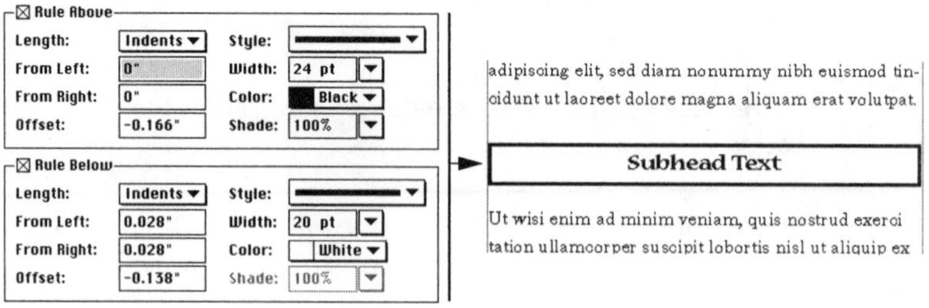

Figure 12.24 *Settings to create paragraph rules that appear to draw a box around a headline.*

Summary

In this chapter, we hope to have provided some insight into the world where text meets graphics. As we mentioned at the beginning of the chapter, the best way to learn is to experiment on your own with converting text to picture boxes, creating text-paths, and working with anchored rules and other graphic elements. Once you learn how to "think" like QuarkXPress does, these features offer exciting creative possibilities limited only by your imagination.

13 Printing Color Separations

The "bottom line" for many QuarkXPress documents is a color document that is ultimately reproduced on an offset press. At some point this process requires separating the color into individual components, whether on film or digitally.

QuarkXPress has become the industry's program of choice for producing files for color separations. Sophisticated controls for output to a wide variety of devices—including imagesetters, direct-to-plate devices, and digital presses—allow for achieving results as reliable and high-quality as that afforded by any existing technologies on the market today.

General Considerations

In order to take advantage of QuarkXPress's excellent capabilities for printing color separations, it's important to understand some of the basics of color printing. With QuarkXPress, designers and production staff have a technology that allows them to directly control the entire color printing process.

No matter what part you play in the process, it's helpful to know about the specifics of the final offset printing for your documents—whether that means talking to a representative from a printing company, or a print production manager in your company, to find out the specifics. The method used, and the best setup for your document, depend on many different factors, and will often be dictated by the economics of time or cost for a specific job.

One of the most basic considerations in preparing your document is whether or not your print job will involve spot or process color, discussed next.

Spot Color versus Process Color

There are generally two ways to prepare film for color printing jobs. One is to create a separate plate for each different color of ink used when printing with *spot colors*. The other is to create four separate plates for each of the four *process colors*—cyan, magenta, yellow, and black. These four basic colors can yield an infinite number of other colors when they are combined on a page.

Spot color printing usually involves preparing film that will be used by a printer when premixed inks will be used in the printing process. PANTONE colors are one of the most common systems for premixing inks. Film prepared for a spot color printing job includes a layer of film output for each premixed ink color.

Process color is made up of four inks—the three subtractive primaries, yellow, cyan, and magenta, plus black—printed one on top of the other in a pattern of halftone dots. Both spot color and process color require separation of color elements, and QuarkXPress lets you specify either type of separations for any color you create.

To understand process color, think about a pointillist painting. The painting actually consists of many minute dots of paint, but the human eye blends the dots into solid tones. Similarly, in four-color process printing, adjacent dots of ink printed in different colors—usually cyan, magenta, yellow, and black—will be interpreted as a single color by the eye. For example, in areas where yellow and cyan are printed together, the eye will perceive green.

The film that must be generated to produce plates for four-color process printing consists of a pattern of halftone dots for each color (cyan, magenta, yellow, and black). Traditional halftone screens are generated by photographing an image through a screen that actually contains dots of various sizes (Figure 13.1). Lighter areas of an image are made up of smaller dots, while darker areas are created by larger dots. The spacing of the lines of dots is called the *screen frequency*, or screen *lines per inch* (lpi).

Figure 13.1 *A traditional halftone screen enlarged.*

If cyan, magenta, yellow, and black were printed directly on top of each other, the result would be muddy and inexact colors. So in traditional color printing, each color is printed at an angle; the combined angles, when printed together, form tiny rosettes of color, which simulate a particular hue.

The algorithms for the necessary angle of rotation, called *irrational angles*, were developed by Dr. Ing. Rudolph Hell GmbH, the parent company of Hell Graphics Systems, now part of Heidleberg, Inc. While new screening technologies are beginning to emerge, most prepress systems in use today have licensed these traditional screen angles for use on their equipment. The traditional screen angles rotate cyan at 105°, magenta at 75°, yellow at 0° or 90°, and black at 45°.

Proofing Color

If you've worked with creating color separations on a personal computer, you know that there are many variables that come into play in getting the results you're looking for. One key challenge is calibrating the color definition on display and output devices so that you can achieve the most predictable results possible.

There are a variety of solutions for monitor calibration, ranging from simple, no-cost solutions to hardware and software solutions that cost thousands of dollars. Some common-sense steps can help ensure consistency in the colors that appear on your monitor:

- Keep the lighting conditions stable in the room where you're working, which usually means using artificial light that has the same brightness at all times of day.
- Use a color swatch book to select colors whenever possible; this is the best way to predict how a color will appear when it's finally printed by an offset press.

Regardless of how carefully you calibrate your monitor, it's important to obtain a quality color proof of your work. In the simplest case, this might be a printout on a 300- or 400-dpi color proofing device, of which there are many on the market today. However, these usually will not suffice as "contract proofs" for your printing company (proofs with color the printer promises to match in the offset process). The most foolproof proof (no pun intended) are traditional proofs made from film, such as those created by PressMatch or Matchprint systems. These proofs can cost anywhere from $30–$100 per page, but they also ensure the quality of your final product once it goes on press.

Trapping Issues

If your printing job uses more than one color, and elements of different colors do not touch each other directly, then printing is fairly simple. But if elements do touch—for example, if you have yellow type in the middle of an orange box—then these elements must meet precisely. Offset printing is not a perfectly exact process, since paper may shift and stretch very slightly on press. Because of this, even if elements do meet exactly, there can be a slight shift in the paper on press, and you will see it in the printed piece, either as a dark line where they overlap or as a white line where they don't overlap (Figure 13.2). In color printing, these registration problems are controlled with *trapping*, generally by causing one color to overprint another very slightly.

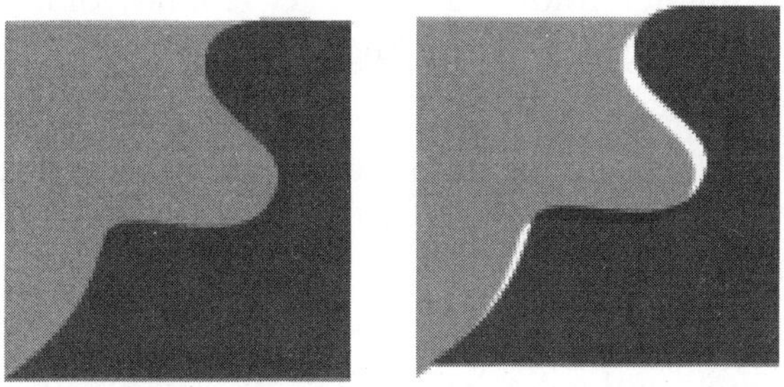

Figure 13.2 *Trapping problems can occur when two colors don't meet exactly, thus exposing the paper underneath.*

You can avoid trapping problems by "designing" your layouts in a way that avoids colors that may have trapping problems. One common way to do this is to ensure that all the colors you use share a common process color. You could, for example, add 5 percent black to all colors, and probably avoid any serious trapping problems.

When you can't avoid problem colors that need to be trapped, you'll find that QuarkXPress has fairly sophisticated built-in trapping functions that help you simplify the process of setting up trapping for your document(s). There are three levels on which you can control trapping—by setting document defaults for automatic trapping, by setting color-specific trapping, or by setting item specific trapping values.

QuarkXPress defines trapping values in terms of an *object* color against a *background* color. Object color is the color applied to any item that is on top of another. Background color is the color applied to any item that is behind an object color. When an object color and a background color meet, QuarkXPress determines the trapping values based on how light or dark each of these colors is—the *luminance* of the color.

There are four basic trapping settings that describe the relationship between the object and background color (shown in Figure 13.3):

- **Spread:** When the object color is lighter (i.e., the object on top is a lighter color than the background color), the object color will spread, or print slightly larger, so that it overlaps the background color.
- **Choke:** When the background color is lighter, the knockout are is slightly smaller so that it prints slightly "underneath" the object item color.
- **Knockout:** Causes the object color to knockout, or not print, the background color behind it.
- **Overprint:** Causes the object color to print without knocking out the background color behind it; the background color prints solid.

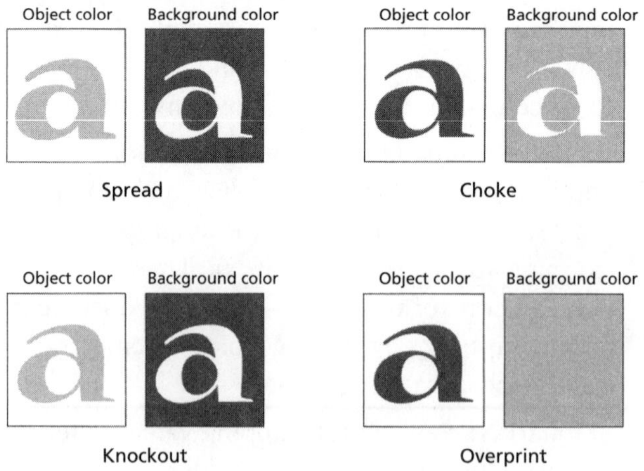

Figure 13.3 *The four basic trapping settings. See "Trapping" page in color plates.*

The exact settings that you need for correct trapping will vary from project to project, and will depend on the paper, ink, and press that are going to be used. QuarkXPress has default settings that are generally acceptable, but setting traps correctly is yet another aspect of color printing that requires communication with your printing company.

Default Trapping Settings

The default method and settings that QuarkXPress uses to trap colors can be defined in the Trapping tab of the Document Preferences dialog box (**Edit ➛ Preferences ➛ Document**) shown in Figure 13.4. As with other Document Preferences, changing the settings with no document open causes them to be applied to all new documents; changing the settings with a document open changes them in that document only.

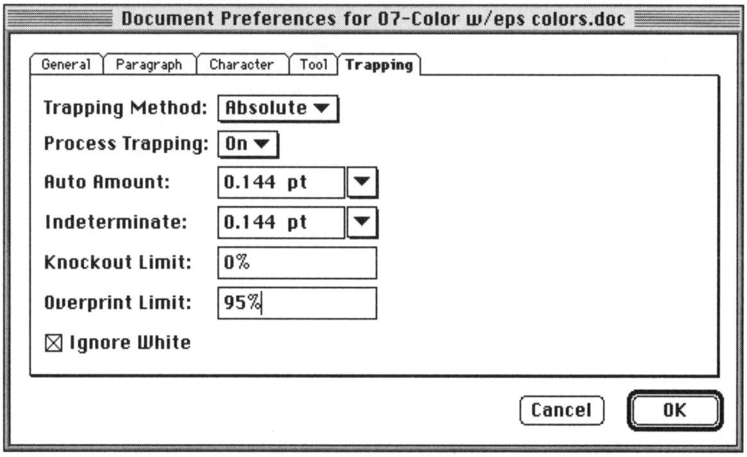

Figure 13.4 *The Trapping tab of the Document Preferences dialog box.*

In the Trapping Preferences dialog box, the settings that can be adjusted are as follows:

- The **Trapping Method** may be specified from a pop-up menu as **Absolute, Proportional** or **Knockout All** (Figure 13.5). If you select **Absolute,** automatic trapping occurs at the absolute value specified in the Auto Amount field. If you specify **Proportional,** QuarkXPress uses a fraction of the value specified in the Auto Amount based on the difference between the luminance of the object and the background color. The formula used is (*value of Auto Amount) x (object luminance - background luminance*). If the object color is lighter than the background color, it will be spread against the background color; if it is darker, it will be choked. Specifying **Knockout All** essentially turns trapping off, setting the trapping values to 0.

Figure 13.5 *The Trapping Method pop-up menu lets you determine the default method used in your document.*

- **Process Trapping** specifies how QuarkXPress handles trapping of process colors. When Process Trap is checked on, each process plate is handled individually; for example, on the cyan plate, the darkness of cyan of an object color is compared against the darkness of cyan in the background color, and trapped accordingly. When Process Trap is unchecked, QuarkXPress traps all process colors equally using the trapping value of the object color against the background color.
- **Auto Amount** is the value used by QuarkXPress for Absolute and Process trapping methods. You can enter a value between 0 and 36 points in .001-point increments. You can also choose **Overprint,** which causes all colors to overprint their backgrounds with no trapping.

- **Indeterminate** specifies the trapping relationship between an object color item and a background consisting of more than one color. If the object color has conflicting trapping relationships with background colors—that is, if it chokes with some and spreads with others—it will trap to the value specified here.
- **Knockout Limit** specifies the shade at which an object color will knockout its background color, expressed as a percentage of the darkness of the object color to the background color. The default setting is zero, which causes all colors to knockout (except black).
- **Overprint Limit** specifies the shade at which an object color overprints its background color. For example, if the value entered in this field is 95% (the preset default), and an object color was shaded 90%, it would not overprint, even if that were the setting defined for that color. Rather, it would knock out the color underneath with the spread or choke specified by the Auto Amount.
- If **Ignore White** is checked (the preset default), QuarkXPress will not take background items that have the color white applied into consideration when determining trapping for an object color over multiple background colors.

Trapping Colors

Normally, QuarkXPress controls trap conditions automatically based on the defaults set in the Trapping tab of Document Preferences (**Edit ➛ Preferences ➛ Document**), discussed in the previous section. However, you can specify the trapping relationships for specific colors—thus overriding the defaults—by using the Trap Specifications dialog box.

First, select **Edit ➛ Colors**; the Colors dialog box appears. In the Colors dialog box, choose the object color for which you want to specify trapping values. Click on the **Edit Trap** button to display the Trap Specifications dialog box (Figure 13.6)

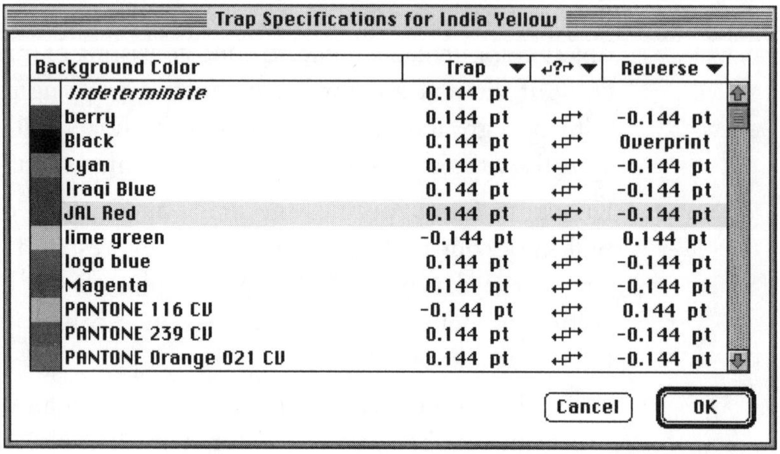

Figure 13.6 *The Trap Specifications dialog box.*

The dialog box shows a list of each of the colors in the color palette in the **Background color** column. The **Trap** column lists the trapping value specified for the object color against each background color in the list. These values can be specified in one of six ways, using the pop-up menu at the top of the column (Figure 13.7):

- **Default** lets QuarkXPress handle the trapping automatically, that is, the object color traps relative to the background color, based on the settings in the Trapping tab of the Document Preferences dialog box. The default settings cause QuarkXPress to utilize the Trapping Method and Auto Amount settings specified in Preferences to determine how much to spread (increase) the object color or choke (reduce) the background color.
- **Overprint** causes the object color to be printed without "knocking out" the background color when you are printing color separation plates, so the object color prints on top of the background color on the press.

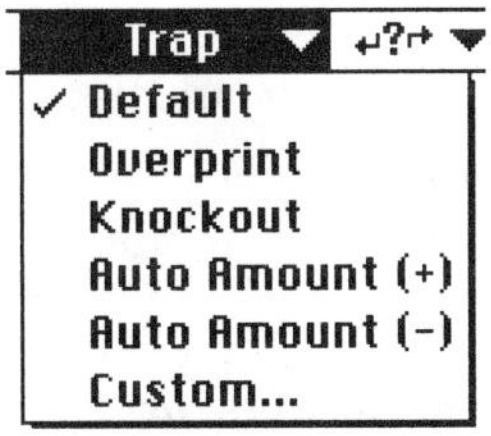

***Figure 13.7** The Trap pop-up menu in the Trap Specifications dialog box lets you define trap relationships at a color-specific level, thus overriding default trap settings.*

- **Knockout** causes the background color knockout to be exactly the same size as the object color item, producing what is sometimes called "butt" registration.
- **Auto Amount** (+) lets you specify that the object color will spread against the background color, by the Auto Amount specified in the Trapping tab of the Document Preferences dialog box.
- **Auto Amount** (-) lets you specify that the object color will be choked by the background color, by the Auto Amount specified in the Trapping tab of the Document Preferences dialog box.
- **Custom** lets you enter a custom value for trapping between the object color and the background color. You can enter a value between –36 points and +36 points, in .001-point increments. After you enter a value, click **OK**. A negative value chokes (reduces) the knockout area of the background color; a positive value spreads (increases) the size of the object against the background color. If you enter a value of zero, no choking or spreading occurs when the object is knocked out from the background, with results the same as those when Knockout is specified.

When you change any of the trap settings from default to any other setting, the values are displayed with an asterisk adjacent (Figure 13.8). This makes it easy to scan the list and see where any variation from the default settings have been made.

Cyan	-0.144 pt	↔	0.144 pt
India Yellow	-0.25 pt*	↔	0.25 pt*
Iraqi Blue	Knockout*	↔	Knockout*

Figure 13.8 *When any setting other than default is specified for color-specific trapping, the values are displayed with an asterisk adjacent.*

The **Dependent/Independent** column of the Trap Specifications dialog box lets you specify that the object color have an Independent or Dependent trapping relationship with the background color and its reverse setting. Choose from the pop-up menu to change the relationship.

The **Reverse** column shows the reverse relationship: the relationship if the background color became the object color. Normally, this is the exact opposite of the setting showing in the Trap column (unless you choose **Independent** in the previous column).

When an object is in front of more than one color, in front of certain color pictures, or if QuarkXPress is unable to identify the background color, the program checks the relationship between the object color and each of the background colors. If there is no conflict, then QuarkXPress traps to the minimum value. If there is a conflict—that is, if the object color would spread into some items and choke others—the item traps to the setting for Indeterminate color.

Trapping Specific Items

In addition to allowing you to set trapping relationships between colors in a document, QuarkXPress allows you to set trapping relationships between individual items via the **Trap Information palette** (**View ➤ Show Trap Information**), thus overriding both the default settings, found in the Trapping tab of the Document Preferences dialog box (**Edit ➛ Preferences ➛ Document**), and the color-specific settings in the Trap Specifications dialog box (**Edit ➛ Colors ➛ Edit Trap**).

To define a trapping relationship for individual items, display the Trap Information palette if it is not already displayed (**View ➛ Show Trap Information**). The palette shows the trapping information for the active item that has been selected. The pop-up menus allow you to control the trapping of box backgrounds, lines (including gap colors), text, pictures, and frames against their background color(s). The appearance of the palette changes based on the active item (Figure 13.9).

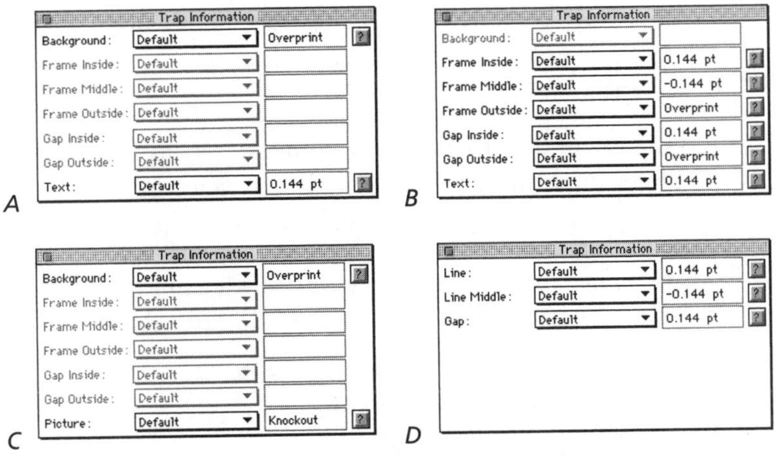

***Figure 13.9** Examples of the Trap Information palette icons when the following are selected: (a) a text box, (b) a framed text box, (c) a picture box, (d) a line.*

Trapping Frames and Lines

When a box contains a custom frame, the frame around the box traps to the background color of the box on the inside, and to any item behind the box on the outside. Since both frame and line styles now contain gaps to which color can be applied, the color of the gap must be taken into consideration. When a box with a frame is selected, the fields in the Trap Information palette include the following:

- **Frame Inside** defines the trapping relationship between the frame color and the box background color.
- **Frame Middle** defines the trapping relationship between the frame color and the gap color.
- **Frame Outside** defines the trapping relationship between the frame and the color of any item behind the box (outside the box).
- **Gap Inside** defines the trapping relationship between the gap color and the box background color.
- **Gap Outside** defines the trapping relationship between the gap color and the color of any item behind the box (outside the box)

A line will trap to any background colors applied to items that are underneath the line. When a line is selected, the following fields become active in the Trap Information palette:

- **Line** specifies the trapping relationship between the line color in relation to any color that falls behind it.
- **Line Middle** specifies the trapping relationship between the line color and gap color.
- **Gap** specifies the trapping relationship between the gap color and any color that falls behind it.

Item-Specific Trapping Values

Trapping values in the Trap Information palette, like those used for default trapping or color-specific trapping, can be specified in one of six ways:

- Choose the **Default** setting on the pop-up menu if you simply want to use the trapping values specified in the Trap Specifications dialog box (**Edit** ➛ **Colors** ➛ **Edit Trap**). The value in the Trap Specifications dialog box is displayed to the right on the pop-up menu on the palette. To obtain more information about the values, click on the question mark to the right of the value and hold down the mouse button. A small window containing information is displayed (Figure 13.10). If **Default** is the setting in the Trap Specifications dialog box, trapping is determined by the settings in the Trapping tab of the Document Preferences dialog box (**Edit** ➛ **Preferences** ➛ **Document**).

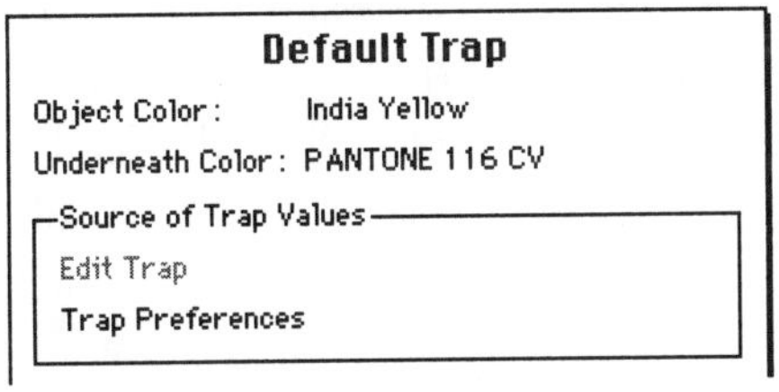

Figure 13.10 *Click on the question mark in the Trap Information palette to obtain more information about Default trapping specifications.*

- Choose **Overprint** if you do not want the object color to knock out or trap the background color. Choosing this option overrides the Overprint Limit value specified in the Trapping Preferences dialog box.
- Specifying **Knockout** causes the object color to knock out the background color with no trapping. This type of trapping is sometimes called "butt" registration.
- **Auto Amount** (+) causes the object color to spread by the amount entered in the Auto Amount field in the Trapping tab of the Document Preferences dialog box.

- **Auto Amount** (–) causes the background color to choke the object color by the amount entered in the Auto Amount field in the Trapping tab of the Document Preferences dialog box.
- **Custom** lets you set a trapping value other than that specified for Auto Amount in the Trapping Preferences dialog box. Enter a value from –36 pt to +36 pt in increments as fine as .001 point. Enter a negative value to cause the background color to choke the object color; enter a positive value to cause the object color to spread.

Remember that the settings used in the Trap Information palette for item-specific trapping override settings for color-specific trapping as specified in the Trap Specification dialog box (**Edit ➛ Colors ➛ Edit Trap**). Settings for color-specific trapping override the document default trapping settings that are specified in the Trapping tab of the Document Preferences dialog box (**Edit ➛ Preferences ➛ Document**). These relationships are illustrated by Figure 13.11.

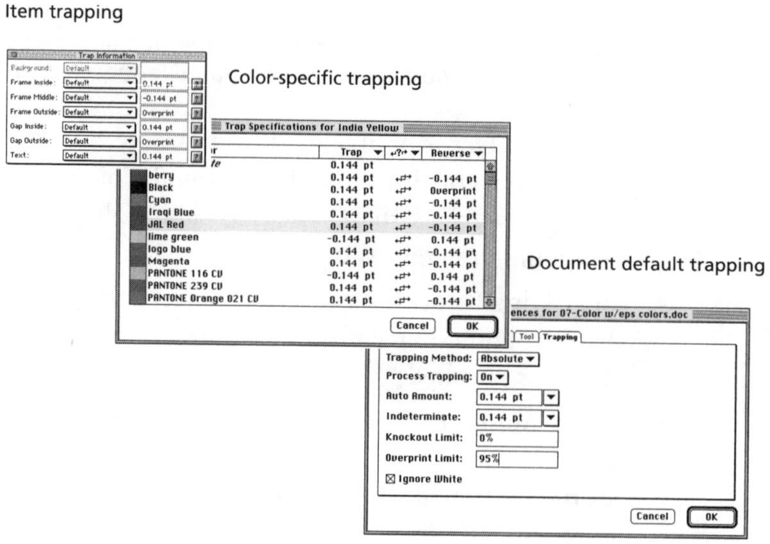

Figure 13.11 *Item trapping overrides color-specific trapping, which overrides the default trapping settings .*

Text always traps as the object color against the color of the background of the text box. If the text box background is specified with a color of **None**, and the text is positioned over another item of a single color, the text traps against the color of the item behind it.

If a transparent text box or other item is positioned over items of more than one color, the trapping relationship varies depending on the colors of the background items:

- If the text or other item of the object color is specified to spread against all the colors of the background items, the object color item spreads by the smallest amount specified.
- If the object color item is specified to be choked by all the background colors, the object color item is choked by the smallest value specified.
- If the object color item is specified to spread against some color and be choked by others, or if Knockout is specified, the object color item traps to the value specified for Indeterminate in the Trapping Preferences dialog box.

Separating Graphics Created in Other Programs

In addition to providing powerful controls for accurate separation and trapping of items created in QuarkXPress, the program also separates graphics created by other applications. QuarkXPress does not, however, trap individual elements in files created in external graphics programs. In order for QuarkXPress to separate a graphic, it must be saved in a format that contains color separation information, such as Encapsulated PostScript (EPS) or color TIFF. The most commonly used applications for preparing graphics to be separated by QuarkXPress are Adobe Illustrator, Macromedia FreeHand or CorelDRAW for illustrations, and Adobe Photoshop for continuous-tone images.

Separating Files Created in PostScript Drawing Programs

In order to separate graphics created by Adobe Illustrator or Macromedia FreeHand, the first step, of course, is to import the graphic. Both Illustrator and FreeHand files must be saved with a screen preview, in Encapsulated PostScript format (EPS). In Adobe Illustrator, these options are selected in the Save As dialog box (Figure 13.12); in FreeHand, you must select the **Export** command from the File menu to save the artwork in EPS format.

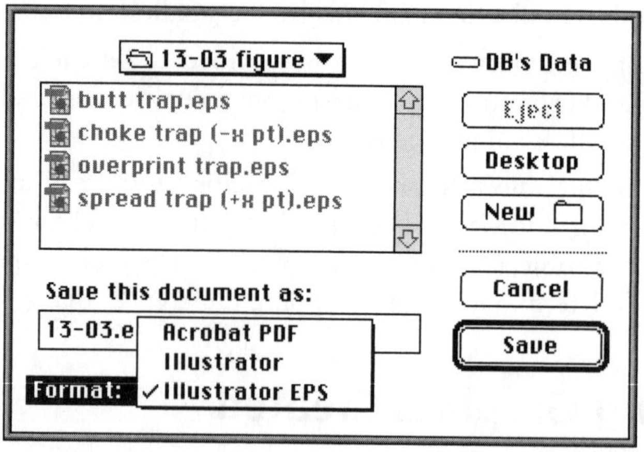

Figure 13.12 *Save Illustrator files in the EPS format to produce color separations.*

QuarkXPress's trapping controls have no direct effect on the Illustrator or FreeHand artwork itself, and trapping issues must be addressed manually in the drawing programs. When a color QuarkXPress item is placed over an imported color graphic, the item traps according to the relationship specified between the item color and Indeterminate background color.

Separating Color Photographs

QuarkXPress can provide high-quality separations of color photographic images. Pages containing color images can be output to a PostScript imagesetter or sent to a high-end system where separations can be stripped into the page digitally.

One of the most common ways that continuous-tone color images are output from QuarkXPress is by preparing the image for color separation using Adobe Photoshop before importing the image into QuarkXPress. This technique puts the burden of the quality of the separations largely on Photoshop, which does an excellent job under the right input (scanning) and output (imagesetter) conditions.

The first step is to use Photoshop to manipulate the image as necessary, to make color corrections, and (if not done already by the scanner), to convert the image to CMYK mode. Then, save the file in Desktop Color Separation (DCS) format, EPS format, or as a color TIFF. With the information contained in these file formats, QuarkXPress can print the appropriate cyan, magenta, yellow, and black components of the continuous-tone image on the correct plate and in position.

The DCS format was developed by Quark, Inc., and adopted by Adobe Systems for facilitating the output of separations for continuous-tone images. Instead of saving an image to one file, DCS images are broken down into five files: four files containing the image's components of cyan, magenta, yellow, and black, plus a fifth file containing a PICT image for previewing on screen (Figure 13.13) and path information. DCS files will yield the same results as EPS files, but tend to print faster, since the separation has essentially already been calculated.

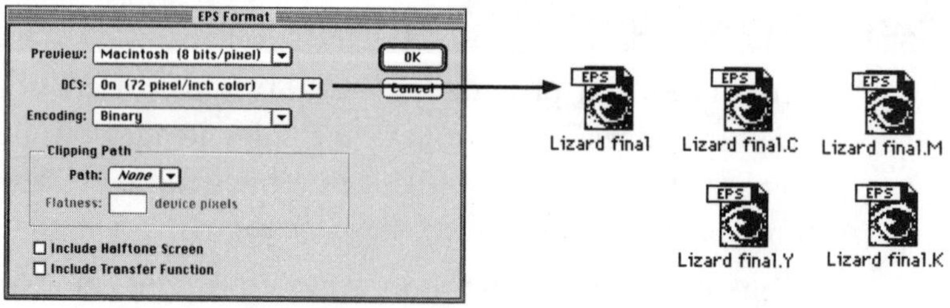

Figure 13.13 *Saving Photoshop files in DCS format creates five files.*

Once you have imported the PICT preview file into a QuarkXPress file, it's important not to move the DCS files to any other folder. If you move the CMYK files, QuarkXPress will not be able to locate them for printing and will use the 72 dpi image instead of the high-resolution files.

Working with Service Bureaus

As we mentioned at the opening of this chapter, the bottom line for many QuarkXPress documents is a color document that is ultimately reproduced on an offset press. For many QuarkXPress users, that means that someone else will output your document to film or some digital device that will produce color separations. Most often, this means you'll be working with your printing company or service bureau.

It would be nice if those responsible for final output of your file could check every little detail of your document file and all the associated picture files, but the simple truth is that it's impossible. Here are a few guidelines that will help make the experience of working with service bureaus more successful. Not all of these tips will apply to your situation, but do read them over, and try to implement the suggestions that will be helpful to your situation:

- **Use the Collect for Output feature of QuarkXPress.** Using Collect for Output (Figure 13.14) ensures that you will have all the high resolution graphics files that are used in your document. As discussed in Chapter 8, "Printing Basics," QuarkXPress imports only a 72-dpi screen preview of your graphics, and must have access to the original picture file to print it correctly. If your service bureau doesn't have your original picture files, there's no amount of magic that will allow them to print correctly.

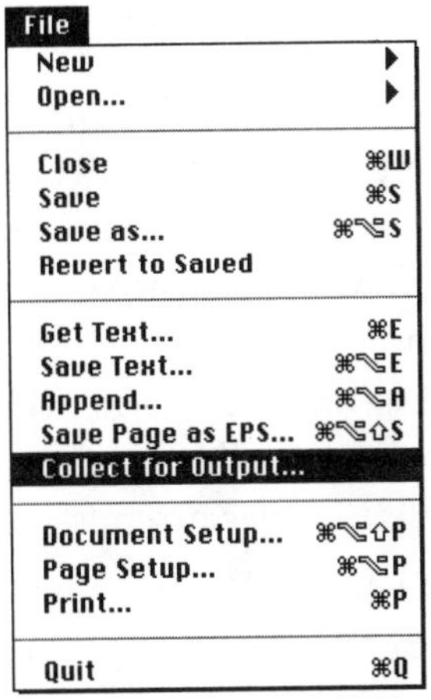

Figure 13.14 *Use the* ***Collect for Output*** *feature to assemble your QuarkXPress documents and all associated picture files.*

- **Make sure your graphics are set up correctly.** Make sure the picture files that you wish to print in color are in CMYK mode, so they'll separate properly. If you try to separate an RGB graphic, the entire graphic will print on the black plate. You can double-check picture file format when you import a picture. Notice the Picture type at the bottom of the Get Picture dialog box (**File ➤ Get Picture**); if the picture type is not CMYK (Figure 13.15), you'll need to re-save the picture in a CMYK format.

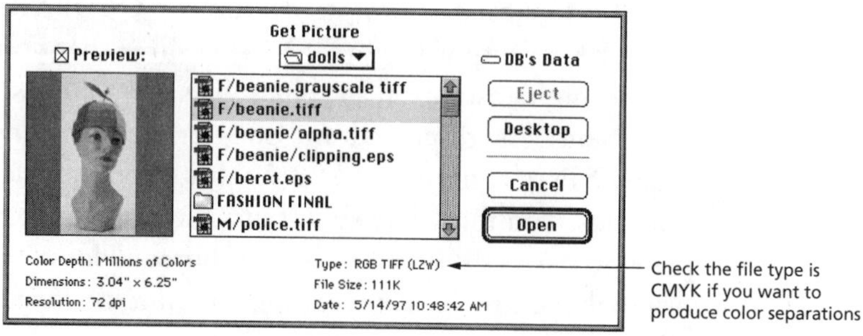

Figure 13.15 *Check that picture files you want to separate are CMYK files, not RGB files, by checking the Picture type in the Get Picture dialog box.*

- **Provide complete information.** Fill out the forms provided by your service bureau, or use the Document Report generated by **Collect for Output.** It's especially important to indicate whether your film should be printed positive or negative, the line screen, and the fonts used, especially those used in EPS graphics (since QuarkXPress only tells you what *document* fonts are missing when you open a file; it does not tell you which fonts contained in *picture files* are missing).
- **Test print your separations first.** When it's practical, print your document, with Separations checked on, and Registration on (in the Setup tab of the Print dialog box). If your page is the same size as your laser printer, reduce the output so you can see the name of each plate as it prints. This simple step can save a lot of headache; while you cannot check subtle features such as screen angles and trapping, you can at least verify that each element is on the correct plate, especially where spot colors are used. If an element prints on the wrong plate when printed to your laser printer, you can rest assured it will print on the wrong plate when output to film!

Summary

This chapter covered some of the issues involved with printing color separations. However, much of the basic information needed to print any QuarkXPress document successfully will be found in Chapter 8, "Printing Basics." Be sure to look over that chapter to familiarize yourself with all the settings available in the Print dialog box, the **Usage** dialog box, and how to use the **Collect for Output** command.

14 Publishing in Other Media

QuarkXPress is best known as a design and production tool for printed media. However, more and more information is becoming available through digital media, including interactive CD-ROMs and the Internet, and QuarkXPress can be a tremendous tool for producing information in interactive digital format, too.

This chapter is quite different from others in the book. Unlike the rest of the book, which is intended to give detailed guidance on how to use QuarkXPress most efficiently in producing printed documents, this chapter provides a very general overview of some of the issues involved in using QuarkXPress as a multimedia design tool and re-purposing QuarkXPress documents for media other than print.

In this chapter, we'll discuss designing original content or re-purposing existing content for digital media using QuarkXPress in combination with the QuarkImmedia XTension. We'll also discuss creating content for the Internet using QuarkXPress and one of the leading QuarkXTensions for doing so, BeyondPress.

Using QuarkImmedia

QuarkImmedia is a sophisticated XTension product that is used in combination with QuarkXPress to produce interactive content, or *multimedia*. QuarkImmedia lets you use QuarkXPress' typography, graphics and layout, tools and adds the ability to include movies, sound, animation, and interactivity. Once complete, QuarkImmedia documents, called *projects*, can be saved out to formats for use on hard disks, CD ROM, or the Internet.

The purpose of this chapter is not to teach you how to use QuarkImmedia, but rather to give you an overview of how it can be used as a tool for multimedia design. A quick skim of this chapter should whet your appetite for some direct, hands-on experience with the product.

Multimedia Basics

Multimedia is a general term that can be used to denote the delivery of information in a variety of digital forms, and which may include elements found in printed material—such as text and graphics—but which also can include sounds, music, digitized video, animation, and interactive objects. Information kiosks, educational or entertainment CD-ROMs, and even the World Wide Web are all examples of multimedia. (Although the Web is sometimes classified separately, it in fact contains all the elements of multimedia).

Designing a multimedia project is quite different from designing a print-based document. The element of interactivity requires the effective use of sound and motion in an easy-to-use interface that conveys informations and holds the user's interest.

Multimedia projects also involve a different set of technical issues than print-based projects do. Many issues are affected by the delivery media—a project will run much more quickly from a hard drive than a CD-ROM for example, and both are usually faster than the Internet. The ability to include sound introduces associated issues such as sampling rates, and video requires designers to make decisions about frame rates and compression. Larger multimedia projects, such as creating a CD-ROM, can often involve many different people in various roles, including not only a designer, but often a producer or project manager, a content provider or writer, and sound and video specialists.

QuarkImmedia Overview

QuarkImmedia is an XTension that must be used in conjunction with QuarkXPress. It uses a page-based metaphor that allows you to create multimedia projects using both the design tools of QuarkXPress and the QuarkImmedia XTension. You can design and create a new project from scratch or you can convert an existing QuarkXPress document to a project. As you work, you can preview the project along the way, using the **QuarkImmedia → Engage** command. Once your project is complete, it is exported, and can be viewed and played using the QuarkImmedia Viewer. The Viewer, available at no cost for both Macintosh and Windows, is required to view a QuarkImmedia project. You can distribute the viewer freely, or you can embed it into the project itself.

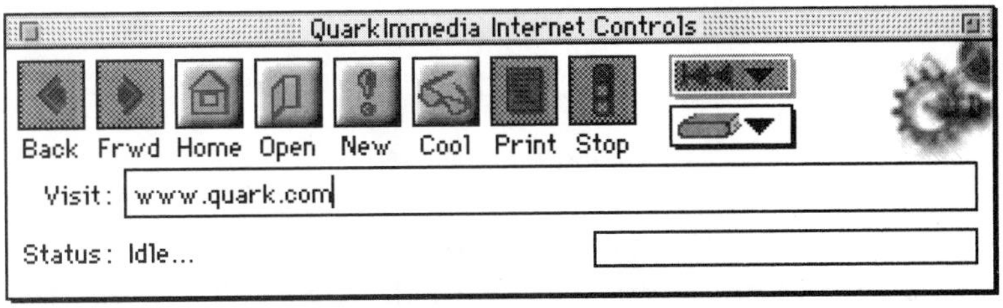

***Figure 14.1** The QuarkImmedia Viewer Internet Controls.*

The QuarkImmedia Viewer is also required to view a QuarkImmedia project on the Internet (Figure 14.1). A QuarkImmedia project is different from most Web pages, which are text files that include hypertext markup language (HTML) code. The QuarkImmedia Viewer downloads QuarkImmedia projects and allows you to view them. The Viewer itself contains Internet navigation controls, and it is compatible with browsers such as Netscape Navigator or Microsoft Internet Explorer.

The QuarkImmedia interface is, as you might expect, consistent with that of QuarkXPress. When the QuarkImmedia XTension is loaded, a new menu—QuarkImmedia—is added to the menu bar

(Figure 14.2). However, most of the controls for designing in QuarkImmedia are found on the QuarkImmedia palette (**View ➛ QuarkImmedia Palette**). The palette contains six tabs: Page, Object, Event, Script, Hot Text, and Keys. Each of these controls is briefly described in the next sections.

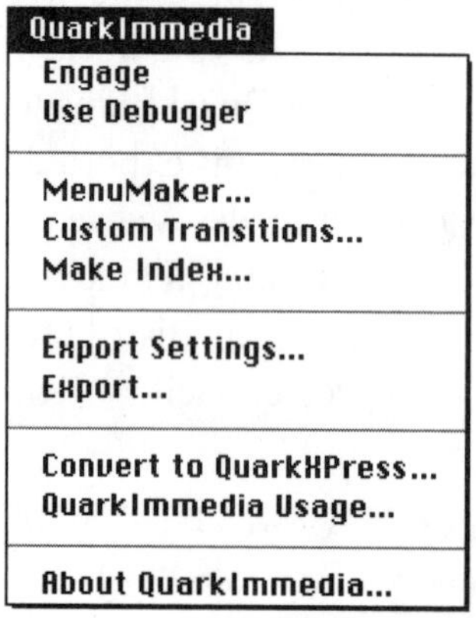

Figure 14.2 *The QuarkImmedia menu.*

With QuarkImmedia, one of the biggest advantages is that designers and production staff who already know QuarkXPress will have a much shorter learning curve than they would with another program. All of QuarkXPress's familiar design features are available.

The QuarkImmedia Palette

The QuarkImmedia palette contains the primary controls for adding sound, movies, animation, and interactivity to your project.

The **Page** tab (Figure 14.3) lists each page in the document by number, and lets you name pages and select page display options, including specifying page transitions. For example, you can make one page fade into another, or make a page slide onto the screen.

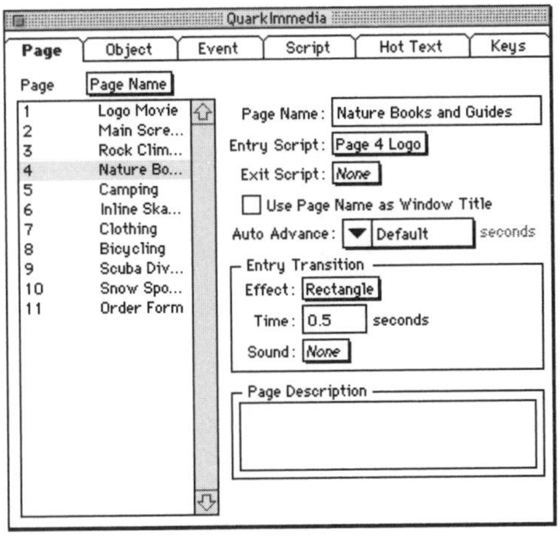

Figure 14.3 *The Page tab of the QuarkImmedia palette.*

The **Object** tab (Figure 14.4) lets you assign a name to any item, thus making it an QuarkImmedia "object" and allowing you to assign events, scripts, and other interactive characteristics. You can specify an object as an Animation, Movie, Pop-up menu, or Window. For example, you could select a picture box, assign it the object type "movie" and then import a QuickTime movie into the picture box.

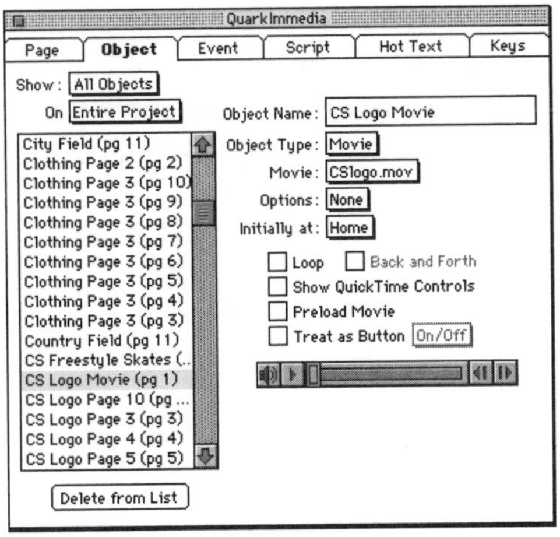

Figure 14.4 *The Object tab of the QuarkImmedia palette.*

The **Event** tab (Figure 14.5) lets you assign user-initiated events, such as a mouse click, and the associated actions, to objects defined in the Object tab. For example, you could specify that upon double clicking a specific picture box, a movie will play.

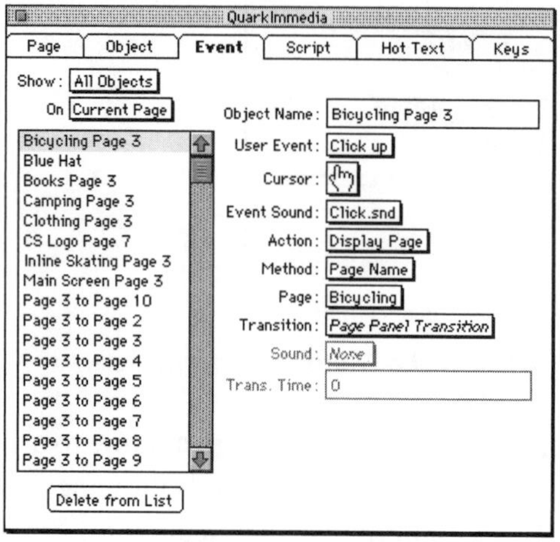

***Figure 14.5** The Event tab of the QuarkImmedia palette.*

The **Script** tab (Figure 14.6) lets you create scripts that can be assigned to an event or to hot text (discussed next). This allows you to automate a complex series of actions using pop-up menus instead of some arcane programming language. Also available are script commands for creating simple animations, such as sliding text across the screen. These will be discussed later in this section.

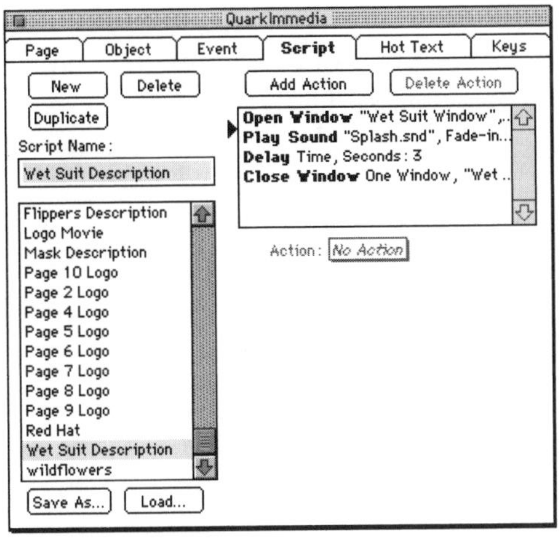

***Figure 14.6** The Script tab of the QuarkImmedia palette.*

The **Hot Text** tab (Figure 14.7) lets you assign events and scripts to text. You could, for example, specify that when the user clicks on a word, a movie will play in an adjacent window.

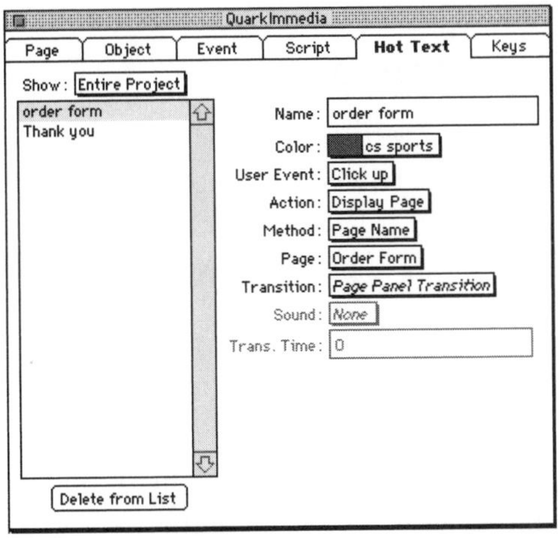

***Figure 14.7** The Hot Text tab of the QuarkImmedia palette.*

The **Keys** tab (Figure 14.8) lets you create keyboard commands that initiate actions or scripts. For example, you could specify that pressing the right arrow key turns to the next page of a project.

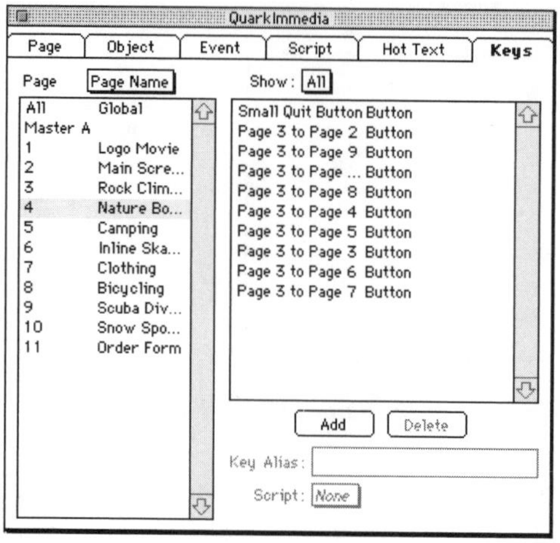

***Figure 14.8** The Keys tab of the QuarkImmedia palette.*

Making Objects Interactive

One of the most powerful features of QuarkImmedia is that it lets you design interactive features. For example, you might link a box containing a picture of a golf ball to a movie of Tiger Woods taking his final putt at the U.S. Open. Here's how to do it:

1. Draw a picture box and import the picture of a golf ball. All the usual QuarkXPress commands for modifying pictures are available.
2. Select the picture box and, using the **Object** tab of the QuarkImmedia palette, assign a name to the picture, thus making it a QuarkImmedia object (Figure 14.9).

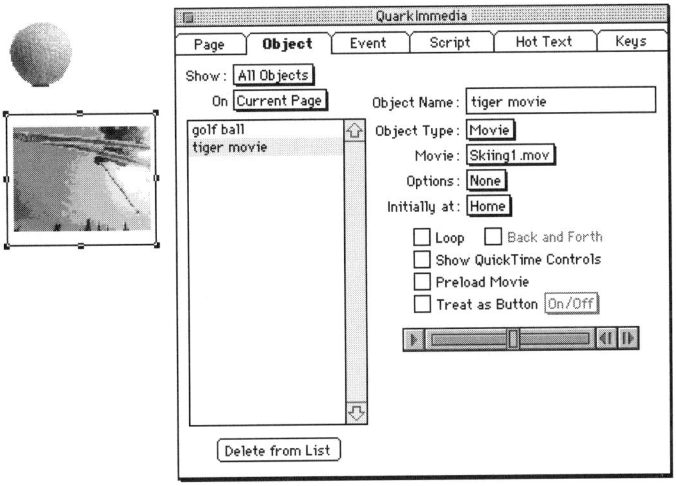

Figure 14.9 *Specify an item as a QuarkImmedia object using the Object tab of the QuarkImmedia palette.*

3. Draw another picture box and use the **Object** tab to specify it as a movie object, indicating that the movie file to be used. The first frame of the movie is imported.
4. To cause a click on the golf ball to play the movie, use the **Event** tab to set the entries for playing the movie when the user clicks on the golf ball, as shown in Figure 14.10.

Figure 14.10 *Event tab settings for specifying a movie to play when a picture is clicked.*

Animation

You can import animation files, but you can also create simple animations directly in your project using QuarkImmedia. Let's take a look at the steps required to slide text across a page when a page is first displayed:

1. Select the text box containing the text you wish to slide and, using the Object tab of the QuarkImmedia palette, assign a name to the text box, so that it becomes an QuarkImmedia object.
2. Click on the **Script** tab and create a new script called **Tiger Power**. Create a one-line script using the **Animation ➝ Slide** pop-up menu, which will cause the text object to slide across the page. The settings for this script are shown in Figure 14.11.

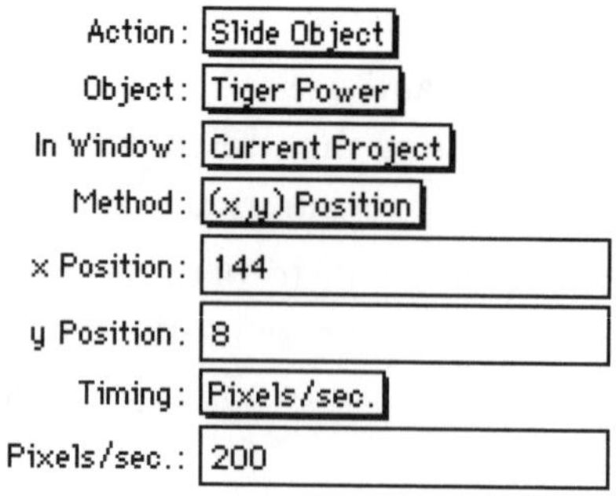

Figure 14.11 *Settings for a script to slide text across a page.*

3. Make this the entry script for a page by clicking on the **Page** tab, selecting the appropriate page from the scroll list on the left, and specifying the script as the entry script (Figure 14.12). When the project is running, the text will slide across the page when it is first displayed.

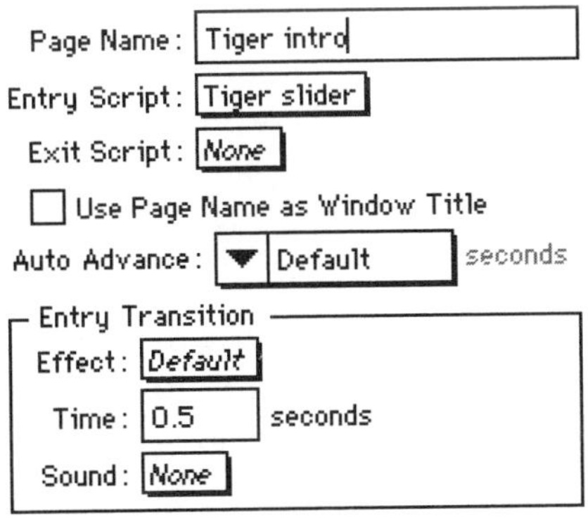

Figure 14.12 *Setting a script as an Entry Script in the Page tab of the QuarkImmedia palette.*

Exporting a Project

Once you've completed your project, you can export it so that it can be viewed by the QuarkImmedia Viewer. There are several options for export, including different formats based on the project's intended use—on a hard drive, on a CD-ROM, or for viewing on the Internet. To export a project, display the Export dialog box (**QuarkImmedia ➛ Export**), as shown in Figure 14.13.

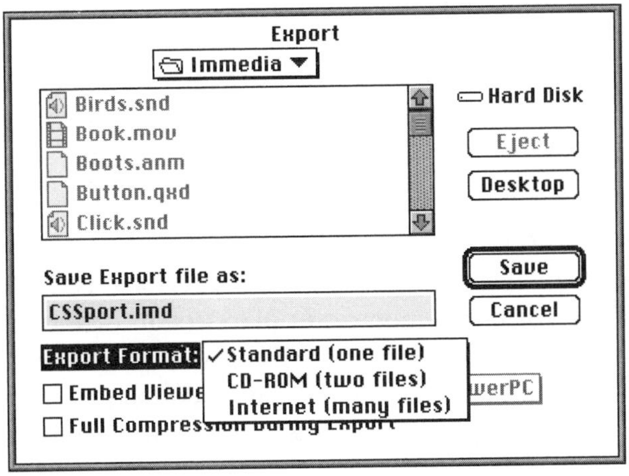

Figure 14.13 *The QuarkImmedia Export dialog box.*

The **Export** Format options include saving the project in **Standard** format, which creates one (usually large) file containing all the sound, movies, and other elements of your project. This format is is best for projects that will run off of a hard drive, such as those found in a kiosk. The **CD-ROM** format creates two files—one for the user to copy onto a local hard drive, the other files to remain on the CD-ROM. Using this option will greatly increase the speed at which the project will run. The **Internet** format creates many files, so that each can be downloaded quickly over the Internet.

You can also opt to embed the Viewer in your project, and you can specify that the viewer be in Macintosh or Windows format.

Converting QuarkXPress Documents to Web Pages

Without question, one of the fastest-growing segments of publishing is the Internet. The staggering growth in this area is well documented. The issue of QuarkXPress and publishing on the Internet is important for several reasons. First, because QuarkXPress has for several years been the leading publishing tool worldwide—it is used for everything from magazines and books to catalogues and corporate policy manuals—an enormous amount of information is stored in QuarkXPress documents. Second, many of the people who are or will be responsible for designing and publishing information on the Internet have also been involved with design and publishing in print, and QuarkXPress is a familiar tool.

As mentioned earlier, QuarkImmedia project can be delivered over the Internet, but doing so requires a special viewer (the QuarkImmedia viewer, discussed in the previous section) in addition to a bandwidth that is not yet in place for most Internet users. In some cases, it may be appropriate to deliver QuarkImmedia projects via the Internet, but currently most Web sites consist of HTML-formatted text-only pages that can be read by popular browser applications, such as Netscape Navigator or Microsoft Internet Explorer.

Any number ofapproaches can be taken to Web site design, just as there are different approaches to publishing content that exists in QuarkXPress documents. There are many standalone tools for both Macintosh and Windows—HTML editors and graphics-processing programs—and any QuarkXPress document can be "pulled apart," resulting in text files and graphics files that can then be processed for the Internet like any other text and graphics.

Several QuarkXTensions offer some interesting options for using QuarkXPress directly as a Web design tool and for converting QuarkXPress documents to HTML documents. One of the most successful Xtensions on the market today is BeyondPress, by AstroByte (www.astrobyte.com). The next section gives a brief overview of how BeyondPress works. Like the discussion of QuarkImmedia, our objective is not to present a detailed how-to-guide but to give you a general idea of how the program works so you can decide whether to investigate further on your own.

We also assume you understand the basic issues involved in publishing on the Web and creating Web sites. Our purpose here is to discuss these issues only as they relate to QuarkXPress and the use of the BeyondPress XTension.

Using BeyondPress

BeyondPress is a Macintosh XTension that lets you design Web pages from scratch and convert existing QuarkXPress documents to Web pages. You can place QuarkXPress items on a document page, just as you want them to appear in a Web browser and use BeyondPress to add multimedia or interactive elements, including QuickTime movies, Java applets, and RealAudio and Shockwave files. BeyondPress also supports Cascading Style Sheets and Bitstream's TrueDoc font technology to maintain font styles, and it allows you to easily create hyperlinks and image maps.

BeyondPress adds two palettes to QuarkXPress's View menu:

- The **Document Content** palette, which includes tabs for both Authoring and Conversion mode.

- The **Elements** palette, which allows you to share images, HTML items, and media files across multiple Web pages.

As you work, you can preview your pages at any time in the browser you specify.

The Authoring tab of the Document Content palette (Figure 14.14) lists the pages in your QuarkXPress document. You can produce a design and layout just as you would in QuarkXPress, then use controls in the Authoring tab of the Document Content palette to preview and export your pages to HTML.

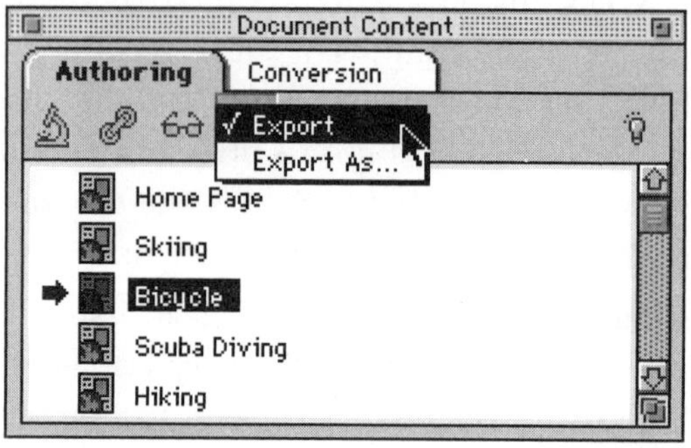

Figure 14.14 The Authoring tab of BeyondPress's Document Content palette.

BeyondPress approximates the layout of QuarkXPress documents using HTML tables. Because of HTML's limitations, some layouts cannot be reproduced exactly, but you can get good results by following a few guidelines such as avoiding overlapping items and rotated items. See the "Converting QuarkXPress Documents to HTML" page of the color plates for an example of a QuarkXPress Layout that has been converted to HTML using BeyondPress.

The Elements palette (Figure 14.15) lets you add elements that will be used throughout your Web site pages. This could be, for example, snippets of HTML code that are used as headers or footers, or media elements such as movie and sound files. To import media files, you must specify the folder in which the files reside, and they will be brought into the Elements palette. Once in the palette, you can drag any element onto your QuarkXPress document page.

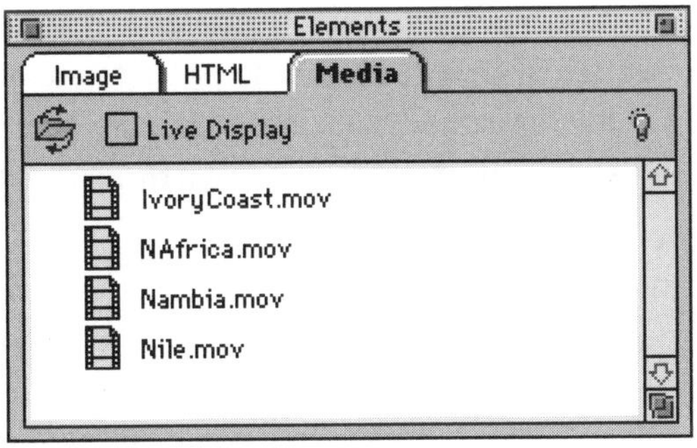

Figure 14.15 The Media tab of BeyondPress's Element palette. Drag an element onto the document page to include it in the final Web page.

For many users, the most valuable feature of BeyondPress is its ability to convert existing QuarkXPress documents to HTML. For this, the Conversion tab of the Document Content palette is used (Figure 14.16).

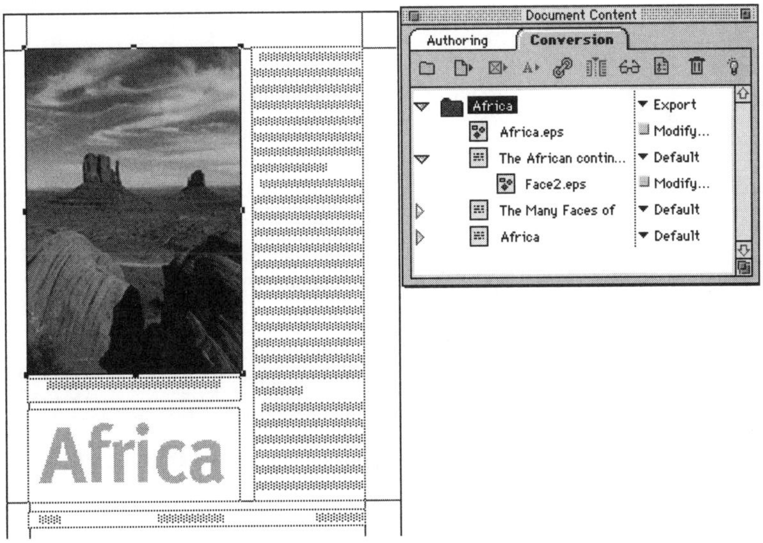

Figure 14.16 The Conversion tab of BeyondPress's Document Content palette.

The palette works by generating a list of the contents of the document. Each item is listed separately in the palette. Stories that run over several pages are listed as one item that can be divided into separate text blocks, and all items can be rearranged in the palette as needed.

Some of the most powerful features in this palette are implemented by setting up preferences.These include specifying default table and list formats and style sheet mapping. For example, you can specify that the text in the QuarkXPress document to which the style sheet *Head 1* has been applied can be mapped to an HTML style (Figure 14.17). When the document is exported, all the text will be automatically formatted in the appropriate HTML style. You can also map styles by font size. For example, you can specify that all text that is 18 points or larger will be formatted in the *Heading 1* HTML style.

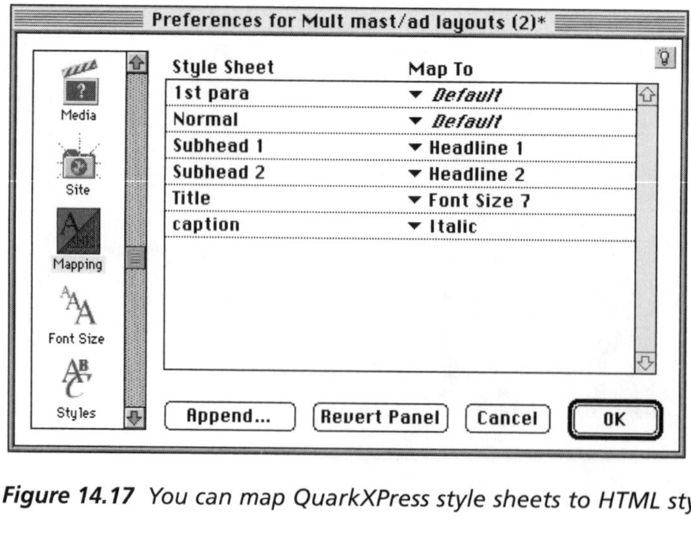

Figure 14.17 *You can map QuarkXPress style sheets to HTML styles.*

Another powerful BeyondPress feature is automatic conversion of picture files. Whether your documents contain picture files in TIFF, EPS, or some other format, BeyondPress will convert them to GIF or JPEG, as you specify. Using the Image Settings dialog box, you can scale graphics, assign ALT tags or assign a color palette (Figure 14.18).

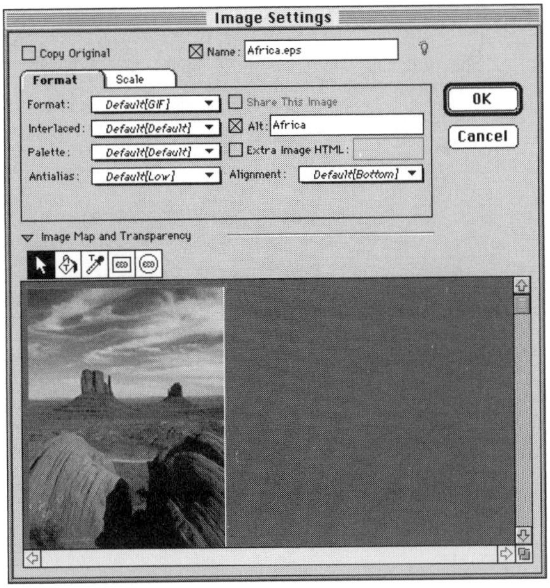

Figure 14.18 *BeyondPress's Image Settings dialog box.*

Summary

QuarkXPress is the world's workhorse for publishing all kinds of printed media, but it can also be a great design tool for other media, offering a familiar set of tools to designers and production staff alike. We've taken a look at two tools that aid that process, but other tools are also available. The important thing is to understand that QuarkXPress is not for print media alone, and it will likely prove to be an important tool as we move further into the age of digital information.

APPENDIX A

USING THE XTENSION MANAGER

An important aspect of QuarkXPress technology is to be found in the world of XTension products. To say "world" is truly appropriate, because today hundreds of third-party XTension products are available for both the Macintosh and Windows versions of QuarkXPress.

An XTension is a software program that extends the capability of QuarkXPress. An XTension can provide one very simple feature, or it can be very powerful and add the dimension of an additional software program, like the QuarkImmedia XTension. Some XTension products are distributed as shareware, while others cost thousands of dollars.

XTension technology is a result of some very smart planning by Quark, Inc. Years ago, Quark began making available, at a relatively low cost, an XTension programming toolkit. This toolkit can be used by any programmer familiar with the C++ programming language to create custom or commercial XTension software. One of the first XTensions, for example, was the Visionary XTension developed by the Scitex Corp., which linked QuarkXPress to Scitex's high-end prepress systems.

Many of the features of QuarkXPress itself are provided through XTension technology. For example, the indexing feature is provided by an XTension. Import filters for word processing programs and some graphics programs are also XTension products.

If you have been using a number of XTensions with QuarkXPress 3.3 on your Macintosh, you will probably be able to use them with 4.0. Quark has built in an emulation layer that supports 3.3 Macintosh XTensions; if the XTension is written properly, it should work with 4.0. Windows XTensions, on the other hand, must be specifically written for 4.0 because they use true 32-bit code, which was not used by the QuarkXPress 3.3 Windows version.

When you install QuarkXPress, the XTensions you choose are copied into the **Xtension**, folder, which is in your **QuarkXPress** program folder (Figure A.1). XTensions that are installed but not enabled to launch with the program are copied into the **XTension Disabled** folder. When you launch QuarkXPress, the XTensions in the **XTension** folder will be launched, too.

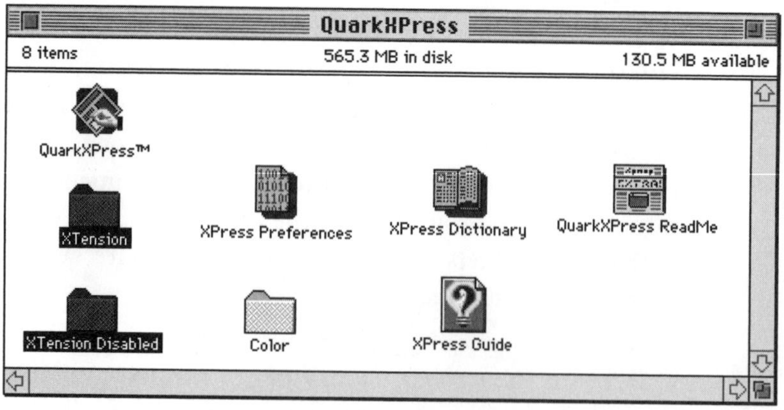

***Figure A.1** XTensions are copied into the XTension folder in your QuarkXPress program folder.*

Because the use of XTension products is so common, Quark has included a new feature in version 4.0 called the XTensions Manager (**Utilities** ➔ **XTensions Manager**), which enables you to control which XTensions are loaded and which are not.

The XTensions Manager, shown in Figure A.2, lists all the XTensions in the **XTension** and the **XTension Disabled** folders. You can enable or disable individual XTensions in the list, or you can create a set of XTensions that can be loaded quickly.

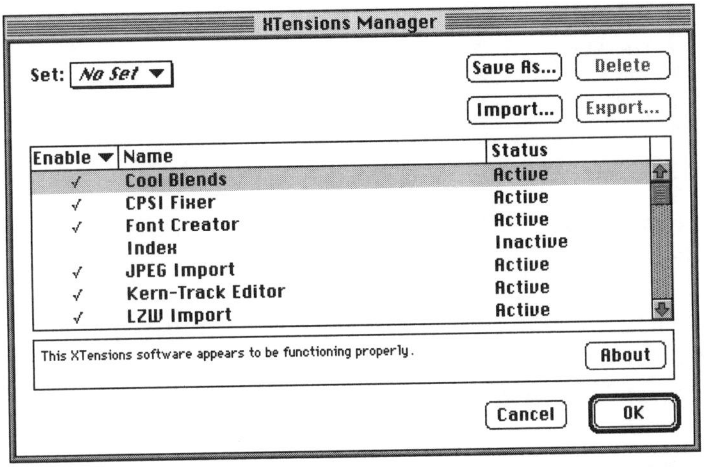

Figure A.2 *The XTensions Manager (Utilities ¤ XTensions Manager).*

The **Enable** column displays a check mark next to every XTension that is enabled. To disable an XTension, click in the Enable column. Click again to enable the XTension. Next to the **Name** of the XTension, the **Status** column lists whether the XTension is active or inactive, or it displays an error message if the XTension is enabled but cannot be loaded for some reason. When you click on the XTension, a message that elaborates on the status appears in the lower part of the dialog box.

The **About** button displays a dialog box with more information about the selected XTension (Figure A.3). This information includes the path name where the XTension is located on your hard disk, whether the XTension is optimized for version 4.0, and, if the manufacturer has provided it, information about what the XTension does.

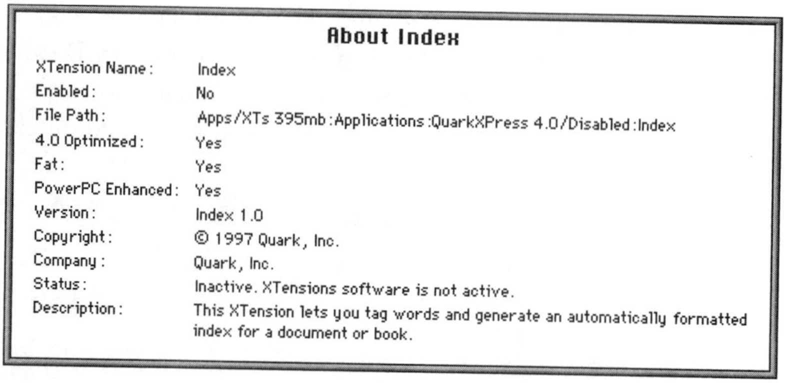

About Index
XTension Name: Index
Enabled: No
File Path: Apps/XTs 395mb:Applications:QuarkXPress 4.0/Disabled:Index
4.0 Optimized: Yes
Fat: Yes
PowerPC Enhanced: Yes
Version: Index 1.0
Copyright: © 1997 Quark, Inc.
Company: Quark, Inc.
Status: Inactive. XTensions software is not active.
Description: This XTension lets you tag words and generate an automatically formatted index for a document or book.

Figure A.3 *The About button displays more information about the selected XTension.*

The **Set** pop-up menu lets you choose predefined sets of XTensions. In addition to the default choices (Figure A.4), you can create your own custom sets.

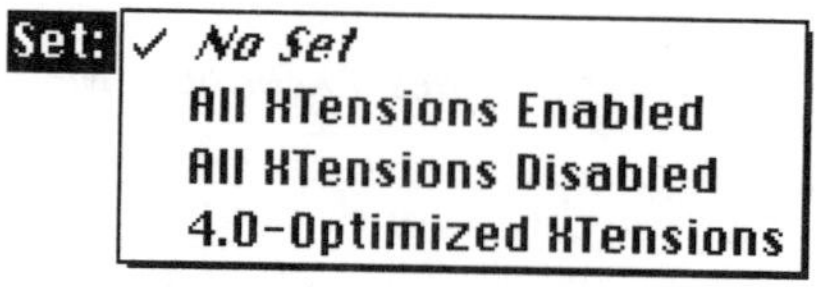

Figure A.4 *The default XTension sets.*

To create a custom XTension set, enable only the XTensions in the list that you wish to be part of the set. Click the **Save As** button and name the set. It will then be available in the Set pop-up menu. When you choose the custom name, only XTensions that are part of the set will be enabled.

TIP: You must restart QuarkXPress for any changes in the XTensions Manager to take effect.

The default setting is that the XTensions Manager will not display unless there is an error loading an XTension. If you wish to change this default, you can do so from the XTensions tab of the Application Preferences dialog box (**Edit → Preferences → Application**), shown in Figure A.5.

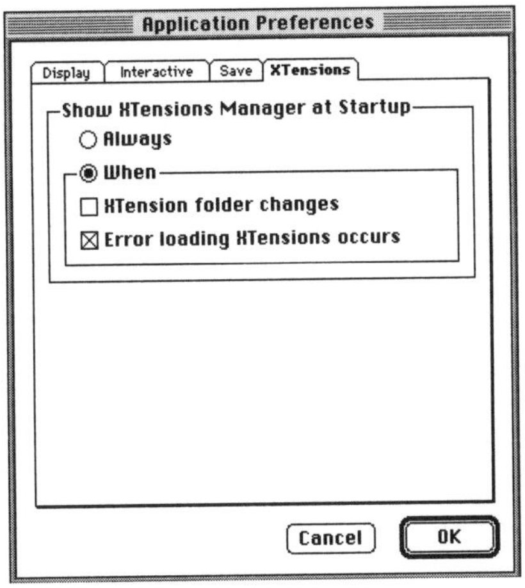

Figure A.5 *The XTensions tab of the Application Preferences dialog box.*

If you'd like the XTensions Manager to display every time you launch QuarkXPress, check **Always.** Check **When XTension folder changes** if you'd like it to display the XTensions Manager when an XTension has been removed from or added to the XTension folder in your QuarkXPress document folder. **When Error loading occurs** is the default setting. And, of course, you can display the XTensions Manager anytime by selecting the **Utilities → XTensions Manager** command.

There are many great on-line resources for XTension products, and many vendors offer demo versions of their products. Three of our favorite Web sites for XTensions include:

- Quark, Inc. (www.quark.com)
- XChange USA (www.xchangeus.com)
- Media-Network (www.xtension.com)

QuarkXPress is a great product on its own, but many other capabilities are available through the wonderful world of XTensions. If you can think of a feature you wish QuarkXPress had, chances are good that someone has provided the very capability you're looking for with an XTension product. When you're using QuarkXPress, "the program just can't do it" is rarely the case!

INDEX